Power, Participation and Ideology

Readings in the Sociology
of American Political Life

Edited by CALVIN J. LARSON
and PHILO C. WASBURN

PURDUE UNIVERSITY

Bringing together outstanding statements concerning three central topics
in political sociology—power, participation and ideology—the editors
present the major divergent views on
basic topics in political sociology and
reveal the complexity and interrelatedness of political structures and
processes through a comprehensive
look at American society and its political system.

Part I presents a common sociological
approach to the study of decision-
making at the national and local
levels. Part II reveals the interplay
of psychological, social-structural and
cultural influences in the determination of patterns of political participation. The interplay of personality,
social structure and culture with
respect to their influence on ideology
is presented in Part III.
behavior and comparative political
sociology.

Power, Participation and Ideology

POWER, PARTICIPATION

AND IDEOLOGY

Readings in the Sociology of American Political Life

Edited by

CALVIN J. LARSON

and

PHILO C. WASBURN

Purdue University

DAVID McKAY COMPANY, INC.

New York, 1969

POWER, PARTICIPATION AND IDEOLOGY

COPYRIGHT © 1969 BY DAVID MCKAY COMPANY, INC.

LIBRARY OF CONGRESS CATALOG CARD NUMBER: 69–17701

MANUFACTURED IN THE UNITED STATES OF AMERICA

To Edith and Mara

PREFACE

To understand the nature of political sociology one must have some familiarity with the particular way in which the sociologist approaches the study of human behavior and how he characterizes political phenomena. A central ingredient of the sociological perspective is the premise that men are dependent upon each other for the fulfillment of a variety of important needs. The postulate of dependence implies to the sociologist the necessity for the development among people of a body of common understandings as to how they are to approach one another for the satisfaction of individual and common objectives. Thus, many sociologists declare the subject matter of their discipline to be human interaction as it is structured by shared and learned behavioral expectations.

One of the major theoretical concerns of sociology is to account for the continuity of patterns of interaction. If relationships among people are to endure, they must develop a system for resolving the various differences and conflicting interests that inevitably arise. They must be able to decide when individual interests are to take precedence over collective interests and vice versa. In essence, any on-going social unit must evolve a shared set of certain fundamental expectations in order to maintain orderly relationships among its members. Agreements as to the manner in which power is to be allocated, obtained, and used are of crucial importance for this purpose.

While the concept of power is an important consideration in general sociological theory, it is of central concern in political sociology. Power has proved to be one of the most difficult terms to define precisely in social science. Included in any comprehensive dicussion of the concept will be reference to the ability of its possessors to establish collective goals, to mobilize the resources to attain them, and to insure social cohesion.[1]

Power has a positive and a negative function in society. It may be used to dominate and constrain people against their will and for the selfish motives of a select few. It can be based upon the possession of coercive capabilities, economic resources, social esteem, personal skills, or virtually any one or any combination of socially scarce and valued qualities. Power can be distributed with relative equality among the members of a social system; it can be concentrated in the hands of one or a few individuals; or its distribution can be somewhere in between these patterns. It can be exercised according to thoroughly democratic principles or in an absolutely totalitarian manner. For reasons such as these, both the formally prescribed methods and the informally developed techniques of acquiring and applying power are analyzed by political sociologists.

Reactions to the exercise of power can be both attitudinal and behavioral. Attitudes can range from belief in the rightness and justness of its exercise to

vii

feelings of the wickedness and injustice of its use. Behavior may range from willing compliance with the decisions of the powerful to violent opposition to the attempted implementation of their policies. Political sociologists are vitally interested in studying the conditions which produce different patterns of power and mark its evolution. As Lewis Coser has put it:

> Political sociology is that branch of sociology which is concerned with the social causes and consequences of given power distributions within or between societies, and with the social and political conflicts that lead to changes in the allocation of power.[2]

Some political sociologists have expressed primary concern with those power relations that take place within the context of the state. To Scott Greer and Peter Orleans:

> The major empirical problem of political sociology today would seem then, to be the description, analysis and sociological explanation of the peculiar social structure called the state.[3]

Political scientists also have a basic interest in the study of the state. According to Francis J. Sorauf:

> Political science . . . studies [the] political system and, where they exist, the institutions of government around which it centers. It is concerned with the authoritative decision-making of the political system and with all of the processes and activities by which a society makes those decisions, chooses men to make them, and influences those who have been chosen. Its concern ranges from the individual's political interests and awareness to the complex operation of large political institutions. Its prime focus is on the processes of policy-making in the political system and on any activity that attempts to influence it. Any behavior concerned with those processes is political.[4]

Some analysts would accept Sorauf's statement as a concise description of the aims of political sociology. This raises the question: How does political sociology differ from political science?

This is a difficult question to deal with for several reasons. First, there is seldom perfect agreement among practitioners in any academic field concerning what is the *central* focus of their subject. Second, definitions of fields usually beg important theoretical questions. Third, attempts to distinguish one field from another often lead to exaggerations of the differences which may exist. Therefore, it is better to distinguish political sociology and contemporary political science by describing differences in the emphasis each places on specific topics than by contrasting formal definitions.

One of the main differences between the two fields can be traced to the different emphases which political scientists and political sociologists place upon the formal political system and the society of which the political system is an integral part. Reinhard Bendix and Seymour M. Lipset have characterized this difference in emphasis as follows:

> Like political science, political sociology is concerned with the distribution and exercise of power in society. Unlike political science, it is not concerned with the institutional provisions for that distribution and exercise, but takes them as given. Thus, political science starts with the state and examines how it affects society, while political sociology starts with society and examines how it affects distribution and exercise of power.[5]

Traditionally, the political scientist focused his attention on the formal political system—its structure and functioning.[6] Sociologists found this approach somewhat unsatisfactory because it promoted a tendency to treat the formal political system as an isolated entity, and, therefore, to overlook its relation to and interdependence with the other societal institutions. While demonstrating a deep interest in the prescribed political ideals of a particular society, the political scientist seemed to the sociologist to give short shrift to the way in which people from all walks of life interpreted and were affected by these ideals. In other words, from the point of view of the sociologist, the political scientist appeared to grant the formally prescribed political institutions of a society greater autonomy and legitimacy than seemed valid.

Interestingly enough, and somewhat ironically, the political sociologist has exhibited a penchant for emphasizing the informal system to the neglect of the formal system. In the area of community power, for example, sociologists have too often conducted studies and drawn inferences about the nature of community decision-making without evidencing a thorough familiarity with, or even much regard for, the nature of the formally prescribed political system. It is for this reason that representatives of the two fields have at times been encouraged to view one another as competitors rather than as allies embarked on a common endeavor.

However, today there are political scientists whose mode of analysis is virtually indistinguishable from that employed by political sociologists. Furthermore, a common intellectual heritage has tended to promote a basic theoretical compatibility between the two fields. Two of the basic concerns of this heritage are the problems of the relationship between individual freedom and collective responsibility, and the dynamics of consensus and dissensus, of order and of change.

The analysis of the kind of systems and elements within systems which make for different types of accommodation between individual and collective needs is to a considerable extent a reflection of a defensive preoccupation with democatic principles. Situations in which the balance between individualism and collectivism is involved (for example, political movements such as fascism and communism) are of basic interest to students in both fields. The subjects of consensus and cleavage have been studied in an attempt to test the theories of two critics of democracy in particular: Karl Marx and Roberto Michels.[7]

Karl Marx asserted that Western democracy was heavily dependent upon the capitalistic mode of production. Certain conditions within capitalism itself would inevitably, Marx argued, lead to a revolutionary conflict between two classes—owners of the means of production and their workers. Since political sociologists recognize Marx as one of the bulwarks of their field, one might expect that "sociologists until fairly recently have been much more involved in studying the conditions facilitating cleavage than studying the requisites of political consensus." [8]

This is not to say that political sociologists necessarily looked with ideological favor upon cleavage, conflict, or revolution. To a great extent, their reading of Marx was quite the reverse, for their reaction to his theories was more in the vein of conservative fear than radical fervor. Many of the initial endeavors of American political sociologists—voting studies, studies of extremist movements, analyses of the locus and distribution of power in all types of organizations— were carried out as much to ascertain the health of American democracy and to critically test Marx as to explore important subjects. Until quite recently, the political sociologist revealed a tendency to emphasize much more than the political scientist the role of the economic institution in structuring political behavior.[9]

Roberto Michels, in his *Political Parties,* introduced the principle of the "iron law of oligarchy." [10] His thesis was that leadership in any organization, regardless of whether or not it was located in a democratic or totalitarian political milieu, would eventually become the prerogative of a select few. In combination with Max Weber's thesis that industrial societies require bureaucratic decision-making structures, and that bureaucracies in time would come to dominate men rather than vice versa, Michels' hypothesis spurred the study of leadership in the private sector of society as well as the public.

In both fields, an important stimulus for investigating the relationship between order and change was provided by the contributions of Alexis de Tocqueville.[11] It was his contention that the maintenance of democratic ideals in large industrial societies could be significantly influenced by the character of and role played by voluntary associations. The line of reasoning followed was that voluntary associations could block the growth of centralized control if their number was sufficiently great and their membership cohesive and aggressive in expressing their ideas and in pursuing the attainment of their goals. A multiplicity of autonomous and competing interest-groups would create, in effect, an informal power bloc to complement as well as offset the influence of the formally prescribed decision-making structure. Seymour M. Lipset succinctly describes his version of the theory in the following statement:

> Democracy is a social mechanism for resolving the problem of societal decision-making among conflicting interest groups with minimal force and maximal consensus. A stable democratic system requires sources of cleavage

so that there will be struggle over ruling positions, challenges to parties in power, and shifts of parties in office; but without consensus—a value system allowing the peaceful "play" of power, the adherence by the "outs" to decisions made by "ins," and the recognition by "ins" of the rights of the "outs" —there can be no democracy.[12]

The study of interest-groups—the bases of their formation, their overt activities as well as internal structure—has been and continues to be an important area of investigation for students of politics.

Unfortunately, too many political sociologists and political scientists have shown a tendency to approach the study of conflict as the physiologist might the study of cancer—that is, as an abnormal growth within a basically sound structure. There simply has not been sufficient attention devoted to the analysis of the legitimate and non-legitimate bases of conflict in society, particularly in so-called democratic societies, and their positive and negative functions for individual freedom and social organization.

In summary, the central concerns of political sociology have been characterized above as (1) the study of the organization and exercise of power, (2) the analysis of factors conducive to consensus and dissensus, and (3) the investigation of the social conditions of democracy. Stated yet another way, political sociology investigates the interrelated phenomena of *power, participation,* and *ideology.*

As noted earlier, power includes the ability of power holders to establish group goals, to garner the facilities necessary to achieve them, and to ensure social cohesion. The term has many dimensions and has been defined and analyzed in a number of ways.[13] The selections in Part I deal with the concept of power and reveal some of the major points of agreement and dispute among those who have examined its exercise in the United States.

Political participation is the process by which individuals, acting singly or through group organization, attempt to influence decision-making, or alter the manner in which power may be distributed and the principles by which it may be exercised in a particular society. Part II contains statements that range from analyses of the motives of individuals to participate to the social and political effects of their participation.

An ideology is a shared body of beliefs and sentiments concerning the proper as well as the actual distribution of power in society and the principles by which it is and should be exercised. In Part III, a variety of theoretical interpretations and empirical studies of the nature and function of ideology in America is presented.

It should be noted that each of the analyses contained in this volume deals primarily with the United States. We have chosen to restrict the selections to the American scene for several reasons. First of all, there have been more studies of political processes in America than in any other nation. Also, the student can get a better idea of the complexity and interrelatedness of political structures and processes through a comprehensive look at one society and its political system. Finally, of course, most of the students who will use this reader will be Americans. Their own experiences and observations should make this particular set of readings all the more meaningful to them.

C.J.L.
P.C.W.

NOTES

[1] These are aspects of power conceived as a facility for the performance of functions in and on behalf of the society as a system. A complementary view of power sees it as distributive and raises questions about how and on what basis it is apportioned to and exercised by subgroups within a society. For a recent attempt to deal with these two perspectives on power within a single theoretical framework see William A. Gamson, *Power and Discontent* (Homewood, Ill.: The Dorsey Press, 1968).

[2] Lewis A. Coser (ed.), *Political Sociology: Selected Essays* (New York: Harper Torchbooks, 1967), p. 1.

[3] Scott Greer and Peter Orleans, "Political Sociology," Chapter 21, pp. 808–851, in Robert E. L. Faris (ed.), *Handbook of Modern Sociology* (Chicago: Rand McNally & Company, 1964), p. 810.

[4] Francis J. Sorauf, *Political Science: An Informal Overview* (Columbus, Ohio: Charles E. Merrill Books, Inc., 1965), p. 5.

[5] Reinhard Bendix and Seymour M. Lipset, "The Field of Political Sociology," Chapter 2, pp. 9–47, in Lewis A. Coser (ed.), *op. cit.,* p. 26.

[6] For some time, of course, there have been a number of political scientists who have been concerned with politically relevant processes which occur outside of formal governmental institutions. Harold Lasswell was among the first and most prominent of these. An influential political scientist, David Easton, wrote in 1953:

"Of the vast variety of activity involved in political situations, that of persons within the governmental and party structure is only a manifest and a small part when compared with the importance of non-governmental social groups."

David Easton, *The Political System* (New York: Alfred A. Knopf, Inc., 1953).

[7] See the discussion on the contributions of these two men by Seymour M. Lipset, "Political Sociology," Chapter 3, pp. 81–114 in Robert K. Merton, Leonard Broom, and Leonard S. Cottrell, Jr. (eds.), *Sociology Today* (New York: Basic Books, Inc., 1959).

[8] Lipset, *ibid.,* pp. 83–84.

[9] See the recent statement by the political scientist William C. Mitchell, "The Shape of Political Theory to Come: From Political Sociology to Political Economy," *American Behavioral Scientist,* November-December, 1967, pp. 8–20.

[10] Roberto Michels, *Political Parties* (New York: The Free Press, 1949).

[11] Alexis de Tocqueville, *Democracy in America,* Two Volumes (New York: Alfred A. Knopf, 1945) and *The Old Regime and the French Revolution* (New York: Doubleday & Company, Inc., 1955).

[12] Lipset, *op. cit.,* p. 92.

[13] Some of the more important discussions of the concept of power include Robert A. Dahl, "The Concept of Power," *Behavioral Science* (July, 1957), pp. 201–215; Herbert Goldhamer and Edward A. Shils, "Types of Power and Status," *The American Journal of Sociology,* Vol. 45 (September, 1939), pp. 171–182; Robert Bierstedt, "An Analysis of Social Power," *American Sociological Review,* Vol. 15 (December, 1950), pp. 730–738; Terry N. Clark, "The Concept of Power: Some Overemphasized and Underrecognized Dimensions," *The Southwestern Social Science Quarterly,* Vol. 58 (December, 1967), pp. 272–287; Robert A. Dahl, "Power," in David L. Sills (ed.), *International Encyclopedia of the Social Sciences* (New York: Macmillan and The Free Press, 1968), Vol. 12, pp. 405–415; and William A. Gamson, *op. cit.*

CONTENTS

Part III

POLITICAL IDEOLOGY IN AMERICA

C. The End of Ideology?

Power, Participation and Ideology

PART I

Power and Decision-Making in America

INTRODUCTION

In the United States, political power at any level is officially the prerogative of certain formally designated individuals. As long as public officals conform to the requirements of their offices, policies and decisions made by them are recognized as legitimate and are expected to be complied with.

While elected decision-makers are subjected to public scrutiny and critical appraisal, those who may influence them to make decisions are not necessarily visible to, or known by, the public. Ideally, however, those who influence decisions should be just as apparent and publicly accountable as formal decision-makers. Theoretically, when a decision must be determined in a non-routine, or controversial matter, all those directly involved or even interested should be encouraged to express their positions. The assumption here is that while there are many possible solutions to any important problem, the "best" solution will most likely be found if all possible alternatives are made known.

Not only must all viewpoints be allowed expression, but also they should be carefully and impartially considered by both the public and their leaders. It is assumed that only in this way can leaders make appropriate and just decisions, and the public adequately evaluate their leaders' performance.

In order for the ideal to be approximated, all those with an interest in affecting a decision must have equal access to the means of influence (the only means necessary in the "ideal" case would be an open platform). Since it is a fact that individuals and groups in America do not have equal access to the means of influence (for example, not everyone can afford a Washington lobby), there has been a great deal of attention devoted to the study of how and by whom decisions are influenced. The question is, what kind of impact does the "latent" structure of influence have on the formally constituted decision-making apparatus?

1

In the first paper in Section A, C. Wright Mills argues that the structure of influence in America takes the form of a pyramid with a "power elite" at the apex. The power elite constitute a triumvirate from the economic, political, and military sectors of society. Although Mills points out that the power elite come together "only on certain coinciding-points and only on certain occasions of 'crisis'," he suggests that they are in effect an oligarchy which is more attuned to its own needs and interests than it is to those of the "masses." Mills analyzes the historical factors which he believes responsible for the concentration of influence in a team of three and examines the implications of his findings for American democracy.

Mills's argument was not new nor his findings particularly surprising to scholars weaned on the political theories of European writers such as Pareto, Mosca, and Michels. However, to those nurtured on the premise that America is a pluralistic democracy, Mills's position was overstated and a distortion of reality. Critics of Mills in this camp asserted that interests were too varied and power too diffused for a power elite to be likely in America. Reasoning along such lines, David Riesman denied the existence of an elite power bloc in America and instead suggested that decisions emanated from the interaction of competing interest-groups.

Where Mills saw the growth of unchecked leadership, Riesman saw the decline of effective leadership in America. To Riesman, power in America had become "other directed"—a mechanism for defense—where it once had been an "inner directed" offensive resource. In answer to the question "Who has the power?" Riesman replied, "The veto groups." [1] The veto groups are the "various business groups, large and small, the movie-censoring groups, the farm groups and the labor and professional groups, the major ethnic groups and major regional groups . . ." In a rather regretful tone, Riesman observed:

The only leaders of national scope left in the United States today are those who can placate the veto groups. The only followers left in the United States today are those unorganized and sometimes disorganized unfortunates who have not yet invented their groups.

In a penetrating examination of the different positions of Mills and Riesman, William Kornhauser pointed out:

Just as Mills is presenting a distorted image of power in America when he fails to consider the pressures on those in high positions, so Riesman presents a biased picture by not giving sufficient attention to power differentials among the various groups in society. [2]

Many other analyses have been made of the interpretations of Mills and Riesman, but it is Mills's work that has attracted the greatest amount of critical attention. [3]

In the third paper, Robert S. Lynd conceives of power as an inevitable by-product of group living and a necessary tool for the maintenance of order in society. In the absence of established mechanisms of social control, individual freedoms cannot be adequately safeguarded and collective goals effectively pursued. The question that Lynd wishes us to consider is not so much what is power, but where does it come from and how is it used.

Lynd begins his analysis by examining the frequent assertion that the ubiquity of power in human society can be traced to an innate power lust in the human organism. In his opinion, this thesis overlooks the elementary fact of the interaction between nature and nurture and serves only to turn attention away from the study of the more plausible and valid sources of power. Clearly, he says, what a person wants and what he does is not only a function of his inherited capacities, but also a consequence of the particular social and cultural milieu in which he was raised. Having reasoned thus, Lynd proceeds by emphasizing the role of "external" sociological factors.

According to Lynd, one can trace the generating source of power to either the institutional patterns or the "social structural" features of society. As he points out, two institutions in particular have been analyzed as the generating sources of power: the state and the economy. While agreeing that significant power is most often displayed in these two institutional sectors, Lynd argues that an underlying, but mostly unrecognized, "social structure" may be the stimulating force behind the display. He defines "social structure" as

. . . the organized relations of groups and categories of people identified within a given society according to kinship, sex, age, division of labor, race, religion, or any other criteria stressed as differentiating people in role, status, access to resources, and authority. This structure establishes durable relations that hold groups of people together for certain purposes and separates them for others. . . . [Footnote 13]

He believes that the hierarchical social structure of the United States permits some people greater access than others to the means to influence the working of the major social institutions. Since power is supposed to reside in institutions rather than "social structures," Lynd feels that the "actual" men of power in America are not necessarily held accountable for its use. Accordingly, he states:

The "problem of democracy" as it exists in our society concerns principally the fact that purportedly democratic political institutions operate upon a factually undemocratic class base appropriate to capitalism.

In the fourth paper, Arnold Rose puts forth a lengthy critique of the works of Mills and Floyd Hunter and offers his own hypothesis concerning the distribution of power in America. He refers to the Hunter-Mills position as the "economic-elite-dominance hypothesis," and his own view as the "multi-influence hypothesis." Rose interprets the Hunter-Mills hypothesis to mean that "the economic elite acts in a more-or-less unified fashion to control the political process of the United States." The "multi-influence hypothesis" conceives of society "as consisting of many elites, each relatively small numerically and operating in different spheres of life, and of the bulk of the population classifiable into organized groups and publics as well as the masses."

In the opening presentation in Section B (number 5), Floyd Hunter found the pattern of decision-making at the local level to be comparable, if not identical, to that claimed by Mills to exist at the national level. In his study of Atlanta, Georgia, Hunter found the "real" leaders to be a "behind-the-scenes" clique of economic dominants with a penchant for manipulating the "legitimate" decision-making structure for other than altruistic reasons. Political scientists were quick to challenge the validity of Hunter's claims and findings. They did so primarily by pointing out certain of his methodological shortcomings. Hunter's methodological approach has come to be termed the "reputational" technique, although it is sometimes referred to as the nominations, stratification, and sociological approach.

Hunter thinks of a power leader as one "who traditionally and consistently exercises independent judgment in formulating policies that affect major segments of the community." [4] In order to identify men of "independent judgment," Hunter's initial procedure is to ask "highly placed functionnaires in business, government, civic, and 'society' organizations who, in their opinion, are the most powerful members of their town." The manner in which this question is phrased has been a central focus of Hunter's critics.

It is claimed that the question is stated in too general and vague a fashion to permit a meaningful or unambiguous response. It is alleged that since Hunter does not indicate that he provides his respondents with a common and comprehensible definition of what is meant by a powerful person, it must be assumed that each respondent must of necessity conjure up his own definition in order to answer the question. Thus, it is argued, Hunter cannot be sure that his respondents have provided him with comparable responses.[5]

Largely in response to the writings of Hunter, a group of political scientists outlined another perspective and methodology which they referred to as the "pluralist alternative." In the second paper of Section B (number 6), Nelson W. Polsby claims that the basic assumption of the pluralistic viewpoint "is that nothing categorical can be assumed about power in any community." Furthermore:

> It rejects the stratification thesis that some group necessarily dominates in a community. If anything, there seems to be an unspoken notion among pluralist researchers that at bottom nobody dominates in a town, so that their first question to a local informant is not likely to be, "Who runs this community"?, but rather, "Does anyone at all run this community?"

The pluralist methodology, says Polsby, is based on the study of "specific outcomes" of issues in order to determine "who actually prevails in community decision-making." More than one issue-area is always studied, but not as many as might be preferred because of the expense and difficulty of field-work.

Both the reputational and pluralistic perspectives attracted adherents, some of whom once engaged in spirited debate.[6] Currently, the tendency is to use a combined approach to study community decision-making.

In the third article (number 7), Linton C. Freeman and his colleagues analyzed the congruity of three approaches used to locate leaders in a single community. They looked for extent of participation in decision-making; they noted extent of voluntary association membership; and they documented the institutional-occupational positions of community actors in Syracuse, New York. They found that these "several procedures for determining leaders did not converge on a single set of individuals." In exploring possible explanations for this finding, the authors hit upon a new index—"organizational participation." It seemed to them that recognition of leadership quite often stemmed more from the reputations of organizations than from those of individuals. They report that a re-analysis of the data supported their hypothesis.

The concluding paper (number 8) by John Walton summarizes the current position of community power research. The findings of some thirty-three studies are presented and compared. An important part of the discussion is that devoted to the testing of nine hypotheses not previously capable of appraisal in such a broad context. Walton's conclusion is that comparative studies are the next logical step in the study of community decision-making.

NOTES

[1] Writing in 1961, some eleven years after the publication of *The Lonely Crowd*, Riesman observed that his book as well as John Kenneth Galbraith's *American Capitalism* agreed "that there is no single coherent, self-conscious power elite, but an amorphous set of would-be elites, bidding for and forming coalitions." Furthermore, he pointed out, "We do not see that this general picture has changed radically; it has changed some." p. xxxvi of the preface to *The Lonely Crowd* (New Haven: Yale University Press, a Yale Paperbound, 1961).

[2] William Kornhauser, "Power Elite" or "Veto Groups"? Chapter 11 in Seymour Martin Lipset and Leo Lowenthal (eds.), *Culture and Social Character: The Work of David Riesman Reviewed* (New York: The Free Press of Glencoe, 1961), p. 264.

[3] A recent publication containing a variety of reviews of *The Power Elite* is G. William Domhoff and Hoyt B. Ballard (eds.), *C. Wright Mills and The Power Elite* (Boston: Beacon Press, 1968).

[4] Floyd Hunter, *Host Community and Air Force Base* (Maxwell A.F.B.: Human Resources Research Institute, 1952), p. 5.

[5] See, for example, Raymond E. Wolfinger, "Reputation and Reality in the Study of 'Community Power'," *American Sociological Review*, 25 (October, 1960), pp. 636–644.

[6] See the discussion by Polsby and Wolfinger writing from the pluralist point of view, and D'Antonio, Ehrlich, and Erickson writing from the reputational viewpoint in the *American Sociological Review*, 27 (December, 1962), pp. 838–854.

A. POWER IN AMERICA: THE NATION

1. THE POWER ELITE

C. Wright Mills

Except for the unsuccessful Civil War, changes in the power system of the United States have not involved important challenges to its basic legitimations. Even when they have been decisive enough to be called "revolutions," they have not involved the "resort to the guns of a cruiser, the dispersal of an elected assembly by bayonets, or the mechanisms of a police state." [1] Nor have they involved, in any decisive way, any ideological struggle to control masses. Changes in the American structure of power have generally come about by institutional shifts in the relative positions of the political, the economic, and the military orders. From this point of view, and broadly speaking, the American power elite has gone through four epochs, and is now well into a fifth.

1

I. During the first—roughly from the Revolution through the administration of John Adams—the social and economic, the political and the military institutions were more or less unified in a simple and direct way: the individual men of these several elites moved easily from one role to another at the top of each of the major institutional orders. Many of them were many-sided men who could take the part of legislator and merchant, frontiersman and soldier, scholar and surveyor.[2]

Until the downfall of the Congressional caucus of 1824, political institutions seemed quite central; political decisions, of great importance; many politicians, considered national statesmen of note "Society, as I first remember it," Henry Cabot Lodge once said, speaking of the Boston of his early boyhood, "was based on the old families; Doctor Holmes defines them in the 'Autocrat' as the families which had held high position in the colony, the province and during the Revolution and the early decades of the United States. They represented several generations of education and standing in the community . . . They had ancestors who had filled the pulpits, sat upon the bench, and taken part in the government under the crown; who had fought in the Revolution, helped to make the State and National constitutions and served in the army or navy; who had been members of the House or Senate in the early days of the Republic, and who had won success as merchants, manufacturers, lawyers, or men of letters." [3]

SOURCE: C. Wright Mills, *The Power Elite* (New York: Oxford University Press, 1959), pp. 269–297. Copyright © 1956 by Oxford University Press, Inc. Reprinted by permission.

Such men of affairs, who—as I have noted—were the backbone of Mrs. John Jay's social list of 1787, definitely included political figures of note. The important fact about these early days is that social life, economic institutions, military establishment, and political order coincided, and men who were high politicians also played key roles in the economy and, with their families, were among those of the reputable who made up local society. In fact, this first period is marked by the leadership of men whose status does not rest exclusively upon their political position, although their political activities are important and the prestige of politicians high. And this prestige seems attached to the men who occupy Congressional position as well as the cabinet. The elite are political men of education and of administrative experience, and, as Lord Bryce noted, possess a certain "largeness of view and dignity of character." [4]

II. During the early nineteenth century—which followed Jefferson's political philosophy, but, in due course, Hamilton's economic principles—the economic and political and military orders fitted loosely into the great scatter of the American social structure. The broadening of the economic order which came to be seated in the individual property owner was dramatized by Jefferson's purchase of the Louisiana Territory and by the formation of the Democratic-Republican party as successor to the Federalists

In this society, the "elite" became a plurality of top groups, each in turn quite loosely made up. They overlapped to be sure, but again quite loosely so. One definite key to the period, and certainly to our images of it, is the fact that the Jacksonian Revolution was much more of a status revolution than either an economic or a political one. The metropolitan 400 could not truly flourish in the face of the status tides of Jacksonian democracy; alongside it was a political elite in charge of the new party system. No set of men controlled centralized means of power; no small clique dominated economic, much less political, affairs. The economic order was ascendant over both social status and political power; within the economic order, a quite sizable proportion of all the economic men were among those who decided. For this was the period —roughly from Jefferson to Lincoln—when the elite was at most a loose coalition. The period ended, of course, with the decisive split of southern and northern types.

Official commentators like to contrast the ascendancy in totalitarian countries of a tightly organized clique with the American system of power. Such comments, however, are easier to sustain if one compares mid-twentieth-century Russia with mid-nineteenth-century America, which is what is often done by Tocqueville-quoting Americans making the contrast. But that was an America of a century ago, and in the century that has passed, the American elite have not remained as patrioteer essayists have described them to us. The "loose cliques" now head institutions of a scale and power not then existing and, especially since World War I, the loose cliques have tightened up. We are well beyond the era of romantic pluralism.

III. The supremacy of corporate economic power began, in a formal way, with the Congressional elections of 1866, and was consolidated by the Supreme Court decision of 1886 which declared that the Fourteenth Amendment protected the corporation. That period witnessed the transfer of the center of initiative from government to corporation. Until the First World War (which gave us an advanced showing of certain features of our own period) this was an age of raids on the government by the economic elite, an age of simple corruption, when Senators and judges were simply bought up. Here, once upon a time, in the era of McKinley and Morgan, far removed from the undocumented complexities of our own time, many now believe, was the golden era of the American ruling class.[5]

The military order of this period, as in the second, was subordinate to the political, which in turn was subordinate to the economic. The military was thus off to the side of the main driving forces of United States history. Political institutions in the United States have never formed a centralized and autonomous domain of power; they have been enlarged and centralized only reluctantly in slow response to the public consequences of the corporate economy.

In the post-Civil-War era, that economy was the dynamic; the "trusts"—as policies and events make amply clear—could readily use the relatively weak governmental apparatus for their own ends. That both state and federal governments were decisively limited in their power to regulate, in fact meant that they were themselves regulatable by the larger moneyed interests. Their powers were scattered and unorganized; the powers of the industrial and financial corporations concentrated and interlocked. The Morgan interests alone held 341 directorships in 112 corporations with an aggregate capitalization of over $22 billion—over three times the assessed value of all real and personal property in New England.[6] With revenues greater and employees more numerous than those of many states, corporations controlled parties, bought laws, and kept Congressmen of the "neutral" state. And as private economic power overshadowed public political power, so the economic elite overshadowed the political.

Yet even between 1896 and 1919, events of importance tended to assume a political form, foreshadowing the shape of power which after the partial boom of the 'twenties was to prevail in the New Deal. Perhaps there has never been any period in American history so politically transparent as the Progressive era of President-makers and Muckrakers.

IV. The New Deal did *not* reverse the political and economic relations of the third era, but it did create within the political arena, as well as in the corporate world itself, competing centers of power that challenged those of the corporate directors. As the New Deal directorate gained political power, the economic elite, which in the third period had fought against the growth of "government" while raiding it for crafty privileges, belatedly attempted to join it on the higher levels. When they did so they found themselves confronting other interests and men, for the places of decision were crowded. In due course, they did come to control and to use for their own purposes the New Deal institutions whose creation they had so bitterly denounced.

But during the 'thirties, the political order was still an instrument of small propertied farmers and businessmen, although they were weakened, having lost their last chance for real ascendancy in the Progressive era. The struggle between big and small property flared up again, however, in the political realm of the New Deal era, and to this struggle there was added, as we have seen, the new struggle of organized labor and the unorganized unemployed. This new force flourished under political tutelage, but nevertheless, for the first time in United States history, social legislation and lower-class issues became important features of the reform movement.

In the decade of the 'thirties, a set of shifting balances involving newly instituted farm measures and newly organized labor unions—along with big business—made up the political and administrative drama of power. These farm, labor, and business groups, moreover, were more or less contained within the framework of an enlarging governmental structure, whose political directorship made decisions in a definitely political manner. These groups pressured, and in pressuring against one another and against the governmental and party system, they helped to shape it. But it could not be said that any of them for any considerable length of time used that government unilaterally as their instrument. That is why the 'thirties was a *political* decade: the power of business was not replaced, but it was contested and supplemented: it became one major power within a structure of power that was chiefly run by political men, and not by economic or military men turned political.

The earlier and middle Roosevelt administrations can best be understood as a desperate search for ways and means, within the existing capitalist system, of reducing the staggering and ominous army of the unemployed. In these years, the New Deal as a system of power was essentially a balance of pressure groups and interest blocs. The political top adjusted many conflicts, gave way to this demand, sidetracked that one, was the unilateral servant of none, and so evened it all out into such going policy line as prevailed from one minor crisis to another. Policies were the result of a political act of balance at the top. Of course, the balancing act that Roosevelt performed did not affect the fundamental institutions of capitalism as a type of economy. By his policies, he subsidized the defaults of the capitalist economy, which had simply broken down; and by his rhetoric, he balanced its political disgrace, putting "economic royalists" in the political doghouse.

The "welfare state," created to sustain the balance and to carry out the subsidy, differed from the "laissez-faire" state: "If the state was believed neutral in the days of T.R. because its leaders claimed to sanction favors for no one," Richard Hofstadter has remarked, "the state under F.D.R. could be called neutral only in the sense that it offered favors to everyone." [7] The new state of the corporate commissars differs from the old welfare state. In fact, the later Roosevelt years—beginning with the entrance of the United States into overt acts of war and preparations for World War II—cannot be understood entirely in terms of an adroit equipoise of political power.

2

We study history, it has been said, to rid ourselves of it, and the history of the power elite is a clear case for which this maxim is correct. Like the tempo of American life in general, the long-term trends of the power structure have been greatly speeded up since World War II, and certain newer trends within and between the dominant institutions have also set the shape of the power elite and given historically specific meaning to its fifth epoch:

I. In so far as the structural clue to the power elite today lies in the political order, that clue is the decline of politics as genuine and public debate of alternative decisions—with nationally responsible and policy-coherent parties and with autonomous organizations connecting the lower and middle levels of power with the top levels of decision. America is now in considerable part more a formal political democracy than a democratic social structure, and even the formal political mechanics are weak.

The long-time tendency of business and government to become more intricately and deeply involved with each other has, in the fifth epoch, reached a new point of explicitness. The two cannot now be seen clearly as two distinct worlds. It is in terms of the executive agencies of the state that the rapprochement has proceeded most decisively. The growth of the executive branch of the government, with its agencies that patrol the complex economy, does not mean merely the "enlargement of government" as some sort of autonomous bureaucracy: it has meant the ascendancy of the corporation's man as a political eminence.

During the New Deal the corporate chieftains joined the political directorate; as of World War II they have come to dominate it. Long interlocked with government, now they have moved into quite full direction of the economy of the war effort and of the postwar era. This shift of the corporation executives into the political directorate has accelerated the long-term relegation of the professional politicians in the Congress to the middle levels of power.

II. In so far as the structural clue to the power elite today lies in the enlarged and military state, that clue becomes evident in the military ascendancy. The warlords have gained decisive political relevance, and the military structure of America is now in considerable part a political structure. The seemingly permanent military threat places a premium on the military and upon their control of men, materiel, money, and power; virtually all political and economic actions are now judged in terms of military definitions of reality: the higher warlords have ascended to a firm position within the power elite of the fifth epoch.

In part at least this has resulted from one simple historical fact, pivotal for the years since 1939: the focus of elite attention has been shifted from domestic problems, centered in the 'thirties around slump, to international problems, centered in the 'forties and 'fifties around war. Since the governing apparatus of the United States has by long historic usage been adapted to and shaped by domestic clash and balance, it has not, from any angle, had suitable agencies and traditions for the handling of international problems. Such formal democratic mechanics as had arisen in the century and a half of national development prior to 1941, had not been extended to the American handling of international affairs. It is, in considerable part, in this vacuum that the power elite has grown.

III. In so far as the structural clue to the power elite today lies in the economic order, that clue is the fact that the economy is at once a permanent-war economy and a private-corporation economy. American capitalism is now in considerable part a military capitalism, and the most important relation of the big corporation to the state rests on the coincidence of interests between military and corporate needs, as defined by warlords and corporate rich. Within the elite as a whole, this coincidence of interest between the high military and the corporate chieftains strengthens both of them and further subordinates the role of the merely political men. Not politicians, but corporate executives, sit with the military and plan the organization of war effort.

The shape and meaning of the power elite today can be understood only when these three sets of structural trends are seen at their point of coincidence: the military capitalism of private corporations exists in a weakened and formal democratic system containing a military order already quite political in outlook and demeanor. Accordingly, at the top of this structure, the power elite has been shaped by the coincidence of interest between those who control the major means of production and those who control the newly enlarged means of violence; from the decline of the professional politician and the rise to explicit political command of the corporate chieftains and the professional warlords; from the absence of any genuine civil service of skill and integrity, independent of vested interests.

The power elite is composed of political, economic, and military men, but this instituted elite is frequently in some tension: it comes together only on certain coinciding points and only on certain occasions of "crisis." In the long peace of the nineteenth century, the military were not in the high councils of state, not of the political directorate, and neither were the economic men—they made raids upon the state but they did not join its directorate. During the 'thirties, the political man was ascendant. Now the military and the corporate men are in top positions.

Of the three types of circle that compose the power elite today, it is the military that has benefited the most in its enhanced power, although the corporate circles have also become more explicitly intrenched in the more public decision-making circles. It is the professional politician that has the most, so much that in examining the events and decisions, one is tempted to speak of a political vacuum in which the corporate rich and the high warlord, in their coinciding interests, rule.

It should not be said that the three "take turns" in carrying the initiative, for the mechanics of the power elite are not often as deliberate as that would imply. At times, of course, it is—as when political men, thinking they can borrow the prestige of generals, find that they must pay for it, or, as when during big slumps, economic men feel the need of a politician at once safe and possessing vote appeal. Today all three are involved in virtually all widely ramifying decisions. Which of the three types seems to lead depends upon "the tasks of the period" as they, the elite, define them. Just now, these tasks center upon "defense" and international affairs. Accordingly, as we have seen, the military are ascendant in two senses: as personnel and as justifying ideology. That is why, just now, we can most easily specify the unity and the shape of the power elite in terms of the military ascendancy.

But we must always be historically specific and open to complexities. The simple Marxian view makes the big economic man the *real* holder of power; the simple liberal view makes the big political man the chief of the power system; and there are some who would view the warlords as virtual dictators. Each of these is an oversimplified view. It is to avoid them that we use the term "power elite" rather than, for example, "ruling class." *

In so far as the power elite has come to wide public attention, it has done so in terms of the "military clique." The power elite does, in fact, take its current shape from the decisive entrance into it of the military. Their presence and their ideology are its major legitimations, whenever the power elite feels the need to provide any. But what is called the "Washington military clique" is not composed merely of military men, and it does not prevail merely in Washington. Its members exist all over the country, and it is a coalition of generals in the roles of corporation executives, of politicians masquerading as admirals, of corporation executives acting like politicians, of civil servants who become majors, of vice-admirals who are also the assistants to a cabinet officer, who is himself, by the way, really a member of the managerial elite.

Neither the idea of a "ruling class" nor of a simple monolithic rise of "bureaucratic politicians" nor of a "military clique" is adequate. The power elite today involves the often uneasy coincidence of economic, military, and political power.

3

Even if our understanding were limited to these structural trends, we should have grounds for believing the power elite a useful, indeed indispensable, concept for the interpretation of what is going on at the topside of modern American society. But we are not, of course, so limited: our conception of the power elite does not need to rest only upon the correspondence of the institutional hierarchies involved, or upon the many points at which their shifting interests coincide. The power elite, as we conceive it, also rests upon the similarity of its personnel, and their personal and official relations with one another, upon their social and psychological affinities. In order to grasp the personal and social basis of the power elite's unity, we have first to remind ourselves of the facts of origin, career, and style of life of each of the types of circle whose members compose the power elite.

* "Ruling class" is a badly loaded phrase. "Class" is an economic term; "rule" a political one. The phrase, "ruling class," thus contains the theory that an economic class rules politically. That short-cut theory may or may not at times be true, but we do not want to carry that one rather simple theory about in the terms that we use to define our problems; we wish to state the theories explicitly, using terms of more precise and unilateral meaning. Specifically, the phrase "ruling class," in its common political connotations, does not allow enough autonomy to the political order and its agents, and it says nothing about the military as such. It should be clear to the reader by now that we do not accept as adequate the simple view that high economic men unilaterally make all decisions of national consequence. We hold that such a simple view of "economic determinism" must be elaborated by "political determinism" and "military determinism"; that the higher agents of each of these three domains now often have a noticeable degree of autonomy; and that only in the often intricate ways of coalition do they make up and carry through the most important decisions. Those are the major reasons we prefer "power elite" to "ruling class" as a characterizing phrase for the higher circles when we consider them in terms of power.

The power elite is *not* an aristocracy, which is to say that it is not a political ruling group based upon a nobility of hereditary origin. It has no compact basis in a small circle of great families whose members can and do consistently occupy the top positions in the several higher circles which overlap as the power elite. But such nobility is only one possible basis of common origin. That it does not exist for the American elite does not mean that members of this elite derive socially from the full range of strata composing American society. They derive in substantial proportions from the upper classes, both new and old, of local society and the metropolitan 400. The bulk of the very rich, the corporate executives, the political outsiders, the high military, derive from, at most, the upper third of the income and occupational pyramids. Their fathers were at least of the professional and business strata, and very frequently higher than that. They are native-born Americans of native parents, primarily from urban areas, and, with the exceptions of the politicians among them, overwhelmingly from the East. They are mainly Protestants, especially Episcopalian or Presbyterian. In general, the higher the position, the greater the proportion of men within it who have derived from and who maintain connections with the upper classes. The generally similar origins of the members of the power elite are underlined and carried further by the fact of their increasingly common educational routine. Overwhelmingly college graduates, substantial proportions have attended Ivy League colleges, although the education of the higher military, of course, differs from that of other members of the power elite.

But what do these apparently simple facts about the social composition of the higher circles really mean? In particular, what do they mean for any attempt to understand the degree of unity, and the direction of policy and interest that may prevail among these several circles? Perhaps it is best to put this question in a deceptively simple way: in terms of origin and career, who or what do these men at the top represent?

Of course, if they are elected politicians, they are supposed to represent those who elected them; and, if they are appointed, they are supposed to represent, indirectly, those who elected their appointers. But this is recognized as something of an abstraction, as a rhetorical formula by which all men of power in almost all systems of government nowadays justify their power of decision. At times it may be true, both in the sense of their motives and in the sense of who benefits from their decisions. Yet it would not be wise in any power system merely to assume it.

The fact that members of the power elite come from near the top of the nation's class and status levels does not mean that they are necessarily "representative" of the top levels only. And if they were, as social types, representative of a cross-section of the population, that would not mean that a balanced democracy of interest and power would automatically be the going political fact.

We cannot infer the direction of policy merely from the social origins and careers of the policy-makers. The social and economic backgrounds of the men of power do not tell us all that we need to know in order to understand the distribution of social power. For: (1) Men from high places may be ideological representatives of the poor and humble. (2) Men of humble origin, brightly self-made, may energetically serve the most vested and inherited interests. Moreover (3), not all men who effectively represent the interests of a stratum need in any way belong to it or personally benefit by policies that further its interests. Among the politicians, in short, there are sympathetic *agents* of given groups, conscious and unconscious, paid and unpaid. Finally (4), among the top decision-makers we find men who have been chosen for their positions because of their "expert knowledge." These are some of the obvious reasons why the social origins and careers of the power elite do not enable us to infer the class interests and policy directions of a modern system of power.

Do the high social origin and careers of the top men mean nothing, then, about the distribution of power? By no means. They simply remind us that we must be careful of any simple and direct inference from origin and career to political character and policy, not that we must ignore them in our attempt at political understanding. They simply mean that we must analyze the political psychology and the actual decisions of the political directorate as well as its social composition. And they mean, above all, that we should control, as we have done here, any inference we make from the origin and careers of the political actors by close understanding of the institutional landscape in which they act out their drama. Otherwise we should be guilty of a rather simple-minded biographical theory of society and history.

Just as we cannot rest the notion of the power elite solely upon the institutional mechanics that lead to its formation, so we cannot rest the notion solely upon the facts of the origin and career of its personnel. We need both, and we have both—as well as other bases, among them that of the status intermingling.

But it is not only the similarities of social origin, religious affiliation, nativity, and education that are important to the psychological and social affinities of the members of the power elite. Even if their recruitment and formal training were more heterogeneous than they are, these men would still be of quite homogeneous social type. For the most important set of facts about a circle of men is the criteria of admission, of praise, of honor, of promotion that prevails among them; if these are similar within a circle, then they will tend as personalities to become similar. The circles that compose the power elite do tend to have such codes and criteria in common. The co-optation of the social types to which these common values lead is often more important than any statistics of common origin and career that we might have at hand.

There is a kind of reciprocal attraction among the fraternity of the successful—not between each and every member of the circles of the high and mighty, but between enough of them to insure a certain unity. On the slight side, it is a sort of tacit, mutual admiration; in the strongest tie-ins, it proceeds by intermarriage. And there are all grades and types of connection between these extremes. Some overlaps certainly occur by means of cliques and clubs, churches, and schools.

If social origin and formal education in common tend to make the members of the power elite more readily understood and trusted by one another, their continued association further cements what they feel they have in common.

Members of the several higher circles know one another as personal friends and even as neighbors; they mingle with one another on the golf course, in the gentleman's clubs, at resorts, on transcontinental airplanes, and on ocean liners. They meet at the estates of mutual friends, face each other in front of the TV camera, or serve on the same philanthropic committee; and many are sure to cross one another's path in the columns of newspapers, if not in the exact cafes from which many of these columns originate. As we have seen, of "The New 400" of cafe society, one chronicler has named forty-one members of the very rich, ninety-three political leaders, and seventy-nine chief executives of corporations.

"I did not know, I could not have dreamed," Whittaker Chambers has written, "of the immense scope and power of Hiss' political alliances and his social connections, which cut across all party lines and ran from the Supreme Court to the Religious Society of Friends, from governors of states and instructors in college faculties to the staff members of liberal magazines. In the decade since I had last seen him, he had used his career, and, in particular, his identification with the cause of peace through his part in organizing the United Nations, to put down roots that made him one with the matted forest floor of American upper class, enlightened middle class, liberal and official life. His roots could not be disturbed without disturbing all the roots on all sides of him." [8]

The sphere of status has reflected the epochs of the power elite. In the third epoch, for example, who could compete with big money? And in the fourth, with big politicians, or even the bright young men of the New Deal? And in the fifth, who can compete with the generals and the admirals and the corporate officials now so sympathetically portrayed on the stage, in the novel, and on the screen? Can one imagine *Executive Suite* as a successful motion picture in 1935? Or *The Caine Mutiny?*

The multiplicity of high-prestige organizations to which the elite usually belong is revealed by even casual examination of the obituaries of the big businessman, the high-prestige lawyer, the top general and admiral, the key senator: usually, high-prestige church, business associations, plus high-prestige clubs, and often plus military rank. In the course of their lifetimes, the university president, the New York Stock Exchange chairman, the head of the bank, the old West Pointer—mingle in the status sphere, within which they easily renew old friendships and draw upon them in an effort to understand through the experience of trusted others those contexts of power and decision in which they have not personally moved.

In these diverse contexts, prestige accumulates in each of the higher circles, and the members of each borrow status from one another. Their self-images are fed by these accumulations and these borrowings, and accordingly, however segmental a given man's role may seem, he comes to feel himself a "diffuse" or "generalized" man of the higher circles, a "broad-gauge" man. Perhaps such inside experience is one feature of what is meant by "judgment."

The key organizations, perhaps, are the major corporations themselves, for on the boards of directors we find a heavy overlapping among the members of these several elites. On the lighter side, again in the summer and winter resorts, we find that, in an intricate series of overlapping circles; in the course of time, each meets each or knows somebody who knows somebody who knows that one.

The higher members of the military, economic, and political orders are able readily to take over one another's point of view, always in a sympathetic way, and often in a knowledgeable way as well. They define one another as among those who count, and who, accordingly, must be taken into account. Each of them as a member of the power elite comes to incorporate into his own integrity, his own honor, his own conscience, the viewpoint, the expectations, the values of the others. If there are no common ideals and standards among them that are based upon an explicitly aristocratic culture, that does not mean that they do not feel responsibility to one another.

All the structural coincidence of their interests as well as the intricate, psychological facts of their origins and their education, their careers and their associations make possible the psychological affinities that prevail among them, affinities that make it possible for them to say of one another: He is, of course, one of us. And all this points to the basic, psychological meaning of class consciousness. Nowhere in America is there as great a "class consciousness" as among the elite; nowhere is it organized as effectively as among the power elite. For by class consciousness, as a psychological fact, one means that the individual member of a "class" accepts only those accepted by his circle as among those who are significant to his own image of self.

Within the higher circles of the power elite, factions do exist; there are conflicts of policy; individual ambitions do clash. There are still enough divisions of importance within the Republican party, and even between Republicans and Democrats, to make for different methods of operation. But more powerful than these divisions are the internal discipline and the community of interests that bind the power elite together, even across the boundaries of nations at war.[9]

4

Yet we must give due weight to the other side of the case which may not question the facts but only our interpretation of them. There is a set of objections that will inevitably be made to our whole conception of the power elite, but which has essentially to do with only the psychology of its members. It might well be put by liberals or by conservatives in some such way as this:

"To talk of a power elite—isn't this to characterize men by their origins and associations? Isn't such characterization both unfair and untrue? Don't men modify themselves, especially Americans such as these, as they rise in stature to meet the demands of their jobs? Don't they arrive at a view and a line of policy that represents, so far as they in their human weaknesses can know, the interests of the nation as a whole? Aren't they merely honorable men who are doing their duty?"

What are we to reply to these objections?

I. We are sure that they are honorable men. But what is honor? Honor can only mean living up to a code that one believes to be honorable. There is no one code upon which we are all agreed. That is why, if we are civilized men, we do not kill off all of those with whom we disagree. The question is not: are these honorable men? The question is: what are their codes of honor? The answer to that question is that they are the codes of their circles, of those to whose opinions they defer. How could it be otherwise? That is one meaning of the important truism that all men are human and that all men are social creatures. As for sincerity, it can only be disproved, never proved.

II. To the question of their adaptability—which means their capacity to transcend the codes of conduct which, in their life's work and experience, they have acquired—we must answer: simply no, they cannot, at least not in the handful of years most of them have left. To expect that is to assume that they are indeed strange and expedient: such flexibility would in fact involve a violation of what we may rightly call their character and their integrity. By the way, may it not be precisely because of the lack of such character and integrity that earlier types of American politicians have not represented as great a threat as do these men of character?

It would be an insult to the effective training of the military, and to their indoctrination as well, to suppose that military officials shed their military character and outlook upon changing from uniform to mufti. This background is more important perhaps in the military case than in that of the corporate executives, for the training of the career is deeper and more total.

"Lack of imagination," Gerald W. Johnson has noted, "is not to be confused with lack of principle. On the contrary, an unimaginative man is often a man of the highest principles. The trouble is that his principles conform to Cornford's famous definition: 'A principle is a rule of inaction giving valid general reasons for not doing in a specific instance what to unprincipled instinct would seem to be right.' "[10]

Would it not be ridiculous, for example, to believe seriously that, in psychological fact, Charles Erwin Wilson represented anyone or any interest other than those of the corporate world? This is not because he is dishonest; on the contrary, it is because he is probably a man of solid integrity—as sound as a dollar. He is what he is and he cannot very well be anything else. He is a member of the professional corporation elite, just as are his colleagues, in the government and out of it; he represents the wealth of the higher corporate world; he represents its power; and he believes sincerely in his oft-quoted remark that "what is good for the United States is good for the General Motors Corporation and vice versa."

The revealing point about the pitiful hearings on the confirmation of such men for political posts is not the cynicism toward the law and toward the lawmakers on the middle levels of power which they display, nor their reluctance to dispose of their personal stock.[11] The interesting point is how impossible it is for such men to divest themselves of their engagement with the corporate world in general and with their own corporations in particular. Not only their money, but their friends, their interests, their training—their lives in short—are deeply involved in this world. The disposal of stock is, of course, merely a purifying ritual. The point is not so much financial or personal interests in a given corporation, but identification with the corporate world. To ask a man suddenly to divest himself of these interests and sensibilities is almost like asking a man to become a woman.

III. To the question of their patriotism, of their desire to serve the nation as a whole, we must answer first that, like codes of honor, feelings of patriotism and views of what is to the whole nation's good, are not ultimate facts but matters upon which there exists a great variety of opinion. Furthermore, patriotic opinions too are rooted in and are sustained by what a man has become by virtue of how and with whom he has lived. This is no simple mechanical determination of individual character by social conditions; it is an intricate process, well established in the major tradition of modern social study. One can only wonder why more social scientists do not use it systematically in speculating about politics.

IV. The elite cannot be truly thought of as men who are merely doing their duty. They are the ones who determine their duty, as well as the duties of those beneath them. They are not merely following orders: they give the orders. They are not merely "bureaucrats": they command bureaucracies. They may try to disguise these facts from others and from themselves by appeals to traditions of which they imagine themselves the instruments, but there are many traditions, and they must choose which ones they will serve. They face decisions for which there simply are no traditions.

Now, to what do these several answers add up? To the fact that we cannot reason about public events and historical trends merely from knowledge about the motives and character of the men or the small groups who sit in the seats of the high and mighty. This fact, in turn, does not mean that we should be intimidated by accusations that in taking up our problem in the way we have, we are impugning the honor, the integrity, or the ability of those who are in high office. For it is not, in the first instance, a question of individual character; and if, in further instances, we find that it is, we should not hesitate to say so plainly. In the meantime, we must judge men of power by the standards of power, by what they do as decision-makers, and not by who they are or what they may do in private life. Our interest is not in that: we are interested in their policies and in the *consequences* of their conduct of office. We must remember that these men of the power elite now occupy the strategic places in the structure of American society; that they command the dominant institutions of a dominant nation; that, as a set of men, they are in a position to make decisions with terrible consequences for the underlying populations of the world.

5

Despite their social similarity and psychological affinities, the members of the power elite do not constitute a club having a permanent membership with fixed and formal boundaries. It is of the nature of the power elite that within it there is a good deal of shifting about, and that it thus does not consist of one small set of the same men in the same positions in the same hierarchies. Because men know each other personally does not mean that among them there is a unity of policy; and because they do not know each other personally does not mean that among them there is a disunity. The conception of the power elite does not rest, as I have repeatedly said, primarily upon personal friendship.

As the requirements of the top places in each of the major hierarchies become similar, the types of men occupying these roles at the top—by selection and by training in the jobs—become similar. This is no mere deduction from structure to personnel. That it is a fact is revealed by the heavy traffic that has been going on between the three structures, often in very intricate patterns. The chief executives, the warlords, and selected politicians came into contact with one another in an intimate, working way during World War II; after that war ended, they continued their associations, out of common beliefs, social congeniality, and coinciding interests. Noticeable proportions of top men from the military, the economic, and the political worlds have during the last fifteen years occupied positions in one or both of the other worlds: between these higher circles there is an interchangeability of position, based formally upon the supposed transferability of "executive ability," based in substance upon the co-optation by cliques of insiders. As members of a power elite, many of those busy in this traffic have come to look upon "the government" as an umbrella under whose authority they do their work.

As the business between the big three increases in volume and importance, so does the traffic in personnel. The very criteria for selecting men who will rise come to embody this fact. The corporate commissar, dealing with the state and its military, is wiser to choose a young man who has experienced the state and its military than one who has not. The political director, often dependent for his own political success upon corporate decisions and corporations, is also wiser to choose a man with corporate experience. Thus, by virtue of the very criterion of success, the interchange of personnel and the unity of the power elite is increased.

Given the formal similarity of the three hierarchies in which the several members of the elite spend their working lives, given the ramifications of the decisions made in each upon the others, given the coincidence of interest that prevails among them at many points, and given the administrative vacuum of the American civilian state along with its enlargement of tasks—given these trends of structure, and adding to them the psychological affinities we have noted—we should indeed be surprised were we to find that men said to be skilled in administrative contacts and full of organizing ability would fail to do more than get in touch with one another. They have, of course, done much more than that: increasingly, they assume positions in one another's domains.

The unity revealed by the interchangeability of top roles rests upon the parallel development of the top jobs in each of the big three domains. The interchange occurs most frequently at the points of their coinciding interest, as between regulatory agency and the regulated industry; contracting agency and contractor. And, as we shall see, it leads to co-ordinations that are more explicit, and even formal.

The inner core of the power elite consists, first, of those who interchange commanding roles at the top of one dominant institutional order with those in another: the admiral who is also a banker and a lawyer and who heads up an important federal commission; the corporation executive whose company was one of the two or three leading war materiel producers who is now the Secretary of Defense; the wartime general who dons civilian clothes to sit on the political directorate and then becomes a member of the board of directors of a leading economic corporation.

Although the executive who becomes a general, the general who becomes a statesman, the statesman who becomes a banker, see much more than ordinary men in their ordinary environments, still the perspectives of even such men often remain tied to their dominant locales. In their very career, however, they interchange roles within the big three and thus readily transcend the particularity of interest in any one of these institutional milieux. By their very careers and activities, they lace the three types of milieux together. They are, accordingly, the core members of the power elite.

These men are not necessarily familiar with every major arena of power. We refer to one man who moves in and between perhaps two circles—say the industrial and the military—and to another man who moves in the military and the political, and to a third who moves in the political as well as among opinion-makers. These in-between types most closely display our image of the power elite's structure and operation, even of behind-the-scenes operations. To the extent that there is any "invisible elite," these advisory and liaison types are its core. Even if—as I believe to be very likely—many of them are, at least in the first part of their careers, "agents" of the various elites rather than themselves elite, it is they who are most active in organizing the several top milieux into a structure of power and maintaining it.

The inner core of the power elite also includes men of the higher legal and financial type from the great law factories and investment firms, who are almost professional go-betweens of economic, political and military affairs, and who thus act to unify the power elite. The corporation lawyer and the investment banker perform the functions of the "go-between" effectively and powerfully. By the nature of their work, they transcend the narrower milieu of any one industry, and accordingly are in a position to speak and act for the corporate world or at least sizable sectors of it. The corporation lawyer is a key link between the economic and military and political areas; the investment banker is a key organizer and unifier of the corporate world and a person well versed in spending the huge amounts of money the American military establishment now ponders. When you get a lawyer who handles the legal work of investment bankers you get a key member of the power elite.

During the Democratic era, one link between private corporate organizations and governmental institutions was the investment house of Dillon, Read. From it came such men as James Forrestal and Charles F. Detmar, Jr.; Ferdinand Eberstadt had once been a partner in it before he branched out into his own investment house from which came other men to political and military circles. Republican administrations seem to favor the investment firm of Kuhn, Loeb and the advertising firm of Batten, Barton, Durstine and Osborn.

Regardless of administrations, there is always the law firm of Sullivan and Cromwell. Mid-West investment banker Cyrus Eaton has said that "Arthur H. Dean, a senior partner of Sullivan & Cromwell of No. 48 Wall Street, was one of those who assisted in the drafting of the Securities Act of 1933, the first of the series of bills passed to regulate the capital markets. He and his firm, which is reputed to be the largest in the United States, have maintained close relations with the SEC since its creation, and theirs is the dominating influence on the Commission." [12]

There is also the third largest bank in the United States: the Chase National Bank of New York (now Chase-Manhattan). Regardless of political administration, executives of this bank and those of the International Bank of Reconstruction and Development have changed positions: John J. McCloy, who became Chairman of the Chase National in 1953, is a former president of the World Bank; and his successor to the presidency of the World Bank was a former senior vice-president of the Chase National Bank.[13] And in 1953, the president of the Chase National Bank, Winthrop W. Aldrich, had left to become Ambassador to Great Britain.

The outermost fringes of the power elite—which change more than its core—consist of "those who count" even though they may not be "in" on given decisions of consequence nor in their career move between the hierarchies. Each member of the power elite need not be a man who personally decides every decision that is to be ascribed to the power elite. Each member, in the decisions that he does make, takes the others seriously into account. They not only make decisions in the several major areas of war and peace; they are the men who, in decisions in which they take no direct part, are taken into decisive account by those who are directly in charge.

On the fringes and below them, somewhat to the side of the lower echelons, the power elite fades off into the middle levels of power, into the rank and file of the Congress, the pressure groups that are not vested in the power elite itself, as well as a multiplicity of regional and state and local interests. If all the men on the middle levels are not among those who count, they sometimes must be taken into account, handled, cajoled, broken or raised to higher circles.

When the power elite find that in order to get things done they must reach below their own realms—as is the case when it is necessary to get bills passed through Congress—they themselves must exert some pressure. But among the power elite, the name for such high-level lobbying is "liaison work." There are "liaison" military men with Congress, with certain wayward sections of industry, with practically every important element not directly concerned with the power elite. The two men on the White House staff who are *named* "liaison" men are both experienced in military matters; one of them is a former investment banker and lawyer as well as a general.

Not the trade associations but the higher cliques of lawyers and investment bankers are the active political heads of the corporate rich and the members of the power elite. "While it is generally assumed that the national associations carry tremendous weight in formulating public opinion and directing the course of national policy, there is some evidence to indicate that interaction between associations on a formal level is not a very tight-knit affair. The general tendency within associations seems to be to stimulate activities around the specific interests of the organization, and more effort is made to educate its members rather than to spend much time in trying to influence other associations on the issue at hand . . . As media for stating and re-stating the over-all value structure of the nation they (the trade associations) are important . . . But when issues are firmly drawn, individuals related to the larger corporate interests are called upon to exert pressure in the proper places at the strategic time. The national associations may act as media for co-ordinating such pressures, but a great volume of intercommunication between members at the apex of power of the larger corporate interests seems to be the decisive factor in final policy determination." [14]

Conventional "lobbying," carried on by trade associations, still exists, although it usually concerns the middle levels of power—usually being targeted at Congress and, of course, its own rank and file members. The important function of the National Association of Manufacturers, for example, is less directly to influence policy than to reveal to small businessmen that their interests are the same as those of larger businesses. But there is also "high-level lobbying." All over the country the corporate leaders are drawn into the circle of the high military and political through personal friendship, trade and professional associations and their various subcommittees, prestige clubs, open political affiliation, and customer relationships. "There is . . . an awareness among these power leaders," one first-hand investigator of such executive cliques has asserted, "of many of the current major policy issues before the nation such as keeping taxes down, turning all productive operations over to private enterprises, increasing foreign trade, keeping governmental welfare and other domestic activities to a minimum, and strengthening and maintaining the hold of the current party in power nationally." [15]

There are, in fact, cliques of corporate executives who are more important as informal opinion leaders in the top echelons of corporate, military, and political power than as actual participants in military and political organizations. Inside military circles and inside political circles and "on the sidelines" in the economic area, these circles and cliques of corporation executives are in on most all major decisions regardless of topic. And what is important about all this high-level lobbying is that it is done within the confines of that elite.

6

The conception of the power elite and of its unity rests upon the corresponding developments and the coincidence of interests among economic, political, and military organizations. It also rests upon the similarity of origin and outlook, and the social and personal intermingling of the top circles from each of these dominant hierarchies. This conjunction of institutional and psychological forces, in turn, is revealed by the heavy personnel traffic within and between the big three institutional orders, as well as by the rise of go-betweens as in the high-level lobbying. The conception of the power elite, accordingly, does *not* rest upon the assumption that American history since the origins of World War II must be understood as a secret plot, or as a great and co-ordinated conspiracy of the members of this elite. The conception rests upon quite impersonal grounds.

There is, however, little doubt that the American power elite—which contains, we are told, some of "the greatest organizers in the world"—has also planned and has plotted. The rise of the elite, as we have already made clear, was not and could not have been caused by a plot; and the tenability of the conception does not rest upon the existence of any secret or any publicly known organization. But, once the conjunction of structural trend and of the personal will to utilize it gave rise to the power elite, then plans and programs did occur to its members and indeed it is not possible to interpret many events and official policies of the fifth epoch without reference to the power elite. "There is a great difference," Richard Hofstadter has remarked, "between locating conspiracies *in* history and saying that history *is*, in effect, a conspiracy . . ." [16]

The structural trends of institutions become defined as opportunities by those who occupy their command posts. Once such opportunities are recognized, men may avail themselves of them. Certain types of men from each of the dominant institutional areas, more far-sighted than others, have actively promoted the liaison before it took its truly modern shape. They have often done so for reasons not shared by their partners, although not objected to by them either; and often the outcome of their liaison has had consequences which none of them foresaw, much less shaped, and which only later in the course of development came under explicit control. Only after it was well under way did most of its members find themselves part of it and become gladdened, although sometimes also worried, by this fact. But once the co-ordination is a going concern, new men come readily into it and assume its existence without question.

So far as explicit organization—conspiratorial or not—is concerned, the power elite, by its very nature, is more likely to use existing organizations, working within and between them, than to set up explicit organizations whose membership is strictly limited to its own members. But if there is no machinery in existence to ensure, for example, that military and political factors will be balanced in decisions made, they will invent such machinery and use it, as with the National Security Council. Moreover, in a formally democratic polity, the aims and the powers of the various elements of this elite are further supported by an aspect of the permanent war economy: the assumption that the security of the nation supposedly rests upon great secrecy of plan and intent. Many higher events that would reveal the working of the power elite can be withheld from public knowledge under the guise of secrecy. With the wide secrecy covering their operations and decisions, the power elite can mask their intentions, operations, and further consolidation. Any secrecy that is imposed upon those in positions to observe high decision-makers clearly works for and not against the operations of the power elite.

There is accordingly reason to suspect—but by the nature of the case, no proof—that the power elite is not altogether "surfaced." There is nothing hidden about it, although its activities are not publicized. As an elite, it is not organized, although its members often know one another, seem quite naturally to work together, and share many organizations in common. There is nothing conspiratorial about it, although its decisions are often publicly unknown and its mode of operation manipulative rather than explicit.

It is not that the elite "believe in" a compact elite behind the scenes and a a mass down below. It is not put in that language. It is just that the people are of necessity confused and must, like trusting children, place all the new world of foreign policy and strategy and executive action in the hands of experts. It is just that everyone knows somebody has got to run the show, and that somebody usually does. Others do not really care anyway, and besides, they do not know how. So the gap between the two types gets wider.

When crises are defined as total, and as seemingly permanent, the consequences of decision become total, and the decisions in each major area of life come to be integrated and total. Up to a point, these consequences for other institutional orders can be assessed; beyond such points, chances have to be taken. It is then that the felt scarcity of trained and imaginative judgment leads to plaintive feelings among executives about the shortage of qualified successors in political, military, and economic life. This feeling, in turn, leads to an increasing concern with the training of successors who could take over as older men of power retire.[17] In each area, there slowly arises a new generation which has grown up in an age of co-ordinated decisions.

In each of the elite circles, we have noticed this concern to recruit and to train successors as "broad-gauge" men, that is, as men capable of making decisions that involve institutional areas other than their own. The chief executives have set up formal recruitment and training programs to man the corporate world as virtually a state within a state. Recruitment and training for the military elite has long been rigidly professionalized, but has now come to include educational routines of a sort which the remnants of older generals and admirals consider quite nonsensical.

Only the political order, with its absence of a genuine civil service, has lagged behind, creating an administrative vacuum into which military bureaucrats and corporate outsiders have been drawn. But even in this domain, since World War II, there have been repeated attempts, by elite men of such vision as the late James Forrestal's, to inaugurate a career service that would include periods in the corporate world as well as in the governmental.[18]

What is lacking is a truly common elite program of recruitment and training; for the prep school, Ivy League College, and law school sequence of the metropolitan 400 is not up to the demands now made upon members of the power elite.[19] Britishers, such as Field Marshall Viscount Montgomery, well aware of this lack, recently urged the adoption of a system "under which a minority of high-caliber young students could be separated from the mediocre and given the best education possible to supply the country with leadership." His proposal is echoed, in various forms, by many who accept his criticism of "the American theory of public education on the ground that it is ill-suited to produce the "elite" group of leaders . . . this country needs to fulfill its obligations of world leadership." [20]

In part these demands reflect the unstated need to transcend recruitment on the sole basis of economic success, especially since it is suspect as often involving the higher immorality; in part it reflects the stated need to have men who, as Viscount Montgomery says, know "the meaning of discipline." But above all these demands reflect the at least vague consciousness on the part of the power elite themselves that the age of co-ordinated decisions, entailing a newly enormous range of consequences, requires a power elite that is of a new caliber. In so far as the sweep of matters which go into the making of decisions is vast and interrelated, the information needed for judgments complex and requiring particularized knowledge,[21] the men in charge will not only call upon one another; they will try to train their successors for the work at hand. These new men will grow up as men of power within the co-ordination of economic and political and military decision.

7

The idea of the power elite rests upon and enables us to make sense of (1) the decisive institutional trends that characterize the structure of our epoch, in particular, the military ascendancy in a privately incorporated economy, and more broadly, the several coincidences of objective interests between economic, military, and political institutions; (2) the social similarities and the psychological affinities of the men who occupy the command posts of these structures, in particular the increased interchangeability of the top positions in each of them and the increased traffic between these orders in the careers of men of power; (3) the ramifications, to the point of virtual totality, of the kind of decisions that are made at the top, and the rise to power of a set of men who, by training and bent, are professional organizers of considerable force and who are unrestrained by democratic party training.

Negatively, the formation of the power elite rests upon (1) the relegation of the professional party politician to the middle levels of power, (2) the semi-organized stalemate of the interests of sovereign localities into which the legislative function has fallen, (3) the virtually complete absence of a civil service that constitutes a politically neutral, but politically relevant, depository of brainpower and executive skill, and (4) the increased official secrecy behind which great decisions are made without benefit of public or even Congressional debate.

As a result, the political directorate, the corporate rich, and the ascendant military have come together as the power elite, and the expanded and centralized hierarchies which they head have encroached upon the old balances and have now relegated them to the middle levels of power. Now the balancing society is a conception that pertains accurately to the middle levels, and on that level the balance has become more often an affair of intrenched provincial and nationally irresponsible forces and demands than a center of power and national decision.

But how about the bottom? As all these trends have become visible at the top and on the middle, what has been happening to the great American public? If the top is unprecedentedly powerful and increasingly unified and willful; if the middle zones are increasingly a semi-organized stalemate—in what shape is the bottom, in what condition is the public at large? The rise of the power elite, we shall now see, rests upon, and in some ways is part of, the transformation of the publics of America into a mass society.

NOTES

[1] Cf. Elmer Davis, *But We Were Born Free* (Indianapolis: Bobbs-Merrill, 1953), p. 187.

[2] For points used to characterize the first and second of these phases, I have drawn from Robert Lamb, "Political Elites and the Process of Economic Development," *The Progress of Underdeveloped Areas* (Edited by Bert Hoselitz) (Chicago: The University of Chicago Press, 1952).

[3] Henry Cabot Lodge, *Early Memoirs,* cited by Dixon Wecter, *The Saga of American Society* (New York: Scribner's, 1937), p. 206.

[4] Lord James Bryce, *The American Commonwealth* (New York: Macmillan, 1918), vol. I, pp. 84–5. In pre-revolutionary America, regional differences were of course important; but see: William E. Dodd, *The Cotton Kingdom* (Volume 27 of the Chronicles of America Series, edited by Allen Johnson) (New Haven: Yale University Press, 1919), p. 41; Louis B. Wright, *The First Gentlemen of Virginia* (Huntington Library, 1940), Chapter 12; Samuel Morison and Henry S. Commager, *The Growth of the American Republic* (New York: Oxford University Press, 1950), pp. 177–8; James T. Adams, *Provincial Society, 1690–1763* (New York: Macmillan, 1927), p. 83.

[5] Cf., for example, David Riesman, in collaboration with Reuel Denney and Nathan Glazer, *The Lonely Crowd* (New Haven: Yale University Press, 1950).

[6] See the Hearings of the Pujo Committee, quoted in Richard Hofstadter, *The Age of Reform* (New York: Knopf, 1955), p. 230; and Louis D. Brandeis, *Other People's Money* (New York: Stokes, 1932), pp. 22–3.

[7] Richard Hofstadter, op. cit., p. 305.

[8] Whittaker Chambers, *Witness* (New York: Random House, 1952), p. 550.

[9] For an excellent introduction to the international unity of corporate interests, see James Stewart Martin, *All Honorable Men* (Boston: Little, Brown, 1950).

[10] Gerald W. Johnson, "The Superficial Aspect," *New Republic,* 25 October 1954, p. 7.

[11] See the Hearings before the Committee on Armed Services, United States Senate, Eighty-third Congress, First Session. On Nominees Designate Charles E. Wilson, Roger M. Keyes, Robert T. Stevens, Robert B. Anderson, and Harold E. Talbot, 15, 16, and 23 January 1953 (Washington, D.C.: U.S. Government Printing Office, 1953).

[12] Hearings before the Subcommittee on Study of Monopoly Power of the Committee on the Judiciary, House of Representatives, Eighty-first Congress, First Session, Serial No. 14, Part 2-A (Washington, D.C.: U.S. Government Printing Office, 1950), p. 468.

[13] Cf. *The New York Times,* 6 December 1952, p. 1.

[14] Floyd Hunter, "Pilot Study of National Power and Policy Structures." Institute for Research in Social Science, University of North Carolina, Research Previews, vol. 2, No. 2, March 1954 (mimeo), p. 8.

[15] Ibid. p. 9.

[16] Richard Hofstadter, op. cit., pp. 71–2.

[17] Cf. Gerth and Mills, *Character and Social Structure* (New York: Harcourt, Brace, 1953).

[18] Cf. Mills, "The Conscription of America," *Common Sense,* April 1945, pp. 15 ff.

[19] Cf. "Twelve of the Best American Schools," *Fortune,* January 1936, p. 48.

[20] Speech of Field Marshall Viscount Montgomery at Columbia University as reported in *The New York Times,* 24 November 1954, p. 25.

[21] Cf. Dean Acheson, "What a Secretary of State Really Does," *Harper's,* December 1954, p. 48.

2. IMAGES OF POWER

David Riesman with Nathan Glazer and Reuel Denney

In the United States the more opulent citizens take great care not to stand aloof from the people; on the contrary, they constantly keep on easy terms with the lower classes; they listen to them, they speak to them every day. They know that the rich in democracies always stand in need of the poor, and that in democratic times you attach a poor man to you more by your manner than by benefits conferred.

Tocqueville, *Democracy in America*

There has been in the last fifty years a change in the configuration of power in America, in which a single hierarchy with a ruling class at its head has been replaced by a number of "veto groups" among which power is dispersed. This change has many complex roots and complex consequences, including the change in political mood from moralizing to tolerance. A clear-cut power structure helped to create the clarity of goals of the inner-directed; an amorphous power structure helps to create the consumer orientation of the other-directed.

I. THE LEADERS AND THE LED

There have been two periods in American history in which a sharply defined ruling class emerged. In the late eighteenth and early nineteenth centuries the Federalist leadership—landed-gentry and mercantilist-money leadership—certainly thought of itself as, and was, a ruling group. Long before its leadership was actually dislodged, its power was disputed and, in decisive instances, overruled in the northern and middle states by yeoman farmers and artisans. These latter, having little time or gift for politics, ordinarily left it to their "betters," but they retained a veto on what was done and occasionally, as with Jackson moved into a more positive command. After the Civil War, however, farmers and artisans lost their capacity to check what was done, and the captains of industry emerged as a ruling class. During their hegemony the images and the actualities of power in America coincided more closely than I think they do today.

Captains of Industry and Captains of Consumption

According to this view of the matter, the election of 1896 appears as an historical watershed: the high point of oligarchic rule. In terms of political style, there were moralizers for Bryan and moralizers for McKinley. And there were groups that, whether or not they saw their interests in moral terms, had a clear picture of themselves and of their interests; they, too, responded to the election in an inner-directed way. Only a few people like Brooks Adams,

27

who supported Bryan out of his hatred for the "gold-bugs," were aware of some of the ambiguities in the positions of both candidates.

Certainly, the victorious leaders—McKinley, Hanna, and Morgan in their several bailiwicks—were not aware of ambiguity. The success of their electoral bid is less important to us than the mood of their undertaking, which was one of conscious leadership, directed by conscious class considerations. This self-conscious leadership took support from the close connection, to which I have already called attention, between politics and work. The world of work was the great world; politics was an extension that could either facilitate work or sabotage it. While bankers and Grangers had different notions as to what work politics should do and what leave undone, they agreed as to the primacy of the production side of life.

Of course, the political sphere was not devoid of entertainment for the inner-directed man: with its opportunity for cracker-barrel argument, beer drinking, and shirt-sleeved good-fellowship by torchlight, it had its occasional uses as a "downward" escape from the dignities of work and the propertied existence. But the great difference from today is that the leaders went into politics to do a job—primarily to assure the conquest of American resources—rather than to seek a responsive audience. As Rockefeller sold his oil more by force or cheapness than by brand, so the late nineteenth-century political leader sold his wares (votes or decisions) to the highest bidder. Either cash or morality might bid—but not "good will" as such.

This situation and these inner-directed motivations gave a clarity to the political and social scene in 1896 that it does not appear to have had in Tocqueville's day and has not had since. The bullet that killed McKinley marked the end of the days of explicit class leadership. Muckraking and savage political cartooning—arts that depend on clarity of line—continued for a time and of course have not quite vanished yet. But as the old-time religion depended on a clear image of heaven and hell and clear judgments of good and evil, so the old-time politics depended on a clear class structure and the clear and easily moralized judgments of good and bad that flow from it. It depended, too, and I cannot emphasize the point too much, on an agreement between leaders and led that the work sphere of life was dominant. And because the goals were clear, the obvious job of the leader was to lead; of the led, to follow. Their political cooperation, like their cooperation in industry and agriculture, was based on mutual interests, whether directly moralized or not, rather than on mutual preferences and likings.

What I have said must be taken as an "ideal-typical" political portrait of the age, useful by way of contrast to our own times. Actually, the changes are, as always, changes in emphasis and degree, and the portrait would be seriously overdrawn if the reader should conclude that no emotional moods, no cravings for charisma and glamor, eddied about the relations between leaders and led. These relations were not built entirely out of sober moralizing and well-understood economic interests, but occasionally, as Veblen described matters, the Captain of Industry served to provide the underlying population with personages to admire "to the greater spiritual comfort of all parties concerned."

Ruling-class theories, applied to contemporary America, seem to be spectral survivals of this earlier time. The captain of industry no longer runs business, no longer runs politics, and no longer provides legitimate "spiritual comfort." Here and there, it is true, there are survivals. In the booming Southwest, Texas still produces men like Glenn McCarthy, and California produced an old-style lion of the jungle in A. P. Giannini (who was, significantly enough, from a family which lacked the opportunity to educate him for the newer business motivations). Yet even these types are touched by traits that were not nearly so evident in the earlier captains of industry who fascinated Veblen as Lucifer fascinated Milton. Like Henry Kaiser, they depend much more than did the older magnificoes on public opinion and, as a corollary to public opinion, on the attitude of government. To this end they tend to exploit their personalities, or allow them to be exploited, in a way that makes the elder Rockefeller's Ivy Lee stunt of dime-giving seem as remote as the Fuggers.

Much more than their pre-World War I predecessors, then, these surviving captains stay within the limits as well as the possibilities of the economy of the glad hand. If they enter politics they do so because it is a sport or obligation for the rich; or simply because they are tied in with government at every step in their ramifying enterprises. These latter-day captains neither see themselves nor are recognized as political leaders who, by their presence and by what they stand for, clarify and thereby moralize politics. The elder Morgan and his friends thought it was up to them to stop Bryan and to stop the depression of 1907. No one has taken their place.

In the focus of public attention the old captains of industry have been re-placed by an entirely new type: the Captains of Non-industry, of Consumption and Leisure. Surveys of content in the mass media show a shift in the kinds of information about business and political leaders that audiences ask for.[1] In an earlier day the audience was given a story of the hero's work-minded rise to success. Today, the ladder climbing is taken for granted or is seen in terms of "the breaks," and the hero's tastes in dress, food, women, and recreation are emphasized—these are, as we have seen, the frontiers on which the reader can himself compete, while he cannot imagine himself in the work role of the presi-dent of the United States or the head of a big company.

What is more, there is a shift in such biographies from an accent on business leaders to an accent on "leaders" in consumption. Proportionately, actors, artists, entertainers, get more space than they used to, and the heroes of the office, hustings, and factory get less. These consumers of the surplus product may, in Veblen's terms, provide "spiritual comfort" by their very skill in consumption. The glamor of such heroes of consumption may reside in their incompetence in the skills of businesslike performance and, as we have seen, in some cases their wholly personal "sincerity" may do duty in place of more objective artistic criteria.

But, of course, these captains of consumption are not leaders. They are still only personalities, employed to adorn movements, not to lead them. Yet the actual leaders have much in common with them.

For an illustration we can turn to a recent American leader—undoubtedly a leader—who shared many characteristics of the artist and entertainer: Franklin

D. Roosevelt. We are accustomed to thinking of him as a man of great power. Yet his role in leading the country into war was very different from that of McKinley or even of Wilson. Think of McKinley pacing the floor of his study, deciding whether or not to ask for a declaration of war on Spain—when he already knew that Spain would capitulate. McKinley felt it was up to him; so did Wilson. Roosevelt felt he could only maneuver within very narrow limits, limits which came close to leaving the decision to the enemy.

Again, if we compare his activities during the war years with those of Churchill, we can see important differences. Churchill led the British in something like the old-time sense of an explicit relation between the leader and the followers. That he led, moreover, as a moralizing leader and not, despite his great personal charm, as a "personality," appeared in the readiness of the electorate to follow him in war and to dispense with him in peace: they were work-minded rather than consumption-minded about him. Roosevelt on the other hand remained throughout the war, as before, a powerful though tolerant persuader, even conniver and stimulator, of changes in public opinion that he followed with deep concern at all times. Churchill exploited his indignation, Roosevelt his charm.

The obviously real differences in the military situation of Britain and the United States during this period are not sufficent to explain these differences in the mood and method of leadership. Much more important than the wartime differences between the two countries are the differing shifts in political pattern during the last half century. America in the 90's could be led politically and morally. Since then we have entered a social and political phase in which power is dispersed among veto groups. These groups are too many and diverse to be led by moralizing; what they want is too various to be moralized and too intangible to be bought off for cash alone; and what is called political leadership consists, as we could see in Roosevelt's case, in the tolerant ability to manipulate coalitions.

This means that the men who, at an earlier historical period, were political leaders are now busy with the other-directed occupation of studying the feedback from all the others—their constituencies, their correspondents, and friends and enemies within influential pressure groups. The revolution in communications makes this attention possible in ways that were not available to the equally assiduous client-cultivator of an earlier day, who could buy a few editors if he wanted favorable things said. And those who were once the followers have learned the arts of lobbying and publicity. The roll call of nineteenth- and early twentieth-century leaders contains many men who refused to follow their flock: Gladstone and Cleveland, Robert Peel and John Stuart Mill (as M.P.), Woodrow Wilson and Winston Churchill. Even today the need to impose unpopular courses brings to the fore inner-directed types: Cripps, for instance, in England; Stimson and Robert Patterson in this country. Of course, political figures in all ages have been dependent on their following, and opportunism and manipulation are not a twentieth-century discovery. The inner-directed leader, however, was quite conscious of discrepancies between his views and those of others; if he shifted his courses, it was still *his* course. Moreover, since he was ambitious, he might well prefer later fame to momentary warmth of response;

in any event he did not need to have everybody love him, but only those who mattered for his fortunes.

In his autobiography, John Stuart Mill tells the following story:

In the pamphlet, "Thoughts on Parliamentary Reform," I had said, rather bluntly, that the working classes, though differing from those of some other countries, in being ashamed of lying, are yet generally liars. This passage some opponent got printed in a placard which was handed to me at a meeting, chiefly composed of the working classes, and I was asked whether I had written and published it. I at once answered "I did." Scarcely were these two words out of my mouth, when vehement applause resounded through the whole meeting.

It is interesting to compare this incident with the practices of certain American public figures who not only would not think of saying anything that might offend an audience but who frequently depart from a prepared text, carefully designed to please a wide audience, in order to mollify the smaller face-to-face group before whom the speech happens to be delivered.

The old-time captain of industry was also a captain of consumption: what standards were set, were set by him. He was also a captain of politics. The new captain of consumption who has usurped his place in the public eye is limited severely to the sphere of consumption—which itself has of course greatly expanded. Today, the personalities from the leisure world, no matter how much loved, lack the strength and the situation for leadership. If a movie star of today tries to put across a political message, in or out of films, he finds himself vulnerable to all sorts of pressures. The movie producer is no more powerful. The Catholics, the Methodists, the organized morticians, the state department, the southerners, the Jews, the doctors, all put their pressure on the vehicle that is being prepared for mass distribution. Piety or decency protects some minority groups that have no lobbies. The movie maker acts as a broker among these veto groups in a situation much too intricate to encourage his taking a firm, moralizing stance. At best, he or someone in his organization may sneak a moral and political message into the film as Roosevelt or someone in his organization sneaked over an appointment or a new coordinating agency. The message, the appointment, the agency—none of them could get very far in the Alice in Wonderland croquet game of the veto groups.

II. WHO HAS THE POWER?

The Veto Groups. The shifting nature of the lobby provides us with an important clue as to the difference between the present American political scene and that of the age of McKinley. The ruling class of businessmen could relatively easily (though perhaps mistakenly) decide where their interests lay and what editors, lawyers, and legislators might be paid to advance them. The lobby ministered to the clear leadership, privilege, and imperative of the business ruling class.

Today we have substituted for that leadership a series of groups, each of which has struggled for and finally attained a power to stop things conceivably inimical to its interests and, within far narrower limits, to start things. The various business groups, large and small, the movie-censoring groups, the farm groups and the labor and professional groups, the major ethnic groups and major regional groups, have in many instances succeeded in maneuvering themselves into a position in which they are able to neutralize those who might attack them. The very increase in the number of these groups, and in the kinds of interests "practical" and "fictional" they are protecting, marks, therefore, a decisive change from the lobbies of an earlier day. There is a change in method, too, in the way the groups are organized, the way they handle each other, and the way they handle the public, that is, the unorganized.

These veto groups are neither leader-groups nor led-groups. The only leaders of national scope left in the United States today are those who can placate the veto groups. The only followers left in the United Staes today are those unorganized and sometimes disorganized unfortunates who have not yet invented their group.

Within the veto groups, there is, of course, the same struggle for top places that goes on in other bureaucratic setups. Among the veto groups competition is monopolistic; rules of fairness and fellowship dictate how far one can go. Despite the rules there are, of course, occasional "price wars," like the jurisdictional disputes of labor unions or Jewish defense groups; these are ended by negotiation, the division of territory, and the formation of a roof organization for the previously split constituency. These big monopolies, taken as a single group, are in devastating competition with the not yet grouped, much as the fair-trade economy competes against the free-trade economy. These latter scattered followers find what protection they can in the interstices around the group-minded.[2]

Each of the veto groups in this pattern is capable of an aggressive move, but the move is sharply limited in its range by the way in which the various groups have already cut up the sphere of politics and arrayed certain massive expectations behind each cut. Both within the groups and in the situation created by their presence, the political mood tends to become one of otherdirected tolerance. The vetoes so bind action that it is hard for the moralizers to conceive of a program that might in any large way alter the relations between political and personal life or between political and economic life. In the amorphous power structure created by the veto groups it is hard to distinguish rulers from the ruled, those to be aided from those to be opposed, those on your side from those on the other side. This very pattern encourages the inside-dopester who can unravel the personal linkages, and discourages the enthusiast or indignant who wants to install the good or fend off the bad. Probably, most of all it encourages the new-style indifferent who feels and is often told that his and everyone else's affairs are in the hands of the experts and that laymen, though they should "participate," should not really be too inquisitive or aroused.

By their very nature the veto groups exist as defense groups, not as leadership groups. If it is true that they do "have the power," they have it by virtue of a necessary mutual tolerance. More and more they mirror each other in their style of political action, including their interest in public relations and their emphasis on internal harmony of feelings. There is a tendency for organizations as differently oriented as, say, the Young Socialists and the 4-H Club, to adopt similar psychological methods of salesmanship to obtain and solidify their recruits.

This does not mean, however, that the veto groups are formed along the lines of character structure. As in a business corporation there is room for extreme inner-directed and other-directed types, and all mixtures between, so in a veto group there can exist complex symbiotic relationships among people of different political styles. Thus a team of lobbyists may include both moralizers and inside-dopesters, sometimes working in harness, sometimes in conflict; and the constituency of the team may be composed mainly of new-style political indifferents who have enough literacy and organizational experience to throw weight around when called upon. Despite these complications I think it fair to say that the veto groups, even when they are set up to protect a clear-cut moralizing interest, are generally forced to adopt the political manners of the other-directed.

In saying this I am talking about the national scene. The smaller the constituency, of course, the smaller the number of veto groups involved and the greater the chance that some one of them will be dominant. Thus, in local politics there is more indignation and less tolerance, just as even the *Chicago Tribune* is a tolerant paper in comparison with the community throwaways in many Chicago neighborhoods.

The same problem may be considered from another perspective. Various groups have discovered that they can go quite far in the amorphous power situation in America without being stopped. Our society is behaviorally open enough to permit a considerable community of gangsters a comfortable living under a variety of partisan political regimes. In their lack of concern for public relations these men are belated businessmen. So are some labor leaders who have discovered their power to hold up the economy, though in most situations what is surprising is the moderation of labor demands—a moderation based more on psychological restraints than on any power that could effectively be interposed. Likewise, it is sometimes possible for an aggressive group, while not belonging to the entrenched veto-power teams, to push a bill through a legislature. Thus, the original Social Security Act went through Congress, so far as I can discover, because it was pushed by a devoted but tiny cohort; the large veto groups including organized labor were neither very much for it nor very much against it.

For similar reasons those veto groups are in many political situations strongest whose own memberships are composed of veto groups, especially veto groups of one. The best example of this is the individual farmer who, after one of the farm lobbies had made a deal for him, can still hold out for more. The farm lobby's concern for the reaction of other veto groups, such as labor unions, cuts little ice with the individual farmer. This fact may strengthen the lobby in a negotiation: it can use its internal public relations problems as a counter in bargaining, very much as does a diplomat who tells a foreign minister that he must consider how Senator so-and-so will react. For, no matter what the other-directedness of the lobby's leaders, they cannot bind their membership to carry out a public relations approach. Many labor unions have a similar power because they cannot control their memberships who, if not satisfied with a deal made by the union, can walk off or otherwise sabotage a job.

In contrast, those veto groups are often weaker whose other-directed orientation can dominate their memberships. Large corporations are vulnerable to a call from the White House because, save for a residual indignant like Sewell Avery, their officials are themselves other-directed and because, once the word from the chief goes out, the factory superintendents, no matter how boiling mad, have to fall into line with the new policy by the very nature of the centralized organization for which they work: they can sabotage top management on minor matters but not, say, on wage rates or tax accounting. As against this, the American Catholic Church possesses immense veto-group power because it combines a certain amount of centralized command—and a public picture of a still greater amount—with a highly decentralized priesthood (each priest is in a sense his own trade association secretary) and a membership organization of wide-ranging ethnic, social, and political loyalties; this structure permits great flexibility in bargaining.

These qualifications, however, do not change the fact that the veto groups, taken together, constitute a new buffer region between the old, altered, and thinning extremes of those who were once leaders and led. It is both the attenuation of leaders and led, and the other-oriented doings of these buffers, that help to give many moralizers a sense of vacuum in American political life.

The veto groups, by the conditions their presence creates and by the requirements they set for leadership in politics, foster the tolerant mood of other-direction and hasten the retreat of the inner-directed indignants.

Is There A Ruling Class Left?

Nevertheless, people go on acting as if there still were a decisive ruling class in contemporary America. In the postwar years, businessmen thought labor leaders and politicians ran the country, while labor and the left thought that "Wall Street" ran it, or the "sixty families." Wall Street, confused perhaps by its dethronement as a telling barometer of capital-formation weather, may have thought that the midwestern industrial barons, cushioned on plant expansion money in the form of heavy depreciation reserves and undivided profits, ran the country. They might have had some evidence for this in the fact that the New Deal was much tougher with finance capital—e.g., the SEC and the Holding Company Act—than with industrial capital and that when, in the undistributed profits tax, it tried to subject the latter to a stockholder and money-market control, the tax was quickly repealed.

But these barons of Pittsburgh, Weirton, Akron, and Detroit, though certainly a tougher crowd than the Wall Streeters, are, as we saw earlier, coming more and more to think of themselves as trustees for their beneficiaries. And whereas, from the point of view of labor and the left, these men ran the War

Production Board in the interest of their respective companies, one could argue just as easily that the WPB experience was one of the congeries of factors that have tamed the barons. It put them in a situation where they had to view their company from the point of view of "the others."

Despite the absence of intensive studies of business power and of what happens in a business negotiation, one can readily get an impressionistic sense of the change in business behavior in the last generation. In the pages of *Fortune,* that excellent chronicler of business, one can see that there are few survivals of the kinds of dealings—with other businessmen, with labor, with the government—that were standard operating practice for the pre-World War I tycoons. Moreover, in its twenty-year history, *Fortune* itself has shown, and perhaps it may be considered not too unrepresentative of its audience, a steady decline of interest in business as such and a growing interest in once peripheral matters, such as international relations, social science, and other accoutrements of the modern executive.

But it is of course more difficult to know whether character has changed as well as behavior—whether, as some contend, businessmen simply rule today in a more subtle, more "managerial" way. In "Manager Meets Union" Joseph M. Goldsen and Lillian Low have depicted the psychological dependence of a contemporary sales manager on the approval of the men under him, his willingness to go to great lengths, in terms of concessions, to maintain interpersonal warmth in his relations with them, and his fierce resentment of the union as a barrier to this emotional exchange.[3] As against this, one must set the attitude of some of the auto-supply companies whose leadership still seems much more craft-oriented than people-oriented and therefore unwilling to make concessions and none too concerned with the emotional atmosphere of negotiations. Likewise, the General Motors-UAW negotiations of 1946, as reported in print, sound more like a cockfight than a Platonic symposium, although in Peter Drucker's *Concept of the Corporation,* a study of General Motors published in the same year, there is much evidence of management eagerness to build a big, happy family.

Power, indeed, is founded, in a large measure, on interpersonal expectations and attitudes. If businessmen feel weak and dependent, they do in actuality become weaker and more dependent, no matter what material resources may be ascribed to them. My impression, based mainly on experiences of my own in business and law practice, is that businessmen from large manufacturing companies, though they often talk big, are easily frightened by the threat of others' hostility; they may pound the table, but they look to others for leadership and do not care to get out of line with their peer-groupers. Possibly, attitudes toward such an irascible businessman as Sewell Avery might mark a good dividing line between the older and the newer attitudes. Those businessmen who admire Avery, though they might not dare to imitate him, are becoming increasingly an elderly minority, while the younger men generally are shocked by Avery's "highhandedness," his rebuff of the glad hand.

The desire of businessmen to be well thought of has led to the irony that each time a professor writes a book attacking business, even if almost nobody reads it, he creates jobs in industry for his students in public relations, trade association work, and market research! While the Black Horse Cavalry of an earlier era held up businessmen by threatening to let pass crippling legislation desired by anti-business moralizers, today many honest intellectuals who would not think of taking a bribe hold business or trade association jobs because their clients have been scared, perhaps by these very men, into taking cognizance of some actual or imaginary veto group. Since a large structure is built up to woo the group, no test of power is made to see whether the group has real existence or real strength. Understandably, ideologies about who has power in America are relied upon to support these amiable fictions which serve . . . to provide the modern businessman with an endless shopping list, an endless task of glad-handing. This is a far cry, I suggest, from the opportunistic glad-handing of the wealthy on which Tocqueville comments at the chapter head; very likely, what was mere practice in his day has become embedded in character in ours.

Businessmen, moreover, are not the only people who fail to exploit the power position they are supposed, in the eyes of many observers, to have. Army officers are also astonishingly timid about exercising their leadership. During the war one would have thought that the army would be relatively impervious to criticism. But frequently the generals went to great lengths to refrain from doing something about which a congressman might make an unfriendly speech. They did so even at times when they might have brushed the congressman off like an angry fly. When dealing with businessmen or labor leaders, army officers were, it seemed to me, astonishingly deferential; and this was as true of the West Pointers as of the reservists. Of course, there were exceptions, but in many of the situations where the armed services made concessions to propitiate some veto group, they rationalized the concessions in terms of morale or of postwar public relations or, frequently, simply were not aware of their power.

To be sure, some came to the same result by the route of a democratic tradition of civilian dominance. Very likely, it was a good thing for the country that the services were so self-restrained. I do not here deal with the matter on the merits but use it as an illustration of changing character and changing social structure.

All this may lead to the question: well, who really runs things? What people fail to see is that, while it may take leadership to start things running, or to stop them, very little leadership is needed once things are under way—that, indeed, things can get terribly snarled up and still go on running. If one studies a factory, an army group, or other large organization, one wonders how things get done at all, with the lack of leadership and with all the featherbedding. Perhaps they get done because we are still trading on our reserves of inner-direction, especially in the lower ranks. At any rate, the fact they do get done is no proof that there is someone in charge.

There are, of course, still some veto groups that have more power than others and some individuals who have more power than others. But the determination of who these are has to be made all over again for our time: we cannot be satisfied with the answers given by Marx, Mosca, Michels, Pareto, Weber, Veblen, or Burnham, though we can learn from all of them.

There are also phenomena in this vast country that evade all of them (and surely, too, evade my collaborators and me). One example is the immense power, both political and economic, possessed by Artie Samish, allegedly the veto-group boss of California. Samish is a new-type lobbyist, who represents not one but scores of interests, often competing ones, from truckers to chiropractors, and who plays one veto group off against others to shake them down and strengthen his own power: he has learned how the other-orientation of the established veto groups will lead them to call still other groups into being through his auspices. Since the old-line parties have little power in California, there is no way of reaching a clear-cut decision for or against a particular veto group through the party system; instead, the state officials have become dependent on Samish for electoral support, or at least nonopposition, through his herded groups of voters and their cash contributions; moreover, he knows how to go directly to the people through the "democratic" plebiscite machinery.[4]

Carey McWilliams has observed that Samish's power rests both on the peculiar election machinery of the state and on the fact that no one industry or allied group of industries, no one union, one ethnic group or region, is dominant. The situation is very different in a state like Montana, where copper is pivotal, and one must be either for the union or for Anaconda. It is different again in Virginia where, as V. O. Key shows in *Southern Politics*, the setup of the state constitution favors control by the old courthouse crowd. In view of these divergences, rooted in local legal niceties as well as in major social and economic factors, it is apparent that any discussion of class and power on the national scene can at best be only an approximation. Yet I would venture to say that the United States is on the whole more like California in its variety—but without its veto boss—than like Montana and Virginia in their particularity. The vaster number of veto groups, and their greater power, mean that no one man or small group of men can amass the power nationally that Artie Samish and, in earlier days, Huey Long, have held locally.

Rather, power on the national scene must be viewed in terms of issues. It is possible that, where an issue involves only two or three veto groups, themselves tiny minorities, the official or unofficial broker among the groups can be quite powerful—but only on that issue. However, where the issue involves the country as a whole, no individual or group leadership is likely to be very effective, because the entrenched veto groups cannot be budged: unlike a party that may be defeated at the polls, or a class that may be replaced by another class, the veto groups are always "in."

One might ask whether one would not find, over a long period of time, that decisions in America favored one group or class—thereby, by definition, the ruling group or class—over others. Does not wealth exert its pull in the long run? In the past this has been so; for the future I doubt it. The future seems to be in the hands of the small business and professional men who control Congress, such as realtors, lawyers, car salesmen, undertakers, and so on; of the military men who control defense and, in part, foreign policy; of the big business managers and their lawyers, finance-committee men, and other counselors who decide on plant investment and influence the rate of technological change; of the labor leaders who control worker productivity and worker votes; of the black belt whites who have the greatest stake in southern politics; of the Poles, Italians, Jews, and Irishmen who have stakes in foreign policy, city jobs, and ethnic religious and cultural organizations; of the editorializers and storytellers who help socialize the young, tease and train the adult, and amuse and annoy the aged; of the farmers—themselves a warring congeries of cattlemen, corn men, dairymen, cotton men, and so on—who control key departments and committees and who, as the living representatives of our inner-directed past, control many of our memories; of the Russians and, to a lesser degree, other foreign powers who control much of our agenda of attention; and so on. The reader can complete the list. Power in America seems to me situational and mercurial; it resists attempts to locate it the way a molecule, under the Heisenberg principle, resists attempts simultaneously to locate it and time its velocity.

But people are afraid of this indeterminacy and amorphousness in the cosmology of power. Even those intellectuals, for instance, who feel themselves very much out of power and who are frightened of those who they think have the power, prefer to be scared by the power structures they conjure up than to face the possibility that the power structure they believe exists has largely evaporated. Most people prefer to suffer with interpretations that give their world meaning than to relax in the cave without an Ariadne's thread.

Let me now summarize the argument. . . . The inner-directed person, if he is political at all, is related to the political scene either by his morality, his well-defined interests, or both. His relationship to his opinions is close, not peripheral. The opinions are means of defending certain principles of politics. They may be highly charged and personal, as in the political discussion in the first pages of Joyce's *Portrait of the Artist as a Young Man,* or they may be highly charged and impersonal—a means of defending one's proper Bostonianship or other class position. In either case one's own opinions are felt to matter and to have some direct relationship to the objective world in which one lives.

As against this, the other-directed person, if he is political, is related to the political scene as a member of a veto group. He leaves it to the group to defend his interests, cooperating when called on to vote, to apply pressure, and so on. These pressure tactics seem to make his opinions manifest on the political level, but they actually help make it possible for him to be detached from his opinions. No longer operating as an "independent voter"—mostly an amiable fiction even in the era dependent on inner-direction—his political opinions, as such, are not felt to be related to his political function. Thus, they can serve him as a social counter in his role as a peer-group consumer of the political news-of-the-day. He can be tolerant of other opinions not only because of his characterological tolerance but also because they are "mere" opinions, interesting or amusing perhaps, but lacking the weight of even a partial, let alone a total, commitment to one's political role or action. They are "mere" opinions, moreover, because so intractable is the political world of the veto groups that opinion as such is felt to be almost irrelevant.

The inner-directed political moralizer has a firm grip—often much too firm—on the gamut of judgments that he is willing to apply anywhere and everywhere. The other-directed inside-dopester is unable to fortify any particular judgment with convictions springing from a summarized and organized emotional tone. It could be argued that the suppressed affect or emotional tone is still there, remaining hidden. Freudian doctrine would predict the return of the repressed. But it seems more likely, social habit being as powerful as it is, that the repeated suppression of such enthusiasm or moral indignation as the inner-directed man would consider natural permanently decreases the capacity of the other-directed man for those forms of response. The other-directed man may even begin as an inner-directed man who plays at being other-directed. He ends up being what he plays, and his mask becomes the perhaps inescapable reality of his style of life.

NOTES

[1] See the excellent article by Leo Lowenthal, "Biographies in Popular Magazines," *Radio Research, 1942–43,* ed. Lazarsfeld and Stanton (New York, Duell, Sloan & Pearce, 1944), p. 507. Dr. Lowenthal links the shift from "heroes of production" to "heroes of consumption" to major social changes in American life.

[2] It should be clear that monopolistic competition, both in business and politics, is competition. People are very much aware of their rivals, within and without the organization. They know who they are, but by the very nature of monopolistic competition they are seldom able to eliminate them entirely. While we have been talking of fair trade and tolerance, this should not obscure the fact that for the participants the feeling of being in a rivalrous setup is very strong. Indeed, they face the problem of so many other-directed people: how to combine the appearance of friendly, personalized, "sincere" behavior with the ruthless, sometimes almost paranoid, envies of their occupational life.

[3] "Manager Meets Union: a Case Study of Personal Immaturity," *Human Factors in Management,* ed. S. D. Hoslett (Parkville, Missouri, Park College Press, 1946), p. 77.

[4] Ironically enough, but typically enough, Samish craves the one power he does not have: social power in the society-page sense. A poor boy in origin, he can make or break businessmen and politicians but cannot get into the more exclusive clubs. And while consciously he is said to despise these social leaders whom he can so easily frighten and manipulate, he cannot purge himself of the childhood hurts and childhood images of power that make him vulnerable to their exclusion of him. In this, of course, he resembles other and better-known dictators.

I have drawn on Carey McWilliams, "Guy Who Gets Things Done," *Nation* CLXIX (1949), 31–33; and Lester Velie, "Secret Boss of California," *Collier's,* CXXIV (August 13, 20, 1949), 11–13, 12–13.

3.   POWER IN AMERICAN SOCIETY AS RESOURCE AND PROBLEM

Robert S. Lynd

The term "power" is customarily used as though everyone knew what it means. It does have clarity in its oldest social meaning, "dominance." Power as "authority" is a more inclusive concept, ranging in reference from what we call "authoritarianism" to controlled, responsible forms of representation in democracy. "Social control" is likewise widely inclusive, notable in its extension into such fluid areas as more or less active public opinion. Conversely, popular reactions to power included under the term "consent" may mean many things: People may consent because their wills have been neutralized by fear or force, or their judgments captured by propaganda. Genuine human impulses may be exploited in a false context in such enforced or contrived consent. Unforced acquiescence may rest upon habit or upon the fact that the issues as presented are too complex for the citizen and he accepts more or less willingly the solutions presented, assuming that those in authority know what they are doing. Or consent may rest upon collaboration involving understanding and informed choice.

Obviously, the term "power" refers to a pervasive phenomenon capable of taking many forms. Bertrand Russell goes so far as to suggest that power is fundamental to all analysis of men's affairs "in the same sense in which energy is the fundamental concept in physics." [1]

Present-day social scientists confront the phenomenon of power in different ways, and with varying degrees of uneasiness. Historians have long used the term "power" in a general sense to describe a wide variety of flows of events: rulers and political parties of different ideological colors come to power and lose power; nations and whole civilizations gain or decline in power; certain ideas are said to gain or to lose power; and some men grow in power and become "great." Economists recognize uneasily the growing concentration of economic power as this affects their traditional competitive model of the economy, while they for the most part avoid the political and social implications of this change in the structure of the economy. Sociologists, confronting as they must the problem of social stratification, seek prevailingly to soften the objective realities of "class," and they turn to the study of status groups and elites, of small groups, and (with the psychologists) of the "authoritarian personality." In view of this seeming avoidance of power it is relevant to note the comment by a sociologist that, while power and the power structure of society are central to sociology, no concept is more troublesome as to what it means. [2]

The general trend in the social sciences today is illustrated by the shift in emphasis in the study of government and politics. Political theorists, accepting the fact of authority "vested in" the state, long sought to find moral reasons to justify the obedience of the subject to authority and to set moral limits to the

SOURCE: Arthur Kornhauser, editor, *Problems of Power in American Democracy* (Detroit: Wayne State University Press, 1959), pp. 1–45. Reprinted by permission of the Wayne State University Press.

competence of the state. More recently, this search for a moral basis of authority and consent has become anachronistic; political philosophers have become political scientists, and their concern focuses upon the operational aspects of politics, or, stated more simply, upon how politics works. But if the earlier approach was too general and moral, the present operational approach tends towards analysis of the tactics of power without a theory of power other than the traditional liberal doctrine of the flux of competing forces. Here we see the haven that refined empiricism can provide for the modern social scientist confronted with the problem of power in society: bits of power may be analyzed in detail as tactical moves in an endless game of competing parties and pressure groups, of trends in opinion polls, of the impact of state and regional issues on voting in national elections, and so on, without ever confronting directly the massive, over-all structure of power as a weighting built into the social structure and the institutional system of the society.

The pervasiveness of power as a social phenomenon does not stem from a native unruliness or anti-social quality in human nature. Our knowledge of man has passed far beyond such earlier over-simplications as those that attributed to him an innate "lust for power" or saw him goaded or lured into action by "stick or carrot." It is not primarily the desire of some men to constrain others that makes power, in one form or another, so universal a phenomenon in society; rather, it is the necessity in each society—if it is to be a society, not a rabble—to order the relations of men and their institutional ways of achieving needed ends. As the following pages will suggest, organized power exists—always and everywhere, in societies large or small, primitive or modern—because it performs the necessary function of establishing and maintaining the version of order by which a given society in a given time and place lives.

Since order stands at the opposite pole from anarchy, it should be readily acknowledged that power in a society necessarily involves control. And as the complexity of a society increases, with specialization of functions performed and resulting intensified interdependence of parts, the prevalence of controls necessarily increases. One needs simply point to the indispensability of traffic lights in an age that values travel by automobile; or to the close and pervasive planning and management of the flow of materials and parts in relation to specialized manpower, machinery, and market that make possible the large industrial corporation. But, as E. H. Carr has remarked, ". . . more nonsense is talked on the subject of [the evils of] controls than on any other in current politics." [3] Controls may be dictated, or collectively imposed. They may be used to hem men in or to liberate them. It is not the fact of controls that endangers men's freedom, but their arbitrary or capricious use. Nor do all controls bear upon living with equal rigor; and a democratic society encourages a wide variety of controls, from formal laws to the more flexible and spontaneous controls of public opinion. The ordering of social life is a manifold process, expressing itself in many forms according to the character of the society.

Much of the confusion regarding power in contemporary society derives from the traditional identification of power with domination. It is true that the law against arson insists that, regardless of the desire of the citizen, he may not under any circumstances dispose of an unwelcome competitor by burning down his shop. In this case the collective entity we call "society" does exercise domination over its members—in the interest of a fundamental type of common welfare. We may not, however, shut our eyes to the fact that domination in the world in which we are living is by no means limited to such collectively serviceable controls. The upsurge of Nazi totalitarianism in a highly developed, civilized nation like Germany warns us of how compliant contemporary tolerance may become to the uses of dominance by means of raw force. We live today with a startled new sense of the tension between liberal democracy and the potential authoritarianism that may lie close to the surface of seemingly civilized life. Some form of power is necessary for orderly living, but where power takes the form of arbitrarily imposed dominance, it is important to recognize it as such.

A central problem here is whether it is conducive either to clear thinking about power or to its effective use to lump together as dominance both arbitrarily imposed power and the uses of organized power by democratic means to achieve democratic purposes. The identification of power with dominance obscures the fact that power in a genuine democracy may be a human resource which can be used for the enlargement of human freedom. It is my purpose to invite clear recognition of power as a social resource and to consider ways in which it may be used and abused. The traditional identification of power with dominance—riveted home in popular thought by the most widely quoted of all statements about power: Lord Acton's dictum that "power corrupts"—renders public reference to organized power in a society professing democratic values furtive and its use awkward. Liberal democracy has, accordingly, tended to resolve the problem of power by quantitative limitation of its use. And the result of this, as I shall note later, has been the progressive transference of this social resource from use for the ends of democratic society to use by private power agencies for their private purposes. If this tendency is to be reversed, it is necessary to remove the concept of power from the dubious limbo in which it now lives, and ask: Under what conditions may this social resource be used in democratic ways for democratic ends?

When I speak, here and elsewhere, of power—or of society and institutions—I do not mean to reify these abstractions. None of the three exists and decides and acts in and of itself. Each of these terms refers to an always more or less organized phenomenon, an interacting structure of people and of organizations concerned with durable interests. Power is, accordingly, a structure of concrete organized powers related, whether in conflict or accommodation, in pursuit of their respective interests. And it is not from single actions but from sustained thrusts in identifiable directions that we can infer that organized power is involved.

It should also be noted that I refer here to democracy in two senses: (1) "liberal democracy" as we know it in our American system, which yokes together a professedly democratic social structure and political system with a capitalist economy; and (2) a version of democracy in which social structure and all institutions would have coherence in expressing and implementing democratic values. To distinguish the second of these from liberal democracy,

I shall use the terms "thoroughgoing democracy" or "a society committed throughout to democratic ends."

Professor R. H. Tawney, the English social historian, says that "power is the most obvious characteristic of organized society, but it is also the most ambiguous." [4] I shall accordingly begin by discussing some of the ambiguities in our current conceptions of power. For "to wander around" (the root meaning of "ambiguous") concerning so central and necessary an ingredient in social living is to confuse both thought and action.

We Americans have an uneasy awareness that organized power, as we know it and use it, and democracy, as we profess it, do not fit well together. And this leaves us for the most part busy with, but reticent about, power. Professor Galbraith, a Harvard economist, in his recent book on "countervailing power," is refreshingly candid about this American combination of ambivalence and reticence about power: "Power," he says, "obviously presents awkward problems for a community which abhors its existence, disavows its possession, but values its exercise." So,

> The role of power in American life is a curious one. The privilege of controlling the actions or of affecting the income and property of other persons is something that no one of us can profess to seek or admit to possessing. No American ever runs for office because of an avowed desire to govern. He seeks to serve—and then only in response to the insistent pressure of friends or of that anonymous but oddly vocal fauna which inhabit the grass roots. . . . The same scrupulous avoidance of the terminology of power characterizes American business.[5]

Paul Appleby writes in similar vein of his administrative experience in Washington: "Public administrators and politicians," he says, "do not like to admit the fact of size [of the administrative agencies they direct]. In self-protection they minimize the size of the agencies they direct and control by finding ways to make them appear smaller than they really are." [6]

And yet—and here I quote again from Professor Galbraith: "Despite this convention [of reticence and understatement], which outlaws ostensible pursuit of power and which leads to a constant search for euphemisms to disguise its possession, there is no indication that, as a people, we are averse to power. On the contrary, few things are more valued and more jealously guarded by their possessors in our society." [7]

This endless playing hide-and-seek concerning so important a factor as power makes no sense. For a democratic society to tolerate such confusion and habitual resort to verbal equivocations exposes that society in all its processses to the risks of a pitchman's shell-game. Democracy is the most difficult form of living together in a large society that modern man has attempted; and one of the fundamental conditions of its existence is the maintenance of clarity and reliability in the meanings of men's relations to each other and to their institutions. But ideas and the meanings given to things—that is, the verbal ways by which we close the gap between reality and ways of thinking about and describing reality—are potent levers of organized power, as much for what they may hide as for what they reveal. One of the oldest tactics of power, now elevated to an applied science in the rapidly growing skills of the public relations industry, is the distraction of attention from awkward problems by means of bread and circuses, by drums and trumpets, or by otherwise encouraging avoidance of, or mis-thinking about, a vital segment of reality. What appears to be needed is to examine the more important of the ambiguities from which our current thinking about power suffers.

Organized thinking about power arose historically in the context of men's political institutions. I shall, therefore, consider first some of the ambiguities we have inherited from this historical circumstance. Man's oldest public pre-occupation has been with the burden of tyrants, oligarchies, and other forms of absolute ruling, and with the resulting struggle to establish the rights and freedoms of the citizen under government. The intensity of this preoccupation has deeply prejudiced—right down into the present—consideration of the nature and uses of organized power in society. Under the resulting narrowing of focus to the political model, the tendency has been to view the whole range of reality concerning organized power as equated to, and comprised within, a society's political institutions. In earlier times this often involved exaggeration of the role of leaders and the locating of the "badness" of power in their persons. Latterly, under liberal democracy, the chief villain has been seen as the state.

Political power has historically operated on a scarcity theory. According to this theory, when somebody has power others do not. Under nineteenth century liberal democracy the doctrine of "man against the state" preserved a version of this theory in what David G. Ritchie called the theory of the "two heaps of a fixed number of stones." [8] According to this theory—which to some extent survives today—every power assumed by the state reduces by precisely that much the power of the people; for whatever is added to the one is assumed necessarily to be taken from the other. Such scarcity versions of power have meant in no uncertain sense that power is power *over* others. The inherited image is one of struggle against others, of winning or losing the right to dominate and to practice against the losers the skills and wiles that go with domination. Machiavelli taught the arts of control—all of which had been known by Aristotle; and Hobbes urged upon the multitude their need to be ruled.

The ambiguity I am discussing raises the question whether it is necessary or appropriate to perpetuate in a democratic society this scarcity conception of power conceived in terms of dominance and submission. A thoroughgoing democracy presumably has a rich resource in the fact that it opens the door to abundance in power by providing opportunity for power *with* others in achieving widely desired ends. I do not underestimate the obvious fact that the exercise of power under any version of democracy involves choices and decisions about which people may differ as to purpose, scope, or detail. Respect for such differences and responsibility regarding them are essential to democracy. Presumably, a genuine democracy exists and grows by providing recognition both for the large areas of common need and concern among men, as well as by recognition of the strength inherent in diversity. Politics in such a society performs the double function of affording full opportunity for men to register their areas of agreement, while also providing occasions for clarifying precisely what it is that is important in the differences among them on concrete issues. It may be that such a democracy is unattainable; but if it is attainable, it will be, not through a politics of dominance and submission, but through a use of power which recognizes the resources inherent in both the common humanity and the diversity in human beings. This is a very different thing from our current American "game of politics," in which differences are recklessly exaggerated or equally recklessly covered over by slogans of false homogeneity, while carefully-tailored persons displace issues, platforms mean less and less, and full-throated commercial propaganda exploits public confusion.

One may suggest that the perpetuation of the scarcity version of politics and the resulting uncandid forms that liberal democratic politics takes reflect a deeper power issue in the society. Modern democracy, as we know it, was founded on a fundamental compromise between business power and state power. The rising urban middle class—by which I mean businessmen—in Britain three hundred years ago pressed for a political form free from the arbitrariness of king and aristocracy and compatible with merchants' expanding opportunities for trade. But this middle-class political system, of which our liberal capitalist democracy is the lineal descendant, has been characterized right down into the present by a double resistance: earliest and most openly to state power disserviceable to business; and, latterly and covertly, also to interferences inherent in the new power of numbers which the extension of the suffrage was to put formally within reach of the masses. This has amounted to a double-locking of the doors to thoroughgoing democratic power against democracy itself: at the top, the growth of state power was discouraged; at the bottom, care was taken to see that the power of the people did not get out of hand.

In its centennial number of September 4, 1943, the London *Economist*, looking back to 1843, the year of its founding, remarked that "the men of 1843 had less courage of their convictions in political matters than in economic. As economists they stood for the radical solution, they were for going the whole hog. But in politics they hesitated." [9] This hesitation is still with us today, in the reticence about organized power Dr. Galbraith describes.

Modern mass society is internally highly interdependent. The maintenance of continuous and reliable webs of relation and of flow may no longer be viewed as primarily private concerns, but are matters of basic concern to our whole society. Many things must be done collectively because they can no longer be done so well—or well enough to be socially dependable—individually and piecemeal. But because of the drag I describe upon the positive exercise of thoroughgoing democratic power, the liberal democratic state has no clear warrant for developing an unambiguous, positive theory of the sustained use of democratic power for collective democratic ends. Action for such ends has, in fact, grown markedly in the last four decades under extreme pressures of wars and depression. Some of this growth is unlikely to be revoked. But it is important to note that such extensions of democratic power have been rationalized and tolerated largely only as emergency deviations from the "American way." And the present Administration's program of what has been called "the great give-away" reveals how essentially private the American conception of the uses of power remains.

The suspicion that surrounds state power has not in general extended so acutely to the growth of organized private powers. The growth in size and effective power of private institutions reflects their relative freedom, in fact if not always in visible form, to adapt to changing needs and opportunities. As a result, great corporate industrial blocs, as well as bodies like the American Medical Association, constitute in some very real sense autonomous empires within our liberal democratic society. "Never since the rise of modern statehood," according to Dr. E. Pendleton Herring, "have there been such great power areas dissociated so clearly from social control." [10]

Efforts are made to rationalize away the threats to democracy inherent in the presence of these large and growing private powers. One such type of effort invokes liberal pluralistic doctrine, which I shall discuss later. Another example attempts to tuck the reality of these powers back under the state's political power. This is attempted by claiming that it is the state, with its monopoly over the law, that confers private rights, and so legitimizes private powers. But to assume this is surely to put the cart before the horse; for it is not legal recognition which creates private power, but power which secures the legal recognition.

So far I have discussed ambiguities in thinking about power to derive from the historical prominence in Western society of identifying power with political power. I have treated this as a serious biasing and limiting factor in our consideration of the nature and uses of power. And I have just suggested that to conceive of power as lying essentially at the level of the state reverses the actual situation. This last point raises the important question of where one locates the generating source or sources of power in society. The answer one gives to this question determines where and how one begins the analysis of power: whether one conceives of it as primarily an attribute of individual persons, or as lying at the level of organized institutional agencies, or in the social structure of society; whether one views it in terms of discrete actions or areas of action, or in terms of continuing lines of related actions; and, ultimately, how and how much change one may see as possible in regard to the "problem" of power in society.

As we look at the forms and uses of power in society, it is apparent that power-in-use is very widely distributed: persons may be said to have it in varying degrees in their direct relation with others, in their social roles, and in their participation in the making and application of public opinion; institutions have it; values that motivate social action may be said to have it; and likewise power appears in the structure of society. And there can be no doubt that many factors—such as size, organization, wealth, initiative, and access to professional skills, to channels of communication and to such subtler resources as secrecy and sophistication, as well as the degree of general dependence of the public on the function performed—may *add to* the power of a given unit, however that power may be generated in any larger sense. In this complex and highly dynamic situation it would appear to be extremely difficult to locate any one generating source from which this pervasive phenomenon may be said to stem. Nevertheless, the fact that certain selected emphases recur again and again in the courses that powers take within a given society, and the persistence these emphases exhibit in penetrating and molding seemingly most unlikely aspects of living, suggest that the least probable hypothesis is the pluralistic one. Rather, it would seem that powers in society do not spring up anywhere and anyhow, nor does each develop thereafter on its own autonomous and idiosyncratic terms. Perhaps some tough, enduring factor may be identified as operating fundamentally and persistently to determine the characteristic functions and intensities of organized powers in each specific society.

I shall examine first perhaps the oldest imputed generating source of power phenomena in society: the individual person and his all too human nature. Long before ordered speculation about power emerged, it is probable that man simply accepted power as a concrete fact manifested in the persons of those who possessed it. The course of political speculation began in reaction against the person of the tyrant, who carried authority "in his own breast"; and it moved outward from this image in search of a generalized principle, the rule of law, founded on reason, God, natural law, and in more recent times the consent of the governed. Throughout the development of Western civilization run two strains of optimism and of despair, reflecting different views of human nature: the one emphasizing man's rational character, the other the predominance of the irrational in him. Historically, these two strains have tended to alternate: reason has groped for the rule of law in the ordering of human affairs; and then—as stubborn circumstances have exposed this oversimplification of human nature—the "dark" qualities in man have been emphasized which, so it has been claimed, render order impossible or at best extremely hazardous and unreliable. Beginning with the image of power in the person of the tyrant, this dark stain of suspicion has been recurrently renewed by the attribution to human nature of an inborn insatiable "lust for power."

I regard this location of the generating source of power phenomena within human nature as the *pons asinorum* of power analysis. (As the reader may recall, this term, "the bridge of donkeys," is the name given to the fifth proposition of the first book of Euclid's geometry: if one could not get over that, one could not master geometry.) There is political, as well as scientific, reason for being more than a little suspicious of this blaming of society's problems concerning power on human nature. It has obvious advantages to a ruling segment of society in that it, by implication, rationalizes the social necessity for man's being ruled. It also conveniently deflects attention from such questions as whether destructive tendencies in society may be blamed upon the underlying social structure of a society or upon inadequacies in institutions. So long as this explanation of power is allowed to stand, rational approach to problems of power is largely blocked: one can simply conclude that man is as he is; we can't change human nature; man will forever disrupt society because it is his nature to do so; and all that reason and the social sciences can do is to attempt to police somewhat the disastrous consequences.

It is worth-while to look more closely at this theory. First, it is useful to distinguish between desire for status and desire for power. Status is a relatively quiet value in those who are not psychologically sick, and it refers to the need in each of us not to become socially lost but, rather, to have social acceptance and recognition of what we are and do. Power, on the other hand, in the sense in which it is customarily used to mean power over others, is a much more active and strident phenomenon which implies conscious and sustained effort. Whereas the need for status is psychologically, in the healthy personality, a by-product of interest and of such things as work well done and life well lived, power over others tends to become a monopolizing end in itself that blocks off the spontaneities of living and to which other values become necessarily secondary.

Three kinds of evidence refute the innate insatiable lust for power theory:

(1) The first is the observable fact that so many people do not exhibit it as the organizing core of their living—and these people are not confined to the weaklings, the culls, the Milquetoasts of society. What does one do, for instance, with the Leonardos, the Beethovens, the Faradays, the Darwins, the Tyndals, the Pasteurs—men who had passionate interest in their work? Michael Faraday, for instance, at thirty-nine was a married man living on £100 from the Royal Institution in two rooms, with free coal included. Two years later (1832) his discovery of magneto-electric induction offered him the possibility of raising his professional income to £5,000 a year. Instead, he chose to continue his modest level of living, supplemented in time by a £200 lectureship at the Woolwich Royal Artillery Academy. He declined an offer of knighthood and of the presidencies of the Royal Society and of the Royal Institution. And almost every year of his life he produced some further substantial contribution to science.

(2) The second kind of evidence to which we may look comes from anthropology's study of comparative cultures, particularly the study of the relation of culture and personality that has developed in the past quarter-century. Here the evidence reveals that societies vary widely in the prevalence within them of aggressive tendencies to power over others, and that where such behavior is largely developed the reasons for it are to be sought in the character of the social and cultural environment into which the members are born.

Professor Sidney Hook is correct in saying that "it is extremely questionable whether there is any such thing as a love of power in the abstract. . . ."[11] This statement occurs in the course of Professor Hook's discussion of widely cited generalizations about the inevitability of the abuse of power which Mosca, Pareto, Max Nomad, and to a lesser extent Michels elevated into social "laws" on the basis of psychological traits they imputed to human nature. And Professor Hook goes on to say that "habits, historical traditions, and social institutions play a much more important role in political behavior, and are more reliable in predicting the future than any set of native impulses, residues [in Pareto's sense], instincts or urges. By isolating the latter from their objective cultural setting, selecting from among them an alleged impulse to dominate, to be selfish, to fight, love or flee, the pattern of human nature can be cut to suit any political myth."[12]

(3) The third source of evidence is the trend in contemporary psychiatry. Here the evidence accumulates that the normal thrust of the growing human personality is, if not too much thwarted by circumstances, towards mental health, *i.e.,* towards constructive meshing with, and also constructive dif-

ferentiation within, his society and its culture; that the person's attitude towards others depends upon the reality and validity of his attitude towards himself; that this reality and validity of one's attitude towards oneself depends upon one's ability to deal with life's situations and upon having relatively secure social recognition among one's fellows therefrom; that a person who is able to achieve this sense of not too ineffective dealing with life and of acceptance among his fellows does not need to gain, and will not tend to seek, power over others; but that, on the other hand, where life repeatedly frustrates and rejects one, a drive for power over others is one of the likely consequences.

All of these terms just used—"realistic and valid attitude towards oneself," "ability to deal with the situations that confront one," "the warmth and security of one's social status," and the "degree of frustration and rejection"—are relative terms; and individual differences in capacity are an important variable. But what this emphasis in psychiatric thinking does, reenforcing the findings from the study of comparative cultures, is to lay the ghost of innate insatiable lust for power. Rather, it directs attention to the fact that what a person values and seeks, including the extent to which he seeks it at the expense of others, depends not only upon his native endowment but also upon the concrete social structure and culture in which he learns and practices the arts of living.

This suggests that the most likely hypothesis regarding those persons who do manifest a seemingly insatiable lust for power is that they have been seriously thwarted or socially damaged, and as a result are out to show "who is really boss around here." As an example of this, it is said of the late John D. Rockefeller, Sr., whose relentless tactics drove his competitors to the wall, that he was one of five children of an impecunious patent-medicine salesman who boasted, "I cheat my boys every chance I get. I want to make 'em sharp. I trade with the boys and skin 'em and I just beat 'em every time I can. I want to make 'em sharp."

It takes a long time for a society to free a convenient scapegoat; but it is possible that as psychologists and psychiatrists increasingly direct their attention to studying human beings more in terms of what they are seeking rather than of what they are defending themselves against, another major source of ambiguity about power in society will disappear. Since, however, one of the chief characteristics of organized power is its tendency to disguise its true character wherever this protects it or otherwise serves its ends, one may always anticipate that, so long as the conditions that generate power striving persist, other rationalization of the inevitability of unlimited power striving may be contrived.

Even though one rejects the theory of the generality of the lust for power in human beings, one may still contend that power lies fundamentally with those individuals who—for whatever reason—lead, and who thus continuously renew in their persons society's sense of what power is and can do. As noted above, one of the biasing effects of the historical association of the concept of power with politics has been the exaggeration of the importance of personal leadership. It would appear that, without derogating the importance of individuals, one may firmly turn one's back on all efforts to locate the primary generating source of power in society at the level of individuals.

Where, then, does one look for the generating source that gives power its characteristic shape, prominence and direction of thrust in a given society? The answer would appear necessarily to lie either at the level of institutions or at the level of the social structure of a society.[13]

The decision as to which of these is the primary generating source of organized power in society has far-reaching consequences. It scarcely requires saying that organized power tends to be most alert and active precisely at the hinge-points of change, where new options, or loss of customary ones, impend. Such options in our type of society may involve potential social gains at the expense of losses to organized private power, or the reverse. One observes this in the current process by which the highly important new resource of atomic energy is being captured by private business, although it was developed at public expense and as a public resource. If effective power—both in the government which gives away such a resource to private business and in organized business which receives the resources—derives from the same effective class power in the underlying social structure, then such exchanges of favors at the *institutional level* become a foregone conclusion—a simple transfer from one pocket to another of the same pair of trousers—and democracy is largely emptied of meaning. One may say, therefore, that correct decision as to whether power is initially and primarily structured at the level of institutions *or* at the level of the more general social structure of the entire society is a crucial pre-condition for effective analysis and prediction regarding organized power and regarding change in society that involves more than minor adaptations of the status quo to new conditions.

Although individual leaders have historically tended to focus the high drama of power in public imagination, it is institutions that have been most widely identified as the place where organized power is and is most truly real. While conditions vary from society to society, the social structure of society has tended to be neither so visible nor so easy to grasp as a whole in its relations to power as have been the institutions that continually exercise control over man's affairs. Reference has already been made to the habit of viewing the state as the great repository of power. From the early Middle Ages to the Reformation and the rise of the nation state, the Church of Rome stood forth as ordering power in Western Europe. More recently attention has focused upon economic institutions as the massive locus of power: Marxism viewed the "mode of production" as determining all other institutions; while liberal capitalism, with its emphasis upon "economic man" in a natural market setting, has factually approached the same end, without directly anticipating it, by largely giving economic institutions their head while reining in the power of the state.

In the United States it has been particularly easy to identify organized power with institutions, rather than with the social structure of American society, because of the absence of an hereditary aristocracy and because of the presence of pronounced individual vertical mobility. Such characteristics, in a setting of formal political democracy preoccupied with its regional differences, have blurred the objective boundaries of classes and thus seemingly emphasized the differentness of American capitalist democracy from that of the older nations of Europe. This climate of opinion has denied a conspicuous role to our social structure in determining the structure of American power.

And yet, in our society as elsewhere, one should be warned by the thrust—from somewhere behind or beneath institutions—that appears to impart common directions and common limitations in movement to quite diverse institutions. This apparently active selecting and controlling factor does not operate at random; rather, there is in any given society a pattern in what it is "for" and "against." Certain emphases, as regards both favored and opposed lines of action, repeat themselves again and again. The persistence of these broad types of thrust and resistance is impressive.

One sees this active selecting and controlling factor operating, for instance, to compromise at the source the efforts of such diverse institutions as the church and democratic government to extend their commitments regarding "equality" among men into concrete institutional action. Men may be equal before God and the law; but religious denominations experience both conflict deep within their own ranks and popular cynicism in society when they attempt to spell out in institutional terms the "social teachings" of religion; while such problems as that of "justice and the poor" constitute a standing reproach to liberal democracy. Only at the expense of fundamental compromise can religious and democratic advocacy of equality be applied in concrete social situations. And it is important for our purposes here to recognize that the axis on which such compromise turns is always basically the same and is largely predictable in advance.

This kind of repeated emphasis in diverse institutions, even in cases where the emphasis is incompatible with the professed aims of a given institution, suggests one of two possibilities: either that institutions do not, so to speak, stand on their own feet and are not primary sources of the power they express but, rather, are agents of something else underlying and controlling them; or that some one institution controls all the others, molding their orientation and actions to support its needs.

The first of these explanations leads directly to the general postulate in contemporary sociology and cultural anthropology that the social structure of a given society conditions and controls the structure and uses of the society institutions. A social structure is, itself, a structure of power. And since one of the pronounced characteristics of organized power is its tendency to extend into, and to maintain itself in, functions relevant to it, it would be the least likely explanation to say that power relations established in the basic social relations of a society would not repeat themselves in the values and institutions by means of which the society lives and maintains itself.

The second explanation, which postulates the "determination" of all other institutions within a society by one dominant institution, is implicit in the historical tendency to accept the power of the state as supreme. But, as noted earlier, such attribution of primary influence to the state confuses the formality of law with the realities of power which secure the enactment of laws. Nor, for the same reason, does the familiar argument from the state's "monopoly over the legitimized use of force" establish the primacy of the state, other than formally, over all other institutions. Accordingly, the case of state power would appear to support the first of the two explanations above, rather than the second.

A clearer warrant for resort to the second explanation would appear to be the dominance of the economic institutions of capitalist societies over other institutions in such societies. But it is important to note that this dominance results not from the inevitable character of economic institutions, but from the special case of capitalism. Capitalism has operated by an ideology that has had no need for the conception of society: economic institutions have been assumed to rest upon free individuals, predominantly economically motivated and devoid of need of, or responsibility to, society because their self-oriented actions had reference only to the natural, *i.e.,* extra-social, ordering mechanism of the market. Under this natural market theory society was invisible and, when it did obtrude into view, it tended to be regarded as an obstructive interruption. This has meant under capitalism that society has been submerged in its economic institutions, while the criteria of "success" in the person and the scope of operation of other institutions has tended to be narrowed to terms of functional serviceability to the economy. But this seeming escape of a single institution into autonomy and dominance overlooks an important factor: though liberal capitalism has theoretically rested upon individuals, it has factually rested upon classes of like-circumstanced individuals—the classes being erected fundamentally on economic interest and power; and it has been the fact that this social structure of classes has been primarily economic—despite the avowed democratic equality in the social structure and the democratic professions of the political institutions—that has made it possible for economic institutions so largely to "determine" the other institutions.

Accordingly, one may conclude that here, too, the first of our two explanations is correct, *i.e.,* the power expressed by institutions is not primarily autonomous but derives from the social structure. To this one may add that if the social structure of a society is erected primarily in terms of the same interest that is the focus of some one institution, then that institution tends to become dominant over other institutions in the society. And to this one may venture to append the following: If the power expressed in the social structure and related dominant institution is secure, the development of the power of minority segments of the social structure, and of powers expressing secondary interests throughout the entire social structure, tends to be allowed to grow; but with the onset of insecurity in the dominant power, these minority or secondary powers tend to lose those parts of their freedom that conflict with the interests of the dominant power. One may illustrate this dynamic relation between dominant and secondary interests by reference to business and democracy, respectively, in our own society: threats to the prestige and security of our economy currently lead to the extension of business control over such things as education, media of communication, freedom of speech, and politics, though it is significant that this tightening control is referred to as a crusade in defense of democracy.

The import of the immediately preceding section is that the generating source of organized power in any society inheres in the social structure of the society; and the locating of this source at the institutional level, however immediately plausible this may seem, tends to confuse both analysis of, and attempts to control the uses of, power. This is particularly true where institutional change is at issue. To attempt fundamental change in institutions, of a kind that affects the basic character of organized power in a given society, without changing the social structure of that society is like trying to drive a car forward with the gears set in reverse.

The guilt and resulting reticence about power in our society, noted earlier, encourage avoidance of identification of its true locus. Since the power built into the underlying structure of social relations by capitalism is more rigid, and more vulnerable because of its arbitrary character, than are the values and institutions that implement this power in the flow of daily living, criticism of the social structure is more dangerous and more awkward to counter than is criticism of values and institutions. Accordingly, it is usually tactically more convenient for organized power in the social structure to deflect such criticism outward from the social base to the more fluid levels of values and institutions. The issue is blurred thereby and counter-maneuverability in the face of criticism increased; and, in the end, the issue may be met and contained by minor remedial legislation or similar moves without yielding substantial ground. At the institutional level a given institution may be defended strictly in terms of other institutions. For instance, the awkwardness of professing "competition" in a situation in which oligopoly is increasing, and of stressing the "private" character of enterprise when the interdependent, collective character of the relation of modern society and its institutions is patent has led to the dropping of the two vulnerable words in the terms "free competition" and "private enterprise," and the tactical substitution of the current term "free enterprise." From then on this "free enterprise system" may be defended in terms of "democratic freedom"; or inequalities at the institutional level may be charged to that convenient whipping-boy, "human nature"; "good" and "bad" leaders may be distinguished; criticism of the rights of property may be opposed on the ground that it involves "criticism of the Constitution," or that it weakens "the national defense agencies"—and so on indefinitely.

This tactical maneuverability at the institutional level illustrates the confusions that result from basing power analysis on that level. Institutions, when seen without reference to their social base, assume an unwarranted fluidity and appear to float free as autonomous entities; the basis of responsibility is lost; power becomes anybody's epithet; and the whole issue becomes merely pragmatic—often degenerating only into the adroit application of public relations tactics. In this shifting scene, the locus of power does not change; but what is done by organized power may now be done more boldly, with the immediate needs of institutions seemingly carrying a large measure of self-justifying legitimacy.

Contributing to these institutional confusions is the most characteristic incompatibility in the values of our type of society: that between the democratic value of equality, which bases power upon the decisiveness of numbers, *i.e.,* majorities, and the capitalist value of effective control, which bases power upon ability to buy what one needs in a purportedly free market. In such a situation democracy waits for the verdict at the polls and in congressional votes, while capitalism buys up the market in advance. I do not refer here to corruption, but simply to the superior initiative that inheres in ability to buy sophisticated skills in order to make serviceable things happen.

One of the major devices for masking this deep power conflict within liberal capitalist democracy is the use of the pluralistic formula to resolve the fundamental incompatibilities this hybrid system involves. This takes the form of extending the liberal natural free-market theory, by uncritical analogy, into other areas than the economic, where this theory is no less unreal and quite as deceptive. This pluralistic doctrine, which purports to resolve the problem of unequal powers through the ceaseless free flux of their interaction, has, for instance been given lyrical expression by Professor Earl Latham, of Amherst College. He refers to the interaction of organizations oriented to different values as comprising "one pluralistic world": "an aggregation, a collection, an assemblage, a throng, a moving multitude of human clusters, a consociation of groups, a plurality of collectivities, an intersecting series of social organisms, adhering, interpenetrating, overlapping—a single universe of groups which combine, break, federate, and form coalitions and constellations of power in a flux of restless alterations."[14] This kind of mysticism begs the whole problem of organized power. It encourages the conclusion that, in effect, the locus of power in society is undiscoverable; and it makes a salutary virtue of its undiscoverability, importing into the situation a natural mechanism which purportedly renders the identification of the locus of power unnecessary. Under this mechanism the competition of disparate powers and of the diverse values they represent is assumed to work out to the best interests of all concerned.

It is worthwhile to note in passing that Professor Galbraith's theory of "countervailing power," in his *American Capitalism* is a plausible, stream-lined contemporary example of this pluralistic doctrine. He recognizes that the competitive model no longer represents the central tendency in our economy; but he re-invokes the social beneficence of this model as achievable through the pressures of organized blocs of power upon each other. His theory correctly recognizes the trend toward the oligopolistic organization of industry; and, in line with this, he postulates the raising of small or unorganized interests to something approximating parity in bargaining power with the industrial oligopolies—where necessary, with government assistance and authority. Thence the game is assumed to go on for the benefit of everybody. One may simply comment that such tolerance by the strong of loss of relative advantage over all weaker powers has never characterized private capitalist power as a general policy. The strong are not accustomed to stand still while the weak catch up with them. And where such tolerance has occurred within or between limited groups it has tended to result in collusion that has operated at the expense of other segments of society.

The power of organization, contrary to traditional democratic assumption, does not necessarily correlate with the scope and priorities of popular needs; and this is increasingly the case now that organizing costs large sums of money and is a professional skill directly dependent upon ability to hire experts in organization. Accordingly, the number and size of going organizations openly or covertly pushing the general values and aims of a given institutional area within our society should be viewed as a power phenomenon, and not necessarily a genuinely democratic phenomenon. Also, sheer multiplicity of organizations in a society may not be assumed to indicate their discreteness and autonomy; for one of the most obvious attributes of power is their tendency to cohere, if not structurally, then in reliable working arrangements. And the fact that formally separate institutions trade back and forth with each other in terms of their respective powers does not indicate that this trading is either voluntary or equal, or that some institutions do not occupy positions of established dependence upon other institutions. One may illustrate this by the cases of education and of the Protestant churches which trade their respective prestige and something of their integrity for financial support from business.

All of this suggests that, instead of being led astray by the multiplicity of powers in our society, one needs to concentrate upon the organization of these powers, as they take the unequal forms of single units and of other units with elaborate clusters, or long kite-tails, of satellite organizations.

This should warn us, also, against over-emphasis on the importance of minority powers and their influence. There are, of course, minority powers; and multiple interests may participate in, and in some sense influence, decisions. Theoretically, in a democratic society all relevant powers, large and small, are assumed to contribute their respective true weights of influence to the society's decisions. But there is a wide difference between the power to draft a basic policy document and the power to insert in it minor dotting of "i's" and crossing of "t's" as any one of us who has ever sat as a lone minority representative on a committee not designed to attend to the minority interest one represented can testify. I was a member of the Consumers Advisory Board of the NRA throughout its lifetime. Here one was among friends, but in the broad setting of the NRA the Consumers Advisory Board was a beleaguered Gideon's band which lived by faith and the meagerest crumbs of influence. In a world of organized power the right to minority organization and presumptive influence may amount to little more than the right to exist as a permanent but largely mute minority.

Nothing that has been said above regarding the fallacy of pluralistic doctrine as a means for resolving conflicts among organized power interests should be interpreted as denying the importance of plural values in social living, particularly in a democracy. The more thoroughgoing democracy is, the more it affirms and encourages diversity in values, on the theory that both persons and society draw strength from such multi-accented living. The pragmatic assumption of our commercial American society is that "people know what they want." But "wanting" in any subtle sense is apt to be a matter of slow maturing. Many values of importance to a democratic society are relatively fragile things. Such values must be granted some measure of genuine freedom as to the areas of experience to which they apply; and they need encouragement and support for what they are and can mean in the society. Above all, it must be recognized by society that the qualities for which values stand and which they, respectively, focus are not mensurable upon any common scale; and that to leave such values, and the development of the publics they require in order to live and to grow, to the accidents of the "market" impairs the very quality of subtle diversity they may provide. This is apparent in our hybrid society, in which business power exerts heavy pressures for conformity to manufactured novelty upon the value-*ing* potentials of our people. This state of things exists in a commercial society because people's wishes can be made to be worth a great deal of money in our luxury and mass markets. Such progressive capturing of a people's valuing operates under a kind of Gresham's law in which superficial values tend to drive out values expressing deeper and subtler ways of viewing human experiences. This cannot but do incalculable damage to democracy, which necessarily relies heavily upon the clarity, integrity and human relevance of people's values. For education, for instance, to have to go hat in hand to business corporations, as it is increasingly doing today, and for it to submit to censorship of its teachers and textbooks cannot fail to impair that independence in thinking which is the particular responsibility of education in a democratic society. Democracy cannot thrive on second-hand values in its people. The thing that makes democratic social relations a distinguishable way of life is the maturing of shared experiences and goals that are evaluated in terms that have direct and unequivocal reference to free, growing human beings.

There is space here to refer only briefly to the importance of the concept "social power." This term is currently used either simply as a synonym for "power," to indicate the obvious fact that power occurs in society; or it is used to indicate the probability that power will be powerful—*e.g.*: "Social power is the probability of the effective control of an individual or other social unit by another, irrespective of the former's wishes." Both of these loose and tautological uses forfeit a much more important and serviceable special reference this term may carry.

We lack a term that refers to the power inhering in norms that are wider in reference than any single class, political party or other institution, and that are accepted in a given society as parts of what one may refer to as the unwritten code of compatible social conduct in that society. The essence of such norms in a given society is that they are accepted as qualities that are not at issue in debates over concrete ways and means; they are not reducible to the accidents or to the conventions associated with single institutions, such as superior tactical force, however contrived, in "the game of politics," or ability to command compliance by use of money. My use of the term "code" does not imply reference only to restrictive norms; for the positive potentialities of such norms for liberating the immediacies of experience for wider reference to other ranges of experience is very important.

Such norms exist to some extent in every society, though societies differ as to their scope, coherence, generality of acceptance, and the resulting relative importance of this social power in relation to the powers associated with specific institutions. Social power, in the sense in which I here use it, is an aspect of the power of public opinion; but it concerns that portion of public opinion which has matured, permeated the institutions of the given society, and, as noted before, become independent of single institutions. It is probably correct to say that social power in Britain is more pervasive, coherent, and stronger—as its influence spreads across British politics, business, press and radio, and so on—than is social power in the United States. It is perhaps indicative of the thinness of social power in our American society that we are largely content to see public opinion in terms of the flotsam and jetsam of "yes's" and "no's" the commercial pollsters collect on a very odd array of questions. "Public opinion" in the United States refers principally to the Sargasso Sea in which the polling industry fishes for the benefit of other industries.

At its best, social power may approach becoming what one commentator has referred to as "the conscience of a nation."

So far I have been concerned with ambiguities regarding power and with identification of sources of these ambiguities. Central to my analysis have been the propositions that power is a term that refers to a continuing process that, in one form or another, society cannot dispense with; that the approach to this process has been historically heavily biased by the identification of power with domination conceived as naturally running to arbitrariness and social irresponsibility; and that this combination of necessary use of power with these traditionally imputed unavoidable but deprecated accompaniments of its concrete use has paralyzed direct approach to power as a major social resource capable of adaptation to the values and institutions of a wide variety of social structures. Clearly, a social system stressing throughgoing democratic social relations is a test case likely to burst the seams of the traditional conception of power, since a genuinely democratic social structure and a structure of power operating in terms of arbitrary and socially irresponsible dominance are incompatible.

What is needed is a re-statement of the concept of power that will not leave the road to the use of power blocked off by such contradictions. It is not a new experience for men to confront and overcome deeply traditional separations of things that belong together. For many centuries human nature was viewed as divided against itself into rational part and irrational part or into God-like and sinful parts. With such an assumed unavoidable yoking together of incompatibles the very process of living was distorted by concentration on the attempt to head off evil by making the one part dominate and repress the other. Modern psychology and related biological sciences have begun to place emphasis, not upon polarities and separate parts in the make-up of a human being, but upon his inter-related wholeness. In this view body is not something to be kept in check by mind; emotion is not something to be held down by reason. Such differing aspects of man need no longer be regarded as deplorable, but both are necessary potentials for health and growth.

A somewhat similar advance is possible in the case of organized power in society. What is here involved is not the discovery of a new way to hold incompatibles together, to "make the best of a bad situation." Power is no more necessarily a destructive force that needs to be avoided when possible, and otherwise repressed as much as possible, than is emotion in man. The need is to recognize that organized society and organized power are not two discrete things; but that an organized society is, *ipso facto*, organized power. For a society to exist it must be a system of power. The orderly structure of men's relations as they daily go about institutionally-channeled ways of achieving needed things also includes ways of resolving differences among them. It is due in part to the unusual visibility of many of these concrete processes of resolving differences that the incidence of power has been associated so largely with that part of social action that concerns men's differences. Power is, of course, no less present in the massive, habitual routines of living. Differences among men are not a regrettable oversight of nature but a continuing source of diversity and growth both in the person and in the society; and surely it is the most unreal and crabbed view of man's long struggle for freedom to interpret it as an effort to replace one version of enforced sameness by another. But where this is the outcome of the processes by which men resolve their differences, it is to the structure of the society, and not to the fact that power is involved, that one must look for the explanation.

The following five propositions are accordingly suggested as a basis for a positive approach to power as a major social resource:

(1) Organized power is not an optional factor in society, but an essential component of social living, always and everywhere present in some form.

(2) It is neither inherently, and therefore necessarily, "bad" nor "good." The controls it provides establish and maintain the continuities by which a given society lives together in the present and lives toward its version of the future. These controls may range in type, depending upon the fundamental structure of a society, from (a) sustained, arbitrary coercion in the presence of which the maintenance of, and resistance to, the manner of its imposition and the results thereof become a major preoccupation in the life of the society; through (b) various mixed types in which arbitrariness is in varying degrees curbed by law but in which coercion remains in intensities that differ according to what is at stake; to (c) voluntary cooperation for commonly-desired ends, in which attention tends to concentrate upon the work itself, while concern over the manner of exercise of control is largely limited to the correction of minor excesses and deficiencies in control as they affect the achievement of the ends sought.

(3) Organized power may accordingly be conceived as the process by which whatever is the version of *order* and *disorder* in a given society is continually defined, redefined, and maintained. Order in this sense is the way the major routines of a population's daily actions are channeled toward selected goals in the use of available institutional means. It is a relative term that carries no implication of "goodness" or "efficiency" other than that of serviceability to the given society, or to the controlling segments of the society, in respect to how they identify opportunity and insecurity in view of the concrete resources and preoccupations of the given era and location. Disorderly, likewise a relative term, refers to types of action that are recognized as obstructive to, or destructive of, the maintenance of order so defined. What is orderly enough not to be viewed as disorder varies from society to society according to the broad type and concrete detail of its social structure. Order and disorder may vary in detail over time within the same society as a result of change in such factors as size, complexity, technology, and so on.[15]

(4) While individual differences in capacities and temperament and the necessarily hierarchical structure of roles in the carrying out of complex social processes will always create some unevenness in ordering society by, for instance, the best conceivable democratic social controls, the issue does not lie at the mercy of such differences among persons and their roles. Different functions, responsibilities and authorities allocated to persons on different levels of a common task need not necessarily create power resentments and antagonisms in

a genuinely democratic society. Nor do differences in remuneration and levels of living necessarily array men against each other, so long as the social service-ability of superior functions performed is clearly apparent, that of the lesser functions is recognized and given social status, and differences in income are clearly appropriate to the demands of the work performed. What does create resentments and antagonisms is capricious authority and irresponsible power, the arbitrary assignment of status, and the resulting institutionalization of un-equal life-chances. Nor does the issue inhere in the sheer fact of controls. Controls that endow private concerns with power to keep prices up and wages down for private benefit are quite different things from public controls that keep prices down and maintain an adequate floor under wages. And they evoke quite different reactions from the people controlled. Ordering controls that stem from the recognition of widely-shared needs and are clearly oriented to commonly-sought goals relevant to these needs may establish substantial counter-weights against tendencies to abuse power.

(5) The fact of the long historical identification of organized power as a corrupting, disordering factor in society may not be interpreted as precluding the possibility of a society in which positive democratic power would be used in democratic ways for collective ends. There is no fundamental incompatibility between democracy and power. Given a system of social relations that expresses unqualified democracy, the structure of power in that society will tend to ex-press similarly unqualified democracy, and likewise the resulting values and modes of operating institutions.

It is important to qualify the implied rational character of organized power in these propositions, and indeed throughout all the preceding discussion. Terms like "order," "control," "structure," and expressions such as "power does," or "power tends to do," so-and-so carry strong implied overtones of rationality; in fact the very term "power," particularly "organized power," tends to suggest that anything that has enough power to control what happens "knows" what it is doing. It should scarcely require saying, however, that it is a mistake to con-ceive of power—even organized power—as acting predominantly with cold rationality, with the longrun view in mind. Most decisions are either habitual or only adjustive in familiar terms of immediate expediencies; and such small decisions not infrequently cumulate into "policies." Even in the face of sudden and markedly new situations, yesterday's powers and ways of using power tend to persist into today's ways of coping with novelty, as even those who have "made" a revolution have discovered to their dismay on the morrow of the revolution. Just as the theory that attributes power striving to man's innate emo-tional propensities was challenged earlier in this lecture, so should the imputa-tion of predominant rationality also be challenged. The very fact that one locates the generating source of power in the social structure, with the large role of shared "interest" this involves—whether within classes or other units of combination of interest—should warn against a theory of power that takes its rational character for granted. All of this suggests the but incompletely rational character of the decisions of even organized powers, while on the level of tactics action may become an elaborate feuding between rival political parties, bureaus or echelons within government or business bureaucracies, or even between large rival business corporations with a common stake in maintaining orderly "competition." [16]

When, however, all due reservation has been made as to the amount and quality of the rationality exhibited in the power relations of any society, it is important to recognize the power resource that access to sophisticated knowledge constitutes. Different historical eras have varied as to the institutional spheres under which, and with reference to which, such knowledge has been relatively most emphasized; and they have also varied as to access by different segments of the population to such knowledge in coping with their problems. Changing reliance upon tradition, revelation, common sense, and latterly ever more refined science, has created important differences as to who—including what organized powers—could use knowledge as an instrument of power. In this connection one must also note the shift over time from largely personal and customary decisions to organized decision-making by skilled administrative bureaucracies with access to modern research techniques and refined data. A major result of such change has been the extension, in the case of *some* organized powers, of calculation of the flow of relative advantage into an indefinitely long future, with resulting superior influence over the direction of change.[17] The fact that the increasing complexities of modern living are probably at least matched by the rate of increase of scientific skills for controlling society, but that different classes have markedly different access, financial and otherwise, to the use of such skills, constitutes one of the outstanding power realities of our society.

The last of the five propositions states that no fundamental incompatibility exists between democracy and power. Democracy is, however, the most difficult form of living together that men have ever attempted, and the growth of large societies of people living in big cities by big technology has added to the difficulties. The development and maintenance of a democratic social order under such conditions undoubtedly requires more time, patience and effort than does a society with a less difficult system of social relations. In view of this, it is ironic that no small part of the reason why organized power has been such a chronic problem in liberal democracy has derived from our assumption that democracy is easy to get and does not require constantly and pervasively to be worked at. It is far too simple and easy-going to assume that by the open-handed device of formally scattering authority among the people the problem of power will disappear and nothing further will need to be done but to protect the citizen from encroachments by the state.

The "problem of democracy" as it exists in our society concerns principally the fact that purportedly democratic political institutions operate upon a factually undemocratic class base appropriate to capitalism. Such a situation creates a built-in, serious and enduring problem of power that cannot but continue so long as these contradictions continue. Indeed, one may suggest that under such circumstances the contest runs increasingly to the disadvantage of democracy. One should not be deceived about this by the growth in the scope of governmental activity in the United States in the past quarter-century. The issue of liberal democracy rests upon the built-in advantages which growing private industry has over government, and the resulting relatively greater initiative and maneuverability the private corporate sphere possesses as compared with the more restricted sphere of officialdom under our Constitution. Control over the future, as already noted, has become a major concern of organized big business. In this respect liberal democratic government is constrained to be both more sluggish and more helpless. Theoretically, the liberal state operates as umpire in the struggle of private interests. But it is handicapped because—and properly so in a democracy—it must operate "in a goldfish bowl," with its actions continually exposed to public scrutiny, while the large corporation has far greater privacy in its planning and actions. Business, as part of the public, for instance, is able to challenge, and to keep, government expenditures for publicity and propaganda to a minimum, while business' own freedom of initiative in public relations and otherwise is to a very large extent unlimited. Also, as the Senate monograph *Economic Power and Political Pressures* remarks, "Cohesion is a characteristic of great advantage to business" and combined with its financial resources gives it large tactical advantage over other pressure groups "and over government itself." "In comparison with business, government appears to be almost completely lacking in cohesion", and this deprives it of the kind of "single-minded purposefulness which business possesses." [18]

Because big business enterprise is more private and free, more concerned with controlling the future, and more highly valued and tolerated than is government enterprise, it is able to innovate at or beyond the legal limits of legitimacy. In this it is greatly aided by the presence of ambiguities and contradictions in the structure and ideology of liberal capitalist democracy. The soft spots in such a hybrid system—including lack of clarity at crucial, contested points or even the co-existence of two or more explanations of what a given thing or quality means—invite the substitution of achievement for public debate. This can be done, under the favoring freedoms granted to business, by setting up *de facto* situations in the twilight zones at the margins of legitimacy which may either rapidly become too well-established to be revoked or may actually command public tolerance because of the prosperity they promise. The references and limits of legal legitimacy may then be stretched to include the innovation. This may amount to a continued forcing of the hand of a democratic government on the defensive. A case in point is the quiet establishment of the business oligopolies of which Professor Galbraith writes so confidently as the new model of American business, with their webs of tacit "understandings" which lie largely beyond the reach of the law. An even more interesting case concerns the current devouring of the concept "democratic welfare." American society has operated with a double definition of welfare: the one, "democratic welfare," has wide reference to the freedoms, the rising standards of education, public opinion and participation, and the diversity in living associated with the concept democracy; and the other, "business welfare," had until recently blunt reference simply to the profitability of business. As part of its recovery of confidence following the financial and ideological shock of the 1929 depression, business saw that it has much to gain from the identification of these two "welfares" under the formula that what is good for business creates thereby democratic welfare. And by now we Americans are well on our way to trusting our future to business welfare. Such subjection of the direct meanings of democracy to the expediencies of one of its institutional means not only weakens men's sense of what it is other than material prosperity that they as men may desire, but also progressively erodes away the basis for any more genuine democratic power.

The central problem of democracy in our time is the need to discover and use the enormous potential of democratic power. But in order to do that, there can be no double-talk about democracy; no bi-focal values; no double standard in our social structure and in the ways our institutions operate. Men of democracy must be confident of their society, know where it is going because they share genuinely in its decisions, and they must be unafraid. It has been said that half the virtue leaves a man when, if he behaves like a man, he may lose his job.

In the centennial issue of the London *Economist* to which I referred earlier, the editors said:

> Consent is an essential prerequisite of any form of democracy; but it is a negative element, and one of the greatest needs of the twentieth century is to transmute it into something more positive. . . . There have been examples in past history of the enormous momentum that can be developed when a whole people feels itself at one with its institutions. . . .
>
> . . . The British citizen *should be* an ardent participant in his public affairs; he *is* little more than a consenting spectator who draws a distinction between "we" who sit and watch and "they" who run the state. . . . Democracy in the twentieth century needs fire in its belly. . . .[19]

If this is to be made to happen it cannot be done by mere additions to, or by re-combinations or intensifications of, liberal democratic assumptions and practices. This is not, for instance, simply a matter of "voting better men into office" or of trying harder to "safeguard our freedoms." For it is precisely the conditions of democratic freedom that are involved. To meet this issue requires the rebuilding of men's social relations from the social structure up and throughout the institutions by which the society lives. And for this to happen will require the development and application of a thoroughgoing, positive theory of democratic power by which free men will be able to control and to order together all institutional means that can contribute to their collective welfare.

NOTES

[1] Bertrand Russell, *Power: A New Social Analysis* (London: Allen & Unwin, 1938), p. 10.

[2] Robert Bierstedt, "An Analysis of Social Power," *American Sociological Review*, 15 (1950), 730–738.

[3] E. H. Carr, *The New Society* (London: Macmillan, 1951), p. 110.

[4] R. H. Tawney, *Equality* (London: Allen & Unwin, 1931), p. 228.

[5] John Kenneth Galbraith, *American Capitalism: the Concept of Countervailing*

Power (Boston: Houghton Mifflin Co., 1952), pp. 30 and 28; quoted with the permission of the author.

⁶ Paul Appleby, *Big Democracy* (New York: A. A. Knopf, 1945), p. 11.

⁷ John Kenneth Galbraith, *op. cit.,* p. 28; quoted with the permission of the author.

⁸ David G. Ritchie, *The Principles of State Interference* (London: Sonnenschein, 1891), pp. 12–13.

⁹ The London *Economist,* 145 (September 4, 1943), 296.

¹⁰ E. Pendleton Herring, "Logomachy and Administration," *Journal of Social Philosophy,* 2 (1937), 95–117.

¹¹ Sidney Hook, *Reason, Social Myths and Democracy* (New York: John Day, 1940), p. 126; quoted with the permission of the author.

¹² *Ibid.,* p. 123; quoted with the permission of the author.

¹³ The term "social structure" refers to the organized relations of groups and categories of people identified within a given society according to kinship, sex, age, division of labor, race, religion, or any other criteria stressed as differentiating people in role, status, access to resources, and authority. This structure establishes durable relations that hold groups of people together for certain purposes and separate them for others. Such a social structure may persist over many generations. Its continuance depends upon its ability to cope with historical changes that involve absorption of new groupings and relations of men without fundamental change in the structure of the society of a kind that involves major transfer of power.

¹⁴ Earl Latham, *The Group Basis of Politics: a Study in Basing-Point Legislation* (Ithaca: Cornell University Press, 1952), p. 49; quoted with the permission of the publishers.

¹⁵ It is important to note that the controls that insure major order of a desired kind may involve tolerance of what may be viewed as disorders according to another version of order within the same society. An example of this within our own society is the frequent slowness and cumbersomeness of democratic processes as compared with engineering criteria of administrative efficiency—*e.g.,* the generally slower maturing of genuinely democratic public opinion as compared with "the engineering of consent." A reverse example is the active tolerance, and even the encouragement, of certain kinds of disorders as an aid in maintaining a dominant version of order. This last is probably one of the oldest tactics of organized power under circumstances that render the direct use of force inexpedient. It may take the form of control over opposition elements by the policy of "divide and rule," or the maintenance of the monopoly of existing political parties within a democracy by the passage of laws making the organization of new popular parties difficult; or general control over the public by holding back information or the propagation of mis-information, or by the organization and financing of specious "front" bodies under ultra-democratic names; or organized "witch-hunting" of scapegoat elements in order to quiet popular unrest or to distract attention from otherwise dubious actions by organized power. All such actions may be rationalized by organized power as aids in the maintenance of order.

¹⁶ An example of this is given by the late Paul T. Cherington, a leading market analyst and former professor of marketing in the Harvard Graduate School of Business Administration, in his *People's Wants and How to Satisfy Them.* On the basis of "a close relationship with more than a hundred concerns" in the drafting of NRA business and industry codes in Washington, he set up a list, to which he gave frankly subjective weighting, of the, to him, seeming "motives" of the firms involved, as revealed in these "serious" code discussions. Over 50 per cent of the total weighting

was assigned to the following seven of the total thirteen "motives" he lists: stealing accounts; demolishing salesmen's rumors; meeting some chiseler; getting some competitor's goat; getting even with a goat-getter; keeping up an appearance of alertness; trying to "pull a fast one" on the trade.—(New York: Harper & Bros., 1935), p. 179.

[17] The extent of the tacit or open control over both the social and the natural sciences by private big business and wealth is most probably increasing the power imbalance within our society. The social sciences and their applied branches are increasingly heavily oriented to the service of these sources of funds and of professional influence. And this "gold rush" has only begun and is capable of indefinite expansion. The case of the natural sciences is equally substantial, though perhaps less spectacular because these sciences do not deal so directly with the immediate "management of men" and the "engineering of society." According to the Senate committee report on *Economic Power and Political Pressures*, "[Business] corporations have marshaled behind them the bulk of the scientific brains of the country, a resource which labor, farmers, and government itself cannot equal. . . . To a great extent industry's political formidability can be traced to its dominant position in scientific research. . . . The controls centralized in the business community extend to both pure and applied science. It is the domination in both fields which gives business its key position. No other group, not even government, controls and enjoys this asset to the same extent. It is a resource of the first magnitude, endowing business with unique influence in the social process, and making its political strength almost unassailable." —Donald C. Blaisdell, *Economic Power and Political Pressures*, Monograph 26 of the Investigation of Concentration of Economic Power by the Temporary National Economic Committee (Washington: Government Printing Office, 1941), pp. 13, 22, 23.

[18] *Ibid.*, p. 18.

[19] The London *Economist*, 145 (September 4, 1943), 297.

4. CONTRASTING THEORIES OF POLITICAL POWER IN AMERICAN SOCIETY

Arnold M. Rose

The belief that an "economic elite" controls governmental and community affairs, by means kept hidden from the public, is one that can be traced at least as far back in American history as the political attacks of some Jeffersonians on some Hamiltonians at the end of the eighteenth century. Scarcely any lower-class political movement in the United States has failed to express the theme that the upper classes successfully used nondemocratic means to thwart democratic processes. Perhaps the widest popular use of the theme was achieved by the Populist movement in the decades following 1890. Anarchism and Marxism were imports from Europe that accepted the theme as one of the essential elements of their ideologies.[1] The history of the United States also provides ample factual examples to strengthen credence in the theme. The literature of exposure, especially that of the "muckrakers" in the first decade of the twentieth century, provides details as to how economically privileged individuals and groups illegally bought and bribed legislators, judges, and executive heads of government to serve their own desires for increased wealth and power.

The belief is not entirely wrong. But it presents only a portion of relevant reality and creates a significant misimpression that in itself has political repercussions. A more balanced analysis of the historical facts would probably arrive at something like the following conclusion: Segments of the economic elite have violated democratic political and legal processes, with differing degrees of effort and success in the various periods of American history, but in no recent period could they correctly be said to have controlled the elected and appointed political authorities in large measure. The relationship between the economic elite and the political authorities has been a constantly varying one of strong influence, co-operation, division of labor, and conflict, with each influencing the other in changing proportion to some extent and each operating independently of the other to a large extent. Today there is significant political control and limitation of certain activities over the economic elite, and there are also some significant processes by which the economic elite uses its wealth to help elect some political candidates and to influence other political authorities in ways which are not available to the average citizen. Further, neither the economic elite nor the political authorities are monolithic units which act with internal consensus and coordinated action with regard to each other (or probably in any other way). In fact there are several economic elites which only very rarely act as units within themselves and among themselves, and there are at least two political parties which have significantly differing programs with regard to their actions toward any economic elite, and each of them has only a partial degree of internal cohesion.[2] On domestic issues, at least, it is appropriate to observe that there are actually four political parties, two liberal ones and two conservative ones, the largest currently being the national Democratic party, which generally

SOURCE: Arnold M. Rose, *The Power Structure* (New York: Oxford University Press, 1967), pp. 1–39. Copyright © 1967 by Oxford University Press, Inc. Reprinted by permission.

has a domestic policy that frustrates the special interests of the economic elite. This paragraph states our general hypothesis, and we shall seek to substantiate it with facts that leave no significant areas of omission. Merely to provide it with a shorthand label, we shall call it the "multi-influence hypothesis," as distinguished from the "economic-elite-dominance" hypothesis.

These two hypotheses are not to be equated with what in the social science literature is often called the "opposing theories of consensus and conflict." Both hypotheses fall under conflict theory, and the difference is that the multi-influence hypothesis depicts social reality as a far more complex conflict than does the economic-elite-dominance hypothesis. The latter sees conflict merely between a more or less unified elite and largely unorganized "masses," and if by some chain of events the latter could become better organized, conduct the conflict more effectively and *win,* there could ensue a society with a substantial consensus (ranging—in the writings of the varying proponents of the theme—from traditional agrarianism to communism). The multi-influence hypothesis sees conflict as often multilateral, with large proportions of the population often not involved, with the sides changing at least partially from issue to issue, and with consensus being achieved only temporarily and on a limited number of issues (except when naked force imposes an apparent consensus). The multi-influence hypothesis holds this to be true at least for heterogeneous, industrialized societies; it begs the question as to whether its own image or the "consensus theory" is more applicable to small, "primitive" societies.[3]

The distinction between the two hypotheses we are considering is also not to be equated with another distinction found in the social science literature—that between "social force" explanations and "powerful men" explanations. Sociologists generally are inclined to adopt the former and reject the latter, whereas proponents of the economic-elite-dominance hypothesis openly embrace the latter, at least much of the time. For example, Ferdinand Lundberg, the author of one study using the economic-elite-dominance hypothesis, wholeheartedly accepts the "powerful men" explanation in attributing complete power in the United States to "sixty families." [4] C. Wright Mills, the author of a more recent and more scholarly exposition of the economic-elite-dominance hypothesis,[5] is too much of a sociologist and too much of a Marxist to reject "social force" explanations completely. After making the distinction between the two sorts of explanations, which he calls the "drift" and the "conspiracy" explanations, Mills comes out in favor of a combination of both of them, while concentrating on the latter for the purposes of the study in hand. In now presenting the multi-influence hypothesis and the evidence for it, I accept the general need for balance between "social force" and "powerful men" explanations, and even recognize that for a study of political power it might be desirable to stress the "powerful men" explanation. I believe it is necessary to use terms like "elite" and "leaders," and to recognize that the truly active and innovative people in any group activity are relatively few in number (although probably not so few as Lundberg and Mills suggest). But it is not necessary to consider all "powerful men" explanations as "conspiracy" or "secrecy" theories, as Lundberg and Mills do. While it may be true that not everything about power meets the eye, it does not follow that most things that are open to observation are false. Conspiracy and secrecy theories of power are theories based on inference, with very little fact, and their authors justify the absence of facts by stating that the important facts are kept hidden. This assertion might have a degree of plausibility if empirically supported explanations were offered as to the means of linking the conspiracy to the observable facts of power. But the conspiracy theorists who adopt the economic-elite-dominance hypothesis do not offer such explanations as far as the observable facts of political power are concerned. If facts regarding means and processes are not to be offered, then plausible and rational hypotheses must be presented; lacking even these, the social scientist must be skeptical about conspiracy and secrecy theories of power. In sum, in the hypothesis of [*The Power Structure*], I am willing to admit a large element of a "powerful men" explanation of power, but not much of a "conspiracy" or "secrecy" explanation.

The multi-influence hypothesis differs from the economic-elite-dominance hypothesis both in its conception of the elite and in its conception of the masses. The latter hypothesis envisages society as a vast pyramid, with the people of wealth in control at the top. They may or may not be seen as interspersed with a military elite. At a somewhat lower level are said to be their "lieutenants"—politicians, hired managers, small businessmen, and perhaps a few lesser categories who accept the orders of the economic elite and operate the control mechanisms and institutions that manipulate the rest of the society. Still lower are the "local opinion-makers," persons who constitute the mechanisms of control, who respond more or less automatically to the will of their superiors and who have a "grass-roots" following. At the bottom is the great bulk of the population, envisaged in the hypothesis as inert masses deprived of their rights and exploited economically and politically to serve the interests of those on top.[6]

There is also a "contrast-conception," an ideal of what an alternative structure of society would be, envisaged by those who hold the economic-elite-dominance hypothesis: this is of a classless, equalitarian society, in which the dominant groups have been eliminated or merged as equals into the masses, and the masses have been organized into functional groups that have a social structure for operating a society without the present controllers.[7] Those who hold this hypothesis usually imagine that their theoretical opponents are setting forth their own contrast-conception as the present reality and that they are declaring that a society without classes presently exists in order to fool the masses and keep them acquiescent.

While there are undoubtedly some among the wealthy who do deny a class system as a means of fooling the "masses" and trying to keep them satisfied with the status quo, this is not the view of most of those who hold the multi-influence hypothesis. The latter hypothesis, which is expounded and empirically supported in the present study, conceives of society as consisting of many elites, each relatively small numerically and operating in different spheres of life, and of the bulk of the population classifiable into organized groups and publics as well as masses. Among the elites are several that have their power through economic controls, several others that have power through political controls, and still others that have power through military, associational, religious, and other controls. While it is true that there are inert masses of undifferentiated individuals without access to each other (except in the most trivial respects) and therefore without influence, the bulk of the population consists not of the mass but of integrated groups and publics, stratified with varying degrees of power. "Integrated groups" are defined as numbers of individuals operating on the basis of common, "traditional" meanings and values, with networks of communication among themselves, with internal divisions of labor in role and function, and resistant to control by any elites who "pressure" them to behave in ways contrary to their common meanings and values. "Publics" are similar, but much less structured internally, more open to ideas from the outside, whether from an elite or from any other idea-generator (including Marxists), and much more specialized in that they have a very small range of common interests about which their members interact. Constituted mainly of integrated groups and shifting publics, as well as of an undifferentiated inert "mass," the bulk of the population is seen as much more differentiated and much less susceptible to control by any elite in the multi-influence hypothesis than in the economic-elite-dominance hypothesis.

Both hypotheses recognize the role of impersonal forces—such as economics and geography—as having significant influence over the course of society, but there is a difference between the hypotheses in how they view the nature and manner of influence of these impersonal forces. The economic-elite-dominance hypothesis holds the economic force as setting the course of history, and at the present time giving predominance to those private owners and managers of the means of production and media of mass communication they call the economic elite. The multi-influence hypothesis recognizes the importance of economic forces but considers that there are also semi-independent forces of social change in technology, cultural contact and conflict, and concrete and diffuse social movements. It further recognizes resistances to social change not only in economic vested interests but also in law and custom and in social structure generally. Both the impersonal forces of social change and of resistance to social change set marked limits to the power of any elite group to control the actions of society. For example, when we later consider the effort, in 1957–65, to institute a federal program for financing medical care through Social Security, we shall see that a most significant new factor that promotes this is improvement in medical technology, which markedly reduces death through acute illness and leaves an increasing number of older people prone to heavy medical expenses through contracting the chronic illnesses. Social movements and elites then come into operation to promote or retard the formation of a federal program, and elements of existing social structure—such as private insurance plans and the committee system of Congress—play their roles in determining the final outcome. Thus, the multi-influence hypothesis holds that each social change or decision occurs in a matrix of social forces and social resistances, of cultural elements and social structures, only some of which are or can be deliberately controlled or manipulated by elites.

While, as we have pointed out, the economic-elite-dominance hypothesis has had a long history, and has had ups and downs of popular acceptance, its recent resurgence is a result of the publication of works by two sociologists. One is Floyd Hunter, who did a study of power structure, first of a single city, then of the entire United States.[8] The other is C. Wright Mills, who wrote a general analysis of elites and social structure in the United States.[9] These books have received both favorable and unfavorable reviews,[10] and the first Hunter study has been favored by a number of replications, some of which come to the same general conclusion that Hunter does while others do not. Our purpose . . . is not primarily to review or even add to the criticisms, but through the presentation of a variety of related empirical researches and observations to demonstrate the inadequacy of the economic-elite-dominance hypothesis which underlies the Hunter-Mills works and to indicate the greater theoretical and empirical viability of the multi-influence hypothesis as an explanation of political power and political processes in American society.

Certainly [*The Power Structure*] is not the first to set forth or to seek to substantiate the multi-influence hypothesis. It is implicit in many treatises and studies of nineteenth- and twentieth-century social historians and political scentists.[11] Particularly as it concerns political structure and processes, the hypothesis has received explicit formulation and empirical support in the writings of Arthur Bentley, E. Pendleton Herring, E. E. Schattschneider, David B. Truman, and V. O. Key, Jr.[12] We shall follow the lead of these latter writers in concentrating on political processes, but differ from them in following two procedures brought into the analysis of power by Hunter and Mills, respectively: (1) we shall use, among other research techniques, the "modern" technique of survey analysis, and (2) we shall analyze the facts of power, not in a "narrow" political context, but in the broader context of sociology. Thus, our theory and approach approximate those of many social historians and political scientists; our analysis and presentation will seem closer to those of Hunter and Mills. This [work] does not deal with the exercise of economic power in areas of purely economic decision-making. It does deal with the exercise of economic power in areas of political decision-making, to show that the political elite are not mere lieutenants of the economic elite, although the economic elite provide one major influence on the political decisions made. It also shows something of the influence of political decisions on the economic sphere, although this is a minor focus.[13] Its main task is to set forth the multi-influence hypothesis . . . as a viable framework for future researches on the power structure of the United States.

The Hunter and Mills works are here treated together, as they both present the viewpoint which we have labeled the "economic-elite-dominance hypothesis." As we now turn to a specific analysis of the contents and methods of the writings of these two authors, we shall find that they differ markedly. Hunter presents his readers with straightforward empirical research, with few or no theoretical underpinnings and with interpretations that might be considered naïve. He claims to arrive at the economic-elite-dominance hypothesis because his facts bring him there. Mills, on the other hand, offers his readers a sophisticated and scholarly work; he is fully conscious of his theoretical framework, and he presents facts to support this hypothesis. Both have produced facts, although these facts do not refer to the processes by means of which power is exercised. On the whole, their facts are not contradicted here: our attitude toward the facts produced by Hunter is that he has misinterpreted them; our attitude toward the facts presented by Mills is that he has not balanced them with other equally relevant facts.[14] Hunter claims to present a picture of the power structure; we say he has presented a partial picture of the *image* of the power structure, as held mainly by the subordinates of the economic elite. Mills claims to present a picture of three elites, with the economic elite (and the military elite recently merged with them) superordinate over the political elite, and all three superordinate over an inert mass; we say he has presented only some of the pertinent facts. We shall now present some of the more specific procedures and findings of Hunter and Hills, along with some specific criticisms.

Hunter states his basic assumptions for *Top Leadership, U.S.A.* in succinct form: "At the beginning this work I assumed that the most influential men in national policy-making would be found residing in the larger cities, manning the larger corporate enterprises, and using their influence to get the government to move according to their interests" (p. 7). While he elaborates on this statement, it provides his basic hypothesis and becomes his main conclusion. His procedures may be summarized as follows:

1. "The first major step was to consult management personnel of the national organizations. I began by calling upon secretaries in the U.S. Chamber of Commerce, the American Medical Association, the American Bankers Association, the American Farm Bureau, the American Meat Institute, the Congress of Industrial Organizations, the National Association of Manufacturers, and the National Federation of Business and Professional Women's Clubs. I moved from these groups and their secretaries to others" (pp. 11–12). This produced a tentative list of 1,093 organizations.

2. Since this was too many to tap for interviews, "With the aid of four other persons who had a working knowledge of national organizations, the list was pared to 106" (p. 13). The 106 included 4 recreational associations, 6 in the category of science and education, 5 veterans' and fraternal associations, 5 in the area of government and civic affairs, 4 women's organizations, 5 associations of lower professional groups, 6 representing organized labor and consumer groups, and 4 representing religious and minority group interests. These 39 apparently represent elites and groups other than economic. Some additional categories are marginal: 4 service club associations (including Rotary and Lions), 3 national foundations, 2 large social welfare organizations (Red Cross and Community Chest), and the American Arbitration Association. The remaining 57 organizations—a clear majority—represented major economic interests. Thus Hunter begins to create the conditions in his method of research which are bound to lead him to the economic-elite-dominance conclusion.

3. Some official in each of these 106 organizations was polled for the names of the top 20 organizations and for "the names of persons known to [him] who might be considered top policy makers at the national level" (p. 16).

4. "The names of persons given in response to the question of nominating top national leaders provided a basic list of leaders, nearly 500, to whom a questionnaire was eventually addressed and with whom I had a sample of interviews designed to relate the activities of individual leaders to other leaders, and leader groups, in turn, to the development of public policy" (p. 16).

This first list was modified by later nominations. The list is very heavily loaded with the names of industrialists, bankers, and other businessmen. Only the category of political and government leaders will be analyzed here. Of the 500 names only 17 (3.4 per cent) can be considered as being in this category: 5 were on the presidential or presidential-candidate level (Hoover, Truman, Eisenhower, Dewey, Stevenson), 4 were senators (Byrd, Flanders, Knowland, Saltonstall), 2 were governors (Lausche, Shivers), 3 were State Department officials (Herbert Hoover Jr., Herter, Lodge), 1 was a lesser official in the Department of Health, Education and Welfare (Schottland), 1 was a mayor (Morrison of New Orleans), 1 a reputed city political boss (Arvey). The 5 in the presidential level seem obvious choices; the others represent obvious biases of selection—there were no representatives, no cabinet officers, no active military leaders, no Northern Democrats (except for Arvey and Lausche, the latter a political maverick).

5. As a result of criticism from a political scientist, Hunter felt it was necessary to make some additions to his 1953 list in 1955. "If one were to have added to the list a few names of ranking, elected and appointed politicians, a sprinkling of news editors and columnists, and a few organization secretaries and lobbyists, the core structure of power at the national level would have been more nearly complete" (p. 59)

6. "Determined to have the study of policy-making completely empirical, I took several polls of national leaders to get their own choices of those whom they consider to be their peers."

"Each new poll added a few names to the list, but also many names were dropped in the process."

"The third and fourth polls of national leaders in 1957 and 1958 revealed that a basic core of names continued to be nominated for national leadership positions. In the 1957 and 1958 polls the names of public politicians were included" (p. 195).

7. The final list was "heavily weighted with industrial leaders (23), followed in order by: 15 U. S. Senators, 10 cabinet members, 6 professionals (3 attorneys, 2 professors, 1 scientist), 5 bankers, 5 publishers, 5 Congressmen, 4 assistant cabinet secretaries, 3 labor leaders, 3 military officers, 4 Presidential assistants, 3 transportation executives (2 air, 1 railroad), 2 ambassadors, 2 governors, 3 United States Presidents (2 retired), and 1 each, chief justice of the Supreme Court, communications executive (radio-TV), religious leader, utilities executive, United Nations representative, and the Vice-President of the United States.

"Of those who could be identified by political party affiliation, 20 were Democrats and 50 were Republicans. Most of them were born in the Northeastern quarter or in the Middle West of the country" (p. 199).

The relationship between this final list and the first list of names (see (3) above), as far as political leaders is concerned, is impossible to discern. It seems that somewhere along the line, Hunter became aware of political leadership. Nevertheless, "Policy . . . rarely originated in the legislative halls. . . . Legislators acted decisively on policy matters that were originated in one constituency or another by those who were the most active in producing goods and services in society" (pp. 210–11).

8. Additional studies were made in two states (South Carolina and North Carolina) and two industries (textiles and housing). While the specific facts re-

ported do not indicate that the textile industry got much of what it wanted from Congress, this in no way modified Hunter's conclusion that industry controls the politicians.

It should be evident from the above summary of Hunter's method of research that he is not engaged in systematic scientific research, but uses a hit-and-miss sequence of techniques almost all of which have a built-in bias toward the industrial and commercial elite. Except when he deliberately and arbitrarily interjects politicians and a few others into his lists, his techniques lead him to the economic elite. He asks the lower economic elite who the top elite is, and of course the answers refer to the top economic elite. From this inherent bias and from interviews with a sample of the economic elite, Hunter derives an *image* of the national power structure which he confuses with the power structure itself. A brief summary of this image follows:

1. "After concluding the more extensive study, I feel that the membership lists of the National Industrial Conference, the Committee for Economic Development, and the Business Advisory Council provide good starting points for anyone interested in a quick and partial rundown of national leadership. . . . Along with a sprinkling of foreign policy associations and educational bodies, they represent top groupings of national leadership" (p. 33).

2. "The role of the professional in most instances is subordinate to that of one or more lay leaders" (p. 39).

3. Lobbying, especially through personal contacts, with important congressmen, is the way to get any bill accepted by Congress and the President (pp. 34, 55, 64, 79, 180).

4. There are local leaders who are primarily interested in local issues, and are extremely powerful in determining their outcome, but who know little about national issues and have little influence over these (pp. 86, 111–12).

5. "The wielding of power in American community life . . . is a combination of powerful individuals willing that things be done or not done and sometimes getting others to believe they thought of the idea in the first place and wanted to do it all along" (p. 137).

6. "It is also apparent that each major, particular power structure is related directly and indirectly, through its personnel, to every other structure. This is not to say that there is a monolithic power structure in the nation moving in willful accord on every national issue, but it may be said with confidence that various groups of power within the nation are interlocked by persons who can and do communicate core policy decisions of a particular power structure to key persons of other structures as occasion demands" (p. 138).

7. The image of power is the power structure itself: "From the point of view of the power structure concept, we are dealing here, in part with a belief system. Because of their observations of acts, positions, or reputations, men begin to believe that power resides in this or that man. Power is imputed to him. He is then observed in the company of others; or, as importantly, he is believed to be in league with others; or, further, it is believed that if he is not consorting with others of his imputed power rank, he could be if he so willed. It is func-

tional to the structured community system of order that men so believe. The man or men, as the case may be, begin themselves to believe their own or others' estimates of themselves and they weigh others in the balance with themselves and others of their kind" (pp. 172–3).

8. Government is secondary—an instrument for the execution of policy, not the formation of policy. "It was abundantly clear that the men interviewed did not think of government officials exclusively as top policy makers in the country. This does not say they did not recognize the important roles played by politicians in the process of getting things done, but universally, government was thought of as an instrument of extending policy rather than a primary source of policy development" (p. 176).

Only the unimportant people in the small towns think political representatives are powerful in getting things done (p. 184).

9. Few in the elite were closely bound up with politics: "The 100 number-one leaders in the research list were not listed in appreciable numbers as members of the national committees of the major political parties, although 15 of them had been members of some political party committee at some stage of their careers. Some of the leaders expressed an interest in one of the two major parties, particularly the Republican party, but by the time they were recognized national leaders they had restricted their activities largely to helping raise political money and to conferring with others on the suitability of national candidates. For the most part, the leaders of the larger enterprises did not wish to put themselves forward as politicians. Although they were policy makers, with rare exceptions they did not wish to run for public office, and they held themselves superior to the men who seek office" (pp. 207–8).

10. Politicians are ordinary people who attend mainly to the wishes of industrial policy makers: "When stripped of the glamour and aura of publicity that often surrounds them, the men who are elected to public office are quite ordinary men going about tasks prescribed by the society around them. There is a routineness in much that the politician does which grows out of the stability of the political structure and the general climate of opinion in which he operates. Because so much activity in society is related to men who organize working groups, the politician is compelled to understand and be sympathetic to employers and labor union officials who are powerful in determining industrial policy which in turn affects public policy as previously shown. He listens sympathetically, of course, to other groups, but his attention is centered most often on industrial policy makers" (pp. 208–9).

Mills's general thesis is that there is a national power elite which forms a self-conscious integrated unity, and "Insofar as national events are decided, the power elite are those who decide them" (p. 18).

The people of the higher circles may also be conceived as members of a top social stratum, as a set of groups whose members know one another, see one another socially and at business, and so, in making decisions, take one another into account. The elite, according to this conception, feel themselves to be, and are felt by others to be, the inner circle of "the upper social classes."

They form a more or less compact social and psychological entity; they have become self-conscious members of a social class. People are either accepted into this class or they are not, and there is a qualitative split, rather than merely a numerical scale, separating them from those who are not elite. They are more or less aware of themselves as a social class and they behave toward one another differently from the way they do toward members of other classes. They accept one another, understand one another, marry one another, tend to work and to think if not together at least alike. [Page 11.]

The unity of the power elite, however, does not rest solely on psychological similarity and social intermingling, nor entirely on the structural coincidences of commanding positions and interests. At times it is the unity of a more explicit co-ordination. To say that these three higher circles are increasingly co-ordinated, and that this is *one* basis of their unity, and that at times—as during the wars—such co-ordination is quite decisive, is not to say that the co-ordination is total or continuous, or even that it is very sure-footed. Much less is it to say that willful co-ordination is the sole or the major basis of their unity, or that the power elite has emerged as the realization of a plan. But it is to say that as the institutional mechanics of our time have opened up avenues to men pursuing their several interests, many of them have come to see that these several interests could be realized more easily if they worked together, in informal as well as in more formal ways, and accordingly they have done so. [Pages 19–20.]

Mills gives the impression of not being consistent in his thesis, however, especially regarding the role of politicians, for he considers them as subordinates to the economic elite (now integrated with the military elite): "What is usually taken to be the central content of politics, the pressures and the campaigns and the congressional maneuvering, has, in considerable part, now been relegated to the middle levels of power" (p. 28). Elsewhere he speaks of the top politicians as the "lieutenants" of the economic elite. His chapter on the political elite (chapter 10) is the shortest in the book, and almost half of it deals with the civil service rather than the superordinate elected or appointed government officials. Even when he deals with the political elite, he considers it to consist only of those in the Executive branch; there are only a few casual references to the Legislative and Judicial branches. Thus, despite Mills's initial reference to three elites, the book portrays the population of the United States as a *single* power pyramid: the economic-military elite are on top, their appointed henchmen plus the politicians form a secondary level of power, and at the large base are the powerless undifferentiated masses (pp. 28–29). This national pattern prevails also in each of the several communities of the United States, at least in the major ones, except that the military may be absent from the local community power structure:

Local society is a structure of power as well as a hierarchy of status; at its top there is a set of cliques or "crowds" whose members judge and decide the important community issues, as well as many larger issues of state and nation in which "the community" is involved. Usually, although by no means always, these cliques are composed of old upper-class people; they include the larger businessmen and those who control the banks who usually also have connections with the major real-estate holders. Informally organized, these cliques are often centered in the several economic functions: there is an industrial, a retailing, a banking clique. The cliques overlap, and there are usually some men who, moving from one to another, co-ordinate viewpoints and decisions. There are also the lawyers and administrators of the solid *rentier* families, who, by the power of proxy and by the many contacts between old and new wealth they embody, tie together and focus in decision the power of money, of credit, or organization.

Immediately below such cliques are the hustlers, largely of new upper-class status, who carry out the decisions and programs of the top—sometimes anticipating them and always trying to do so. Here are the "operations" men— the vice-presidents of the banks, successful small businessmen, the ranking public officials, contractors, and executives of local industries. This number two level shades off into the third string men—the heads of civic agencies, organization officials, the pettier civic leaders, newspaper men and, finally, into the fourth order of the power hierarchy the rank and file of the professional and business strata, the ministers, the leading teachers, social workers, personnel directors. [Pages 36–7.]

Actually, Mills is not quite as inconsistent about the existence of *three* power elites as he at first appears to be, for later in his book he explains that, in his view, the economic-military elite have taken over the top "command" positions in the political elite. Thus his view is that a political elite might be said to exist, but it is manned and controlled by certain members of the economic-military elites. Nevertheless his initial statement that there are three power elites is quite misleading; it does not reflect his true views, and it allows his thesis to appear more acceptable than it should in view of the facts about the distribution of power.

Mills does not assume that the unity and integration of the power elite rests on elite consciousness or on deliberate co-ordination among all its members. He thus departs from European aristocratic theories of the elite and from conspiracy theories circulated in both Europe and the United States. Nevertheless, Mills's conception of the power elite is that it is more or less integrated and unitary, but he considers this integration and unity to be based on three other factors: "psychological similarity," "social intermingling," and "coinciding interests." The main *empirical* evidence he brings to these points is on "social intermingling"; he offers no data on "psychological similarity" and little on "coinciding interests," but infers that these result from extensive social interaction from childhood on. While our own inclination is to believe that the United States is too large and too heterogeneous to permit the economic leadership to be as integrated, in any of the three respects, as Mills says it is, we shall not present any direct data on these matters. We shall, however, consider how the *political* elite is subject to diverse pressures, to external limitations not subject to control by the economic elite, and to tendencies which on many occasions resist the interests of the economic elite.

But even at this early stage of our analysis we must express our amazement at the rationalistic nature of Mills's interpretation that an economic elite can control American society. In the first place, there are large-scale historical forces—often of an economic character—which constrain, limit, push, and direct any society in ways beyond the control of any segment in it. If Mills was a student of Marx and Veblen, among others, he apparently did not learn his lesson well. The substructure of any society—its geography, technology, economic organization, and basic institutions of family and religion—are only to a very limited extent manipulable by any one group, no matter how powerful or rational it is in the pursuit of its material interests. Related to this, but somewhat more manipulable, are the demands and requirements of that large-scale organization, the government. Perhaps Mills took these as given, and did not feel the need even to mention them.

In the second place, there are cultural values—both on the high plane of ideals and the low plane of everyday norms—which are also subject to only limited manipulation. The "American creed" of liberty, equality, fair play, justice, etc., and the more universal religious and humanistic ideals are not mere words which can be completely twisted and distorted to serve the interests of any group, even though man's ability to rationalize them away while pursuing his individual or sub-group interests is considerable. The everyday norms of mutual expectations in interpersonal relations set further limits on rational behavior, and these norms also are internalized by power elites no less than by the masses. Rational manipulation can take place within their framework, but not in spite of it, and if Mills wished to point out the facts of manipulation and the "higher immorality" in American society, he would be required to start from the general cultural framework of values and norms. Thirdly, there are the constraints on power, embodied in the Constitution and other forms of law, that are supported by public opinion in principle if not always in detail. Powerful leaders can sometimes get around basic law or change it, but not with ease or speed. In the fourth place, there are limits on rational pursuit of individual and group interests imposed by counter-elites (such as civil-rights groups, youth groups, and trade unions), kinship and friendship loyalties, public opinion, and voluntary associations. Mills explicitly denies the importance of these factors in American society, but we shall later adduce evidence that they are not without significance. Even if Mills were correct on this last point, we should have to consider his analysis sociologically inadequate through his neglect of the first three considerations. If the economic elite uses its power to make decisions for its own advantage in many instances, it lacks alternatives in other instances, and does not always behave rationally where there are alternatives.

It is because of the great social imperatives—that is, the physical, institutional, and cultural forces—that there is a certain similarity of action among the contending groups within a society (and sometimes even across national lines). Mills interprets this as the imposition on the political elites and other "secondary" leaders of the dominant will of the top economic elite, whereas usually it is nothing more than the lack of alternatives. That is, when leaders of the major political parties, or the leaders of the Western nations, or even the leaders of the United States and the Soviet Union came to an agreement, it is usually a case of reason bowing to the inevitable, rather than of lieutenants bowing to a hidden economic elite. Of course, there are the extremists—said to be at both ends—who refuse to believe this, and who, if they accede to political power, use that power to fly in the face of the inevitable. They either get smashed or reverse course without any directions from the economic elite. In world affairs we see this in the actions of Communist China; in the United States we see it in the local communities where right-wing extremists have been elected to public office.

Mills accepts the Marxist assumption of "false consciousness" in the masses—arising out of ignorance, apathy, and deliberate distortion (often with the aid of the mass media). He is supported here by much sociological research on anomie in an urbanized and mass culture, voting and non-voting patterns, alienation from work, the effects of the mass media, individualistic forms of social pathology, and the findings of vast body of research since Durkheim's study of suicide (1897). But, as we shall also attempt to show later, Mills's use of the facts of false consciousness in the mass suffers from two defects. First, Mills assumes that it is avoided by the economic elite, whereas the facts show that this is true only in degree. The economic power elite also has contracted some of the "illness" of the mass society. It sometimes deliberately and consciously works against its own interests, although perhaps less frequently than do the lower classes. Even its incidence of mental illness, addiction, and irrational crime is only somewhat lower than that found in the lower classes. Second, there are certain "reactions to the mass society" developing in all strata of American society which can be expected to operate against false consciousness to some extent. For example, mass education has some effect in immunizing people against ignorance and the distortions of the mass media; some voluntary associations bring their members into realistic participation in politics. Mills gives the impression that the inert masses in the United States are the great majority, whereas studies of participation in voluntary associations suggest that they are not over 40 per cent of the population, and are probably slowly decreasing in proportion. . . .

Mills's rebuttal to arguments about mass participation in voluntary associations and social movements rests on his opinion that such things are not important. This is not only a personal value judgment; it also leads to circular reasoning: the only important things in American life are those things the economic elite successfully seeks; since the economic elite has shown little interest in the civil-rights movement, either for or against it, then *ipso facto,* the civil-rights movement is not important, even though it involves the social energies and life chances of a sizable minority of the population.

Whereas Hunter says nothing regarding the means by which the economic elite control the government, Mills lists three such means (pp. 165–70 of *The Power Elite*).

He states, first, that the Constitution, particularly since the adoption of the Fourteenth Amendment, gives free rein to the corporate rich to run the economy. I would not basically quarrel with this statement standing alone, for the American economy is overwhelmingly one of free private enterprise and semi-monopoly capitalism, rather than of state capitalism or guild socialism. However, when Mills carries this over to the political realm, he cites only evidence that supports his view: "In virtually every case of [governmental] regulation that we examine the regulating agency has tended to become a corporate outpost" (p. 166).[15] He ignores the numerous and powerful governmental restraints and limitations on corporations—through the power to tax, to license, to set rates in interstate commerce, to control conditions of marketing (of securities as well as of products), to control the accuracy of labeling and advertising, to set the conditions of collective bargaining and the labor contract, and dozens of lesser governmental powers. It is of course true that in some of these areas (particularly rate-setting and licensing), the economic elite has found means of influencing the government administrators, but even here the fact that they must work through the government administrators (appointed by the President with the consent of the Senate) is a limitation on their power. It is simply incorrect to consider that the relation of government to the economy is the same in 1960 as it was in 1860 except insofar as the government today is even more controlled by the interests of the economic elite than it was then—which is Mills's position. The difficulty lies with Mills's contrast-conception, which is one of state capitalism, or guild socialism, or populism; for implicit in his remarks about the lack of government interference with the economy is his belief that the only real alternative to complete private enterprise is complete state or "worker" ownership, control, and operation of the economy.

The second means by which Mills considers that the economic elite controls the government is that of the large political campaign contribution. I agree that this is a major means of influence, though not of control. . . . However, Mills pays very little attention to this factor, which could provide the main factual basis for his thesis. I do not know why Mills considers it so unimportant, but I suspect it is probably because he has little understanding of how politics works.

The third means of elite control over government, which Mills considers the most important of all, he states in the following words: "As the corporate world has become more intricately involved in the political order, these executives have become intimately associated with the politicians, and especially with the key 'politicians' who form the political directorate of the United States government" (p. 167). More specifically:

During World War II they served on innumerable advisory committees in the prosecution of the war. They were also brought into the military apparatus more permanently by the awarding to many businessmen of commissions in the reserve officer corps. All this has been going on for a long time and is rather well known, but in the Eisenhower administration the corporate executives publicly assumed the key posts of the executive branch of the government. Where before the more silent power and the ample contract was there, now there was also the loud voice. [Pages 167–8.]

During the last three decades, since the First World War in fact, the distinction between the political and the economic man has been diminishing; although the corporation managers have, in the past, distrusted one of their own who stays too long in the political arena. They like to come and go, for then they are not responsible. Yet more and more of the corporate executives have entered government directly; and the result has been a virtually new political economy at the apex of which we find those who represent the corporate rich. [Page 169.]

I understand these and other statements by Mills to mean that the economic elite has taken over control of the Executive branch of the government. But just exactly how they have done that, he does not say. To point to many specific businessman appointments in the Eisenhower Administration does show a major (not exclusive) reliance of a Republican Administration on businessmen. It does not explain the means of control, and it does not prove that the businessman appointees are running the government for the benefit of business. I suspect that businessmen who go to work for the government develop a quite different point of view toward government from that of businessmen who never have government experience. The latter, I would hypothesize, remain largely alienated from, and hostile to, government even when it is in Republican hands. Mills himself acknowledges this when he states that the business elite become suspicious of their colleagues who remain in government service "too long." Part of the businessmen's antagonism to even Republican administrations, I suspect, is toward the permanent top civil servants, but mainly it is due to a lack of understanding of political processes. The Kennedy Administration made some major business appointments too; it made even more appointments of college professors. Despite the facetious observations, this does not mean that Harvard University (or the academic profession in general) has assumed political control of the nation. The activities of the Executive branch suggest that President Kennedy was mainly in control of his businessman and professor appointees. [The process by which Kennedy achieved the nomination for the presidency] was a political process, involving very little special dependence on the economic elite.

Mills does not give much consideration to the Congress, and does not claim that any significant number of businessmen have entered the Congress. Rather he holds, without evidence, that Congress is subordinate to the Executive branch and consists of persons who take orders from the economic elite. I do not doubt that a small number of congressmen have been "bought" by the economic elite, and that a larger number have viewpoints identical to those of the economic elite and contrary to the wishes of the majority of their constituencies. But I believe political processes are such that most congressmen are most of the time responsive to the wishes of the majority of their constituents.[16] And I believe, contrary to Mills, that congressional action is important to the outcome of key national issues. I do not claim to "prove" that these statements are correct, nor do I claim that congressmen or other elected officials are mere passive registers of the wishes of their constituencies. I seek . . . to illustrate the complexity of political processes, and to show how largely independent they are of controls from the economic elite. I seek to show this for the selection of the political elite in certain states . . . and for the passage of a specific piece of federal legislation. . . . Insofar as the facts presented about the political process in these studies are representative, they do not confirm Mills's portrayal of economic elite control, although they are not inconsistent with a statement that the economic elite has political influence considerably beyond its proportion in the population.

Mills specifies the theories of others to which he is opposed. He considers Ferdinand Lundberg's attribution of power to "America's Sixty Families" [17] as incomplete and partly out-of-date, although based on a fundamental truth. This propertied class, Mills believes, has been merged with the managerial elite "into a new corporate world of privilege and prerogative" (p. 147). This point explains also his criticism of James Burnham's *The Managerial Revolution*.[18] In Mills's view, there is no opposition of ownership and management; rather, these two groups have merged into a new class with continuity of interest from the time when there was no distinct managerial type. In other words, he accepts the theory of economic elitism of Lundberg and Burnham, but denies that the economic elite consists only of the propertied rich or of the executive managers. Mills holds that these two economic elites are really one, which he calls the "corporate rich": "They are a corporate rich because they depend directly, as well as indirectly, for their money, their privileges, their securities, their advantages, their powers on the world of the big corporations" (p. 148).

Another predecessor from whom Mills diverges is Robert Brady. Brady's thesis was that (1) in capitalistic societies control over means of production is increasingly centralized within a small number of giant corporations; (2) these corporations set up "peak associations" (like the National Association of Manufacturers) to speak for them on national political policy; (3) business and its peak associations tend to "shake off all popular restraints on such cumulative powers" as they acquire, and eventually they emerge as the controllers of totalitarian states, as in Italy and Germany. Brady believed that war accelerates economic concentration and economic power and feared that the end of World War II would see the United States become a totalitarian state along some fascist line. Mills did not believe that the economic elite was organized in such a conscious way, nor did he believe that it had to transform the state into a totalitarian form, since it more or less achieved its goals by "Madison Avenue" techniques and by controlling the popularly elected political elite. A prosperous economy (in terms of the interests of the economic elite) and the absence of an internal revolutionary threat along communist lines would keep the economic elite from setting up a totalitarian state. It can be seen that Mills follows the general theme of Lundberg, Burnham, and Brady, but has a more complex and sophisticated analysis which leads him to a different image of the way the economic elite controls American society.

Mills is in much more fundamental disagreement with the theories of A. A. Berle [19] and John Kenneth Galbraith.[20] He asserts that Berle believes in a "restraining corporation conscience," that is, a voluntary relinquishment of power on the part of the modern economic elite in the interests of the masses. Mills criticizes Berle by saying he mistakes expedient public relations and a liberal rhetoric of defense for a corporate soul (page 126). This is unfair to Berle, whose chief point is not that corporations have acquired a conscience or soul, but that the economic elite of today is more restricted in the exercise of arbitrary economic and political power than it was in the days of the "robber barons." Mills evaluates the power elite and finds its typical member is characterized by "intellectual mediocrity" and "higher immorality." We have no way of comparing the present elites with past ones in these respects, but we doubt that Mills does either. At any rate, it is in this particular characterization that Mills attacks Berle.[21]

Galbraith's thesis is that there are diverse economic interests, which check each other's power in an equilibrium of "countervailing power." Mills has many criticisms of this: (1) economic interests—including unions—are often in fact integrated or in collusion; (2) as Galbraith himself recognizes, "countervailing power" does not work in periods of inflation, when each economic interest seeks to outbid the other in pushing up the price of its product or service; (3) markets do not actually "generate" countervailing powers, except in a few unconcentrated fields such as food supply; (4) government does not in fact help the weaker economic interests. In general, Mills criticizes Galbraith for setting forth a theory which "is more ideological hope than factual description, more dogma than realism" (p. 126). This is somewhat unfair to Galbraith, who presents both facts and a proposal for government policy.

The thesis of the present book [*The Power Structure*] has little or nothing to do with the theories of Lundberg, Burnham, Brady, Berle, or Galbraith. It could agree with Mills regarding the limitations of Lundberg, Burnham, and Brady, and, while it is not incompatible with the theories of Berle and Galbraith, its validity is not dependent on the validity of those theories. This book [*The Power Structure*] limits itself to the political processes, and considers that Mills has presented so oversimplified a picture of the relation between the economic elite and the political processes as to be false. Specifically, this study presents evidence against the following statements of Mills:

There is no effective countervailing power against the coalition of the big businessmen—who, as political outsiders, now occupy the command posts—and the ascendant military men—who with such grave voices now speak so frequently in the higher councils.

While the professional party politicians may still, at times, be brokers of power, compromisers of interests, negotiators of issues, they are no longer at the top of the state.

The executive bureaucracy becomes not only the center of power but also the arena within which all conflicts of power are resolved or denied resolution. Administration replaces electoral politics. [Page 267.]

Implicit in these and other remarks are Mills's political assumptions that (1) voting means little or nothing; (2) there is no significant difference between the two major political parties; (3) the economic-military elite has an interest in all major political issues against the interest of the masses, and that the former interest is always victorious over the latter; (4) the Legislative branch of government is subordinate to the Executive branch. There are other political assumptions of Mills with which we shall not be concerned: " . . . the virtually complete absence of a civil service that constitutes a politically neutral, but politically relevant, depository of brainpower and executive skill, and the increased official secrecy behind which great decisions are made without benefit of public or even Congressional debate" (p. 296).

Mills adopts an economic determinism which we cannot accept. He points to the fact that most congressmen are of upper-class or middle-class origin (p. 248), and assumes that they must therefore reflect the economic interests of businessmen and other members of the economic elite. Even when a congressman does not have an upper-class or middle-class background, he is assumed to take orders from the economic elite. These assumptions neglect the vast amount of social welfare legislation, particularly since the 1930's, and of other legislation designed to protect the interests of the working classes. They neglect the fact that some of the wealthiest of elected government officials have been among those leading in the fight for such legislation. The aristocratic Franklin Roosevelt doubtless represented the interests of the working masses better than his "average man" political opponent of 1936, Alfred Landon; and a similar comparison could be made between the wealthy John Kennedy and his opponent of more nearly average wealth, Richard Nixon. Of course, Mills can consider Landon and Nixon as "lieutenants" of the economic elite, but he cannot get around the fact that Roosevelt, Kennedy, and such other liberal politicians as W. Averill Harriman, Joseph Clark, Herbert Lehman, Stuart Symington, and G. Mennen Williams are members of the upper economic class. It may be true that military leaders have growing power in government circles, but they have not succeeded in getting much of the legislation they have asked for, nor has any President allowed them to speak freely in public. It is not illuminating to be told by Mills that "a small group of men are now in charge of the executive decisions" (p. 231), for there has always been, and must continue to be, leadership in a democracy; this is even part of the definition of "executive." The significant question is in whose interests the political elite acts and whether it is checked by the mass of voters and of interest groups. There is every evidence that the masses of the American people today are better off economically, both absolutely and relatively, than they were in the past, and that this has been largely due to government intervention, supported by the majority of the voters.

It is explicit in Mills's and Hunter's analyses that the elected legislators have no power in and of themselves. At most, they are "lieutenants" who carry out the orders of the economic elite, who—Mills claims—have taken over the direction of the government through appointment to the top policy-making offices in the federal Executive. In fact, a considerable number of statutes originate in the Congress rather than in the Executive branch—more than in European parliamentary regimes—and many of these are responses to the wishes of private pressure groups, including those of the economic elite. Yet, there are also some bills that are originated by the congressmen themselves, sometimes in opposition to the wishes of both the Executive branch and the pressure groups. Congress also controls the purse strings, and the areas of taxation and appropriations involve far more creative opportunities than is generally understood.

Administrations since 1933 have been diligent in efforts to solve social problems, and have sought enabling statutes and appropriations from the Congress, a large number with success, some after a delay, and others with failure. In most cases Congress has "improved" the bills submitted to it by the Executive before passing them, and that has been its chief role. But in some outstanding instances, it has initiated or expanded legislation on its own when it felt the Executive branch was evasive or dilatory. The Civil Rights Act of 1964 and the Medicare Act of 1965 provide examples of liberal legislation enacted by Congress with provisions that went much beyond what the Administration requested. Congress's annual allocation of funds for medical research and often for medical facilities is usually greater than that requested by the President, and in 1965 Congress doubled the educational program for veterans that the President requested, and made a special allocation, that the President did not request, for schools in areas of high federal employment.[22]

There are a number of other general points to be made against the Mills-Hunter thesis. . . .

1. The important facts of political power and political influence are not "secret" or "hidden" or "behind the scenes" most of the time. Pressure groups —of which many represent economic interests—and public opinion operate on legislative and executive branches of government. But only a small proportion of federal legislators and executives are "in the control of" an economic elite. At state and local levels, a larger proportion of legislators seek their positions to serve special economic interests, but even when they do, many of their votes are in accord with their ideological conception of what the public interest is.

There is a circularity in Mills's reasoning because of his beliefs that the top economic elite effects its control of American society secretly and that the political elite consists of lieutenants of the commanding economic elite. From these premises he deduces that the *actions* of the political elite are generally the only means by which the wishes and interests of the commanding economic elite can be ascertained by the outside observers, and that the *words* of the political elite are mere window dressing to mislead the masses into voting for them. There are several factual questions at issue here—the extent to which there is a discrepancy between the words and deeds of the political elite, and the extent to which the deeds of the political elite do not reflect the interests and wishes of the public. But aside from these factual questions, there is dubious logic in reasoning that the political elite constantly proves its subordination to the economic elite by its actions, when there is no independent way of ascertaining what the commanding economic elite really wants because of its secret modes of operating. The economic elite in fact does often expound its wishes—in the programs and campaigns of the National Association of Manufacturers, the United States Chamber of Commerce, and more specialized groups such as the American Medical Association. As we shall see [elsewhere] the President and the majority of the Congress more often go against these programs than support them, although the businessmen are more likely to get their way when they seek narrow economic advantages from the independent regulatory commissions and the military procurement agencies. Are the National Association of Manufacturers, the Chamber of Commerce, and the American Medical Associaton merely engaging in window dressing to fool the public as to their true wishes when they come out with a program or campaign?

Secrecy in politics has many functions other than the desire to hide the control that may be exercised by the economic elite on the politicians. The New York Reform Democratic party leader, Edward U. Costikyan,[23] says:

The nature of politics and politicians is to reach decisions privately. This often leads the public to believe that secrecy is a screen to shield wrongdoing. It usually isn't. Generally it shields a desire for privacy, as well as some confusion, and some selfishness.

He acknowledges that the closed doors must usually simply protect a process that cannot function as well at a public hearing, yet he argues that the doors should be opened—at least more than they now are.

What goes on behind is normally perfectly exposable to the light of day. Only the mystery is destroyed. But, like magicians, politicians like to smile enigmatic smiles after a startling political result. For mystery breeds respect. And respect breeds power. And power is the principal asset and persistent natural goal of the politician.

Thus, the existence of secrecy in some political actions cannot by itself be taken as evidence that it hides business control of politics. Just how much secrecy there is in politics is an open question on which there is little evidence. Public ignorance of certain actions taken by politicians does not mean that there is secrecy; it often simply reflects the failure of the news media to report actions that were taken openly. Politicians interviewed by this author invariably stated, when asked about the frequency of the decisions they take in secret, that they occasionally found it expedient to act in secret, but that the secret usually "leaked out" in a matter of days or weeks. They all averred that the value of secrecy to them was temporary, and that they assumed, when they took secret actions, that the secret would likely ultimately become public. They also stated that many of the supposedly secret actions they took were not secret at all: newspaper and other mass media reporters were just not present, and when the news releases were finally issued, the reporters excused their own failure to be present by asserting that the decison-making had occurred secretly.

2. Granted there has been a deviation from the principle of "one man, one vote" because legislatures have failed to redistrict (federal court decisions are now changing this situation); because of gerrymandering, legislators still are fairly representative of the ideological distributions of their constituents. Most of the American people are basically conservative, although regularly willing and even anxious to support specific "reforms." Among the masses of the American people, there is a good deal of ignorance about politics and "false consciousness" about their interests. But so also is there among the economic elite. We have sought to illustrate the false consciousness of the economic elite in an analysis of the politics of the Medicare legislation before Congress in the period 1957–65. But in a far more important sense, the economic elite has demonstrated its false consciousness in its ideological commitment to a balanced federal government budget, which during the 1950's reduced the rate of national

economic growth and created several economic recessions. It was the federal Executive, in the persons of President Kennedy and Johnson acting on the advice of economists, that adopted governmental measures to create the sustained prosperity of the 1960's which worked to the benefit of the economic elite along with most other sectors of the American society. Similarly, social welfare measures inaugurated by President Franklin Roosevelt, and sustained and extended by all federal administrations since his, have usually been opposed by large segments of the economic elite (though not by all). Yet they have provided a floor under poverty which has prevented social unrest from reaching revolutionary proportions (particularly during the 1930's) and have also contributed to the total prosperity of the country. The facts would seem to favor a thesis quite different from that of Marx or Mills—that false consciousness is occasionally found in all segments of society, and, in the most important respects, is found in the economic elite more often than in the lower classes.

3. Mills holds that there are practically no ideological or policy differences between the two major political parties. There were occasions in which this seemed to be true before the 1930's, but since then they have been becoming increasingly different. Systematic studies show that party affiliation explains more congressional voting than any other single variable.[24] The divergence between the two major political parties has especially increased since the late 1940's, as a two-party system has developed in the Northern states and as some leading Republicans have challenged the loyalty of many Democratic leaders. Political partisans, such as former Secretary of State Dean Acheson, often express the antithesis of Mills' position on the facts:

> In 1919–20 the attack on the Democrats was savage and malicious. In 1950–52 the ferocity of the Republican attack knew no limits. It went beyond the policies involved and the competence of leaders. It struck at the character and patriotism of those who devised and executed policies. It assaulted institutions of government, and, as in the Bricker Amendment, even government itself. Nor did it stop at the water's edge. It involved the motives and character of nations and peoples associated with us. It is hardly too much to say that the whole conception of trust and confidence, including the confidence of the people in their own judgment, was brought into doubt. . . . When the ignorant are taught to doubt they do not know what they safely may believe.[25]

In the 1960's, the parties have diverged so sharply that the question can be raised whether the national consensus which holds the country together is not in jeopardy. By 1964, the Republican party was largely controlled by a group that considered most Democratic party leaders, and some of its own former leaders, subversives. Up to 1964 there was a coalition in Congress between the majority of the Republicans and the majority of the Southern Democrats, based on opposition to bills favoring civil rights for Negroes and welfare programs for the poor. With the growth of a two-party system in the South and the weakening of the Republican party in the North, as well as the adroit political leadership of President Johnson, this was no longer an effective coalition in the 1964–65 sessions of Congress, and a great number of "reform" bills passed which had previously been vigorously opposed by the majority of the economic elite. The weakening of the congressional "coalition" sharpened the division between the two major political parties, but it is premature to say that the coalition is entirely dead until the South completes its transition to a two-party system on the pattern of the North.

4. Mills and his followers have been critical of those political scientists like Dahl who hold that political power is pluralistic in the United States. Our position is not simply that power is pluralistic in American society, but that the society itself is pluralistic. The different spheres of life do not interpenetrate each other in the way that in India, for example, religious values and institutions permeate the average man's political, economic, family, artistic, educational, and other spheres of life. Or in the way that, in Hitler's Germany, or Stalin's Russia, political values similarly permeated all the other spheres of life. In the United States (and many other countries), practically every person has differentiated roles and values for the various spheres of life, and so power too usually does not significantly cross the boundaries of each sphere in which it is created. As Merton has put it: "Men with power to affect the economic life-chances of a large group may exert little interpersonal influence in other spheres: the power to withhold jobs from people may not result in directly influencing their political or associational or religious behavior." [26]

5. Since 1933, Democrats have won the great majority of the elections, naming all the Presidents but one (Eisenhower), dominating all the Congresses but two (1946–48, 1952–54), and electing a considerable majority of the governors and state legislatures. Yet the majority of businessmen have strongly supported the Republican party. Businessmen have not only not dominated the political scene, but have shown an increasing sense of frustration and bitterness at being "left out" in political decisions.

In 1960, the Committee on Economic Development conducted an attitude survey of bankers. One of the findings was that they felt that Congress ignored them and their interests. They pointed to the much lighter controls on their competitors, the savings and loan associations and the credit unions. In their belief this could be attributed to the "fact" that Congressmen were more likely to place their savings in these latter associations than in banks, and that, because of the high rate of bank failures in the early 1930's, banks were still regarded with suspicion—in spite of the many reforms in procedure that banks had made since then.

The brief two years (1952–54) when the Republicans controlled both the presidency and the Congress must have seemed like a "Restoration" for the majority of businessmen, and it was during this atypical period that C. Wright Mills must have written the bulk of *The Power Elite*. But alienation from government increased during the late years of the Eisenhower presidency as the Administration proved unable to achieve any of the major goals of the businessmen. They became even more antagonistic and truculent toward government when President Kennedy forced back the steel price rise, . . . and they went so far as to pull the Business Advisory Council out of its semiofficial relationship to the government. It was not until a politically extremist minority seized control of the majority of the Republican state organizations that a significant group of big businessmen exhibited a desire to take an accommodating position toward the Democrats. Big businessmen worked out a pragmatic relationship with President Lyndon Johnson [27]—which they had refused to do with Presidents Roosevelt, Truman, and Kennedy—but their subordinate role in the Johnson Administration was shown by the fact that more welfare and "reform" legislation was passed by the 1964–65 Congress, under Johnson's stimulation, than by any Congress since 1933.[28]

6. Mills contends that the American top elite has a common provenance: He says that they are upper-class people, who attend the same preparatory schools and private colleges, associate with each other throughout their lives, and pass on their power to their offspring. This picture is certainly not true for the top elected government officials. Very few sons of presidents, governors, and congressmen ever achieve top political positions. The men in these positions have the most diverse social origins. Of presidents in the twentieth century, only the two Roosevelts (sixth cousins to each other) were from the upper upper class, and only one came from a very wealthy family (Kennedy, whose family background is *nouveau riche*); Truman, Eisenhower, and Johnson could be said to have come from the lower middle class, and the others had somewhat higher middle-class family backgrounds. The Middle West provided as many presidents as did the East, and the small towns provided more than the opulent cities or suburbs. The majority did not attend the upper-class private schools or colleges. The great majority of the top elected officials of the United States have experienced a considerable amount of upward social mobility in comparison with their parents, not only in prestige and power, but also in education and wealth.

Studies by Newcomer, and by Warner and Abegglen, suggest that there is more social mobility in the economic elite than Mills claims.[29] In Newcomer's sample of big business executives in the early 1950's, 7.5 per cent were sons of workers, as compared to 4.2 per cent for the executives of 1900; in Warner and Abegglen's study of 8,562 businessmen from 1900 to 1950 there was an increase of 8 per cent in the proportion of executives whose fathers were laborers and a decrease of 10 per cent in those whose fathers were owners of businesses. But Mills is almost completely wrong about the absence of social mobility among the political elite.

Dwight D. Eisenhower, General of the Armies and President of the United States, appointer of many top-level business executives to the leading decision-making posts in government, must have been considered by Mills a leading member of the power elite. Yet he was one of the few in top decision-making posts who publicly warned against a "military-industrial complex" as a threat to the United States. On the significant occasion of his Farewell Address, this leader of the Establishment seemed to give support to one of C. Wright Mills's central theses:

In the councils of Government, we must guard against the acquisition of unwarranted influence, whether sought or unsought, by the military-industrial complex. The potential for the disastrous rise of misplaced power exists and will persist. We must never let the weight of this combination endanger our liberties or democratic processes.

Many individuals not persuaded by the scholar Mills were persuaded by the President Eisenhower.[30] Yet a closer reading of Eisenhower's speech shows that he was on a different track than Mills. In the first place, Eisenhower placed the danger in the future; Mills had the economic-military power elite already in control of the nation. Secondly, Eisenhower was arguing for the autonomy of government; Mills identified the government as a tool of the elite. Thirdly, Eisenhower—a leading figure in Mills's elite—was publicly denouncing the threat posed by that presumed elite, whereas Mills held that the members of the elite were like-minded and operated more or less in secret.

It is clear that Eisenhower was worried about the huge size of the armaments industry, and its consequent potential for using its great economic power to influence many areas of government, education, and science. . . .

Eisenhower may also have been worried about conflict of interest on the part of the nation's military leaders: As direct purchasers from the armaments industry, and as relatively low-paid government servants who could "retire" at an early age, were they not in danger of making decisions influenced by the fact that they could go into high-salaried jobs in one or another munitions firm after they retired? When Eisenhower made his statement, Congress was considering a bill to require retiring military procurement officers to wait two years before accepting a position in one of the supplying firms. But this may not be a long enough waiting period to prevent conflict of interest, and the law could not apply to civilians working for the Defense Department or to military officers not directly engaged in procurement. There were all sorts of ways of unduly influencing a military procurement officer: The military supply firms even set up [a] trade association, called the National Security Industrial Association, which has been in existence since World War II, to enhance their relationships with military leaders. Provision of information and gossip, wining and dining, and other standard techniques of lobbying were used on the military procurement officers. General Eisenhower was concerned about the conflict of interest on the part of his brother officers, and anxious to maintain the tradition of military independence and service.

Yet Eisenhower's conception of his role as President, as a mere enforcer of laws and mediator of the various conflicting forces in the Executive branch, did much to enhance the very dangers he called attention to. It was his successors, Kennedy and Johnson, because they had a conception of the dominant and decisive role of the presidency, who set industry back several times when it sought an inflationary rise in prices, and whose appointed Secretary of Defense, Robert McNamara, maintained his dominance over the military in all matters. These Presidents were political leaders, who saw a superordinate government as the check on any potential military-industrial complex.

There are some successors to Mills who recognize several defects in his analysis, yet hold to his central theme that there is a economic-military power elite which controls American society. Perhaps the most sophisticated of these are Pilisuk and Hayden,[31] who use the Eisenhower term "military-industrial complex," and define it as "an informal and changing coalition of groups with vested psychological, moral, and material interests in the continuous development and maintenance of high levels of weaponry, in preservation of colonial markets and in military-strategic conceptions of international affairs." These authors have at the same time narrowed Mills's conception to make it primarily operative in the fields of defense and foreign affairs (saying nothing about domestic matters), and broadened it to make it an intrinsic part of American culture and social structure.

> Our concept is not that American society contains a ruling military-industry complex. Our concept is more nearly that American society is a military-industrial complex. It can accommodate a wide range of factional interests from those concerned with the production or utilization of a particular weapon to those enraptured with the mystique of optimal global strategies. It can accommodate those with rabid desires to advance toward the brink and into limitless intensification of the arms race. It can even accommodate those who wish either to prevent war or to limit the destructiveness of war through the gradual achievement of arms control and disarmament agreements. What it cannot accommodate is the type of radical departures needed to produce enduring peace (pp. 98–9).

The problem, then, is not so much in a business elite or a military elite, as in "core beliefs" found among most Americans. These include: (1) "Efficacy is preferable to principle in foreign affairs. In practice this means that violence is preferable to non-violence as a means of defense." (2) "Private property is preferable to collective property." (3) ". . . the particular form of constitutional government which is practiced within the United States is preferable to any other system of government." When the attack is on such fundamental aspects of American culture, and the demand is for such a revolutionary set of changes, it is not possible to refute it by marshaling empirical facts about American life. . . . Therefore, we shall confine ourselves to the data which relate to Mills's more specific attack on American society. It should be noted, however, that the fact that some of the more sophisticated of Mills's successors have felt it necessary to go much beyond his arguments suggests that they find these arguments inadequate.

NOTES

[1] That the orthodox communist viewpoint regarding power in the United States today is still in terms of dominance by an economic elite was made evident in a series of interviews Walter Lippmann had with Premier Nikita Khrushchev in April 1961. When Lippmann said that decisions regarding foreign policy would be made by President Kennedy, "Khrushchev insisted that the forces behind the President would determine his policy. These forces behind the Kennedy administration he summed up in the one word: Rockefeller." It was also Khrushchev's opinion that Kennedy could not accelerate American economic growth "because of Rockefeller" and then added, "DuPont. They will not let him." (Walter Lippmann, syndicated columns, *Minneapolis Morning Tribune,* April 17, 18, 1961).

[2] The two political parties sometimes agree on almost identical specific pieces of

legislation, but mainly in the areas of foreign policy and national defense, practically never in regard to their programs or actions with respect to an economic elite.

[3] The functionalists in anthropology have used a consensus theory to explain the societies they typically study. When they, or the functionalists in sociology, use a consensus theory to explain heterogeneous, industrialized societies, our multi-influence hypothesis is opposed to theirs as well as to the economic-elite-dominance hypothesis. But we shall not deal here with the consensus or functionalist theory. I have considered sociological functionalism in three other publications: *The Institutions of Advanced Societies* (Minneapolis: University of Minnesota Press, 1958), ch. 1; "On Merton's Neo-Functionalism," *Alpha Kappa Deltan,* 30 (Spring 1960), 14–17; and "A Current Theoretical Issue in Social Gerontology," *The Gerontologist,* 4 (March 1964), 46–50.

[4] *America's Sixty Families* (New York: Vanguard, 1937).

[5] *The Power Elite* (New York: Oxford University Press, 1956); see esp. pp. 24–7.

[6] There is some difference of opinion as to the nature of the masses among the various proponents of the economic-elite-dominance hypothesis. C. Wright Mills depicts them as inherently passive and disorganized in the American system, completely unable and unwilling to resist their exploitation. The theorists of a communist bent, however, see them constantly resisting and struggling against their exploiters, but unable to take effective action because they have no access to the instruments of control. This theoretical difference is well expressed in the book by the communist theoretician Herbert Aptheker, *The World of C. Wright Mills* (New York: Marzani and Munsell, 1960).

[7] This contrast-conception ranges from the "communist stage" of Marx through the guild socialism of Mills (best expressed in his 1948 book, *The New Men of Power*) to the "social fascism" of some of the latter-day populists like Representative William Lemke of North Dakota, who, with the Catholic priest Charles Coughlin, sought in the mid-1930's to build a political movement around the goal of "social justice."

[8] *Community Power Structure* (Chapel Hill: University of North Carolina Press, 1953); *Top Leadership, U. S. A.* (Chapel Hill: University of North Carolina Press, 1959).

[9] *The Power Elite.* We shall occasionally make reference to other works by Mills, but it is the one which sets in fullest fashion the economic-elite-dominance hypothesis. Our criticism of this work does not necessarily imply criticism of other works by Mills that do not deal with the political power structure and processes.

[10] Among the best reviews of Mills's *The Power Elite* are those by C. A. Anderson and H. L. Gracey in the *Kentucky Law Journal,* vol. 46, no. 2 (Winter 1958), 301–17; Daniel Bell, "The Power Elite Reconsidered," *American Journal of Sociology,* 64 (November 9, 1959), 238–50; Robert A. Dahl, "A Critique of the Power Elite Method," *American Political Science Review,* 52 (June 1958), 463–9; and Talcott Parsons, "The Distribution of Power in American Society," *World Politics,* 10 (1957), 123–43. Among the best reviews of Hunter's *Top Leadership U.S.A.* are those of C. Arnold Anderson in the *American Journal of Sociology,* 65 (November 1959), 311; and of Robert O. Schulze, in the *Administrative Science Quarterly,* 4 (December 1959), 373–7. See also Robert A. Dahl in *The Journal of Politics,* 22 (February 1960), 148–51. On Hunter's earlier *Community Power Structure,* see Raymond E. Wolfinger, "Reputation and Reality in the Study of Community Power," *American Sociological Review,* 25 (October 1960), 636–44.

[11] For example, Alexis de Tocqueville, *Democracy in America* (1835).

[12] *The Process of Government* (Chicago: University of Chicago Press, 1908); *The*

Politics of Democracy (New York: W. W. Norton, 1940); *Party Government* (New York: Farrar and Rinehart, 1942); *The Governmental Process* (New York: Knopf, 1953); and *Politics, Parties and Pressure Groups* (New York: Knopf, 1959).

[13] For a consideration of how governmental processes affect economic life in the United States, see such works as Marshall Dimock, *Business and Government* (New York: Henry Holt 1949); and Robert E. Lane, *The Regulation of Businessmen* (New Haven: Yale University Press, 1954).

[14] Anderson and Gracey (see n. 10) say of the Mills book: "Whether or not its conclusions are valid, they cannot be derived from the data offered. The few bits of new data are handled incautiously. . . . At no time does he examine the precise operations of any single elite in any actual situation."

[15] To support this statement, Mills cites "Hearings before the Subcommittee on Study of Monopoly Power of the Committee on the Judiciary," House of Representatives, 81st Congress, 1st Sess. Ser. No. 14, Part 2-A (Washington: U.S. Government Printing Office, 1950), pp. 468–9. These hearings show the persistence of business monopolies in the face of antitrust legislation; they do not show that there is no effective regulation and limitation of business and industry in other spheres.

[16] If the majority of congressmen do not favor state capitalism or socialism, that is because their constituencies also do not. I speak of the fact of state capitalism or socialism, not the name. A significant minority of congressmen and of the American people probably favor some degree of state capitalism or socialism in fact, though not in name.

[17] New York: Vanguard, 1937. Mills also criticizes Lundberg on methodological grounds (p. 377).

[18] New York: John Day, 1941.

[19] *The Twentieth-Century Capitalist Revolution* (New York: Harcourt, Brace, 1954).

[20] *American Capitalism* (Boston: Houghton Mifflin, 1952).

[21] See Berle's review of Mills's *The Power Elite, The New York Times Book Review,* April 22, 1956, pp. 3, 22.

[22] *The New York Times,* April 5, 1966, p. 21.

[23] *Behind Closed Doors: Politics in the Public Interest* (New York: Harcourt, Brace and World, 1966), Preface.

[24] Julius Turner, *Party and Constituency: Pressures on Congress* (Baltimore: Johns Hopkins Press, 1951); H. Bradford Westerfield, *Foreign Policy and Party Politics* (New Haven: Yale University Press, 1955).

[25] Dean Acheson, *A Democrat Looks at His Party* (New York: Harper, 1955), p. 65.

[26] Robert K. Merton, "Patterns of Influence: A Study of Interpersonal Influence and of Communication Behavior in a Local Community," in Paul F. Lazarsfeld and Frank N. Stanton (eds.), *Communication Research: 1948–1949* (New York: Harper, 1949), p. 217.

[27] David T. Bazelon, "Big Business and the Democrats," *Commentary,* 39 (May 1965), 39–46.

[28] Throughout this book [*The Power Structure*] we leave in abeyance the situation before 1933. Certainly a strong case can be made for the thesis that much of the political leadership then was of a like mind with the economic elite. But this does not say that the latter dominated the former, in Mills's terms. An instructive study—both of the pro-business orientation of a dominating political leader and of his personal power independent of any outside influence—is Blair Bolles's political biography of House Speaker Joseph Cannon, *Tyrant from Illinois* (New York: W. W. Norton, 1951).

[29] Mabel Newcomer, *The Big Business Executive* (New York: Columbia University Press, 1955); W. Lloyd Warner and James C. Abegglen, *Big Business Leaders in America* (New York: Harper, 1955).

[30] I do not know if Mills welcomed Eisenhower's statement. Among those who accepted it as verification of Mills's thesis were Fred J. Cook, *The Warfare State* (New York: Macmillan, 1962); and Marc Pilisuk and Thomas Hayden, "Is There a Military Industrial Complex which Prevents Peace?" *Journal of Social Issues,* 21 (July 1965), 67–117. The latter mentions many others.

[31] *Op. cit.;* see esp. pp. 91–2, 98–9.

B. POWER IN AMERICA: THE LOCAL COMMUNITY

5. THE STRUCTURE OF POWER IN REGIONAL CITY

Floyd Hunter

One of the first tasks in making a theoretical analysis of the community is that of delimiting and defining it as a structure.[1] The task of delimitation may take into account four basic elements, namely (1) personnel (members), (2) test(s) of admission and membership, (3) distinctive roles or functions of the members, and (4) norms regulating the conduct of the personnel.[2] The physical limits of the structure with which this study is concerned have been set, or at least an awareness of such limits has been indicated. We shall presently be concerned with all of the elements suggested here, and most particularly with the first three, but only in relation to a segment of the community—the power element. The fourth item, norms regulating conduct within the community of Regional City, presents problems with which the present study does not deal, except in a passing fashion. All of the norms of behavior of power personnel in Regional City are not known, but some specifications of men which may indicate norms will be outlined.

The personnel with which the current discussion is concerned represents but a minute fraction of the community in which it moves and functions. It does represent a definite group, however, and a very important one in Regional City. No pretense is made that the group to be discussed represents the totality of power leaders of the community, but it is felt that a representative case sample is presented, and that the men described come well within the range of the center of power in the community.

It will be recalled that the leaders selected for study were secured from lists of leading civic, professional, and fraternal organizations, governmental personnel, business leaders, and "society" and "wealth" personnel suggested by various sources. These lists of more than 175 persons were rated by "judges" who selected by mutual choice the top forty persons in the total listings. These forty were the object of study and investigation in Regional City. Some data were collected about the total number. Twenty-seven members of the group were interviewed on the basis of a prepared schedule plus additional questions as the investigation proceeded. Any figures used in the study will need to be tied fairly rigidly to the twenty-seven members on whom there are comparable data.

SOURCE: *Floyd Hunter, Community Power Structure* (Chapel Hill: The University of North Carolina Press, 1953), pp. 60–113. Reprinted by permission.

93

. . . The fourteen under-structure professionals in civic and social work who were interviewed have also provided data which may be considered comparable.

The top leaders, the under-structure professionals, and the Negro community leaders represent community groups. They are identifiable groups. Since they are definitely groups, I shall rely to a considerable extent, in this portion of the discussion, upon George C. Homans for certain hypotheses he has put forward on group structure.[3]

The system of power groups which is being examined may not be called a closed system. The groups are links in a total pattern, which may offer suggestive clues to total power patterns in the operating system of Regional City. There are gaps in the power arc which investigation may not be able to close. Actually the discussion here is primarily concerned with the structuring of power on a policy-making level. Only a rudimentary "power pyramid" of Regional City will be presented. One may be content to do this because I doubt seriously that power forms a single pyramid with any nicety in a community the size of Regional City. There are *pyramids* of power in this community which seem more important to the present discussion than *a* pyramid. Let me illustrate this point.

In the interviews, Regional City leaders were asked to choose ten top leaders from the basic list of forty. The choices of the twenty-seven persons answering this question showed considerable unanimity of opinion. One leader received twenty-one votes out of a possible twenty-seven. Other leaders received nearly as many votes. Some received no votes at all. One could pyramid the forty leaders on the basis of the votes cast for them, as has been done in Table 1, but the pyramid is not a true expression of the existing relationships between the top leaders of the community. George Delbert, for example, was chosen eight times more than Charles Homer, and Homer is consequently six places down the scale from Delbert. Delbert is considered a "big man" in Regional City affairs, but he is not as big as Homer, according to most of the informants in answer to the simple question, "Who is the 'biggest' man in town?"

The question on which Delbert came to the top of the voting poll was phrased, "If a project were before the community that required *decision* by a group of leaders—leaders that nearly everyone would accept—which *ten* on the list of forty would you choose?" Delbert came out on top in this question, but not on the one related to who is the biggest man in town. Thus the pyramid scheme suggested by the voting poll of leaders, related to making projects move, must be modified in relation to the factors which weigh in Homer's favor in other areas related to power. Quite possibly some of these factors are Homer's wealth, his social position, and his business position. Homer is from an old family of wealth in Regional City. He is the wealthiest man in the community according to most reports. He is chairman of the board of the community's largest industry in volume of sales. Delbert, on the other hand, is the president of a large corporation but is a salaried man—with a very large reputed salary. There is a distinction made between salaried personnel and owners of enterprises in Regional City whether the salary be large or small. Delbert's family background is also not comparable to Homer's.

This is not to say that Delbert is not a powerful man. He is. He can command

TABLE 1. REGIONAL CITY LEADERS RANKED ACCORDING TO NUMBER OF VOTES RECEIVED FROM OTHER LEADERS IN LEADERSHIP POLL *

Leaders	Number of Votes
George Delbert	21
Cary Stokes	19
Ray Moster	18
Peter Barner	17
James Treat	15
Fargo Dunham	14
Charles Homer	13
Adam Graves, Joseph Hardy, Luke Street, Harry Parker, Jack Williams	12
Avery Spear	11
Elsworth Mines	10
Percy Latham	9
Mabel Gordon, Arthur Tarbell	5
Truman Worth, Edna Moore, Mark Parks	4
Harvey Aiken, Epworth Simpson, Bert Tidwell, Grover Smith, Edward Stokes	3
Phillip Gould, Harold Farmer, Brenda Howe, Gary Stone, Ralph Spade, Herman Schmidt	2
John Webster, Samuel Farris, Norman Trable, Claudia Mills, Horace Black, Howard Rake	1
Hetty Fairly, Gloria Stevens, Russell Gregory	0

* Code numbers used in analyzing data and corresponding to fictional names of leaders are as follows:

1. Latham	14. Delbert	28. Mills
2. Graves	15. Farris	29. Spade
3. Dunham	16. Stevens	30. Gregory
4. Mines	17. Trable	31. Parker
5. Smith	18. Schmidt	32. Williams
6. Fairly	19. Moore	33. Black
7. Webster	20. Farmer	34. Tidwell
8. Worth	21. Barner	35. Tarbell
9. C. Stokes	22. Parks	36. Moster
10. Stone	23. Gould	37. Treat
11. Simpson	24. E. Stokes	38. Street
12. Aiken	25. Gordon	39. Rake
13. Howe	26. Spear	40. Homer
	27. Hardy	

the services of more than 50,000 employees, and he has a very large voice in community matters—a larger voice perhaps than Homer's, since he uses it oftener. Delbert is willing to serve on top-flight community committees and boards. Homer is not. Homer says of himself, "I will work on no boards or committees. I work entirely through other men." His attitude on this matter is well known in the community, and consequently he was chosen fewer times than Delbert on the question under discussion. In spite of his methods of work he was chosen by almost half the men voting on the question.

The validity of the question concerning who might be chosen to "decide" on a community project cannot be measured purely in terms of a pyramid-structuring. Its validity for this study lies in the fact that the question determined, in some degree, "how near the center" this group was that could "move things" in the affairs of the community. Each man interviewed was asked to add names of persons he considered as powerful as or more powerful than the men listed. Sixty-four names were added to the list. Thirty-seven of the additional names were mentioned but once by informants. Sixteen were mentioned twice; five, three times; five, four times; and one, five times. Eleven informants added names, but there was general agreement that the list was a fairly comprehensive one as it stood, with the exceptions mentioned.

The high consensus regarding the top leaders on the list of forty, plus the lack of any concerted opinion on additional individuals, would indicate that the men being interviewed represented at least a nucleus of a power grouping.

The question was also put to interviewees, "How many men would need to be involved in a major community project in Regional City 'to put it over'?" The answers to this question varied from, "You've got the men right here on this list —maybe ten of them," to "fifty or a hundred." One informant said, "Some of the men on this list would undoubtedly be in on getting the project started. After it got moving, perhaps six hundred men might be involved either directly or indirectly." This was the largest figure any informant gave. The informant elaborated on the answer by saying that a large fund-raising campaign was the thing he had in mind, and he illustrated the point by speaking of a fund drive for a hospital building program that had recently been completed in Regional City. He said that he could count the men on his hands who had "sparked" the drive, but hundreds of volunteers had been used from the civic associations and the general community to "put the drive over the top." He felt that any project for civic improvement would likely involve the same type of organization.

In the above illustration of structured action, the "men of independent decision" are a relatively small group. The "executors of policy" may run into the hundreds. This pattern of a relatively small decision-making group working through a larger under-structure is a reality, and if data were available, the total personnel involved in a major community project might possibly form a pyramid of power, but the constituency of the pyramid would change according to the project being acted upon.

In other words, the personnel of the pyramid would change depending upon what needs to be done at a particular time. Ten men might, for example, decide to bring a new industry into the community. Getting the industry physically established and operating might take the disciplined and coordinated action of a few more men or several hundred men, depending on the size of the project. Some of the same decision men in another instance might be involved in starting a program for some local governmental change, but another group of men would be involved in carrying out the decisions reached. Both projects are power oriented, but each requires different personnel in the execution. The men in the under-structure may have a multiplicity of individual roles within the totality of the community structure which can be set in motion by the men of decision.

As I became familiar with the list of forty names through the interviewing process, it became evident that certain men, even within the relatively narrow range of decision leaders with whom I was dealing, represented a top layer of personnel. Certain men were chosen more frequently than others, not only in relation to who should be chosen to decide on a project, as has already been indicated, but the same men interacted together on committees and were on the whole better known to each other than to those outside this group. Through analyzing the mutual choices made by those interviewed, it will be shown that there is an *esprit de corps* among certain top leaders, and some of them may be said to operate on a very high level of decision in the community; but this will not necessarily mean that one of the top leaders can be considered subordinate to any other in the community as a whole. On specific projects one leader may allow another to carry the ball, as a leader is said to do when he is "out front" on a project which interests him. On the next community-wide project another may carry the ball. Each may subordinate himself to another on a temporary basis, but such a structure of subordination is quite fluid, and it is voluntary.

In a scale of mutual choices among twenty of the top leaders (that is, when two leaders chose each other in the leadership poll), there is indication of a selective process in leadership choices made by the men of decision. Again, these choices were made on the basis of "who might best decide on a project." The fact that the mutual choices remain well within the upper limits of the ranking scale (Table 1) indicates definite selectivity.

A sociogram, adapted from Lundberg and Lawsing's work in a Vermont community, was constructed to show graphically the interrelationships of the choices indicated in Table 2.[4] The Vermont study indicated "friendship choices" made by 256 persons interviewed and showed in sociometric form both single and mutual choices of friends of the respondents.[5] Our sociogram shows only the mutual choices among forty persons who were asked to choose ten top leaders from the list of forty. Figures 1 through 4, to follow, are drawn from data collected from twenty-seven of the total list of forty. With one exception,[6] the leaders receiving a high number of votes as leaders were interviewed, and

TABLE 2. LEADERSHIP AS DETERMINED BY NUMBERS OF MUTUAL CHOICES AMONG 40 POWER LEADERS

Leaders	Number of Mutual Choices
Delbert, Hardy	6
Barner, Moster, Street, Dunham	5
Graves, Homer, Mines, Williams	4
Latham, Tidwell	3
Parker, E. Stokes Parks, Spade, Stone, Tarbell, Webster	1

scheduled data were gathered from them. The group receiving the largest number of votes will be designated an upper-limits group in contradistinction to a lower-limits group which received fewer votes from the leaders interviewed. Mutual choices of leaders are shown only among the twenty-seven persons interviewed and do not include their choices among the forty leaders. The sociogram of the mutual choices of twenty-seven leaders is illustrated in Figure 1.[7] The usefulness of the sociogram lies in the fact that it does indicate that the

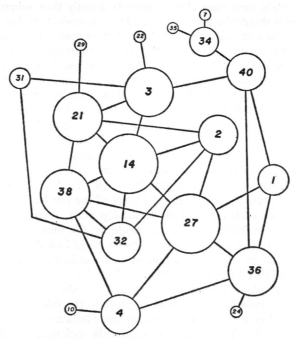

FIG. 1. Mutual Choices Made by Leaders in Regional City Leadership Poll. (Each circle represents a leader involved in one or more mutual choices with another leader. Size of the circle in each instance indicates a relative number of choices received by the individual leader. For key to numbers, see footnote to Table 1.)

FIG. 2. Mutual Choices of 27 Leaders in Regional City Leadership Poll. (For key to numbers, see footnote to Table 1.)

leaders who were most frequently chosen as the very top leaders tended to choose one another more frequently than they chose persons who received the fewest number of votes. Aside from this point, the sociogram was not found to be particularly useful.

The principal objection to the sociogram may be illustrated in this way: Number 14, George Delbert, in the sociogram may be considered the "star," since he has the highest number of mutual choices. However, the study of Regional City was convincing on the point that number 40, Charles Homer, was the more powerful man. Thus the same objection obtains that was found

FIG. 3. All Choices of Upper-Limits Group of 12 Leaders in Leadership Poll. (For key to numbers, see footnote to Table 2.)

to hold true in pyramiding the total votes cast for all leaders. It was also felt that any one of the men who surround the "star," number 14, could be just as powerful and influential in initiating and carrying through a particular project in the community. The sociogram does not show a true working relationship between the persons described. F. Stuart Chapin, in discussing "star isolates," has voiced some of the same objections.[8] The dimension of status is lacking in the flat-surfaced sociogram presented.

The leaders named in mutual choices as indicated in Table 2 do, however, represent a majority in the upper limits of the group of forty men and women in the Regional City decision-leader group. By using this group as an upper-limits group, and comparing it with the remaining leaders interviewed in relation to committee interaction, the hard core of leadership represented by the former group may be shown more clearly. And for clarity, it may be repeated that here an attempt is being made to isolate decision leaders from other elements of personnel in the community, in order that they may be discussed as a structural grouping.

In order to present another visual picture of the differentiation of choices among the leadership group interviewed, Figures 2, 3, and 4 have been prepared.[9] The top half of the circle in each figure shows by code number those leaders who received the highest number of votes from other leaders for their position as a leader. The bottom half of the circle shows the leaders who received the lowest number of leadership choices.

Figure 2 represents the mutual choices among all leaders responding to the question on this item. It may be clearly seen that most of the mutual choices occur among members of the upper-limits group. This clustering of choices obtains also in Figure 3, in which all choices of the upper-limits group of leaders are shown. Relatively few times did the top leaders go outside the upper-limits group to choose leaders. Contrariwise, Figure 4 shows that the lower-limits group often looked to the upper group in choosing top leaders.

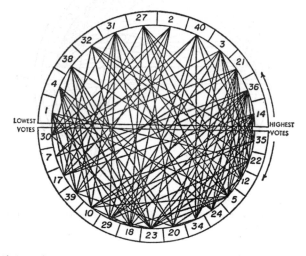

FIG. 4. All Choices of Lower-Limits Group of 15 Leaders in Leadership Poll. (For key to numbers see footnote to Table 1.)

The question was also asked each person interviewed, "Indicate how many persons (in the list of forty) you have worked with on committees within the past five years?" The upper-limits group indicated that they have worked with an average of twenty-nine persons on the list. The lower-limits group indicated that they had worked with an average of only twenty-one persons on the list. The professional under-structure of civil and social workers were asked the same question and indicated that they had worked with an average of only ten persons on the list. There is a definite drop, therefore, in the rate of interaction between each of the three groups and the group of forty leaders. Each group has access to the other, but those in the upper-limits group are in contact with other leaders more frequently, in committee work, at least. The under-structure professionals, with few exceptions, interact with persons immediately above them and with other professionals close to them in the power scale.

Another index used to discover the degree of relationship existing between the leaders interviewed and the total group of forty leaders was based upon a question which asked, on a six-point scale, how well known each person on the list of forty was to the interviewee. The scale read: "How well do you know each person (on the list of forty): (1) related____ , (2) know socially____, (3) know well____, (4) know slightly____, (5) heard of him____, (6) not known____." By again utilizing the upper-limits and lower-limits groups of leaders, and through comparison of these two groups with the professional under-structure personnel, we see a definite differentiation between the groups. In order not to present too confusing an array of figures, we shall indicate only the average number of persons known well or better in each group.

The upper-limits group knew well or better an average of thirty-four persons in the list of forty. The lower-limits group of top leaders knew an average of 28.7 leaders well or better. The professional under-structure averaged only 7.3 persons for this same degree of acquaintance. Obviously the upper-structure is better acquainted with the total group of top leaders, in addition to having a higher rate of committee interaction with this same group. The professional persons who carry out the decisions of the policy-making group are definitely differentiated from the top leaders in rates of interaction and in degree of acquaintance with the top leaders.

Our rudimentary statistical conclusions on the degrees of relationship among the persons named were borne out in qualitative interviewing. Over and over, the same persons were named as influential and consequently able to "move things" in Regional City. The significance of a high degree of interaction is suggested by Homans' hypothesis, "The more nearly equal in social rank a number of men are, the more frequently they will interact with one another." [10] Our findings bear out this hypothesis.

One other index was used to determine how closely integrated the upper-limits group was in relation to the lower-limits group. By ranking the leaders according to the number of leadership choices received from other leaders and analyzing how far up the scale or how far down the scale each went in making his choice, one finds a differentiating picture of the two groups. Members of the upper-limits group would go both up and down the scale from their own position in their choices, but not very far. They would go up an average of 5.4 places. They would go down an average of 4.9 places in their choices. These figures indicate a tendency to choose persons as leaders who are fairly close to the choosers in the scale.

The lower-limits personnel, on the other hand, tended almost entirely to choose men above them in rank. They would go up the scale an average of 13.1 places, and would go down only 0.6 places in their choices. It would seem from this evidence that the under group defers to the upper group, and that there is some solidarity in the upper echelons of policy-makers.

As shown earlier, power has been defined in terms of policy leadership, and the data given in the present chapter make a beginning at defining structural power relations. A group of men have been isolated who are among the most powerful in Regional City. It has been shown that they interact among themselves on community projects and select one another as leaders. Their relations with one another are not encompassed in a true pyramid of power, but some degree of ranking, even in the top-level policy leadership group, has been indicated. Let us now look at policy personnel patterns in another way.

In sizing up any individual one often asks, "What do you do for a living?" The reply to this question allows one rather quickly to rank another in a rough scale of social values. The men under discussion hold commercial, industrial, financial, and professional positions in Regional City that tend to classify them in the minds of any observer. In order to make a beginning at seeing the relations among the men of power in more personal terms than statistics will allow, let us examine a list of positions held by some of the leaders of the policy-determining group in Regional City (Table 3).

It can be seen at a glance that most of the leaders hold positions as presidents of companies, chairmen of boards, or professional positions of some prestige. Generally speaking, the companies represented in the listing are of major enterprise proportions. More than half the men may be said to be businessmen, if the term is used broadly. The major economic interests of the community are overwhelmingly represented in the listing. The pattern of business dominance of civic affairs in Regional City is a fact. No other institution is as dominant in community life as the economic institution, and this phenomenon will be dealt with at greater length under an appropriate heading.

Figure 5 represents those leaders who are related to one another as directors on boards of corporate enterprises in Regional City. The figure is intended to show that the economic interests of the leaders are in some measure coordinate. Again, one cannot rely too heavily upon a schematic diagram to understand the interrelations of leadership patterns, but such configurations as have been shown cumulatively tend to lend credence to the fact that there are structural relations among the members of the leadership group. All interviews with leaders helped to fill in some of the structural gaps. The sources of data for this figure give only a partial sample of existing corporate board relationships. Comparable data could be obtained only from fifteen out of the total leadership group of forty.

One of the first interviews had in Regional City was with James Treat of the Southern Yarn Company. He gave a great deal of information concerning power relations in the community. Among other things, he supplied a clue to certain existing clique relationships and considerable information about them which was later verified. Several times in his conversation he had used the term "crowds" in describing how certain men acted in relation to each other on community projects, and he was asked to explain the term. His reply ran in this vein:

"I simply mean that there are 'crowds' in Regional City—several of them— that pretty well make the big decisions. There is the crowd I belong to (the Homer Chemical crowd); then there is the First State Bank crowd—the Regional Gas Heat crowd—the Mercantile crowd—the Growers Bank crowd—and the like."

Mr. Treat was asked to give the names of some of the men who were active in each crowd, and he said:

"Sure! The biggest man in our crowd is Charles Homer. I belong to his crowd along with John Webster, Bert Tidwell, Ray Moster, Harold Jones, James Finer,

TABLE 3. POLICY-MAKING LEADERS IN REGIONAL CITY
BY OCCUPATIONAL POSITION

Type of Occupation	Name of Leader	Name of Organizational Affiliation	Position
Banking, Finance, Insurance	Hardy	Investment Company of Old State	President
	Mines	Producer's Investments	President
	Schmidt	First Bank	President
	Simpson	Second Bank	Vice-President
	Spade	Growers Bank	President
	Tarbell	Commercial Bank	Executive Vice-President
	Trable	Regional City Life	President
Commercial	Aiken	Livestock Company	Chairman, Board
	Black	Realty Company of Regional City	President
	Delbert	Allied Utilities	President
	Dunham	Regional Gas Heat Company	General Manager
	Grave·	Refrigeration, Incorporated	President
	Parker	Mercantile Company	Executive Manager
	Parks	Paper Box Company	Chairman, Board
	Smith	Cotton Cloth Company	Manager
	C. Stokes	Oil Pipe Line Company	President
	Webster	Regional City Publishing Company	Managing Editor
	Williams	Mercantile Company	Chairman, Board
Government	Barner	City Government	Mayor
	Gordon	City Schools	Superintendent
	Rake	County Schools	Superintendent
	Worth	County Government	Treasurer
Labor	Gregory	Local Union	President
	Ston_	Local Union	President
Leisure	Fairly	None	Social Leader
	Howe	None	Social Leader
	Mills	None	Social Leader
	Moore	None	Social Leader
	Stevens	None	Social Leader
Manufacture and Industry	Farris	Steel Spool Company	Chairman, Board
	Homer	Homer Chemical Company	Chairman, Board
	Spear	Homer Chemical Company	President
	E. Stokes	Stokes Gear Company	Chairman, Board
	Treat	Southern Yarn Company	President
Professional *	Farmer	Law Firm	Attorney
	Gould	Law Firm	Attorney
	Latham	Private Office	Dentist
	Moster	Law Firm	Attorney
	Street	Law Firm	Attorney
	Tidwell	Law Firm	Attorney

* Attorneys' affiliations not given. Without exception they are corporation lawyers.

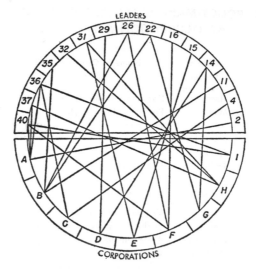

FIG. 5. Interlocking Directorates of Corporate Leaders in Regional City. (For key to numbers, see footnote to Table 1.)

Larry Stroup, and Harold Farmer. There are others, but they would be on the edges of this crowd. These would be the ones to be brought in on anything.

"In the State Bank crowd there would be Herman Schmidt, Harvey Aiken, Mark Parks, and Joseph Hardy. Schmidt used to be the biggest man in that crowd, but young Hardy is coming up fast over there.

"In the Regional Gas Heat crowd there is Fargo Dunham, Elsworth Mines, Gilbert Smith, and Percy Latham maybe. George Delbert might be said to belong to that crowd, but he is a pretty independent fellow. He moves around [from crowd to crowd] quite a bit.

"The Mercantile crowd is made up of Harry Parker, Jack Williams, Luke Street, Adam Graves, Cary Stokes, and Epworth Simpson.

"The Growers Bank crowd would be Ralph Spade, Arthur Tarbell, and Edward Stokes. They are kind of a weak outfit, but they come in on a lot of things. Spade is probably the most aggressive of the lot, but he's not too much at that!"

With this information given, Mr. Treat was asked to tell how these crowds would operate in relation to one another on a community-wide project, and he outlined the procedure very clearly. This type of action will be given in fuller detail in connection with the techniques of power wielding, but it may be said here that representatives from each crowd are drawn into any discussion relative to a major community decision. Each man mentioned as belonging to a crowd also belongs to a major business enterprise within the community—at least the clique leader does. His position within the bureaucratic structure of his business almost automatically makes him a community leader, if he wishes to become one. The test for admission to this circle of decision-makers is almost wholly a man's position in the business community in Regional City. The larger business enterprises represent pyramids of power in their own right, as work units within the community, and the leaders within these concerns gather around them some of the top personnel within their own organization. They then augment this nucleus of leadership by a coterie of selected friends from other establishments to form knots of interest called "crowds" by Mr. Treat. The outer edges of any crowd may pick up such men as Percy Latham, the dentist, who in turn picks up others in relation to any specific activity in which the crowd may be interested. The top men in any crowd tend to act together, and they depend upon men below them to serve as intermediaries in relation to the general community.

The crowds described by Mr. Treat were also mentioned by numerous other informants. These crowds did not, however, exhaust the possibilities of clique relations within the larger group of policy leaders. Twenty-one distinct groupings were picked up within the forty persons on the list, as the study proceeded, but the crowds mentioned by Treat seemed to be the most generally recognized groupings. Several of the top leaders within the crowds would "clear with each other" informally on many matters. The older men, as mentioned earlier, tended to get their heads together on most matters, as did the younger group, but such relationships were not completely stable. Each man at the top of a "crowd pyramid" depended upon those close to him in business to carry out decisions when made. An older man, for example, could not command another older man to do something, but within his own crowd there would be a hierarchy he could put to work. In most instances decision-making tended to be channeled through the older men at some point in the process of formulation, but many things may be done on the initiative of any combination of several powerful leaders in the crowds named. None of the leaders indicated that he could work alone on any big project, nor did any feel that there was any man in the community with such power. The individual power leader is dependent on others in Regional City in contrast to mill or mining company towns where one man or one family may dominate the community actions which take place.

Society prestige and deference to wealth are not among the primary criteria for admission to the upper ranks of the decision-makers according to the study of Regional City. The persons who were included in the listing of forty top leaders purely on the basis of their wealth or society connections did not, with three or four exceptions, make the top listing of persons who might be called upon to "put across a community project." As has been mentioned before, a distinction is made between persons of wealth and social prestige who engage in work and those who do not. The persons of wealth are perhaps important in the social structure of the community as symbolic persons. They may be followed in matters of fashion and in their general manner of living. Their money may be important in financing a given project, but they are not of themselves doers. They may only be called decisive in the sense that they can withhold or give money through others to change the course of action of any given project. Gloria Stevens spends large sums of money on Regional City projects, but the expenditures are made through her lawyer, Ray Moster. She does not interact with any of the top leaders whom we interviewed, other than Moster, so far as could be ascertained. Hetty Fairly, another woman of wealth, spends her charitable monies through a foundation handled by a lawyer not on the list of leaders. The lawyers may be vigilant in serving the interests of their clients in both instances, and a part of the vigilance exercised is in keeping abreast of possible tax incursions on the "frozen wealth" of the foundations. In this there may be some connection with power, but it is rather obscure in terms of the definition of power as being the ability of persons to move goods and services toward defined goals. If there is power in the charitable foundation structures, it resides in the lawyers who operate them, rather than in the donors who are largely inactive in the affairs of the foundations.

Political eminence cannot be said to be a sole criterion for entry into the policy echelons of Regional City's life, generally speaking. The two exceptions to this statement are embodied in Mayor Barner and County Treasurer Truman Worth. Both Barner and Worth were successful businessmen before becoming involved in local politics to the point of seeking public office. Their interests may be said to be primarily business in the strict sense of the word. Both have a popular following that has kept them in office, but their close associates are businessmen. Mayor Barner had only one picture in his office—that of Charles Homer, the biggest businessman in the community. Both Barner and Worth look to businessmen constantly for advice before they make a move on any project concerning the whole community. Furthermore, they do not ordinarily "move out front" on any project themselves, but rather follow the lead of men like Delbert, Graves, or any one of the other leaders of particular crowds.

The point made at this turn of the discussion is not a new one. Businesssmen are the community leaders in Regional City as they are in other cities. Wealth, social prestige, and political machinery are functional to the wielding of power by the business leaders in the community. William E. Henry puts the matter this way:

> The business executive is the central figure in the economic and social life of the United States. His direction of business enterprise and his participation in informal social groupings give him a significant place in community life. In both its economic and its social aspects the role of the business executive is sociologically a highly visible one.[11]

The "visibility" suggested by Henry is a highly applicable concept in connection with an analysis of Regional City leadership. One need not labor the point. This study has already shown that busines leaders take a prominent position in Regional City civic affairs.

In the general social structure of community life social scientists are prone to look upon the institutions and formal associations as powerful forces, and it is easy to be in basic agreement with this view. Most institutions and associations are subordinate, however, to the interests of the policy-makers who operate in the economic sphere of community life in Regional City. The institutions of the family, church, state, education, and the like draw sustenance from economic institutional sources and are thereby subordinate to this particular institution more than any other. The associations stand in the same relationship to the economic interests as do the institutions. We see both the institutions and the formal associations playing a vital role in the execution of determined policy, but the formulation of policy often takes place outside these formalized groupings. Within the policy-forming groups the economic interests are dominant.

The economic institution in Regional City, in drawing around itself many of the other institutions in the community, provides from within itself much of the personnel which may be considered of primary influence in power relationships. A lengthy discussion on institutions per se is not proposed. Their existence as channels through which policy may be funneled up and down to broader groups of people than those represented by the top men of power is easily recognized. Some of the institutions would represent imperfect channels for power transmission, however. For example, the family as an institution is not a channel of itself for bringing about general community agreement on such a matter as the desirability of building a new bridge across Regional River. On the other hand, the church might represent a more potent force on this question. The preacher could preach a sermon on the matter in any given church, and the members could sign petitions, attend meetings at the behest of the church bureaucracy, and go through a whole series of activities motivated by the institution in question.

It may be noted here that none of the ministers of churches in Regional City were chosen as top leaders by the persons interviewed in the study. The idea was expressed several times by interviewees that some minister *ought* to be on the listing, but under the terms of power definitions used in the study they did not make "top billing." It is understood, however, that in order to get a project well under way it would be important to bring the churches in, but they are not, as institutions, considered crucial in the decision-making process. Their influence is crucial in restating settled policies from time to time and in interpreting new policies which have been formed or are in the process of formulation. Church leaders, however, whether they be prominent laymen or professional ministers, have relatively little influence with the larger economic interests.

One cannot, in Regional City at least, look to the organized institutions as policy-determining groupings, nor can one look to the formal associations which are part of these institutions. But let us briefly be specific concerning the role of organizations. There is a multiplicity of organized groups in Regional City. The Chamber of Commerce lists more than 800 organizations from bee-keeping societies to federated industrial groups. The membership lists of some of these organizations often run into the hundreds. In this study organizations were considered as being influential in civic affairs and some ranking of the most important was deemed necessary. Consequently, all persons interviewed were asked to give their opinion on a selected list of supposedly top-ranking organizations in the community. An initial selection of thirty organizations was made by a panel of judges from lists supplied by the Chamber of Commerce and the local Community Council. The persons interviewed in the list of forty leaders narrowed their selections of organizations to seven—organizations to which the majority of these top leaders belonged. They were (in rank order of importance) the Chamber of Commerce, Community Chest, Rotary Club, Y.M.C.A., Community Council, Grand Jurors' Association, and Bar Association. There was a scattering of votes for the Christian Council and for one of the larger labor organizations. The Retail Merchants Association was added to our list by two merchants. The under-structure professional personnel in civic and social work who were interviewed indicated that they recognized the influence of the same organizations chosen by the top leaders. It may be noted that they generally belonged to only the Community Chest and the Community Council in conjunction with the top leaders.

Some of the top leaders may hold board positions within the associational groupings to lend prestige to the organization, but such members are more noted for their absence than for their attendance at meetings of the respective boards. They can be called upon in an organizational crisis or emergency, and at such times they may function decisively. One leader explained his position in this way: "If I attend meetings too regularly, I am asked to be chairman of this or that committee. I don't have time for that kind of work, but you hate to refuse before a bunch of people. There are usually two or three listening posts, people who can keep me in touch with things, on these boards. I get reports from them from time to time and that way keep a hand in. I also read the minutes of important meetings. Most of the time I know about where any board I belong to stands on various matters. I attend meetings only when I'm really needed."

Occasionally a top leader will take the presidency of one of the associations, but such position is usually unsought and avoided if possible—particularly by the older leaders. The younger leaders may be pushed to take some of the top associational posts as training assignments. They take on such duties, they say, with reluctance and make feeble protests of being terribly busy and pressed for time. The less powerful understructure associational personnel may scramble (in a dignified way, of course) for the top positions in these groupings.

In crisis situations, such as during World War II, many of the older leaders were called to active duty on civic boards. This was particularly true in the large fund-raising organizations where campaign goals were doubled or tripled over previous ones and the prestige of the older leaders was needed to insure the success of particular drives. During the crisis of depression in the 1930's several of the older leaders served on the local welfare board, but as the economic situation improved, they were replaced by "second-rate" and "third-rate" community leaders.[12]

Many of the persons interviewed belonged to many more organizations than those previously indicated, but the groups listed represent those that the power leaders consider most important in carrying out or interpreting a community-wide project. Two formal organizations were mentioned which are not generally known to the community at large but which are considered quite influential by the men of power. One is called the "49 Club" and the other the "Committee of 101." The 49 Club is a highly selective group organized in Regional City at the turn of the century. It is composed of a group of men who are prominent in community life and who have in some instances inherited a place on the membership roster. The club discusses major issues before the community and the general body politic seeking agreement on general policy matters. Its meetings are not formal and are often held in the homes of members. When a member dies, his vacancy is not filled for a considerable time. The one chosen to fill the vacancy is highly honored. Several of the top men on our list belonged to this club.

The Committee of 101 is almost exclusively devoted to a discussion of political matters. It discusses candidates and issues but takes no action on any matter which comes before it, nor are any formal records kept of the meetings. These latter stipulations also apply to the 49 Club. Membership in the Committee of 101 is considered a privilege, but it does not rank as high as the 49 Club. Both have high dues, the proceeds of which are spent on entertainment of the members.

Comparable data were gathered on twenty-four Regional City leaders concerning club memberships. Figure 6 shows the interlocking nature of these

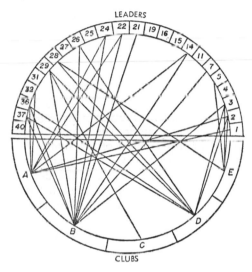

FIG. 6. Interlocking Club Memberships of 24 Regional City Leaders. (For key to numbers, see footnote to Table 1.)

memberships. Attention may be called to Club C. This club is comparable to Club B. Both are civic luncheon clubs, but Club B has a higher status in the community than Club C, as indicated by its apparent popularity among the top leaders. Clubs A, D, and E are social clubs of prominence. None of the under-structure professional personnel interviewed belong to any of these clubs.

None of the men interviewed considered any of the associational groupings crucial in policy determination. Their role, like that of the organized institutional groupings, is one of following rather than leading. They may provide a forum for discussing and studying community issues, needs, and policies; but, when decision is called for, another structure must come into play before action becomes the order of the day. The organizations may serve as training grounds for many of the men who later become power leaders. Most of the leaders had "graduated" from a stint in the upper positions of the more important organizations. Most associational presidents, however, remain in the under-structure of the power hierarchy. The organizations are not a sure route to sustained community prominence. Membership in the top brackets of one of the stable economic bureaucracies is the surest road to power, and this road is entered by only a few. Organizational leaders are prone to get the publicity; the upper echelon economic leaders, the power.

It was indicated at the beginning of this chapter that there would be a discussion of leadership groupings in a framework developed by E. T. Hiller, and by implication, at least, two of his criteria for analyzing community structure have been touched upon, namely, personnel and tests of admission of members. In a sense the third criterion has been bordered upon, that is, the distinctive roles of members. It has been said that the leading personnel in community power situations in Regional City tend to be businessmen. The personnel factor has been isolated to a definite group. One of the critical tests of membership in the policy-making group is prior membership in one of the commercial or industrial bureaucracies in the community. Kingsley Davis has indicated that because a man occupies a certain status and office, he enjoys power.[13] The men under discussion for the most part hold offices within powerful economic units in Regional City. Definite roles are played by these men in moving goods and services within each of the enterprises of which they are a part, but if their roles were limited to only one community unit we would be speaking of economic power and not community power. The composite power relations of men in the community are the primary object of this study.

Neither the institutional, associational, nor economic groupings comprise the totality of the power scheme in Regional City. The difference between policy-making and policy-execution has been stressed and it has been shown that the various organizations in the community may be very important in carrying out policy decisions. Segments of structure including individuals and cliques, particularly those related to the upper decision-making groups, have been identified. One more organizational component must be analyzed before tying together the units of the community structure. This component is what may be termed a fluid committee structure.

The committee is a phenomenon which is inescapable in organized community life in American hamlets, villages, small cities, and great metropolitan centers. Almost every activity of any importance in our culture must be preceded by committee work, carried on by committee work, and finally posthumously evaluated by a committee. Regional City is no exception to the general rule. Day after day the hotel, club, and associational meeting rooms are packed with men going through the familiar motions of calling meetings to order and dismissing them. Committees may have short lives or they may go on for years. An example of the latter is the Committee of 101 previously discussed. Committees may be quite formally organized, utilizing parliamentary rules of order, or they may be loosely organized and informal in their procedures. They may be accompanied by food and drink or they may be devoid of such amenities. They may have serious or light purposes, and consequently solemn or gay occasions as the case may be. Withal, each is accompanied by a certain degree of ritual befitting the occasion. Men used to committee work are sharp to detect poorly conducted meetings. No meeting, for example, can be said to have amounted to much if at least one motion is not put, passed, or put down—that is, in the more formally organized meetings. Men trained in conducting meetings are in demand, and such a person may display rare skills in ordering a group as it goes about its business.

Meetings are often a substitute for group action. As one Regional City professional phrased it, "There are those who believe in salvation by luncheon!" There is a great faith manifest in certain quarters of our society that if people can just be got together in a meeting all problems will be solved. And there is some justification for this faith, since so many matters of community business, as well as private transactions, are brought to successful conclusions in meetings.

Meetings have the functions of clarifying objectives of a group and of fixing and delegating responsibilities for action on any matter. They may in like manner hold action in abeyance. Decisions reached in meetings may be solemnly binding, or they may not be. Decisions arrived at in one meeting may be changed in the next meeting. Responsibilities may be shifted and membership changed according to the will of the group as a series of meetings proceeds. Rarely are committee meetings bound by "constitutional" prohibitions or heavy legalistic trappings which characterize so many associational and institutional gatherings. The outstanding characteristic of the ordinary committee meeting is its fluidity and its adaptability in adjusting to changing conditions, which are so essentially a part of our modern urban culture. The importance of the committee in power relations cannot be overstressed.

While it is important to stress the fluidity of committee structure, it must also be pointed out that there is a stable base of personnel who are seen time and again in a variety of committee meetings. There are men in any community who devote large portions of their waking hours to attendance at one meeting or another. Public-relations men in industry and associational secretaries are paid to devote considerable of their time to meeting attendance. It becomes commonplace among this latter personnel group to see one another at committee meetings, and such personnel become familiar with community leaders who operate on a similar level with them. There is a tendency to judge the importance of these meetings by who is in attendance.

Most of the top personnel of the power group are rarely seen at meetings attended by the associational under-structure personnel in Regional City. The exception to this general statement may be found in those instances in which a project is broad enough so that the "whole community needs to be brought in on the matter." Such meetings as bring in the under-structure personnel are usually relatively large affairs, rather than the smaller, more personal meetings which characterize policy-determination sessions. The interaction patterns of the two groups discussed here have shown a much higher rate of interaction among the top group than between the top and lower groups.

In matters of power decision the committee structure assumes keystone importance. The committee as a structure is a vital part of community power relationships in Regional City. Let us illustrate graphically in Figure 7 the place of two hypothetical policy committees in relation to institutional, associational, and corporate groups.

Not all the institutions and associations in Regional City were identified as being related to the power leaders studied. For example, none of the leaders in a power relationship could be identified as representing the institution of the family or a cultural association. This does not mean that either of these groupings was unimportant for some of the top leaders, but in the specific power relations studied no identification could be made of persons within these groupings as such. Because of this, in Figure 7 the cultural association is indicated as a pyramid grouping for under-structure power personnel only. No family institutional pyramid is shown. On the other hand, some of the institutions and associations could be identified with both upper-limits and lower-limits power personnel, and these pyramids show this by contrasting shaded portions for the two types of power leaders. We have also indicated in the figure that some institutions and associations are more frequently drawn upon for power personnel than others. The dotted lines represent those groups that are potential contributors to the policy-making structure. The cultural association group has been so designated, for example, since policy is formulated around some cultural activities which may have bearing on power relations. As an illustration, the status factor operating when a leader becomes a patron of the arts may have some relation to his general power position.

A few generalized remarks may be made concerning Figure 7, using a hypothetical example, after which it will be illustrated concretely how the structure worked in relation to a specific community project in Regional City.

If a project of major proportions were before the community for consideration—let us say a project aimed at building a new municipal auditorium—a policy committee would be formed. This may be called Project Committee A. Such a policy committee would more than likely grow out of a series of in-

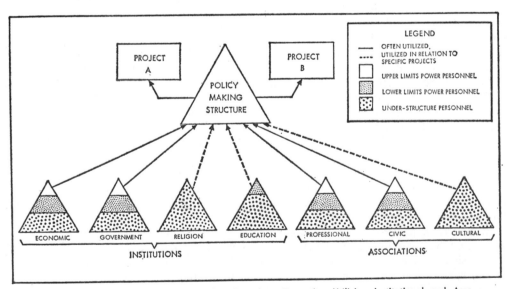

FIG. 7. Generalized Pattern of Policy Committee Formation Utilizing Institutional and Associational Structures.

formal meetings, and it might be related to a project that has been on the discussion agenda of many associations for months or even years. But the time has arrived for action. Money must be raised through private subscription or taxation, a site selected, and contracts let. The time for a policy committee is propitious. The selection of the policy committee will fall largely to the men of power in the community. They will likely be businessmen in one or more of the larger business establishments. Mutual choices will be agreed upon for committee membership. In the early stages of policy formulation there will be a few men who make the basic decisions. As the project is trimmed, pared, and shaped into manageable proportions there will be a recognition that the committee should be enlarged. Top-ranking organizational and institutional personnel will then be selected by the original members to augment their numbers, i.e., the committee will be expanded. The civic associations and the formalized institutions will next be drawn into certain phases of planning and initiation of the project on a community-wide basis. The newspapers will finally carry stories of the proposals, the ministers will preach sermons, and the associational members will hear speeches regarding plans. This rather simply is the process, familiar to many, that goes on in getting any community project under way.

Project B might be related to changing the tax structure of the community. Much the same organizational procedure will be repeated, but different associations may be drawn into the planning and execution stages. The policy-making personnel will tend to be much the same as in Project A and this is an important point in the present discussion. There will be a hard core of policy leadership on Policy Committee B that was also present on Project Committee A. This relative stability of the top policy-making group is a pattern quite apparent in Regional City civic affairs. A similar pattern of stable committee membership exists in the under-structure of the associational and corporate bureaucracies in the community which interact in a chain of command with the top power leaders on given projects.

It must be stressed that the same policy leaders do not interact repeatedly with the same under-structure personnel in getting projects put over. The interaction is based entirely upon a given project that is under consideration at a given time. The under-structure personnel may be likened to a keyboard over which the top structure personnel play, and the particular keys struck may vary from project to project. The players remain the same or nearly so, however.

A variation in the pattern of structuring a top-decision committee may be found in those policy committees in which the decision is made by individuals who are not to be out front on the project. In other words, the men of policy may wish to remain anonymous in relation to the action phases of the program in question. In such cases, the policy group remains informally intact, and "second-rate" or "third-rate" men are advertised as the sponsors of the particular project. This pattern may occur when a project is somewhat questionable as to its success. The policy-forming group is just as real, however, as if it were named publicly. The men upon whom falls the burden of carrying the project into its action stages are well aware of the persons who chose them.

Projects that are not originated in the policy-determining group are often allowed to proceed with a tentative blessing of a few of the men of decision if their interests and dominant values are not threatened by the proposed activity. If such a project goes sour, the men of decision cannot be blamed. This is another variation of structure and represents a real behavioral pattern in civic affairs in Regional City.

The leaders interviewed indicated that one of the projects which has current top priority in the community is known as "The Plan of Development." . . . Here we are interested in two things: (1) Which community leaders were identified as related to the project on the level of policy decision; and (2) which community leaders were identified with activating the project. It can be seen in an examination of Figures 8 and 9 that a different group was concerned with policy from that concerned with activating the project. Both the power leaders we have been discussing and the secretary for the official Committee for the Plan of Development were interviewed in relation to leadership utilized in formulating and activating the program. Consequently, it is clear that the leadership identified with this project represents a relatively closed and inclusive group.

The Plan of Development has been a controversial project in the community. It is a project that has a history of some ten years. One of the top policy leaders was quite active over a period of time in getting the interest of other leaders in this particular case. The leaders he interested on a policy level are indicated by code numbers in Figure 8. These numbers correspond to the upper- and lower-limits groups of personnel earlier identified. No under-structure personnel, so far as could be determined, participated in the informal policy committee which laid the groundwork for the program and determined its major outlines.

As the program moved toward the action stage, however, the structural picture changed. Three of the power leaders, numbers 31 and 1 in the upper-limits group and number 5 in the lower-limits group, were designated from the policy group as a nucleus around which an official operations committee was to be built. These leaders are subordinate to number 14, the leader who largely initiated the project.

The dominance of the business leaders may be noted. Out of thirteen policy leaders active in the project, nine were identified as belonging to the business group, six of whom were in the upper-limits category, and three in the lower-limits group. The government leader identified with the movement was very anxious to see the program get under way and succeed. He had a personal power interest in the matter, but his interest could not be made public. Publicly he maintained a hands-off policy in relation to the project, but in policy formulation he was quite active. In the professional group, numbers 38 and 23 were legal advisors to the policy group as a whole. Number 1, in the professional category, acted as an informal liaison person between several organizations and the policy-makers.

After the policy line had been set and before the project could be activated, it was necessary to go to the state legislature for enabling legislation. In this process the legislators bargained with the policy group concerning the membership of the proposed official committee. During the horse-trading, some of the names proposed by the policy-makers were dropped in favor of local politicos agreeable to the state political leaders. The local "politicians" might be classified as semi-politicians. They have business connections which are their primary interest, but in at least four instances these businesses involve contracting or motor transport in which it is profitable to have good political relations with state officials.

Figure 9 identifies the institutions and associations with which the leaders were involved in getting the project activated. With the exception of numbers 1, 5, 8, 31, and 39, the leaders named to the official committee operate outside the policy-making power group. These men have been given code numbers above 40 to distinguish them from the policy-making group. None of them operate businesses that can be favorably compared in size or influence with the policy leaders'. The remaining business leaders operate small establishments that might be compared in size to local insurance or auto sales agencies. The religious leader in this group is a minister of one of the larger churches in Regional City. He is a man who may be characterized as a community gadfly and a person upon whom the policy leaders depend for a certain amount of civic information.

Two of the persons identified in the professional association grouping, numbers 43, 44, are lawyers from the outlying sections of the city. It was considered good strategy to have these men identified with the official group concerned with activating the project, since the areas adjacent to Regional City were affected by the proposals. Number 45 in the professional grouping is a secretary of a local dry cleaning association. The reasons for his inclusion on the project committee are not clear. It was mentioned by one informant that he had "good labor connections," but I could not ascertain the scope of these connections.

One labor representative from a relatively weak union was put on the com-

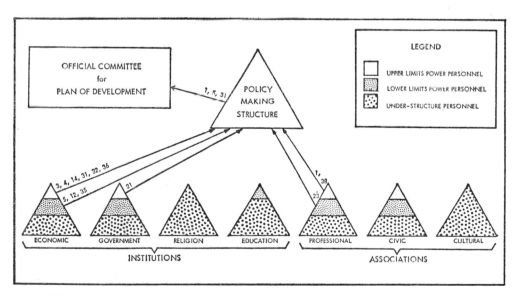

FIG. 8. Pattern of Participation of Three Strata of Institutional and Associational Personnel in Policy Formulation of Regional City's Plan of Development.

mittee. He was chosen because he was identified with a joint union committee on community affairs devoted to interpreting welfare projects to the various labor groups. It does not seem desirable or necessary to describe all of the leaders of the activating committee, but mention will be made of one more individual, since his position in the scheme of project operation seems significant. This leader is identified with code number 31.

Number 31 is a top policy leader. He represents the upper-limits power leaders in the policy group. He is also a person identified with big business in the community. When the Plan of Development project was to be officially launched, number 31 was asked to take the presidency of one of the more powerful civic associations for a year to "swing that group into line." He was given an impressive build-up by the newspapers for his broad civic interests and for a year he devoted a great deal of time to getting the Plan of Development under way. His leadership was well received generally, and apparently he was well supported, for the project has been put across successfully.

By comparing Figures 8 and 9, it may be clearly seen that the policy-makers generally move out of the picture at the stage of project execution. This pattern holds true generally for major community projects. The men in the understructure of power become the doers and are activated by the policy-makers—the initiators.

The project discussed above is one related to Regional City *as a community*. Of course the affairs of the community do not stop at its borders. There are relationships between personnel in the city and persons in state and national power groups. Robert K. Merton observed in a recent study that community

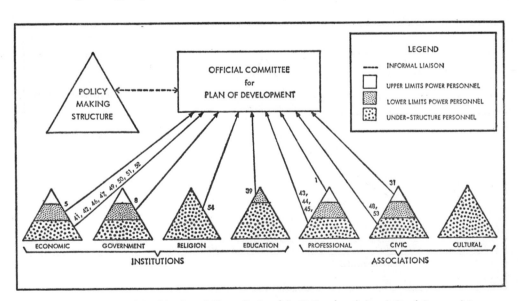

FIG. 9. Pattern of Participation of Three Strata of Institutional and Associational Personnel in Activating Program of Regional City's Plan of Development.

leaders fall into "cosmopolitan" and "local" groupings.[14] This generalized concept seems to hold true in Regional City. Some men tend to confine their activities almost entirely within the community, while others are active on state and regional matters.

Homer, Parks, Hardy, Aiken, Parker, and Rake appear to be the men in Regional City who act largely as liaison persons between the community and national policy-making groups. These men average three committees each on the national level, in comparison to 1.2 for the group as a whole. Hardy claims to belong to the most national policy-making boards and committees, with ten as his total. Homer and Aiken are definitely more interested in national than in local affairs. This fact came out strongly in interviews with them. Aiken said, "There are plenty of men who can keep an eye on things here at home. Some of these matters like inflation and national defense need to be got at in Washington, and my interest is in these things."

On the state level of operations in relation to the city, Hardy is also active along with Stone, Rake, and Parker. These men average four state committees each in comparison with an average of 1.3 for the remainder of the group. Stone confines his policy-making committee work entirely to the state, He belongs to a few local committees but is not active on them. The other persons interested in state affairs tend to divide their remaining committee time between local and national groups. The majority of the top leaders belong to an average of six policy-making boards or committees in comparison to an average of 1.3 in the state and 1.2 nationally.

The professional under-structure persons belong to fewer local committees and boards on a policy-making level than do the top leaders, but they compare favorably with the leaders on the national and state levels. They average 4.7 local committees, 1.0 state committees, and 1.3 national committees. Qualitatively their committees and boards differ from the upper power group. They most generally belong to professional association groupings which are different from the trade and other economic groupings of the top leaders.

The community politicians almost entirely operate locally on boards and committees, but the Mayor has many individual contacts with the two levels of government above him on a less formalized basis than boards and committees of policy would imply. During an interview with the Mayor he was interrupted by a phone call which he had put through to Washington regarding a project which concerned the community, and one cannot say that he is not an influential man in national and state affairs. On the phone he sounded influential. He is not the most influential man in Regional City in local-national policy matters, and when the dynamics of the power structure is elaborated upon, this will become apparent. The Mayor denies much influence in state matters. When questioned on this area he said, "I was saying to Rafferty Jones [a state politician] the other day, 'Rafferty, I'll bet that I could not be elected to the lowest job in state government'" State and local politics are differentiated, but not entirely distinct. As in other states where a large metropolitan center is located there is much friction and conflict of interest between the two political groupings. The two are joined often at that point at which major economic interests are involved, and the leaders of economic bureaucracies have much personal influence in bridging the formal structural gaps between the levels of government on specific matters.

In one of our postulates it is stated that, "Power is structured socially, in the United States, into a dual relationship between governmental and economic authorities on national, state, and local levels." In the light of the present analysis, there is less of a "dual" relationship than had been assumed. This is particularly true in Regional City, where the dominant factor in political life is the personnel of the economic interests. It is true that there is no formal tie between the economic interests and government, but the structure of policy-determining committees and their tie-in with the other powerful institutions and organizations of the community make government subservient to the interests of these combined groups. The governmental departments and their personnel are acutely aware of the power of key individuals and combinations of citizens' groups in the policy-making realm, and they are loathe to act before consulting and "clearing" with these interests.

Brady is enlightening on this point when he says that the same interests tend to dominate politics and business, particularly in the realm of policy. "The same individuals, the same groups and cliques, [and] the same interests dominate each sphere [of property and politics]," he says.[15] One is compelled to agree with him from observations of the two groups in Regional City. There is evidence, too, that the local economic interests tie into larger groupings of like interests on the state and national levels which tend to overshadow the policy-making machinery of government at all levels. The structure is that of a dominant policy-making group using the machinery of government as a bureaucracy for the attainment of certain goals coordinate with the interests of the policy-forming group. The description of the structure of the "third house" mentioned in the discussion of Gary Stone, a labor leader, may be recalled in this connection.

The structural relationship between the economic policy-determining groups and the operating units of government have often been looked upon as inherently immoral. The ethical implications of the domination by one set of men in manipulating government for specific and limited purposes may be avoided, but some concern must be expressed in relation to a functional difficulty which such domination presents in our society. "Common to all the national, social, and economic crises of our day," says von Beckerath, "is the fundamental problem of rebuilding a constant workable connection between the political structure . . . and its economic structure."[16] A consistent and workable connection between the political and economic structures appears to be an extremely pertinent concept, which highlights a weakness of the power structure of Regional City as it relates to other units on the political level. There are gaps in the power arc which are closed on many issues by the narrower-interest groups. In other words, it has been pointed out that the power personnel do not represent a true pyramid of political power. The power personnel may decisively influence most policies that concern legislative groups, and they are acutely aware of their own interests in such policy matters. However, on many issues they are not interested, and there is consequently no continuing structure which may transmit to the legislative bodies the general interests of the underlying groups within the body politic. This is no new problem, but it is a structurally significant one. If the formalized structures of government are under the domination of a group of policy leaders who are isolated from direct responsibility to the mass of people in a democratic society, then, values aside, the scheme is at best dysfunctional. No patent remedy is suggested in this writing but there is a structural weakness in the policy-making machinery and power-wielding mechanism as it has been observed in a particular locality. Correction of the difficulty may come from an open recognition of actual operating elements in power relations unobscured by abstract value descriptions which do not fit reality. Simply put, power structure is looked at here, not from the point of view of what one may think we have, or what one may think we ought to have, but rather in terms of what we've got. Although [in the concluding chapter of *Community Power Structure*] there will be a brief discussion of ways in which community democratic processes may be strengthened, the central intention of the entire study is to describe what actually *is* in community power relations.

The Mayor of Regional City says, "We have got a citizen-run town here." And one can agree with him, but policy is controlled by a relatively small group of the citizenry. In such a situation an obvious question is, "What holds the system together?" This question was asked of our informants. The question was put in this way: "It is evident that we are dealing with a small group of policy leaders in this study, but the whole community of Regional City is comprised of some half million persons. What holds the whole group together in relation to the influence exerted by so few leaders?"

Boiled down, the more significant answers ran along the following lines: "It is a sense of obligation which some men have toward others which keeps the system operating." "It is obligation plus confidence in the ability of some men to get things done, while other men cannot get things done." "Some men are interested in working on community projects, others are not." "Money holds them together." "Some people just naturally work together better than others." "You get to know certain people and when anything comes up you tend to call on the same men over and over to work on community projects." "You watch to see who is moving—when you see a man on the move, pick him up. He'll work for you!"

There is merit in all of these answers. Within the primary groups, or separate crowds clustered around specific interests, it is evident that similar interests and resulting common sentiments have a great deal to do with holding the groups together. Men who work together over a long period of time become comfortable in their working relationships with one another. Mutual sentiments of liking will grow up between them, and these sentiments in turn will lead to further interactions.[17] The ability of a top leader to retain a position of prestige depends to some extent on how well he conforms to the norms of the group he leads. The men of Regional City tend to be exponents of the "common man" in appearance and manner of speech, at least during the workday. Some of the men of top wealth and position are spoken of as "common as an old shoe." Their private lives hidden from the general mass of people may be uncommon, but their everyday behavior tends toward a confirmation of what one Regional

City professional in the understructure has called the "patched pants theory." "The biggest ones act like they have patches on their pants," he said. "The higher the rank of the person within a group, the more nearly his activities conform to the norms of the group," says Homans.[18]

Common interests, cutting across the lines of all separate crowds, tend to hold the community structure intact. James Treat said, "If you want to know what is going on, you have to be where the money is. It is capitalism, I suppose you would say. The men who make things move are interested in the larger issues—making money, keeping power." Joseph Hardy and Harvey Aiken agreed with Treat, but Aiken modified his statement by saying, "Money is only good so long as it is backed up by material goods. Inflation can ruin money, and it can ruin all the people who have money." He told of being in France recently where he inquired of some of the banking men who lived along one of the old boulevards whether their neighbors had suffered from post-war inflation. They indicated that most of their neighbors were the newly rich who had profited in the black markets resulting from World War II, and many of the new men of power were those who had been able to hold goods during the inflation rather than depend upon income from securities. The writer shares Aiken's caution about money as a sole source of power. It represents power in a stable economy when it is backed by tangible resources. With this limitation noted, it must be admitted that money still has meaning in power terms in Regional City. It is an important element.

Force is also an element of power but it is not an independent element. Von Beckerath says, "A state built upon *mere* force of a minority against the will of the majority is never possible in the long run." [19] One must look deeper than the elements of money or force to analyze adequately the power structure of Regional City. Both of these elements have their place, but both are interconnected with a complex set of habitual relationships of men which are described in terms of group relations.

Homans says, "The higher a man's social rank, the larger will be the number of persons that originate interaction for him, either directly or through subordinates." Also, "The higher a man's social rank, the larger number of persons for whom he originates interaction, either directly or through intermediaries." [20] The actions indicated are a two-way process. The men of high social rank—in this discussion, policy-makers—are acted upon and they act upon others, and because of their position they influence large numbers of people. Homans also says that high social rank presages a wide range of interactions. If Homans were to leave the matter at the latter point, I should have to disagree with him, since I found that the men of power tended to act within a limited range of contacts in Regional City, but Homans has an answer to this:

An increasing specialization of activities will bring about a decrease in the range of interaction of a person . . . and will limit the field in which he can originate action. . . . Thus an increase in the size of the group and in the specialization of activity will tend to increase the numbers of positions in the chain of interaction between the top leader and the ordinary member [in our case, citizen].[21]

The group of men dealt with here have a specialized function, namely, policy-making. It would not be physically possible for the men of decision to interact with great numbers of citizens on a face-to-face basis in Regional City. The contacts with the average citizen must be limited, but there must be channels of interaction open for decisions to flow down, and for issues to rise, at times, from the underlying population. These channels are open through the institutions and associations previously outlined in this chapter. The men of decision will not go far up or down the scale of leadership to choose others with whom to work, and these findings are in conformity with another of Homans' theories: "If a person does originate interaction for a person of higher rank, a tendency will exist for him to do so with the member of his own subgroup who is nearest him in rank." [22]

The tendency works the other way, too. Persons in the higher ranks most often work with persons close to them and rely on men immediately below them to originate interaction with persons in turn below them. As a matter of custom and practice, the person of higher rank originates interaction for those below him more often than the latter originate interaction for him.[23] This process has the following results:

Channels of interaction will become established, and the leader will not become overburdened with interaction. The relative frequency of interaction with immediate superiors and interaction with the top leader must differ from group to group according to the number of circumstances, two of which are the size of the group and the severity of the environment. . . . The more severe the environment in which the group must survive—ships and armies [for example]—the more likely it is that interaction will be strictly channeled.[24]

The channels of interaction are established in Regional City to conserve the time of the men of power. Even with the channels that are opened, there is still considerable burden of responsibility placed upon these men. In discussing this point with George Delbert, the question was asked, "With so few men in policy positions, isn't there a tendency to choke off many projects which may be of equal merit with those being given consideration?" He thought the question over for a moment and replied, "Yes, I suppose that may be true; but there's only so much time in a year, and we can only handle a certain number of things. Then there's not money enough to go around for everything that comes up. There is always anywhere from one to two million being raised in this community for one purpose or another. It takes time to get around to everything!"

The power leaders do get around with considerable facility in the area of economic activity. When a new corporation is started, as for example a new television company, or a multimillion dollar apartment building project recently established in the city, one or more of the leaders were observed to "find time" to be identified with such developments. Certainly, the top leaders would appear to have time for policy considerations of such economic projects, if one takes into account the reports in the business section of the local press. The day-to-day working arrangements of the corporations are put into the hands of trusted under-structure administrative personnel. The pattern of power implicit in the situation matches that of civic enterprises in formation and development.

"If two institutions," says Hughes, "draw upon the same people . . . they may compete in some measure, for people have but a limited amount of time and money to expend." [25] The leaders of Regional City tend to protect themselves from too many demands by channeling policy execution through an under-structure on matters of policy. This under-structure is not a rigid bureaucracy, as has been pointed out, but is a flexible system. It has elements of stability and tends to operate by levels. The men at each level are spoken of as first, second, third and fourth rate by the power leaders, who operate primarily in conjunction with individuals of the first two ratings. The types of personnel which may be found in each rating by a sample classification are as follows:

EXAMPLES OF PERSONNEL FROM FIRST TO FOURTH RATE IN REGIONAL CITY

FIRST RATE: Industrial, commercial, financial owners and top executives of large enterprises.

SECOND RATE: Operations officials, bank vice-presidents, public-relations men, small businessmen (owners), top-ranking public officials, corporation attorneys, contractors.

THIRD RATE: Civic organization personnel, civic agency board personnel, newspaper columnists, radio commentators, petty public officials, selected organization executives.

FOURTH RATE: Professionals such as ministers, teachers, social workers, personnel directors, and such persons as small business managers, higher paid accountants, and the like.

These ratings might be expanded. They are given simply to indicate a suggested ranking of selected personnel who operate below the policy-making leaders in Regional City. The first two ratings are personnel who are said to "set the line of policy," while the latter two groups "hold the line." The ratings are very real to the under-structure professional personnel. One of these men said: "I know that the top boys get together on things. This community is divided into tiers. You can't get the first-tier men to work on anything originating in the second- and third-tier level. The top ones may put their names on second- and third-tier projects, but you cannot get them to work with you. They will not attend your meetings, but you know they are attending their own meetings all the time." The top leaders are conserving their time and energies for the primary role they play—policy-determination. They are also interested in holding a balance of power in the community.

In discussing the men in the lower group of the top leadership hierarchy, one of the informants said: "When you see one of the little fellows move, you know he is not moving on his own. Somebody is moving him, and it is the bigger fellow who is moving him that you need to watch, if you want to know what is going on.

"My father, who was a farmer, used to chop wood with me. He'd say, 'Son, when you see a chip in the woodpile move, look under the chip. You probably will find something interesting under it.' I've always remembered that. I've always looked to see what makes the 'chips' move."

The "little fellows" are continually moved to perform their proper tasks by those above them. The roles defined for the under-structure of power personnel are carefully defined in keeping with the larger interests. Their movements are carefully stimulated and watched at all times to see that their various functions are properly performed.

Stability of relationships is highly desirable in maintaining social control, and keeping men "in their places" is a vital part of the structuring of community power. Andrew Carnegie expressed the idea of every man in his place in this manner: "It is the business of the preacher to preach, of the physician to practice, of the poet to write, the business of the college professor to teach. . . ." [26] Each of these professions also has a role to play in the community activities consistent with its economic or professional role. Such roles do not ordinarily include policy-making. If one of these under-structure men should be presumptuous enough to question policy decisions, he would be immediately considered insubordinate and "punished," first by a threat to his job security, followed possibly by expulsion from his job if his insubordination continued. To quote Homans:

> A social system is in a moving equilibrium and authority exists when the state of the elements that enter the system and the relations between them, including the behavior of the leader(s), is such that disobedience to the orders of the leader(s) will be followed by changes in the other elements tending to bring the system back to the state the leader(s) would have wished to reach if the disobedience had not occurred.[27]

There may be isolated dissatisfactions with policy decisions in Regional City, but mainly there is unanimity. The controversial is avoided, partly by the policy-making group's not allowing a proposal to get too far along if it meets stiff criticism at any point in decision-making. A careful watch is kept for what "will go" and what "will not go." Luke Street says, "Most of the carping comes from people who are envious of some of the bigger crowds. When there is such envy, the crowds are talked about and criticized." Such criticism usually is not open. When criticism is open it is generally directed toward some of the under-structure men who are fronting for the larger interests. If criticism is directed toward the top leaders, the critic is liable to job dismissal in extreme cases or more subtle pressures in less flagrant cases. The omnipresent threat of power sanctions used against recalcitrant underlings is recognized by the lower echelons of power, and they generally go along with most decisions, grumbling in private with close associates, if at all. Most of these third- or fourth-rate leaders rationalize their behavior—particularly when upper decisions are in conflict with their professional or private value systems. . . .

Two of the hypotheses of the study have been discussed in some measure in the preceding analysis. These hypotheses, restated, are as follows:

1. The exercise of power is limited and directed by the formulation and extension of social policy within a framework of socially sanctioned authority.

2. In a given power unit a smaller number of individuals will be found formulating and extending policy than those exercising power.

A corollary of the latter hypothesis was also touched upon: All policy-makers are men of power, but all men of power are not, per se, policy-makers.

The top group of the power hierarchy has been isolated and defined as comprised of policy-makers. These men are drawn largely from the businessmen's class in Regional City. They form cliques or crowds, as the term is more often used in the community, which formulate policy. Committees for formulation of policy are commonplace, and on community-wide issues policy is channeled by a "fluid committee structure" down to institutional, associational groupings through a lower-level bureaucracy which executes policy.

It has been pointed out that intra-community and extra-community policy matters are handled by essentially the same group of men in this city, but there is a differentiation of functional activity within this policy group. Some men operate on different levels of policy decision, particularly in matters concerning governmental action. Some structural weaknesses in the power structure have been touched upon but at no great length. Finally, it was found that the structure is held together by common interests, mutual obligations, money, habit, delegated responsibilities, and in some cases by coercion and force.

NOTES

[1] E. T. Hiller, "The Community as a Social Group," *American Sociological Review,* VI (April 1941), 191–92.

[2] *Ibid.,* p. 189.

[3] *The Human Group* (New York: Harcourt, Brace and Company, 1950).

[4] George A. Lundberg and Margaret Lawsing, "The Sociography of Some Community Relations," *American Sociological Review,* II (June 1937), 318–35.

[5] *Ibid.,* pp. 328–29.

[6] This man was out of the city for an extended period working with the Federal Government on defense mobilization plans.

[7] The numbers used in all figures correspond to code numbers used in analyzing data.

[8] "Sociometric Star Isolates," *American Journal of Sociology,* LVI (November 1950), 263–67.

[9] These figures were adapted from schematic diagrams used by Seymour Louis Wolfbein in depicting "interlocking directorates" in a field study of a mill community. See Wolfbein, *The Decline of a Cotton Textile City* (New York: Columbia University Press, 1944), pp. 93–95.

[10] *Op. cit.,* p. 184.

[11] "The Business Executive: The Psycho-Dynamics of a Social Role," *American Journal of Sociology,* LIV (January 1949), 286.

[12] This classification is explained later in the chapter.

[13] "A Conceptual Analysis of Stratification," *American Sociological Review,* VII (June 1942), 316.

[14] Paul Lazarsfeld and Frank N. Stanton (eds.), *Communications Research* (New York: Harper and Brothers, 1949), p. 192.

[15] R. A. Brady, *Business as a System of Power* (New York: Columbia University Press, 1938), p. 314.

[16] Herbert von Beckerath, "Economics and Politics," *Social Forces,* XIV (October 1935), 42.

[17] Homans, *op. cit.,* p. 112.

[18] *Ibid.,* p. 141.

[19] "Economics and Politics," *loc. cit.,* p. 52.

[20] *Op. cit.,* p. 145.

[21] *Ibid.,* p. 406.

[22] *Ibid.,* p. 184.

[23] *Ibid.,* p. 145.

[24] *Ibid.,* p. 184.

[25] Everett C. Hughes, "Ecological Aspects of Institutions," *American Sociological Review,* I (April 1936), 186.

[26] *The Empire of Business* (New York: Doubleday, Page and Company, 1902), p. 189.

[27] *Op. cit.,* p. 422.

6. HOW TO STUDY COMMUNITY POWER: THE PLURALIST ALTERNATIVE *

Nelson W. Polsby

Political scientists are beginning to view certain major contributions to the study of community politics less favorably than one would have expected after hearing the fanfare surrounding the original acceptance of these works.[1] Often billed as studies of "community power structure," these works have been produced mostly by sociologists, whose orientation has been to study the politics of American communities as a subsidiary aspect of social structure.[2] "The political organization of Jonesville," writes one such scholar, "fits the rest of the social structure . . . curving or bulging with the class outlines of the body politic." [3]

The faults which critics have found with studies following this general conception of politics as an epiphenomenon of social stratification are many, varied and serious. They include the charges that this conception encourages research designs which generate self-fulfilling prophecies,[4] and that it leads to the systematic misreporting of facts [5] and to the formulation of ambiguous and unprovable assertions about community power.[6] It would be gratuitous for me to re-explore these criticisms here. It would be more profitable, instead, to describe some of the ways in which students have evaded—apparently with success—the various disabilities of the stratification approach to the study of community power. With judicious unoriginality, I shall call the alternative research strategy to be outlned here the "pluralist" approach. Old, familiar pluralistic presumptions [7] about the nature of American politics seem to have given researchers strategies for the study of community power which are both feasible to execute and comparatively faithful to conditions in the real world.[8] What follows is an attempt to explain why this seems to be the case for pluralist studies, but not for stratification studies.

The first, and perhaps most basic presupposition of the pluralist approach, is that nothing categorical can be assumed about power in any community. It rejects the stratification thesis that *some* group necessarily dominates a community.[9] If anything, there seems to be an unspoken notion among pluralist researchers that at bottom *nobody* dominates in a town, so that their first question to a local informant is not likely to be, "Who runs this community?," but rather, "Does anyone at all run this community?" It is instructive to examine the range of possible answers to each of these questions. The first query is somewhat like, "Have you stopped beating your wife?," in that virtually any response short of

* This article is a paper of the New Haven Community Leadership Study, and owes a great deal to Robert A. Dahl and Raymond E. Wolfinger. I am also grateful to George M. Belknap, Norton E. Long and Robert O. Schulze, but none of these gentlemen should be held responsible for the notions presented here.

SOURCE: *The Journal of Politics,* 22 (August, 1960), pp. 474–484. Reprinted by permission. This article forms the major part of Chapter 6 of *Community Power and Political Theory* (Yale University Press, 1963) pp. 112–221.

total unwillingness to answer will supply the researchers with a "power élite" along the lines presupposed by the stratification theory.[10] On the other hand, the second question is capable of eliciting a response which *could* lead to the discovery of a power élite (*i.e.,* "Yes"), or any of an infinite number of stable, but non-élitist patterns of decision-making (*i.e.,* "No, but . . ."; "Yes, but . . ."), or total fragmentation, or disorganization (*i.e.,* "No").

What sort of question is likely to follow "Who runs the community?" in a questionnaire? Obviously, something like "*How* do the people named in the above response run the community?" This entirely probable pattern of investigation begs the question of whether or not those said to rule actually do rule. In the pluralist approach, on the other hand, an attempt is made to study specific outcomes, in order to determine who actually prevails in community decision-making. Consonant with the desire to study actual outcomes, which requires arduous and expensive field work, outcomes in a few (but, for reasons of expense, usually only a few) issue-areas are studied closely. More than a single issue-area is always chosen, however, because of the presumption among pluralist researchers that the same pattern of decision-making is highly unlikely to reproduce itself in more than one issue-area. In this expectation, pluralist researchers have seldom been disappointed.[11] They recognize, however, the possibility that the same pattern *could* reproduce itself in more than one issue area. Since actual behavior is observed, or reconstructed from documents, witnesses, and so on, it is possible to determine empirically whether or not the same group rules two or more issue-areas. The presumption that the existence of a power élite is unlikely does not, in other words, prevent the finding of such an élite if the data so indicate.

A superficially persuasive objection to this approach might be phrased as follows: "Suppose research in a community discloses different patterns of decision-making in each of three issue-areas. This does not rule out the possibility that all other issue-areas in the community are dominated by a single power élite." How can pluralists meet this objection? First, it is necessary to acknowledge the *possibility* that this is the case. However, pluralists can (and do) protect themselves in part by studying significant issues. In the New Haven study, for example, of which this paper is an outgrowth, we studied (1) nominations by the two political parties, which determine which persons hold public offices; (2) the New Haven Redevelopment program, which is the largest in the country (measured by past and present outlay per capita); (3) public education, which is the most costly item in the city's budget; and (4) a campaign to revise the city charter.[12] In Bennington, Scoble studied political nominations and elections, the issue of consolidation of various municipal governments, the formation of a union high-school district, and the construction of a new high-school building.[13] A pilot study by Long and Belknap, of a large eastern city embraced the problems of transportation, race relations, traffic, urban redevelopment and recreation,[14] whtile, in the San Francisco Bay area, Belknap studied the issues of urban redevelopment, transportation and race relations.[15] None of these issues was trivial; they probably were, in fact, the most important issues before these communities during the time these studies were being carried out. What sort of a power élite is it—it may appropriately be asked—which asserts itself in relatively trivial matters, but is inactive or ineffective in the most significant areas of community policy-making?

Stratification theory holds that power élites fail to prevail only on trivial issues.[16] By pre-selecting as issues for study those which are generally agreed to be significant, pluralist researchers can test stratification theory without searching endlessly in one issue-area after another, in order to discover some semblance of a power élite. After all, it cannot be reasonably required of researchers that they validate someone else's preconceived notions of community power distributions. If the researcher's design is such that any power distribution has an equal chance of appearing in his result, his result may not properly be criticized on the grounds that it did not conform to expectations. The burden of proof is clearly on the challenger in such a case to make good his assertion that power is actually distributed otherwise.[17]

Another presumption of the pluralist approach runs directly counter to stratification theory's presumption that power distributions are a more or less permanent aspect of social structure. Pluralists hold that power may be tied to issues, and issues can be fleeting or persistent, provoking coalitions among interested groups and citizens ranging in their duration from momentary to semi-permanent. There is a clear gain in descriptive accuracy involved in formulating power distributions so as to take account of the dimension of time, as pluralists do,[18] since it is easily demonstrated that coalitions *do* vary in their permanency. To presume that the set of coalitions which exists in the community at any given time is a timelessly stable aspect of social structure is to introduce systematic inaccuracies into one's description of social reality.

Why do pluralists reject the idea that *some* group necessarily dominates every community? The presumption that communities are likely to be less rather than more permanent in their patterns of decision-making is no doubt part of the answer, but another part is an even more fundamental conception of human behavior as governed in large part by inertia. This view leads pluralists to put a high value on overt activity as indicative of involvement in issues and to look upon the collection of "reputations" for leadership as a much less desirable research procedure.[19]

Pluralists consider as arbitrary the inclusion of certain groups as being "implicated" in decisions when these groups themselves reject such involvement.[20] For pluralists, "false class consciousness" does not exist, because it implies that the values of analysts are imposed on groups in the community. They reject the idea that there is any particular issue or any particular point in the determination of an issue where a group must assert itself in order to follow its expressed values. Rather, the pluralist assumes that there are many issues and many points at which group values can be realized. Further, pluralists presume that there are certain costs in taking any action at all. This refers not simply to the possibility of losing, of making political enemies, and so on, but also to the costs in personal time and effort involved in political mobilization, in becoming informed, in lobbying or campaigning and in taking the trouble to vote.[21]

It is a demonstrated fact that public activity of all sorts is a habit more characteristic of the middle and upper classes than of the lower classes.[22] Vidich and Bensman, for the first time in a community study, depicted the life of the lowest-class groups in the community sufficiently well so that the personally functional aspects of withdrawal from the community were revealed.[23] The presumption of inertia permits the researcher to regard the public sector of activity as but one facet of behavior capable of giving people satisfaction, and discourages the inappropriate and arbitrary assignment of upper and middle-class values to all actors in the community.

The presumption of inertia also helps put economic and social notables into perspective, If a man's major life work is banking, the pluralist presumes he will spend his time at the bank, and not in manipulating community decisions. This presumption holds until the banker's activities and participations indicate otherwise. Once again, it is very important to make the point that this assumption is not scientifically equivalent to its opposite. If we presume that the banker is "really" engaged in running the community, there is practically no way of disconfirming this notion, even if it is totally erroneous. On the other hand, it is easy to spot the banker who really *does* run community affairs when we presume he does not, because his activities will make this fact apparent. In the absence of the requisite activities, we have no grounds for asserting that the banker, in fact, does run the community.[24]

The pluralist emphasis on the time-bounded nature of coalitions and on the voluntary aspect of political participation leads to a further contrast with stratification theory, since pluralists hold that the "interest group" and the "public" are the social collectives most relevant to the analysis of political processes. In the sociologist's patois, politically important groups would be called phenomena of "collective behavior" rather than of "social structure." [25] Social classes in stratification theory are populations differentially ranked according to economic or status criteria, which embrace the entire community. Everyone in a community is a member of at least one but no more than one class at any given moment, and no one in the community falls outside the system. This is a legitimate heuristic construction; however, it is a mistake to impute to the apparently inescapable fact of class membership any sort of class consciousness. This sociologists have long recognized.[26] But they seem less willing to grant that it is equally incorrect to presume that those sharing similar market or status positions are also equidistant to all the bases of political power, or in fact share class interests. American society has never been noted for its interclass warfare, a fact often reported with a great show of surprise in stratification studies of American communities.[27]

Pluralists, who see American society as fractured into a congeries of hundreds of small "special interest" groups, with incompletely overlapping memberships, widely differing power bases, and a multitude of techniques for exercising influence on decisions salient to them,[28] are not surprised at the low priority which Americans give to their class membership as bases of social action. In the decision-making of fragmented government—and American national, state and local governments are nothing if not fragmented—the claims of small, intense minorities are usually attended to.[29] Hence it is not only inefficient but usually unnecessary for entire classes to mobilize when the preferences of class-members are pressed and often satisfied in a piecemeal fashion. The empirical evidence supporting this pluralist doctrine is overwhelming,[30] however much stratification theorists may have missed its significance for them, namely, that the fragmentation of American governmental decision-making and of American society makes class consciousness inefficient, and, in most cases, makes the political interests of members of the same class different.

Pluralist research is not interested in ascertaining an actor's ranking in a system presumed to operate hierarchically. Rather, pluralists want to find out about leadership *roles,* which are presumed to be diverse and fluid, both within a single issue-area over time, and as between issue-areas. Long and Belknap, for example, identify the following leadership roles in community decision-making: Initiation, Staffing and Planning, Communication and Publicity, Intra-élite Organizing, Financing and Public Sanctioning.[31]

By describing and specifying leadership roles in concrete situations, pluralists are in a position to determine the extent to which power structure exists. If there exist high degrees of overlap among issue-areas in decision-making personnel, or of institutionalization in the bases of power in specified issue-areas, or of regularity in the procedures of decision-making, then the empirical conclusion is justified that some sort of a "power structure" exists. By specifying leadership roles and activities, the pluralist research strategy makes it possible for an empirical determination of the bounds and durability of a community "power structure"—if one exists—to be described, and the stratification theory presumption that community power is necessarily general and relatively immutable can be discarded as arbitrary.

The final contrast I want to make between the pluralist and stratification methods has to do with their differing conceptions of what is meant by "power." I have already noted that stratification theorists emphasize the cataloguing of power bases, meaning the resources available to actors for the exercise of power.[32] Pluralists, on the other hand, concentrate on power exercise itself. This leads to two subsidiary discoveries. First, there are a great many different kinds of resources which can be turned to use in the process of community decision-making—many more resources, in fact, than stratification theorists customarily take account of. One list, for example, includes: money and credit; control over jobs; control over the information of others; social standing; knowledge and expertness; popularity, esteem and charisma; legality, constitutionality and officiality; ethnic solidarity; and the right to vote.[33]

The second product of the pluralist emphasis on power exercise is the discovery that resources are employed only with variations in degree of skill. The elaboration of the ways in which resources are employed enables the pluralist researcher to pay attention to what practical politicians customarily see as the heart of their own craft: the processes of bargaining, negotiation, salesmanship and brokerage, and of leadership in mobilizing resources of all kinds. This approach also makes possible a more realistic evaluation of the actual disposable resources of actors. A corporation may be worth millions of dollars, but its policies and liquidity position may be such that it cannot possibly bring those monetary resources into play in order to influence the outcome of a community decision—even one in which the corporation is vitally interested. And interest itself, as noted above, is differentially distributed in a pattern which pluralists assume is rational for most actors, most of the time. For example, Long and Belknap observe:

> Just as business organizations may be disinterested in community affairs because of the national scope of its (sic) operations, individual businessmen who move or are shifted from city to city may have little opportunity or incentive to participate in community affairs. Some businesses have strong pressures on them to give attention to community and metropolitan problems. Large department stores are particularly tied up with the destiny of the city and must decide whether to keep to the central city or decentralize in suburban shopping centers. Businessmen with a "metropolitan view" would thus be expected to be found here rather than in the branch office of a national corporation.[34]

What practical recommendations emerge from this comparison of stratification and pluralist approaches to the study of community power?[35] First, the researcher should pick issue-areas as the focus of his study of community power. Second, he should be able to defend these issue-areas as being very important in the life of the community. Third, he should study actual behavior, either at first hand, or by reconstructing behavior from documents, informants, newspapers and other appropriate sources. There is no harm in starting with a list of people whose behavior the researcher wishes to study *vis-à-vis* any issue-area. The harm comes, rather, in attributing some mystical significance to such a list, so that the examination of activity and of actual participation in decision-making becomes superfluous. This recommendation is not meant to discourage the researcher from collecting information about the reputation of actors, or their intentions with respect to community issues, or their evaluations about the "meanings" of community incidents. All of these kinds of data are of immeasurable value in tracing patterns of decision-making. However, these cultural data must be accompanied by information about behavior so that the researcher has some way of distinguishing between myths and facts.

The final recommendation is of the same order: researchers should study the outcomes of actual decisions within the community. It is important, but insufficient, to know what leaders want to do, what they intend to do, and what they think they can do. The researcher still has to decide on the basis of his own examination of the facts what actually emerges from these various intentions, and not conclude prematurely that the combination of intentions and resources inflexibly predetermines outcomes.

NOTES

[1] For indications that disenchantment is setting in among political scientists, see the following. Robert A. Dahl, "A Critique of the Ruling Elite Model," *American Political Science Review,* 52 (June, 1958), 463–469; Herbert Kaufman and Victor Jones, "The Mystery of Power," *Public Administration Review,* 14 (Summer, 1954), 205–212; Norton E. Long, "The Local Community as an Ecology of Games," *American Journal*

of Sociology, 64 (November, 1958), 251–261; Nelson W. Polsby, "The Sociology of Community Power: A Reassessment," *Social Forces,* 37 (March, 1959), 232–236 and "Three Problems in the Analysis of Community Power," *American Sociological Review,* 24 (December, 1959), 796–803; Raymond E. Wolfinger, "Reputation and Reality in the Study of 'Community Power,'" *American Sociological Review,* 25 (December, 1960), in press. Sociologists also seem to be re-examining studies of community power: Reinhard Bendix and Seymour M. Lipset, "Political Sociology," *Current Sociology,* 6 (1957), 79–99; Peter H. Rossi, "Community Decision-Making," *Administrative Science Quarterly,* 1 (March, 1957), 415–443. Writings praising community power studies are quite extensive, and include the following: Gordon Blackwell, "Community Analysis," in Roland Young (ed.), *Approaches to the Study of Politics* (Evanston, 1958), 305–317; William J. Gore and Fred S. Silander, "A Bibliographical Essay on Decision-Making," *Administrative Science Quarterly,* 4 (June, 1959), 106–121; Lawrence J. R. Herson, "The Lost World of Municipal Government," *American Political Science Review,* 51 (June, 1957), 330–345.

[2] For example, Robert S. Lynd and Helen M. Lynd, *Middletown* (New York, 1929) and *Middletown in Transition* (New York, 1937); Floyd Hunter, *Community Power Structure* (Chapel Hill, 1953); August B. Hollingshead, *Elmtown's Youth* (New York, 1949); W. Lloyd Warner *et al., Democracy in Jonesville* (New York, 1949); C. Wright Mills, the Middle Classes in the Middle-Sized Cities," *American Sociological Review,* 11 (October, 1946), 520–529; Robert O. Schulze, "Economic Dominants and Community Power Structure," *American Sociological Review,* 23 (February, 1958), 3–9; Roland Pellegrin and Charles H. Coates, "Absentee-Owned Corporations and Community Power Structure," *American Journal of Sociology,* 61 (March, 1956), 413–419; Delbert C. Miller, "Industry and Community Power Structure," *American Sociological Review,* 23 (February, 1958), 9–15 and "Decision-Making Cliques in Community Power Structure," *American Journal of Sociology,* 64 (November, 1958), 299–310.

[3] Warner *et. al., op. cit.,* p. xviii.

[4] See, *e.g.,* Kaufman and Jones, *op. cit.*

[5] See Polsby, *op. cit.*

[6] See *ibid.,* Dahl, *op. cit.,* and Kaufman and Jones, *op. cit.*

[7] I am well aware that for other purposes the "pluralist" approach can be divided into several schools of thought. However, all variations of pluralist theory contrast effectively with stratification theory. Pluralist presumptions can be found, for example, in the writings of de Tocqueville and Madison, and in Arthur Bentley, *The Process of Government* (Chicago, 1908); E. Pendleton Herring, *The Politics of Democracy* (New York, 1940); David B. Truman, *The Governmental Process* (New York, 1953); V. O. Key, Jr., *Politics, Parties and Pressure Groups* (New York, 4th ed., 1959).

[8] Among the researchers who have found pluralist presumptions about the nature of the political system useful are Robert A. Dahl ("The New Haven Community Leadership Study," Working Paper Number 1, December, 1957, mimeo); Harry Scoble ("Yankeetown: Leadership in Three Decision-Making Processes," presented at the meeting of the American Political Science Association, 1956); and George Belknap and Norton E. Long. See Long, *op. cit.;* Long and Belknap, "A Research Program on Leadership and Decision-Making in Metropolitan Areas" (New York, Governmental Affairs Institute, 1956), mimeo; Belknap and John H. Bunzel, "The Trade Union in the Political Community," *PROD,* 2 (September, 1958), 3–6; Belknap, "A Plan for Research on the Socio-Political Dynamics of Metropolitan Areas" (presented before a seminar on urban leadership of the Social Science Research Council, New York,

August, 1957). See also a paper presented to this same seminar by Peter H. Rossi, "The Study of Decision-Making in the Local Community."

[9] I present some of the characteristics of a stratification theory of community power in other papers, *e.g.,* "Power in Middletown: Fact and Value in Community Research" (March, 1960), mimeo.; "Power as a Variable of Social Stratification" (November, 1959), mimeo.

[10] See Kaufman and Jones, *op. cit.*

[11] Wolfinger, *op. cit.,* has summarized findings on this point, pp. *7 ff.*

[12] See Dahl, "The New Haven . . .," *op. cit.,* Polsby, *op cit.,* and Wolfinger, *op cit.,* and forthcoming publications of the New Haven Community Leadership Study.

[13] Scoble, *op cit.*

[14] Long and Belknap, *op. cit.*

[15] Belknap, *op. cit.*

[16] See, for example, Pellegrin and Coates, *op. cit.,* and Lynd, *Middletown in Transition, op. cit.,* p. 89.

[17] See Dahl, "Critique . . .," *op. cit.*

[18] See, for example, Belknap, *op. cit.,* for an explicit discussion of this point. One stratification writer who has attempted to take account of the time factor is Jerome K. Myers, "Assimilation in the Political Community," *Sociology and Social Research,* 35 (January-February, 1951), 175–182. Myers plots a secular trend which indicates slow increases in the number of Italians and Italian descended persons employed by New Haven municipal government over a fifty year period ending in 1940. Myers claims to have discovered "discrimination" against Italians, because they did not participate in city government jobs to an extent proportional with their representation in the total population of the city. His conclusion was that "the early or quick assimilation of New Haven Italians in the political system does not seem very probable. . . . All indications are that political assimilation is inevitable, although it is at least several generations away."

By taking account of shorter-term cyclical movements within the allegedly "basic" structure, we may be able to explain the delay in the political assimilation of Italians.

First, New Haven Italo-Americans were and are predominantly Republican in local politics, because in New Haven the Republican organization early and energetically courted the Italo-American vote. From 1920 to 1940, years in which that ethnic group would "normally" have been expected to come into their own as a politically significant minority group, the city government was in Democratic hands two-thirds of the time. It might be expected, therefore, that Italo-Americans would be less well represented among officeholders than if these circumstances were reversed. Second, in 1945, a Republican of Italian descent was elected Mayor, whereupon Italian-Americans invaded the top echelons of city government to such an extent that the Mayor pleaded in vain with one who was a candidate for President of the City Council to withdraw to favor of a Yankee Republican, on the grounds that there were "too many Italians" in City Hall, and that the Yankee members of the Republican coalition should have some recognition.

[19] See, especially, Wolfinger, *op. cit.*

[20] See C. Wright Mills, "The Middle Classes . . . ," *op. cit.,* and my "The Sociology of Community Power," *op. cit.,* on this point.

[21] See Anthony Downs, *An Economic Theory of Democracy* (New York, 1957); Robert E. Lane, *Political Life: How People Get Involved in Politics* (Glencoe, 1959); Samuel Stouffer, *Communism, Conformity and Civil Liberties* (New York, 1955), pp. 58*ff.*

[22] Lane, *op. cit.*, pp. 220–234.

[23] Arthur J. Vidich and Joseph Bensman, *Small Town in Mass Society* (Princeton, 1958), pp. 69–70, 290–291. Studies of social status have been hampered by a similar problem of upper-class-centeredness. See the criticism of Warner on this point by Seymour M. Lipset and Reinhard Bendix, "Social Status and Social Structure," *British Journal of Sociology,* 2 (June, 1951), esp. pp. 163*ff*.

[24] See Bentley, *op. cit.,* pp. 175–222. Note, at p. 202: "If we can get our social life stated in terms of activity, and of nothing else, we have not indeed succeeded in measuring it, but we have at least reached a foundation upon which a coherent system of measurements can be built up. . . . We shall cease to be blocked by the intervention of unmeasurable elements, which claim to be themselves the real causes of all that is happening, and which by their spook-like arbitrariness make impossible any progress toward dependable knowledge."

[25] Only one sociologist seems to have realized what this implies for the methods and conclusions of political analysis. See Rudolf Heberle, *Social Movements* (New York, 1951). The relevant theory is compactly expounded by Herbert Blumer in "Collective Behavior," in Alfred M. Lee (ed.), *Principles of Sociology* (New York, 1953), pp. 167–220.

[26] Indeed, Max Weber, the most important "founding father" of modern stratification analysis, makes just this point. See Weber's "Class, Status, Party," in H. H. Gerth and C. W. Mills (eds.), *From Max Weber: Essays in Sociology* (New York, 1946), pp. 180–195, esp. p. 184.

[27] See, for example, Lynd and Lynd, *Middletown in Transition, op. cit.,* pp. 454–455, 509; Alfred W. Jones, *Life, Liberty and Property* (Philadelphia, 1941), pp. 336–354; Warner *et al., op. cit.,* p. 27; C. Wright Mills, "The Middle Classes," *op. cit.* Compare also Richard Centers, *The Psychology of Social Classes* (Princeton, 1948), and note the extent to which his conclusions outrun his data.

[28] See, for example, Truman, *op. cit., passim.* Alexis de Tocqueville, *Democracy In America* (New York, 1954), esp. Vol. I, pp. 181–205, 281–342, Vol. II, pp. 114–135.

[29] See Robert A. Dahl, *A Preface to Democratic Theory* (Chicago, 1956).

[30] Truman, *op. cit.,* summarizes a tremendous amount of this material.

[31] Long and Belknap, *op. cit.,* pp. 9–11. See Polsby, "The Sociology of Community Power," *op. cit.,* and Edward C. Banfield, "The Concept 'Leadership' in Community Research" (delivered at the meeting of the American Political Science Association, 1958), for similar lists.

[32] In papers cited in note 9 above.

[33] Robert A. Dahl, "The Analysis of Influence in Local Communities" (May, 1959), mimeo., p. 10.

[34] Long and Belknap, *op. cit.,* pp. 13–14. This corresponds to the findings—but not the interpretations—of Schulze, *op. cit.,* and of Pellegrin and Coates, *op. cit.*

[35] This presumes that the researcher wants to make some generalizations about the "normal" distributions of power in community decision-making.

7. LOCATING LEADERS IN LOCAL COMMUNITIES: A COMPARISON OF SOME ALTERNATIVE APPROACHES *

Linton C. Freeman, Thomas J. Fararo, Warner Bloomberg, Jr., and Morris H. Sunshine

Most investigators would probably agree that leadership refers to a complex process whereby a relatively small number of individuals in a collectivity behave in such a way that they effect (or effectively prevent) a change in the lives of a relatively large number. But agreement on theoretical details of the leadership process or on how it is to be studied is another matter. Much of the recent literature on community leadership has been critical.[1] Gibb has suggested that there are a great many *kinds* of leadership—many different ways in which changes may be effected. He has proposed that leaders be assigned to various types including "the initiator, energizer, harmonizer, expediter, and the like." [2] Banfield has stressed the importance of the distinction between intended and unintended leadership.[3] And both Dahl and Polsby have called attention to the desirability of considering the *extent* of the effect a given leader has in expediting a particular change and the *range* of changes over which his effect holds.[4] It seems evident, then, that although these critics might agree with the minimum definition presented above, they would all like to see some additional factors included within its scope.

Polsby has translated the comments of the critics into a set of operational guides for research.[5] He has suggested that a satisfactory study of community leadership must involve a detailed examination of the whole decision-making process as it is exhibited over a range of issues. Here we should have to specify each issue, the persons involved, their intentions, and the extent and nature of their influence if any. Such a program represents an ideal that might be used to think about the process of community leadership. But as a research strategy, this plan raises many problems.

In the first place, both influence and intention are concepts presenting great difficulty in empirical application. Both require that elaborate observational and interviewing procedures be developed, and both raise reliability problems.[6] May we, for example, take a person's word concerning his intentions, or must they be inferred from his behavior? And even when two persons interact and one subsequently changes his stated position in the direction of the views of the other, it is difficult to *prove* that influence has taken place. But even if these questions were eliminated, a practical problem would still remain. To follow the prescriptions listed above would be prohibitively expensive, requiring detailed observation of hundreds (or thousands) of individuals over an extended period. To record all interaction relevant to the decisions under study, it would

* Support for this study was provided by a grant from the Fund for Adult Education to the University College of Syracuse University.

SOURCE: *American Sociological Review*, 28 (October, 1963), pp. 791–798. Reprinted by permission of the authors and the American Sociological Association.

be necessary to observe each person in a large number of varied situations, many of them quite private. Even then it would be difficult to evaluate the impact of the process of observation itself. Given these considerations, Polsby's ideal has never been reached. All existing studies of community leadership represent some compromise.

Most authors of community leadership studies would probably agree that the critics are on the right track. But most have been willing (or perhaps forced by circumstances) to make one or more basic assumptions in order to achieve a workable research design. Four types of compromise have been common. They will be discussed below.

Perhaps the most realistic of the compromise studies are those based on the assumption that active participation in decision making *is* leadership. Typically, in such studies, one or a series of community decisions are either observed or reconstructed. In so doing, an attempt is made to identify the active participants in the decision-making process. These decision-making studies frequently are restricted to a small number of decisions, and they usually fail to present convincing evidence on the questions of intent and amount of impact. But they do provide a more or less direct index of participation. If they err it is by including individuals who, though present, had little or no impact on the decision. On the face of it this seems preferable to the likelihood of excluding important influentials.[7]

A second compromise approach is to assume that formal authority *is* leadership. Aside from arbitrarily defining which positions are "on top," these studies underestimate the impact of those not in official positions on the outcomes of the decision-making process.

The third approach assumes that leadership is a necessary consequence of social activity. This assumption leads to studies of social participation. Such studies have used everything from rough indexes of memberships in voluntary associations to carefully constructed scales of activity in such associations. In each case it is reasoned that community leadership results from a high degree of voluntary activity in community affairs. The social participation approach is thus the converse of the study of position. While the former stresses activity, the latter is concerned only with formal authority. But to the extent that activity in voluntary associations leads to having an impact upon community change, activists are leaders.

The final approach assumes that leadership is too complex to be indexed directly. Instead of examining leadership as such, proponents of this approach assess reputation for leadership. Their reasoning suggests that all of the more direct approaches neglect one or another key dimensions of the leadership process. They turn, therefore, to informants from the community itself. Often rather elaborate steps have been taken to insure that the informants are indeed informed. For example, positional leaders may be questioned in order to develop a list of reputed leaders or influentials; then the reported influentials are polled to determine the top influentials. In such cases it is reasonable to suppose that the grossly uninformed are ruled out.

Various critics have condemned the indeterminancy and subjectivity of this procedure.[8] But its defenders reason that the reputational approach is the only way to uncover the subtleties of intent, extent of impact, and the like in the leadership process. What, they ask, but a life-long involvement in the activities of a community could possibly yield sophisticated answers to the question "Who are the leaders?" The reputational approach, then, assumes the possibility of locating some individuals who unquestionably meet the criteria of community leadership, and who in turn will be able to name others not so visible to the outside observer.

Currently, the controversy continues. Proponents of one or another of these competing points of view argue for its inherent superiority and the obvious validity of its assumptions. Others take the view that all of these approaches get at leadership. But these are empirical questions; they can be answered only on the basis of comparison, not by faith or by rhetoric. A number of partial contrasts have been published, but so far no systematic overall comparison of these procedures has been reported. The present report represents such an attempt. An effort is made to determine the degree to which these several procedures agree or disagree in locating community leaders.

The data presented here represent a part of a larger study of leadership in the Syracuse, N.Y. metropolitan area. Two reports have been published,[9] and several additional papers are forthcoming.

Decision-Making

The study of participation in the decision-making process was of central concern in the Syracuse study. The first major task of the project team was to select a set of community problems or issues which would provide a point of entry into a pool (or pools) of participants in the decision-making process. Interviews were conducted with 20 local specialists in community study and with 50 informants representing diverse segments of the city's population. Care was taken to include representatives of each group along the total range of interest and institutional commitment. These 70 interviews provided a list of about 250 community issues. The list was reduced to a set of 39 issues according to the following criteria:

1. Each issue must have been at least temporarily resolved by a decision.
2. The decision must be perceived as important by informants representing diverse segments of the community.
3. The decision must pertain to the development, distribution, and utilization of resources and facilities which have an impact on a large segment of the metropolitan population.
4. The decision must involve alternative lines of action. It must entail a certain degree of choice on the part of participants; and the outcome must not be predetermined.
5. The decision must be administered rather than made by individuals in "the market." For the purpose of this study, an administered decision was defined as one made by individuals holding top positions in organizational structures which empower them to make decisions affecting many people.
6. The decision must involve individuals and groups resident in the Syracuse

Metropolitan Area. Decisions made outside the Metropolitan Area (e.g., by the state government), were excluded even though they might affect residents of the Metropolitan Area.

7. The decision must fall within the time period 1955–1960.

8. The set of decisions as a whole must affect the entire range of important institutional sectors, such as governmental, economic, political, educational, religious, ethnic, and the like.[10]

The next step in the research required the determination of positional leaders or formal authorities for each of the set of 39 issues. The study began with those individuals who were formally responsible for the decisions. The element of arbitrary judgment usually involved in the positional approach was thus avoided. Here, the importance of a position was derived from its role in determining a choice among alternative lines of action rather than of being the consequence of an arbitrary assumption.

The responsible formal authorities were determined on the basis of documents pertinent to the 39 decisions. In addition, several attorneys were consulted to insure that correct determinations were made. The number of authorities responsible for making each of these decisions ranged from two to 57.

The interviews started with authoritative persons. Respondents were presented with a set of 39 cards, each of which identified a decision. They were asked to sort the cards into two piles: (1) "Those in which you participated; that is, where others involved in this decision would recognize you as being involved," and (2) "Those in which you were not a participant." For those issues in which they claimed participation, individuals were then asked to name all the others who were also involved. Here they were instructed to report on the basis of first-hand knowledge of participation rather than on hearsay. Respondents were also given a questionnaire covering their social backgrounds.

When the interviews with authorities were completed, their responses for those decisions on which they possessed authority were tabulated. Then, any person who had been nominated as a participant by two authorities for the same issue was designated as a first zone influential. Two nominations were deemed necessary in order to avoid bias due to accidental contacts, mistakes of memory, or a tendency to mention personal friends. In the final tabulations this same rule of two nominations was applied to authorities also. Therefore, no person is counted as a participant unless he has two nominations by qualified nominators.

As the next step, all first zone influentials were interviewed using exactly the same procedures as those used for authorities. Their responses were tabulated for the decisions in which they had been involved, and any person nominated by one authority and one first zone influential was also classified as a first zone influential and interviewed. Then any person nominated by two first zone influentials was designated a second zone influential—two steps removed from formal authority but still involved. We did not interview beyond these second zone influentials. We might have continued with third and fourth zones and so on; but on the basis of qualitative data gathered during the interviews, we suspected we were moving well into the periphery of impact on the outcome of decision making.

In all, 628 interviews were completed. Of these, 550 qualified as participants. These participants, then, are the leaders as determined by the decision-making phase of the Syracuse study. They were ranked in terms of the number of decisions in which they were involved. For the present analysis the 32 most active participants are considered.

Social Activity

Each of the 550 participants uncovered by the decision-making study was asked to complete a questionnaire covering his social background and current activities. These questionnaires were returned by 506 informants. The answers included responses to a set of questions designed to elicit as much information as possible about voluntary association memberships. Specific questions were included to determine memberships in the following areas:

1. Committees formed to deal with community problems.
2. Community service organizations.
3. Business organizations.
4. Professional organizations.
5. Union organizations.
6. Clubs and social organizations.
7. Cultural organizations.
8. Religious organizations.
9. Political parties, organizations and clubs.
10. Veterans' and patriotic organizations.
11. Other clubs and organizations.

Memberships in these organizations were tabulated, and a rough overall index to voluntary activity was calculated by simply summing the number of memberships for each person. The respondents were ranked in terms of number of memberships, and the 32 most active organizational members were included in the present analysis.

Reputation

Each questionnaire also invited the respondent to list the most influential leaders in the community. Eight spaces were provided for answers. Nominations were tabulated and, following traditional procedures, the top 41 reputed leaders were listed. The responses of those 41 repondents were then tabulated separately. The top 32 were derived from their rankings. This was done in order to maximize the chances that our nominators would be informed. As it turned out, however, the top 32 nominations of the whole group and the top 32 provided by the top 41 were exactly the same persons and in the same order. For Syracuse these nominations showed remarkable consistency all along the line.

Position

In determining the top positional leaders it seemed desirable to avoid as much as possible making the usual arbitrary assumptions. Traditional usage of the positional approach dictated the determination of the titular heads of the major organizations in business, government, the professions, and the like. Within each of these institutional areas choice could be made in terms of size, but it was difficult to determine how many organizations should be selected in each area.

An empirical resolution for this problem was provided in a recent report by D'Antonio et al.[11] These authors provided data on the proportions of reputed leaders representing each of the seven relevant institutional areas in 10 previous studies. Since agreement on these relative proportions was reasonably close for the six middle-sized American communities reported, they were used to assign proportions in each institutional area in the present study. The proportions derived from D'Antonio and those used in the present study are reported in Table 1. In this case positional leaders are the titular heads of the largest organizations in each of the institutional areas, and each area is represented according

TABLE 1. PERCENTAGE OF LEADERS IN EACH INSTITUTIONAL AREA

Institution	Six Cities	Syracuse
Business	57	59
Government	8	9
Professions	12	13
Education	5	6
Communications	8	6
Labor	4	3
Religion	5	3
Total	99	99

to the proportion listed in Table 1. Thirty-two organizations were chosen in all. As a check on its validity, the list of organizations was shown to several local experts in community affairs. They were in substantial agreement that the organizations listed seemed consistent with their perceptions of the "top" organizations in Syracuse. The heads of these organizations might be expected to have formal control over much of the institutional system of the community.

These, then, are the raw materials of the current study. An attempt was made to determine the degree to which these several procedures would allocate the same persons to the top leadership category.

Results

The several procedures for determining leaders did not converge on a single set of individuals. Top leaders according to one procedure were not necessarily the same as those indicated by another. An index of agreement for each pair was constructed by calculating the ratio of the actual number of agreements to their total possible number. Results are listed in Table 2.

It is possible that any of the methods used, if modified enough, would have yielded significantly different results.[12] The procedures we followed seem in their essentials to be like those followed in most of the studies so far published. (Those who believe they have altered the use of positions, nominations, memberships, or other indexes in such a way as to obtain a major difference in the output of the technique have only to demonstrate this by empirical comparisons.) Our impression is that most versions of each approach represent only vernier adjustments of the same device and thus can have only marginally differing results.

Table 2 suggests that there is far from perfect agreement in determining leaders by means of these four methods. In only one case do two of these methods concur in more than 50 per cent of their nominations. Reputation and position seem to be in substantial agreement in locating leaders. To a large

TABLE 2. PERCENTAGE OF AGREEMENT IN DETERMINING LEADERS BY FOUR TRADITIONAL PROCEDURES

Participation			
25	Social activity		
33	25	Reputation	
39	22	74	Position

degree, therefore, reputed leaders are the titular heads of major community organizations. They are not, however, themselves active as participants in decision making to any great extent.

Reputation for leadership seems to derive primarily from position, not from participation. But it appears unlikely that position itself constitutes a sufficient basis for reputation. The reputations, however, might belong to the organizations and not the individuals. In such a case, when an informant named John Smith as a leader what might have been intended was the fact that the Smith Snippel Company (of which John Smith was president) is influential in community decisions. Smith would thus have been named only because we had asked for a person's name. Our hypothesis, then, is that reputation should correspond with the participation rate of organizations rather than the participation rates of individuals.

On the basis of this hypothesis, the data on participation were retabulated. Each participant was classified according to his organization or place of employment. Then the head of each organization was credited not only with his own participation, but with the sum of the participation of his employees. In this manner an index of organizational participation was constructed and the top 30 organizational leaders were determined. Individuals so nominated were compared with those introduced by the earlier procedures. The results are shown in Table 3.

TABLE 3. PERCENTAGE OF AGREEMENT BETWEEN ORGANIZATIONAL PARTICIPATION AND FOUR TRADITIONAL PROCEDURES

Traditional Procedure	Percentage of Agreement
Participation	33
Social activity	25
Reputation	67
Position	80

The proportions shown in Table 3 support our hypothesis. Organizational participation seems to uncover substantially the same leaders as reputation and position. The top reputed leaders, therefore, though not active participants themselves, head up the largest organizations, and the personnel of these organizations have the highest participation rates.

This result accounts for a great deal of participation in community decision making. Since organizational participation provides a workable index, many participants must be employees of large community organizations. But this does not explain the most active class of individual participants—those who were picked up by the individual participation index. These people seem to be virtually full-time participants in community affairs. We know that they are not organizational heads, but we have not determined who they are.

In view of the sheer amount of their participation, the top participants must be professional participants of some sort. And, as a class, professional participants in community affairs should be government officials and employees or full-time professional executives of non-governmental agencies formally and primarily committed to intervention in community affairs. With this as our hypothesis, the individuals nominated as leaders by the four traditional indexes were all classified into either government and professional or non-professional categories. Then percentages of government personnel and professionals were calculated for all four indexes. The results are shown in Table 4.

Again the results support our hypothesis. The most active individual participants are typically government personnel.

The participation index thus gets at personnel quite different from those selected by reputational or positional indexes, or by social activity. These differing cadres of people seem to represent *different kinds* of leadership behavior with respect to the local community.

Summary and Discussion of Results

These results indicate that at least in Syracuse "leadership" is not a homogeneous category. Which "leaders" are uncovered seems in large part to be a function of the mode of study. The several traditional indexes allow us to locate one or another of three basic types of "leaders."

First, there are those who enjoy the reputation for top leadership. These are

TABLE 4. PERCENTAGE OF LEADERS ACCORDING TO FOUR TRADITIONAL PROCEDURES WHO ARE GOVERNMENT OFFICIALS OR EMPLOYEES OR PROFESSIONAL PARTICIPANTS

Traditional Procedure	Percentage of Government Personnel or Professional Participants
Participation	66
Social activity	20
Reputation	20
Position	28

very frequently the same individuals who are the heads of the largest and most actively participating business, industrial, governmental, political, professional, educational, labor and religious organizations in Syracuse. They are uncovered by studies of reputation, position, or organizational participation. In view of their formal command over the institutional structure and the symbolic value of their status as indexed by reputation, these individuals may be called the *Institutional Leaders* of Syracuse.

These Institutional Leaders, however, are for the most part not active participants in community affairs. There is no evidence that they have any direct impact on most decisions which take place. Their activity may be limited to that of lending prestige to or legitimizing the solutions provided by others. They might conceivably be participating decision makers in secret, but more likely they serve chiefly to provide access to the decision-making structure for their underlings: the *Effectors*.

The Effectors are located by studying participation. They are the active workers in the actual process of community decision making. Many of the most active Effectors are government personnel and professional participants, and the others are the employees of the large private corporations directed by the Institutional Leaders. In some cases, the Effectors are in touch with their employers, and it seems likely that their activities are frequently guided by what they view as company policy; but, judging from our data, they are often pretty much on their own. At any rate, these men carry most of the burden of effecting community change.

The third type of leader might be called the *Activists*. These people are active—and often hold office—in voluntary organizations, community service organizations, and clubs. Although they are not involved as often as the Effectors, the Activists do participate in decision making. For the most part they seem to lack the positional stature to be Institutional Leaders. Furthermore, they often work for or direct smaller organizations in the community. They lack the power base provided by association with government or one of the major industrial or business firms. Yet, seemingly by sheer commitment of time and effort to community affairs, these Activists do help shape the future of the community.

In conclusion, the various differing approaches to the study of community leadership seem to uncover different types of leaders. The study of reputation, position or organizational participation seems to get at the Institutional Leaders. Studies of participation in decision making, on the other hand, tap the Effectors of community action. And studies of social activity seem to seek out the Activists who gain entry by dint of sheer commitment, time, and energy.

In part, our results are dependent upon the Syracuse situation. It is likely that 25 years ago, when Syracuse was smaller and less diversified, the Institutional Leaders and the Effectors were the same people.[13] And 25 years from now this description will probably no longer hold. Other communities, in other stages of development and diversification will probably show different patterns. But until more comparative studies are done, conclusions of this kind are virtually guesses.

NOTES

[1] Cecil A. Gibb, "Leadership," in Gardner Lindzey (ed.), *Handbook of Social Psychology,* Vol. 2, Cambridge, Mass.: Addison-Wesley, 1954, pp. 877–920; Edward C. Banfield, "The Concept 'Leadership' in Community Research," paper read before the Annual Meeting of the American Political Science Association, St. Louis, Missouri, 1958; Robert A. Dahl, "A Critique of the Ruling Elite Model," *American Political Science Review,* 52 (June, 1958), pp. 463–469; Nelson W. Polsby, "The Sociology of Community Power: A Reassessment," *Social Forces,* 37 (March, 1959), pp. 232–236; Nelson W. Polsby, "Three Problems in the Analysis of Community Power," *American Sociological Review,* 24 (December, 1959), pp. 798–803; Raymond E. Wolfinger, "Reputation and Reality in the Study of 'Community Power'," *American Sociological Review,* 25 (October, 1960), pp. 636–644.

[2] Cecil A. Gibb, *op. cit.*

[3] Edward C. Banfield, *op. cit.*

[4] Nelson W. Polsby, "The Sociology of Community Power: A Reassessment," *op. cit.* and Robert A. Dahl, *op. cit.*

[5] Nelson W. Polsby, "The Sociology of Community Power," *op. cit.*

[6] Herbert A. Simon, "Notes on the Observation and Measurement of Political Power," in his *Models of Man,* New York: John Wiley and Sons, 1957; James G. March, "An Introduction to the Theory and Measurement of Influence," *American Political Science Review,* 49 (June, 1955), pp. 431–451; James G. March, "Measurement Concepts in the Theory of Influence," *Journal of Politics,* 19 (May, 1957), pp. 202–226.

[7] Numerous examples of this and other approaches to the study of leadership may be found in Wendell Bell, Richard J. Hill, and Charles R. Wright, *Public Leadership,* San Francisco: Chandler, 1961.

[8] See the articles by Dahl, Polsby, and Wolfinger cited above.

[9] Linton C. Freeman, Warner Bloomberg, Jr., Stephen P. Koff, Morris H. Sunshine, and Thomas J. Fararo, *Local Community Leadership,* Syracuse: University College of Syracuse University, 1960; Linton C. Freeman, Thomas J. Fararo, Warner Bloomberg, Jr., and Morris H. Sunshine, *Metropolitan Decision-Making,* Syracuse: University College of Syracuse University, 1962.

[10] The entire set of 39 issues is described in the earlier publications of the study group, *op. cit.*

[11] William D'Antonio, William Form, Charles Loomis, and Eugene Erickson, "Institutional and Occupational Representatives in Eleven Community Influence Systems," *American Sociological Review,* 26 (June, 1961), pp. 440–446.

[12] The choice of the top 32 leaders in each category, is, for example, somewhat arbitrary. When another number is used, the *absolute* percentages of agreement vary, but their standings *relative* to one another remain stable.

[13] For an interesting discussion of the development of a community leadership structure, see Robert O. Schulze, "The Bifurcation of Power in a Satellite City," in Morris Janowitz (ed.), *Community Political Systems,* Glencoe, Illinois: Free Press, 1961.

8. SUBSTANCE AND ARTIFACT: THE CURRENT STATUS OF RESEARCH ON COMMUNITY POWER STRUCTURE [1]

John Walton

In the twelve years since the publication of Floyd Hunter's classic, *Community Power Structure*,[2] sociology and political science have experienced a vigorous revival of interest in community studies. Certainly one of the major explanations for this resurgence is to be found in the fact that Hunter introduced a method that promised wide application and a procedure for the verification of particular results. Yet at the same time Hunter's method aroused considerable skepticism, especially among political scientists, for what was alleged to be a misplaced focus on reputation rather than actual influence and, perhaps as a result, an overly monopolistic description of the community power structure. In these twelve years the debate over the relative merits of the (Hunter) reputational method, as opposed to the analysis of decision-making processes, has been joined by numerous scholars of various persuasions and shows little sign of abatement.[3] There is, however, one point on which researchers and commentators are nearly unanimous: the need for truly comparative studies.

The purpose of this paper is to review a substantial portion of the existing literature on community power in order to identify what generalizations, if any, can be drawn concerning the methodological and substantive correlates of various types of community power structure. Once this has been done we should be in a position to suggest some guidelines for comparative studies. Rossi, commenting on the diversity of findings and persistent gaps in our knowledge of the community, has observed that "little progress has been made in putting things together in a systematic way."[4] This review is an attempt to "put things together" in such a way.

Summary of the Literature

Table 1 summarizes thirty-three studies dealing with fifty-five communities.[5] The information that it contains regarding research method, community characteristics, and type of power structure has been distilled from each separate study and, for that reason, loses somewhat in comparability. This difficulty has been met in two ways. When studies are not explicit on certain aspects, no entry is made in the table. Second, it is believed that the categories used in the summary are sufficiently general to provide reasonable comparability for present purposes.

A brief description of the variables with which we will be concerned should demonstrate the point.

A. Community Characteristics

The demographic and economic characteristics in Table 1—region, popu-

SOURCE: *The American Journal of Sociology*, LXXI (January, 1966), pp. 430–438. Copyright 1966 by The University of Chicago. Reprinted by permission of the University of Chicago Press.

lation size and composition, extent of industrialization and economic base —are self-explanatory.

B. Method

Studies of community power have relied on three distinct methods: the reputational, the decision-making, and the case study. Actual use of these three usually involves some variations which are more definitively encompassed with the following fivefold classification.

1. Reputational methods
   a) Reputational—informants are asked to identify the most influential people in the community when it comes to getting things done. Here leaders are nominated directly in a one-step procedure.
   b) Reputational, two-step—informants are given lists, assembled by various means, of purportedly influential leaders and asked to evaluate them in terms of influence (usually by narrowing the list or ranking its members).
2. Positional methods
   a) Positional—leaders are taken to be those persons occupying important positions in formal and/or informal organizations.
   b) Positional and Reputational—a combination of 1 b and 2 a.
3. Decision-making approach (event or issue analysis)
   a) Decisions—the focus is on specific community issues, and leaders are those persons active or instrumental in the resolution.
4. Case-study method
   a) Case study methods are less explicit; usually the community and leadership are analyzed as a process.
5. Combined approaches
   a) Combined—simultaneous use of the above, especially 1 b and 3.

C. Issues

This category designates the area of influence with which the study is chiefly concerned.

1. Governmental—influence in matters of public jurisdiction, for example, nominations and campaigns, bond issues, public works.
2. Non-governmental—influence in matters of private jurisdiction, for example, general community policy, new industry.

D. Community Power Structure [6]

1. Pyramidal—monolithic, monopolistic, or a single concentrated leadership group.
2. Factional—at least two durable factions.
3. Coalitional—fluid coalitions of interest usually varying with issues.
4. Amorphous—absence of any persistent pattern of leadership.

Hypotheses

The organization of studies provided in Table 1 enables us to test, at least on the basis of a substantial portion of the literature, a number of hypotheses that have been advanced in more limited contexts. The nine hypotheses employ community power structure as the dependent variable and are arranged under

TABLE 1. COMPARATIVE OUTLINE OF STUDIES OF COMMUNITY POWER STRUCTURE *

Community	Region	< 10,000	10,000–50,000	50,000–100,000	> 100,000	Industrialized	Non-industrialized	Diversified Economy	Narrow Economy	Absentee Ownership	Increasing Population	Stable Population	Heterogeneous Population	Homogeneous Population	Integration	Cleavage	Reputational	Two-step	Positional	Decision-making	Combined	Case Study	Non-governmental	Governmental	Pyramidal	Factional	Coalitional	Amorphous	Leadership Group (N)
1. Regional City	S				X	X		X				X	X			X	X	X					X		X				40
2. Loraine	NC†			X		X		X		X			X		X		X					X	X			X		X	
3. Red Wing	NC		X			X		X				X		X	X		X					X	X		X			X	
4. Big Town	NC				X	X		X			X		X				X	X					X		X	X			75
5. Community A	S				X	X		X			X		X				X	X					X		X				25
6. Bakerville	NE	X					X		X	X				X		X	X					X			X			X	69
7. Bennington	W				X	X		X			X		X				X	X					X		X				59
8. Pacific City						X		X	X		X		X				X	X					X		X				47
9. English City	NC				X	X		X			X		X				X	X		X			X		X				35
10. Cibolia	W				X		X		X		X		X			X	X	X		X		X			X				76
11. Seattle	NE				X		X		X		X		X			X	X	X						X	X				5
12. Springdale	NE	X					X	X			X		X			X	X	X	X			X		X	X		X		415
13. New Haven	S			X			X	X			X		X			X	X	X		X			X	X			X		61
14. El Paso					X	X		X			X		X			X	X								X				60
15. C. Juarez					X		X		X		X		X			X	X								X				30
16. Tia Juana	W	X				X		X			X		X			X	X	X				X	X			X		X	16
17. Northville															X		X											
Miami (Dade County)	W																											
18. Sanford	S				X	X			X		X		X				X	X				X	X	X	X			X	
Amory	S			X		X		X		X		X					X	X				X		X	X			X	
Algona	S				X	X		X		X		X					X	X				X	X	X	X			X	
Gretna	NC				X	X			X		X		X				X	X				X	X	X	X			X	
Milton	NE					X		X			X			X		X	X	X			X		X		X				
19. Norwood	W			X		X			X		X		X				X	X		X			X		X			X	
Service City	NE		X		X	X		X				X		X		X	X	X				X		X	X			X	
20. Syracuse	NE					X		X		X		X		X		X	X	X				X		X	X				
Syracuse						X		X		X		X		X		X	X		X			X		X	X				
21. Dixie City	S		X	X		X			X		X		X			X	X	X				X		X	X		X	X	
22. Community A	NC			X		X			X		X		X		X		X			X			X		X		X		49
23. Cerebrille	NC		X		X	X		X			X		X		X		X			X		X			X		X		49
24. Burlington	S		X			X		X				X		X		X	X	X				X	X		X	X			16

* See n. 4.   † North central region.

TABLE 1—Continued

Community	Region	<10,000	10,000–50,000	50,000–100,000	>100,000	Industrialized	Non-industrialized	Diversified Economy	Narrow Economy	Absentee Ownership	Increasing Population	Stable Population	Heterogeneous Population	Homogeneous Population	Integration	Cleavage	Reputational	Two step	Positional	Decision-making	Combined	Case Study	Non-governmental	Governmental	Pyramidal	Factional	Coalitional	Amorphous	Leadership Group (N)
25. Watertown	S				X		X	X						X			X	X					X		X				74
Centralia	S				X		X	X						X			X	X					X		X				61
26. Orange Point	S	X					X		X		X	X	X			X					X		X		X			
Floriana	S		X				X		X			X				X					X		X			X		
Center City	S			X			X		X							X					X		X		X			
Eastborne	S						X		X		X					X					X		X			X		
Westborne	S								X		X			X		X					X		X			X		
Dorado	S											X									X		X			X		
Hiberna	S													X							X		X					
Estiva	S													X							X		X					
Dallas	S		X									X									X		X		X			
27. Wheelsburg	NC				X	X			X		X		X	X		X	X	X	X			X		X	X	X			67
28. Edgewood	NE	X				X		X			X			X				X	X			X		X	X	X			78
29. Riverview	NE	X				X		X						X					X			X		X	X		X		36
30. Midway County	S						X		X						X				X			X		X	X				35
River County	S			X						X			X						X					X	X				20
Beach County	S						X												X					X	X				38
Southern County	S						X												X					X	X				18
31. Atlanta	S				X	X		X	X	X	X	X		X	X		X	X	X			X			X	X		X	8
32. Farmdale	W		X			X		X			X		X		X			X	X			X			X			X	133
Oretown	W						X	X			X								X			X		X	X	X		X	14
Petropolis	S			X		X		X			X		X				X		X			X		X	X				38
Metroville	S			X		X		X			X		X				X		X			X		X	X	X			61
33. Oberlin	NC		X				X														X			X	X	X	X		41

three categories of independent variables. They are derived from a number of sources with occasional modification in order to keep the list to a manageable size and to provide conceptual equivalence with the data.

A. Methodological Characteristics
  1. The reputational method tends to identify pyramidal power structures, while the decision-making approach discovers factional and coalitional power structures.[7]
  2. The two-step reputational method tends to produce a pyramidal description of power structure more frequently than the direct-nomination procedure.[8]
  3. Studies focusing on governmental issues tend to find factional and coalitional structures, while a focus on non-governmental issues more frequently results in a pyramidal description.[9]
  4. Comparative studies tend to find factional and coalitional power structures.
B. Demographic Characteristics
  1. Socially integrated, heterogeneous populations have less concentrated power structures.[10]
  2. Regional differences obtain.[11]
C. Economic Characteristics
  1. The more industrialized the community, the less concentrated its power structure.[12]
  2. Communities with a high proportion of absentee ownership tend to have less concentrated power structures.[13]
  3. The more diversified the economic base, the less concentrated the power structure.[14]

Results

Table 2 illustrates the association between research and power structure.[15]

Hypotheses A1, A2 and A3 are confirmed. The reputational method tends to identify pyramidal structures while decision-making and combined methods reflect factional, coalitional, and amorphous types.[16] Further, when the reputational method is used, either exclusively or in combination with some other, the two-step procedure indicates pyramidal structures. Third, when non-governmental areas of influence are of chief concern, pyramidal structures more frequently obtain than when the focus is on governmental areas.[17] Hypothesis A4 is rejected, comparative studies showing no significant departure from the results of single case studies.

Hypotheses B1 and B2 are not clearly supported although the data in Table 3 show tendencies in that direction. A socially integrated population may tend to be associated with a less concentrated power structure. Regional differences are somewhat clearer with the northeast and north central regions, reflecting less concentration of power than is found in the South.

Although the levels of significance are not striking, mere inspection of the data on the economic variables provides some support for hypotheses C1 and C2, although in the case of C3 the data are inconclusive.[18]

TABLE 2. RESEARCH METHOD AND COMMUNITY POWER STRUCTURE

	Pyramidal	Factional	Coalitional Amorphous *	Total †
Method:				
Reputational	13	7	7	27
Decision-making-combined	2	4	8	14
Total	15	11	15	41
	$\chi^2(2 \times 2)$ $p < .05$‡			
Reputational method: §				
One-step	2	5	3	10
Two-step	13	5	7	25
Total	15	10	10	35
	Fisher exact $p - .072$			
Area of Influence:				
Non-governmental	11	4	3	18
Governmental	5	9	12	26
Total	16	13	15	44
	$\chi^2(2 \times 2)$ $p < .02$			
Scope of study:				
One community	7	7	11	25
Two or more communities	12	10	8	30
Total	19	17	19	55
	Not significant			

* The coalitional and amorphous categories are combined because of frequent small N's in the latter and because both represent the absence of any concentration of power, thereby satisfying the purposes of this analysis.

† The N's here and in the table that follows vary because the studies do not uniformly provide data on each variable.

‡ The χ^2 test is employed here with the recognition that the assumption of independent cell frequencies is not fully met, since over half of the communities were investigated in conjunction with at least one other. This consideration did not seem important enough to dispense with an otherwise useful technique.

§ The N here is inflated because studies employing either the one-step or two-step reputational method in combination with the decision-making approach are included in the analysis.

TABLE 3. COMMUNITY CHARACTERISTICS AND COMMUNITY POWER STRUCTURE

	Pyramidal	Factional	Coalitional-Amorphous	Total
Social integration:				
Integration	0	2	4	6
Cleavage	8	4	3	15
Total	8	6	7	21

Fisher exact $p = .032$

	Pyramidal	Factional	Coalitional-Amorphous	Total
Region:				
Northeast	1	2	5	8
North Central	1	5	3	9
South	14	8	7	29
West	3	0	3	6
Total	19	15	18	52
Industrialization:				
Industrialized	7	7	11	25
Non-industrialized	10	6	3	19
Total	17	13	14	44

$\chi^2 .10 < p < .05$

	Pyramidal	Factional	Coalitional-Amorphous	Total
Industry ownership:				
Absentee owned	0	2	6	8
Locally owned	7	5	5	17
Total	7	7	11	25

Fisher exact $p = .040$

	Pyramidal	Factional	Coalitional-Amorphous	Total
Economic base:				
Diversified	10	5	9	24
Narrow	6	7	3	16
Total	16	12	12	40

Summary of Results

1. The type of power structure identified by studies that rely on a single method may well be an artifact of that method.[19]

2. Social integration and region, variables which reflect something of the political life of the community, show some association with power structure.[20]

3. Economic variables reflecting patterns characteristic of increasing industralization are moderately associated with less concentrated power structures.

Suggestions for a Comparative Method

The findings presented here must be regarded as tentative. The tests that have been employed on a sample of studies are scarcely a substitute for tests based on a large sample of communities.

To come to grips with the diverse social and political facets of community life in a comparative design remains the chief problem in this field. Yet this sharpening of our focus on the problem has several procedural implications which should be instructive guidelines for future research. Specifically, comparative studies should employ samples stratified with regard to demographic and economic characteristics. Considerably more attention should be devoted to change, especially vis-à-vis metropolitan development and larger governmental units.[21] An abbreviated combination of the reputational and decision-making techniques needs to be developed to guard against the type of bias we have considered.[22]

In summary, the absence of comparative methods continues to be the major obstacle to an adequate sociology of community power. This review documents the need for more attention to this problem.

NOTES

[1] I am especially grateful to David Gold for the advice and encouragement he has given in the preparation of this paper. For their comments on an earlier version, I also wish to thank Robert Agger and Albert Pierce.

[2] Chapel Hill: University of North Carolina Press, 1953.

[3] Key issues and contributions to the debate are summarized in Raymond Wolfinger, "Reputation and Reality in the Study of Community Power," *American Sociological Review,* XXVII (October, 1960), 636–44; and M. Herbert Danzger, "Community Power Structure: Problems and Continuities," *American Sociological Review,* XXIX (October, 1964), 707–17.

[4] Peter H. Rossi, "Theory, Research and Practice in Community Organization" in Charles R. Adrian (ed.), *Social Science and Community Action* (East Lansing: Michigan State University, 1960).

[5] The identifying names of each community in Table 1 are those used in the study; frequently they are pseudonyms. The original studies, listed roughly in order of publication, are as follows: (1) Floyd Hunter, *op. cit.;* (2) James B. McKee, "Status and Power in the Industrial Community: A Comment on Drucker's Thesis," *American Journal of Sociology,* LVIII (January, 1953), 364–70; (3) Donald W. Olmstead, "Organizational Leadership and Social Structure in a Small City," *American Sociological Review,* XIX (June, 1954), 273–81; (4) Roland J. Pellegrin and Charles H. Coates, "Absentee-owned Corporations and Community Power Structure," *American Journal of Sociology,* LXI (March, 1956), 413–19; (5) George Belknap and Ralph Smuckler, "Political Power Relations in a Mid-West City," *Public Opinion Quarterly,* XX (Spring, 1956), 73–81; (6) Alexander Fanelli, "A Typology of Community Leadership Based on Influence and Interaction within the Leader Sub-system," *Social Forces,* XXXIV (May, 1956), 332–38; (7) Harry Scoble, "Leadership Hierarchies and Political Issues in a New England Town," in Morris Janowitz (ed.), *Community Political Systems* (Glencoe, Ill.: Free Press, 1961), pp. 117–45; (8) Del-

bert C. Miller, "Decision-making Cliques in Community Power Structures: A Comparative Study of an American and an English City," *American Journal of Sociology,* LXIV (November, 1958), 299–310; (9) Robert O. Schulze, "The Bifurcation of Power in a Satellite City," in Janowitz, *op. cit.,* pp. 19–80; (10) William J. Gore and Robert L. Peabody, "The Functions of the Political Campaign," *Western Political Quarterly,* XI (March, 1958), 55–70; (11) Arthur J. Vidich and Joseph Bensman, *Small Town in Mass Society* (Princeton, N.J.: Princeton University Press, 1958); (12) Robert A. Dahl, *Who Governs: Power and Democracy in an American City* (New Haven, Conn.: Yale University Press, 1961); (13) William H. Form and William V. D'Antonio, "Integration and Cleavage among Community Influentials in Two Border Cities," *American Sociological Review,* XXIV (December, 1959), 804–14; (14) Orion Klapp and Vincent Padgett, "Power Structure and Decision-making in a Mexican Border City," *American Journal of Sociology,* LXV (January, 1960), 400–406; (15) Ted C. Smith, "The Structure of Power in a Suburban Community," *Pacific Sociological Review,* III (Fall, 1960), 83–88; (16) Edward Sofen, "Problems of Metropolitan Leadership: The Miami Experience," *Midwest Journal of Political Science,* V (February, 1961), 18–38; Thomas J. Wood, "Dade County: Unbossed, Erratically Led," *Annals of the American Academy of Political and Social Science,* CCCLIII (May, 1964), 64–71; (17) Ernest A. T. Barth, "Community Influence Systems: Structure and Change," *Social Forces,* XL (October, 1961), 58–63; (18) Robert C. Stone, "Power and Values in Trans-Community Relations," in Bert E. Swanson, *Current Trends in Comparative Community Studies* (Kansas City, Mo.: Community Studies, Inc., 1962); (19) Linton C. Freeman *et al., Local Community Leadership* (Syracuse, N.Y.: University College, 1960); (20) Roscoe C. Martin *et al., Decisions in Syracuse* (Bloomington: Indiana University Press, 1961); (21) Jackson M. McClain and Robert Highsaw, *Dixie City Acts: A Study in Decision Making* (Birmingham: Bureau of Public Administration, University of Alabama, 1962); (22) David A. Booth and Charles R. Adrian, "Power Structure and Community Change: A Replication Study of Community A," *Midwest Journal of Political Science,* VI (August, 1962), 277–96; (23) Delbert C. Miller, "Town and Gown: The Power Structure of a University Town," *American Journal of Sociology,* LXVIII (January, 1963), 432–43; (24) Charles M. Bonjean, "Community Leadership: A Case Study and Conceptual Refinement," *American Journal of Sociology,* LXVIII (May, 1963), 672–81; (25) Ivan Belknap and John Steinle, *The Community and Its Hospitals* (Syracuse, N.Y.: Syracuse University Press, 1963); (26) Gladys M. Kammerer *et al., The Urban Political Community: Profiles in Town Politics* (Boston: Houghton Mifflin Co., 1963); (27) Carol Estes Thometz, *The Decision-makers: The Power Structure of Dallas* (Dallas, Texas: Southern Methodist University Press, 1963); (28) Donald A. Clelland and William H. Form, "Economic Dominants and Community Power: A Comparative Analysis," *American Journal of Sociology,* LXIX (March, 1964), 511–21; (29) Robert Presthus, *Men at the Top: A Study in Community Power* (New York: Oxford University Press, 1964); (30) Ralph B. Kimbrough, *Political Power and Educational Decision Making* (Chicago: Rand McNally & Co., 1964); (31) M. Kent Jennings, *Community Influentials: The Elites of Atlanta* (New York: Free Press, 1964); (32) Robert E. Agger, Daniel Goldrich, and Bert E. Swanson, *The Rulers and the Ruled: Political Power and Impotence in American Communities* (New York: John Wiley & Sons, 1964); (33) Aaron Wildavsky, *Leadership in a Small Town* (Totowa, N.J.: Bedminster Press, 1964). (Owing to the recency of its publication, only a portion of the available information has been drawn from the Wildavsky study.)

[6] Except for some difference in emphasis in types 2 and 3, this typology closely

resembles that offered by Peter H. Rossi, "Power and Community Structure," *Midwest Journal of Political Science,* IV (November, 1960), 390–401.

[7] Dahl, *op. cit.*; Nelson Polsby, "The Sociology of Community Power: A Reassessment," *Social Forces,* XXXVII (March, 1959), 232–36; and Polsby, "Community Power: Some Reflections on the Recent Literature," *American Sociological Review,* XXVII (December, 1962), 838–41; Wolfinger, *op. cit.*; David Rogers, "Community Political Systems: A Framework and Hypotheses for Comparative Studies," in Bert E. Swanson (ed.), *op. cit.*

[8] William H. Form and William V. D'Antonio, *op. cit.*; Nelson Polsby, "Three Problems in the Analysis of Community Power," *American Sociological Review,* XXIV (December, 1959), 796–803.

[9] Thomas J. Anton, "Power, Pluralism and Local Politics," *Administrative Science Quarterly,* VII (March, 1963), 425–57; Robert E. Agger, in private correspondence. The converse to each of these first three hypotheses, i.e., that "the reputational approach does not predetermine conclusions in the way which critics suggest," has recently been put forth. See Baha Abu-Laban, "The Reputational Approach in the Study of Community Power: A Critical Evaluation," *Pacific Sociological Review,* VIII (Spring, 1965), 35–42.

[10] Presthus, *op. cit.*

[11] Suggestions in Paul A. Miller, *Community Health Action* (East Lansing: Michigan State College Press, 1953).

[12] Rogers, *op. cit.*

[13] Agger *et al., op. cit.*; Barth, *op. cit.*; Schulze, *op. cit.*

[14] Rogers, *op. cit.*; Delbert C. Miller and William H. Form, *Industry, Labor and Community* (New York: Harper & Bros., 1960).

[15] Where, for purposes of statistical analysis, the categories have been collapsed, pyramidal forms one and factional, coalitional, and amorphous the other.

[16] The decision-making and combined methods are taken as one category here since the intention is to contrast the reputational approach with alternative ones.

[17] Problems in the interpretation of this finding result from the fact that the reputational method characteristically is concerned with influence in non-governmental matters of general community policy. Looking only at reputational studies, there are not enough cases dealing with influence in governmental matters to provide support for hypothesis A3, although the available data reflect a more even distribution among power-structure types.

[18] In addition to these five variables, four others were investigated: type of city government, population, population growth, and population composition (homogeneous-heterogeneous). No significant relationship was observed in any of these; however, because of the low quality of the data, these findings are inconclusive. Generally speaking, the lower the quality of the data, the more difficult it is to demonstrate statistically significant relationships and the more likely it is that such relationships may be obscured.

[19] The relationship between method and power structure is stronger when the "combined" cases are left out of the analysis.

[20] An attempt was made to get at the political life of the community with a variable designated "public involvement in civic affairs," which was found to be highly associated with power structure irrespective of method (the less concentrated power being characteristic of towns with high public involvement). However, in terms of the data, this finding is very nearly tautologous. Future research might do well to explore this question on the basis of an independent assessment of "political life."

[21] In twenty-four studies which dealt with changes, eighteen (75 per cent) reported that power had become more dispersed, while only one reported more concentration.

[22] Systematic comparisons between methods and implications for a parsimonious combination of them are provided in the following: Robert O. Schulze and Leonard Blumberg, "The Determination of Local Power Elites," *American Sociological Review,* LXIII (November, 1957), 290–96; John M. Foskett and Raymond Hohle, "The Measurement of Influence in Community Affairs," *Research Studies of the State College of Washington,* XXV (June, 1957), 148–54; Linton C. Freeman *et al.,* "Metropolitan Decision Making," in Publications Committee of University College (Syracuse, N.Y.: Syracuse University, 1962); Irwin T. Sanders, "The Community Social Profile," *American Sociological Review,* XXV (February, 1960), 75–77; David A. Booth and Charles R. Adrian, "Simplifying the Discovery of Elites," *American Behavioral Scientist,* V, No. 2 (October, 1961), 14–16; Bonjean, *op. cit.;* Presthus, *op. cit.;* Agger *et al., op. cit.;* L. Vaughn Blankenship, "Community Power and Decision Making: A Comparative Evaluation of Measurement Techniques," *Social Forces,* XLIII (December, 1964), 207–16.

PART II

Political Participation
in America

INTRODUCTION

The political beliefs, attitudes, and behavior patterns of most Americans are quite different from those which classical social and political philosophers envisaged for the citizens of a political democracy. Numerous studies have shown that the majority of Americans are not seriously concerned about politics, are not well informed on the major political issues which confront their society, and have little inclination to take an active role in public affairs.

Research does indeed indicate that the concerned, informed, and active citizen is more frequently found in the successful than in the unsuccessful democracies of the world. All stable political democracies require that their citizens have some degree of awareness of their legal obligations to the state, feel that the obligations are legitimate, and meet them. They also require that, for the most part, their citizens evaluate their political system and government positively. They require some material support, generally in the form of the payment of taxes, obedience to laws and regulations, some degree of political participation, and some deference to public authority. In short, they require some awareness of obligations and a willingness to meet them, some knowledge of rights and an inclination to utilize them, some readiness to ascribe legitimacy to the political system, and an overall positive evaluation of it.[1]

On the other hand, modern, enduring political democracies require neither a constant, high level of citizen interest and concern in political affairs, nor a population which is well informed on all major political issues, nor a citizenry most of whom are continually ready to actively perform political roles. Political democracy in America is such that intense involvement in policy-making is not demanded of the citizen.

In our urban-industrial society, political roles are highly differentiated and specialized. The vast majority of these are performed by individuals who devote themselves full-time to their enactment. Such persons or political "elites" deal

157

at different levels of administration with the political problems which flow from the conditions of modern life (e.g., security, welfare, education) and from America's historical experience (e.g., civil rights, apportionment of representation, international relations). Such problems are numerous, are often complex, and are frequently far removed from the experience of large sectors of our population.

Central to the American political system are political parties which are competing bodies of men seeking elite positions at various levels of political administration but which do not consistently represent any given set of interests.[2] Parties may be viewed as alternative sets of leaders for the given political unit. V. O. Key, Jr., noted:

> Political parties constitute a basic element of democratic institutional apparatus. They perform an essential function in the management of succession to power, as well as in the process of obtaining popular consent to the course of public policy. They amass sufficient support to buttress the authority of governments; or, on the contrary, they attract or organize discontent and dissatisfaction sufficient to oust the government. In either case they perform the function of the articulation of the interests and aspirations of a substantial segment of the citizenry, usually in ways contended to be promotive of the national weal.[3]

So long as America's party system operates effectively, so long as political elites are perceived to be reasonably successful in dealing with political problems, and do so in ways acceptable to the majority of citizens, and so long as political elites remain responsive to the wishes of the majority of their constituents, the stability of our democratic political system will remain relatively secure.

The readings included in Section A of this part concern who gets involved in politics and why. While America's present political system does not correspond to the classical conceptions of political democracy, clearly many citizens do discuss politics, many do vote, many do contribute financially to political parties. Obviously some Americans do attempt to become political elites.

The concept of political participation, like the concepts of power and ideology is quite complex, as Lester Milbrath indicates in the first article of this part (number 9). Political participation refers to many different forms of behavior: voting, petitioning political leaders, attending party meetings, campaigning, etc. Milbrath systematically considers this wide variety of behavior and indicates factors associated with engaging in each type.

Patterns of political participation are commonly influenced by perceptions that political activity may be instrumental for the achievement of certain nonpolitical goals. Robert Lane (in number 10) considers a variety of "needs" which are served by political participation: economic well-being, social adjustment, and understanding.

Robert Dahl's article (number 11) contains findings about varying degrees of "involvement" in politics, ranging from a discussion of the "apolitical strata," i.e., those who have relatively little, if any, interest in, concern about, or information relevant to their political system, to a consideration of the "powerful strata," i.e., elites of a political system.

Gabriel Almond and Sidney Verba (in number 12) compare the sense of civic obligation felt by most Americans with the attitudes of citizens of four other Western political democracies: The United Kingdom, Germany, Italy, and Mexico. Their conclusion that a democratic political system is most likely to be sustained when citizens feel they have some obligation to participate in political matters is basic to an understanding of the dynamics of any political democracy.

Direct participation by the indivdual citizen is one of the two main ways of exerting political influence in America. The second method is through the medium of a group, or voluntary association. While citizens of a democracy may have a formal obligation to participate in political affairs, it has been found that various non-political social forces may provide considerable impetus for political participation. For example, the prevalence of political interest groups as well as other voluntary associations in America has been examined as the consequence of the products of rapid industrialization and urbanization—complex occupational specialization and high geographical and social mobility. The selections in Section B are concerned not only with the identification of the non-political social stimuli behind voluntary association affiliation, but also with the social functions and political role of "secondary groups" in a democracy.

In the first presentation (number 13), Robert A. Nisbet discusses the relationship between "loss of community" and contemporary unrest. It is his view, and that of many others as well, that current expressions of political and social discontent reflect a search for new institutional forms to provide the social and psychological support previously obtained from the family, neighborhood, church, and local communty. Many, of course, have used this theory to account for the number and variety of voluntary associations in America. According to Nisbet, although it is true that traditional groups have been considerably weakened, the evidence does not suggest that new forms of organization have adequately taken their place. In his words, "Despite the appeal of the older sociological stereotype of the urban dweller who belongs to various voluntary associations, all of which have progressively replaced the older social unities, the facts so far gathered suggest the contrary: that a rising number of individuals belong to no organized association at all, and that, in the large cities, the unaffilated persons may even constitute a majority of the population." In effect, then, Nisbet suggests that the "quest for community" will continue because "it springs from some of the powerful needs of human nature—needs for a clear sense of cultural purpose, membership, status, and continuity."

The implications of Nisbet's thesis for political theory are many. One of the more important of them has been discussed by Erich Fromm in his *Escape from Freedom*.[4] The line of reasoning followed in this book is that the human need for psychological and social support engendered by stable group bonds may at times take precedence over the quest for freedom and autonomy. One of Fromm's main points is that political extremism is in good measure related to the psychological consequences of social isolation. In any event, both Fromm and

Nisbet view political participation as inextricably involved with social-psychological variables.

In pursuing the theoretical position of writers such as Nisbet and Fromm, inversely one might expect the ostensibly communal, highly family-centered population of suburban America to exhibit a great deal of social and political participation. In the next two papers, Scott Greer explores the nature of participation in suburbia. Greer presents a theoretical scheme for the analysis of social and political participation in a suburban community. His goal is to determine what unique impact, if any, suburban living may have on an individual's type and rate of community participation. In developing his theory, Greer took pains to identify possible external factors that could interfere with the independence of his design. He was particularly concerned with the matter of occupational position because Riesman and Whyte had argued persuasively that suburban man is basically "other directed" and organizationally dominated.[5] Generally speaking, one looks for the other-directed person to be less socially and politically active than his inner-directed counterpart.

Greer delineates three structural levels in the analysis of the suburban community: the neighborhood, the local residential area, and the municipality or political unit. He presents a typology of community roles based upon possible combinations of activity at the three levels. In concludng his paper, Greer lists a number of hypotheses concerning the nature of social and political participation in the suburban community which are in need of further examination. His second paper (number 15) reports the results of a test of the theory.

Overall, Greer feels that his empirical test tended to support the expectations of the constructed theory. Some of the important findings of his study are the following: (1) as the social rank (measured by occupation, education, and income) of a residential area rises, the proportion of "community actors" in a population increases; (2) apartment house districts produce fewer "community actors" than regions of homeowners; and (3) "organizational behavior is by far the most powerful differentiator in local political behavior." Elsewhere, Greer has summarized the results of his analysis in the following manner:

. . . most of the public affairs in a community of limited liability are carried on by a self-selected fraction of the population. When local voluntary organizations are spokesmen for corporate interests, it is for the community actors they speak. The latter are also disproportionately important in the outcome of local elections. But they are, in one sense, representatives of the total population. Insofar as they have the same household, neighborhood, and community commitments as those who are isolated or confine their lives to the neighborhoods, their actions stand for the whole community. They are virtual representatives. They may not always represent these interests in an unbiased fashion, but their organizational advantage assures them a strong voice, collectively, in the polity of the local area. They are a form of ruling class, a "Coxey's army" drawn from local businessmen and bureaucrats, small property owners, clubwomen, aspiring young lawyers, and the League of Women Voters.[6]

In the fourth selection (number 16) Lipset, Trow, and Coleman discuss the relationship between oligarchic leadership and democratic institutions. The topic is an important one, as it has been claimed that leadership in any ongoing organization will inevitably tend toward closure about a few who determine their own tenure and replacements. If, in fact, this trend is a manifestation of what Michels called the "iron law of oligarchy," those concerned with the perpetuation of democratic values must examine its dynamics. It should be recognized, however, that oligarchic leadership does not automatically imply totalitarian or dictatorial rule, nor must it be essentially undemocratic in its tactics. Oligarchs may satisfy many, if not most, of the prime requisites of democratic leadership by attempting to meet the needs of their constituency by constant communication with them and responsiveness to their demands. A fundamental consideration is, to be sure, whether or not citizens are accorded the right to challenge the decisions and activities of leaders if they deem a situation requires this response.

While accepting the general finding that voluntary associations in America tend to be dominated by oligarchs, the authors outline the factors that give rise to oligarchic leadership and show that its emergence is not inevitable and can be avoided. Their example of an exception to the "iron law of oligarchy" is the International Typographical Union and it is this "deviant case" that is their subject.

William Kornhauser (in number 17) presents his conception of political democracy and describes the role of intermediate groups in the theory. In his view, an effective pluralistic democracy requires that there be a balance in decision-making between the contributions of leaders and their constituents. From his vantage point, a healthy democracy requires both elites and non-elites to recognize each other's autonomous needs while remaining accessible to each other's requests.

According to Kornhauser, direct confrontations between elites and non-elites are generally detrimental to a democratic system. Thus, interest groups and other voluntary associations are assigned the task of mediating and tempering contacts between the two "bodies." Specifically, they are expected to protect non-elites from spontaneous and direct manipulations by elites, and vice versa.

To Kornhauser, when non-elites are directly available to the intrusions of elites, a totalitarian regime is a possibility; conversely, when elites are directly accessible to the demands of non-elites, mob rule is a likelihood. Groups intermediate to elites and non-elites serve to diffuse and moderate the demands of each upon the other and make a pluralistic system possible. Kornhauser reasons:

> Pluralistic society requires accessible elites and unavailable non-elites if it is to sustain its freedom and diversity—as in certain liberal democracies. Elites are accessible in that competition among independent groups opens many channels of communication and power. The population is unavailable in that people possess multiple commitments to diverse and autonomous groups. The mobilization of a population bound by multiple commitments would require the breaking up of large numbers of independent organizations, as totalitarian movements have sought to do.[7]

Kornhauser's highly influential thesis thus emphasizes the facilitating effects of primary and secondary groupings for the maintenance of political pluralism. But under certain circumstances such groupings can operate so as to hinder rather than sustain pluralism.

In the final selection of this section (number 18) Maurice Pinard criticizes mass society theory for failing to recognize that intermediate groupings can exert mobilizing effects for mass movements. Pinard argues that under conditions of severe social strain, mobilizing and communicating effects of primary and secondary groupings will tend to predominate over restraining effects, at least in the early phases of a mass movement, and that integrated individuals and pluralist societies will prove more prone to political movements than atomized individuals and mass societies.

NOTES

[1] For a review of several analyses of the demands placed upon political systems and the supports required by them, see H. V. Wiseman, *Political Systems: Some Sociological Approaches* (New York: Frederick A. Praeger, Publishers, 1966), especially pages 154–163.

[2] For an elaboration of this view of political parties, see Joseph Schumpeter, *Capitalism, Socialism, and Democracy* (New York: Harper, 1947), p. 269.

[3] V. O. Key, Jr., *Politics, Parties and Pressure Groups* (New York: Thomas Y. Crowell Company, Fifth Edition, 1964), p. 9.

[4] Erich Fromm, *Escape from Freedom* (New York: Holt, Rinehart and Winston, 1960).

[5] See David Riesman, Nathan Glazer, and Reuel Denney, *The Lonely Crowd* (New York: Doubleday & Company, Inc., 1950) and William H. Whyte, Jr., *The Organization Man* (New York: Doubleday & Company, Inc., 1956).

[6] Scott Greer, *The Emerging City* (New York: The Free Press of Glencoe, 1962), p. 122.

[7] William Kornhauser, *The Politics of Mass Society* (New York: The Free Press of Glencoe, 1959), pp. 40–41.

A. POLITICAL PARTICIPATION AND THE CITIZEN

9. CONCEPTUAL PROBLEMS OF POLITICAL PARTICIPATION

Lester W. Milbrath

The first task is to find a way to think about political participation. Participation must be defined; variables relating to it must be specified; and the subject must be bounded so that it is kept to manageable size. A model to facilitate thinking about participation is sketched later in this article.

Clarity in social science research is facilitated by specifying a level of analysis. The distinction is usually made between macro and micro levels. In social science, the macro level refers to large social units such as a nation, or political system, or organization. The micro level refers to individuals and their behavior. "Micro" and "macro" are comparative rather than absolute terms, however, and in other sciences may have a different specific meaning. In biology, for example, "macro" means unusualy large and "micro" means unusually small.

Although the emphasis here is on micro political behavior, some attention is given to macro characteristics as well. The behavior of the two systems is often interrelated; individual (micro) political behavior affects the behavior of the larger political system (macro); macro characteristics, in turn, affect micro behavior. The level of inquiry adopted by the analyst is determined partially by the kinds of questions he wishes to ask. The question, "How does a system of political parties affect the stability of a political regime?" requires a macro level of analysis. The question: "How and why do people get involved in politics?" requires emphasis on the micro level. Certain questions require a bridging of the two levels. Two such questions are: "How do the characteristics of the political system affect the manner and extent of citizen participation in politics?" and "How do the participation patterns of citizens affect the functioning of the political system?"

DECISIONS ABOUT PARTICIPATION

Taking any political action generally requires two decisions: one must decide to act or not to act; and one must also decide the direction of his action. For example, a person not only decides to vote or not to vote, but also decides

SOURCE: Lester W. Milbrath, *Political Participation* (Chicago: Rand McNally & Co., 1965), pp. 5–38. Reprinted by permission.

whom to vote for. Usually, the decision to perform an action like voting precedes the decision about the direction of the action, but the time sequence could be reversed. Sometimes, a person decides that he likes a candidate or a party before he makes up his mind to cast a vote. Certain actions do not involve a directional choice; for example, one cannot choose the government to which one wishes to pay taxes (without changing one's residence).

Decisions to act in a particular way often are accompanied by a third decision about the intensity, duration, and/or extremity of the action. Persons may lend political support mildly or vigorously, in a single instance or repeatedly. This third choice is intimately related to the other two. A person who takes vigorous and sustained political action very probably is strongly attracted in a certain direction. The very fact that he feels intensely makes it more likely that he will participate. This article focuses mainly on decisions to act or not to act and on decisions about the intensity and duration of the action.

Decisions about the direction of political action are properly another topic, and this paper would be unduly expanded and complicated if an attempt were made to cover them here. Research findings about directional political choices are quite voluminous; furthermore, they are difficult to summarize, since the directions are specific as to setting and time. Generalizations applicable in one setting very likely are not applicable in other settings. For example, explanation of the factors leading some persons to prefer Eisenhower and others to prefer Stevenson in the 1956 presidential election in the United States [1] has little generalizability to the choice the voters made between candidates in the 1960 or 1964 presidential elections.

Settings have one thing in common, however—the concept of *status quo*. Persons can defend or try to change the *status quo*. Its defenders often are called conservatives, and those trying to change it often are called liberals. Liberal-conservative contention about what should be done with the *status quo* is a familiar theme through many centuries of political writing. Unfortunately, many directional choices cannot be fitted to this general liberal-conservative dimension; they are even more specific as to setting and time and, therefore, are even more difficult to summarize.

We have learned to be very cautious in generalizing about liberal-conservative directional choices. Although rational deliberation plays some role in a person's choosing a liberal or conservative direction, the rational aspect of such a choice should not be overemphasized. We shall see that relatively few people have sufficient information or sufficient understanding of the political system to be able to make a completely rational political choice. Furthermore, personality predispositions incline a person to screen out uncongenial stimuli from the mass that impinge on his sensory system. Research evidence suggests that at least some persons have personalities which are inclined either liberally or conservatively. Presumably, persons inclined liberally or conservatively would adopt a corresponding position with respect to the *status quo* no matter what setting or era they lived in. For lack of empirical evidence, this assumption must remain purely speculative.

But one can ask, in turn, where liberal or conservative personalities come from. In part, a liberal or conservative inclination comes from environment:

certain environments tend to produce liberals, and other environments tend to produce conservatives. It is a well-known generalization, for example, that lower-class environments tend to produce status-changers (liberals), and that upper-class environments tend to produce status-defenders (conservatives). But environment does not seem to account for all the variance in political personality; persons coming from very similar environments may have quite different personalities. This suggests that heredity also is a factor inclining some persons liberally and others conservatively. It is likely that there is a very complex interaction between heredity and environment which produces a personality inclined in a certain political direction. Social scientists, at this point, have only a very dim understanding of that interaction.

Many other factors can intervene between personality inclination and choice of political direction. Pressures from family or peer groups are very important. Predominant community beliefs tend to structure the way a person sees his political world. The presence of a certain configuration of information about a current political choice (in contrast to an alternative configuration of information) can strongly influence that choice.

The complex interaction of these multiple factors influencing direction of political choice produces decisions that may seem rather inconsistent to the political analyst. Studies of the American electorate show, for example, that a "liberal" position on foreign policy (internationalism in contrast to isolationism) is not related to a "liberal" position on domestic economic policy (welfare state in contrast to laissez faire). These two positions, in turn, seem to show no correlation with a "liberal" posture favoring integration in contrast to segregation. In the United States, the issue of the welfare state versus laissez faire most clearly and consistently distinguishes the Democratic (liberal) party from the Republican (conservative) party. It is only in this very limited way that two American parties can be characterized as liberal or conservative. If the political setting should change, one could anticipate that labels about the political direction of a party might also change.

The point of this short digression concerning the factors involved in making choices about political direction is to suggest to the reader the complexity and magnitude of the problem of trying to explain such choices. It would take us too far afield to attempt a full explanation here. The reader need only be aware that a choice to take action nearly always requires a second choice about direction. Most of the findings to be discussed in this article are valid, no matter what directional choice the political actor makes.

THE ACTIVE-INACTIVE DIMENSION

Acting politically seems to have two types of contrasts: inactive and passive. Most citizens have both active and passive postures toward politics. Every person participates at least passively in the political system in which he lives. Mere compliance gives support to the existing regime and, therefore, is a type of political behavior.[2] There are other essentially passive responses to the political system: obeying laws, paying taxes, experiencing order and security. These passive behaviors are to be distinguished from the inactive counterparts to political action: nonvoting versus voting, noncontributing versus contributing, nonattending versus attending, and so forth.

Activity generally can be graded into quantities: some persons do more of a given thing than other persons. They may engage in an activity with greater frequency or regularity; they may give more hours or money at a time; they may participate in a wider repertoire of activities. Some persons are almost totally inactive; some are active in one type of behavior but passive in others; some are active in a wide variety of behaviors. Inactivity may be thought of as a zero or base point from which quantities of action can be measured.

Some additional characteristics of this general active-inactive dimension are discussed later in this paper, but it might be helpful first to discuss several subdimensions of political action. Certain of these subdimensional characteristics may make the prospect of taking an action attractive or unattractive to a potential participant. Learning theory tells us that if the costs of the action outweigh the anticipated rewards, the person is unlikely to perform the action.

Overt versus Covert

Some political actions are taken in full public view with exposure to the possibility of criticism and acclamation, while other actions are essentially private. A particular act, e.g., writing a letter, may be private in one context (a letter to a friend) and public in another (a letter to an editor). A discussion about politics with friends in a private home is quite different from a discussion of the same subject before the public media (such as a television discussion program). It is clear that in most cases the overt action has higher costs than the covert and thus requires high rewards before persons engage in it.

Autonomous versus Compliant

All action is a response to a stimulus of some sort, but there is an important difference between a person who responds to an inner or general environmental stimulus (e.g., awareness that a campaign is in progress) and a person who responds to solicitation. Action taken in response to a request is certainly action rather than inaction, but it has passive overtones when compared to autonomous action. If the stimulus becomes virtually irresistible, such as a governmental order to pay taxes, action in compliance with the order may be seen as more passive than efforts to avoid compliance. It also is possible for a person to receive a request not to take an action; inaction, in this case, should be seen as compliance. Although the boundary between autonomy and compliance may be indistinct, there is an important difference in emphasis. Compliant behavior should, in most cases, be seen as the route of least cost or greatest reward.

Approaching versus Avoiding

Approaching behavior is characterized by a positive valence between actor and object, in contrast to avoiding behavior, characterized by a negative valence between actor and object. A valence is a relationship of either attraction or repulsion. If one likes ice cream, for example, he has a positive valence toward it. If one hates giving speeches, he has a negative valence toward the action. A valence is a property characterizing the actor and must have an object referent of which the actor is aware. The mere absence of action is not necessarily avoidance; the actor must withdraw or consciously abstain from an object or action before his behavior can be characterized as avoidance. For example, a person who does not make a political contribution because he is unaware that anyone wants him to contribute is not avoiding, but a person who does not contribute when he is requested to do so is. Avoiding behavior probably flows from anticipation of high costs, whereas approaching behavior probably follows the anticipation of high rewards.

Episodic versus Continuous

Some political action, such as voting, takes place only at specified times. The decision to take the action usually is conscious and often is preceded by a build-up period such as a campaign. Other actions, such as contacting a politician, holding an office, supporting a party, can be taken up at any time and for extended periods of time. Actions that can be continuous often become part of living patterns and may take on a routine character with little conscious decision to act or not to act. Continuous action generally has higher costs than episodic action, and a significant reward structure, preferably built in (like a salary) is needed to insure performance of the action. When measuring quantities or magnitudes of political action, it is important to note the episodic or continuous character of the action.

Inputs versus Outtakes

Certain behaviors constitute inputs to the political system (voting, campaigning, contacting officials, seeking office), in contrast to those which are outtakes or withdrawals from the system (services, public order, conflict resolution, justice). Scientists often speak of inputs and outputs when analyzing systems. Our concern here is to classify behavior of an individual with respect to a system; therefore, we speak of inputs and outtakes. This distinction can characterize the orientations or postures of individuals as well as characterize specific acts; some individuals emphasize outtakes in their orientation to the system and others emphasize inputs. It would be a little oversimple to classify inputs simply as costs and outtakes simply as rewards; many inputs carry auxiliary rewards (e.g., pleasure in voting), and many outtakes carry auxiliary costs (e.g., court costs in seeking justice).

Expressive versus Instrumental

Expressive political action focuses on symbol manipulation; mere engagement in the behavior is satisfying or drive-reducing. Instrumental action, in contrast, is oriented primarily toward manipulating and changing things. This subdimension of action is a motivational distinction, and the classification is made by looking at the situation and motivation of the actor. Consequently, it is difficult to classify specific acts as expressive or instrumental in every case. Casting a vote, for example, may be primarily expressive in one situation or for one person but primarily instrumental for another situation or person.

A person who behaves politically to satisfy expressive needs seems to consume the experience of engaging in the action. As his needs are satisfied by engaging in the action, his drive reduces, and the behavior ceases until a new need for expressive consumption arises. Participating in a demonstration, shouting a protest, engaging in political argument, pledging allegiance, are examples of specific acts that in most situations are expressive. The classification is one of motivation and emphasis; such acts also may have instrumental consequences.

Instrumental action typically follows through a long chain of events and intermediary goals leading to a final goal. Although participation in the action may be immediately satisfying to the actor, mere participation is not sufficient reward to produce the action; rather, reaching the goal is the source of drive reduction. Participating in a campaign, collecting information, volunteering for a job, are examples of acts that are primarily instrumental in orientation and emphasis, even though their performance may provide expressive rewards as well.[3]

Verbal versus Nonverbal

Most political acts require the use of verbal symbols, but some (talking about politics, writing letters, making speeches) demand much more verbal ability than others (stuffing envelopes, marching in parades). A person who does not possess verbal skills has a barrier to verbal participation; the cost of participating in the activity may be so great that he avoids or withdraws from verbal activities.

Social versus Nonsocial

This subdimension of action is closely related to the verbal-nonverbal subdimension, but the two are not identical. Writing a letter or a speech, for example, is highly verbal but does not require social interaction. Nearly all political acts entail some minimal kind of social interaction, but it is useful to distinguish the amount required. Soliciting political funds or campaigning from door to door, for example, requires much more social interaction than voting, attending a meeting, joining a party, or making a monetary contribution. The cost of participating in activities requiring a good deal of social interaction is very high for persons who are not skilled or at ease socially. Contrariwise, persons with a strong need for social interaction may find sociable political activities very rewarding.

SUMMARIZING BEHAVIORAL DIMENSIONS

Unless the political analyst has thoroughly conceptualized the dimensions of political action, his ability to think about antecedent conditions for that action is limited. This is especially important if one wants to be sure that he has measured behavior in all its richness, or if one wishes to measure all the relevant antecedent conditions. On the other hand, some means must be found for summarizing or classifying these dimensions to facilitate thinking about them. Classifications alert us to the ways that specific acts are similar or different and thus facilitate the search for variables that explain the occurrence of acts.

If one is concerned with only two or three dimensions of specific political acts, one possible way of summarizing these dimensions is shown in Figure 1, where the active-passive dimension is modified by the expressive-instrumental subdimension and by the input-outtake subdimension. The six-celled table or abstract map shown in Figure 1 suggests pigeonholes into which political behavior

		Inputs to the System by Individuals	Outtakes from the System by Individuals
Active	Instrumental	Leader selection (vote) Party activity Contributing money Keeping informed Volunteering Disobedience	Stewardship Communication opportunitie Services Economic opportunities Conflict resolution Justice
	Expressive	Allegiance Demonstrations Protests (vote) Political argument	National symbols Sense of identification Governmental protests Sense of superiority
Passive		Obedience Compliance Conscription Paying taxes Indifference	Public order Security

[a] I am indebted to Professor David W. Minar, Northwestern University, for suggesting an earlier version of this figure.

FIG. 1. Abstract Map of an Individual's Political Behavior.[a] The political acts shown in the various cells are illustrative for a hypothetical individual; for another individual, certain specific acts might appear in different cells.

might be classified for certain analytical purposes. The acts shown in the various cells are illustrative for a given individual and are not analytically exclusive. The classification shown is from the perspective of the individual actor rather than of the political system. A given act (a vote, a protest, a contribution) may be primarily expressive in one setting or for a given individual but may be primarily instrumental in another setting or for another individual. Similarly, a specific act, such as making a contribution, may be primarily passive in one setting and primarily active in another.

A drawback of the type of map shown in Figure 1 is that it cannot be used for more than three, or possibly four, dimensions at one time. If one should try to draw a map that would categorize acts on nine dimensions at once, it would become so complicated and cumbersome as to lose all its utility. If, however, one can focus on a given act, he might turn to the profile method used by psychologists to summarize personality traits. A sample profile showing how a specific political act (making a monetary contribution to a party) might be sketched is shown in Figure 2. Although more information about a given political act is shown in such a profile than in the abstract map shown in Figure 1, the profile makes an assumption that is difficult to sustain. It assumes that the distance between the two extremes of a dimension can be measured and quantified, thereby enabling the assignment of a midpoint between them. In many cases, this assumption cannot be met. Certain dimensions (e.g., input-outtake) should more accurately be called categories, because there is no quantifiable

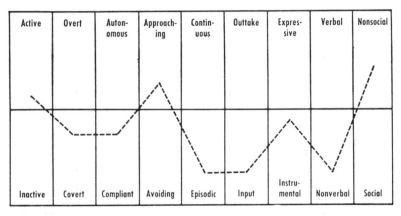

Active	Overt	Auton- omous	Approach- ing	Contin- uous	Outtake	Expres- sive	Verbal	Nonsocial
Inactive	Covert	Compliant	Avoiding	Episodic	Input	Instru- mental	Nonverbal	Social

FIG. 2. Illustrative Profile of a Political Contribution.

distance between them. For other dimensions, political science has no reliable yardstick showing equal distance between units. Since the quantifiability assumption can be met only poorly or not at all for certain dimensions, such a profile may imply more precision than really exists.

The summarizing methods illustrated in Figures 1 and 2 have greater utility, at this point, for thinking about political behavior than for measuring it. They alert us to dimensions that may be overlooked in research. Most of these dimensions have been overlooked in research to date. In fact, a good deal of the research on political behavior has, so far, focused on a single active input: voting. Almost no attention has been given to outtakes. The discussion that follows focuses on the general active-inactive dimension (active inputs, to be more accurate) for two reasons: (1) it is a more general dimension than the subdimensions just discussed; (2) most research to date has asked simply whether a given active input occurred or not. A more elaborate dimensional framework would have no corresponding data to report.

THE GENERAL DIMENSION OF INVOLVEMENT

Political activity seems to have a patterning or clustering characteristic. This seems to be true in two senses: (1) variables that correlate with a specific political act tend to correlate with other political acts as well; (2) there seems to be a hierarchy of political involvement, in that persons at a given level of involvement tend to perform many of the same acts, including those performed by persons at lower levels of involvement. Each of these points is discussed in turn.

A broad generalization about political participation, which is widely supported in research findings, is that the same independent variables are related to a variety of political acts. For example, higher socioeconomic status (SES) is positively associated with increased likelihood of participation in many different political acts; higher SES persons are more likely to vote, attend meetings, join a party, campaign, and so forth. There are some minor exceptions to the above generalization, but the repetitiveness with which a given independent variable correlates significantly with different political acts is impressive.

In addition to the above, research findings show that variables which are associated with political activity also are associated with nonpolitical community activity. Furthermore, persons who are active in community affairs are much more likely than those not active to participate in politics. A comparative survey of five countries shows that in the United States and Great Britain, where levels of political participation are higher than in Germany, Italy, and Mexico, there is also a much higher level of social and organizational activity.[4] This same study shows that participation in decisions in nonpolitical organizations is cumulative: persons participating in decisions in one organization are very likely to participate in decisions in other organizations as well. This pattern of behavior carries over to politics. This evidence suggests that political participation can be thought of as a special case of general participation in social and community activities. Not everyone who is active socially is likely to become active in politics, but *it is probably easier for a person who enjoys social activity to enter politics than it is for a person who shuns social and community participation.*

Political participation is often spoken of as being cumulative; persons who engage in one political action often engage in others as well. Figure 3 shows a hierarchical ranking of behaviors; with those most often engaged in at the bottom, and those least often engaged in at the top. The cumulative characteristic arises from the fact that persons who engage in the topmost behaviors are very likely to perform those lower in rank also. The hierarchy includes most, but not all, common political activities that characterize the normal process of a democracy. Although political demonstrations are considered a legitimate expression of political feeling in a democracy and are widely held, it is a behavior used by only certain sectors of society. Many other sectors look upon demonstrations as undignified and refuse to use them. Thus, this type of behavior does not fit into the hierarchy of political involvement in the United States. The hierarchy also does not apply to behavior designed to disrupt the normal operation of democratic political processes or to dislodge a regime from office by violent means; a general strike is an example of the former, and a palace revolt or *coup d'état* are examples of the latter.[5]

Another general characteristic of the levels of participation shown in Figure 3 is that they constitute a hierarchy of costs. Time and energy costs are least for the activities at the bottom of the hierachy. Behaviors higher in the hierarchy obviously require a greater expenditure of energy and probably require a greater personal commitment. The particular ranking shown in the figure is based on percentages of Americans who engage in the behavior. Probably less than 1 per cent of the American adult population engage in the top two or three behaviors. Only about 4 or 5 per cent are active in a party, campaign, and attend meetings. About 10 per cent make monetary contributions, about 13 per cent contact public officials, and about 15 per cent display a button or sticker. Around 25 or 30 per cent try to proselyte others to vote a certain way, and from 40 to 70 per cent perceive political messages and vote in any given election.[6]

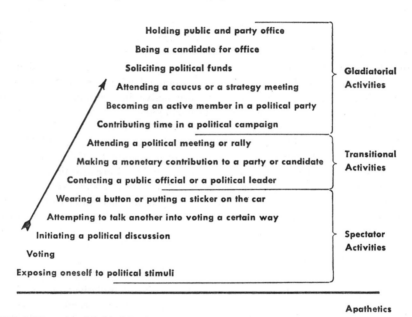

FIG. 3. Hierarchy of Political Involvement.

The ranking of a given item in the hierarchy may vary from election to election, from decade to decade, and from country to country. Since it is a hierarchy of costs, however, one would not expect the variation to be more than a shift of a rank or two. One must be cautious in comparing percentages of persons performing acts with the same name across political cultures. The political setting or context may put different content into the acts in the cultures being compared. For example, joining a political party seems to have a different social-psychological meaning in the United States than it does in Norway.[7] (See the section on party membership later in this article.) Provided the acts have similar psychological meaning in the cultures being compared, one could expect the ranking of the acts in the hierarchy to be similar.

The hierarchy semes to have a kind of internal logic, a natural progression of becoming involved in active politics. Although persons engaging in the topmost behaviors are likely also to engage in those behaviors ranking lower, the obverse does not hold. Minimally involved persons confine their actions to those acts ranking low in the hierarchy. As a person becomes more involved in politics, he engages in a wider repertoire of political acts and moves upward in the hierarchy from the more frequent to the less frequent behaviors.

Although this implies a smooth progression from less to more participation, data on the American citizenry suggest that persons cluster into three general types or roles along the active-inactive dimension. One group participates only passively in the political process; they do not engage in any of the political acts shown in Figure 3. The second group is minimally involved in some or all of the first five activities shown in the hierarchy: seeking information, voting, discussing, proselyting, and displaying preference. A third, and quite small, group not only participates in the above activities but also is drawn into the political fray; they attend meetings, campaign, become active in a party, solicit money, run for and hold public and party office.

This division is reminiscent of the roles played at a Roman gladiatorial contest. A small band of gladiators battle fiercely to please the spectators, who have the power to decide their fate. The spectators in the stands cheer, transmit messages of advice and encouragement, and, at given periods, vote to decide who has won a particular battle (election). The apathetics do not bother to come to the stadium to watch the show. Taking a cue from the roles played in gladiatorial contests, the three political participation roles will be called "apathetics," "spectators," and "gladiators."

One of the striking things about these roles is their stability. From time to tme, a gladiator who no longer enjoys the contest may withdraw to the role of spectator or even to apathetic. Occasionally, a spectator jumps into the political fray. But, by and large, personality and environmental factors encourage persons to stay in their roles. There seems to be a kind of threshold that must be crossed before a person changes role; this is especially characteristic of the transition from spectator to gladiator. A person needs an extra strong push from the envronment (e.g., earnest solicitation from a friend) or needs to feel very strongly about an issue or a candidate before he will cross the threshold and become a political combatant.[8] Once the threshold is crossed and the new team member becomes integrated in his role, he usually participates in a wide repertoire of political acts.

Transitions between roles seem to occur at two points of the hierarchy shown in Figure 3. A person in transition from apathetic to spectator probably would seek information as a way of orienting himself as spectator and voter. Similarly, a person who chooses to lend more support than a cheer for his side in a political contest is likely to contact public officials, attend meetings, and make a monetary contribution as first transitional steps to becoming a full-fledged gladiator.

An additional role differentiation might be made within the gladiatorial category. Just as the political participation of spectators is nearly always in their leisure (nonwork) time, leisure-time participation characterizes a certain proportion of gladiators. Some gladiators, however, make politics their profession. In most settings, one should think of the professional politician as the most involved of all political roles.

About one-third of the American adult population can be characterized as politically apathetic or passive; in most cases, they are unaware, literally, of the political part of the world around them. Another 60 per cent play largely spectator roles in the political process; they watch, they cheer, they vote, but they do not do battle. In the purest sense of the word, probably only 1 or 2 per cent could be called gladiators. In order to have enough cases to analyze statistically, the definition of gladiator is expanded a bit in the following pages to include any person doing any of the acts in the top part of the hierarchy. Even by this expanded definition, the percentage of gladiators does not exceed 5 to 7. The proportions apply mainly to elections at which a President is chosen in the United States. The apathetic ranks probably are even larger in strictly state and local elections; they are also larger in the American South. The five-nation study suggests that the apathetic ranks are also large in many other countries.[9]

CHARACTERISTICS OF SPECIFIC POLITICAL ACTS

It might be helpful to discuss here as concretely as possible the characteristics and dimensions of specific acts that go to make up the general dimension of active participation in politics. We shall follow the hierarchy of specific acts shown in Figure 3.

Exposure to Stimuli Perceived as Political

The person who hopes to deal effectively with his political environment must devote some energy to collecting information about it. This activity is elemental and fundamental to all other political activity, yet persons vary a good deal in the extent of their exposure to stimuli about politics. Despite the great flood of political stimuli available through the mass media, some persons are remarkably clever in exposing themselves to little or none of it. Variation in such exposure is a function of a person's predispositions and of the environment in which he lives. The senses of some persons are tuned to and pick up large amounts, whereas others seem to tune out all stimuli about politics. The environments of a few individuals are filled with political talk and political events (e.g., the son of a public office-holder) to the point where they could not avoid politics even if they tried. Other environments have so few stimuli about politics that an interested person has to seek them out deliberately. Generally, the more political stimuli received by a person, the more likely he is to be active in politics.

Voting

This most thoroughly researched of all political behaviors requires two decisions: first, the decision to engage in the act or not; and, second, the decision of which candidate or party to support. It is episodic in that it can occur only on days specified by law. These days are known well in advance, so that a person can gather relevant data and make a preliminary decision. Voting research also investigates the time of this decision and the frequency, regularity, and stability (in terms of direction) of the voting act.

Discussion and Opinion Leadership

Of all the stimuli about politics which a person may encounter, those which come through personal discussions are probably the most influential. Nearly everyone gets caught in a political discussion once in a while; some persons studiously avoid them, while others enjoy them and seek them out. Therefore, in thinking about discussions, it is important to distinguish initiator from recipient, leader from follower, missionary from unconvinced. A certain proportion of the population (about 20 per cent in the United States) regularly exercises political leadership in face-to-face interactions. These persons may be called opinion leaders. Opinion leadership may not be directed toward support of a party or candidate and, therefore, in many cases is a spectator rather than a gladiatorial activity. *Opinion leaders,* however, *are much more likely than followers to become gladiators.*

Wearing a Button or Putting a Sticker on the Car

Displaying one's partisan or candidate preference with a button or a sticker is another, but relatively weak, form of opinion leadership. Persons doing this often do not engage in additional proselyting activity to bring home their point. In many communities, it becomes a children's game to wear buttons displaying the candidate preference of their parents. The desire of children to conform to the button-wearing pattern and to have some preference to display instills party identification at an early age and helps make the adoption of partisan preference an accepted thing.

Petitioning Political Leaders

Only a relatively small proportion of citizens takes the step of contacting political leaders and public officials.[10] This may be done by letter, telegram, telephone, or direct personal contact. A few persons, as a function of their position in the social and political structure, have normal daily interaction with political leaders and find it natural and useful to communicate their views to these men. This may constitute an easy transitional step to becoming a gladiator. Most persons, however, must take special pains to communicate with political leaders; seemingly, a large majority of them do not wish to take the trouble or may feel uncomfortable in attempting to do so. This barrier can be partially overcome by institutional intervention. A still larger proportion of citizens [11] belong to special-interest groups which represent them before government, often by hiring full-time lobbyists.

Making a Monetary Contribution

This act may be the first transitional step to becoming a gladiator, or it may be the extreme of spectator activity beyond which a citizen refuses to go. Like voting, it requires a decision to perform the act or not, and a second decision as to the direction of the act. Some busy and wealthy persons look upon monetary contributions as a substitute for their personal participation in gladiatorial activity. *Most contributions,* however, *come from gladiators themselves.* They see political money as another weapon in their battle with the opposition. A few persons feel monetary contributions to politics are immoral, but this attitude is not widespread.[12]

Attending a Political Meeting

This is a spectator activity for some persons; they merely come to watch the show. No commitment of support is implied by their presence. For others, however, attending meetings is a gladiatorial activity, and this is especially likely if they attend them more often than once or twice a year. Perhaps they are officials who have responsibility for organizing or participating in the meetings; perhaps they wish to show support of their party by helping to swell the turnout. Highly involved partisans also regularly attend caucuses and strategy meetings.

Campaigning

Political campaigns are episodic, but working in them can continue for several weeks. Some campaign work, like typing or stuffing envelopes, may be routine and boring. Most, however, requires considerable social interaction with other people, some of it in a pleading or salesman-like posture. This is especially true of canvassing from door to door or of making speeches. Evidence shows that *self-confidence and a feeling of social ease are important prerequisites to participation in the socially interactive phase of campaigning.*

Active Party Membership

There are three ways in which a person could be said to be a party affiliate or member: (1) psychological identification with a party; (2) formal membership through payment of dues; and (3) active participation in party affairs. Psychological identification means that the person likes the party and is inclined to support it with a vote at election time. Identification can be ascertained by a survey question such as this: "Generally speaking, do you usually *think of yourself as* a Republican, a Democrat, an Independent, or what?" [13] A fairly large proportion of citizens identify with a political party (about 75 per cent in the United States). When a person says he thinks of himself as a Democrat or Republican, however, he very likely does not mean that he has a formal membership in the party.

Formal membership means that a person's name is entered on the party rolls and that possibly he has been issued a membership card. Even this formal membership is loosely and variously defined. Some parties require only a declaration of support as a membership requirement; more commonly, dues or a monetary contribution are required.[14] In many instances, formal membership is not a commitment to activity on behalf of the party, and little is done to engage the "member" in party affairs. This is especially true of some European labor parties affiliated with labor unions and cooperative organizations. A formal institutional arrangement is worked out, whereby union members pay party dues along with their union dues and are blanketed into party membership unless they take the special trouble to "contract out." At the state and local level in the United States, there are party clubs to which citizens can belong and which constitute the effective working organizations of the parties. National parties, per se, have no provision for formal membership; a citizen can belong to a national party only through a state party.

The most meaningful kind of party membership is active party work. Party actives participate in meetings, caucuses, and conventions; they hold precinct, township, or ward office; they do the multitude of chores required around party or campaign headquarters; they canvass voters at election time; and so forth. Many party actives are leaders or aspire to be leaders, but, as in all organizations, there are also many followers. Active followers and leaders, taken together, constitute a relatively small cadre in most countries; usually less than 5 per cent of the citizenry are active party members.

Soliciting Political Funds

Relatively few persons have the position or the talent for soliciting money for parties or candidates. Some soliciting takes the form of door-to-door canvassing, usually for small contributions. Solicitors responsible for raising large sums of money not only need a talent for soliciting but also must be in a position (social, professional, commercial) that enables them to approach persons of wealth and prominence to request money. Any kind of soliciting requires social interaction, and a sociable personality trait is an important prerequisite to taking the action. Solicitors are important middlemen in politics who have ready access to official decision-makers and thus can transmit the desires of persons giving money.

Office-Seeking and Holding

At the center of the political structure are the party and public office-holders. A special set of talents generally is required just to seek office. In certain party structures, where party discipline is strong and many jobs are filled by patronage, the main talent required for holding lesser office is the ability to carry out orders effectively. In other structures, or for holding higher office, it is important for a person to have strong initiative and great ego strength. These differences in talent requirements for different kinds of offices point up the analytical importance of distinguishing party and public office, appointive and elective office, lesser and higher office.

Protests and Demonstrations

Whether or not protest demonstrations are used seems to be affected more by political environment than most other political acts. They are, almost by definition, extraordinary rather than normal, and thus are difficult to place on Figure 3. Citizens with ready access to officials, and whose needs are routinely handled within the political system, tend to look upon demonstrations as undignified and not very effective. Persons in certain minorities who do not have ready access to decision-makers or who feel that the system does not respond to their demands have quite a different perspective on protest demonstrations. The very extraordinary character of the demonstrations helps get their message of dissatisfaction across to the public as well as to officials. Demonstrations also provide an important expressive outlet for pent-up feelings of resentment and dissatisfaction. In other words, people who find demonstrations rewarding (usually deprived minorities) use them.

A CONCEPTUAL DIAGRAM OF POLITICAL
BEHAVIOR VARIABLES

So far, we have been discussing ways of classifying and describing political behavior. Now we will try to think about its roots. We want to understand why people perform political acts and why they choose to perform some acts and not others. Description and explanation are not totally separate enterprises, but a shift to an emphasis on explanation leads to a search for relationships between variables that an emphasis on classification often does not.

Figure 4 shows a conceptual diagram that is useful for thinking about the causes of behavior. Designed to analyze behavior at the individual level, the model is largely based on concepts developed by learning theorists in psychology.[15] Although it is not irrelevant to the analysis of group or organizational behavior, more serviceable models could be developed for them. The diagram incorporates a time dimension. Those factors to the left of the diagram are presumed to have had their effect on behavior earlier in time than those factors to the right, which are presumed to precede behavior immediately. The explanation of the diagram is most parsimonious if we begin at the right and work back from decision and its immediate antecedents to factors that affect behavior at progressively earlier points in time.

Behavior is by definition continuous: there is no such thing as not behaving. Deciding to do nothing (make no change) or to sleep are still modes of behaving. An organism does not have the option of choosing not to choose. For analytical purposes, however, continuous behaving might be sliced into arbitrary units of time that can be called decisional units. The behaving organism constantly is choosing to do some one thing rather than another. The analysis of the factors that produce political behavior must begin with the immediate factors that produce a given decision.

The decision of an organism about its next act may be seen as a function of the interaction between the stimuli coming from the environment and the particular pattern of predispositions possessed by the organism at a given point in time. At any moment, several predispositions may be competing to take command of the organism, and several stimuli are available in the environment with the potentiality of interacting with those predispositions. The difficult task for the analyst of human behavior is to try to understand why a given set of stimuli and predispositions take precedence over several competing sets. Before speaking directly to that point, it is necessary to discuss the nature of pre-

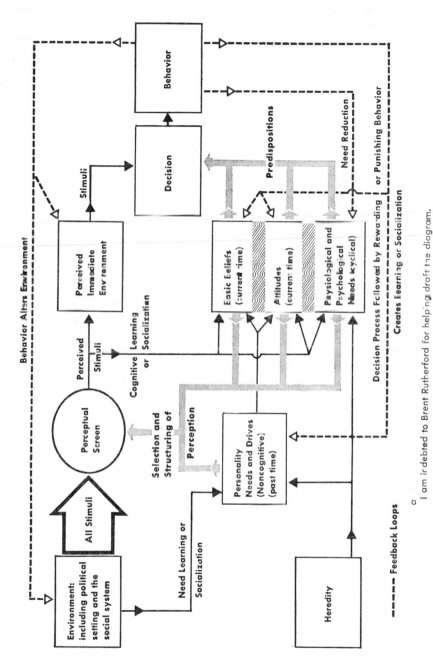

FIG. 4. Model for Analysis of Individual Behavior.[a]

[a] I am indebted to Brent Rutherford for helping draft the diagram.

179

dispositions and to introduce two concepts: a threshold concept and a selective perception concept.

Predispositions have been categorized analytically into three types in Figure 4: physiological and psychological needs, beliefs, and attitudes. This particular breakdown is most serviceable for explaining political behavior, but for other types of behavior, another classification might be more useful. The strength of a given predisposition is a function of the needs of the organism and of the amount of reinforcement that predisposition has received. Psychologist Abraham Maslow has listed five main categories of human needs: (1) physical (food, water, sex, sleep, etc.); (2) safety (order, predictability of the environment); (3) love, affection, belongingness; (4) self-esteem; (5) self-actualization.[16] Some of these needs, especially the physical ones, rise and fall in strength cyclically. At times of great physical need, the organism becomes completely absorbed in filling that need. It is only when these needs can be satisfied somewhat routinely or readily that the organism can turn to social and political behavior. This tendency for physical needs to override all others when they are not satisfied is the main reason they are included as part of the predispositional complex in a diagram (Figure 4) which is primarily oriented toward analyzing social and political behavior.

The strength of more strictly political predispositions, such as beliefs and attitudes, is largely a function of a learning mechanism called reinforcement. If an individual performs a certain act and is rewarded for it, the predisposition to perform that act is reinforced. If the reward helps to satisfy a basic human need, such as that for food or affection, we say the predisposition has received a primary reinforcement; thus, rewards that satisfy basic human needs are known as primary reinforcers. If a certain stimulus is repeatedly present when primary reinforcement (reward) is received, the stimulus itself becomes rewarding; this is called secondary reinforcement. (The reader is reminded of Pavlov's classical experiment with a dog who heard a bell each time food was given him; eventually the dog salivated at the sound of the bell even though no food was present.) This principle of secondary reinforcement is very important, because many social behavior patterns are established by it. In addition, the concept helps us understand another very important mechanism, to be discussed shortly, called selective perception. If a certain behavior pattern has been reinforced again and again (the principle holds for both primary and secondary reinforcement), that behavior pattern, or predisposition, is said to have developed habit strength. The greater the habit strength, the greater the likelihood that that habit or predisposition will take command of the organism when several habits or predispositions are competing for command.

Figure 4 sets forth beliefs and attitudes as important political predispositions. Beliefs are defined as cognitions with an extra feeling of credibility which distinguishes them from cognitions which are not believed. I can cognize myself taking a trip in a spaceship to the moon, but I do not believe I will take such a trip. It is the *feeling* of credibility that makes a cognition believable; the cognition doesn't have to be true by some objective standard. People believe many things about which they have very poor information. Beliefs are expectancies and are close to what was called habit strength above. Attitudes are defined as feelings of like or dislike toward some object. A person may feel a duty to vote, or he may enjoy discussing politics, or he may feel an obligation to support his party with money or work. In these examples there is a positive valence between actor and object. There also can be a negative valence between them; a person may dislike door-to-door campaigning, he may be frightened of making speeches, he may dislike reading about politics.

Many cognitions are both beliefs and attitudes simultaneously. A person may believe very strongly that he is afraid to make a speech, that his party will win, or that it is his duty to vote. In fact, there is a tendency for persons to believe or expect those things they like or value. But it also is possible to have beliefs which are affectively neutral. One believes such things as "two plus two equals four," "there is an Africa," "steel is strong and hard," without necessarily having feelings of either like or dislike for them. Contrariwise, it is possible to like or dislike things one does not believe: "I would like to fly like a bird." Both beliefs and attitudes are included in the diagram because it is important to be aware that cognitions are affected by two kinds of feelings—credibility or incredibility and like or dislike. Another reason is that beliefs and cognitions have been relatively neglected in political behavior research, while there is already a good deal of research on attitudes. It is important to emphasize that political behavior is very dependent on the cognitions, and their credibility, that political actors hold about the political system in which they operate.

A threshold concept is helpful in understanding how predispositions compete to command the organism. The strength of a predisposition needed to take command of an organism is relative to the strength of the stimulus calling up the predisposition. Take, as an example, a person who has played mainly a spectator role in politics. None of the stimuli encountered in his daily environment have been strong enough to surmount his predispositional threshold and elicit active inputs to the system other than voting. The action of a personal friend in becoming a candidate for office, however, changes his personal environment. A request from his friend to help out in the campaign is sufficient to surmount his threshold and elicit new active political inputs. The stimulus which breaks the threshold is one which has previously received many primary reinforcements. The general predisposition to become active in politics has changed very little, but a particularly strong stimulus crosses the threshold. In this case, the stimulus not only acts upon the weak predisposition to become active in politics, but also activates a predisposition to help out a friend. A stimulus, then, need not be physically stronger or louder to activate a dormant behavior pattern (although the physical quality of the stimulus also is important); it may produce the relevant behavior by calling up additional predispositions until their combined force is sufficient to take command of the organism.

Returning to our example, suppose the man has some rewarding experiences while participating in his friend's campaign; he receives both primary and secondary reinforcement. The primary reinforcement strengthens his predisposition to campaign. The secondary reinforcement makes the stimuli associated with campaigning more attractive; they start to carry secondary rewards. The next time a political campaign starts up, a personal request may not be needed to elicit campaign behavior. The stimuli coming from the campaign will seem stronger to him, the strengthened predisposition to campaign will have lowered the stimulus threshold, and this is sufficient to get him to volunteer his services without a personal request.

The threshold concept is intimately related to a second concept we shall call the selective effect of predispositions upon perceptions. It is essential to the psychic economy of organisms that they perceive selectively. They have a perceptual screen which passes some stimuli and blocks others (see Figure 4.). An organism would be overwhelmed if it attempted to attend to every stimulus impinging on its sensory organs. An organism may shift attention from one stimulus to another rather rapidly, but at any given instant the focus is upon relatively few.

How does the organism select the stimuli it will attend to? The answer to that is so difficult to study that psychologists speak of it as the "black box" which their methods cannot penetrate. Very generally, we can say that the choice of the stimulus seems to be a function both of the strength of the stimulus and of the strength of the predisposition with which that stimulus interacts. Very intense stimuli (loud sounds, bright lights, penetrating odors) are likely to get through the screen no matter how hard the individual tries to attend to something else. Also, stimuli that have been secondarily reinforced will be attractive and more likely to pass through the screen than those not so reinforced.

Stimuli also are screened for credibility. The judgment about credibility largely depends on how well the stimulus fits with the tightly woven pattern of cognitions already held as credible. Rokeach has told of hearing on a newscast one day that a camera had been invented that would take a picture of something that wasn't there; he rejected it as incredible. Later, he read that it took pictures of the heat remaining on a given spot after the object creating the heat had been moved. This fitted into his pattern of believed cognitions, and he could accept the new invention as credible.[17] Credibility is determined not only by fit with things already believed but also by what a person wishes to believe. It is a natural human failing to perceive selectively and to distort perception so that it bolsters cherished beliefs.

The stimulus attended to also depends on the state of the organism, so to speak. A strong predisposition will incline an organism to pick up stimuli relevant to that predisposition. This interaction can be illustrated by the example of the man campaigning for his friend. One evening after dinner, he is calling on voters door to door. As the evening progresses, his earlier satiation with food gives way to hunger. Stimuli associated with food, such as the smell of food or the sight of a restaurant sign, which earlier in the evening were ignored, now become relevant. The predisposition to eat interacts with the sight of a restaurant, and the man turns away from campaigning to eat a hamburger. With partial satiation, the predisposition to campaign once more takes command, until increasing fatigue inhibits the response. The organism must allow sleep to take over and replenish the predisposition for campaigning.

The way that an individual selectively attends to stimuli is in many ways analogous to the way a radio tuner functions. If the tuner responded at once to all the stimuli in its environment, it would produce an unintelligible garble. If the set is tuned to an appropriate frequency and the gain (volume control) is set sufficiently high, a usable response is emitted. Similarly, the human organism must be tuned to a stimulus (have a relevant predisposition), and the predisposition must be strong enough to lower the threshold so that the stimulus can cross it. The strength of the stimulus needed to activate a radio is relative to the gain setting (predisposition level); a strong stimulus activates the receiver at even a low gain setting, but a higher gain setting is needed for a weak signal. If the environmental stimulus ceases, the receiver ceases to respond. Similarly, the human organism cannot make a given response unless the appropriate stimulus calling it forth is available in the environment. If several stimuli are at about the same frequency (desireability), the stronger crowds out the weaker.

It was asked several pages back why a given set of stimuli and predispositions take precedence over several competing sets. With the threshold and selective perception concepts in mind, the answer should now be more intelligible. It is a function of the need of the organism, the stimuli available in the environment, and the strength of the various predispositions relevant to those stimuli. The organism responds only to stimuli that are present. It selects from those stimuli according to its needs and according to the strength of various competing predispositions, as these have been built up through numerous past reinforcements. Social science has not advanced sufficiently for us to be more precise at this time.

One can gain a bit more understanding, however, by asking where and how predispositions are developed? What are their roots? Figure 4 shows that beliefs and attitudes are a product of three factors: (1) personality needs and drives; (2) cognitive learning (getting to know the world one lives in), and (3) learning which comes from behaving and then being rewarded or punished for that behavior. Physiological and psychological needs are developed partially from heredity and partially from personality needs and drives. The cyclical intensity of physiological needs is affected by the behavior of the organism in filling those needs; thus, a need-reduction arrow is drawn from behavior to that predispositional box.

Moving back a step in time, personality needs are a product of heredity, of need learning or socialization coming from the environment, and of rewards or punishments following from the various decisions of the organism. The reader will note that affective need learning has been conceptually distinguished from cognitive learning in the diagram; in real life, however, the two kinds of learning take place simultaneously.

Often, when explaining social and political behavior, we distinguish personality factors from environmental factors. . . . According to such a distinction, personality would include all five of the following boxes on the diagram: heredity, personality needs and drives, physiological and psychological needs, beliefs, and attitudes.

Environmental impact on behavior is indirect, meaning that it is always mediated by personality. In past time, it has had its impact by forming the personality and belief system of the actor. Rewards and punishments, by which learning takes place, had come out of the environment. In addition, environment had produced nearly all the stimuli (the only exception being kinetic stimuli from inside the organism) for cognitive learning. In current time, environment provides the stimuli from which the individual selects his perceived environment; thus, current environment also is mediated by personality. Personality is not totally determinative, however, since it selects only from stimuli presented. Environmental stimuli not only incite action but also provide information about boundaries, barriers, norms, and costs which help the organism to choose among alternatives.

The behavior model presented in Figure 4 is dynamic. The current behavior of an organism feeds back and has an impact on its future behavior (feedback loops are dotted lines on the diagram). Behavior alters the environment and thus changes the stimulus complex presented to the organism. In a discussion situation, for example, sending a message to one or more of the other actors usually stimulates a new message back to the first actor. An actor can move from one setting to another and thereby alter his stimulus complex. In a more long-range sense, lending or withholding political support partially determines whether a given set of officials win an election; this surely has an impact on environment. Behavior also can alter the organism's internal environment by satisfying a drive; when satiation occurs, the drive-fulfilling behavior ceases.

Another way that behavior feeds back and affects future behavior is through the learning mechanism. Nearly all decisions have rewarding or punishing consequences through which the organism learns habits, beliefs, attitudes, and drives. The complex mechanisms by which learning occurs are a central theoretical preoccupation of modern psychology, and a thorough description of them would be too elaborate for inclusion here. We can say, however, that an explanation of political behavior must include an examination of the stimuli present, of the impact of personality on selecting from those stimuli, and of the needs and predispositions competing for command of the organism. When we examine connections between environmental factors and political behavior, either we are indirectly measuring the impact of environment in shaping personality or we are seeing how the current environment presents opportunities and barriers to the actor. Finding the key to full understanding lies in our ability to unravel the complex learning process that mediates between the person and his environment.

The conceptual diagram sketched in Figure 4 does not have the predictive power expected of a full-fledged model. It does not, for example, enable us to predict which precise set of antecedent factors will produce one complex of predispositions and which set is needed to produce a differing complex. The major utility of the diagram is in locating and tentatively relating the variables that seem to determine behavior.

NOTES

[1] For a very sophisticated analysis of these factors, see Angus Campbell, Philip Converse, Warren Miller, and Donald Stokes, *The American Voter* (New York: Wiley, 1960).

[2] Almond and Verba have distinguished three roles: "Participant," "subject," and "parochial." They have made the valuable point that each citizen plays all three roles at one time or another. "Participant" and "subject roles" (similar to the active-passive

distinction made here) are both essential to a viable political regime. The "parochials" are similar to the inactives or those we later call the "apathetics." See Gabriel Almond and Sidney Verba, *The Civic Culture* (Princeton, N. J.: Princeton University Press, 1963).

[3] The most elaborate statement of expressive-instrumental orientation to politics has been made by Ulf Himmelstrand in his *Social Pressures, Attitudes and Democratic Processes* (Stockholm, Sweden: Almqvist and Wiksell, 1960). See also Ulf Himmelstrand, "Verbal Attitudes and Behavior: A Paradigm for the Study of Message Transmission and Transformation," *Public Opinion Quarterly,* XXIV (Summer, 1960), pp. 224–250. Allusion to a similar classification was made earlier by David Riesman in his *Faces in the Crowd* (New Haven: Yale University Press, 1952).

[4] Gabriel Almond and Sidney Verba, *op. cit.*

[5] In another sense, no political activity could be considered normal or routine for everyday existence. Persons turn to politics only when their basic physical needs, such as food, sex, sleep, safety, affection, have been met. The democratic processes listed in Figure 3 become normal, or even possible, only in societies where more basic needs are routinely satisfied. See James Davies, *Human Nature in Politics* (New York: Wiley, 1963), Chapters 1 and 2.

[6] Figures are drawn from Campbell, *et al. (op. cit.)*; Robert E. Lane, *Political Life: Why People Get Involved in Politics* (Glencoe, Ill.: The Free Press, 1959); and Julian Woodward and Elmo Roper, "Political Activity of American Citizens," *American Political Science Review,* XLIV (December, 1950), pp. 872–885.

[7] Stein Rokkan and Angus Campbell, "Norway and the United States of America," in *Citizen Participation in Political Life,* issue of *International Social Science Journal,* XII, no. 1 (1960), pp. 69–99.

[8] George Robert Boynton and Lewis Bowman, "The Recruitment of Political Activists: A Case Study," unpublished manuscript, 1964, found in a study of recruitment to office in two cities that 26 percent of local officials had been asked by someone else to become a candidate; another 24 percent were strongly moved by some policy concern; only 25 percent could be accounted for by general involvement and interest.

[9] They were especially large in Italy and Mexico, but Germany also had more apathetics than the United States and Great Britain. Gabriel Almond and Sidney Verba, *op. cit.*

[10] Woodward and Roper, *op. cit.,* found 21 percent in the United States.

[11] Woodward and Roper, *op. cit.,* found 38 percent in the United States.

[12] See Alexander Heard, *The Costs of Democracy* (Chapel Hill, N. C.: University of North Carolina Press, 1960) and Lester W. Milbrath, "The Motivations and Characteristics of Political Contributors, North Carolina General Election, 1952" (unpublished doctoral dissertation, University of North Carolina, 1956).

[13] This question, developed by Campbell, *et al. (op. cit.)* has been used repeatedly in a variety of surveys. Emphasis has been added.

[14] See Kenneth Janda, "A Comparative Study of Political Alienation and Voting Behavior in Three Suburban Communities," in *Studies in History and the Social Sciences: Studies in Honor of John A. Kinneman* (Normal, Ill.: Illinois State University Press, 1965). Janda has studied the basis of affiliation of parties in all parts of the world. Of the 140 parties coded on this variable, 26 percent have no formal membership requirement: a person merely needs to indicate support as in American parties. Half of the parties have an open requirement which grants membership to anyone who signs a form or pays dues. The remaining 24 percent not only require a signature and dues but also require the potential member to go through a proba-

tionary period or have his application approved by party officials before membership is granted.

[15] Two leading learning theorists have had the greatest impact on my own thinking about these matters: Clark L. Hull and Burrhus F. Skinner. The discussion here merely borrows some of their concepts; it is not an exposition of their very complex and much more precise theories.

[16] For a stimulating discussion of the way these needs affect political behavior, see James Davies, *op. cit.*, especially Chapters 1 and 2.

[17] Milton Rokeach, *The Open and Closed Mind* (New York: Basic Books, 1960). Part I, on the theory of belief systems, is very good.

10. WHAT CONSCIOUS NEEDS ARE SERVED BY PARTICIPATION IN POLITICAL LIFE?

Robert E. Lane

ECONOMIC, SOCIAL, AND INTELLECTUAL NEEDS

Of what use to a man is his politics? As Graham Wallas points out, it is unfruitful to say that men in politics are self-interested.[1] That only leads to the further question: which interests? He criticizes the over-rational approaches of the utilitarians, and deals instead with the political expression of such "impulses" as affection, fear, laughter, the desire for property, the "fighting instinct," "suspicion, curiosity, and the desire to excel." [2] Lasswell concurs in the impulse theory, but believes that their expression in politics represents a displacement from areas of private life.[3]

Another possible approach is through the study of values: Which values do men pursue through political instruments? Lasswell suggests that these values are: power, wealth, well-being, skill, enlightenment, affection, rectitude and respect—and it is true that men do seek these values in politics.[4] It is said that men join social movements because some object, person, or idea has become "ego-involved"—and this idea of the extension of the self to include selected features of society is useful.[5] Smith, Bruner, and White believe that men develop their political opinions to meet three needs: (1) to understand the world and to control events, (2) to get along well with others, and (3) to express psychic tensions.[6]

While all of these views are partially true, and frequently useful, it has served our purposes to develop the following grammar of political motives. These are the needs served by men's political activity.

1. Men seek to advance their economic or material well-being, their income, their property, their economic security through political means.
2. Men seek to satisfy their needs for friendship, affection, and easy social relations through political means.
3. Men seek to understand the world, and the causes of the events which affect them, through observing and discussing politics.
4. Men seek to relieve intra-psychic tensions, chiefly those arising from aggressive and sexual impulses, through political expression.
5. Men seek power over others (to satisfy doubts about themselves) through political channels.
6. Men generally seek to defend and improve their self-esteem through political activity.

These are not mutually exclusive motives, they are overlapping and leave lacunae, but they are "real" in the sense that their connection with political acts can be traced, and they are at the focus of attention of those who have discussed human nature in politics in the last thirty or forty years.

SOURCE: Robert E. Lane, *Political Life* (New York: The Free Press of Glencoe, 1959), pp. 101–114. © by The Free Press, a corporation, 1959. Reprinted with permission of the Macmillan Company.

POLITICS AND THE PURSUIT OF ECONOMIC GAIN

Here lies the substance of the older economic interpretations of politics: a man adopts those opinions and undertakes those activities which advance his material well-being. He protects his property by an interest in governmental economy implemented by a contribution to the local taxpayers' research bureau. He advances his security (certainly of income) by writing a letter to the President urging an extension of social security for the self-employed. He votes for a candidate because that candidate seems to be "for people like me"—a motive which combines many elements but includes the hope that the voters' economic interests will be favored. There is no doubt that, along with the political pursuit of other needs, men pursue economic gain through political activity.

Conceptualization in this area is clouded by certain irrelevancies which confuse the issue. Problems regarding the relation of the "cultural superstructure" to the economic basis of society, dialectical materialism in history, rationality of economic choice, etc., must be set aside as only tangential to the study of economic needs served by political activity. What is needed at this point is something less ambitious, a classification of the nature of the gratifications to be achieved by political pursuit of economic gain.

Perception of Economics in Politics: From survey material there accumulates evidence that relatively few people believe that national elections will "affect me personally"—only three out of ten in 1944.[7] Observers and interpreters of the political scene, relying on more impressionistic material, have come to the same conclusion. "We must not ignore the fact that political involvement may supply the individual with . . . the practical gratification of satisfying some material need. But psychologically speaking, the less obvious 'meanings' of politics are probably more influential in determining political behavior." [8] The articulation in the mind of the individual voter of economc life and political affairs is loose. But it is not altogether missing, and it takes devious routes.

One reason for this low perception is the individualized means whereby men in America satisfy their needs. If a man wants housing, lower prices, or other material satisfactions, he generally tries to gratify these needs individually by shopping around in the existing market, rather than through political organization. As one Ithaca citizen said, "I don't think politics or election results will or do affect my own life very much. Regardless of who is in power, I'll keep my job and my home." [9] Even Tocqueville noted something of this sort when he said, "The discharge of political duties appears to them [Americans] to be a troublesome impediment, which diverts them from their occupation and business. These people think they are following the principle of self-interest, but the idea they entertain of that principle is a very crude one. . . ." [10] Thus, in at least one crucial respect, the interpretation of economic man in the political arena is different from the view of the species in the marketplace. The relations of his acts to his needs in politics are even more obscure than usual to him.

Level of Economic Need: Economic theory tells us that the more money a person has, the less will each additional dollar contribute to his total satisfaction; money, like everything else, has a diminishing marginal utility. That is, for those with more money a 10 per cent increase in spendable income has less utility than has a 10 per cent increase for those with less, although the range within which this is true has never been specified. In any event, one cannot account for political activity on this basis since such activity shows a positive correlation with income. The less money a person has, the less likely he is to pursue economic or any other gain through political activity. The possibility exists, however, that the economic rewards of politics are more salient for the lower income groups: to the extent that they are interested at all in politics, they may see it more in economic terms. There is some evidence that this is true from a study of public attitudes toward Roosevelt, in which personal economic gain was more salient for the lower income groups than for the middle income groups.[11] This relatively greater salience of personal economic gain and loss for lower income groups is also supported by analysis of values in senatorial mail on the conscription issue. Here it was found that while 32 per cent of the low income group referred to conscription in terms of its effect upon their economic situation, only 16 per cent of the high income group made this kind of reference. The high income group was, on the other hand, much more likely to refer to "freedom," or civil liberties, or other generalized social values.[12] This greater focus of interest on personal-economic problems in lower income groups not only reflects greater marginal utility of money but also lower interest in general policy matters, lower capacity for handling abstractions, and generally lower horizons of knowledge and awareness.

There are, on the other hand, reasons for believing that lower income groups, instead of relating their economic well-being to political decisions more closely than others, in fact are less likely to perceive this relationship. At least in 1944 fewer lower status than upper status people expected the presidential election of that year to affect them personally.[13] And for a very good reason. Businessmen receive more individualized benefits from government: contracts, tariffs, tax abatements, etc. For them, therefore, there is an opportunity to relate personal gain to individual effort. Others, and especially workers, receive benefits only as members of larger groups and therefore see the rewards of effort as more tenuous and less probable. Under these circumstances, the salience of personal economic stakes in political decisions would be greater for businessmen (and to some extent farmers) than for urban laborers and white collar workers. Thus, there are both theoretical and empirical reasons for believing that the political perspectives of lower income persons have a higher than average economic content and reasons for believing the opposite.

From these findings, combined with our evidence [given elsewhere], that electoral turnout is not in the least related to economic depression, it seems clear that level of income, awareness of economic implications of political decisions, and individualized incidence of economic benefit are so intertwined as to make a *general* relationship between economic need and political participation unlikely.

Reference Groups and the Perception of Economic Need: Almost everyone is better off than someone he knows and worse off than someone else. Almost everyone has unfulfilled desires which might be fulfilled if he had greater income. How, then, does he determine, in his own mind, whether he is underprivileged or privileged, whether he is economically deprived or not. Of course, such a determination is a complex matter to which personality variables make a contribution, as do a host of circumstantial factors. Among these factors, however, the location and relative wealth of the individual's significant reference groups make considerable difference. In the armed services it was found that a person's estimate of his deprivation depended upon whom he compared himself with. If he was behind the lines overseas, his sense of deprivation was greater if he compared himself with others back home, and less if he compared himself with those in the front lines.[14] The perception of economic deprivation undoubtedly follows the same pattern. Those who compare themselves with parents who were or are less well off, or with their own status in their years of apprenticeship, may be less likely to perceive politics as a means of satisfying economic needs. Those who compare their status with more prosperous college friends, or with the image of exaggerated success their parents held out to them, may see everything, including politics, in terms of their economic needs.

Self and Group: Most, but not all, political decisions which re-allocate resources affect selected classes of the population: importers, owners of natural gas wells, the unemployed, and so forth. Thus, when a person appraises politics in terms of the satisfaction of his economic needs, he is confronted with a group gain or loss and his perception of the group, and his identification or disidentification with the group, will color his attitudes toward the politico-economic decisions involved. When Beard reports that of the members of the Constitutional Convention of 1787, "The overwhelming majority of members, at least five sixths, were immediately, directly, and personally interested in the outcome of their labors at Philadelphia," [15] a mixture of motives is apparent: loyalty to the class of men who were involved and satisfaction in the group gain along with the personal satisfaction in the individual's own gain.

Individual economic gain from political activity, of course, still persists in the form of patronage positions, assured contracts, or legal protection. In this form, however, the sanctions of the society tend to be brought to bear upon the individual, for the difference between group gain and individual gain usually coincides with the boundaries of what is loosely called political morality. With respect to individual gain, then, the desire for economic gain must be strong enough to cross the threshold imposed by concepts of unethical practice and hence a stronger economic orientation is likely to be implied.

When considering the decisions of group members on group-related issues, not only ethics but conflicting group memberships and political beliefs must be considered. In a study dealing with public attitudes toward government personnel problems, it was found that veterans were only slightly more in favor of veterans' preference provisions than were the general public.[16] Similarly, college educated respondents were only a little more favorable than respondents with less education to preference for educated persons in government hiring policies. Herring points out that cultural items favoring equality of opportunity interfere here with the college graduates' self-interest.

Economic Values as Instrumental to Other Values: One of the great difficulties in the kind of politico-economic analysis which has prevailed in this area of politics and economics is the illusion of economic gain as a terminal value. Beyond certain minima, economic gain is inevitably associated with prestige and status, self-validation called "success," opportunities for assertion against others, autonomy from disliked persons, tasks, or situations, and so forth. What gives economics its power to command such energy as is invested in the pursuit of gain is often its instrumental value as a means to some other objective. Money buys more than commodities; it buys psychic gratifications of all sorts—although never so completely as the money-seeker thinks it will. The pursuit of income through politics, then, may be preliminary or auxiliary to the gratification of other needs mentioned in this section.

The Dynamics of Politico-Economic Pursuits: We have said that money and wealth often become libidinized, so to speak, because of their instrumental values. There are two ways in which this investment of wealth with high priority may be achieved. Society may do it by making certain equations between income and success or income and prestige. In some instances, as may be seen in the favored position of the middle-class child in public schools, income and morality tend to be equated [17]—a hideous perversion of the Calvinist doctrine first applied to the Puritan adult. Thus, social transfusion of value takes place, creating economic needs where there were none before.

The second method is the psychic process of displacement or generalization which will be discussed more systematically below. We need not accept, nor deny, the identification of thrift and miserliness with early training in cleanliness, though there is considerable case material to support this view. But considering only the processes of displacement in the mature adult, we may find that an individual substitutes pursuit of economic gain for the pursuit of sex objects, or of aggressive activity forbidden by the society. In this latter regard there are social gains, as Keynes notes in remarking that it is better for a man to tyrannize over his bank account than over other people.[18] We shall discuss below Lasswell's formula for political displacement, but we may note here that one might express this displacement in the economic sphere in similar terms: private emotions displaced onto an economic object and rationalized into an economic theory equals Economic Man. The explanation of the pursuit of economic needs through political activity, then, might examine the terms of the rationalization (human nature requires the profit motive), or the economic object (oil wells, pensions), or the private emotions (a desire to defeat the father in cross-generational competition). Out of such material, in the abundant society, are fashioned economic drives which may be pursued through political participation at every level.

That they are so pursued needs little documentation. Perhaps it is most clearly seen in the stakes of the ward leader or precinct committeeman. In King County, Washington, about an eighth of the group worked for the government and therefore had economic stakes in electoral outcomes; in Elmira, New York, about a third of the ward leaders were in this position.[19] The precinct and ward leaders in Chicago in the late thirties and forties freely admitted their economic interests in their political work, and in Detroit volunteer workers included "several hundred paid workers" in 1952.[20] On certain kinds of issues, notably the tariff, the mail tends to emphasize economic self-interest or thinly disguised generalizations about the welfare of those whose jobs are jeopardized by low tariffs.[21] And in the various analyses of financial contributions to campaign funds, the economic self-interest of the contributors is stressed by most authors on the subject.[22]

In summary, then, we may say:

Political participation in pursuit of economic needs is impeded by the obscure relation of political decisions to the gratification of these needs. Paradoxically, this obscurity may be more characteristic of the American political system, where economic orientation is said to be high, than other cultures.

Political participation to satisfy economic needs is unrelated to level of income in the American culture.

Political participation to satisfy economic needs is related to the perception of needs mediated by the selection of reference groups.

Political participation to satisfy economic needs is usually associated with group gain or loss and the gratifications involved are related to attitudes toward the group. Where the gains and losses from political activity are individual, rather than group, the culture usually attributes some immorality to the transaction and hence motivation must be strong enough to overcome this cultural stigma.

Economic needs motivating political participation are usually instrumental to the gratification of some other psycho-social needs, such as status, power, or self-validation.

The investment of economic goals with emotional intensity is a product of (a) cultural equations between economic success and other values, and (b) the displacement onto economic objects of emotions and drives arising from unconscious needs and wishes of the individual.

SOCIAL ADJUSTMENT

Political interests and activity may facilitate easy interpersonal relations, and so satisfy a person's needs for social adjustment. Common political beliefs lay the groundwork for sharing equivalent emotions of anger, sympathy, and distress; common interests improve the opportunities for small talk; common activities create bonds of friendship. Politics may offer to the lonely man new opportunities for association with others—the excuse may be politics, the need may be fear of isolation. In short, political interests and activity may "lubricate" social relations and create opportunities for association in many areas.[23]

The effect of political disagreement is just the reverse. Interests or attitudes which diverge from those held by a person's friends may cause him to withdraw from politics and turn his attentions elsewhere. It is possible, at least, that one reason for American political apathy is that American political preferences frequently cut across class, religious, and ethnic lines so that without a clear orientation on the attitudes of one's social groups, the expression of political opinions offers risks of social friction rather than opportunities for social adjustment.

How strong is the need for agreement! The "strain toward agreement" (for most, but not all, people), and the fear of disagreement has been examined in experiments and field observations for over twenty years.[24] Persons viewing *together* an illusory movement of a fixed point of light give estimates of movement within a narrow range, whereas when persons view the illusion *separately*, there is a much broader range of reported movement. Furthermore, those who have established a standard in viewing the illusion alone, adjust their standard when they hear the reports of others in a second trial so that their standards come closer to the group norms.[25] Opinions on relative lengths of real objects, where there is no illusory effect, are subject to group pressure in such a way that many people will refuse the evidence of their senses in order to avoid an isolated opinion—although when given even a small minority with which to agree they become much more resistant to this pressure.[26] College students who are oriented toward the college group adopt the favored attitudes of the college community;[27] members of a cooperative housing project have been shown to adjust their views on Russia to what they conceive to be the group mode.[28]

The facts of the situation seem clear. But the private meanings of these acts of opinion adjustment for social purposes may differ in each individual. Among these meanings, perhaps the instrumental need of the group's support for some personal project or goal, say election to office, is the most "objective." Other such needs turn directly upon the manner in which interpersonal relations are interpreted by the individual himself. Fear of conflict may be the motivating force in the politicization of a non-political person in a political group. Or social adjustment may serve as a needed counterweight to a nagging sense of personal inadequacy, perhaps as a reminder that one's private idiosyncratic behavior does not cut one off from other people as much as is sometimes feared. Whatever it is, it has a private meaning deriving from the individual's experiences and personality structure.

To some extent, perhaps, the problem of adequate integration in a human group is universal: all adults have experienced in some manner the "separation anxiety" which comes with growing up.[29] But in different societies this expresses itself in different ways. The mode of life and cultural pressure of the times creates, among most Americans, a need to "get along" with other people in a superficially harmonious manner but without deep personal emotional commitments.[30] This is the "other-directed" person, low in affect and high in facile competence in interpersonal relations. In a sense, this is a corollary to Lewin's diagnosis of American personality—a relatively small core of private "self" surrounded by a larger area of public "self" which is exposed to view and not so easily hurt. (This is in contrast to the German personality where the public area is much smaller and the private area larger).[31] The needs which such personality constellations reveal in abundant measure are adjustment needs; not the need for personal integrity, not the need of propitiating a stern super ego, but the need to get along socially without friction.

Horney makes this point in her discussion of the relation between culture and neurotic symptoms in the present era. She says, "One of the predominant trends of neurotics of our time is their excessive dependence on the approval and affection of others," a condition partly attributable to the highly competitive terms of existence in a laissez-faire industrialized society.[32] If this is true, group life will reflect these mutual demands for affection, or at least acceptance, to an unusual degree. The social adjustment function of politics will, in such a period, serve needs which have been culturally intensified.

The history of the past four hundred years is a history of increasing "individuation," the destruction of the primary group bonds of the individual.[33] This is true of the individual's family connections, religious connections, his class and status connections, his occupational connections, and, with the kind of mobility in America, the ties which bind him to a town or region. It is also true of political connections, particularly in America where "independence" is so highly valued. Fromm believes that man cannot endure such negative freedom, the loosening of old institutional bonds, and he seeks constantly to establish new ones which will relate him to his friends and his work and his beliefs either in a "positive" autonomous manner, or, failing that, in a destructive or dependent manner. Many persons do not have the capacity to make such bonds for themselves, to create a relationship which was once created ready made in the order of things. For them political life may serve acute needs for social adjustment and integration.

Toward whom does a person need to adjust? Authoritarians seek adjustments with people of higher status and power, content to ignore those with relatively less of these qualities. In much the same manner the ethnocentric, the snob, and often the merely insecure, define their adjustment needs in such a way that much of the population is excluded. The question of social adjustment is intricate in detail and specific in content for each individual.

We have suggested that such social adjustment needs may lead people to join political parties—although they may also lead them to avoid joining where this might antagonize others who are important. In a similar manner, the need for social adjustment, the need to make friends and keep their friendship on an easy frictionless plane, may lead them to join other organizations and to contribute to the political process in this way. Indeed the pluralistic basis of American politics may be dependent upon the prevalence of acute social adjustment needs in the population. Joining organizations and seeking friends, in turn, will lead to political discussion where this is not divisive, the kind of discussion referred to above as a reinforcement of mutually agreed upon views. Furthermore, social adjustment needs may lead to other forms of political behavior, such as financial contributions to parties. For some donors to political parties, the salient motive is to be a "good fellow" combined with a fear of the impression which refusing to "go along with the boys" may make upon friends and acquaintances.[34] Similarly, for party workers, door to door canvassing may be a "social event" whose primary meaning lies in the increased rate of visiting and gossiping.[35]

In summary, then, the following hypotheses reflect the ideas set forth.

Participation is a function of the individual's need for social adjustment with others in his community, although such adjustment has a variety of idiosyncratic meanings and functions for each person.

In all societies, some common ends and directives contribute to the mental health of the members of that community; hence behind the adjustment function there lies the powerful pressure towards consensus in some significant areas of life.

Persons brought up in the American culture are more likely to employ their participation as an aid to social adjustment than persons socialized in other Western cultures.

Gemeinschaft politics (particularly totalitarian movements) serve as especially suitable vehicles for participation for those with social adjustment needs arising from feelings of alienation.

Historically, the individualization or atomization of persons in society has tended to leave unsatisfied the drives for social adjustment, leaving available a powerful unfulfilled need for political movements.

Participation based upon the need for social adjustment will be differentiated according to the nature of the adjustment needs toward (a) people of differing status and power, (b) inclusively or exclusively defined groups.

Periods of crisis for societies, as for individuals, are likely to produce a "regressive" mode of satisfying social adjustment needs in politics.

THE NEED TO UNDERSTAND

"On *a priori* grounds one might suppose that a person's attitudes toward any topic serve the important function of sorting out his world of experience into a predictable order that can provide the background for an orderly existence." [36] An understanding of political events is a tool for living, an instrument whereby other goals are achieved. But, more than that, there is satisfaction in understanding which does not depend upon its utility in achieving further goals. "Quite apart from the pressure of particular emotions, we continually seek to extract meaning from our environment. There is, so to speak, intellectual pressure along with the emotional. To find a plausible reason for a confused situation is itself a motive. . . ." [37] An interest in public affairs and opinions about the world around us serves this motive and represents a response to this pressure. The results may be grotesque, as Lippmann's discussion of stereotypes suggests, but it is the very need to understand that partially accounts for the oversimplified image which causes "Mrs. Sherwin of Gopher Prairie" to think of a world war in terms of a personal duel.[38]

The pressure to have opinions on remote political topics is not just the vestige of days when opinions and influence went hand in hand. It is not just social pressure; it is, even for the ignorant, internal and personal.[39]

The nature of the "meanings" extracted from the environment varies. In a study of attitudes toward Russia, some people were more projective than others in their interpretation of events, making the meanings and opinions serve their wishes; others did not.[40] Some seek syntheses of many variables in an over-all world view, and nothing short of a comprehensive ideology is satisfactory. Others extract extremely limited meanings. As shown in recent studies, rational arguments are assimilated by some individuals relatively easily; others are blocked in their understanding of such arguments by overriding emotional needs. Furthermore, persons fearful that their interpretations, if stated aloud, will reveal their ignorance, will be inhibited from exercising their curiosity and asking questions about politics.[41]

The basis of this curiosity, like its products, has many facets. Animal psychologists, finding that rats who have satisfied all of the so-called "basic" drives (hunger, thirst, sex, relief from pain, etc.) may still be active, have included curiosity as an additional drive. This interpretation would give the phenomenon a biological basis. Good maternal care is said to be the basis for developing curiosity, and therefore educability, in the human child. Freud found sexual curiosity to be the beginning of intellectual curiosity. And it is said that "High school and college foster an abstract orientation and an involvement in the superpersonal. Hence educated people feel at home in the company of political ideas which partake of the abstract." [42] No doubt all these factors (and many more) may explain differential efforts to extract meaning from the political environment.

What does this pursuit of meaning lead people to do in the political sphere? People who seek to satisfy this need are undoubtedly more attentive to the media and are relatively well informed. An example of this behavior is the following response from a person who was deprived of his daily paper by a strike of newspaper dealers.[43]

> I don't have the details now, I just have the results. It's almost like reading the headlines of the newspaper without following up the story. I miss the detail and the explanations of events leading up to the news. I like to get the story behind the news and the development leading up to—it's more penetrating. . . . I like to analyze for myself why things do happen and after getting the writers' opinions of it from the various newspapers, in which each one portrays the story in a different manner, I have a broader view and a more detailed view when I formulate my own opinion.

Does the pursuit of meaning lead beyond this to active political behavior? One study of the factors associated with participation in grass roots civic meetings on a college campus shows that both a superior academic record and a capacity for critical thinking (as measured by a special test) were positively related to such participation.[44] This does not necessarily mean that going to civic or political meetings was prompted by the need to think through a problem, but this is at least a possible interpretation.

In a broader sense, it seems to have other results. In one analysis the pursuit of meaning forms one of the two most important psychological bases for participation in social movements (the other being the need for self-esteem).[45] It is reflected in almost all the interviews and psychoanalytic material dealing with Communists and former Communists.[46] Thus it seemed to be a feature of both modal and deviant politics, of both active and "spectator" political participation.

Although political opinions may be functional, they may be dysfunctional as well. Ignorance has psychic utility too, and there are at least five circumstances in which a man will cling tenaciously to ignorance of public affairs. The first of these, *conflict-avoidance ignorance,* is illustrated by the businessman who remarked that he preferred not to study economics because it might undermine his faith in a system with which he had to work. Such a businessman is, of course, in a position similar to the Catholic who permits his reading to be guided by the Index, or a Communist who studies only Marxist social science. All of them are avoiding mental conflict before it begins to work upon them, rather than wait and, possibly, withdraw from the painful conflict after it has been initiated.

The second variety of useful ignorance exists when a person has discovered some tension relief in a belief which would be threatened by new knowledge, a variety which may be thought of as *cathartic ignorance.* For those to whom Red Russia has provided a legitimate target for the discharge of hostile emotions, a scientific treatment of the Soviet Union must be threatening—not because such a treatment would not provide evidence to feed their hatred, but the balanced tone of the discussion would suggest that their emotional investment was inappropriate. Similarly, the anti-intellectualism of the ethnocentric serves to ward off any study of ethnic relations which would jeopardize his, to him, useful hostilities. The very term selected by the anti-aliens of the 1850's— "Know-nothings"—although chosen for another reason, reflects a frame of mind where ignorance is positively valued.

In the third place, those who defend the status quo do not need to go to the trouble of producing evidence about it to the same extent as those who propose a reform. If this is an economic conviction they can rest upon the assumption that the challenger must make the case. If it is a psychic conviction that whatever it is best, inquiry is dangerous and should be suppressed. "A man who is prone to identify himself *a priori* with the world as it is has little incentive to penetrate it intellectually and to distinguish between essence and surface." [47]

A variation of this view, and an additional set of reasons for ignorance, is suggested by the fact that political affairs, for many people, meet few direct and urgent needs; they are "remote from the direct concerns of daily life." [48] Thus the person who is immersed in getting along in his own world from day to day avoids the political. His own private status quo, like the larger social status quo, does not require him to be politically informed. This kind of drive to exclude political information from what is learned may be termed *apathetic ignorance.*

Fourth, political views may alienate friends, neighbors, customers, and group members, as we have noted before. Better then, not to hold them. Ignorance from such a motive may be termed *socializing ignorance.* And a fifth situation, where ignorance of public affairs serves some personal function, occurs when the drive to politicize men and saturate their lives with community, partisan, or social meaning becomes fatiguing and a person experiences the longing to privatize his life. This suggests a kind of *privatizing ignorance.*[49]

To summarize these views on the pursuit of meaning, the following hypotheses may be set forth:

Political participation and involvement are products of the need for meaning, both as a source of satisfaction in itself and as a means of satisfying other needs.

The pursuit of meaning is said to be based on (a) a physiological drive apparent in animals, (b) early socializing experiences and particularly the treatment of sexual curiosity, (c) education and other experiences awakening interests and developing skills for handling abstractions.

The pursuit of meaning leads to exposure, attention, and absorption of knowledge (with feedback effects) and, in some circumstances, to civic and political participation.

The reverse of the pursuit of meaning, clinging to ignorance, serves other needs: (a) avoidance of knowledge which might create internal conflict (conflict-avoidance ignorance), (b) avoidance of knowledge which might deprive a person of needed tension-releasing opinions (cathartic ignorance), (c) apathy about knowledge which fulfills no useful purpose (apathetic ignorance), (d) avoidance of knowledge which would disrupt social relations (socializing ignorance), and (e) avoidance of knowledge in order to protect interest and attention in other, and private affairs (privatizing ignorance).

NOTES

[1] This is the Benthamite formula. Even the critics of Bentham, like Macaulay, assumed that men adapted their politics to serve conscious self-interest. "When we see the actions of a man, we know with certainty what he thinks his interest to be," quoted in Graham Wallas, *Human Nature in Politics* (Boston: Houghton Mifflin, 1909), p. 22. On this see David Riesman's discussion of "self-interest: death of a motive," in his *Faces in the Crowd* (New Haven: Yale University Press, 1952), p. 33.

[2] Wallas, *op. cit.,* pp. 21–38.

[3] Harold D. Lasswell, "Psychopathology and Politics," reprinted in *The Political Writings of Harold D. Lasswell* (Glencoe, Ill.: Free Press, 1951), pp. 74–77.

[4] Harold D. Lasswell, *The World Revolution of Our Time* (Stanford, Cal.: Stanford University Press, 1951), p. 6.

[5] Hadley Cantril, *The Psychology of Social Movements* (New York: Wiley, 1941); Muzafer Sherif and Hadley Cantril, *The Psychology of Ego-Involvements* (New York: Wiley, 1941).

[6] M. Brewster Smith, Jerome Bruner, and Robert White, *Opinions and Personality* (New York: Wiley, 1956), p. 41; see also Smith, "The Personal Setting of Public Opinions: A Study of Attitudes Toward Russia," *Public Opinion Quarterly, 11* (1947), pp. 516–23.

[7] Gerhart H. Saenger, "Social Status and Political Behavior," *American Journal of Sociology, 51* (1945), p. 104.

[8] Morris Rosenberg, "The Meaning of Politics in Mass Society," *Public Opinion Quarterly, 15* (1951), p. 8.

[9] Morris Rosenberg, "Some Determinants of Political Apathy," *Public Opinion Quarterly, 18* (1954–55), p. 363.

[10] Alexis de Tocqueville, *Democracy in America,* The Henry Reeve Text, edited by Phillips Bradley (New York: Knopf, 1945), p. 141.

[11] Fillmore Sanford, "Public Orientation to Roosevelt," *Public Opinion Quarterly, 15* (1951), pp. 189–216.

[12] Rowena Wyant and Herta Herzog, "Voting via the Senate Mailbag, Part II," *Public Opinion Quarterly, 5* (1941), p. 607.

[13] G. H. Saenger, *op. cit.,* p. 104.

[14] Robert K. Merton and Alice S. Kitt, "Contributions to the Theory of Reference Group Behavior," in Merton and Paul F. Lazarsfeld, eds., *Studies in the Scope and Method of "The American Soldier"* (Glencoe, Ill.: Free Press, 1950), pp. 42–70.

[15] Charles A. Beard, *An Economic Interpretation of the Constitution of the United States,* rev. ed. (New York: Macmillan, 1948), p. 149.

[16] E. Pendleton Herring, "How Does the Voter Make Up His Mind?" *Public Opinion Quarterly, 2* (1938), pp. 32–33.

[17] August de B. Hollingshead, *Elmtown's Youth* (New York: Wiley, 1949).

[18] John Maynard Keynes, *The General Theory of Employment, Interest, and Money* (New York: Harcourt, Brace, undated [c. 1936]), p. 374.

[19] Hugh A. Bone, *Grass Roots Party Leadership: A Case Study of King County* (Seattle, Washington: University of Washington, 1952, mimeographed); Bernard R. Berelson, Paul F. Lazarsfeld, William N. McPhee, *Voting* (Chicago: University of Chicago Press, 1954), p. 164.

[20] H. Gosnell, *Machine Politics, Chicago Model* (Chicago: University of Chicago Press, 1937); Sonya Forthal, *Cogwheels of Democracy, A Study of the Precinct Captain* (New York: William Frederick Press, 1946); Peter J. Turano, *Organization and Operation of the Democratic Party in Wayne County, Mich.* (Ann Arbor, Mich.: Edwards, 1953, (paper bound), p. 103.

[21] Lewis A. Dexter, "What Do Congressmen Hear? The Mail," *Public Opinion Quarterly, 20* (1956), pp. 16–27; Frank Bonilla, "When is Petition Pressure?" *Public Opinion Quarterly, 20* (1956), pp. 39–49.

[22] James K. Pollack, *Party Campaign Funds* (New York: Knopf, 1926), pp. 113, 126, Louise Overacker, *Money in Elections* (New York: Macmillan, 1932), pp. 169–93; V. O. Key, *Politics, Parties, and Pressure Groups,* 3rd ed. (New York: Crowell, 1952), pp. 537–42.

[23] See Rosenberg, "The Meaning of Politics in Mass Society," pp. 6, 11.

[24] See Theodore M. Newcomb, "The Prediction of Interpersonal Attraction," *American Psychologist, 11* (1956), pp. 575–86.

[25] Muzafer Sherif, *The Psychology of Social Norms* (New York: Harper, 1936).

[26] Solomon E. Asch, "Effects of Group Pressure upon the Modification and Distortion of Judgments," reprinted in Dorwin Cartwright and Alvin Zander, eds., *Group Dynamics* (Evanston, Ill.: Row, Peterson, 1953), pp. 151–62.

[27] Theodore M. Newcomb, *Personality and Social Change* (New York, Dryden, 1943).

[28] Raymond L. Gorden, "Interaction between Attitude and the Definition of the Situation in the Expression of Opinion," *American Sociological Review, 17* (1952), pp. 50–58.

[29] See Sebastian de Grazia, *The Political Community* (Chicago: University of Chicago Press, 1948).

[30] Riesman, *op. cit.*

[31] Kurt Lewin, *Resolving Social Conflicts* (New York: Harper & Bros., 1948), pp. 1–31.

[32] Karen Horney, *The Neurotic Personality of Our Time* (New York: Norton, 1937), pp. 35, 284.

[33] Erich Fromm, *Escape from Freedom* (New York, Rinehart, 1941).

[34] Overacker, *op. cit.,* pp. 169–95.

[35] Berelson and associates, *op. cit.,* p. 165.

[36] Smith, *op. cit.,* p. 521.

[37] Gordon W. Allport and Leo Postman, "An Analysis of Rumor," *Public Opinion Quarterly, 10* (1946–47), p. 503.

[38] Walter Lippmann, *Public Opinion* (New York: Macmillan, 1922), p. 8.

[39] David Riesman and Nathan Glazer, "The Meaning of Opinion," *Public Opinion Quarterly, 12* (1948), pp. 631–48.

[40] Smith, *op. cit.,* pp. 516, 521.

[41] Rosenberg, "Some Determinants of Political Apathy," p. 353.

[42] Rosenberg, "The Meaning of Politics in Mass Society," p. 7.

[43] Bernard R. Berelson, "What 'Missing the Newspaper' Means," in Paul F. Lazarsfeld and Frank N. Stanton, eds., *Communications Research, 1948–49* (New York: Harper and Bros., 1949), pp. 111–29.

[44] Everett K. Wilson, "Determinants of Participation in Policy Formation in a College Community," *Human Relations, 7* (1954), pp. 287–312.

[45] Cantril, *op. cit.,* pp. 53–77.

[46] Gabriel Almond, *The Appeals of Communism* (Princeton: Princeton University Press, 1954).

[47] T. W. Adorno and associates, *The Authoritarian Personality* (New York: Harper & Bros., 1950), p. 658.

[48] Rosenberg, "Some Determinants of Political Apathy," p. 363.

[49] Ernst Kris and Nathan Leites, "Trends in Twentieth Century Propaganda," in Geza Roheim, ed., *Psychoanalysis and the Social Sciences* (New York: International Universities Press, 1947), pp. 393–410.

11.   POLITICAL MAN

Robert A. Dahl

An elementary starting point for all political theory is the existential fact that members of the human species live together. With few exceptions human beings do not carry on their lives in complete isolation. Whatever may be the elements of instinct, habit, necessity, or choice that induce people to form societies, man has amply demonstrated for thousands of years that he is a social animal. Yet though man is a social animal, neither by instincts nor by learning is he necessarily a political animal—at least not in quite the same sense. Even though they live in a society, men need not concern themselves with the politics of that society, nor participate actively in political life, nor cherish the political institutions and values of their society. Some people do, to be sure; but many, as we have seen, do not.

Nonetheless, simply because human beings are social they also develop political systems. Evidently they cannot dwell together without entering into relationships of influence; whenever these relationships become stable and repetitive, political systems exist.

In this looser sense, then, one might say (with Aristotle) that man *is* a political animal. Whatever his own values and concerns as a social being man is inevitably enmeshed in political systems—whether or not he likes or even notices the fact.

However, the individuals who find themselves within the boundaries of a political system are by no means equally concerned with political life. Some people are indifferent to politics, others are more deeply involved. Even among those who are heavily involved in politics, only some actively seek power. And among the power-seekers, some gain more power than the rest.

These four groups—the apolitical strata, the political strata, the power-seekers, and the powerful—can be illustrated in this way:

THE POLITICAL STRATA

The political strata consist of individuals who are psychologically "involved" in governmental decisions. There are various ways in which individuals may be psychologically "involved" in decisions; these different forms of involvement usually run together, but they need not. Four dimensions of involvement in a decision are:

1. Interest—how curious one is to know what is happening.
2. Concern—how important one feels the decision is.
3. Information—how much knowledge one has about the decision.
4. Activity—how much one overtly participates in the decision.

In the United States, and probably in most societies, these four dimensions are correlated. For example, a person who has little interest in a presidential

SOURCE: Robert A. Dahl, "Political Man," in *Modern Political Analysis* (Englewood Cliffs, N. J.: Prentice-Hall, Inc., 1963), pp. 55–71. © 1963. Reprinted by permission of Prentice-Hall, Inc.

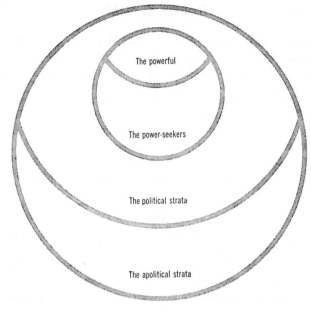

FIGURE 1

campaign and little concern about the outcome of the election is less likely to acquire information about the campaign and the issues involved, and is also less likely to vote in the election itself, than a citizen who has a great deal of interest and concern.[1] Tables 1 and 2 show how interest, concern, and voting turnout were related in the 1956 presidential campaign.

TABLE 1. RELATION OF DEGREE OF INTEREST IN CAMPAIGN TO VOTING TURNOUT, 1956

	Degree of Interest in Campaign [a]		
	Not Much Interested	Somewhat Interested	Very Much Interested
Voted	58%	72%	87%
Did not vote	42	28	13
	100%	100%	100%
Number of cases	540	695	520

Source: A. Campbell, *et al., The American Voter* (New York: Wiley, 1960), p. 103.

[a] Respondents were classified according to their responses to the following question: "Some people don't pay much attention to the political campaigns. How about you? Would you say that you have been very much interested, somewhat interested, or not much interested in following the political campaigns so far this year?"

TABLE 2. RELATION OF DEGREE OF CONCERN ABOUT ELECTION OUTCOME TO VOTING TURNOUT, 1956

	Degree of Concern over Election Outcome [a]			
	Don't Care at All	Don't Care Very Much	Care Somewhat	Care Very Much
Voted	52%	69%	76%	84%
Did not vote	48	31	24	16
	100%	100%	100%	100%
Number of cases	230	367	627	459

Source: Ibid., p. 104.

[a] Respondents were classified according to their responses to the following question: "Generally speaking, would you say that you personally care a good deal which party wins the presidential election this fall, or that you don't care very much which party wins?"

Table 3 illustrates the relationship between activity and information in the 1956 election. It is hardly surprising, of course, that those who participated most in the 1956 campaign were more familiar with the issues than those who participated less.

TABLE 3. RELATION OF POLITICAL PARTICIPATION TO LEVEL OF ISSUE FAMILIARITY, 1956

Issue Familiarity		Level of Participation		
		Low	Medium	High
High	4	16%	30%	45%
	3	17	27	27
	2	18	19	16
Low	1	49	24	12
		100%	100%	100%
	N	394	770	515

Source: V. O. Key, Jr., *Public Opinion and American Democracy* (New York: Knopf, 1961), Table 8.1, p. 185.

Voting, of course, is only one kind of activity. A study of registered voters in New Haven, Connecticut, included a wide variety of activities in addition to voting—nine having to do with campaigns and elections and four having to do with activities outside campaigns. When both interest and concern were combined into a single measure, the relationship with activity was very strong. As might be expected, citizens who were the most active in local affairs were also likely to be better informed.

TABLE 4. RELATION BETWEEN ACTIVITY IN LOCAL AFFAIRS, INTEREST, CONCERN, AND INFORMATION (NEW HAVEN, CONN., 1959)

	Extent of Activity				
	Least	Low	Medium	High	Highest
Highly interested and concerned	16%	27%	47%	64%	72%
Highly informed	20%	17%	21%	39%	62%
Number of cases (total)	188	148	89	68	29

THE APOLITICAL STRATA

Because there are several dimensions of involvement, and because each dimension is more or less continuous, the political stratum shades off gradually into the apolitical strata; an exact boundary between the political strata and the apolitical strata must, therefore, be arbitrary. Nonetheless, it is probably true that in most political systems those who display great political interest, concern, information, and activity are not a large proportion of the adults; generally, no doubt, they are a minority. Even in a democratic society the political strata do not include all citizens, for even in democracies a sizeable number of citizens are apathetic about politics and relatively inactive. There are, to be sure, variations from one democracy to another and from time to time; but the existence of political apathy and indifference among many citizens in a democracy seems to be nearly universal. Even the Greek city-states, which are sometimes held up as models of democratic participation (aside from the slaves), were not immune. In Athens, for example, the *demos* was often indifferent. Aristotle wrote of fourth century Athens:

> Payment for attendance at the assembly was, at first, a step which they (i.e., the restored democrats, once more in control after the perturbations at the end of the Peloponnesian War) refused to take. The citizens, however, failed to attend; and the presidents of the assembly were driven to one device after another in order to induce the populace to present themselves for the purpose of ratifying measures. In these circumstances Agyrrhius began by providing an obol a day for attendance: Heraclides . . . increased it to two obols; and Agyrrhius afterward advanced it to three.

By Aristotle's time, citizens received 6 obols a day for attending the Assembly, the town meeting of Athens.[2]

Sometimes, too, New England town meetings are regarded as a model. But just as in Athens, in New England towns many citizens were unconcerned about exercising their rights or fulfilling their political obligations. In New Haven, for example, the problem seems to have been a persistent one. In

1642 the General Court of the Colony "voted that any freeman who after due warning, should fail to appear in the General Courts before the Secretary finished the roll-call, should be fined 1s. 6d; and that any of the rest of the planters who should be absent after their names were read, should be fined one shilling. The novelty of the first few years had worn away, and attendance at the General Courts seemed, to many, burdensome." A century later the problem was still unsolved in New Haven. In 1784 the old colonial town officially became a city, and the first city elections were held. Of some 600 adult males living in the city, about 250 were excluded as voters either because they could not meet the property requirements or because they had been loyal to Great Britain. Of the 343 eligible males, about one-fourth failed to take the oath and hence could not vote in the first election. Although most of those who were qualified to vote did actually vote for the mayoralty candidates, two days later only about a hundred citizens (out of 261 eligible) showed up to vote for the councilmen.[3]

The problem is still acute today. Only a minority of adult American citizens vote regularly and participate in other ways. In 1950 two well-known pollsters reported the results of a survey of political activities among a cross-section sample of 8,000 adult Americans. The results are shown in Table 5. Except for voting once or more in the preceding four years, only a minority—usually a small minority—of the respondents had engaged in the forms of political activity listed.

Obviously man is not instinctively a political animal. It is true that few people ever live outside a political system; it is also true that by the standards of most of us the benefits of living in political systems far outweigh the disadvantages. Nonetheless, though human beings must and do live in political

TABLE 5. POLITICAL ACTIVITIES OF AMERICAN CITIZENS

Voting	
Once or more in last four years	75%
Three times or more	47
Five times or more	21
Discussing public issues with others	
Discusses frequently and takes an equal share in the conversation	21
Discusses frequently and usually tries to convince others he is right	6
Belonging to organizations that take stands on public issues	
Belongs to one or more such organizations	31
Belongs to two or more	7
Written or talked to congressman or other public official to give own opinion on a public issue	
One or more times in past year	13
Two or more times in past year	7
Worked for election of a political candidate in last four years	11
Contributed money to a party or candidate in last four years	7

Source: Julian L. Woodward and Elmo Roper, "Political Activity of American Citizens," *The American Political Science Review,* Vol. 44 (December, 1950), pp. 872–885.

systems and share the benefits of political life, they do not necessarily participate in political life; they are not necessarily interested in politics, nor do they always care what happens in politics, know much about political events, or share in making decisions. In most political systems, in fact, the political stratum is a minority of the adult population. Moreover, those who are *highly* interested, concerned, informed, and active are an even smaller minority within the political stratum.

Why is it that even in modern societies with widespread education, universal suffrage, and democratic political systems the apolitical stratum is so large? To answer this question would require much more space than can be given here, but a short if somewhat formal answer can be indicated. Essentially there seem to be three reasons why an individual does not become involved in politics.

1. *An individual is unlikely to get involved in politics if he places a low valuation on the rewards to be gained from political involvement relative to the rewards expected from other kinds of human activity.* For many people political activity is a good deal less gratifying than other outlets—family, friends, recreation, and the like. For many, political involvement yields far less affection, income, security, respect, excitement, and other values than working at one's job, watching television, reading, fishing, playing with the children, attending a football game, or assembling a new hi-fi set. For many, the rewards of political involvement are distant and vague, whereas the rewards of other activities are more immediate and concrete. In short, for many people the opportunity costs of political involvement are simply too high to make it worthwhile. These people are unwilling to forego immediate, certain, and concrete benefits or gratifications derived from non-political activities in order to obtain the more remote, uncertain, and abstract benefits that might ensue from political participation.

Just why political involvement is not more rewarding for more people is a question for which no short or easy answer is possible. The explanation, no doubt, turns on the fact that man is not by instinct a reasonable, reasoning civic-minded being. Many of his most imperious desires and the source of many of his most powerful gratifications can be traced to ancient and persistent biological and physiological drives, needs, and wants. Organized political life arrived late in man's evolution; today man learns how to behave as a political man with the aid and often with the hindrance of instinctive equipment that is the product of a long prior development. To avoid pain, discomfort, and hunger; to satisfy drives for sexual gratification, love, security and respect—these needs are insistent and primordial. The means of satisfying them quickly and concretely generally lie outside political life.

2. *An individual is unlikely to get involved in politics if he thinks that the probability of his influencing the outcome of events, of changing the balance of rewards by means of his political involvement, is low.* Individuals do not engage in activity merely because the *possible* rewards are high, if the *probability* of gaining the rewards is very low. Even though the pay-off to Irish Sweepstakes winners is very high, not everyone buys a ticket, for many people feel that the chance of winning is so slight that they would be throwing their money away. In the same way, citizens who are pessimistic about their capacity to influence political events may eschew politics on the ground that

what they do won't matter anyway. Voters sometimes neglect to vote because they feel that one vote won't change the outcome; citizens often fail to press their views on public officials because they believe that public officials won't pay attention to people like themselves.

Surveys show a strong relationship between a person's sense of political efficacy (the confidence that what one does really matters) and the extent of his political involvement. The weaker one's sense of political efficacy, the less likely one is to become involved. Table 6 is a typical illustration of this relationship. The table shows a strong relation between a sense of political efficacy and voting turnout in the 1956 presidential election. Of those with the highest confidence, 91 per cent voted, compared with only 52 per cent among those with the lowest degree of confidence.

TABLE 6. RELATION OF SENSE OF POLITICAL EFFICACY TO VOTING TURNOUT IN THE 1956 PRESIDENTIAL ELECTION

	Sense of Political Efficacy				
	Low				High
Voted	52%	60%	75%	84%	91%
Did not Vote	48	40	25	16	9
	100%	100%	100%	100%	100%
Number of cases	263	343	461	501	196

Source: Campbell, *et al., op. cit.,* Table 5–6, p. 105.

Figure 2 shows another example. This table shows the relationship among a sample of voters in New Haven between the sense of political efficacy and a general index of local action. The index of local action combines a large variety of campaign, electoral, and non-campaign activities and thus is a more comprehensive measure of political involvement than mere voting.

The confidence one has in one's capacity to be effective in political life depends on many factors. In the United States the sense of efficacy rises with income, social standing, political experience, and, most of all, education. Of course, a person's sense of confidence may also simply reflect a realistic appraisal of his influence. Thus it is hardly surprising that among sub-leaders in various political organizations in New Haven, more than 8 out of 10 possess a relatively high sense of efficacy (Fig. 3). Probably one's "personality" has some bearing on one's sense of efficacy. Optimism or pessimism about one's chances of influencing policy is probably related to deeper personality factors, such as an underlying sense of confidence or lack of confidence that pervades a person's entire outlook.

3. *An individual is unlikely to get involved in politics if he believes that the outcome will be relatively satisfactory to him without his involvement.* A citizen who believes that some political decision is important might nevertheless not become involved if he feels quite confident that the decision will turn out well anyway. Just as low confidence in one's political efficacy discourages par-

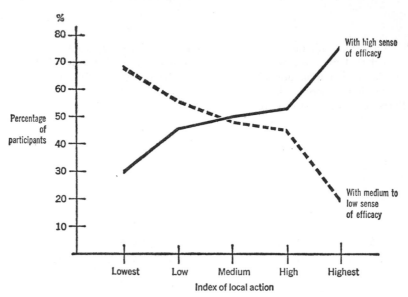

FIG. 2. *The more a person participates in local affairs, the more likely he is to have a high sense of political efficacy.* (Source: Robert A. Dahl, *Who Governs? Democracy and Power in an American City* (New Haven: Yale University Press, 1961), p. 288.)

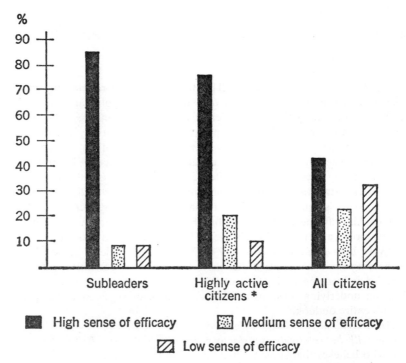

* Highest on index of local action. Those who did not answer are omitted from the graph.

FIG. 3. *Subleaders have a very high sense of political efficacy.* (Source: Dahl, *op. cit.*, p. 289.)

ticipation, so high confidence in the all-round justice, legitimacy, stability, and fairness of decisions in one's political system may make one's own participation seem unnecessary. One might expect political involvement to decrease during periods of prosperity and rise during depressions. A comparison of the turnout in United States presidential elections and major periods of depression and prosperity does indeed show some relation; though so many factors influence voting turnout that the results must be interpreted cautiously. However, the percentage of eligible voters who voted in presidential elections climbed to a sharp peak in 1876 during the depression that lasted from 1873–1878. The Greenback Movement and Populism were undoubtedly stimulated by the depressions of 1873–1878 and 1893–1897. The percentage of eligible voters who went to the polls rose during the Great Depression of 1929–1939.

POWER-SEEKERS AND LEADERS

Within the political strata, some persons seek power much more actively than others. And some persons gain much more power than others. Within the political strata, then, there is a sub-stratum of *power-seekers* and a sub-stratum of powerful *leaders*.

What we have just said is a restatement of two propositions set forth [earlier] as empirical characteristics of political systems:

1. Some members of the political system seek to gain influence over the policies, rules, and decisions enforced by the government.

2. Political influence is distributed unevenly among adult members of a political system.

Now to seek power and to gain power are by no means the same thing. Although the two phenomena—seeking power and gaining power—are sometimes confused, clearly they are distinguishable. Not only are some power-seekers unsuccessful in their efforts to gain power; some people who gain power may not actually seek it. This might occur, for example, among those who, like a monarch or a feudal lord, acquire their power by inheritance. In Table 7 the two different dimensions are combined to yield four categories.

We have, then, two important questions: Why do some people seek more power than others? And why do some people gain more power than others?

TABLE 7. SEEKING POWER AND GAINING POWER

		Extent of Seeking Power	
		Little or No Active Search	Highly Active Search
Extent of power gained	Much	Powerful leaders who do not seek power	Successful power-seekers
	Little or none	Non-leaders who do not seek power	Unsuccessful power-seekers

THE POWER-SEEKERS

Every human being has access to resources of some kind. His resources may be pitifully meager—a tiny barren patch of land that barely yields enough food to sustain his life, the labor-time he sells to a landlord for a pittance, a primitive wooden hoe. Or his resources may be enormous and varied—the wealth of a pasha, a famous family name, control over means of communication, a high public position, widespread popularity, a disciplined and loyal band of associates and followers, a far-flung bureaucracy for acquiring intelligence and analyzing information.

These resources could, in principle, nearly always be applied to more than a single purpose. The poor half-starved peasant in his wintry hour of need could burn his wooden hoe in a last desperate struggle to survive; he could use it to club an intruder or drive off an animal; or he and his fellows could use their labor-time and their hoes to overpower the landlord and rob his grain bin.

Nearly always, too, these resources could, in principle, be applied to change the expected behavior of someone else, in a word: to influence others. Frequently, in fact, these resources could be used to create a threat of severe penalties and thus offer the chance of gaining power over others.

Generally, then, human beings have access to some political resources, however paltry these may be. But human beings have many goals. Often, too, they can employ different means to achieve a given goal. Not all men apply their resources to gaining power. Yet some, the power-seekers, do. Why?

The answers to this question can be grouped into three categories.

1. Men seek power, it is said, in order to achieve the collective good. They wish to protect the interests of all citizens, achieve justice for all, benefit the state, or provide for life, liberty, and the pursuit of happiness. This is the argument attributed to Socrates in Plato's *Republic*:

> So far as arts are concerned, then, no art ever studies or enjoins the interests of the superior or stronger party, but always that of the weaker over which it has authority.
>
> Thrasymachus assented to this at last, though he tried to put up a fight. I then went on:
>
> So the physician, as such, studies only the patient's interest, not his own . . . ; and the ship's captain . . . will study and enjoin the interests of his subordinates, not his own.
>
> He agreed reluctantly.
>
> And so with government of any kind: no ruler, insofar as he is acting as ruler, will study or enjoin what is for his own interest. All that he says and does will be said and done with a view to what is good and proper for the subject for whom he practises his art.[4]

Now the difficulty with this debate between Socrates (or Plato) and Thrasymachus is that the two men are talking right past one another. This often happens in political controversy; each opponent vigorously flails an argument the other did not make, and thereby fails to meet head-on the precise point the other did make. In this case Socrates was making a *normative* argument, Thrasymachus an *empirical* one. Socrates met Thrasymachus' attempt to describe how rulers generally *do* act by indicating how good rulers ought to act.

Socrates and Plato knew perfectly well that rulers of states do not in fact always rule in the interests of their subjects. Indeed, to both Socrates and Plato the very meaning of a bad or perverted state was that the rulers did not seek the good of those over whom they ruled. Later on in the *Republic* Plato undertakes a description of the tyrant:

> . . . In every one of us, even those who seem most respectable, there exist desires, terrible in their untamed lawlessness, which reveal themselves in dreams. . . . Thus, when nature or habit or both have combined the traits of drunkenness, lust, and lunacy, then you have the perfect specimen of the despotic man. . . . When the number of such criminals and their hangers-on increases and they become aware of their strength, then it is they who, helped by the folly of the common people, create the despot out of that one among their number whose soul is itself under the most tyrannical despotism.[5]

In sum, many political philosophers have argued that leaders *should* seek power in order to exercise authority for the good of all. But probably no student of politics has ever really argued that this is the only reason, or even the principal reason, why men *do* in fact seek power.

2. Men seek power, it has been argued, in conscious pursuit of their self-interest. This was the argument of Thrasymachus that Socrates purported to attack. Thrasymachus had said (according to Plato):

> What I say is that "just" or "right" means nothing but what is to the interest of the stronger party. . . . In every case the laws are made by the ruling party in its own interest; a democracy makes democratic laws, a despot autocratic ones, and so on. By making these laws they define as "right" for their subjects whatever is for their own interest, and they call anyone who breaks them a "wrongdoer" and punish him accordingly. This is what I mean: in all states alike "right" has the same meaning, namely what is for the interest of the party established in power, and that is the strongest.[6]

Thrasymachus may well have represented an early Greek attempt to find naturalistic explanations for political behavior. Since nearly all we know of him comes from his enemy Plato, his argument in the *Republic* is probably somewhat distorted. Evidently Thrasymachus was trying to explain how it is that although rulers always proclaim that they are seeking justice, different rulers impose different ideas of justice on their states. To Thrasymachus the obvious explanation of the paradox was that each ruler was simply pursuing his own self-interest; "justice" as it was actually defined in the laws of each state was a mere ideological rationalization for the self-interest of the rulers. It is quite possible that Thrasymachus used his analysis to uphold traditional

Athenian democratic institutions against subversion by supporters of oligarchy who insisted that they and they alone were concerned for the good of the state. Undoubtedly he also employed his analysis to undermine the appeal of Plato's elaborate defense of aristocracy, which Thrasymachus probably believed was no more than a brilliant rationalization for the anti-democratic ambitions of the oligarchical faction in Athens.[7]

Thrasymachus' hypothesis that men deliberately seek power for reasons of self-interest has been restated many times. Hobbes, for example, held that men were impelled by their passions and guided by their reason. Passion is the wind that fills the sails, reason the hand on the rudder. Man, to use another metaphor, is a chariot pulled by the wild horses of passion and steered by reason. Men's desires are insatiable, but reason dictates prudence. With the aid of his reason, man can discover the general rules or precepts that will enable him to improve his chances of gaining the ends his passsions dictate. All men, then, seek power in order to satisfy their passions. But reason tells them *how* to seek power so as to reduce frustration, defeat, and the chances of violent death.

One difficulty with this hypothesis, as Plato rightly saw, is that the notion of "self-interest," which seems transparently obvious, is actually very complex. What one views as his "self" depends on one's identifications, and evidently these vary a good deal. How one perceives the "self" is not wholly instinctive, it seems, but also a matter of social learning. Likewise, what one considers to be in the "interest" of the self is shaped by learning, experience, tradition and culture. Consequently, to attribute an act to self-interest does not explain very much. As a distinguished modern psychologist has said:

> . . . the self comprises all the precious things and persons who are relevant to an individual's life, so that the term selfish loses its original connotation, and the proposition that man is selfish resolves itself into the circular statement that people are concerned with the things they are concerned with.[8]

Jones' self-interest can mean Jones' pursuit of advantages for himself alone. Or it can mean his attempt to obtain advantages of all kinds for himself and his family. The Jones family now becomes the "self" and its "interests" run from acquisitiveness to zoology. Or Jones' self-interest can mean his attempt to obtain advantages for larger strata with which he identifies—his neighborhood, region, class, religion, ethnic group, race, nation. Thus both the "self" with which Jones identifies and the range of ends he regards as in the "interests" of the self may be extremely narrow or very wide, depending on learning, experience, tradition and culture. Anthropological studies testify to the fact that notions of "self," "interest," and "self-interest" vary widely among human beings.

A second objection to rational self-interest as an explanation is posed by post-Freudian psychology. Thrasymachus, Hobbes, Jeremy Bentham, and Marx all interpreted the search for power as "rational" and conscious pursuit of self-interest. But Freud showed that the "desires, terrible in their untamed lawlessness," of which Socrates spoke did more than drive human beings into conflict with one another (as Hobbes argued); they also drive human beings into conflict with themselves. These inner conflicts, according to Freud, are fierce gales that often blow out the flickering light of reason. Reason, as Freud saw it, cannot always guide the chariot drawn by passion, for these violent steeds turn on one another and in their battle the reins of reason become entangled.

Freud discovered, analyzed, and stated what those keen students of human psychology, the great playwrights and novelists, had always known. But since Freud's day, several social scientists have attempted to develop systematic theories dealing with the search for power.

3. Men seek power, some recent students of politics argue, from unconscious motives. One of the most influential contemporary explanations of power-seeking is Lasswell's. His theory can be summarized as follows. The power-seeker pursues power as a means of compensating for psychological deprivations suffered during childhood. Typical deprivations that engender power-seeking are a lack of respect and affection at an early age. The self, then, suffers damage; the individual acquires a low estimate of the self. (The self usually includes more than the "primary ego," the "I" or "me"; it includes parents, wife, children, friends, countrymen, co-religionists and others.) In childhood, adolescence or perhaps later, the power-seeker learns to compensate for this low estimate of the worth of his "self" by pursuing power. He comes to believe that by acquiring power he can either make the self better, and hence more loved and respected, or he can change the attitudes of others about his "self." With power he will become important, loved, respected, admired. He hopes, then, to acquire through power relationships the affection and respect he failed to acquire in his family relationships. None of this behavior, of course, need be impelled by conscious, "rational" thought. On the contrary, a great deal of the motivation is likely to be unconscious. The power-seeker does not necessarily have much insight into why he seeks power; he rationalizes his power-seeking in terms acceptable to his conscious values and perhaps the prevailing ideology among those with whom he identifies. In comparison with other people, then, the power-seeker is a person who:

a. Places a high value on gaining power.

b. Demands power (and other values) for the self (the primary ego plus incorporated symbols of other egos).

c. Has relatively high confidence that he can gain power.

d. Acquires at least a minimum proficiency in the skills of power.[9]

Lasswell himself has questioned whether his power-seeker is likely to be very effective in *achieving* power, since he is likely to stimulate too much dislike and distrust to acquire much support. Robert Lane also argues that a number of recent findings suggest that a strong desire to gain power over other people is not correlated with political activity, at least in democratic systems. Lane furnishes several explanations for this paradox:

a. "To be successful in politics a person must have sufficient interpersonal skills to relate himself effectively to other men and must not be so consumed with power drives that he loses touch with reality. A person with a raging desire for power . . . will constantly alienate his supporters, thereby making the achievement of power impossible for him."

b. "One of the most common sources of the need for power over others is the deeper need for reassurance about the self. . . . This need for reassurance is, of course, related to lack of self-confidence, feelings of unworthiness, or low esteem. (But) . . . a feeling of personal effectiveness is highly related to participation."

c. "The power-seeker may find his needs sublimated in other ways than political activity, at least as this term is ordinarily defined." [10]

Conclusion

Of the three explanations for seeking power that we have explored, none seems entirely satisfactory. However, our discussion does suggest several conclusions:

First, whatever the reasons may be, some people do seek power more intently than others.

Second, scientific knowledge about the personalities and motives of power-seekers is still scanty. Everyone agrees that some people seek power more ardently than others, but authorities disagree over why they do.

Third, it seems evident that men seek power not only for its own sake but because of its instrumental value. Power can be used to gain a great variety of ends. Depending on culture, society, economy, and political system, power (as Lasswell and many others have pointed out) can be used to acquire fame, reverence, security, respect, affection, wealth and many other values. It is not surprising, then, that men should seek power; nor should we necessarily assume that power-seeking is abnormal or pathological. In its instrumental character, power is like money. Some men invest more effort in gaining money than others do; they do not necessarily do so because they value money, as such, more highly than others but because they see money as an instrument to other goals.

Fourth, power-seeking, like other behavior, is no doubt usually a compound of conscious and unconscious motives. Men who seek power may know some of the reasons why they do so; we can hardly expect them to know all the reasons.

Fifth, it seems unlikely that all power-seekers have substantially similar personalities. There are too many different reasons, conscious and unconscious, why one might want power, and too many variations in the costs and benefits of power from one political system to another and from one time to another. Undoubtedly both Caligula and Abraham Lincoln sought power. Yet it is highly implausible to suppose that Caligula and Lincoln had even approximately the same kind of personality.

THE POWERFUL

Not all power-seekers, we have said, gain power. Indeed, though it is probably uncommon, some men who do not seek to gain and wield power may nevertheless exercise it. Why do some people gain more power than others?

In principle, if one gains more power than another (over X, with respect to Y)[11] then we may look to two possible sources of explanation to account for differences in the amount of power—to differences in the amount of resources used, and to differences in the skill or efficiency with which the resources are applied. Some people use more resources to gain power than others do. Some people use what resources they have more efficiently, more skillfully.

Why do some people use more resources than others do to gain power? Presumably because they expect to "gain more" by doing so. I may "gain more" than you from a given action either because the action is "less costly" to me or because the outcome of the action is "more valuable" to me. If A has more resources than B—if, say, A is wealthier than B—then a given outlay is less costly for A than for B (all other things being equal) because A has to forgo fewer alternatives than B. Or, in the language of the economist, A's opportunity costs are lower.

A man of wealth and a good deal of leisure can devote 60 hours a week to non-paying political activities at considerably lower opportunity cost than the man who has to work long hours to make a living. In short, if A has more resources than B, the opportunity costs of allocating a given amount of those resources to gaining power are less for A than for B. A can make the same outlays as B at less opportunity cost or more outlays at the same opportunity cost. In general, then, some people use more resources to gain power than others do because they have access to more resources. And, all other things being equal, it is reasonable to expect that people with more resources would gain more power. To this extent, then, differences in power and power-seeking are related to differences in objective circumstances.

However, "all other things" are not usually equal. Even if their resources were objectively identical, A might allocate a greater share of his resources in order to gain power if he places a higher value on the results. Why might A place a higher value than B on the results of an outlay of resources to gain power?

Because A might expect different results from B.

Because, though both expect the same results, A and B use different values or different scales to appraise the results.

Because, though they expect the same results, A feels more confident about the outcome than B does.

However, A's application of more resources may not result in more power if B has more skill than A. A deft politician may accomplish more with little than a clumsy politician can accomplish with a great deal. Why then do some people have more skill in politics than others?

This is a difficult question to answer. To try to do so would carry on beyond the limits of this article. In brief, however, there are three possible explanations for a difference in skill between two persons, whatever the skill may be, whether walking a tightrope over the Niagara, playing the part of Mimi in "La Boheme," or serving as majority leader in the United States Senate. These are:

1. Genetic differences.
2. Differences in opportunities to learn.
3. Differences in incentives to learn.

The first two are differences in situations, the third is a difference in motivations.

The question we started out to answer a moment ago, you may remember, was, Why do some people gain more power than others? Let us now summarize our explanation.

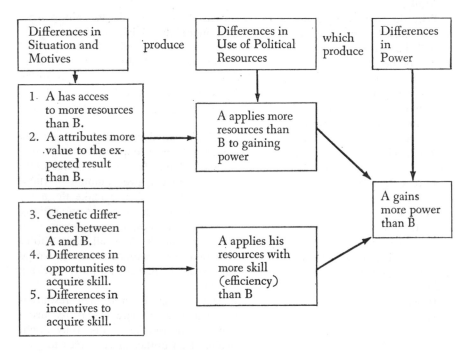

Once again, the argument points to the conclusion that men who gain power need to be similar to one another only in certain formal respects. In fact, the concrete characteristics of leaders seem to vary a good deal in different political systems, different times, and different situations. Leaders have different social origins, different resources, different skills, different personalities. Among those who have sought and gained power, the range of human types runs from Napoleon Bonaparte, the Corsican upstart, to Winston Churchill, descendant of seven Dukes of Marlborough; from Caesar, the military genius, to Woodrow Wilson, historian, political scientist, and college president; from the detached and reflective Hadrian to Savonarola, the fanatic; from the regal Elizabeth the First to Madame de Pompadour, the witty mistress of Louis XV; from the serene stoicism of the philosopher Marcus Aurelius to the neurosis of Hitler and the paranoia of Stalin; from Caligula to Lincoln.

NOTES

[1] Robert Lane, *Political Life* (New York: The Free Press, 1959), 143 ff., and Angus Campbell *et al., The American Voter* (New York: Wiley, 1960), pp. 101 ff.

[2] Aristotle, *On the Constitution of Athens,* Appendix IV, in Ernest Barker (ed.), *Reflections on Government* (New York: Oxford University Press, 1942), pp. 379, 383.

[3] Charles H. Levermore, *The Republic of New Haven* (Baltimore: Johns Hopkins University Press, 1886), pp. 44, 231.

[4] *The Republic of Plato,* translated with introduction and notes by F. M. Cornford (New York: Oxford University Press, 1945), pp. 23–24. The English translations of Plato's *Republic* often vary somewhat, but in the passages quoted here the differences are not significant. The student may wish to compare *The Dialogues of Plato,* translated by B. Jowett (New York: Random House, 1937), Vol. I, pp. 607–608; and *Plato, The Republic,* translated by P. Shorey (New York: Putnam, The Loeb Classical Library, 1930), p. 63.

[5] *The Republic of Plato,* in Cornford, trans., *op. cit.,* pp. 297, 298 and 300.

[6] *Ibid.,* p. 18.

[7] On this point see Eric A. Havelock, *The Liberal Temper in Greek Politics* (New Haven: Yale University Press, 1957), p. 231 and *passim.*

[8] Gardner Murphy, "Social Motivation" in G. Lindzey (ed.), *Handbook of Social Psychology* (Cambridge, Mass.: Addison-Wesley, 1954), 2 Vols., Vol. 2, p. 625. On the influence of social learning on the self, see also E. H. Erikson, *Childhood and Society* (New York: Norton, 1950).

[9] Harold Lasswell, *Power and Personality* (New York: Norton, 1948), Ch. 3, "The Political Personality," *passim.*

[10] Lane, *op. cit.,* pp. 126–128.

[11] For convenience, the clause in parenthesis will be dropped from time to time, though [as we saw earlier] it would be formally necessary to give more precise meaning to the sentence.

12. THE OBLIGATION TO PARTICIPATE

Gabriel A. Almond and Sidney Verba

The citizen, unlike the subject, is an active participant in the political input process—the process by which political decisions are made. But the citizen role does not replace the subject role or the parochial role: it is added to them. Only the rare individual considers his role as citizen more important and salient than his role as subject or parochial, for whom politics is a matter of first priority. This has been corroborated in many surveys of political opinion. When asked general questions about what worries them, or what they consider important, people usually mention family problems, job problems, economic problems, but rarely political problems.[1] Furthermore, if the ordinary man is interested in political matters, he is more likely to be interested in the output than in the input process. He is concerned about who wins the election, not about how it is carried on; he cares about who is benefited by legislation, not about how legislation is passed. Even in relation to his vote—an act that is designed to make him an active participant in the decision-making processes of his nation—he may behave routinely, voting for a party because of traditional allegiance or for other reasons not connected with a desire to guide the course of policy.

That most men orient themselves more as subjects than as citizens is a familiar theme. Much has been written describing this fact, sometimes deploring it. Interest in and criticism of the role of the ordinary man in his political system is especially characteristic of those writers and thinkers concerned with the problems of democracy—from the ancient Greeks to current writers on American civic affairs; for it is in a democracy that the role of the ordinary man as a participant in the political affairs of his country is significant. The man whose relation to his government is that of a subject—a passive beneficiary or victim of routine governmental actions—would not not be found wanting in a traditional, nondemocratic society. Moreover, this relationship would exhaust what is expected of him. What the government does affects him, but why or how the government decides to do what it does is outside his sphere of competence. He has obligations, but the obligations are passive—he should be loyal and respectful of authority. "All that is necessary for salvation is contained in two virtues, *faith* in Christ and *obedience* to law." [2] As a subject he may be more or less competent, but his competence will be "subject competence." He will not attempt to influence the decisions of his government, but will try to see that he is treated properly once the decision is made. It is not in his sphere of competence to say what taxes should be levied, but once these are decided the competent subject will see that he is treated fairly within the boundaries of that decision. The law is something he obeys, not something he helps shape. If he is competent, he knows the law, knows what he must do, and what is due him.

SOURCE: Gabriel A. Almond and Sidney Verba, *The Civic Culture* (Princeton: Princeton University Press, 1963), pp. 161–179. Reprinted by permission of the Princeton University Press.

In democratic societies, on the other hand, his role as subject does not exhaust what is expected of him. He is expected to have the virtues of the subject—to obey the law, to be loyal—but he is also expected to take some part in the formation of decisions. The common thread running through the many definitions of democracy is that a democracy is a society in which ". . . ordinary citizens exert a relatively high degree of control over leaders." [3] Democracy is thus characterized by the fact that power over significant authoritative decisions in a society is distributed among the population. The ordinary man is expected to take an active part in governmental affairs, to be aware of how decisions are made, and to make his views known.

The fact that the ordinary man does not live up to the ideal set by the normative theory of democracy has led to much criticism of his passivity and indifference. Our goal is to describe and analyze, however, and not to assign praise or blame. In any case, normative questions about the role of the individual in his political system are by no means unrelated to more descriptive and analytic questions. Certainly the political moralist in describing what an individual *should* do will probably not be unaffected by what individuals actually *do*, and certainly he will consider what he believes that *can* do. The three types of questions are not identical, but they affect one another, especially if we switch our perspective to that of the ordinary man himself. So far we have talked about the gap between what scholars, philosophers, and teachers have said the ordinary man ought to do in a democracy and what in fact he does. But what about the ordinary man himself? What does *he* think he *should* do? And how does this compare with what he thinks he *can* do and with what he does?

This selection will deal with the first question: What does the ordinary man think he should do? Philosophers and democratic ideologists have writtten at length about the obligations of the citizen, but what is the ordinary man's conception of his role in politics? If the model democratic citizen is active, participating, and influential, is this what the ordinary man aspires to be? And, what may be more important, does he think of himself as capable of influencing and participating in the decisions of his government?

WHAT IS THE GOOD CITIZEN?

The good citizen does not equal the good man. No zealous advocate of good citizenship would argue that political participation ought to be pursued to the neglect of all other obligations. The active influential citizen described in normative political theory is not excused from the obligations of the subject. If he participates in the making of the law, he is also expected to obey the law. It has, in fact, been argued that he has greater obligation to obey because of his participation. Nor would one want his civic activity to be at the expense of his private obligations. Surely the lady described by Riesman who left her screaming children locked in their room while she attended a meeting of a neighborhood improvement association does not represent the ideal toward which the advocates of good citizenship are striving.[4] There will, of course, always be conflicts between the demands of different roles, but the obligations of one role do not replace those of another.

This point is stressed here because it introduces a complexity into our attempt to measure the extent to which the ideal of the participating citizen exists in the minds of men; for the man who believes that he should be upright in his personal life—work for the good of his family or, to quote one of our respondents, "If he is a carpenter, he should be a good carpenter"—may also believe that he should be a participating and active citizen. Similarly, the man who believes that he should pay taxes and obey the laws is a "good subject." The same man may also be a "good citizen." It is only when the individual thinks of his family's advantage as the only goal to pursue, or conceives of his role in the political system in familistic terms, that he is a parochial and not also a citizen. And it is only when an individual thinks of his relationship to his state as being exhausted by his role as subject that he is subject and not also citizen.

Attempting to see how much the role of participant has been added to those of parochial and subject in our five countries, we examined our respondents' relationships with their local community. We were interested in the extent to which respondents considered themselves to have some sort of responsibility to be active in their community—either in a formal or an informal way; either in relation to local government or in relation to fellow citizens. The local community seemed to be a good place to begin, since political and governmental problems tend to be more understandable, the organs of government less distant, the chances of effective participation for the individual citizen greater on the local level than on the level of national government. In fact, it has often been argued that effective democracy rests on the ability of the individual to participate locally, for it is only here that he can develop some sense of mastery over political affairs. As Bryce put it (and as defenders of local autonomy have constantly argued), "An essential ingredient of a satisfactory democracy is that a considerable proportion should have experience of active participation in the work of small self-governing groups, whether in connection with local government, trade unions, cooperatives or other forms of activity." [5]

NATIONAL DIFFERENCES IN THE CHARACTERISTICS OF LOCAL GOVERNMENT

In this article . . . we shall deal with attitudes toward the local government. In interpreting the responses to questions about the local government, we are faced with the problem that the structures of local government differ from nation to nation and within the nations as well. And these differences in structure partially explain differences in attitudes found among the nations. It is important that these differences be kept in mind. Though it would be impossible to describe fully the patterns of local government within the five nations—there are numerous levels of local government in all five nations and substantial variations among regions—one can specify certain similarities and differences among them.

In the first place, all five nations have some form of local government. (It is important to note here that we are dealing with the most local governmental units: units below the level of state, or *Land,* or province.) And the local unit, whether it be a commune, *municipio, Gemeinde,* township, or non-county borough, almost invariably has some sort of locally elected council or set of officials. Thus in each country there is a set of locally elected units on which we can focus.

But despite this similarity, local government differs sharply among the five nations. From the point of view of respondents' attitudes toward participation within the local community, there are two types of structural differences that are particularly significant: the degree of local autonomy and the degree to which local structures foster citizen participation. It is difficult to measure precisely the extent of autonomy of local governmental units within nations; there are variations within nations, the criteria of autonomy are not clear, and the data are often lacking. Nevertheless, the five nations do differ so substantially in this respect—and the variations among the nations are generally larger than the variations within each nation—that one can rank the nations with some confidence according to local autonomy. It is clear that at one extreme the pattern of local government in the United States represents the greatest amount of local autonomy. The range of subject matter over which the local communities have control—the police and schools are two important examples, and the communities not only handle administration of the schools, but in many cases they actually formulate educational policy—as well as the extent of the local governments' freedom from external control appear to be much greater in the United States than elsewhere.

It would appear that Great Britain ranks next to the United States in degree of local autonomy. The range of issues over which the local government has control is smaller—educational policy, for instance, is controlled by central government agencies to a much larger degree—and within the unitary British system of government, local autonomy is not provided for formally by home rule provisions, as it is in the constitutions of a number of American states. Nevertheless, the British have a long tradition of local self-government. And local councils are active in administrative work as well as in some limited areas of legislation where permission is given by the central government.[6]

It is difficult to rank the other three nations precisely. As to the formal structure of local government, however, it is relatively easy to specify which ranks lowest. The existence of the prefect system in Italy limits substantially any opportunity for local self-government. The communes in Italy have locally elected councils, but they have little freedom of action. All acts must be submitted to the centrally appointed prefect of the province, who passes on their legality; and certain significant matters, such as the municipal budget and the levying of taxes, must be approved by the provincial administrative committee (*Giunta Provinciale Amministrativa*), which passes on both the legality and the merit of the act. It is quite unlikely that a local government structure of this sort, in which there is a centrally appointed official with powers to oversee the activities of the locality, would foster a high level of autonomous local activity. Though there is some evidence of more local autonomy than one would expect, given the formal structure, the degree of autonomy is probably least of all the five nations.[7]

As in most cases when one is trying to array a series of units along a scale, it is the units near the middle of the scale that present the more difficult problems in categorization. In terms of the degree of local governmental autonomy, it is probably accurate to place Germany and Mexico between the United States and Britain on the one hand and Italy on the other. But one must approach the characterization of these two nations with somewhat more caution. One reason is the wide range of variation possible within a federal system, a situation heightened in Germany by differing regional traditions and by the somewhat different heritages from the three occupying powers. There is in many areas of Germany a strong tradition of local autonomy, as well as a tendency for local communities to engage in a wide range of activities, especially among many of the older northern German cities, which have long histories of local self-government.[8] It is, however, difficult to estimate in any precise way the extent to which local self-government is firmly entrenched in other areas in Germany.

Mexico, unlike Italy but like the other three nations, has legal provision for relatively autonomous local governments on the level of the *municipio*. In actual practice, however, these local governments have been relatively uninfluential and relatively nonautonomous, largely because of central control over local finances and the pervasive influence of the PRI, the single important Mexican political party. Local government in Mexico has rarely been of great significance.[9]

The nations also differ in the extent to which the local decision-making apparatus is accessible to participation by local residents. In some communities —and again this varies within nations, but perhaps more sharply among nations —there will be greater opportunity for the individual to participate in decisions. It is somewhat more difficult to compare the nations in this respect than it was to compare them in respect to local autonomy. There are fewer studies of the degree to which individuals actually participate in local affairs, for such participation depends largely upon informal as well as formal channels of participation. In general, one would expect that the extent to which the local government is open to citizen participation in decisions would be closely related to the extent of local autonomy; and impresssions of community life in these five nations, as well as other data presented in *The Civic Culture,* support this proposition.[10]

Consequently, in interpreting the data . . . we shall have to keep in mind that one reason why individuals differ in the frequency with which they adhere to participatory norms is that the structure of government and community organization changes from one nation to another. This does not make the attitudinal data any less significant. . . . Even if the attitudes we describe are in part determined by the structure of government and social system in each nation, this does not remove the fact that these attitudes in turn affect these same structures. The norms to which an individual adheres are largely determined by the role that the system allows him to play (though the fit between norms and structure will rarely be perfect); but these norms in turn have a feedback effect on the structure, reinforcing the structure if the fit between norms and structure is a good one; introducing strain into the system if norms and structure fit less well. And lastly, as we shall attempt to demonstrate below, attitudes toward the local government cannot be explained solely by the relationship between the individual and the local governmental structure (and the same point can and will be made about the national government as well). We shall attempt to show, for instance, that the extent to which individuals believe they can influence the government, and in particular the ways in which they would attempt to exert that influence, depend, not only on the governmental system, but upon certain social and attitudinal characteristics of the individuals.

NATIONAL DIFFERENCES IN SENSE OF CIVIC OBLIGATION

Our question to the respondents dealt with participation in local affairs. We were interested not only in political participation, but also in any sort of outgoing activity the individual might mention. We wanted to know the extent to which individuals believe they have any sort of obligation to the community— to care about more than the personal problems of the family life and job.[11]

Table 1 summarizes the responses we received as to the role individuals should play within their local community. We have classified our respondents into those who believe that the ordinary man should take some active part in

TABLE 1. HOW ACTIVE SHOULD THE ORDINARY MAN BE IN HIS LOCAL COMMUNITY; BY NATION

Percentage who say the ordinary man should	U.S.	U.K.	Germany	Italy	Mexico
Be active in his community	51	39	22	10	26
Only participate passively*	27	31	38	22	33
Only participate in church affairs*	5	2	1	*	—
Total who mention some outgoing activity	83	72	61	32	59
Only be upright in personal life*	1	1	11	15	2
Do nothing in local community	3	6	7	11	2
Don't know	11	17	21	35	30
Other	2	5	1	7	7
Total percentage	100	100	100	100	100
Total number of cases	970	963	955	995	1,007

* Multiple answers were possible, but we have eliminated them from this table by listing respondents' *most active* response only (i.e., the response that would fall highest on the table). Thus an individual who mentioned active as well as passive participation would be listed under active participation only; one who mentioned church activities as well as an upright private life would be listed under the former and not the latter.

his community (this includes those who say the ordinary man should attend meetings, join organizations involved in community affairs, and the like); those who believe that one ought to participate more passively in community activities (for example: one ought to be interested in local affairs, try to understand them and keep informed, vote); those who feel that the ordinary man ought to participate only in church and religious activities; and those who do not think the ordinary man has any responsibility that involves him in the affairs of his community (here we include the respondents who feel that the ordinary man ought to maintain an upright personal life; who say that he ought to take no part in the affairs of his community; and who do not know what role the individual ought to play in his community).

Clearly, from this table the image of the citizen-as-participant is more widespread in some countries than in others. In the United States and Britain a large number of respondents believe that the individual should be an active participant in the affairs of his community. Half of the Americans interviewed and 39 per cent of the British mention some active role that the individual ought to play. In Italy, at the other extreme, there are few who conceive of the citizen as active participant. Only one in ten Italians believes that the ordinary man has an obligation to take an active role in his community. The proportions of German and Mexican respondents who have some image of the active citizen lie between the American and British proportions on the one hand and the Italian on the other. One out of five of our German respondents and one out of four of our Mexicans conceive of the ordinary man as having some obligation to participate.[12]

"One ought at least to take an interest in what goes on in the community"; or, "One ought to be active in church and religious affairs": if we consider these statements an indicator (albeit a weaker one) of the existence of some norm of participation, then the contrasts among the nations are still striking. In the United States 83 per cent of the respondents talk of the ordinary man as having some commitment to his community that takes him out of involvement in purely personal affairs—even if the responsibility is minimal. The proportion in Britain is somewhat smaller at 72 per cent; in Mexico and Germany about 60 per cent talk of some outgoing role for the individual, whereas in Italy only 32 per cent do.

What sorts of community activities do our respondents have in mind when they say the ordinary man ought to play some part in his local community? As Table 2 shows, only a small number of respondents in each country mention partisan activity as the responsibility of the individual to his community. In the United States and Britain respondents frequently mention taking part in local government bodies, attending meetings, and the like. In Germany and Mexico this is less frequently mentioned, but is mentioned more frequently than in Italy. Active community participation in a nongovernmental sense—participation in civic groups and organizations, or informal activity to help the community—is quite frequently mentioned in the United States. Such nongovernmental activity is again least mentioned in Italy, with Germany and Mexico trailing Britain. In active participation, then, the five countries can be roughly grouped: the United States and Britain are the countries in which the image of the active participating citizen is most often the normative ideal; in Germany and Mexico the ideal receives mention, but less often; and in Italy this ideal is least widespread.

Some illustrations may be useful in making explicit the specific areas of activity respondents had in mind:

TABLE 2. WHAT ROLE SHOULD THE ORDINARY MAN PLAY IN HIS LOCAL COMMUNITY; BY NATION

Percentage who choose	U.S.	U.K.	Germany	Italy	Mexico
Active participation in local community [a]					
Take part in activities of local government	21	22	13	5	11
Take part in activities of political parties	6	4	4	1	5
Take part in nongovern- mental activity and in organizations Inter- ested in local affairs	32	17	9	5	10
More passive community activities [a]					
Try to understand and keep informed	21	11	24	6	29
Vote	40	18	15	2	1
Take an interest in what is going on	3	13	6	15	4
Participation in church and religious activities [a]	12	2	2	—	—
Total percentage of re- spondents who mention some outgoing activ- ity [b]	83	72	61	32	59
Total number of re- spondents	970	963	955	995	1,007

[a] The percentages in these categories are somewhat larger than in Table 1, since this table contains all the responses of individuals, rather than their most active responses.

[b] Total percentages are less than the total of the individual cells, since the latter involve multiple responses.

A British Housewife: "He should take some part in public life and have a say in town-planning, education, and religion."

An American Housewife: "Everyone should take part in church and community affairs. . . . We should take an active part in making our schools better."

A Mexican Housewife: "People should have diversion, but have enough free time to occupy themselves with political and social things."

A German Worker: "Organizations should be formed that would enable [people] to discuss their problems together—for instance, parents' advisory councils [*Elternbeiräte*] at schools."

An Italian Teacher: "Each individual should be interested in an active way and should criticize justly and severely when it is necessary."

An American Postmaster: "A citizen should play an active part. . . . He might hold a local office. Other civic work such as drives, such as Red Cross. Here we have a volunteer fire company; he could help out with that."

The last quotation, from an American postmaster, suggests how the existence of structures in which one can participate affects the norms of participation that individuals hold. One would certainly not expect an individual to feel an obligation to participate in such activities as "drives," the Red Cross, and volunteer fire companies in communities where such activities were non-existent.

One theme running through many of the answers that stress active participation in the local community—a theme found largely among activists in the United States and Britain—is that the individual ought to be active as a participant in decisions; that he ought, in a rather independent way, to take part in the running of the community:

An English Female Worker: "Everyone should take a part. . . . They should get together and give opinions as to why and how this and that should be worked."

An American Housewife: "I think a person should vote. If there are any town meetings he should attend them. . . . If everyone does things in his own small way, it would add up to something big. Many people sit back and let others do things for them, then complain."

A German Farmer: "He should discuss politics, but shouldn't just accept everything, but [should] speak up too."

On the other hand, local activity means for some respondents more informal social participation, perhaps to help out one's neighbors:

A German Chauffeur: "He should not just talk, but should act too. For instance, during hay harvesting time, one should not just stick his hands in his pockets and watch the farmers exerting themselves, but should pitch in. After all, it's a matter of community welfare."

An English Businessman: "He should help in local organizations—children's clubs, boy scouts. He should help his neighbors and be a good living person."

A number of respondents, as shown in Table 2, thought of the individual as having a more passive sort of obligation to participate in his community; this usually involved some obligation to be informed of what is going on or to be interested in it:

A Mexican Housewife: "[He should] be interested in how the government is formed, and be active by studying books and newspapers."

An English Housewife: "He ought to know what is going on. Go to the occasional meeting to find out."
An Italian Worker: "Simply be interested."

Though the degree of autonomy of local government differs from nation to nation, in all five nations there are elections for some sort of local or communal council. For many respondents, as Table 2 indicates, voting in these elections was considered a responsibility of the individual to his community. But insofar as the individual considered his local responsibility to be exhausted by the act of voting, we have listed this as a relatively passive form of participation in community life—though a form of participation it certainly is. In some cases, particularly among those German respondents who mention voting as an obligation, this interpretation is made explicit. The responsibility to vote is explicitly stated as exhausting the individual's responsibility and, in fact, is invoked as an act that absolves one of all other community responsibilities.

An American Disabled Worker: "I think they should do their part. Outside of voting there isn't too much the average fellow can do. . . . You ought to vote and then support any worthwhile thing your community is trying to do."
An Italian Veterinarian: "What should an individual do? Elect his representatives. That's all."
A German Retired Worker: "Choose a mayor at election time. That's all one need to do. The mayor takes care of everything."
A German House Painter: "He should vote—that's the most important thing. But he should not be politically active himself."
A German Housewife: "I don't understand that. We have to work. The people in the council are cleverer after all. They'll do a good job. You just have to vote for the right ones."

As was pointed out earlier, not all respondents think of the individual as having any outgoing responsibility within his local community. As Table 1 indicated, there were a substantial number of respondents in Germany and Mexico, and particularly in Italy, who admitted to no sense of local civic obligation. In this sense, the norms that they accept in relation to their community are certainly not those of the participating citizen. They are quite probably oriented to their communities as subjects or parochials. These can be found in all five nations, but they are most frequent in Italy (where 15 per cent of the respondents invoke these parochial values—a larger group than those who think the individual ought to be an active participant) and in Germany (where 11 per cent of the respondents talk of such parochial values). The following are some examples of the ways in which one's responsibility to the community is interpreted as an essentially parochial or subject responsibility to one's personal life:

An English Housewife: "It's as much as my husband can do to go to work, never mind taking part in local affairs. We appoint councillors and leave everything to them."

A German Mechanic: "Take care of one's family by working. Make one's children into decent people."

A German Farmer: "I pay my taxes, go to my church, and do my work as a farmer."

A German Mechanic: "Work and support one's family decently. If everyone did that, the state would have less trouble and expense."

A German Housewife: "Everyone should do his work."

An Italian Worker: "[He] should attend to his work . . . be a good citizen, and take care of [his] family."

An Italian Artisan: "[He should be] honest and concerned about his work."

One important point about the relationship among civic, subject, and parochial norms is suggested by the data in Table 2. If the values of active participation are widespread in a country, this does not mean that the valuation of more passive participation is missing, or that subject and parochial values are missing. In the United States, for instance, where active participation is most frequently mentioned, the more passive political participation of voting is also frequently mentioned, as is participation in church and religious activities. And many respondents who mention active participation also mention the more parochial norms. This accords with our notion that the citizen role is built on but does not replace the roles of subject and parochial.

Our data clearly suggest sharp differences among the nations in the roles that respondents think individuals ought to play in their local communities. However, our data do not suggest that all those who think the individual ought to take an active part do in fact take such active roles. The gap between civic norms and civic behavior is, as we all know, large. As one American businessman who stressed the obligation to participate actively put it, "I'm saying what he ought to do, not what I do." We are not saying that one out of two Americans is an active participant in the affairs of his local community or that four out of ten Britons are. Rather, we suggest that in these countries the norm of

TABLE 3. PERCENTAGE WHO SAY THE ORDINARY MAN SHOULD BE ACTIVE IN HIS LOCAL COMMUNITY; BY NATION AND EDUCATION

Nation	Total (%)	(No.)*	Prim. or less (%)	(No.)	Some sec. (%)	(No.)	Some univ. (%)	(No.)
United States	51	(970)	35	(339)	56	(443)	66	(188)
Great Britain	39	(963)	37	(593)	42	(322)	42	(24)
Germany	22	(955)	21	(792)	32	(123)	38	(26)
Italy	10	(995)	7	(692)	17	(245)	22	(54)
Mexico	26	(1,007)	24	(877)	37	(103)	38	(24)

* Numbers in parentheses refer to the bases upon which percentages are calculated.

active citizenship is widespread. And this is congruent with the structure of government. The actual opportunities to participate and the norms that one ought to participate mutually reinforce each other to foster a high level of citizen participation. In Italy, on the other hand, the relative lack of opportunity to participate in an autonomous local community is accompanied by the absence of a set of norms favoring such participation.

DEMOGRAPHIC PATTERNS

Who within each country hold to the ideal of the citizen as participant? The middle class? or those with higher education? As Table 3 indicates, in each of the five nations it is those with some higher education who are most likely to express adherence to the norms of participation; and the least likely to report that the individual has some responsibility to participate actively in his local community are those with primary school education or less. Nevertheless, despite the fact that the distribution of adherence to participatory norms is similar in the five nations, the differences in absolute levels of such expressed adherence are still great even within similar educational groups. And within each educational group the relationship among the nations is roughly the same —American respondents tend most frequently to express adherence to such norms, followed by British, Mexican, German, and Italian respondents in that order. Furthermore, unlike some other variables, where the differences among nations tend to disappear when the all-important characteristic of education is controlled, differences still remain in the frequency of adherence to the norms of participation. In fact, a university-educated person in Germany or Mexico is no more likely to express adherence to these norms than is a primary-educated person in the United States or Britain; and the Italian university-educated respondent is less likely to do so.

If a democratic political system is one in which the ordinary citizen participates in political decisions, a democratic political culture should consist of a set of beliefs, attitudes, norms, perceptions, and the like, which support participation. Of course, the frequency of adherence to this norm will be affected by the structures of the local community. But if the norm of participation is not widespread, institutional change in the direction of fostering participation will not in itself create a participatory democracy.

It is impossible to say what is the requisite level of participatory norms and of participation in political affairs for an effective democracy. Americans more often accept norms of participation than do individuals in the other four countries, yet they have often been accused of not being civic enough. But while our findings cannot tell us whether the level of participation in the United States or Britain is "good enough," they do tell us that it is certainly higher than in Germany, Mexico, and Italy. And as this and other data on participation will suggest, where norms of participation, perceived ability to participate, and actual participation are high, effective democracy is more likely to flourish.

That an individual believes he ought to participate in the political life of his community or nation does not mean that he will in fact do so. Before the norm that one ought to participate can be translated into the act itself, the individual will probably have to perceive that he is able to act. And though the two are related, they are by no means identical. One can believe he ought to participate, but perceive himself as unable to do so. Or one can perceive himself as able to participate but not feel any obligation to do so. Certainly a great source of political discontent is the acceptance of the norms of participation coupled with the belief that one cannot in fact participate. This, it has been suggested, is the danger of overselling the norms of political democracy in the schools. When the myth of democracy comes into serious conflict with the realities of politics, the results are cynicism. The society in which individuals do in fact participate in decisions—that is, the democratic society—is likely to be the society in which individuals believe they ought to participate. It is also likely to be the society in which they think they can participate and know how to go about it. . . .

NOTES

[1] In our survey, when respondents were asked what they spent their free time on, no more than 3 per cent in any of the five nations mentioned something to do with politics; and in most cases the percentage was smaller. Other survey results show almost universally that politics is not uppermost in the minds of people.

[2] Thomas Hobbes, *Leviathan,* London, 1945, Book III, p. 385.

[3] Robert A. Dahl, *A Preface to Democratic Theory,* Chicago, 1956, p. 3.

[4] David Riesman, *Faces in the Crowd,* New Haven, 1952, pp. 82–83.

[5] James Bryce, *Modern Democracies,* New York, 1921, I, p. 132.

[6] See, for instance, W. Eric Jackson, *Local Government in England and Wales,* London, 1960. This is not to argue that in the United States and Britain there is no external control over local government. There is obviously a large amount of external control and this control is steadily growing—a point whose implications will be discussed below. But relatively speaking, local government in these two nations has a vigor missing in the other three.

[7] See Samuel Humes and Eileen M. Martin, *The Structure of Local Governments Throughout the World,* The Hague, 1961, pp. 319–24; Harold Zink et al., *Rural Local Government in Sweden, Italy and India,* London, 1957, and Edward Banfield, *The Moral Basis of a Backward Society,* Glencoe, Ill., 1958. See, also, Robert C. Fried, *The Italian Prefects,* unpublished Ph.D. dissertation, Yale University, 1961.

[8] See, for instance, Lorenz Fischer and Peter Van Hauten, "Cologne," in William A. Robson (ed.), *Great Cities of the World,* London, 1957, pp. 645–82.

[9] For a consideration of the influence of the PRI in the politics of one Mexican city, see Scott, *Mexican Government in Transition,* pp. 44–55; and William H. Form and William V. D'Antonio, "Integration and Cleavage Among Community Influentials in Two Border Cities," *American Sociological Review,* XXIV (1959), pp. 804–14. If our knowledge of and ability to measure this dimension were more precise it is possible that we might rank Mexico close to, or even below, Italy. However, more precise descriptions will depend on more precise research.

[10] But the degree of local self-government and the degree to which individuals can participate within that government may be independent of each other. It would be possible, for instance, to draw the conclusion from John Gimbel's study of *A German Community Under American Occupation: Marburg, 1945–1952,* Stanford, 1961, that the American Occupation's attempt to introduce local democracy failed for the simple reason that, though they gave power to local elites, these elites were not committed to furthering citizen participation.

[11] The question read: "We know that the ordinary person has many problems that

take his time. In view of this, what part do you think the ordinary person ought to play in the local affairs of his town or district?" The interviewer attempted to find out as closely as possible what the respondent specifically felt one ought to do in his community.

[12] The Mexican pattern is interesting here, and we shall return to it later. Mexican respondents mention an obligation to participate more frequently than do German respondents and much more frequently than do Italian respondents. This relatively high sense of obligation, coupled, as we shall discuss, with lower activity and information, is an aspect of the civic aspirational tendency among the Mexicans.

B. POLITICAL PARTICIPATION AND SOCIAL ORGANIZATION

13. THE PROBLEM OF COMMUNITY

Robert A. Nisbet

This is an age of economic interdependence and welfare States, but it is also an age of spiritual insecurity and preoccupation with moral certainty. Why is this? Why has the quest for community become the dominant social tendency of the twentieth century? What are the forces that have conspired, at the very peak of three centuries of economic and political advancement, to make the problem of community more urgent in the minds of men than it has been since the last days of the Roman Empire?

The answer is of course complex. Any effort to resolve the conflicting imperatives of an age into a simple set of institutional dislocations is both vapid and illusory. The conflicts of any age are compounded of immediate cultural frustrations and of timeless spiritual cravings. Attempts to reduce the latter to facile sociological and psychological categories are absurd and pathetic. Whatever else the brilliant literature of political disillusionment of our day has demonstrated, it has made clear that efforts to translate all spiritual problems into secular terms are fraught with stultification as well as tyranny.

The problem before us is in one sense moral. It is moral in that it is closely connected with the values and ends that have traditionally guided and united men but that have in so many instances become remote and inaccessible. We do not have to read deeply in the philosophy and literature of today to sense the degree to which our age has come to seem a period of moral and spiritual chaos, of certainties abandoned, of creeds outworn, and of values devalued. The disenchantment of the world, foreseen by certain nineteenth-century conservatives as the end result of social and spiritual tendencies then becoming dominant, is very much with us. The humane skepticism of the early twentieth century has already been succeeded in many quarters by a new Pyrrhonism that strikes at the very roots of thought itself. Present disenchantment would be no misfortune were it set in an atmosphere of confident attack upon the old and search for the new. But it is not confident, only melancholy and guilty. Along with it are to be seen the drives to absolute skepticism and absolute certainty that are the invariable conditions of rigid despotism.

The problem is also intellectual. It cannot be separated from tendencies in Western thought that are as old as civilization itself, tendencies luminously re-

SOURCE: Robert A. Nisbet, *Community and Power* (New York: Oxford University Press, 1953), pp. 45–74. Copyright 1953 by Oxford University Press, Inc., under the title *The Quest for Community*. Reprinted by permission.

vealed in the writings of Plato, Seneca, Augustine, and all their intellectual children. These are profound tendencies. We cannot avoid, any of us, seeing the world in ways determined by the very words we have inherited from other ages. Not a little of the terminology of alienation and community in our day comes directly from the writings of the philosophical and religious conservatives of other centuries. The problem constituted by the present quest for community is composed of elements as old as mankind, elements of faith and agonizing search which are vivid in all the great prophetic literatures. In large degree, the quest for community is timeless and universal.

Nevertheless, the shape and intensity of the quest for community varies from age to age. For generations, even centuries, it may lie mute, covered over and given gratification by the securities found in such institutions as family, village, class, or some other type of association. In other ages, ages of sudden change and dislocation, the quest for community becomes conscious and even clamant. It is this in our own age. To dismiss the present quest for community with vague references to the revival of tribalism, to man's still incomplete emancipation from conditions supposedly 'primitive,' is to employ substitutes for genuine analysis, substitutes drawn from the nineteenth-century philosophy of unilinear progress. Moral imperatives, our own included, always hold a significant relation to *present* institutional conditions. They cannot be relegated to the past.

It is [my view] that the ominous preoccupation with community revealed by modern thought and mass behavior is a manifestation of certain profound dislocations in the primary associative areas of society, dislocations that have been created to a great extent by the structure of the Western political State. As it is treated here, the problem is social—social in that it pertains to the statuses and social memberships which men hold, or seek to hold. But the problem is also political—political in that it is a reflection of the present location and distribution of power in society.

The two aspects, the social and the political, are inseparable. For, the allegiances and memberships of men, even the least significant, cannot be isolated from the larger systems of authority that prevail in a society or in any of its large social structures. Whether the dominant system of power is primarily religious, economic, or political in the usual sense is of less importance sociologically than the *way* in which the power reveals itself in practical operation and determines the smaller contexts of culture and association. Here we have reference to the degree of centralization, the remoteness, the impersonality of power, and to the concrete ways in which it becomes involved in human life.

We must begin with the role of the social group in present-day Western society, for it is in the basic associations of men that the real consequences of political power reveal themselves. But the present treatment of the group cannot really be divorced from political considerations, which will be dealt with . . . later . . .

Two

It has become commonplace, as we have seen, to refer to social disorganization and moral isolation in the present age. These terms are usually made to cover a diversity of conditions. But in a society as complex as ours it is unlikely that all aspects are undergoing a similar change. Thus it can scarcely be said that the State, as a distinguishable relationship among men, is today undergoing disorganization, for in most countries, including the United States, it is the political relationship that has been and is being enhanced above all other forms of connection among individuals. The contemporary State, with all its apparatus of bureaucracy, has become more powerful, more cohesive, and is endowed with more functions than at any time in its history.

Nor can the great impersonal relationships of the many private and semipublic organizations—educational, charitable, economic—be said to be experiencing any noticeable decline or disintegration. Large-scale labor organizations, political parties, welfare organizations, and corporate associations based upon property and exchange show a continued and even increasing prosperity, at least when measured in terms of institutional significance. It may be true that these organizations do not offer the degree of individual identification that makes for a deep sense of social cohesion, but disorganization is hardly the word for these immense and influential associations which govern the lives of tens of millions of people.

We must be no less wary of such terms as the 'lost,' 'isolated,' or 'unattached' individual. However widespread the contemporary ideology of alienation may be, it would be blindness to miss the fact that it flourishes amid an extraordinary variety of custodial and redemptive agencies. Probably never in all history have so many organizations, public and private, made the individual the center of bureaucratic and institutionalized regard. Quite apart from the innumerable agencies of private welfare, the whole tendency of modern political development has been to enhance the role of the political State as a direct relationship among individuals, and to bring both its powers and its services ever more intimately into the lives of human beings.

Where, then, are the dislocations and the deprivations that have driven so many men, in this age of economic abundance and political welfare, to the quest for community, to narcotic relief from the sense of isolation and anxiety? They lie in the realm of the small, primary, personal relationships of society—the relationships that mediate directly between man and his larger world of economic, moral, and political and religious values. Our problem may be ultimately concerned with all of these values and their greater or lesser accessibility to man, but it is, I think, primarily social: social in the exact sense of pertaining to the small areas of membership and association in which these values are ordinarily made meaningful and directive to men.

Behind the growing sense of isolation in society, behind the whole quest for community which infuses so many theoretical and practical areas of contemporary life and thought, lies the growing realization that the traditional primary relationships of men have become functionally irrelevant to our State and economy and meaningless to the moral aspirations of individuals. We are forced to the conclusion that a great deal of the peculiar character of contemporary social action comes from the efforts of men to find in large-scale organizations the values of status and security which were formerly gained in the primary associations of family, neighborhood, and church. This is the fact, I believe, that is as revealing of the source of many of our contemporary discontents as it is ominous when the related problems of political freedom and order are considered.

The problem, as I shall emphasize later . . . , is by no means restricted to the position of the traditional groups, nor is its solution in any way compatible with antiquarian revivals of groups and values no longer in accord with the requirements of the industrial and democratic age in which we live and to which we are unalterably committed. But the dislocation of the traditional groups must form our point of departure.

Historically, our problem must be seen in terms of the decline in functional and psychological significance of such groups as the family, the small local community, and the various other traditional relationships that have immemorially mediated between the individual and his society. These are the groups that have been morally decisive in the concrete lives of individuals. Other and more powerful forms of association have existed, but the major moral and psychological influences on the individual's life have emanated from the family and local community and the church. Within such groups have been engendered the primary types of identification: affection, friendship, prestige, recognition. And within them also have been engendered or intensified the principal incentives of work, love, prayer, and devotion to freedom and order.

This is the area of association from which the individual commonly gains his concept of the outer world and his sense of position in it. His concrete feelings of status and role, of protection and freedom, his differentiation between good and bad, between order and disorder and guilt and innocence, arise and are shaped largely by his relations within this realm of primary association. What was once called instinct or the social nature of man is but the product of this sphere of interpersonal relationships. It contains and cherishes not only the formal moral precept but what Whitehead has called 'our vast system of inherited symbolism.'

It can be seen that most contemporary themes of alienation have as their referents disruptions of attachment and states of mind which derive from this area of interpersonal relations. Feelings of moral estrangement, of the hostility of the world, the fear of freedom, of irrational aggressiveness, and of helplessness before the simplest of problems have to do commonly—as both the novelist and the psychiatrist testify—with the individual's sense of the inaccessibility of this area of relationship. In the child, or in the adult, the roots of a coherent, logical sense of the outer world are sunk deeply in the soil of close, meaningful interpersonal relations.

It is to this area of relations that the adjective 'disorganized' is most often flung by contemporary social scientists and moralists, and it is unquestionably in this area that most contemporary sensations of cultural dissolution arise. Yet the term disorganization is not an appropriate one and tends to divert attention from the basic problem of the social group in our culture. It has done much to fix attention on those largely irrelevant manifestations of delinquent behavior which are fairly constant in all ages and have little to do with our real problem.

The conception of social disorganization arose with the conservatives in France, who applied it empirically enough to the destruction of the guilds, the aristocracy, and the monasteries. But to Bonald and Comte the most fundamental sense of the term was moral. The Revolution signified to them the destruction of a vast moral order, and in their eyes the common manifestations of individual delinquency became suddenly invested with a new significance, the significance of social disorganization, itself the product of the Revolution. The term disorganization has been a persistent one in social science, and there is even now a deplorable tendency to use such terms as disintegration and disorganization where there is no demonstrable breakdown of a structure and no clear norm from which to calculate supposed deviations of conduct. The family and the community have been treated as disintegrating entities with no clear insight into what relationships are actually disintegrating. A vast amount of attention has been given to such phenomena as marital unhappiness, prostitution, juvenile misbehavior, and the sexual life of the unmarried, on the curious assumption that these are 'pathological' and derive clearly from the breakdown of the family.[1]

But in any intelligible sense of the word it is not disorganization that is crucial to the problem of the family or of any other significant social group in our society. The most fundamental problem has to do with the *organized* associations of men. It has to do with the role of the primary social group in an economy and political order whose principal ends have come to be structured in such a way that the primary social relationships are increasingly functionless, almost irrelevant, with respect to these ends. What is involved most deeply in our problem is the diminishing capacity of organized, traditional relationships for holding a position of moral and psychological centrality in the individual's life.

Three

Interpersonal relationships doubtless exist as abundantly in our age as in any other. But it is becoming apparent that for more and more people such relationships are morally empty and psychologically baffling. It is not simply that old relationships have waned in psychological influence; it is that new forms of primary relationships show, with rare exceptions, little evidence of offering even as much psychological and moral meaning for the individual as do the old ones. For more and more individuals the primary social relationships have lost much of their historic function of mediation between man and the larger ends of our civilization.

But the decline of effective meaning is itself a part of a more fundamental change in the role of such groups as the family and local community. At bottom social organization is a pattern of institutional functions into which are woven numerous psychological threads of meaning, loyalty, and interdependence. The contemporary sense of alienation is most directly perhaps a problem in symbols and meanings, but it is also a problem in the institutional functions of the relationships that ordinarily communicate integration and purpose to indivduals.

In any society the concrete loyalties and devotions of individuals tend to become directed toward the associations and patterns of leadership that in the long run have the greatest perceptible significance in the maintenance of life. It is never a crude relationship; intervening strata of ritual and other forms of crystallized meaning will exert a distinguishable influence on human thought.

But, at bottom, there is a close and vital connection between the effectiveness of the symbols that provide meaning in the individual's life and the institutional value of the social structures that are the immediate source of the symbols. The immediacy of the integrative meaning of the basic values contained in and communicated by the kinship or religious group will vary with the greater or less institutional value of the group to the individual *and to the other institutions in society.*

In earlier times, and even today in diminishing localities, there was an intimate relation between the local, kinship, and religious groups within which individuals consciously lived and the major economic, charitable, and protective functions which are indispensable to human existence. There was an intimate conjunction of larger institutional goals and the social groups small enough to infuse the individual's life with a sense of membership in society and the meaning of the basic moral values. For the overwhelming majority of people, until quite recently the structure of economic and political life rested upon, and even presupposed, the existence of the small social and local groups within which the cravings for psychological security and identification could be satisfied.

Family, church, local community drew and held the allegiances of individuals in earlier times not because of any superior impulses to love and protect, or because of any greater natural harmony of intellectual and spiritual values, or even because of any superior internal organization, but because these groups possessed a virtually indispensable relation to the economic and political order. The social problems of birth and death, courtship and marriage, employment and unemployment, infirmity and old age were met, however inadequately at times, through the associative means of these social groups. In consequence, a whole ideology, reflected in popular literature, custom, and morality, testified to the centrality of kinship and localism.

Our present crisis lies in the fact that whereas the small traditional associations, founded upon kinship, faith, or locality, are still expected to communicate to individuals the principal moral ends and psychological gratifications of society, they have manifestly become detached from positions of functional relevance to the larger economic and political decisions of our society. Family, local community, church, and the whole network of informal interpersonal relationships have ceased to play a determining role in our institutional systems of mutual aid, welfare, education, recreation, and economic production and distribution. Yet despite the loss of these manifest institutional functions, and the failure of most of these groups to develop any new institutional functions, we continue to expect them to perform adequately the implicit psychological or symbolic functions in the life of the individual.

Four

The general condition I am describing in Western society can be compared usefully with social changes taking place in many of the native cultures that have come under the impact of Western civilization. A large volume of anthropological work testifies to the incidence, in such areas as East Africa, India, China, and Burma, of processes of social dislocation and moral insecurity. A conflict of moral values is apparent. More particularly, it is a conflict, as J. S. Furnivall has said, 'between the eastern system resting on religion, personal authority, and customary obligation, and the western system resting on reason, impersonal law, and individual rights.' [2]

This conflict of principles and moral values is not an abstract thing, existing only in philosophical contemplation. It may indeed be a crisis of symbolism, of patterns of moral meaning, but more fundamentally it is a crisis of allegiances. It is a result, in very large part, of the increasing separation of traditional groups from the crucial ends and decisions in economic and political spheres. The wresting of economic significance from native clans, villages, and castes by new systems of industry, and the weakening of their effective social control through the establishment of new systems of administrative authority has had demonstrable moral effects. The revolutionary intellectual and moral ferment of the modern East is closely connected with the dislocation of traditional centers of authority and responsibility from the lives of the people.

The present position of caste in India is a striking case in point. During the past twenty-five or more centuries various efforts have been made by political and religious leaders to abolish or weaken this powerful association through techniques of force, political decree, or religious persuasion. Whether carried out by ancient religious prophets or by modern Christian missionaries, the majority of such efforts have been designed to change the religious or moral *meaning* of caste in the minds of its followers. But such efforts generally have been fruitless. Even attempts to convert the untouchables to Christianity, to wean them away from the caste system of which they have been so horribly the victims, have been for the most part without success. The conversion of many millions to the Muslim creed led only to the creation of new castes.

But at the present time in widening areas of India there is a conspicuous weakening of the whole caste system, among the prosperous as well as among the poverty-stricken. Why, after many centuries of tenacious persistence, has the massive system of caste suddenly begun to dissolve in many areas of India?

The answer comes from the fact of the increasing dislocation of caste *functions*—in law, charity, authority, education, and economic production. The creation of civil courts for the adjudication of disputes traditionally handled by caste *panchayats;* the growing assumption by the State and by many private agencies of mutual-aid activities formerly resident in the caste or subcaste; the rising popularity of the idea that the proper structure of education is the formal school or university, organized in Western terms; and the intrusion of the new systems of constraint and function in the factory and trade union—all of these represent new and competing values, and they represent, more significantly, new systems of *fuction* and *allegiance*.

When the major institutional functions have disappeared from a local village government or from a subcaste, the conditions are laid for the decline of the individual's allegiance to the older forms of organization. Failing to find any institutional substance in the old unities of social life, he is prone to withdraw, consciously or unconsciously, his loyalty to them. They no longer represent the prime moral experiences of his life. He finds himself, mentally, looking in new directions.

Some of the most extreme instances of insecurity and conflict of values in native cultures have resulted not from the nakedly ruthless forces of economic exploitation but from most commendable (by Western standards) acts of humanitarian reform. Thus the introduction of so physically salutary a measure as an irrigation district or medical service may be attended by all the promised gains in abundance and health, but such innovations can also bring about the most complex disruptions of social relationships and allegiances. Why? Because such systems, by the very *humaneness* of their functions, assume values that no purely exploitative agency can, and having become values they more easily serve to alienate the native from his devotion to the meanings associated with obsolete functional structures. The new technology means the creation of new centers of administrative authority which not infrequently nullify the prestige of village or caste groups, leading in time to a growing conflict between the moral meaning of the old areas of authority and the values associated with the new.

The beginnings of the welfare State in India, for example, along with the creation of new private agencies of educational, charitable, and religious activity, have led inevitably to the pre-emption of functions formerly resident (in however meager or debased manner) in the kinship and caste groups. It is irrelevant, for present purposes, that many of these pre-emptions have been responsible for physical improvement in the life of the people. What must be emphasized here are the social and moral effects irrespective of intent—whether accomplished by predatory mining and factory interests or by the liberal humanitarian. What is crucial is the invasion of the area of traditional function by new and often more efficient functional agencies—in charity, law, education, and economics. The consequence is a profound crisis in meanings and loyalties.

It is no part of my intent to offer these observations in any spirit of lament for the old. It is an evident conclusion that for technical as well as moral reasons much of the old order is inadequate to the demand constituted by population density and other factors. It is important to insist, however, that the solution by new administrative measures of technical and material problems does not carry with it any automatic answer to the social and moral difficulties created by the invasion of ancient areas of function. For all their humanitarian sentiments, a large number of native reformers, as well as Western, have been singularly insensitive to the moral problems created in such countries as China and India by the advent of Western techniques. The displacement of function must lead in the long run to the diminution of moral significance in the old; and this means the loss of accustomed centers of allegiance, belief, and incentive. Hence the widely observed spectacle of masses of 'marginal' personalities in native cultures, of individuals adrift, encompassed by, but not belonging to, either the old or the new. New associations have arisen and continue to arise, but their functional value is still but dimly manifest for the greater number of people, and their moral and psychological appeal is correspondingly weak. Hence the profound appeal of what the great Indian philosopher, Tagore, called 'the powerful anesthetic of nationalism.' Hence also the appeal, among a significant minority of intellectuals, of communism, which makes central the ethos of organization and combines it with therapeutic properties of concerted action.

What is to be observed so vividly in many areas of the East is also, and has been, for some time, a notable characteristic of Western society. The process is less striking, less dramatic, for we are directly involved in it. But it is nonetheless a profoundly significant aspect of modern Western history and it arises from some of the same elements in Western culture which, when exported, have caused such dislocation and ferment in foreign areas. We too have suffered a decline in the institutional function of groups and associations upon which we have long depended for moral and psychological stability. We too are in a state that can, most optimistically, be called transition—of change from associative contexts that have become in so many places irrelevant and anachronistic to newer associative contexts that are still psychologically and morally dim to the perceptions of individuals. As a result of the sharp reduction in meaning formerly inherent in membership, the problems of status, adjustment, and moral direction have assumed tremendous importance in the East as well as the West.

Five

Nowhere is the concern with the problem of community in Western society more intense than with respect to the family.[3] The contemporary family, as countless books, articles, college courses, and marital clinics make plain, has become an obsessive problem. The family inspires a curious dualism of thought. We tend to regard it uneasily as a final manifestation of tribal society, somehow inappropriate to a democratic, industrial age, but, at the same time, we have become ever more aware of its possibilities as an instrument of social reconstruction.

The intensity of theoretical interest in the family has curiously enough risen in direct proportion to the decline of the family's basic institutional importance to our culture. The present 'problem' of the family is dramatized by the fact that its abstract importance to the moralist or psychologist has grown all the while that its tangible institutional significance to the layman and its functional importance to economy and State have diminished.

It is doubtless one more manifestation of the contemporary quest for security that students of the family increasingly see its main 'function' to be that of conferring 'adjustment' upon the individual, and, for the most part, they find no difficulty at all in supposing that this psychological function can be carried on by the family in what is otherwise a functional vacuum. Contemporary social psychology has become so single-mindedly aware of the psychological gratification provided by the group for individual needs of security and recognition that there is an increasing tendency to suppose that such a function is primary and can maintain itself autonomously, impervious to changes in *institutional* functions which normally give a group importance in culture. For many reasons the contemporary family is made to carry a conscious symbolic importance that is greater than ever, but it must do this with a structure much smaller in size and of manifestly diminishing relevance to the larger economic, religious, and political ends of contemporary society.

Historically the family's importance has come from the fact of intimate social cohesion united with institutional significance in society, not from its sex or blood relationships. In earlier ages, kinship was inextricably involved in the processes of getting a living, providing education, supporting the infirm, caring for the aged, and maintaining religious values. In vast rural areas, until quite recently, the family was the actual agency of economic production, distribution, and consumption. Even in towns and cities, the family long retained its close relation to these obviously crucial activities. Organized living was simply inconceivable, for the most part, outside of the context provided by kinship. Few individuals were either too young or too old to find a place of importance within the group, a fact which enhanced immeasurably the family's capacity for winning allegiance and providing symbolic integration for the individual.

The interpersonal and psychological aspects of kinship were never made to rest upon personal romance alone or even upon pure standards of individual rectitude. Doubtless, deviations from the moral code and disillusionment with romance were as common then as now. But they did not interfere with the cultural significance of the family simply because the family was far more than an interpersonal relationship based upon affection and moral probity. It was an indispensable institution.

But in ever enlarging areas of population in modern times, the economic, legal, educational, religious, and recreational functions of the family have declined or diminished. Politically, membership in the family is superfluous; economically, it is regarded by many as an outright hindrance to success. The family, as someone has put it, is now the accident of the worker rather than his essence. His competitive position may be more favorable without it. Our systems of law and education and all the manifold recreational activities of individuals engaged in their pursuit of happiness have come to rest upon, and to be directed to, the individual, not the family. On all sides we continue to celebrate from pulpit and rostrum the indispensability to economy and the State of the family. But, in plain fact, the family is indispensable to neither of these at the present time. The major processes of economy and political administration have become increasingly independent of the symbolism and integrative activities of kinship.

There is an optimistic apologetics that sees in this waning of the family's institutional importance only the beneficent hand of Progress. We are told by certain psychologists and sociologists that, with its loss of economic and legal functions, the family has been freed of all that is basically irrelevant to its 'real' nature; that the true function of the family—the cultivation of affection, the shaping of personality, above all, the manufacture of 'adjustment'—is now in a position to flourish illimitably, to the greater glory of man and society. In a highly popular statement, we are told that the family has progressed from institution to companionship.

But, as Ortega y Gasset has written, 'people do not live together merely to be together. They live together to do something together.' To suppose that the present family, or any other group, can perpetually vitalize itself through some indwelling affectional tie, in the absence of concrete, perceived functions,

is like supposing that the comradely ties of mutual aid which grow up incidentally in a military unit will long outlast a condition in which war is plainly
and irrevocably banished. Applied to the family, the argument suggests that
affection and personality cultivation can somehow exist in a social vacuum, un-
supported by the determining goals and ideals of economic and political society.
But in hard fact no social group will long survive the disappearance of its
chief reasons for being, and these reasons are not, primarily, biological but
institutional. Unless new institutional functions are performed by a group—
family, trade union, or church—its psychological influence will become minimal.

No amount of veneration for the psychological functions of a social group,
for the capacity of the group to gratify cravings for security and recognition,
will offset the fact that, however important these functions may be in any given
individual's life, he does not join the group essentially for them. He joins the
group if and when its larger institutional or intellectual functions have relevance
both to his own life organization and to what he can see of the group's relation
to the larger society. The individual may indeed derive vast psychic support and
integration from the pure fact of group membership, but he will not long
derive this when he becomes in some way aware of the gulf between the moral
claims of a group and its actual institutional importance in the social order.

All of this has special relevance to the family, with its major function now
generally reduced by psychologists to that of conferring adjustment upon
individuals. Yet in any objective view the family is probably now less effective
in this regard than it has ever been. It is plain that the family is no longer the
main object of personal loyalty in ever larger sections of our population, and
it is an overstrain on the imagination to suppose that it will regain a position of
psychological importance through pamphlets, clinics, and high-school courses
on courtship and marriage. How quaint now seems that whole literature on
sexual adjustment in marriage with its implicit argument that sexual incompatibility is the basic cause of the reduced significance of marriage. Some of
the solemn preoccupations with 'family tensions' which now hold the field of
clinical practice will one day no doubt seem equally quaint.

The current problem of the family, like the problem of any social group,
cannot be reduced to simple sets of psychological complexes which exist universally in man's nature, or to an ignorance of sexual techniques, or to a lack
of Christian morality. The family is a major problem in our culture simply
because we are attempting to make it perform psychological and symbolic
functions with a structure that has become fragile and an institutional importance that is almost totally unrelated to the economic and political realities of
our society. Moreover, the growing impersonality and the accumulating demands
of ever larger sections of our world of business and government tend to throw
an extraordinary psychological strain upon the family. In this now small and
fragile group we seek the security and affection denied everywhere else. It is
hardly strange that timeless incompatabilities and emotional strains should, in
the present age, assume an unwonted importance—their *meaning* has changed
with respect to the larger context of men's lives. We thus find ourselves increasingly in the position of attempting to correct, through psychiatric or spiritual

techniques, problems which, although assuredly emotional, derive basically from a set of historically given institutional circumstances.

Personal crises, underlying emotional dissatisfactions, individual deviations from strict rectitude—these have presumably been constant in all ages of history. Only our own age tends to blow up these tensions into reasons for a clinical approach to happiness. Such tensions appear more critical and painful, more intolerable to contemporary man, simply because the containing social structures of such tensions have become less vital to his existence. The social structures are expendable so far as the broad economic and political processes of our society are concerned and, consequently, they offer less support for particular emotional states. Not a few of the problems that give special concern to our present society—sex role, courtship and marriage, old age, the position of the child—do so because of the modified functional and psychological position of the family in our culture.

The widely publicized problems of the modern middleclass woman do not result, as certain Freudians have seemed to suggest, from a disharmony between her innate psychological character and the present values of feminism. Whatever may be the neurological nature of the female, as compared with that of the male, the special and distinctive problem of the woman in our culture arises from certain changes in social function and conceptualized role. What has been called women's emancipation from patriarchalism is, in a highly relevant sense, an emancipation from clear, socially approved function and role within the institutionalized family group. To put it in these terms does not lessen the intensity of the problem in many quarters, but it takes it out of the vague realm of supposed innate complexes and places it within the determinable context of historical changes in social position. It puts the psychological problems of women in exactly the same context in which lie contemporary problems of the role of the father and the child. The former problems may be more intense, more explicit, but they do not differ in kind from those besetting the existences of other members of the family.

The oftentimes absurd worship of the female, especially the mother, in contemporary American society, has frequently been interpreted by ardent feminists as a reflection of her recent rise to eminence after centuries of subordination to the male. But it reflects rather an unconscious overcompensation for the historical fact of her release from any clear and indispensable *social role* within the family.[4] And this is a part of the historical change in the function to society of the whole family group.

The sharp discrepancy between the family's actual contributions to present political and economic order and the set of spiritual images inherited from the past intensifies the problem of definition of sex role. From this basic discrepancy proceed all the elaborate, and frequently self-defeating, techniques of the 'rational' cultivation of the family tie, the stunting dosages of scientific mother-love for the child, and the staggering number of clinics, conferences, lectures, pamphlets, and books on the subject of relations between parent and child, between husband and wife. It is this riot of rational techniques that has led to the bland and unexamined assumption that the family is today a more 'affectionate' organization than it was a century ago.

In our society most of the period of storm and stress that is adolescence has little to do with the biological changes the child is undergoing. It has almost everything to do with the problem of role in the family and the clarity of the family's relation to society. In all past ages, and in many contemporary societies today, the development of the child into manhood or womanhood is attended, if not by actual lengthy and intense ceremonial rites, by relatively clear communications of value and purpose. And these have been possible only when there have been concrete institutional functions to symbolize and hence communicate. Today adolescence is the period, we are justified in saying, when the appalling discrepancy between shadow and substance in contemporary kinship first becomes evident to the child. It is then, in a profound if largely unconscious way, that he becomes aware of the gulf between inherited authority patterns and the actual functional contribution of the family. For in any group it is only the latter that can give effective meaning to the former.

Far more tragic in our culture is the position in which more and more of the aged find themselves. To interpret the present problem of old age as the consequence of living in a 'youth-dominated' society is somewhat deceptive. All periods of culture have been characterized by great rewards for the young military leader, statesman, merchant, and writer. The age of some of the most distinguished members in the long history of Parliament in England is a case in point, and we may suppose that the brilliant young Pitt would find it far more difficult today to lead the House of Representatives in supposedly youth-dominated America than he did Parliament in eighteenth-century England. Conversely there is no clear evidence to indicate that the proportion of the aged who are now prominent in business, professions, and government is any smaller than in earlier times.

Since Cicero's *De Senectute* there has probably never been a period in which men have not faced the onset of old age with the feeling that its consolations must be compensatorily set down in writing in order to lessen the pathos of their enforced separation from previous activities. Today it is not the separation from wonted activities that is so painfully manifested in thought and behavior but the widening sense of alienation from family and society, a sense of alienation that is reflected not only in the staggering increase of the so-called senile neuroses and psychoses but in the old-age political movements.

In many instances the root causes are plainly economic, but the contemporary incidence of economic problems of the aged must itself be seen in relation to changes in social structure. To leave out of present consideration those whose position is purely the result of financial strain, there is obviously a growing number of elderly people whose estrangement comes from the altered social status and psychological role in which they find themselves. It is not always that they find themselves physically outside of a family group. In the most pathetic manifestations of this problem it is that such people find themselves *in* but not *of* the group. The change in the structure of the family has led to a change in the significance of individual members, especially of the aged.

The fantastic romanticism that now surrounds courtship and marriage in our culture is drawn in part no doubt from larger contexts of romanticism in modern history and is efficiently supported by the discovery of modern retail business that the mass-advertised fact of romance is good for sales. But the lushness of such advertising obviously depends on a previously fertilized soil, and this soil may be seen in large part as the consequence of changes in the relation of the family to the other aspects of the social order. The diminution in the functional significance of the family has been attended by efforts to compensate in the affectional realm of intensified romance. Probably no other age in history has so completely identified (confused, some might say) marriage and romance as has our own. The claim that cultivation of affection is the one remaining serious function of the family is ironically supported by the stupefying amount of effort put into the calculated cultivation of romance, both direct and vicarious. Whether this has made contemporary marriage a more affectionate and devoted relationship is a controversy we need not enter here.

The social roles of adolescence, old age, and affection have been profoundly altered by changes in the functional positions of the members of the family. Such states are *perceived* differently, both by the individuals immediately concerned and by others around them. So are the recurrent 'crises' of personal life —birth, marriage, and death—regarded differently as a consequence of changes in the structure and functions of the family. Except from the point of view of the biologist, death, for example, is not the same phenomenon from one society to another, from one age to another. Death also has its social role, and this role is inseparable from the organization of values and relationships within which the physical fact of death takes place. Death almost everywhere is ritualized, ritualized for the sake of the deceased, if we like, but far more importantly for the sake of those who are left behind. Such ritualization has immensely important psychological functions in the direction of emotional release for the individuals most closely related to the dead person and in the direction, too, of the whole social group. But these death rites are not disembodied acts of obeisance or succor; they are manifestations of group life and function. They are closely related, that is, to other aspects of the family which have no immediate connection with the fact of death.

In our society we find ourselves increasingly baffled and psychologically unprepared for the incidence of death among loved ones. It is not that grief is greater or that the incomprehensibility of death is increased. It is in considerable part perhaps because the smaller structure of the family gives inevitably a greater emotional value to each of the members. But, more than this, it is the result, I believe, of the decline in significance of the traditional means of ritual *completion* of the fact of death. Death leaves a kind of moral suspense that is terminated psychologically only with greater and greater difficulty. The social *meaning* of death has changed with the social *position* of death.

Six

The problems arising from the diminished institutional and psychological importance of the family in our society also extend into wider areas of social and economic behavior. We find ourselves dealing increasingly with difficulties that seem to resolve themselves into matters of human motivation and incentives. An older economics and politics and educational theory took it for granted that all the root impulses to buying and selling and saving, to voting, and to learning lay, in prepotent form, in the individual himself. The relation between crucial economic motivations and the social groups in which individuals actually lived was seldom if ever heeded by the classical economists.

The late Harvard economist, Joseph Schumpeter, wrote tellingly on this point. 'In order to realize what all this means for the efficiency of the capitalist engine of production we need only recall that the family and the family home used to be the mainspring of the typically bourgeois kind of profit motive. Economists have not always given due weight to this fact. When we look more closely at their idea of the self-interest of entrepreneurs and capitalists we cannot fail to discover that the results it was supposed to produce are really not at all what one would expect from the rational self-interest of the detached individual or the childless couple who no longer look at the world through the windows of a family home. Consciously or unconsciously, they analyzed the behavior of the man whose motives are shaped by such a home and who means to work and save primarily for wife *and children*. As soon as these fade out from the moral vision of the business man, we have a different kind of *homo economicus* before us who cares for different things and acts in different ways.' [5]

Much of the predictability of human response, which the classical economists made the basis of their faith in the automatic workings of the free market, came not from fixed instincts but from the vast conservatism and stability of a society that remanied deeply rooted in kinship long after the advent of the capitalist age. Had it not been for the profound incentives supplied by the family and, equally important, the capacity of the extended family to supply a degree, however minimal, of mutual aid in time of distress, it is a fair guess that capitalism would have failed before it was well under way. The extraordinary rate of capital accumulation in the nineteenth century was dependent, to some extent at least, on a low-wage structure that was in turn dependent on the continuation of the ethic of family aid, even when this involved child labor in the factories. [6]

The same point may be made with respect to the relation of kinship symbolism and population increase. What Malthus and his followers regarded as embedded in the biological nature of man, the almost limitless urge to procreate, has turned out to be inseparable from the cultural fact of kinship, with its inherited incentives and values. As long as the family had institutional importance in society, it tended to maintain moral and psychological devotions which resulted in high birth rates—rates that invited the alarm of a good many sociologists. But with the decline in both the functional and psychological importance of kinship, and with the emergence of a culture based increasingly on the abstract individual rather than the family, there has resulted a quite different birth rate and a quite different set of population problems.

To be sure we are dealing here, in this matter of motivations and incentives, not merely with the effects of the changed significance of the family but with those of the changed significance of other social cohesions upon which our economy and political order depended for a long period of time. What has happened to the family has happened also to neighborhood and local community. As Robert S. Lynd has written: 'Neighborhood and community ties are not only optional but generally growing less strong; and along with them is disappearing the important network of intimate, informal, social controls traditionally associated with living closely with others.' [7] Within all of these lay not merely controls but the incentives that supplied the motive force for such pursuits as education and religion and recreation.

The point is that with the decline in the significance of kinship and locality, and the failure of new social relationships to assume influences of equivalent evocative intensity, a profound change has occurred in the very psychological structure of society. And this is a change that has produced a great deal of the present problem of incentives in so many areas of our society. Most of our ideas and practices in the major institutional areas of society developed during an age when the residual psychological elements of social organization seemed imperishable. No less imperishable seemed the structure of personality itself. Educational goals and political objectives were fashioned accordingly, as were theories of economic behavior and population increase.

But we are learning that many of the motivations and incentives which an older generation of rationalists believed were inherent in the individual are actually supplied by social groups—social groups with both functional and moral relevance to the lives of individuals.

Modern planners thus frequently find themselves dealing, not simply with the upper stratum of decisions, which their forebears assumed would be the sole demand of a planned society, but with often baffling problems which reach down into the very recesses of human personality. [8]

Seven

Basically, however, it is not the position of the family or of any other single group, old or new, that is crucial to the welfare of a social order. Associations may come and go under the impact of historical changes and cultural needs. There is no single type of family, any more than there is a single type of religion, that is essential to personal security and collective prosperity. It would be wrong to assume that the present problem of community in Western society arises inexorably from the modifications which have taken place in old groups, however cherished these may be. But irrespective of particular groups, there must be in any stable culture, in any civilization that prizes its integrity, functionally significant and psychologically meaningful groups and associations lying intermediate to the individual and the larger values and purposes of his society. For these are the small areas of association within which alone such values and purposes can take on clear meaning in personal life and become the vital roots of the large culture. It is, I believe, the problem of intermediate association that is fundamental at the present time.

Under the lulling influence of the idea of Progress we have generally assumed until recently that history automatically provides its own solution to the basic problems of organization in society. We have further assumed that man is ineradicably gregarious and that from this gregariousness must come ever new and relevant forms of intermediate association.

It is tempting to believe this as we survey the innumerable formal organizations of modern life, the proliferation of which has been one of the signal facts in American history, or as we observe the incredible number of personal contacts which take place daily in the congested areas of modern urban life.

But there is a profound difference between the casual, informal relationships which abound in such areas and the kind of social groups which create a sense of belonging, which supply incentive, and which confer upon the individual a sense of status. Moreover, from some highly suggestive evidence supplied by such sociologists as Warner, Lazarsfeld, and especially Mirra Komarovsky, we can justly doubt that all sections of modern populations are as rich in identifiable social groups and associations as we have heretofore taken for granted.

The common assumption that, as the older associations of kinship and neighborhood have become weakened, they are replaced by new voluntary associations filling the same role is not above sharp question. That traditional groups have weakened in significance is apparently true enough but, on the evidence, their place has not been taken to any appreciable extent by new forms of association. Despite the appeal of the older sociological stereotype of the urban dweller who belongs to various voluntary associations, all of which have progressively replaced the older social unities, the facts so far gathered suggest the contrary: that a rising number of individuals belong to no organized association at all, and that, in the large cities, the unaffiliated persons may even constitute a majority of the population.[9]

As for the psychological functions of the great formal associations in modern life—industrial corporations, governmental agencies, large-scale labor and charitable organizations—it is plain that not many of these answer adequately the contemporary quest for community. Such organizations, as Max Weber pointed out, are generally organized not around personal loyalties but around loyalty to an office or machine. The admininstration of charity, hospitalization, unemployment assistance, like the administration of the huge manufacturing corporation, may be more efficient and less given to material inequities, but the possible gains in technical efficiency do not minimize their underlying impersonality in the life of the individual.

Much of the contemporary sense of the impersonality of society comes from the rational impersonality of these great organizations. The widespread reaction against technology, the city, and political freedom, not to mention the nostalgia that pervades so many of the discussions of rural-urban differences, comes from the diminished functional relationship between existent social groups in industry or the community and the remote efficiency of the larger organizations created by modern planners. The derivative loss of meaning for the individual frequently becomes the moral background of vague and impotent reactions against technology and science, and of aggressive states of mind against the culture as a whole. In spatial terms the individual is obviously less isolated from his fellows in the large-scale housing project or in the factory than was his grandfather. What he has become isolated from is the sense of meaningful proximity to the major ends and purposes of his culture. With the relatively complete satisfaction of needs concerned with food, employment, and housing, a different order of needs begins to assert itself imperiously; and these have to do with spiritual belief and social status.

'The uneasiness, the malaise of our time,' writes C. Wright Mills, 'is due to this root fact: in our politics and economy, in family life and religion—in practically every sphere of our existence—the certainties of the eighteenth and nineteenth centuries have disintegrated or been destroyed and, at the same time, no new sanctions or justifications for the new routines we live, and must live, have taken hold. . . . Among white-collar people, the malaise is deep-rooted; for the absence of any order of belief has left them morally defenseless as individuals and politically impotent as a group. Newly created in a harsh time of creation, white-collar man has no culture to lean upon except the contents of a mass society that has shaped him and seeks to manipulate him to its alien ends. For security's sake he must attach himself somewhere, but no communities or organizations seem to be thoroughly his.' [10]

The quest for community will not be denied, for it springs from some of the powerful needs of human nature—needs for a clear sense of cultural purpose, membership, status, and continuity. Without these, no amount of mere material welfare will serve to arrest the developing sense of alienation in our society and the mounting preoccupation with the imperatives of community. To appeal to technological progress is futile. For what we discover is that rising standards of living, together with increases in leisure, actually intensify the disquietude and frustration that arise when cherished and proffered goals are without available means of fulfillment. 'Secular improvement that is taken for granted,' wrote Joseph Schumpeter, 'and coupled with individual insecurity that is acutely resented is of course the best recipe for breeding social unrest.' [11]

The loss of old moral certainties and accustomed statuses is, however, only the setting of our problem. For, despite the enormous influence of nostalgia in human thinking, it is never the recovery of the institutionally old that is desired by most people. In any event, the quest for the past is as futile as is that of the future.

The real problem is not, then, the loss of old contexts but rather the failure of our present democratic and industrial scene to create new contexts of association and moral cohesion within which the smaller allegiances of men will assume both functional and psychological significance. It is almost as if the forces that weakened the old have remained to obstruct the new channels of association.

What is the source of this failure? The blame is usually laid to technology, science, and the city. These, it is said, have left a vacuum. But the attack on these elements of modern culture is ill-founded, for no one of these is either logically or psychologically essential to the problem at hand. Neither science, nor technology, nor the city is inherently incompatible with the existence of moral values and social relationships which will do for modern man what the extended family, the parish, and the village did for earlier man.

Here, our problem becomes inevitably historical. For the present position of the social group in political and industrial society cannot be understood apart from certain historical tendencies concerned with the location of authority and function in society and with certain momentous conflicts of authority and function which have been fundamental in the development of the modern State.

NOTES

[1] This approach is, happily, less common now than a generation ago. The writings of such men as R. M. MacIver, Talcott Parsons, Kingsley Davis, and Howard Becker, among others, have done much to place the study of the family in a more coherent perspective.

[2] *Colonial Policy and Practice* (Cambridge University Press, 1948), p. 3.

[3] There is a kind of historical awareness implicit in this focusing upon the family, for the overwhelming majority of communal or sacred areas of society reflect the transfer, historically, of kinship symbols and nomenclature to non-kinship spheres. We see this in the histories of religion, guilds, village communities, and labor unions. Kinship has ever been the archetype of man's communal aspirations.

[4] Margaret Redfield has pointed out that 'Mother's Day, originally promoted by the florists, and still a source of profit to them, has its whole point in an organization of society in which parents and children lose touch with one another.' "The American Family: Consensus and Freedom," *The American Journal of Sociology* (November 1946).

[5] *Capitalism, Socialism, and Democracy* (New York, 1942), p. 160.

[6] E. H. Norman, in his *Japan's Emergence as a Modern State* (Institute of Pacific Relations, 1940), p. 153, has pointed out the value of the extended family in Japan in making possible a relatively low-wage structure and, derivatively, greater profits and capital expansion.

[7] *Knowledge For What?* (Princeton University Press, 1939), p. 83.

[8] Throughout modern economic society the problem of incentives has become explicit. Both business and governmental planners find themselves with difficulties which, although economic in nature, begin in a structure of motivations that is non-economic. The almost total absence in earlier economic thought, socialist as well as orthodox, of concern for the problem of incentives is some indication of the changes that have taken place in the institutional framework and psychological substructure of capitalism.

[9] This paragraph is a paraphrase of Mirra Komarovsky's penetrating study, "The Voluntary Associations of Urban Dwellers," *American Sociological Review* (December 1946).

[10] *White Collar: The American Middle Classes* (New York, 1951), p. xvi.

[11] *Op. cit.,* p. 145

14. THE SOCIAL STRUCTURE AND POLITICAL PROCESS OF SUBURBIA *

Scott Greer

Three aspects of suburban society are emphasized in the recent literature: the demographic characteristics of the population, the associational structure, and the political structure. Suburban population tends to be more middle-class, ethnic, and family-centered than that of the central city; in the suburb the neighborhood and perhaps the local community are more important *loci* of association than in the city; and suburbia characteristically has smaller governmental units than the cities, and has more of them.

General theory is hazy, unarticulated, and incomplete with respect to the manner in which these three aspects of suburban society are related. Those committed to each approach neglect the others, or assume a non-existent integration. Duncan and Reiss, who emphasize differences in population composition, accept political boundaries as meaningful for their analyses.[1] Those who are more concerned with ecological processes derive demographic differences from ecological position and the economic dependence of suburbs upon the central city, paying little attention to the political structures which contain and define their data.[2] On the other hand, Robert Wood's recent treatment of suburban political structure emphasizes the political form of the municipality in the suburbs as a determinant for both recruitment to suburbia and the staying power of the suburban governmental enclaves.[3] Wood does not, however, explore the interrelations between political structure and the variables emphasized by the demographers and ecologists; again, a "loose fit" is assumed. Finally, recent work by Bell postulates a "quest for community" which implies that associational structure is a major selective factor in migration to suburbia and a stabilizing factor in the suburban trend, but one which cannot be subsumed under the "housing market" or the "political climate" of suburbia.[4]

In this paper an effort is made to integrate and order these three aspects of suburbia and to develop a systematic theory of the relationships among population type, associational patterns, communication system, and political structure congruent with the present state of research findings and capable of further test and evaluation. The paper emphasizes the organizational level of analysis, and concentrates upon the explanation of the immediate organizational structure—that is, the spatially defined group as it exists in the suburbs.

This strategy differs from several current and traditional approaches. It does

* An expanded and revised version of a paper read at the annual meeting of the American Sociological Association, September, 1959. I wish to thank, for their critical reading and creative suggestions, Aaron Cicourel and Harold Guetzkow of Northwestern University, and Wendell Bell of the University of California, Los Angeles.

SOURCE: *American Sociological Review* (August, 1960), pp. 514–526. Reprinted by permission of the author and the American Sociological Association.

251

not move directly from the most general levels of societal structure to the observables (ordinarily the person-to-person relationship) or *vice versa,* as is common in the work of Durkheim, Parsons, Riesman, Weber, and other analysts of large-scale society.[5] Nor does this approach assume away the nature of interaction, as in much work by contemporary ecologists.[6] Both general theory and ecology are "macroscopic" approaches which emphasize the congruity and interdependence of social trends at a high level of abstraction. If, however, one takes seriously the intermediate-level constructs implied by these approaches—social class, bureaucracy, and occupational strata—one finds striking anomalies when studying the local community. Thus suburbanites, disproportionately made up of white-collar bureaucrats (the "organization men" and the "other directed"), are precisely the people who cling most fiercely to the autonomy of the small municipalities when merger with the central city is in question. Their involvement in large-scale organizational systems does not determine their behavior in the community. In view of the viability or staying power of the suburban communities, one must ask: To what extent is this behavior appropriate to occupational scenes transferred, if at all, to the residential area? To raise this question is to require that the relevant area of social action, the residential community itself, be approached with a conceptual scheme appropriate to its own characteristics as a field for social action.

Thus, the strategy adopted here is to move from the macro-level, using census data for an aggregate description, but spelling out the steps by which one reaches the micro-level of household organization. This procedure provides a method of analyzing the social structure of the suburb—neighborhood, local residential community, and municipality. Such an approach then leads back to the macro-level. Indexes based upon census data, however, now become measures of conditions under which spatially defined social groups become probable.[7]

POPULATION TYPE AND LIFE STYLE

The transformation of a predominantly agricultural and rural nation into an increasingly metropolitan nation may be summarized as an increase in societal scale. Many sequences of change are fundamental causes of this process and many secondary changes ensue.[8] For present purposes, changes in the kind of *differentia* which cut across the societal unit are emphasized. Occupation, for example, is a rather unimportant differentiator within small-scale society, and ethnic variations are usually absent. In modern cities, however, nothing is more impressive than the differences in culture, life chances, deference, and power associated with variations in occupation and ethnic identity.

A third dimension emphasized here is urbanism, or life style. By urbanism we refer to the life-ways of sub-segments which have become differentiated on a continuum ranging from a familistic to an extremely urban mode of life.[9] Such a continuum first emerged from the analysis of census tract populations, and the indexes developed to measure it apply to such aggregates.[10] Toward the urban end of the continuum are neighborhoods of apartment houses with single persons, childless couples, and one-child families predominating; toward the other end are single-family dwelling units inhabited by families with several children, in which the woman, not a member of the labor force, plays the role of wife and mother. This definition of urbanism, emphasizing household organization and its consequences, excludes much that is usually encompassed in the term, but this limited meaning appears to be especially relevant to the present analysis of spatially defined groups in the metropolis.

The familistic type of neighborhood approximates, of course, the typical image of suburbia. Although suburbs have no monopoly of such populations, they tend to be more consistently inhabited by familistic households than any other part of the urban agglomeration. One important reason for such concentration lies in the demand and supply of sites for family living. Studies of suburban residents indicate the high evaluation they place on the physical and social facilities for child-rearing and home-making, including the prerequiste for this life, private space, indoors and out. The site demanded is one which allows for the play of children in safe and "pleasant" places, space for growing flowers, vegetables, and grass, for keeping pets, for patio exercise, and the like.[11] With the existing patterns of land allocation in urban regions, however, a large area per person is available at moderate price only on the outskirts of the built-up districts. To be sure, the relationship between demand and supply is far from perfect; as Schnore implies, many persons might settle for equivalent lodgings in the middle of the city.[12] But the point is moot—until new, single-family dwellings, rather than high-rise public housing developments, replace the tenements and row-houses near the centers, we will not know how many "suburbanites" are fleeing the city and how many are forced to move outward because no other acceptable housing is available. Meanwhile, the family-oriented population continues to seek and find its sites on the growing edge of the city.

The local associational structure of a population can be derived from such sociological characteristics as family-orientation, for contiguity indicates the likelihood of contact, homogeneity indicates the likelihood of similar interests, and population type indicates the specific content which may plausibly be inferred for those interests.[13] Thus the use of indexes which aggregate persons by geographical sub-areas implies contiguity and the relative homogeneity of the residential neighborhood. Specifically, the urbanism index developed by Shevky and Bell as a measure of average life-style yields social attributes of the geographically defined subpopulation, hypothesized here as crucial for spatially-based social interaction.[14] The less urban and more familistic the neighborhood, the more important is the dwelling unit as a site for everyday life, and for a particular kind of life.

The type and rate of interaction, however, is not specified in detail by this set of statements. All that is proposed, at this point in the argument, is that spatially defined interaction is related to the familistic character of the suburban population. In order to translate such interaction into social structure and political process, it is necessary to relate the gross variations in population type to a theory of spatially defined organization.

THE ORGANIZATIONAL STRUCTURE
OF THE SUBURBS

The bifurcation of work and residence is sometimes taken as one of the defining characteristics of the suburban population.[15] But this bifurcation holds for most of the population in a metropolis; any local residential area is segmental in nature. Because a living area is the site for some, but not all, of the basic social activities of its residents, Janowitz calls it the "community of limited liability." [16] Such a community, however, encompasses some very crucial structures and therefore has constraining force—which allows the social scientist some predictive and explanatory power.

The definition of social organization used in the present discussion emphasizes functional interdependence. As the unit of analysis, we shall emphasize the spatially defined group. The locality group, or community, is thus viewed as a special case of the social form elsewhere defined as "an aggregate in a state of functional interdependence, from which emerges a flow of communication and a consequent ordering of behavior." [17]

Geographical contiguity, however, has no self-evident sociological meaning. It may become the basis for interdependence only when it constitutes a field for social action. We consider below three such fields, concentric in scope: the neighborhood, the local residential community, and the municipality. Using the definition of the group stated above, we ask three questions about each of these levels of organization: What constitutes the functional interdependence of the members? What are the channels of communication and the contents of the communication flow? What kind of ordered behavior results?

The neighborhood.—If the residents of a neighborhood consist of households with familistic ways of life (and consequently similar interests) existing in close proximity, there is a high probability of intersecting trajectories of action. Since surrounding households constitute important and inescapable parts of any given household's organizational environment, there emerge problems of social order, maintenance, and aid. Specifically, it is necessary to regulate the play of children, child-adult relations, and adult-adult relations to the degree that these represent possible blocks to the orderly performance of the household's way of life. To the extent that contiguous sites overlap visually, aurally, and (sometimes) physically, it is also necessary to regulate the use of the sites. The unsightly yard, the noises of the night, the dangerously barricaded sidewalk may constitute such blocks. Finally, similarity of life routines indicates a probable similarity of equipment and tasks: thus the interchangeability of parts is possible. This may range from the traditional borrowing of a cup of bourbon to the baby-sitting pool.

To be sure, similar problems arise in the apartment house districts characterized by a highly urban way of life, but the structure of the neighborhood and the nature of the population result in different kinds of order. The lower rate of communication, due to lack of common or overlapping space, and the separation of routines in time, result in a greater dependence upon formal norms (rules of the building, laws of residency) and upon formal authorities. Thus the

apartment house manager, or even the police, may be useful for the maintenance of order and the site. (Their utility, from household to *concierge* to
police, is evident in the reliance placed upon such organizations by the state in
various European countries.) In the suburbs, however, life-style and the relationships among the sites force inter-household communication.

Communication in the neighborhood may take place at many levels, but in
viewing the suburban neighborhood as an organizational unit we shall emphasize casual interaction among those whose paths necessarily intersect. In the
adjoining backyards, at bus stops, and local commercial facilities, considerable
social interaction is well nigh unavoidable. This interaction may become elaborated into relatively permanent cliques—kaffeeklatsch groups, pools, and the
like—and frequently results in a network of close friendships. These differ from
"neighboring," or participation in the neighborhood organization, just as friendship within any organization differs from the ongoing structure of activity common to the aggregate.

The resulting patterns of behavior, the structured action, probably vary a good
deal according to the type of neighborhood; however, the ubiquity of the phrase
"the good neighbor" seems to indicate some generalized role system and normative structure.[18] Orderliness, accessibility in time of need, and cleanliness are
salient characteristics rooted in the functional interdependence discussed above.
Individual members conform to such norms (whether or not they love their
neighbors) because the norms facilitate their ongoing household enterprises.

But the neighborhood is a microcosm. Nor is it the only spatially based social
structure mediating between the household and the metropolis. The neighborhood then is a precipitate of interacting households; participation in it does not
necessarily indicate a role in the larger local area as community or as political
unit. The neighborhood produces, at the least, some order among the small
enclave of residents, and communication relevant to the nearby scene.

The local residential area.—Neighbors in the suburbs tend to have similar interests, for their ways of life have similar prerequisites, while in the local residential area interdependence results when similar interests are transformed into
common interests, based upon the common field in which they operate. Spatial
aggregates are the distributing units for many goods and services—public
schools, commercial services, and various governmental aids and are frequently
available to the individual only through his residence in a geographically delimited aggregate. To the degree that this is true of vital resources, the population
of a local residential area is functionally interdependent.[19] At the same time
space, as the site of common activities (street, sidewalk, park, playground), is
a base of interdependence, as in the neighborhood.

The local residential community as here defined includes a number of neighborhoods. It may or may not be coterminous with a political unit. What is its
minimal organizational structure? Communication relevant to the area ordinarily takes place through two channels, the community press and voluntary
organizations. While each is a communication channel, we shall stress the communications function of the press and the action function of the voluntary
organization.

The local community press in the suburbs, widely distributed and widely read, is a medium available to almost all residents of most local areas.[20] Its utility stems directly from the interdependence of activities within the local area; supported by local merchants, it provides support in turn for the various formal organizations which constitute the "community." To be sure, all areas are not now serviced by a community press, but so useful is the medium (and consequently, so lucrative) that it is rapidly "covering" the suburban areas of contemporary cities. As the press develops where there is a market for its services, this should occur most consistently and widely among the familistic populations.

The suburban paper is quite similar to that described by Janowitz—parochial in its interests, reporting almost exclusively upon local happenings, translating metropolitan events into their effects on the local area, seldom reporting national events.[21] Such local personages as merchants, bureaucrats, and organizational leaders constitute the actors on this stage. Insofar as the local area is a social fact, the latter is reflected in the press and at the same time reinforced in the process of reflection, for the press in perpetuating lines of communication stabilizes norms and roles. If it is chiefly a merchandising mechanism in its economic function, it is also a public platform for the area in its social and political functions.

But what of the local area without a separate government? In this case, what kind of structured action is indicated as the third term in the definition of the area as a social structure? Noting again that spatially defined organization in the residential area is loose, unstructured, and does not engage all of the residents, here we emphasize participation in the local formal organizations. Such organizations are segmental in their membership and purposes; they include those residents who are dependent upon them for basic necessities to their way of life. Community-oriented organizations, improvement associations, child-centered organizations, some fraternal and service clubs are examples. They are particular to the area, their membership is largely limited to those living there, and they are instruments of persuasion and control with respect to various community problems, projects, and festivals. Furthermore, if there is no political structure they are the *only* existing structures through which an interdependence specific to the area (issuing in local problems), communicated through the press (as "community issues"), become manifested in social action.

The suburban municipality.—The typical political structure of metropolitan suburbia viewed as a whole is a crazy-quilt of many small municipalities having various eccentric shapes and displaying little obvious order in their boundaries. It is likely, however, that many of these municipalities are roughly coterminous with one or more social communities of the kind discussed above. To the degree that this is the case, the seemingly arbitrary lines on the map may come to represent social communities. The congruence of municipal boundaries with a local residential community permits the translation of common interests into a polity. The common field of activity (and the various segmental interests sited in this field) is contained within a formal organizational structure having the power to control, within wide limits, some of the basic goods and services of the residents. Thus streets, parks, schools (and, to a degree, commercial and residential development) are not only sources of interdependence—their control is so structured as to allow effective action by the interdependent population. Furthermore, taxation, police power, and other governmental attributes are assigned to the local municipality.

Where such is the case, an additional level is added to the structured action which results from interdependence and the flow of communication within the residential community: political action, within a political community.[22] Communication now incorporates well defined political norms and roles, the latter including the government official, political leader, voter, local taxpayer, and so on. But this type of organizational structure does not displace the kinds of voluntary community organizations indicated earlier. Certain modes of action tend to become allocated to the governmental organization; others remain the functions of private and semi-private groups (including the neighborhoods).

The organizational structure of suburbia may be summarized as follows: (1) The overlapping activities of households result in the neighborhoods, which exist as a kind of network spreading throughout the familistic population (for neighborhoods overlap as do households, and the neighborhood structure of a metropolis frequently resembles St. Augustine's definition of God, an infinite circle whose center is everywhere and whose periphery is nowhere). (2) Larger residential areas with a degree of functional interdependence constitute "communities of limited liability." They exhibit communication through informal relations and the community press, and action through voluntary private and semi-private organizations. (3) In many cases, political units are roughly coterminous with, or include, one or more social communities. Neighborhoods are probably nearly omnipresent, though a network need not include all households; so are communities, but they vary widely in degree of organization; political communities may or may not exist. In the summary presented in Table 1, each analytical category is sketched in for each organizational level.

TABLE 1. SOCIAL-POLITICAL STRUCTURES OF SUBURBIA

	Source of Interdependence	Channels of Communication	Structured Action
Neighborhood:	Overlapping field Similar interests	Informal interaction Casual visiting	Regulated interaction Maintenance of the site Mutual aid
Local Area	Common field Common interests	Community press Local organizations Informal interaction	Segmental interests protection Diffuse community action (outside political structure)
Municipality	Common field Common interests Common organizational structure coterminous with both	Local governmental functions Local political organizations Local non-political organizations Community press Informal interaction	Law-abiding (local), tax paying Voting, holding office Attending meetings Use of bureaucratic structure for complaints and appeals Organization of electoral campaigns

RELATIONS BETWEEN ORGANIZATIONAL
LEVELS IN SUBURBIA

The four types of organization discussed above—household, neighborhood, local residential area, municipality—are, generally, of ascending order as to size and descending order as to the probability of face-to-face or "primary" relations. They are also arranged in an order which indicates an increasing possibility of common "public" interest and action and, therefore, of policy relevance. Thus as formal policy becomes possible, representation rather than universal participation is a necessity.

The neighborhood, as the first level beyond the individual household, is very likely to generate interhousehold friendships and visiting patterns; neighboring then may be part of the informal communication flow of the area. The neighborhood, however, is not apt to form polity beyond the conventional "rules of the road," nor is it apt to be a representational unit for any larger collectivity. The social products of the neighborhood *per se* are small-scale order, mutual aid, and friendship. The lack of a formal structure oriented to the collective needs and problems of the inhabitants probably facilitates the performance of those minimal tasks discussed earlier: the informal and, indeed, often unspoken norms relevant to the group allow for considerable flexibility and effective control of deviation. But unformalized norms and unspecialized roles are suitable only for a given routine, and preferably one requiring little precision. The self-ordering of the neighborhood is an ordering of routine interaction, with wide limits of tolerance.

For these reasons, the neighborhood is not formally related to any other level of spatially based organization: it is too small to constitute an administrative sub-unit of a larger system and too informal to constitute a base for independent representation in a larger system. The interaction of households produces a luxuriant network of neighborhoods in the suburbs, but these have little direct significance for the polity.[23] Their chief contribution to other organizational systems is one of communication: they are a site for conversational ferment.

The household is related to the larger local area through formal organizations sited in the area. These include public and business structures and such "auxiliary" voluntary formal organizations as PTA and service club, as well as voluntary organizations built upon independent functional bases. In general, local organizations are concerned with common activities of specific segments of the residential population in the area.[24] The same household activities and interests which produce involvement in these area-wide segmental organizations also produce interest in the flow of local communication through informal relationships and the community press. Thus household members are differentially related to local formal organizations, while their reading of the press (and conversation with others) permits a familiarity with the organizations and actors of the local area as a whole.

In the present approach, the agencies of local government, although they possess distinctive political functions, are also viewed as segmental structures. For, despite its conventional identity with a geographical space and its population, local government has only limited powers and duties and affects only a small part of the residents' activities.

The non-governmental organizational structure of the local area is related to the suburban municipality through the congruence of fields of action (and convergence or conflict of interests) between voluntary organizations and governmental agencies. Possible interrelations of the two kinds of structures include, for example, the use of private organizations as representatives of community interests before the government, the overlapping leadership role within both government and private organizations, and the private organization as a political faction or party. Each of these would strengthen the argument that the local government is "truly representative of the community;" at the same time, each would have important consequences for the effectiveness of, and the constraints upon, local governmental agencies in dealing with problems and issues.

Thus, we should expect an overlapping membership between voluntary organizations and the municipal electorate. If the members of local organizations are exceptionally sensitive to community news as reported in the press, and if at the same time the community press reports governmental affairs extensively and frequently, the persons most active in local voluntary organizations should be highly informed about the dramatis personae of community polity. Insofar as they are committed members of common interest organizations, they would be particularly aware of governmental decisions, for these frequently affect voluntary organizations. And, even though they do not read the local paper, they should be unusually aware of information concerning the local residential community through their organizational activities, neighboring, and local friendships.

In short, neighborhood structures involve a large proportion of the suburban population, are loosely related to the local area communication system, but are not formally related to larger organizational networks. The local residential community and the municipality both involve a smaller proportion of the population (and one that is largely composed of the same individuals), but their scale and functions are such that they "stand for" the total population with respect to many basic activities.

TYPES OF RELATIONSHIP TO COMMUNITY ORGANIZATION

If there are predictable and orderly relationships between households, neighborhoods, residential communities, and municipalities, we can spell out the possible logical combinations, and can examine the distribution of community roles and the consequences for forms of behavior other than those built into the typology. In constructing types we emphasize neighborhood, local area, and governmental structure.

From the previous discussion may be deduced three levels of relationship to local social structure: (1) involvement in the small-scale system of the neighborhood, (2) a role in segmental structures based upon certain interests common to some people in the local area, and (3) a place in the flow of communication representing the local area "as a whole."

Dichotomizing each attribute for simplicity yields eight logically possible combinations. Some of these, however, are inconsistent with the framework sketched out earlier. If we consider separately the possible relations between neighborhood interaction, community roles, and access to the communication flow, the theory, with its emphases upon the communication functions of neighboring and of the local press and the social consequences of roles in local organizations, leads to the conclusions that there are no necessary relationships between (1) neighboring and community roles and (2) neighboring and reading the local press, but that there *is* a necessary relationship between a community role and participation in the communication network, either through neighboring or the press or both. A person with a role in the local organizational network but who neither reads the paper nor visits with his neighbors behaves inconsistently with the general hypothesis.

Following the procedures and qualifications discussed above results in the "organizational types" presented in Table 2. The rubrics in the right-hand column

TABLE 2. "ORGANIZATIONAL TYPES" IN SUBURBIA

	Neighborhood Interaction	Local Community Role	Access to Communication Flow	Type
I.	Yes	Yes	Yes	Multi-level participator
II.	Yes	Yes	No	Community actor (A)
III.	No	Yes	Yes	Community actor (B)
IV.	Yes	No	Yes	Neighborhood actor (A)
V.	Yes	No	No	Neighborhod actor (B)
VI.	No	No	Yes	Voyeur
VII.	No	No	No	Isolate
VIII.	No	Yes	No	Error

of the table are something more than summaries and something less than fully explicated types. The local "isolate," on the one hand, and the "multi-level participator," on the other, are clearly extremes. "Neighborhood actors" have defined positions only within the neighborhood system (although they may read the paper for gossip and entertainment). "Voyeurs" read the papers only as spectators of the community; they do not hold positions in role-systems and are otherwise comparable to isolates. "Community actors" may avoid their neighbors but, through common commitments, may still participate in area-wide formal organizations.

Population type and organizational type.—Certain associations are implied by the theory. Life style as the basis for similar interests at the neighborhood level and for common interests at the local area level should be a key variable in producing associational patterns. Thus, considering the urbanism dimension of the geographical sub-area as a rough measure of life style among contiguous populations, we expect neighboring to increase consistently as urbanism declines. Within a sample from neighborhoods at a given level of urbanism, however, variation in neighboring should be a result of variation in the life style of individual households: neighboring should increase with homeownership, number of children in the family, presence of wife in the household during the day. (The opposite extreme is the single person or childless couple with a working wife, who live in a rented apartment.)

One may object that the latter attributes of individual households would be a simpler and more reliable index than the urbanism of the geographical sub-area, clearly a possibility. However, neighborhoods are aggregates of persons in given sub-areas, and such aggregates cannot be inferred from a sample that is random with respect to neighborhood. If individual household attributes are the only data, we cannot allow for "the neighboring type of people" who live in areas where most women work, there are few children, and neighboring is difficult.[25] Contrariwise, considering only the average nature of the neighborhood, we lose the deviants within it. For these reasons, both aggregate and household attributes are significant.

The same logic should lead to similar relationships between the urbanism of the residential population and membership in local organizations. Commitment to the area, as measured by commitment to home, public schools, and other household investments, should increase as urbanism declines. Within the households residing in given types of area, however, those who are most concerned with the local residential area should be most apt to belong to formal organizations of a "community" nature.

The prediction of discrepancy between neighboring and activity in community organizations is based upon the hypothesis that in some familistic areas the neighborhood interaction system includes persons whose interests are deviant (for example, the post-parental couple, the non-family female), but that such interaction does not necessarily lead to a concern with broader community interests. And, *vice versa*, persons may be "good citizens" in the community at large although they are not involved with immediate neighbors. Thus urbanism should be related to both neighboring and community participation, but not necessarily through the identical group of actors.

Finally, the urbanism of the neighborhood should be associated with access to the local communication flow. The same variations in household commitment producing increased participation in neighborhood and local area organizational networks should increase the value of communication relevant to the residential community. As a consequence of these relationships, the constructed types of local "actors" (see Table 2) should vary with the urbanism of the neighborhood. Moving from urban districts towards familistic suburbs, we should find an increasing proportion of the adult population involved in the small-scale neighborhood and in the larger residential area as organizational systems—with isolates becoming a decreasing proportion.

A note on social rank.—A relationship is often postulated between participation in formal community organizations and social rank (occupation, education, and income levels of the respondents or their neighborhoods or both). With social rank, however, as with age and sex, we are dealing with role variations which cut across the larger society, and these should have about the same effect *within* each type of neighborhood and, within the neighborhood, within each category of local actors. When social rank is controlled, therefore, community participational type should remain a major differentiator with respect to involvement and competence in the affairs of the local residential area.

Nevertheless, we would expect more community actors in upper-status neighborhoods, and among persons with more education, income, and with higher prestige occupations, for these persons may be expected to have more organizational memberships. At each level of social rank, however, the urbanism of the neighborhood should be salient, for it reflects the variations in life style relevant to spatially defined organization. Thus isolates should vary little by social rank, once the urbanism of the neighborhood is controlled. The chief effect of decreasing social rank would then be a decrease in community-level actors and an increase in neighborhood-level actors. Lower-status neighborhoods of low urbanism would be, not so much "massified and fragmented," as organized on the small-scale basis of the neighborhood. At each level of social rank, urbanism should make a major difference in the distribution of participational types.

This theory leads then to the proposition that urbanism *as such* has an independent predictive power for the identification of types of community actors because it indicates aspects of the population conducive to a greater or lesser generation of spatially defined groups. A corollary proposition is that type of community actor is a more powerful predictive instrument for many kinds of *local* organizational behavior than the social rank of the resident or his neighborhood and municipality.

Governmental structure.—It was indicated above that governmental structure adds another organizational level, provides a "mold" for community activity, a focus for the policy-oriented, and a set of roles for the actors on the stage of the local community press. As an additional segmental organization, local government is a voluntary formal organization in that it provides further opportunities for involvement in the residential area's affairs. Therefore, if residential sub-areas are classified by organizational and governmental structure, we should expect the following rank order of competence and involvement in local affairs: areas with (1) autonomous organizational and governmental structures, (2) autonomous organizational but not governmental structures, (3) autonomous governmental but not organizational structures, and (4) areas with neither structure. Type (1) would include the suburban municipality which is a "social fact" as well as a governmental artifact; (2) would include the "local communities" in the unincorporated suburbs; (3) would probably be found in the areas now surrounded by the central city but still retaining political autonomy or in the areas immediately contiguous to the more urban neighborhoods of the city; (4) would be found, for the most part, in the central city.

Such a scheme points up the probability that incorporation will tend to increase public communication and action within a familistic area, for government summarizes many segmental common interests. If we consider the further possibility of applying the organizational types presented earlier to the probabilities of interaction within the political system, the analysis becomes more pertinent to the general problem of relating political and non-political social systems.

POLITICAL SYSTEM AND RESIDENTIAL COMMUNITY

Three general types of actors summarize the seven types presented in Table 2: isolates, neighborhood actors, and community actors. These terms are used below as shorthand for the description of organizational conditions and memberships producing each type.

With respect to the political and proto-political processes in suburbia, we may ask: To what degree does the suburban population participate in a local political system? Participation here refers to *competence* (the possession of adequate and accurate information on the political process) and *involvement* (including voting in local elections).

Interaction within the community-wide system is a clue to probable involvement in the polity (and, consequently, voting, electioneering, standing for office, and other manifestations). We assume that the action role is pursued only within a group context, and that the membership groups available in the suburbs are the various community-wide organizations. Such membership is thus considered a prerequisite to involvement in community politics; similarly involvement emerges from a functional commitment to the local area at other levels. Involvement, however, does not necessarily imply competence. We consider competence as the probable result of participation in the flow of communication *relevant to the community-wide system*. This may result from informal interaction (friendship or neighboring) or the community press or both. The general types of community actors should behave quite differently within the role system of the local municipality.—These hypotheses are suggested by the following tabular presentation:

	Involvement	Competence
Isolates	Low	Low
Neighborhood actors	Higher	Higher
Community actors	Highest	Highest

The difference between political settings is crucial for testing the general hypothesis of organizational scale. If the three types of actors are further categorized by the political structure of their residential areas, isolates should differ little in their competence, whether they live in unincorporated or incorporated areas: they should be largely incompetent. Neighbors should be relatively incompetent in each area. But community actors in the incorporated areas should have more knowledge about community organization, for there is more to know. For example, they should know a larger number of leaders, for their governmental structure provides such parochial leaders. When political leaders are subtracted from their knowledge, however, they should have a general backlog of information on local leadership quite similar to those who live in unincorporated areas: organization type should be a predictor when political structure is controlled.

Two implications may be drawn from this discussion which are relevant to the current controversy about metropolitan governmental reform. First, the areas in which a viable, small-scale, local governmental process is likely are those of familistic populations, within which there are many community actors and few isolates—whether or not such areas are now incorporated. Second, the strength of the resistance to the "merger" of the central city and the suburbs should be found concentrated in those areas with a strong organizational network involving a large proportion of the adults in the residential community. In fact, the rank order of opposition should be correlated with the rank order, stated above, of competence and involvement in local affairs by areal attributes. At the low end of the resulting continuum would be those who live in the highly urban neighborhoods of the central city, for whom the local residential community has little meaning—and these persons are usually strong supporters of metropolitan "integration."

SOME DERIVED HYPOTHESES

Further applications of the theoretical scheme are possible and tempting. It is desirable at this point, however, to apply the theory to some derived observational requirements. The following hypotheses, implicit or explicit in the above discussion, merely illustrate a much larger number of possibilities. They are now being tested against data from a large-scale survey of the suburban population of one of the major metropolitan areas.[26] The hypotheses are stated briefly, but are consistent with the foregoing theoretical presentation.

Urbanism, life-style, and organizational participation.—Thirty-four specific hypotheses under this category may be presented as the following six propositions:

(a) Despite the varying effects of social rank, ethnicity, and the characteristics of individual municipalities, urbanism is negatively related to neighboring, participation in formal organizations situated in the area, readership of the local press for local community news, and the incidence of community actors; urbanism is positively related to the incidence of isolates and voyeurs (hypotheses 1 through 6).

(b) When urbanism is controlled, social rank is positively related to the incidence of community actors, and negatively related to the incidence of neighborhood actors (hypotheses 7 and 8).

(c) Despite the varying effects of unit characteristics, the presence of children in the household is positively related to neighboring, participation in formal organizations situated in the area, and the incidence of community actors; it is negatively related to the incidence of isolates and voyeurs (hypotheses 8 through 11).

(d) When the presence of children in the household is controlled (and despite the varying effects of other unit characteristics), urbanism continues to have discriminating power with respect to the six participational variables indicated in (a) above (hypotheses 12 through 17).

(e) When the urbanism of the census tract of residence is controlled (and despite the varying effects of other unit characteristics), the presence of children in the household has discriminating power with respect to the participational variables indicated in (a) above (hypotheses 17 through 22).

(f) Despite the varying effects of other unit variables, urbanism and the presence of children in the household are conducive to the same types of organizational participation. Specifically, extremely high participation rates characterize those who live in low urban areas and have children, with respect to neighboring, belonging to local organizations, and reading the local press; the opposite holds for those without children in highly urban areas. With respect to the constructed types, the most community actors and the fewest isolates and voyeurs inhabit low urban neighborhoods with children in the households; the opposite holds for high urban neighborhoods among childless households (hypotheses 23 through 34).

Organizational participation and political behavior.—Forty additional specific hypotheses are stated as the following seven more general formulations:

(a) Because it indicates involvement in the local area as an organizational system, participation in local organizations is positively related to voting, naming local leaders, and knowing the electoral rules. Because it indicates participation in the flow of communication in the area, readership of the press is related to naming leaders and knowing the rules. This also holds for neighboring with respect to naming leaders and knowing the rules. Neither neighboring nor readership of the press has a strong relationship with voting when organizational membership and the other unit of the pair is controlled (hypotheses 35 through 43).

(b) When the logically possible combinations are reduced to five, isolates (who neither read, neighbor, nor belong), voyeurs (who neither neighbor nor belong but who read the press), neighborhood actors (who neighbor but do not belong), deviants (who belong but neither neighbor nor read the press), and community actors (who belong and either neighbor, read, or do both), the following relative distributions result:

	Competence		
Type	Names	Knows Rules	Involvement Votes
Isolates	—	—	—
Voyeurs	+	+	—
Neighbors only	+	+	+
Community actors	++	++	++
Deviants	—	—	+
(Hypotheses 44 through 58).			

(c) When age, sex, and education (as an index of social rank) are controlled, each age, sex, and educational category will manifest the same variation by organization type (hypotheses 59 through 64).

(d) If competence and involvement are considered simultaneously, those competent and not active should be concentrated among the voyeurs, those active and not competent among the deviants, those active and competent among the community actors, those neither active nor competent, among the isolates (hypotheses 65 through 68).

(e) The rank order of the distribution of community actor types should be (1) local area coinciding with municipality, (2) local area without municipality, (3) municipality without local area, and (4) district with neither residential area organization nor political structure (hypothesis 69). This, in turn, should result in a similar rank order of ability to name leaders (hypothesis 70). The same rank order should hold for resistance to metropolitan integration movements (hypothesis 71).

(f) With incorporation controlled, the organizational types should have similar ability to name local leaders (hypothesis 72).

(g) If political office-holders and past office-holders are eliminated, organizational types in incorporated and unincorporated areas should have similar abilities to name local leaders, although a somewhat larger number should be able to do so in the incorporated areas. Therefore, naming of nonpolitical leaders should be related to the urbanism of the area (hypotheses 73 and 74).

NOTES

[1] Otis Dudley Duncan and Albert J. Reiss, Jr., *Social Characteristics of Rural and Urban Communities: 1950*, New York: Wiley, 1956.

[2] E.g., Walter T. Martin, "The Structuring of Social Relationships Engendered by Suburban Residence," *American Sociological Review*, 21 (August, 1956) pp. 446–453.

[3] Robert C. Wood, *Suburbia, Its People and Their Politics*, Boston: Houghton Mifflin, 1959. See especially Chapter 4, "The Nature of Suburbia."

[4] Wendell Bell, "Social Choice, Life Styles, and Suburban Residence," in W. A. Dobriner, editor, *The Suburban Community*, New York: Putnam's, 1958, pp. 225–247.

[5] Emile Durkheim, *Suicide*, translated by John A. Spaulding and George Simpson, edited with an Introduction by George Simpson, Glencoe, Ill.: Free Press, 1951; Talcott Parsons, *The Social System*, Glencoe, Ill.: Free Press, 1952; David Riesman, Reuel Denney, and Nathan Glazer, *The Lonely Crowd*, New Haven: Yale University Press, 1950; Max Weber, *The Theory of Social and Economic Organization*, translated by A. M. Henderson and Talcott Parsons, edited with an Introduction by Talcott Parsons, New York: Oxford University Press, 1947. To bring matters up to date, see the work of the Detroit Area Study, which moves immediately from individual characteristics to such societal dimensions as the stratification system: *A Social Profile of Detroit, 1956, A Report of the Detroit Area Study of the University of Michigan*, Ann Arbor: Detroit Area Study, Department of Sociology and the Survey Research Center of the Institute for Social Research, 1957.

[6] Amos H. Hawley, *Human Ecology: A Theory of Community Structure*, New York: Ronald, 1950; Otis Dudley Duncan and Beverly Duncan, "Residential Distribution and Occupational Stratification," *American Journal of Sociology*, 60 (March, 1955) pp. 493–503; Leo F. Schnore, "The Growth of Metropolitan Suburbs," *American Sociological Review*, 22 (April, 1957), pp. 165–173.

[7] In the exposition of the theory that follows, the author has assumed the dogmatic but simplifying device of expressing many discrete hypotheses as valid propositions. These hypotheses, couched in testable form, conclude this paper.

[8] See, e.g., Fred Cottrell, *Energy and Society,* New York: McGraw-Hill, 1955; Godfrey and Monica Wilson, *The Analysis of Social Change,* Cambridge: At the University Press, 1954; Eshref Shevky and Wendell Bell, *Social Area Analysis,* Stanford: Stanford University Press, 1955.

[9] The term *urbanism* is used to refer to a concept Shevky has denoted as "urbanization" and Bell as "family status" or "familism." In general, urbanism implies that the higher the index reading, the nearer the approach to an ideal typical "urbanism as a way of life." Both the earlier terms are awkward, have disturbing connotations in the literature, and are sometimes downright misleading.

[10] The index of urbanism is discussed in Shevky and Bell, *op. cit.,* pp. 17 and 55–56. For evidence of the independence and importance of this dimension, see the factor analysis studies: Wendell Bell, *A Comparative Study of the Methodology of Urban Analysis,* unpublished Ph.D. thesis, University of California, Los Angeles, 1952; Maurice D. Van Arsdol, Jr., Santo F. Camilleri, and Calvin Schmid, "The Generality of Urban Social Area Indexes," *American Sociological Review,* 23 (June, 1958), pp. 277–284. For a test of the index, using sample survey data, see Scott Greer and Ella Kube, "Urbanism and Social Structure," in Marvin Sussman, editor, *Community Structure and Analysis,* New York: Crowell, 1959, pp. 93–112.

[11] See the findings reported by Bell (in Dobriner, *op. cit.*) and by Richard Dewey in "Peripheral Expansion in Milwaukee County," *American Journal of Sociology,* 53 (May, 1948), pp. 417–422. Seventy-two per cent of Bell's respondents who had moved from Chicago into two middle-rank suburbs listed physical characteristics as a reason for moving to the suburbs; 50 per cent of their responses reflected improvement in privacy and geographical space. Dewey's respondents gave as reasons for their move, in order, "better for children," "less congested," "cleaner," and "larger lot," as the four most popular ones.

[12] Schnore, *op. cit.* A polemical statement of the possibility is found in William H. Whyte, Jr., "Are Cities Un-American?" in Editors of *Fortune, The Exploding Metropolis,* Garden City, N. Y.: Doubleday, 1958.

[13] This argument is presented in another context by Wendell Bell in "A Probability Model for the Measurement of Ecological Segregation," *Social Forces,* 32 (May, 1954), pp. 357–364.

[14] By relative homogeneity we mean no more than the probability that differences by a chosen criterion are greater between areas than is true within each area.

[15] See, e.g., Martin, *op. cit.*

[16] Morris Janowitz, *The Community Press in an Urban Setting,* Glencoe, Ill.: Free Press, 1952. See esp. Chapter 7, "The Social Dimensions of the Local Community."

[17] Scott Greer, *Social Organization,* New York: Random House, 1955. The spatially defined group and the changing nature of the urban sub-community are discussed in Chapters 4 and 5.

[18] The norms may vary of course by social rank and ethnicity; to simplify the argument the effects of these dimensions are considered irrelevant to the major hypotheses. Social rank is discussed in a later section.

[19] The reader may question the existence of such "local areas" as social fact. However, scattered evidence indicates that the map of the city breaks down into sub-units for the residential population, whether or not these are congruent with ecologically defined "natural areas." The nature and consequences of economic decentralization are explored by Foley, of social and economic decentralization by Janowitz. See Donald L. Foley, "The Use of Local Facilities in a Metropolis," *American Journal of Sociology,* 56 (November, 1950), pp. 238–246, and *Neighbors or Urbanites? The Study of a Rochester Residential District,* Rochester, N. Y.: University of Rochester,

1952; and Janowitz, *op. cit.* A more recent study reports a strong definition of sub-areas among residents of Boston. See Laurence Ross, *The Local Community in the Metropolis,* unpublished Ph.D. thesis, Harvard University, 1959. Furthermore, 98 per cent of the residents of suburban St. Louis County accept the notion and give a distinctive name to their residential area (unpublished research report, Metropolitan St. Louis Survey).

[20] Thus 84 per cent of Janowitz's respondents were readers of their local press (*op. cit.*). Similar findings are reported for a Los Angeles suburban sample: of those who received the paper (85 per cent) over 92 per cent were regular readers; see Scott Greer and Ella Kube, *Urban Worlds: A Comparative Study of Four Los Angeles Areas,* Los Angeles: Laboratory in Urban Culture, 1955 (processed).

[21] Janowitz, *op. cit.*

[22] This does not imply an automatic evolution which presumes that through time interdependence must result in communication and order. The precise processes by which organizational structures evolve are not spelled out here; they would be desirable but are not essential to the purposes of the present paper.

[23] The reader will recall the widely reported relationship between the voting of respondents and their neighbors; however, the significant variables in the present discussion are quite different. Reference here is to *participation* (not direction of vote) in *local* elections, while neighbors are distinguished from friends (the latter is a sub-category). Near-dwellng friends may indeed influence voting in Presidential elections; this is not the proposition presented above.

[24] They may be coded as: child-centered, community-political, and fraternal-service, for those most intimately related to the affairs of the local residential area. The remaining voluntary organizations may be usefully coded as either work-related or church-related.

[25] Greer and Kube, *op. cit.,* report a diminution in neighboring among non-working women, as the proportion of working women in a neighborhood increases. They explain this as a consequence of declining opportunities for neighboring.

[26] The results of this analysis are to be reported in a forthcoming paper.

15. THE SOCIAL STRUCTURE AND POLITICAL PROCESS OF SUBURBIA: AN EMPIRICAL TEST *

Scott Greer

The author recently presented a systematic theory outlining the nature of suburban social structure conceived in organizational terms.[1] This structure was then related to (a) population types distributed in space and (b) the political process. The discussion concluded with a long list of specific hypotheses. This paper will present the results of empirical analysis based upon the theory and including most of the hypotheses.

THE THEORY

The theory will be stated in as brief a fashion as possible; for a detailed explication the reader is referred to the earlier article.

1. In contemporary metropolitan areas spatially defined social groups occur at three levels: the neighborhood, the residential enclave (or "local community" as it has been termed), and the political unit.

2. These social forms vary in their incidence according to the type of population mix which resides in the area. This is because the forms derive from the functional necessities of households. Thus the familistic population is particularly prone to intensive neighboring, as well as participation in locally based formal organizations, for both structures are useful to the household in its everyday tasks. Contrariwise, as the urbanism of the population increases, neighborhood and local community decline in average importance to the average resident of an area.

3. Neighborhood, local community, and municipality are concentric in scope; therefore one can conceive of variation in the *scale* of an individual's commitment and participation in spatially defined groups. Specifically, a number of types are constructed, based upon participation: these include, for example, Isolates, Neighbors, and Community Actors. Isolates participate in neither neighborhood nor larger local community; Neighbors participate only in the neighborhood; Community Actors participate at the local community level.

4. These participational types are important predictors of political activity and competence, for they summarize involvement and access to the communication flow of the local polity. Those most involved and informed are disproportionately concentrated among the Community Actors; these are the people who "run the railroad."

5. Thus the types will be disproportionately concentrated in the different sub-

* For support in gathering the original data, I wish to thank the Metropolitan St. Louis Survey, a large-scale study of metropolitan government sponsored by the Public Affairs Division of the Ford Foundation and the McDonnel Aircraft Company Charitable Trust. For support in analysis I wish to thank the Graduate School, Northwestern University.

SOURCE: *Rural Sociology*, 27 (December, 1962), pp. 438–459. Reprinted by permission of the author and publisher.

areas of the metropolis. Community Actors will be most common in the familistic neighborhoods, Isolates in the urban neighborhoods of single persons and childless marriages.

6. Involvement in the local area's polity will, in turn, vary with population type. In the absence of a municipality (i.e., in the unincorporated suburbs) the Community Actors will still maintain a "local community" based upon voluntary organizations. Spatially defined social groups are much more than artifacts of political boundaries.

THE RESEARCH DESIGN

In the spring of 1957 the author carried out an extensive sample survey to determine political participation and political opinion. The survey included a systematic areal random sample of the residents in St. Louis County—the suburban county to the west of the city of St. Louis. One randomly selected adult in every one-hundredth household in the county was interviewed. Interviewing was halted at the 86 per cent response level, and the final sample was 1,285 interviews.

St. Louis County includes most of the "suburbia" of the area. Analysis of census data, using the Shevky-Bell typology, indicates (1) that the county is overwhelmingly familistic, with very few census tracts above the 50 percentile on the Shevky-Bell urbanization index, (2) that tracts with a disproportionate concentration of nonwhite or foreign-born populations are very rare in the county, (3) that the county census tract populations range from near the bottom to the top in social rank.[2] Although there are large areas inhabited chiefly by well-paid and highly educated professionals and managers, there are also many areas housing clerical workers, craftsmen, and operatives.

The observations upon which the present analysis rests were produced by the sample survey. The schedule of questions includes a rough inventory of social participation, with particular emphasis upon the spatially defined social group on the one hand and suburban political processes on the other. Thus the existing social structure can be studied as it impinged upon and controlled the responses of the scattered sample: specific groups cannot be studied.

The strategy of analysis is based upon the use of constructed types which, as empirically defined, roughly approximate those mentioned above. These types simultaneously indicate (1) the ways people are involved in the structure and (2) the structure as evidence in the behavior of a sample of people. The materials for constructing the types are those objective indicators logically related to organizational involvement and information at the various levels. Such a strategy aims at a high differentiation of behavior for highly specified types, and therefore a high degree of "prediction," even though a set of constructed types may stop far short of exhausting the *people* in a sample. (For use in a more extensive kind of prediction, one develops grosser categories which demand less of the individual case and which will include all or most of a population—though with lower predictability in the main.)

Seven participational types and an error category were developed through logical permutation and combination of (1) neighborhood interaction, (2) a role in the organizational structure of the local community, and (3) access to the communication flow of the local community. Table 1 summarizes these types.[3]

TABLE 1. "ORGANIZATIONAL TYPES" IN SUBURBIA

	Neighborhood interaction	Local community role	Access to communication flow	Type
I.	Yes	Yes	Yes	Multilevel Participator
II.	Yes	Yes	No	Community Actor (A)
III.	No	Yes	Yes	Community Actor (B)
IV.	Yes	No	Yes	Neighborhood Actor (A)
V.	Yes	No	No	Neighborhood Actor (B)
VI.	No	No	Yes	Voyeur
VII.	No	No	No	Isolate
VIII.	No	Yes	No	Error

The next step in the analysis was the construction of objective indicators for neighborhood interaction, local community role, and access to communication flow. At this point it was crucial that the indicators be developed independently of their use as a test of the theory, for the analysis aims at verification, rather than simply exploration. For this reason, the sample (after the elimination of 89 people who were ineligible to vote) was divided into a "laboratory sample" of 196 cases and a "testing sample" of 1,000 cases. The laboratory sample was analyzed by various possible indicators, and three were finally selected. Both the items selected and the discriminating categories of answers were determined with the small sample: they were not changed in the analysis of the testing sample. In short, a subsample was used as a pretest of the analysis; this sample was not allowed to contaminate the larger test sample.

The indicators finally selected were these: (1) for neighborhood interaction, those were defined as interactors who answered the question "How often do you visit with any of your neighbors? Is it once a week or more, a few times a month, once a month, a few times a year or less, or never?" by saying either "once a week or more" or "a few times a month"; (2) for local community role, those were defined as role players who answered the question "Which organizations or clubs do you belong to?" by naming one or more voluntary organizations and, further, in answer to the question "And does that organization meet in (local community)?" indicated that one or more met locally; (3) for access to communication flow, those were defined as having access who, in answer to the question "Do you get any local community paper or shopping news?" said "Yes" and, to the further question, "What do you like best in it?" said "local community news."

Of the 196 in the laboratory sample, 44 per cent were neighborhood inter-actors, 49 per cent were local community role players, and 49 per cent had access to the local communication flow by these criteria. One's immediate suspicion is that there are the same persons in each case. This is far from true, however, as the analysis of the sample in Table 2 indicates. To be sure, an association is evident between the three indexes, but those who belong to local organizations are about as likely *not* to neighbor as the reverse, and nearly half of those who read the local press for local news do not neighbor. Contrariwise, of those who do neighbor, 36 per cent do not belong to a local organization and 40 per cent do not read the local paper for local news.

TABLE 2. PERCENTAGE DISTRIBUTION OF THE LABORATORY SAMPLE BY INDICATORS OF SOCIAL PARTICIPATION
(N = 188)*

	Neighbors			Does not neighbor		
	44			56		
	Reads local paper	Does not read local paper	Total	Reads paper local	Does not read local paper	Total
Belongs to local organizations	20	8	28	10	11	21
Does not belong to local organizations	6	10	16	13	22	35

* Omitted are 8 cases which do not receive local paper.

The analysis thus justifies the use of the three indicators and would substantiate the notion that the organizational levels of suburbia are separate structures, with less overlap in personnel than one might have supposed. Neighborhoods include active members whose participation in the larger local community is negligible; vice versa, the local community system includes actors who do not neighbor at all intensively. It also includes a small number of those whom we have called "error" types.

The relationship of these levels to that of the political unit is apparent in Table 3. Here the typology is used as a predictor, with voting in local elections ("Have you ever voted for any local officials since you've been living here?") and ability to name local leaders ("In your opinion, who are the people who are leaders in [local community] and can get things done around here?") as the effect variables. The first generalization we can make is that the ability to name local leaders varies more consistently by participational type than does voting. (The latter, in fact, is high for the first three types and the last, and about the same for all others.) The second is that Multilevel Actors and the two types of Community Actors can be combined into one category since they behave in a similar fashion; the same is true of Neighborhood Actors on the one hand and Isolates and Voyeurs on the other. This simplifying scheme yields the types hypothesized previously and would seem to lose very little predictive power (the chief loss is the difference in knowledge between Voyeurs and

Isolates). There is good reason for holding the "Error" category out; having a community role (as in the case of the Community Actors), these people are as apt to be local voters as any, but lacking access to the communication flow through either neighboring or readership of the papers, they are as uninformed as are the Isolates. Their behavior, in fact, supports the separate importance of involvement and information.

TABLE 3. PERCENTAGE OF PARTICIPATIONAL TYPES WHO HAD VOTED IN MUNICIPAL ELECTIONS AND COULD NAME LOCAL LEADERS FOR THE LABORATORY SAMPLE

Types	% who had voted	No. of type	% who named leader	No. of type
I. Multilevel Actor	77	31	71	38
II. Community Actor (A)	85	13	78	14
III. Community Actor (B)	76	14	72	18
IV. Neighborhood Actor (A)	42	12	46	13
V. Neighborhood Actor (B)	36	14	47	19
VI. Voyeur	45	20	37	24
VII. Isolate	45	31	22	40
VIII. Error	78	18	23	22
Total number		153*		188†

* Omitted are 8 persons who do not receive local paper and 35 persons who live in unincorporated areas and cannot vote in municipal election.

† Omitted are 8 persons who do not receive a local paper.

A third generalization is simply that the typology has considerable predictive power. Extreme theoretical types (Isolates, Neighbors, and Multilevel Actors) vary sharply with respect to naming leaders, and the first two and the third differ sharply in their voting. An important question, however, must be answered before the typology is accepted: What is the independent predictive power of each level or organization as measured by these indicators? Tables 4 and 5 provide a partial answer.

With respect to voting, the most striking association is that between belonging to local organizations and having voted. Neighboring is slightly related to voting, but the relationship disappears when controlled for membership in organizations. The same is true with respect to readership of the press. All in all, we might operate more efficiently through using membership in local organizations *only* to predict voting. (This is consistent with the earlier finding that the sample dichotomizes between Community Actors [and Errors] and all others with respect to voting.)

However, the story is different with respect to the naming of local leaders. Here each indicator has power. The theoretically extreme cases go from 62 versus 34 per cent, considering neighboring only, to 73 versus 28 per cent when organizational membership is added, and 71 versus 22 per cent when all three are considered simultaneously. Those who neighbor are, in all categories

TABLE 4. PERCENTAGE VOTING IN LOCAL ELECTIONS BY NEIGHBORING, BELONGING TO LOCAL ORGANIZATION, READING LOCAL PAPER (N = 153)*

	Neighbors			Does not neighbor		
% voting	64†			58		
Total no.	(70)			(83)		
	Reads local paper	Does not read local paper	Total	Reads local paper	Does not read local paper	Total
Belongs to local organizations:						
% voting	77	85	80	86	78	81
Total no.	(31)	(13)	(44)	(14)	(18)	(32)
Does not belong to local organizations:						
% voting	42	36	38	45	45	45
Total no.	(12)	(14)	(26)	(20)	(31)	(51)

* Omitted are 8 who do not receive local paper and 35 who did not live in an incorporated area.

† Percentages are of the basic N's (in parentheses) for each cell.

TABLE 5. PERCENTAGE NAMING LOCAL LEADERS BY NEIGHBORING, BELONGING TO LOCAL ORGANIZATIONS, READING LOCAL PAPER (N = 188)*

	Neighbors			Does not neighbor		
% naming	62†			34		
Total no.	(84)			(104)		
	Reads local paper	Does not read local paper	Total	Reads local paper	Does not read local paper	Total
Belongs to local organizations:						
% naming	71	78	73	72	23	45
Total no.	(38)	(14)	(52)	(18)	(22)	(40)
Does not belong to local organizations:						
% naming	46	47	47	37	22	28
Total no.	(13)	(19)	(32)	(24)	(40)	(64)

* Omitted are 8 who did not receive local paper.

† Percentages are of the basic N's (in parentheses) for each cell.

but one, more able to name leaders. Similarly, those who belong to organizations are, in all categories but one, more able. Those who read the paper, however, are no different from those who do not, *if* they both neighbor and belong to organizations.

These three exceptions, however, are easily derivable from one of the earlier hypotheses, for neighboring and reading the local press are considered to be functional equivalents with respect to the local communications process. Therefore neighboring makes no difference in the ability of those who both belong to local organizations and read the local community press for local news. The one category in which belonging to an organization makes no difference in competence (those who neither read nor neighbor) is the one predictable from the hypothesis. Finally, if one neighbors intensively, the press is redundant; but if one does *not* neighbor, readership of the press makes a very striking difference, even among those who do not belong to organizations.

In summary: through the intensive analysis of the laboratory sample, a set of objective indicators was selected and used in the construction of eight analytical types. These types were then combined into grosser types, since a number of them seemed to fall into clusters, both empirically and theoretically. Thus the Multilevel Actor and the two types of Community Actor were combined in one category—hereafter to be called "Community Actors." Such Actors (1) belong to local organizations and (2) *either* neighbor, read the local paper, or both. The three options under (2) seemed to make little difference in relevant behavior. Similarly, the two types of Neighbors are combined into one category, with the assumption that, if they neighbor, reading the paper makes little difference. Finally, Isolates and Voyeurs are combined for convenience; though Voyeurs are somewhat more able to name leaders, they are a very small population in any sample. "Errors" are carried as a separate category, the "Deviants"; they cannot be logically combined with any of the three major types. Their status is, for the time being, that of a puzzle.

THE FINDINGS

The findings will be presented in this order: (1) the differential concentration of the organizational types in certain neighborhoods by average population type, (2) differential political behavior of the organizational types, (3) the effects of certain conventional controls upon the differential political behavior of the types, and (4) the relationship between political incorporation, local community, and political competence.

Since much of this analysis was preceded by analysis of the laboratory sample of 196 cases, the findings of the pilot analysis will also be presented. Although these analyses were the basis for decisions with respect to indicators, cutting points, and dichotomies, which were then used in the test sample of 1,000 cases, they constitute something of an independent verification of the findings in the latter. Further, comparison of the two sets of findings both reinforces certain conclusions and indicates some of the traps for the unwary when *post hoc* analysis of a small sample leads to large generalizations.

Population type and organizational type: As noted above, the neighborhoods of suburban St. Louis County are predominantly familistic in character; few census tracts measure as much as the 50 percentile score of the Shevky-Bell index of urbanism. Nevertheless, there should be enough variation to influence (1) the predominance of given types of households and, consequently, (2) the type of spatially defined social organization which prevails. In dividing the sample, it seemed necessary to limit the use of the urbanism index to a dichotomy in order to protect the size of the more highly urban sample. Therefore the sample was divided into individuals living in census tracts with scores of 29 or lower on the urbanism index (this was about the middle of the range for most suburban tracts) and in tracts with higher scores. The results are presented in Table 6 (see the "Total" column). The salient finding is that Community Actors are more common in the low urban neighborhoods—47 as compared with 38 per cent—and Isolates more common in the more highly urban tracts —36 as compared with 27 per cent. (These differences are significant by chi-square test at the .05 level of confidence. All differences mentioned in the test in numerical terms are of similar reliability except as otherwise noted.) There is no variation in either Deviants or Neighbors. The census tract score, however, summarizes two aspects of "organizational preconditions." It tells

TABLE 6. PERCENTAGE IN PARTICIPATIONAL TYPES BY TYPE OF NEIGHBORHOOD AND HOUSEHOLDS WITH AND WITHOUT CHILDREN

Participational types	1. Low urban			2. High urban			3. Sample total
Sample no. 1	With child	W/o child	Total	With child	W/o child	Total	
(N = 188)							
I. Isolates	24	39	29	34	64	51	34
II. Neighbors	17	17	17	21	14	17	17
III. Community Actors	48	35	44	21	9	15	37
IV. Deviants	11	9	10	24	13	17	12
Total	100	100	100	100	100	100	100
	(86)	(56)	(142)	(24)	(22)	(46)	(188)*
Sample no. 2 (N = 943)							
I. Isolates	20	40	27	29	43	36	29
II. Neighbors	17	20	18	13	23	18	18
III. Community Actors	55	30	47	50	26	38	44
IV. Deviants	8	10	8	8	8	8	9
Total	100	100	100	100	100	100	100
	(458)	(272)	(730)	(106)	(107)	(213)	(943)†

* Omitted are 8 persons who do not receive paper.
† Omitted are 57 persons who do not receive paper.

the character and requirements of the average households in the area, and as such is an indirect indicator of individual household attributes, and it also indicates the nature of the *environment* for any household regardless of its particular attributes. The relative importance of the two is visible when we control for "children in the household," one of the major theoretically defined household attributes.

For households with and without children, there tend to be more Community Actors and few Isolates in the low urban areas. There are thus grounds for speaking of an independent "areal attribute." However, the presence or absence of children is a much more powerful differentiator in the distribution of types; in low urban areas Isolates are twice as likely in the childless households (40 compared with 20 per cent), and Community Actors almost twice as common (55 versus 3 per cent). Although differences by urbanism of the area, with children in the household controlled, are in the predicted direction, they are not statistically significant. In the more highly urban neighborhood matters are similar. When household attributes and census tract attributes are taken together, however, there is even more differentiation. Actors from households with children in the low urban areas are Isolates in only 20 per cent of the cases; those from childless households in the more urbanized areas are Isolates in 43 per cent of the cases. And 55 per cent of the former are Community Actors, compared with only 26 per cent of the latter.

The results of the two samples are quite similar; it should be noted, however, that the smaller sample yielded more extreme differences. This is particularly true of the high urban category, where subsamples were very small. Finally, the reader should bear in mind the generally familistic nature of this sample: no truly "urbane" neighborhoods are included and the sample is loaded against the urbanism index. It still proves to be a very useful differentiator.

Participational type and political behavior: It is clear from the earlier discussion that participational types, as first defined, have considerable discriminating power with respect to voting in local elections and ability to name local leaders. Table 7 presents the results of (1) combining the eight types into three, with the category of Deviants handled separately, and (2) using the analysis for the test sample of 1,000 cases (which dwindles to 763 when those ineligible to vote in municipal elections are omitted).

Community Actors are by far the most likely to have voted in local elections (71 per cent) with Deviants next (50 per cent) and Neighbors and Isolates about equally likely to vote (41 and 44 per cent). Thus organizational membership still seems to be the chief predictor of voting. With respect to naming local leaders, however, there is a clear progression from Isolate to Neighbor to Community Actor (33, 42, and 62 per cent could name leaders)—and the Deviants are no more competent than Neighbors.

Once again, differences were more extreme in the smaller, pilot sample. Community Actors, particularly, were far more competent and substantially more apt to vote. Although the over-all pattern is unchanged, theoretically extreme types are less dramatic (there are differences of 35 per cent for voting compared with 27, and of 41 compared with 29 per cent for naming leaders).

Controls—Background variables and participational types: At this point

TABLE 7. PERCENTAGE VOTING AND NAMING LOCAL LEADERS AMONG PARTICIPATIONAL TYPES

Organizational type	Votes in municipal elections		Names local leaders	
Sample no. 1 (N = 188)	%	No.	%	No.
I. Isolates	46	(51)	34	(64)
II. Neighbors	40	(26)	44	(32)
III. Community Actors	81	(58)	75	(70)
IV. Deviants	80	(18)	17	(22)
Total number		(153)*		(188)*
Sample no. 2 (N = 763)				
I. Isolates	44	(208)	33	(279)
II. Neighbors	41	(153)	42	(174)
III. Community Actors	71	(343)	62	(417)
IV. Deviants	50	(59)	40	(73)
Total number		(763)†		(943)‡

* Omitted are those listed in the note to Table 4a.
† Omitted are 237 who either did not receive local paper or else lived in unincorporated areas (or both).
‡ Omitted are 57 who did not receive local paper.

the reader may suspect that the participational types conceal bundles of conventional sociological variables—that they are, in fact, spurious. The theory, however, prescribes that organizational participation is by far the most powerful differentiator in local political behavior. While background variables may affect the probability of a person's falling into a given participational type, once he has taken the requisite position he will tend to behave like others in the type.

Three variables are consistently important, across the society, in differentiating voters and nonvoters, the competent and the incompetent. These are age, sex, and social rank. Adults aged 30 or under are less apt to vote than older persons; women are less apt to vote than men; and the low-income, less-educated persons in the blue-collar labor force are less apt to vote than those with more income and education.[4]

When the sample is divided at these points, with education taken as an index of social rank (and the sample divided roughly into grammar school, high school, and college), the distributions presented in Table 8 result. The results are very similar for both samples, with no difference as great as 10 per cent. Community Actors, as would be hypothesized, have fewer people under 30, fewer persons with an eighth-grade education or less, and more with college education than do the other categories. However, they are the category second most heavily weighted with women. (Here, perhaps, is some evidence for the proposition that the policy of suburbia is disproportionately matri-centered.) When Community Actors are compared with the remainder of the sample

TABLE 8. DISTRIBUTION WITHIN PARTICIPATIONAL TYPES BY SELECTED SOCIOECONOMIC ATTRIBUTES

Socioeconomic attribute	Type			
	I. Isolates	II. Neighbors	III. Community Actors	IV. Deviants
Age: % 21–30				
Sample no. 1	14	25	10	13
Sample no. 2	16	24	10	14
Sex: % Female				
Sample no. 1	53	60	53	45
Sample no. 2	50	63	57	48
Education: %				
0–8th grade				
Sample no. 1	35	25	17	32
Sample no. 2	34	32	22	34
9–12th grade				
Sample no. 1	44	49	46	50
Sample no. 2	46	52	46	42
13th grade+				
Sample no. 1	21	16	37	18
Sample no. 2	20	16	32	24
Total N:				
Sample no. 1 (N = 188)*	(64)	(32)	(70)	(22)
Sample no. 2 (N = 943)*	(279)	(174)	(417)	(73)

* Omitted are only those who do not receive local papers, 57 cases.

combined, they are of significantly higher age and education, but there is no significant difference by sex.

Isolates and Deviants are quite similar, having the next lowest proportions of the young, having the lowest proportions of women (about half), but having the highest proportions of eighth graders and the next to highest proportions of the college educated (after the Community Actors). Neighbors, like Community Actors, have a heavy weighting of women (63 per cent); they have the largest proportion of the young (24 per cent); and they have the highest proportion with a high school education and the lowest proportion with a college education. These differences do not appear, a priori, to account for the variation between participational types in their political behavior. First, they are not consistent in direction and, second, they are not nearly extreme enough to account for variations of 30 per cent and more.

When the sample is stratified by these control variables, the results presented in Tables 9 and 10 are obtained for voting and naming leaders, respectively. Younger persons consistently vote less in each participational category. With

TABLE 9. PARTICIPATIONAL TYPE AND VOTING IN MUNICIPAL ELECTIONS CONTROLLED FOR AGE, SEX, AND EDUCATION

	% who have voted by control category for:			
	Type I. Isolates	Type II. Neighbors	Type III. Community Actors	Type IV. Deviants
	Sample no. 1 (N = 153)*			
Age:				
21–30	14	00	33	50
31 +	50	55	86	82
Sex:				
Female	26	32	71	66
Male	66	46	93	88
Education:				
0–8	35	50	78	80
9–12	45	33	76	78
13 +	58	40	87	75
Number	(51)	(26)	(58)	(18)
	Sample no. 2 (N = 763)*			
Age:				
21–30	31	27	47	43
31 +	46	58	73	52
Sex:				
Female	36	41	66	43
Male	52	66	77	58
Education:				
0–8	39	50	59	50
9–12	42	52	66	56
13 +	56	50	82	43
Number	(208)	(153)	(343)	(59)

* Omitted are those ineligible to vote in municipal elections and those who do not receive local papers.

age controlled, however, the participational types discriminate *more consistently*. Thus, of those 31 and older, the percentage voting goes from 46 for Isolates to 58 for Neighbors and 73 for Community Actors. Furthermore, with age controlled Community Actors in each category are more likely to have voted than are the Deviants. While variation by age is somewhat greater than variation by participational type, the young are a small proportion of each category. And the young Community Actors are as likely to vote as the older Isolates.

Women who are Community Actors are more likely to vote than male Isolates or Deviants, and as likely as male Neighbors (though only the difference with male Isolates is significant). In general, differences by sex average about 15 per cent, with men more likely to vote in each case (significantly, the difference is least among Community Actors); the differences by participational types, however, at the theoretical extremes are 30 per cent for women and 20 per cent for men (Isolates as compared with Community Actors).

Education is a consistently important differentiator for Isolates and Community Actors; the proportion voting goes from 39 to 42 to 56, among the former, and from 59 to 66 to 82 among the latter. (The only significant differences are between the college educated and each of the other levels, however). Education makes no consistent difference among either Neighbors or Deviants. And, at each educational level, participational type is a strong differentiator, with a variation range of about 20 per cent. Community Actors with an eighth-grade education or less are more likely to have voted than are any of the other three types with college educations.

Turning now to those who named local leaders in each participational type, with similar controls exercised, we find very similar results. Age, however, is much less important than participational type in differentiating ability to name leaders. The average difference by age is about 10 per cent, but by participational type the range is from 23 to 48 per cent for the young, 30 to 60 per cent for those 31 and over. The same is true for sex, with a range (from Isolate to Community Actor) of 28 per cent for women, 25 per cent for men. And for this variable there is no important difference between the sexes in the Community Actor category. The results obtained after controlling for education show that there is no consistent difference in ability to name leaders except among Community Actors, where the proportion naming leaders goes from 51 to 57 to 67 per cent. (Only the difference between Isolates and Community Actors is significant.) Other differences are slight and inconsistent. Within each educational level, however, variation is striking, with a difference between Isolates and Community Actors of 23 per cent for the lower educational classes and 47 per cent for those with college education.

Young Community Actors are more competent than older persons in all other categories; female Community Actors are more competent than males in all other categories; Community Actors with grade-school educations are more competent than the college educated in all other categories.

Some further controls: The discussion thus far has presented the results of analysis of the test sample, based in every case upon prior analysis of the laboratory sample. In order to give more degrees of freedom to the data (and therefore require more of the theory) it was decided to select some independent measures of political action and information, as well as an independent measure of social rank. These were the variables selected:

1) For political action, voting in school board elections was selected; this is an electorate coterminous with the population sampled—all residents have a school district in which to vote.

2) For political information, reliance was placed upon a measure of ignorance of the electoral rules. In questioning the informant about voting in local elec-

TABLE 10. PARTICIPATIONAL TYPE AND NAMING OF LOCAL LEADERS, CONTROLLED FOR AGE, SEX, AND EDUCATION

	% who could name a local leader by control category for:			
	Type I. Isolates	Type II. Neighbors	Type III. Community Actors	Type IV. Deviants
		Sample no. 1 ($N = 188$)		
Age:				
21–30	22	50	70	00
31 +	29	46	73	26
Sex:				
Female	23	42	62	30
Male	33	55	84	17
Education:				
0–8	14	60	66	28
9–12	43	44	69	18
13 +	23	40	81	25
Number	(64)	(32)	(70)	(22)
		Sample no. 2 ($N = 943$)*		
Age:				
21–30	23	37	48	33
31 +	30	42	60	43
Sex:				
Female	22	35	60	31
Male	37	51	62	50
Education:				
0–8	28	32	51	52
9–12	34	45	57	31
13 +	20	43	67	44
Number	(279)	(174)	(417)	(73)

* Omitted are those who do not receive a community paper, 57 cases.

tions, in order to minimize inflation of reported voting the following procedure was used; first, the individual was shown a card with a list of local governmental officials on it (officials in a city government, members of a school board, officials in a fire district, officials in a county government); second, he was asked, "Which of these officials can people vote for here?" A substantial proportion of the people living in the incorporated municipalities did not know people there voted for municipal officials, and another substantial proportion did not know whether they could vote for school board officials. (Only those who knew were asked if they had voted.) Those persons who could vote in either kind of election but either said they could not or they did not know were considered to be incompetent—or to have incomplete information.

3) For an independent control, individuals were divided into professionals, managers, proprietors, and officials, clerical and sales workers (all termed white collar), and all others.

The results of these analyses are presented in Table 11 for the larger sample only.

With respect to voting in school board elections, the range is from 30 per cent for Isolates to 56 per cent for Community Actors; the range for the white-collar portion of the sample is from 25 to 57 per cent, for the blue-collar workers from 34 to 56 per cent. Thus the blue-collar Community Actors are more likely to vote than white-collar workers in the other three categories. The same is true with respect to correct knowledge of school board and municipal electorates· 21 per cent of the Community Actors are ignorant with respect to school board elections compared with 37 per cent of the Isolates, and 12 per cent are ignorant of municipal elections compared with 25 per cent of the Isolates. Although blue-collar workers are consistently more ignorant, the differences are slight compared with differences between participational types. In each occupational category Community Actors are significantly higher

TABLE 11. VOTING IN SCHOOL BOARD ELECTIONS AND INFORMATION ON THE ELECTORAL PROCESS BY PARTICIPATIONAL TYPE, CONTROLLED FOR OCCUPATION

Participational type	% voting, school board election	% with incorrect information for:	
		School bd. election	Municipal election
I. Isolates (279)	30	37	25
White Collar	25	36	20
Blue Collar	34	38	29
II. Neighbors (174)	35	36	24
White Collar	39	37	19
Blue Collar	31	35	27
III. Community Actors (417)	56	21	12
White Collar	57	20	11
Blue Collar	56	24	16
IV. Deviants (73)	50	29	31
White Collar	51	27	21
Blue Collar	50	31	50
Total number = 943 *			

* Omitted are those who do not receive the local paper, 57 cases.

in competence than any other type. They are similarly more apt to vote—with the exception of Deviants—than any other.

In summary: not one of the standard background variables invalidates the importance of the participational types as predictors of political action and political information. In certain cases, controlling for background variables strengthens and clarifies the relationship between participational type and political behavior.

Social community and political community: A large proportion of the St. Louis suburban area is unincorporated; that is, no municipal level of governmental organization exists. If the general theory here applied is correct, however, there should be a form of spatially defined social organization at both the neighborhood and the residential enclave (or local community) level. In order to test this proposition, the sample was divided into those living in incorporated and unincorporated areas. Distribution of participational types for the two kinds of local area are presented in Table 12.

There is only one striking difference between the two kinds of local areas; a significantly larger proportion of the population in the unincorporated areas is made up of Isolates, and a smaller proportion is made up of Neighbors. The proportions of Community Actors and of Deviants are, however, almost identical. This is strong evidence for the existence of a local community at the nonpolitical level.

In order to test the importance of this community, the following hypotheses were formulated: (1) there will be more people in the incorporated area who can name local leaders, for there are more organizational platforms upon which leaders can stand, (2) when, however, political leaders are differentiated from nonpolitical leaders, those in the unincorporated areas will be able to name the

TABLE 12. DISTRIBUTION OF PARTICIPATIONAL TYPES BY POLITICAL ORGANIZATION, INCORPORATED AND UNINCORPORATED

Participational type	Incorporated areas		Unincorporated areas	
	%	N	%	N
Type I Isolates	27	208	40	71
Type II Neighbors	20	153	12	21
Type III Community Actors	45	343	41	74
Type IV Deviants	8	59	7	14
Total * (943)	100	763	100	180

* Omitted are those who do not receive a local paper, 57 cases.

latter in as many cases as will persons living in municipalities, and (3) participational type will be an important differentiator of ability to name leaders in each kind of local area. The results of these analyses are presented in Table 13.

TABLE 13. POLITICAL LEADERS AND COMMUNITY LEADERS NAMED BY PARTICIPATIONAL TYPE IN UNINCORPORATED AND INCORPORATED AREAS

Participational type	Unincorporated				Incorporated			
	% who named:			No.	% who named:			No.
	Any leader	Political leader	Non-political leader		Any leader	Political leader	Non-political leader	
I. Isolates	31	13	21	(71)	46	39	17	(208)
II. Neighbors	40	14	29	(21)	52	42	16	(153)
III. Community Actors	53	13	41	(74)	73	52	33	(343)
IV. Deviants	50	21	36	(14)	52	41	24	(59)
Total N * (943)				(180)				(763)

* Omitted are those who do not get a local paper, 57 cases.

There seems little doubt that persons in the incorporated areas are better able to name one or more local leaders. This was true for every class of actor. This is entirely accounted for, however, by the *political leaders* named. Persons living in the unincorporated areas were, in each category, more likely to be able to name nonpolitical leaders. Community Actors were far more likely to be able to name leaders in each type of area: 73 per cent could do so, compared with 46 per cent of the Isolates in the incorporated areas, 53 compared with 31 in unincorporated areas. The same was true for political and nonpolitical leaders separately in the incorporated areas, but it only held for nonpolitical leaders in the unincorporated ones. There was such a paucity of leaders to name that there is no significant variation in the unincorporated areas by participational type.

CONCLUSIONS

The analysis has supported the major hypotheses derived from the general theory presented earlier.[5] It has, further, established some bench marks indicating the quantitative importance of the relations hypothesized—those between population type and household type and those between participational type and political behavior. It has, incidentally, indicated the utility of combining analysis of census data with analysis of sample survey data; the key operation in each case was aggregation by position in attribute space. The interposition of organizational theory between the regularities of mass data at the census tract level and of individual data at the sample survey level has resulted in a considerable increase of explanatory and predictive power.

However, differences between categories of 30 per cent or so certainly do not indicate that explanation is near completion. Further discrimination is necessary—at the level of theory and at the level of objective indicators. The latter have been crude and simple, a first approximation, nor have the different explanatory levels been combined as they could be; the major purpose of this analysis has been to demonstrate the *chain* of relationships between social structure and politics. Further refinement and combination of the variables will result in much sharper discriminations (or predictions).

Finally, it should be remembered that any study of a given metropolitan area is a case study. It is the writer's conviction that the variables considered in this theory are general enough to apply to any American metropolitan population.

NOTES

[1] Scott Greer, "The Social Structure and Political Process of Suburbia," *American Sociological Review*, XXV (1960), 514–526.

[2] For a description of the metropolitan area in these terms, see The Metropolitan St. Louis Survey (8157 Delmar Blvd., University City, Mo., *Background for Action, First Public Report of the Metropolitan St. Louis Survey*, 1957. For an explanation of the Shevky-Bell typology, see Eshref Shevky and Wendell Bell, *Social Area Analysis* (Stanford, Calif.: Stanford University Press, 1955).

[3] Reprinted from Greer, *op. cit.*

[4] Cf. the author's extensive analyses of these variables, as related to participation in local elections, in John C. Bollens, ed., *Exploring the Metropolitan Community* (Berkeley: University of Calif. Press, 1961).

[5] Greer, *op cit.*

16. DEMOCRACY AND OLIGARCHY IN TRADE UNIONS

Seymour Martin Lipset, Martin Trow, James Coleman

In recent years political democracy has proved so vulnerable to changes in social structure that the better understanding of these processes has become one of the major tasks of social science. Few still believe (as the American negotiators in Paris in 1919 seemed to believe) that formal guarantees and written constitutions can insure democracy. The most carefully worded guarantees have been swept aside, and the most intelligent of constitutions ignored, until now men seem liable to the opposite error of considering guarantees and constitutions worthless.

In few areas of political life is the discrepancy between the formal juridical guarantees of democratic procedure and the actual practice of oligarchic rule so marked as in private or voluntary organizations such as trade unions, professional and business associations, veterans' groups, and cooperatives. In fact, as many observers have noted, almost all such organizations are characterized internally by the rule of a one-party oligarchy. That is, one group, which controls the administration, usually retains power indefinitely, rarely faces organized opposition, and when faced with such opposition often resorts to undemocratic procedures to eliminate it. This is especially true for national organizations.

There is, however, one trade union—the International Typographical Union (ITU), the organization of the men who set type in the print shops of North America—which does not fit this pattern. It is the only American trade union in which organized parties regularly oppose each other for election to the chief union posts, and in which a two-party system has been institutionalized. Since the beginning of this century, the officers of the international union and of most of the larger locals have been chosen in biennial elections, in which two or more political parties have offered a complete slate of candidates for all offices. The two major parties of the union operate much as do the Democratic and Republican Parties in American politics, though they have no connection with any group or party outside the union. The parties have been of roughly equal strength in the international since 1920, so that turnover in office occurs at least as frequently as in national politics. In the thirty-five years since 1920, five incumbent presidents of the international have been defeated for re-election. In the New York local of the union, the largest local of the ITU, containing 10% of the membership, seven out of the last fourteen elections have resulted in defeat for the incumbent president. Probably nothing like this has happened in any other trade union or other of the private governments (as we may call voluntary organizations) anywhere in the world.

source: Seymour Martin Lipset, Martin Trow, and James Coleman, *Union Democracy* (New York: The Free Press of Glencoe, 1956), pp. 1–16. © by The Free Press, a corporation, 1956. Reprinted with permission of The Macmillan Company.

THE THEORY OF OLIGARCHY

The pattern which characterizes almost all voluntary organizations was generalized over forty years ago by the German sociologist, Robert Michels, when he laid down his famous "iron law of oligarchy" in the following terms: "It is organization which gives birth to the dominion of the elected over the electors, of the mandataries over the mandators, of the delegates over the delegators. Who says organization says oligarchy." [1]

The experience of most people as well as the studies of social scientists concerned with the problem of organization would tend to confirm Michels' generalization. In their trade unions, professional societies, business associations, and cooperatives—in the myriad nominally democratic voluntary organizations —men have learned, and learn again every day, that the clauses in the constitutions which set forth the machinery for translating membership interests and sentiments into organizational purpose and action bear little relationship to the actual political processes which determine what their organizations do. At the head of most private organizations stands a small group of men most of whom have held high office in the organization's government for a long time, and whose tenure and control is rarely threatened by a serious organized internal opposition. In such organizations, regardless of whether the membership has a nominal right to control through regular elections or conventions, the real and often permanent power rests with the men who hold the highest positions.

Since Michels first wrote, many books and articles have been written about oligarchy in voluntary organizations, but almost invariably they have documented the operation of his iron law in another set of circumstances. They have shown how control of the organizational machinery, combined with membership passivity, operates to perpetuate oligarchic control. From these studies it is clear that unions and other voluntary organizations more closely resemble one-party states in their internal organization than they do democratic societies with organized legitimate opposition and turnover in office. Indeed, the pattern of one-party oligarchy is so common in the labor movement that one defender of the Soviet Union has pointed to it as a justification of the one-party regime in that country:

> What is totalitarianism? A country that has a totalitarian government operates like our union operates. There are no political parties. People are elected to govern the country based upon their records. . . . That is totalitarianism. If we started to divide up and run a Republican set of officers, a Democratic set, a Communist set and something else we would have one hell of a time.[2]

Oligarchy becomes a problem only in organizations which assume as part of their public value system the absence of oligarchy, that is, democracy. In societies or organizations in which the self-perpetuation of the governing elite is the norm few people will raise questions regarding the determinants or consequences of oligarchy. In such organizations oligarchy is a thing given, not a phenomenon to be explained. However, when one finds an organization ostensibly devoted to the extension of democracy which is nevertherless itself undemocratically governed, some explanation seems demanded. Thus in his *Political Parties* Michels, himself a socialist at the time he was writing, raised the question of why the German Social-Democratic Party and the German labor movement, though ideologically committed to a completely democratic society and actively engaged in fighting for democratic rights within Germany, were themselves oligarchic in their internal structures. To Michels, oligarchy within the democratic socialist movement was significant because it was an "unintended consequence" of organization. For him, the fact that the conservative German political parties or other organizations were also oligarchic was not a problem, since they did not believe in democracy to the same degree as the socialists, and in fact often upheld the principle of oligarchy for the larger society. In the same way and at about the same time the oligarchic structure of American political parties attracted the interest of some observers such as Moise Ostrogorski, who were struck by the apparent contradiction between American democratic ideals and the reality of the boss and the machine.[3]

The problem had been recognized earlier, of course, but until Michels, European socialists took a generally optimistic view of the problem of machine domination of workers' organizations. Marx and Engels themselves viewed oligarchy as part of the early stage of the political emergence of the working class. They believed that the workers could come to control their institutions as soon as large numbers of them acquired class consciousness and political sophistication. Clique domination of socialist groups could not survive when workers really understood the facts of political life.[4]

American political scientists, with their generally liberal and optimistic outlook, took a similar point of view. They saw the boss and the machine as social problems which would gradually be solved as democracy advanced, the immigrant was assimilated, and education was extended. They viewed the American political party as progressively moving out of close control of a small group of leaders, first to the caucus, then to open conventions, and finally to the ultimate stage of the preferential primary. During the first period of this century, this point of view found expression in a movement to extend formal popular control through the direct primary, initiative, referendum, and recall.

In Europe where the idea of a popular democracy did not actually come to fulfillment in terms of universal adult or male suffrage without class restrictions until after World War I, few efforts were made to formally democratize the structure of political parties. But the left and labor groups, which were concerned with achieving a more complete democracy, invariably set up formal blueprints which provided for a high degree of popular control over the selection of leaders and formation of policy by way of regular conventions, discussion periods, and elections.

Despite the optimistic hopes of early socialist bodies and the institution of formal democratic control, the problem remained. As the trade-union and the socialist movement grew in size and power, members who came to disagree with the policies of incumbent leaders found, with rare exceptions, that it was impossible to dislodge those leaders from office. They discovered that offices whose authority originally and formally derived from the consent of the members gave officials power over the members. In most cases, however, the opponents of an existing oligarchy did not generalize from their own experience, nor did they raise the question, is there something in the nature of large-scale organizations which engenders oligarchic control?[5] Rather, like Karl Marx they tended to view the problem in terms of evil or weak men who were corrupted by power, and to place the democratic solution in a change of personnel.

By itself the existence of oligarchy in voluntary organizations rarely leads to great concern even in democratic societies and organizations. In most cases where men have forcefully and articulately opposed oligarchy, their concern has usually arisen from disagreement with the policies of a specific oligarchy. Thus the critics of the American party machine were not basically incensed by boss control *per se,* but rather by the fact that the machine was linked to corruption and inefficient government or refused to support the various social and economic reforms favored by the critics. In the pre-World War I socialist movement Lenin, for example, attacked the leadership of the German Social Democratic Party, not primarily for being oligarchic, but for having betrayed "Marxism." The CIO critics of AFL leadership in the mid-1930's in the United States were obviously not concerned with the lack of democracy within the AFL, but with the fact that the AFL was not organizing the mass production industries. Two American books which first brought Michels' analysis to the attention of the American labor movement were written by supporters of left-wing labor groups, and they objected more to the fact that many union leaders were restraining the post-World War I strike wave than to the fact that they were dictatorial.[6]

Occasionally the criticism of oligarchic control within the labor movement led to successful attempts to further democratize the constitutional structure of unions so as to reduce the power of the officials. A favored remedy introduced in some unions before World War I was to replace convention election of officers by a direct vote of the membership and to require referenda for constitutional changes, as well as to make it possible for members to directly initiate referenda. The Industrial Workers of the World (IWW) tried to insure turnover in office by limiting the number of years that a man might hold office and requiring that he return to the shop after his term as an official.

With very few significant exceptions all the efforts to reduce oligarchic control by formal mechanisms have failed. In those cases where an entrenched oligarchy was finally dislodged, the new leaders soon reverted to the same tactics as they had denounced in the old in order to guarantee their own permanent tenure in office and reduce or eliminate opposition. Even anarchist political and labor groups, whom we might expect to be highly sensitive to the dangers of oligarchy on the basis of their ideology, have succumbed to the blight. In pre-Franco Spain and in other countries where the anarchists had large organizations, a small semipermanent group of leaders maintained itself in power and selected its own replacements through a process of cooptation (selection by the leaders themselves). There is no more persuasive illustration of the unanticipated consequences of men's purposeful social actions than the recurrent transformations of nominally democratic private organizations into oligarchies more concerned with preserving and enhancing their own power and status than in satisfying the demands and interests of the members.[7]

What are the factors that account for the lack of democracy in labor unions? Why do opposition groups find it so difficult to survive? Michels and others who have dealt with the problem have summed it up in broad generalizations: The nature of large-scale organizations is such as to give the incumbent officials overwhelming power as compared with that of the opposition; the situation of the leaders of most unions is such that they wish to stay in office and will adopt dictatorial tactics to do so; and the relationship of the members to their union results in a low level of participation by the members. These factors have been discussed in considerable detail in another publication by the senior author.[8] Some of these generalizations are deserving of treatment here.

Large-scale organizations give union officials a near monopoly of power.

(a) Unions, like all other large-scale organizations, tend to develop a bureaucratic structure, that is, a system of rational (predictable) organization which is hierarchically organized. Bureaucracy is inherent in the sheer problem of administration, in the requirement that unions be "responsible" in their dealings with management (and responsible for their subordinate units),[9] in the need to parallel the structures of business and government, in the desire of workers to eliminate management arbitrariness and caprice, and in the desire of the leaders of unions to reduce the hazards to their permanent tenure of office.

The price of increased union bureaucracy is increased power at the top, decreased power among the ordinary members. With the increase in the power of the top officials over local units and members, the sources of organized opposition are controlled or reduced. Most unions have given their executive boards the right to suspend local officials for violating policies of the central bodies. Whether they follow a conciliatory tone (as when they call for intraunion discipline and responsibility) or a militant one (as when they call for union solidarity in a dispute with management) union leaders strengthen their own hands and justify their monopolization of internal power in the course of articulating organizational needs and purposes.

(b) Control over the formal means of communication within the organization is almost exclusively in the hands of the officials. The individual member's right of free speech is not an effective check on administrative power if the union leaders control all public statements made by members of the administrative or field staff and the union newspaper. Since the only viewpoints about union matters that are widely available to the members are those of the administration, even widespread discontent which might result in organized opposition cannot be effectively expressed.[10]

(c) In most unions, one of the chief factors perpetuating the power of the incumbents is the administration's almost complete monopoly of political skills and the absence of those skills among the rank and file.[11] Within a trade union the principal source of leadership training is the union administrative and political structure itself. The union official, to maintain his position, must become adept in political skills. The average worker, on the other hand, has little opportunity or need to acquire them. Rarely if ever is he called upon to make a speech before a large group, put his thoughts down in writing, or organize a group's activities.[12] To the extent that union officers possess a monopoly of political skills, they inhibit the rise of an effective opposition.

The Leaders Want to Stay in Office

There is a basic strain between the values inherent in society's stratification system and the democratic values of the trade-union movement. With few significant exceptions, every trade-union official has moved up in the status hierarchy by becoming an official. The leader of a large local or national union has the income and prestige of a member of the upper-middle class,[13] and often wields more power than the average upper-middle class person. Most high-status positions carry with them some security of tenure. Democracy, on the other hand, implies permanent insecurity for those in governing positions: the more truly democratic the governing system, the greater the insecurity. Thus every incumbent of a high-status position of power within a democratic system must of necessity anticipate a loss of position.

It is hard for the persons in such positions to accept this insecurity with equanimity. Once high status is secured, there is usually a pressing need to at least retain and protect it.[14] This is particularly true if the discrepancy between the status and the position to which one must return on losing the status is very great. In other words, if the social distance between the trade-union leader's position as an official and his position as a regular worker is great, his need to retain the former will be correlatively great.[15]

The strenuous efforts on the part of many trade-union leaders to eliminate democracy (the possibility of their defeat) from their unions are, for them, necessary adaptive mechanisms. The insecurity of leadership status endemic in democracy, the pressures on leaders to retain their achieved high status, and the fact that by their control over the organizational structure and the use of their special skills they can often maintain their office, all help in the creation of dictatorial oligarchies.

The Members Do Not Participate in Union Politics

Although high participation is not necessarily a sign of democracy (dictatorships also find participation useful), the maintenance of effective opposition to incumbent leaders requires membership participation and interest. Ordinarily, however, few members show much interest in the day-to-day political process within the union; apathy of the members is the normal state of affairs. There are good reasons for this. Most union members, like other people, must spend most of their time at work or with their families. Their remaining free time is generally taken up by their friends, commercial entertainment, and other personally rewarding recreational activities.[16]

Most trade unions in addition are concerned with technical administrative matters, which cannot be of deep interest to the average member. The typical union appears to its members as an administrative agency doing a specific technical job for them. Union leaders will often attempt to sustain this image to prevent "interference" with their conduct of their job. Consequently only a small minority finds the rewards for participation in union affairs great enough to sustain a high level of interest and activity.

The leaders of the trade unions and other formally democratic organizations must in some way explain and justify the suppression, and to do so they make two points: that trade unions are organized for political or industrial conflicts; and that their membership is more homogeneous in background and interests than the citizens of a nation or some other civic political unit. Officials of trade unions have argued that since the group is engaged in perpetual conflict with management, internal opponents only serve the objective interests of the external enemy. They argue further that there is no basis for factionalism in their organization (other than the illegitimate selfish desire for office of ambitious individuals, or the outside interference of Communists) since all the members are workers and have common interests and objectives. According to this thesis, organized political conflict should take place only among classes, not within them. These same two arguments are, of course, used by the Communists to justify the contradiction between the one-party state and democratic values in the Soviet Union. They explain that since the Soviet Union is surrounded by the capitalist enemy any domestic opposition is in effect treason; and that in any case in a one-class workers' state there is no legitimate basis for disagreement.

Strengthening the force of these arguments is the fact that the political decisions of trade unions and of other groups which are totally or in part political pressure groups, such as the American Legion or the American Medical Association, often fall into the realm of "foreign policy": that is, they involve the tactics and relations that these groups should adopt towards outside groups or the state. And just as in national politics there are many pressures toward a unified bipartisan foreign policy, so in trade unions and other voluntary groups we find similar pressures. Potential oppositionists are consequently faced with the likelihood that if they exercise their constitutional democratic rights, they will be denounced for harming the organization and helping the enemy.

The fact remains, however, that the democratic political system of the International Typographical Union does exist. It is obviously no temporary exception, for the party system of the union has lasted for half a century, and regular political conflict in North American printing unions can be dated back to 1815. As we shall note . . . later . . . there are also a few other unions which deviate from the iron law of oligarchy. Up to now almost all analysts of the political systems of private governments have devoted their energies to documenting further examples of oligarchy. Rather than do this we have undertaken an analysis of the major deviant case. From the point of view of the further development of social research in the area of organizational structure, and indeed, the general expansion of our understanding of society, these deviant cases —cases which operate in ways not anticipated by theory—supply the most fruitful subjects for study. Kendall and Wolf have noted that the analysis of deviant cases

can by refining the theoretical structure of empirical studies, increase the predictive value of their findings. In other words, deviant case analysis can and should play a *positive* role in empirical research, rather than being merely the "tidying up" process through which exceptions to the empirical rule are given some plausibility and thus disposed of.[17]

In the course of our analysis of the ITU we have systematically looked for the various *oligarchic mechanisms*—the elements and processes which Michels and others found operative in the organizations which they studied. Many of these mechanisms—for example, the monopolies of power, status, funds, and communications channels which the officials of most unions ordinarily possess —are not found in the ITU, or if present their effects are greatly mitigated by other elements in the system. A large part of our analysis is directed at specifying those elements in the structure of the ITU and the printing industry which work against oligarchic mechanisms, and at spelling out the processes by which they contribute to the maintenance of the union democracy. And as we look for those attributes and patterns in the ITU which work to nullify the oligarchic tendencies present in large organizations, we are implicitly or explicitly setting forth the conditions necessary for the maintenance of democratic politics within private organizations. In this our purpose is not, of course, to "refute" Michels or other previous workers in this area, but rather to refine and build on their insights and findings, paying them the respect of using them more often than we quote them.

A THEORY OF DEMOCRACY

The problem of democratic or oligarchic political institutions may be approached from two vantage points. We may ask, as we have asked [previously], what are the conditions which are responsible for the development and institutionalization of oligarchy, or alternatively we may ask under what conditions democracy arises and becomes institutionalized. All the literature that deals with political institutions in private governments deals with the determinants of oligarchy. We have found only one article that raises the question of under what conditions democracy, the institutionalization of opposition, can exist in voluntary organizations.[18] There is of course a voluminous literature discussing democracy as a system of civil government, but we must ask ourselves whether a variable which seems related to the existence of democracy in states is relevant to the existence of democracy in organizations.

Aristotle, for example, suggested that democracy can exist only in a society which is predominantly middle class.[19] In essence he and later theorists argued that only in a wealthy society with a roughly equal distribution of income could one get a situation in which the mass of the population would intelligently participate in politics and develop the self-restraint necessary to avoid succumbing to the appeals of irresponsible demagogues. A society divided between a large impoverished mass and a small favored elite would result either in a dictatorship of the elite or a dictatorship of demagogues who would appeal to the masses against the elite. This proposition still appears to be valid. Political democracy has had a stable existence only in the wealthier countries, which have large middle classes and comparatively well-paid and well-educated working classes. Applying this proposition to trade-union government, we would expect to find democracy in organizations whose members have a relatively high income and more than average security, and in which the gap between the organizational elite and the membership is not great.

A second proposition which has been advanced about democracy is that it works best in relatively small units, in which a large proportion of the citizenry can directly observe the operation of their governments: [20] for example, the small Greek city-states, the New England town meetings, and the Swiss cantons. While historical research has indicated that much of the popular mythology about the democratic character of these societies is untrue, it is probably true that the smaller a political unit, the greater the possibility of democratic control. Increased size necessarily involves the delegation of political power to professional rulers and the growth of bureaucratic institutions. The translation of this proposition to the level of private government is clear: The smaller the association or unit, the greater membership control. There can be little doubt that this is true in the trade-union movement. [21]

Both of these approaches to democracy, that in terms of internal stratification, and that in terms of size, however, are somewhat unsatisfactory as solutions to the problem of democracy in complex societies or large private organizations. Clearly democratic political institutions do exist in large, complex, and bureaucratically run societies and in societies which have wide variations in the distribution of income, status, and power. There is a third proposition about the conditions that favor democracy that seems to be of greater value for our understanding of democracy in large private organizations. We know it under two names, the theory of political pluralism, and the theory of the mass society. Writers in English-speaking countries, trying to explain why democracy exists in these countries, have developed the theory of political pluralism. European writers, trying to explain why democracy seems so weak in Germany and other countries, have developed the theory of the mass society. Both theories say in essence the same thing. They argue that in a large complex society the body of the citizenry is unable to affect the policies of the state. If citizens do not belong to politically relevant *groups,* if they are "atomized," the controllers of the central power apparatus will completely dominate the society. Translated to the realm of the internal politics of private organizations, this theory suggests that democracy is most likely to become institutionalized in organizations whose members form organized or structured subgroups which while maintaining a basic loyalty to the larger organization constitute relatively independent and autonomous centers of power within the organization. Or to put it in another way, democracy is strengthened when members are not only related to the larger organization but are also affiliated with or loyal to subgroups within the organization. [22] Since it is this approach which we have found most useful in understanding the internal political system of the ITU, we will briefly characterize it here.

Democratic rights have developed in societies largely through the struggles of various groups—class, religious, sectional, economic, professional, and so on —against one another and against the group which controls the state. Each interest group may desire to carry out its own will, but if no one group is strong enough to gain complete power, the result is the development of tolerance. In large measure the development of the concept of tolerance, of recognition of the rights of groups with whom one disagrees to compete for adherents or power, arose out of conflicts among strong and indestructible groups in different societies. There were a number of processes through which tolerance became legitimate. In some situations groups such as the Catholic and the Protestant churches attempted to destroy the opposing faction, but finally recognized that the complete victory of one group was impossible or could occur only at the risk of destroying the very fabric of society. In these conflicts minority or opposition groups developed a democratic ideology, an insistence on specific minority rights, as a means of legitimating their own right to exist. These groups might then force the dominant power group to grant these rights in order to prevent a revolutionary upsurge or achieve power themselves. For them to reject their own program may then mean a considerable loss of support from adherents who have come to hold the democratic values.

Once democracy is established in a society, private organizations continue to play a positive role. These organizations serve as channels of communication among different groups in the population, crystallizing and organizing conflicting interests and opinions. Their existence makes more difficult the triumph of such movements as Communism and Fascism, for a variety of groups lay claim to the allegiance of the population, reinforcing diversity of belief and helping mobilize such diversity in the political arena.[23] This brief discussion of theories of political pluralism and of mass society does not pretend to be an adequate summary. . . . We have discussed them here to sensitize the reader to the type of factors which we were looking for in our analysis of the political system of the ITU.

NOTES

[1] Robert Michels: *Political Parties,* Glencoe, Ill., Free Press, 1949, p. 401. This book was first published in Germany in 1911.

[2] Harry Bridges, in *Proceedings of the Seventh Biennial Convention I.L.W.U., April 7–11, 1947* (San Francisco, 1947) p. 178. See opposite page.

[3] Moise Ostrogorski: *Democracy and the Organization of Political Parties,* New York, The Macmillan Company, 1902. Bryce, examining the oligarchy endemic to political organizations, considers boss control normal. Cf. James Bryce: *Modern Democracies,* New York, The Macmillan Company, 1921, Vol. 2, Chap. 75.

[4] "The fact that here too [in the British Independent Labour Party] people like Keir Hardy, Shaw Maxwell, and others are pursuing all sorts of secondary aims of personal ambition is, of course, obvious. But the danger arising from this becomes less as the Party itself becomes stronger and gets more of a mass character."—Engels to Sorge, in Karl Marx and Frederick Engels: *Selected Correspondence,* New York, International Publishers Co., Inc., 1942, p. 507. Cf. also Nicolai Bukharin: *Historical Materialism,* New York, International Publishers Co., Inc., 1925, Chap. 8.

[5] Bukharin, *op. cit.,* pp. 306–7, explicitly notes this fact that critics of oligarchy are concerned only with policy, not with oligarchy.

[6] Sylvia Kopald: *Rebellion in Labor Unions,* New York, Boni & Liveright, 1924; William Z. Foster: *Misleaders of Labor,* Chicago, Trade Union Educational League, 1927.

[7] It is, of course, true that the leaders' objectives of personal power and permanent tenure need not conflict with the needs of the members. Most voluntary organizations do in fact represent their members' interests in conflicts with other groups. But there may arise a situation in which the needs and goals of the leaders or simply their desire for peace and quiet as they remain in office lead them to oppose or not fight for membership objectives. In an organization in which the members cannot vote on alternative procedures or courses of action, it is impossible to know whether a leadership decision is in fact something that the members desire.

[8] "The Political Process in Trade Unions: A Theoretical Statement," in Morroe Berger *et al., Freedom and Social Control in Modern Society,* New York, D. Van Nostrand Company, Inc., 1954, pp. 82–124; cf. also Philip Selznick: "An Approach to the Theory of Bureaucracy," *American Sociological Review,* 8:47–54 (1953).

[9] Cf. Joseph Shister: "The Laws of Union Control in Collective Bargaining," *Quarterly Journal of Economics,* 60:513–545 (August 1946).

[10] Cf. in this connection P. F. Lazarsfeld and R. K. Merton: "Mass Communication, Popular Taste and Organized Social Action," in Lyman Bryson (ed.), *The Communication of Ideas,* New York, Harper & Brothers, 1948, pp. 95–118.

[11] Cf. Max Weber: "Politics as a Vocation," in H. Gerth and C. W. Mills (eds.), *From Max Weber: Essays in Sociology,* New York, Oxford University Press, 1946, pp. 77–128.

[12] The history of the British labor movements testifies to the value of such training. Many of its early leaders were men who first served as officers or Sunday-school teachers in the Methodist or other nonconformist churches. Cf. A. P. Belden: *George Whitefield the Awakener,* London, S. Low, Marston & Co., Ltd., 1930, pp. 247 ff.

[13] Cf. Cecil C. North and Paul K. Hatt: "Jobs and Occupations: A Popular Evaluation," in Logan Wilson and William A. Kolb (eds.), *Sociological Analysis,* New York, Harcourt, Brace and Company, Inc., 1949, pp. 464–73.

[14] Furthermore, as Shepard points out, "The demands on leadership are heavy and their positions precarious. . . . To survive, leaders must be extraordinarily able, and able leaders are capable of consolidating their positions." Cf. Herbert A. Shepard: "Democratic Control in a Labor Union," *American Journal of Sociology,* 54:311–316 (1949).

[15] Public officials in a democratic society are also faced with this problem. Most of them, however, come from occupational positions or social strata which permit them to return to private life without a sharp decline in income.

[16] Cf. Bernard Barber: "Participation and Mass Apathy in Associations," in A. W. Gouldner, *Studies in Leadership,* New York, Harper & Brothers, 1950, pp. 477–504.

[17] Patricia Kendall and Katherine Wolf: "The Analysis of Deviant Cases in Communications Research 1948–1949," in Paul F. Lazarsfeld and Frank Stanton (eds.), *Communications Research, 1948–1949,* New York, Harper & Brothers, 1949, p. 153.

[18] Philip Selznick, "The Iron Law of Bureaucracy," *Modern Review,* January, 1950, pp. 157–165.

[19] Aristotle: *Politics,* IV, 11.

[20] Thomas Jefferson advocated "general political organization on the basis of small units, small enough so that all members could have direct communication with one another and take care of all community affairs."—John Dewey: *Freedom and Culture,* New York, G. P. Putnam's Sons, 1939, p. 159. Cf. also Gunnar Myrdal: *An American Dilemma,* New York, Harper & Brothers, 1944, pp. 716–19; John Dewey: *The*

Public and Its Problems, New York, Henry Holt and Company, Inc., 1927, Chap. 5; "The Federalist, No. 10," in *The Federalist,* New York, Modern Library, Inc., 1937.

[21] It has been pointed out as well that in small homogeneous societies a political democracy often succumbs to the danger of extreme democracy: intolerance of the minority by the majority. The authors of the *Federalist Papers* were well aware of this and pointed out the dangers of a small "pure" democracy. See *The Federalist,* pp. 57–59.

[22] "The stability of any democracy depends not on imposing a single unitary loyalty and viewpoint but on maintaining conflicting loyalties and viewpoints in a state of tension."—R. H. S. Crossman: "On Political Neuroses," *Encounter,* 2:66 (May 1954).

[23] Calhoun thought these factors so important he wanted to institutionalize faction by means of the concept *concurrent majority.* Cf. John C. Calhoun: *A Disquisition on Government,* New York, Political Science Classics, 1947.

17. MASS SOCIETY AND DEMOCRATIC ORDER

William Kornhauser

. . . [We have] examined conditions in Western society that favor mass politics. Mass politics occurs when large numbers of people engage in political activity outside of the procedures and rules instituted by a society to govern political action. Mass politics in democratic society therefore is anti-democratic, since it contravenes the constitutional order. The extreme case of mass politics is the totalitarian movement, notably communism and fascism. Less extreme examples of mass politics are McCarthyism and Poujadism.

Modern democratic systems possess a distinct vulnerability to mass politics because they invite the whole population, most of which has historically been politically quiescent, to engage in politics. However, this does not mean that all or even most democratic systems succumb to mass politics. The problem is to identify those factors that increase the vulnerability of democratic systems to mass politics, and those that decrease it, in order to be able to specify the conditions that may strengthen democratic politics and civil liberty.

The most satisfactory theory of the vulnerability of social systems to mass politics is the theory of mass society. This theory has two major versions. One, which may be called the aristocratic criticism, asserts that the primary cause of mass politics lies in the loss of exclusiveness of elites as a result of the rise of popular participation in the critical centers of society. According to this version of the theory of mass society, the main danger to political order and civil liberty is the domination of elites by masses. The other version, which may be called the democratic criticism, stresses the vulnerability of masses to domination by elites. This danger to political order and civil liberty is believed to result from the atomization of society and the rise of elites capable of mobilizing isolated and unattached people. A combination of these two versions produces a stronger theory than either one alone. This integrated theory of mass society locates the causes of mass politics in the condition of both elites and non-elites, that is, in the total social structure and especially in the structure of groups intermediate between the state and the family.

"Mass society," then, is treated as an abstract type. It is always a question of the *degree* to which an actual society is a "mass society." A society is a "mass society" to the extent that both elites and non-elites are directly accessible to one another by virtue of the weakness of groups capable of mediating between them. Insofar as these conditions prevail, neither elites nor non-elites are capable of preventing frequent political activity outside of established channels. Other types of society are more capable of minimizing mass politics (and other forms of mass behavior). Since both elites and non-elites are bound by fixed status in communal (e.g., feudal) society, there is little mass behavior in this kind of

source: William Kornhauser, *The Politics of Mass Society* (New York: The Free Press of Glencoe, 1959), pp. 227–238. © by The Free Press, a corporation, 1959. Reprinted by permission of The Macmillan Company.

system. Since non-elites are bound by multiple group affiliations of their own choosing in pluralist (e.g., liberal) society, there is relatively little mass politics in this kind of system. Since non-elites are subject to extensive control by the political elite in totalitarian (e.g., Communist and Fascist) society, there is little mass politics in this kind of system.

By means of this theory of mass society, a large number of observations on political phenomena in particular organizations, classes, communities, and whole societies can be fitted together to form a coherent picture of the conditions that favor mass behavior in politics. Groups which are particularly vulnerable to mass movements manifest major discontinuities in their structure during periods of change. Thus, communism and fascism have gained strength in social systems undergoing sudden and extensive changes in the structure of authority and community. Sharp tears in the social fabric caused by widespread unemployment or by major military defeat are highly favorable to mass politics. Social classes which provide disproportionate support for mass movements are those that possess the fewest social ties among their members. This means above all the lower social classes. However, since there are sections of all social classes which tend to be socially atomized, members of all social classes are to be found among the participants in mass politics: unattached (especially freelance) intellectuals, marginal (especially small) businessmen and farmers, and isolated workers have engaged in mass politics in times of crisis.

. . . We have stated conditions which favor mass movements destructive of political order and civil liberty. We now shall summarize our analysis by assessing what it implies about the conditions favorable to liberal democracy. This should help to dispel fears that a theory of mass society necessarily is antagonistic to liberal democratic values, or that it is a prophecy of doom.

The theory of mass society stresses the need for the autonomy of certain social units if order with freedom is to be secured. The various versions of this theory tend to divide into two camps according to whether primary stress is placed on the autonomy of elites or on the autonomy of non-elites. The aristocratic view stresses the need for the independence of elites on the premise that constitutional liberty above all requires leadership with the capacity to define, exemplify, and defend it. The democratic view stresses the need for the independence of non-elites on the premise that constitutional liberty above all requires safeguards against the accumulation of power by any group, especially elites. In this fundamental matter, the two views are not incompatible; on the contrary, each is strengthened when it is combined with the other. Civil liberty requires considerable social autonomy of *both* elites and non-elites. This means specifically that elites and non-elites must have the following characteristics:

    (a) There must be extensive self-government, private as well as public, and individuals must belong to several self-governing units.

    (b) There must be extensive opportunities for elites to formulate policies and take action without *ad hoc* interference from the outside.

However, democracy entails a fundamental restriction on the autonomy of elites, especially in politics. This restriction is twofold: first, elites will be restricted by one another in that they will be constrained to compete with one another for leadership; and secondly, elites will be restricted by non-elites in that they will be constrained to compete for the people's votes. An implication of this conception of democracy also involves a restriction on non-elites: the electorate will accept the leadership that they have selected, until the time when it may be rejected according to duly constituted procedure.[1]

In summary, a liberal democracy requires widespread participation in the selection of leaders, and a large amount of self-governing activity on the part of non-elites. It also requires competition among leaders and would-be leaders, and considerable autonomy for those who win positions of leadership. The basic question arises, what kind of social structure will meet these conditions of liberal democracy? The theory of mass society expounded in the present study implies that social pluralism is a social arrangement which performs this function. A plurality of independent and limited-function groups supports liberal democracy by providing social bases of free and open competition for leadership, widespread participation in the selection of leaders, restraint in the application of pressures on leaders, and self-government in wide areas of social life. Therefore, where social pluralism is strong, liberty and democracy tend to be strong; and conversely, forces which weaken social pluralism also weaken liberty and democracy.

In the transition from medieval to modern society, the extent to which pluralist forms emerged as substitutes for communal forms was one decisive factor which determined the fate of liberal democracy. Social pluralism flourished in Northwestern Europe and in North America, and these are the areas where liberty and democracy have found their greatest strength. In seventeenth century England, for example, a plurality of class and religious groups already were developing strong roots. As a consequence, it was possible for new social forms adapted to the requirements of urban-industrial life to emerge from older relations. For a long time, it has been widely feared that urban-industrial conditions would destroy an independent group life. But in the modern world, it is among the highly urbanized and industrialized societies that social pluralism and liberal democracy have achieved their fullest and firmest expression. The Communist movement, for example, has won its widest following within the less industrialized societies of the Western world—in Italy and France,[2] rather than in such nations as Britain or the United States. Liberal democracy is strongest in countries possessing the highest per capita output of industrial energy and personal income (for example, among Western countries, the correlation between size of Communist vote and per capita energy is—.83; and the correlation between size of Communist vote and per capita income is —.93).

But the fact that countries like the Soviet Union are attaining high levels of economic development without liberty or democracy shows that the extent of industrialization alone is not decisive. More important is the mode of economic development, especially whether that development is accomplished through pluralist as well as bureaucratic agencies. Where economic development takes place by means of a variety of social forms, including private as well as public enterprises, liberty and democracy are more likely to grow than where it occurs under the exclusive aegis of the state.

In any case, Marx was wrong: it is not the most highly developed capitalist systems which reveal the greatest social unrest and revolutionary tendencies.

Instead, this has been the fate of the less developed countries of Europe (and, even more, of Asia and Africa).

But if Marx is wrong, will Weber prove to be right? For Weber, bureaucratization, not the class struggle, provides the central dynamic of the modern world. It is widely believed that bureaucracy constitutes the strongest threat to social pluralism and liberal democracy in the highly industrialized countries. This view raises important issues about the future development of American society. Several of these issues are briefly noted in the remaining pages.

One of the most prominent arguments which attribute mass consequences to the rationalization of organization focuses on the transformation of the middle classes: the advent of large corporate organization at the expense of small productive property transforms the bases of middle-class power and undermines the capacity of this class to continue as a major pluralist force in the contemporary social order. If an independent middle class served to support democratic rule prior to the emergence of large-scale urban-industrial organization, it is believed that the ascendancy of bureaucratic organization now threatens to atomize the middle classes and as a result weaken the social foundations of liberal democracy. The shift from the old to the new middle classes is fraught with peril, according to this line of reasoning.

The trouble with this argument is that it is based on too narrow a conception of the bases of social participation and social power. It may be granted that the property basis of social power and participation is weakened by the shift from an entrepreneurial to an employee society. But at the same time new forms of organization, such as professional associations and civic groups, have been developing to take its place. As a result, members of the new middle class have high rates of participation in voluntary associations, political affairs and community life.

A burgeoning literature of social criticism is directed toward the meaning of this heightened participation of the new middle classes, especially in the United States. Some social critics of the new middle class argue that far from being non-participants, members of this class engage in group activity to such an extent that they lose their autonomy as individuals. This is the major characteristic imputed to the "organization man," who is absorbed by the organization for which he works and whose family is absorbed by the (suburban) community in which he lives.[3] The threat to individual autonomy is believed to lie not in the lack of organization but in the inclusiveness of relations to the organization: the hold of the modern corporation over its members begins to resemble that of the medieval corporation over its members. A closely related issue concerns the quality of many community,[4] religious,[5] and other social ties of members of this class: these relations are often alleged to mask an underlying passivity and lack of commitment, and to feed on a widespread disposition to overconform. These issues remain to be settled, but in any case, the evidence does not support the contention that the new middle classes are composed of atomized masses.

A second prominent argument that attributes mass consequences to the ascendancy of large-scale organization focuses on the transformation of the public realm. It is frequently asserted that the expanding scale of bureaucratic organization tends to *centralize* public activities and to substitute administration for politics, and therefore to undermine the basis for political participation. But if many people feel ineffective in public affairs, it is in no small part due to the complexity of public problems and events, rather than the result of the lack of opportunity to engage in political activities. In many ways, national politics are more accessible than they have been in the past (although the secrecy surrounding matters of national security is a major force decreasing access). But the growing scope and complexity of the public realm have made distant decisions and events more decisive for private life and simultaneously less manageable. The local community is less and less the locus of major decisions, so that local self-government cannot have the same significance today that it once did. However, it continues to play an important role in some spheres, for example, in public education in the United States.

Commensurate with the nationalization and even internationalization of the public realm is the comparable shift in the locus of communication. The major media of communication tend to be highly sensitive to their audiences (witness the spread of public opinion polls, market research, etc.). They seek to reflect as well as shape nation-wide opinion, and thereby increase its influence on national policies. Thus there arises the paradox of high *aggregate* access combined with low *individual* access—so that the individual who is responding as an individual feels isolated, and participates psychologically in the power of the aggregate only to the extent that he (along with his personal associates) is capable of identifying himself with his anonymous fellows.

A feeling of political impotence does not stem from the powerlessness of the individual alone. When, after all, have most individuals *qua* individuals been able to readily affect the outcome of public issues? The sense of ineffectiveness results also from the difficulty for citizens to meet and speak together in a public realm dominated by issues of great complexity and by impersonal means of communication. Political apathy would appear to be in large part a response to the resulting distance between the citizen and the locus of major events. However, there are important differences among subgroups in the degree of political apathy and powerlessness. Certain kinds of people, by virtue of their training and position in society, are in relatively better positions to hear and be heard as individuals. This is especially true for professional leaders in government, in business, and, to a lesser extent, in labor—men who are believed to be and consider themselves qualified to head up major institutions by virtue of their education and training. It is also true for the rapidly increasing proportion of the population that is receiving a higher education and going into professional occupations.

Closely related to the question of the impact of large-scale organization on participation in politics is the issue of its consequences for pluralist authority. There are those who believe that American elites are becoming increasingly responsive, even hypersensitive, to public demands and to one another, so much so that leadership and authority are seriously weakened. Thus Lippmann is concerned that the great complexities and needs of foreign policy in the nuclear age are being denied by virtue of public pressures on foreign-policy makers. There are those, on the other hand, who believe that American elites increasingly constitute a closed and unified group, so much so that liberty and democracy are seriously weakened. Thus Mills is concerned that the great consequences of foreign policy are being suffered by a public which has little hand in their determination.

The present study [*The Politics of Mass Society*] has sought to show that directly accessible elites make ready targets for mass movements. Constitutions and other appropriate institutional devices are needed to regulate access to elites, and to reduce pressures on them. But this does not mean that the mere insulation of elites protects liberty and democracy. Ultimate control over elites must be lodged in the community, even as elites are needed to set specific standards and to propose and implement detailed policies. If democratic institutions are to remain salient, even the complex and perilous nature of international relations cannot justify the abrogation of free competition for national leadership. But is it true that the main drift is toward a closed and unified elite? Such a view cannot account for the increasing social representativeness of national elites, nor for the myriad of conflicts among them; and still less can it be made consistent with the growth of powerful organizations among previously unorganized segments of the community (for example, among industrial workers and among Negroes in the United States).

Furthermore, the power of government cannot be viewed merely defensively, as a danger to the community which therefore must take all precautions to limit it. Power also is the capacity to achieve goals, and therefore must be granted to and assumed by those who possess special competence to use it. The very concept of elite is distasteful to many democrats, so much so that those who are elite often feel illegitimate and those who are not elite feel resentful. Herein lies a fundamental dilemma for democracy, the adaptation to which requires widespread appreciation of *the necessary tension between elites and non-elites.*

The major guarantee against the aggrandizement of power by elites is the existence of a plurality of groups that are equal enough in power to generate genuine competition for leadership on the several levels of political society. A danger of bureaucratization is that it will undermine the bases for a plurality of group interests and organizations. For example, it may undermine class organization, so that people in a similar class situation, who therefore have certain economic interests in common, will despair of improving those interests through joint action, and consequently attach themselves to mass movements subversive of all groups, including classes. The nihilism of masses tends to be a greater threat to liberal democracy than the antagonism between classes. Actions taken for economic interests tend to be moderate; whereas mass actions tend to be extremist. A good part of the response to mass appeals is an expression of social atomization, rather than action oriented toward either self interest or the public interest. *Differences in receptivity to mass symbols and leaders are due primarily to the strength of social ties, and not to the influence of class, or any other social status, by itself.*

The central problem posed by the theory of mass society is that of *social alienation,* or the distance between the individual and his society. Social alienation may occur on all levels of society. The mark of mass society is the alienation of elites as well as the alienation of non-elites. Social alienation has increased with the dissolution of medieval society. Aristocratic critics of mass tendencies offer no solution when they beckon us back to a society based on status: certain social processes are irreversible, and among them is the growing equality of condition. Democratic critics of mass society also do not consider alternative outcomes of the modernization of the world when they assert that urbanization and industrialization, and the correlative spread of large-scale organization entail alienation; for in this case, too, we are confronted with irreversible social processes. The present study [*The Politics of Mass Society*] has sought to argue that these conditions of modern life carry with them both the heightened possibility of social alienation *and* enhanced opportunities for the creation of new forms of association. Modern industry destroys the conditions for a society of small enterprises, but it also provides the condition of abundance which frees people to seek new ways of life. Modern urban life atomizes traditional social groups, but it also provides a variety of contacts and experiences that broaden social horizons and the range of social participation. Modern democracy diminishes the legitimacy of elites, but it also encourages a multiplicity of competing elites. By enlarging our understanding of such diverse potentialities in the modern world, concepts of mass society and social pluralism promise to stimulate further studies of the social bases of political integration and autonomy.

NOTES

[1] See Joseph Schumpeter, *Capitalism, Socialism, and Democracy*. New York: Harper and Bros., 1947, pp. 269–96.

[2] However, France is now undergoing a rapid industrial expansion.

[3] See William H. Whyte, *The Organization Man*. New York: Doubleday, 1957.

[4] See Whyte, *op. cit.*, Part VII.

[5] See Will Herberg, *Protestant, Catholic, Jew*. New York: Doubleday, 1955.

18.   MASS SOCIETY AND POLITICAL MOVEMENTS: A NEW FORMULATION [1]

Maurice Pinard

In the contemporary social sciences, the theory of mass society has become a very popular theoretical perspective for the analysis of political movements. For many, this theory is held to be the most pertinent and comprehensive statement of the genesis of modern mass movements. The purpose of this paper is to summarize some of the claims of this theory and to present a critique of these views. This will lay the ground for a reformulation of the model, which will take into account a wider range of theoretical as well as empirical concerns.

THE CLAIMS OF MASS THEORY

According to mass theory,[2] the source of the proliferation of mass behavior and mass movements [3] in modern society has to be sought in the characteristics of its social structure, more specifically, in the weakness of modern societies' integrative functions. The local community, a primary source of integration in feudal or communal society, has lost its functions; the occupational community is weak, when not altogether absent; religious, political, and other voluntary associations play an integrative role—and a weak one, at that—for relatively few people. For some, even primary attachments are weaker, and atomization of the individual prevails.[4]

RESTRAINING EFFECTS

But what are the mechanisms through which strong intermediate structures are assumed to prevent the growth of political movements? Many can be suggested, but let me summarize them immediately under a single heading: strong attachments and identification to social groupings produce *restraining effects* on people. The mechanisms through which this is achieved can be enumerated briefly.[5] First, if there is a strong network of secondary groups, these groups will tend to check one another, and their members will be more selective in their political participation.[6] Second, intermediate organizations are likely to create a structure of social attachments and loyalties between the elites and the non-elites and thus lead to social restraints in the latter's demands from the elites and in their evaluation of the elites' decisions.[7] Third, secondary groups are likely to socialize their members to accept the rules of the game and to struggle for their goals through discussions, negotiations, and compromises, rather than through the use of radical means. Fourth, organizations enlarge the range of proximate concerns of their members and are the source of various cross-pressures with regard to the latter's objectives; they thus prevent the development

SOURCE: *American Journal of Sociology*, Volume 73, Number 6 (May, 1968), pp. 682–690. Copyright 1968 by The University of Chicago. Reprinted by permission of The University of Chicago Press.

of a single overriding goal and ideology so characteristic of a social movement.[8] Fifth, organizations can be a source of sanctions for members who might be tempted to engage in a social movement to secure their objectives outside the routine channels approved by the organization. Sixth, participation in an elaborate set of intermediate groups is likely to foster the development of a sense of political efficacy, while the opposite engenders alienation and anxiety and the search for political ventures.[9] Finally, secondary groups can be the source of rewarding primary attachments and thus procure a more satisfactory life and a greater readiness to accommodation with the status quo.[10]

In short, the main proposition of mass theory states that a society with mass tendencies, because it lacks restraining mechanisms, cannot prevent its members from turning to mass behavior and to mass movements.

A CRITIQUE OF MASS THEORY

This theory has already been subjected to serious criticisms.[11] We would like to recast some of these criticism and present additional ones, in a way which permits a reformulation of the theory. As it now stands, it seems that the theory suffers from some observational and theoretical biases.

To start with, a specification must be entered. Mass theory seems to assume that all the groupings of a strong intermediate structure would always and in all areas of their members' lives act as important *reference groups*. Research indicates, however, that a large number of organizations do not actually represent reference points for their members, even in small rural communities.[12] In this regard, a pluralist society, with a proliferation of autonomous intermediate groupings, could be relatively little more restraining than a mass society. It would seem, in fact, that if restraining effects are to be ascribed to the intermediate structure, primary groups and the social networks of small communities, rather than most associations and organizations, are the groupings to be considered, since they are more likely to act as reference points.

MOBILIZING EFFECTS

Even if we assume that the various components of the intermediate structure are taken as reference points, we must still raise a major criticism: It seems to us that the claim that primary and secondary groups exert restraining effects on their members implies a one-sided view of the role of intermediate groupings. To be sure, no sociologist would question the fact that these groups may exert such effects. But with regard to new political ventures, they may also exert just the opposite type of effects: The intermediate structure may actually, under circumstances discussed below, exert *mobilizing,* rather than restraining, effects. By this, we mean that certain intermediate groups, because of their positive orientations to the means and goals of a social movement, can be a strong force acting to *motivate* and *legitimate* individual as well as group participation in a movement. Between these two extremes, certain groupings can maintain neither a positive nor a negative stand, but simply a neutral, indifferent stand, toward a new movement. In short, the effects of primary and secondary groups can empirically be located at any point on a continuum, ranging from strong restraining to strong mobilizing effects, with an intermediate neutral point.

Mass theorists do not always deny the possibility that primary attachments in fact can play a mobilizing role. Actually, this is the main effect some assign to primary groups.[13] But this is a bias in the opposite direction; it neglects the potential restraining effects of primary groups, which must also be considered.

But what constitutes a major shortcoming of mass theory is its failure to recognize that secondary groupings can also exert neutral or mobilizing functions. It may be empirically true that a large number of organizations in affluent societies will usually exert restraining effects, but not all organizations under any circumstances will do so. There are always certain components of the intermediate structure which exhibit a diffuse orientation of alienation vis-à-vis most or all features of the larger society, and there are certain other components which are alienated against specific aspects of the society, that is, which perceive their subjective interests as well as their norms and goals in harmony with those of a social movement. Obviously, such groups will stimulate rather than restrain participation in social movements.[14]

Still, this only implies a static view of organizational life. All organizations are not necessarily *always,* and to the same degree, conformist *or* alienated. Under certain conditions, some organizations, or sections of them, may *become* alienated, at least with regard to specific social arrangements, and they will then positively sanction non-routinized ways of behavior.

In short, whenever pre-existing primary and secondary groupings possess or develop an ideology or simply subjective interests congruent with that of a new movement, they will act as mobilizing rather than restraining agents toward that movement. And their members will be, not late joiners, but the early joiners of the movement, much earlier than the atomized masses.[15]

DIFFUSION THEORY

These are not the only functions of the intermediate structure which have to be taken into consideration in a reformulated model. The theory of mass society also disregards the accumulated propositions of diffusion studies [16] as well as some propositions of the theory of conflict; both sets of propositions, however, would lead one to make predictions which in important respects are opposite to those of the former theory.[17]

With regard to diffusion theory, mass society theorists overlook the fact that a social movement is basically a new item in a culture and that as such its adoption implies the processes of diffusion. But as the studies of diffusion have shown, the adoption of new ideas and practices, and therefore of new social movements, does not take place in a social vacuum.[18] If there is in that field one firm empirical generalization which can be made, it is that the higher the degree of social integration of potential adopters, the more likely and the sooner they will become actual adopters, and that, on the other hand, near-isolates tend to be the last to adopt an innovation.

Two important mechanisms of the intermediate structure overlooked by mass theory would seem to account for the proposition that social integration is conducive to diffusion. First, of course, are what we have called the mobilizing effects of social groupings, that is, their motivation and legitimation effects, given, presumably, a state of dissatisfaction with prior arrangements.[19]

COMMUNICATING EFFECTS

But a second mechanism can be fruitfully distinguished from the former one at the analytical level. I suggest that one important mechanism which produces the positive association between integration and adoption is what I shall call the *communicating effects* of the intermediate groupings. Organizations and social networks are excellent channels of communication, transmitting information about new ideas and practices; more generally, they contribute in developing among their members a certain degree of sophistication: They enlarge their members' field of attention and perception, as well as contributing to the development of leadership and other organizational skills. Thus, participants in various social groupings, particularly in primary groups, should be more likely to learn about a new social movement—its leadership, its goals, its successes in recruiting members—than atomized people.[20] It is important to note that here we do not distinguish whether the intermediate groupings have a positive or a negative orientation toward the new movement; all groupings, whether characterized by a restraining, mobilizing, or neutral potential, can exert communicating effects and as such can be conducive to the rise of new movements.[21]

Similarly, certain aspects of the theory of community conflict are at odds with mass theory.[22] Notice first that community conflicts are typically uninstitutionalized ways of coping with a given problem, as are social and political movements.

But Coleman describes a community conflict as something that usually originates between the administration of a community and some center of active opposition while the majority of the people remain passive.[23] Moreover, he states that the *more* integrated among these people will be the *first* to join in the controversy; lower-status people, for instance, lacking identification with and attachment to the community and its leaders, will less often and less easily be drawn into a conflict.[24] This is in direct contradiction with what mass theory would predict.

Notice, however, that Coleman also states that "when and if" the least integrated are drawn into a controversy, they are likely to make it degenerate into a "fight to the finish," while the more integrated citizens, though more easily recruited, are more likely to be restrained because of various cross-pressures.[25] This is apparently more in agreement with mass theory; the reason is that, while conflict theory distinguishes between *attraction* to a conflict and *intensity of participation* in it, mass theory fails to make such a distinction. Basically we think the propositions of mass theory are sound to account for what happens after—but only after—the least attached are drawn into a conflict or a social movement: [26] Communicating and mobilizing effects are no longer effective, but the restraining effects of other groups could still affect their modes of participation. What primarily concerns us here, however, is attraction to a new movement, not the modes of participation in it.[27]

THE ROLE OF STRAINS

So far it has been claimed that under certain circumstances, components of the intermediate structure can exert mobilizing effects rather than restraining ones. The specification of one major set of such circumstances leads us to another major criticism of mass theory. Basically, mass theory, with or without the qualifications made above, deals only with some of the *conditions of conduciveness* for the rise of social movements and as such is a more limited model than it pretends to be: The intermediate structure can limit or foster the rise of political movements, but it is not, in itself, a sufficient condition for their appearance. In particular, the presence of strain is a crucial condition.[28]

Once this distinction is made, one soon realizes that the crucial and necessary element of strain, as distinct from that of conduciveness, tends to be seriously underestimated in mass theory. To be sure, some sources of strain are considered—economic crises, for instance—but they are only part of a larger set of forces, such as the processes of democratization, industrialization, and urbanization, and these forces all lead to mass movements, not primarily because they produce deprivations of various sorts but above all because they weaken the system of attachments of the non-elites to the elites.[29]

Contrary to this, we subscribe to the idea that strains are per se a necessary independent factor and a more important one than the conditions of conduciveness mass theory deals with.[30] Moreover, and this is theoretically important, we claim that strains will affect the various functions of the intermediate structure which have been discussed so far, or, to put it differently, that *strain will affect the conduciveness of the intermediate structure.* Under severe strains, and given that no other institutionalized channels for the redress of grievances are available (another condition of conduciveness to be discussed below [31]), conformist components of the intermediate structure can become elements which encourage, rather than limit, the growth of a new movement.

On the one hand, under severe strains, individuals may withdraw psychologically and/or physically from the intermediate groups likely to exert restraining effects on them [32] and turn toward more neutral or mobilizing agents as reference groups, while at the same time becoming very susceptible to the communicating effects [33] of all the groups they participate in.[34] On the other hand, and of greater consequences, the secondary groups themselves, under severe strains, can develop some degree of alienation, oppose some aspects of the status quo and, if no other alternatives are opened, adopt a neutral or even a positive orientation to new movements.[35] This brings us back to an earlier point. We have seen that intermediate groupings can become a source of positive, rather than negative, sanctions regarding non-routine politics. We now add that the appearance of strains is a major determinant of such changes.

STRAINS AND TYPES OF MOVEMENTS

Before we conclude, two additional points must be clarified. It should be emphasized that the severity or mildness of the strains should be considered relative to the strength of the restraining effects of conformist organizations. Obviously, strong restraining effects will need more severe strains to break them than will weak ones. Conversely, the strength of the restraining effects will in large measure depend on the evaluation made of the new movement: The more negative the evaluation of its ideology, of its means and goals, the stronger will be the restraining effects. Hence, an extremist or a "mass" movement may require more severe strains to attract the integrated segments of the population than a mildly reformist movement. But this does not mean that one must have different models to deal with these two types of movements.

ORGANIZATIONS AS CHANNELS FOR THE REDRESS OF GRIEVANCES

Finally, when the mechanisms which, according to mass theory, lead to restraining effects were enumerated, an important one was temporarily put aside. Let us return to it. It can be argued that an elaborate intermediate structure constitutes a barrier against social movements for the simple reason that it provides channels for the redress of grievances. For instance, associations and organizations can act as pressure groups or otherwise help people to work routinely toward the solution of their problems.[36]

From what precedes, it should already be clear that we do not mean to disregard this function of the intermediate structure. If mass theory simply stated that in a mass society movements arise because of the lack of channels for the redress of grievances, then the theory, though incomplete, would be sound in that respect.[37] But mass theory states much more than that, and this is where it fails, as we have tried to show. Not all components of the intermediate structure are fit to work toward the redress of a given set of grievances (think of the primary groups, the community social networks, leisure and religious associations when a modern society is facing an economic depression), while potentially all can act as communication and mobilization centers for a new movement. More importantly, even those groupings who might act as channels will not necessarily be effective in that role; they may fail in their efforts and turn with their members to non-routine means. It is our claim that a society which has a highly pluralist structure, but no channel, or no effective channel, for the redress of a given set of grievances will turn faster and more easily to social movements than a society with a mass structure. A mass society may be more likely to lack effective channels for the redress of grievances, but it will also lack the extensive networks of attachments and organizations on the basis of which new movements arise.

A REFORMULATED MODEL

On the basis of these ideas, it is possible to make some general propositions regarding the fate of social movements in societies or among individuals varying according to their degree of integration. These propositions, however, cannot be as simple as the previous ones.

The outcome, obviously, depends on the relative strength of the various, and opposite, types of effects discussed above. And it seems that one of the crucial variables here will be the severity and the generality of the existing strains.

If the strains are severe and widespread, alienated groups will tend to be particularly active; moreover, either conformist groups will tend to move from a restraining position to a more neutral or even to a mobilizing position, or their members will tend to elude their restraining effects. Their communicating role, on the other hand, will be working fully. To the extent that this prevails, I would predict that integrated individuals and pluralist societies will be more prone to social and political movements than atomized people and mass societies. This prediction, of course, is just the opposite of that made by mass theorists.

If, on the other hand, strains are not severe or widespread, then restraining effects will tend to predominate over mobilizing effects, and communicating effects will be weak since there is no need for a new movement. Under such circumstances, any new movement, if it should appear, will of course be weak; but to the extent that it succeeds in recruiting some people, the basic proposition of mass theory should hold: the lower the degree of integration, the greater the proneness to social movements. So far, therefore, mass theory appears to be sound, paradoxically, only when strains are limited, that is, when the success of a movement is highly problematic to start with.

At this point, however, a final qualification must be entered. In their study of the diffusion of a new drug, Coleman, Katz, and Menzel identified an interesting process of diffusion: They found that the social networks in which doctors were integrated contributed to the adoption process only in the early stages of the diffusion of the new drug; later on, they seemed "completely *inoperative* as chains of influence. The social structure seemed to have exhausted its effect." [38] This would suggest that the communicating and mobilizing effects which we have postulated should be particularly effective during the early stages of a new movement, but should become inoperative during later stages when the movement has become well known and has gained a large degree of legitimacy in the population. To the extent, and only to the extent, that the permanent restraining effects of some intermediate groupings might still prevail at these later stages, one would then predict, with mass theorists, a negative relationship between social integration and the success of social movements at that stage.

Finally, let us repeat that this model is primarily concerned with the processes of recruitment to new movements. It is consistent, however, with the idea that the least integrated, once members of a movement, may be more extremist in their behavior than more integrated people.

NOTES

[1] A paper read at the 62d Annual Meeting of the American Sociological Association, San Francisco, August, 1967. I owe much to both Jerome Kirk and Donald Von Eschen, with whom some of the ideas presented here were developed while engaged in a study of the sit-in movement. James Coleman and Arthur Stinchcombe made very useful comments on an earlier draft. The paper is adapted from the author's *The Rise of a Third Party: The Social Credit Party in Quebec in the 1962 Federal Election* (Englewood Cliffs, N.J.: Prentice-Hall, forthcoming).

[2] We are relying mainly on William Kornhauser's *The Politics of Mass Society* (Glencoe, Ill.: Free Press, 1959). But see also Philip Selznick, *The Organizational Weapon* (Glencoe, Ill.: Free Press, 1960) For a concise statement of the theory, see Joseph R. Gusfield's critique of it: "Mass Society and Extremist Politics," *American Sociological Review*, XXVII (1962), 19–30, esp. 19–22.

[3] In this paper we shall make no distinction between different kinds of political movements, as, for instance, between reform, mass, and totalitarian movements (see Kornhauser, *op. cit.* [n. 2 above], p. 50). The reason for our decision will be presented later.

[4] Though Kornhauser does not see personal isolation as conducive to mass movements (see *op. cit.* [n. 2 above], pp. 90–93, 217–218), he differs on this with others. See, for instance, Hannah Arendt, *The Origins of Totalitarianism* (Cleveland, Ohio: World Publishing Co. [Meridian Books], 1958), chap. x, esp. pp. 318, 323–24.

[5] For a summary of many of these mechanisms, see Donald Von Eschen, Jerome Kirk, and Maurice Pinard, "Organizations and Disorderly Politics: The Case of the Negro Sit-In Movement," a paper read at the 59th Annual Meeting, American Sociological Association, Montreal, 1964. The present paper is a complement to that paper in two main respects: While the first paper examined the relevance of mass theory for an incipient movement with strong cadres but a weak following, the present paper is concerned with social movements having a mass support; moreover, the first paper was primarily concerned with the role of alienated organizations, while this paper considers as problematic the role of the entire intermediate structure.

[6] Kornhauser, *op. cit.* (n. 2 above), p. 82.

[7] *Ibid.*, p. 67; see also James S. Coleman, *Community Conflict* (Glencoe, Ill.: Free Press, 1957).

[8] Kornhauser, *op. cit.* (n. 2 above), p. 64.

[9] *Ibid.*, p. 32; see also Arthur G. Neal and Melvin Seeman, "Organizations and Powerlessness: A Test of the Mediation Hypothesis," *American Sociological Review*, XXIX (1964), 216–26.

[10] Another important effect of organizational integration must be mentioned: Organizations can act as channels for the redress of their members' grievances and thus prevent the recourse to non-routine means of solving their problems. But this is a different function of secondary groups and will be dealt with later.

[11] See in particular Gusfield, *op. cit.* (n. 2 above); Daniel Bell, "America as a Mass Society: A Critique," in his *The End of Ideology* (rev. ed.; New York: Collier Books, 1962), chap. i; Von Eschen *et al.*, *op. cit.* (n. 5 above).

[12] See David E. W. Holden, "Associations as Reference Groups: An Approach to the Problem," *Rural Sociology*, XXX (1965), 63–74.

[13] Kornhauser writes that: "the individual is more likely to engage in new ventures when he receives support from his close associates" (*op. cit.* [n. 2 above], p. 93). In an excellent case study of a hysterical contagion, the authors also distinguished the two opposite types of effects; the primary groups were seen as both "resistors" and "conductors" (see Alan C. Kerckhoff, Kurt W. Back, and Norman Miller, "Sociometric Patterns in Hysterical Contagion," *Sociometry*, XXVII [1965], pp. 2–15).

[14] That this should have been overlooked is in fact surprising, given the often made observation that social movements and revolutions are built upon the foundations of elites and organizations displaying some form of alienation against the larger society. This was as true in the great revolutions of the nineteenth century as it is now in the civil rights movement in the United States, to mention but two examples. See S. M. Lipset, *Agrarian Socialism* (Berkeley: University of California Press, 1950), chap. x. Lipset wrote that "the rapid acceptance of new ideas and movements in Saskatchewan can be attributed mainly to the high degree of organization" (p. 206). See also Crane Brinton, *The Anatomy of Revolution* (New York: Vintage Books, 1960), esp. pp. 41 ff., 106 ff.; Neil Smelser, *Theory of Collective Behavior* (New York: Free Press, 1963), pp. 274 ff., 282 ff.

[15] Von Eschen *et al., op. cit.* (n. 5 above).

[16] Surprisingly, the sociology of diffusion and that of collective behavior, though both are concerned with the appearance of new items in a culture, tend to develop independently of one another. For a notable exception, however, see Kerckhoff *et al., op. cit.* (n. 13 above). Their conclusions are not very different from ours.

[17] For two syntheses of empirical generalizations in the field of diffusion, see Herbert F. Lionberger, *Adoption of New Ideas and Practices* (Ames: Iowa State University Press, 1960); and Everett M. Rogers, *Diffusion of Innovations* (New York: Fress Press, 1962). With regard to conflict theory, we have in mind some of the propositions in Coleman, *op. cit.* (n. 7 above).

[18] A similar idea, from a different point of view, is expressed by Lewis M. Killian (see his "Social Movements," in Robert E. L. Faris, *Handbook of Modern Sociology* [Chicago: Rand McNally, 1964], p. 431).

[19] On the basis of their empirical evidence, students of diffusion tend to overlook the fact that restraining effects can theoretically predominate over mobilizing effects (for instance, under relative satisfaction with existing arrangements).

[20] In at least one case study the failure of a new movement was actually attributed in part to communication failure due to the lack of pre-existing organizational networks complementing the primary groups and the mass media (see Maurice Jackson, Eleanora Petersen, James Bull, Sverre Monsen, and Patricia Richmond, "The Failure of an Incipient Social Movement," *Pacific Sociological Review*, III [1960], 35–40).

[21] Indeed, among collective behavior theorists, mass theorists are an exception in their oversight of the importance of communication for the development of collective behavior. Consider, for instance, Blumer's stress on circular reaction, milling, collective excitement, and social contagion, or Smelser's stress on the necessity of communication channels for the development of collective behavior. Herbert Blumer, "Collective Behavior," in Alfred M. Lee (ed.), *Principles of Sociology* (rev. ed.; New York: Barnes & Noble, 1951), esp. 170–77; and Smelser, *op. cit.* (n. 14 above), *passim*. See also Ralph H. Turner's review of the field, "Collective Behavior," in Robert E. L. Faris, *Handbook of Modern Sociology* (Chicago: Rand McNally, 1964), pp. 382–425, esp. 397–409.

[22] See Coleman, *op. cit.* (n. 7 above).

[23] *Ibid.*, pp. 8–9.

[24] *Ibid.*, pp. 21–22. This model was substantiated in routine politics: It was found

that more integrated communities were more likely to back a fluoridation referendum than less integrated ones, presumably because of the greater restraining effects in the former; but when communities of the first type defeated the proposition, they were more likely to do so with greater unanimity than those of the second type, presumably because of greater mobilizing and informing effects. See Maurice Pinard, "Structural Attachment and Political Support in Urban Politics: The Case of Fluoridation Referendums," *American Journal of Sociology*, LXVIII (1963), 513–26.

[25] Coleman, *op. cit.* (n. 7 above).

[26] Indeed, Kornhauser quotes Coleman, stressing his proposition on the degree of participation, which he implicitly applies to the attraction to the movement, though not making any distinction between the two (see Kornhauser, *op. cit.* [n. 2 above], pp. 66–67).

[27] Suffice it to say that it is indirectly supported by findings of the sit-in movement study: It was found that the least integrated participants, as revealed by their lower social status, were late joiners, but once they had joined they were the most active participants. See Maurice Pinard, Jerome Kirk, and Donald Von Eschen, "The Growth of the Sit-In Movement: Some Processes" (McGill University, Dittoed). See also Lipset, *op. cit.* (n. 14 above), p. 167.

[28] For the distinction between strain and conduciveness as necessary conditions for the appearance of collective behavior, see Smelser, *op. cit., passim.* To be sure, the lack of social participation, but above all the lack of primary group ties, can itself be a source of strains. However, I suggest that the frequency and severity of such strains are often grossly overestimated.

[29] See Kornhauser, *op. cit.* (n. 2 above), pp. 119–74, esp. 162–67.

[30] I would not go as far as Bell (*op. cit.* [n. 11 above]), who seems to discount completely the role of the intermediate structure: "It is not the mass society, but the inability, pure and simple, of any society to meet impatient popular expectations that makes for a strong response to radical appeals" (p. 32).

[31] Smelser, *op. cit.* (n. 14 above), *passim.*

[32] Turner mentions the possibility of "neutralization or inapplicability of existing norms" (*op. cit.* [n. 21 above], p. 390).

[33] Students of diffusion tend to overlook the role of strain or to assume their existence, though Lionberger explicitly states that "for adoption of new practices to take place . . . , there must be a feeling that the present situation is not necessarily the best way or the only way to reach their goal. Dissatisfaction with conditions as they exist . . . is presequisite to change" (*op. cit.* [n. 17 above], p. 14).

[34] For a study which exemplifies these processes, see Jeffrey K. Hadden and Raymond C. Rymph, "The Marching Ministers," *Trans-Action* (September–October, 1966), pp. 38–41.

[35] An excellent case study of such a process, which was instrumental in our rethinking of this problem, is Alvin W. Gouldner's *Wildcat Strike* (Yellow Springs, Ohio: Antioch Press, 1954). Notice that the wildcat strike was started, not by atomized workers, but by a disenchanted clique of the workers' union.

[36] Kornhauser, *op. cit.* (n. 2 above), p. 82.

[37] According to Smelser (*op. cit.* [n. 14 above], *passim*), the lack of routine channels for the redress of grievances is an important condition of conduciveness for collective behavior.

[38] James S. Coleman, Elihu Katz, and Herbert Menzel, "The Diffusion of an Innovation among Physicians," *Sociometry*, XX (1957), 266. The authors found that social networks seemed inoperative if no distinctions between stages were made.

PART III

Political Ideology in America

INTRODUCTION

The present American political scene is becoming increasingly dramatic. The country resounds with the voices of some who feel that America has grossly failed to meet its promises of social justice and equality of opportunity for all of its citizens. Others express deep concern about the role which the world's most materially prosperous and militarily powerful nation is to play in relation to the other nations of the world. New questions concerning the relations between the public and the private sectors of the economy are being raised.

Despite the fact that many Americans may believe that the United States is a "classless" society, a society in which the opportunities for the attainment of positions of power and privilege are more or less equitably distributed among all sectors of the population, countless studies have shown that this is not the case.[1] Despite the apparently widespread belief that virtually all Americans have a similar understanding and evaluation of "democracy," this too is a mistaken notion. This section investigates the senses in which there are divergent, popularly supported political ideologies in the United States and locates some of the social and psychological sources of their support.

In the first article (number 19) of Section A, Robert E. Lane points out that "ideology" has been defined in a variety of ways by lexicographers, psychologists, and sociologists. Lane develops his own concise analysis of the conceptual components of all political ideologies and indicates a sense in which the average citizen may be thought of as maintaining a political ideology.

The second selection (number 20) is also taken from Lane's *Political Ideology*. The work is based on extensive interviews with fifteen men of "Eastport," a city of over 100,000 population on the Atlantic Seaboard. Lane presents the understanding of some "common men" of democracy and investigates those experiences of ordinary citizens which may increase the likelihood of their support for democratic methods.

Seymour M. Lipset discusses (number 21) those factors which contribute to the stability of any democratic political system. Stability, he notes, is closely tied to the perceived legitimacy of the political system. Legitimacy, in turn,

317

depends in a large measure upon the ways in which the basic issues which have traditionally divided the society have been resolved. Those conditions which serve to reduce the intensity of partisan conflict are among the most important conditions of democratic government. In this connection Lipset notes the importance of broadly representative political parties, a social structure which facilitates the interaction of individuals and groups with different political views, and "political cosmopolitanism." Lipset concludes his analysis with a consideration of those political issues which remain important in modern Western democracies, in spite of the fact that he feels there is relatively little difference between the democratic left and right.

The authors of number 22 question the extent to which the terms "liberal" and "conservative" can be meaningfully applied to the sets of political attitudes maintained by most Americans. Their nationwide study revealed that there is no consistent relationship between the positions people take on domestic issues and their attitudes on foreign affairs. The typical American lacks a broad, clearly patterned political ideology. He may feel strongly about a variety of individual issues, but the ability to predict his position in one issue-area from his position in another is severely limited. The authors attempt to account for such discontinuity.

If Americans do not systematically organize their political attitudes along the familiar liberal-conservative continuum, is there some other dimension underlying their apparently unrelated attitudes? Using recently developed statistical techniques, Robert Axelrod (in number 23) finds a suggestion that a modern version of populism may be the widely shared ideology used by the public to relate domestic and foreign issues to each other. He notes, however, that this dimension is not equally distinct for all segments of the population.

Section A of this part contains evidence which indicates the lack of widely supported, clearly defined, antithetical political ideologies in the United States. Some of the conditions that account for the absence of a clash of ideologies of the political left and right are also considered. Section B investigates the relatively persistent political cleavages that do exist in America and their social and psychological foundations.

The most widely discussed, politically relevant personality variable is "authoritarianism." While a considerable amount of research has focused on the notion of "authoritarian character," there has been only limited analysis of the counterpart, "democratic character." The first selection (number 24) in Section B clarifies many of the issues arising in literature on the "authoritarian character" and considers some aspects of the complex connections between personal character and political belief, political action, and the functioning of political institutions.

In addition to characterological factors, the social roles individuals play are significant in the determination of their politics. An important instance of this is reported in the second selection (number 25). Samuel A. Stouffer found that libertarianism is associated with occupying community leadership positions. Community leaders are more likely than the rank and file to give serious consideration to the dangers involved in denying civil liberties to those whose views they dislike. Stouffer notes that this can be of great significance for America's future, for, if the reverse had been found, there would be an enormous threat to the continuation of America's historic liberties.

Broad societal characteristics also influence a nation's political life. The high level of economic development of America associated with industrialization and urbanization has produced conditions which facilitate political democracy. Considerable evidence indicates that the more well-to-do a nation, the greater the chances it will sustain democracy.[2] However, continuing industrialization and certain concomitant social changes may introduce strains in a social system as well as factors which enhance political democracy. Some analysts, such as Talcott Parsons, have viewed McCarthyism of the 1950s and the John Birch Society of the 1960s as political-ideological expressions of such strains. Parsons argues (in number 26) that continuing industrialization has not only brought about rapid change in American society, but has also significantly altered America's relations with other nations. Such changes have produced vehement protest against the fact and the direction of that change.

Strains generated by changes in American society have also produced reactions at the other end of the political spectrum. Gary T. Marx has examined one of these: black nationalism (number 27). He finds, however, a general rejection of this separatist ideology by American Negroes. This rejection, he feels, is indicative of a real desire for integration into American society. Such a finding tends to support American historian David Potter's thesis:

> European radical thought is prone to demand that the man of property be stripped of his carriage and fine clothes; but American radical thought is likely to insist, instead, that the ordinary man is entitled to mass-produced copies, indistinguishable from the originals. Few Americans feel entirely at ease with the slogan 'Soak the rich,' but the phrase, 'Deal me in' springs spontaneously and joyously to American lips.[3]

Conservatives of the John Birch Society variety comprise but a small fraction of American conservatives. There are few Black Nationalists among American Negroes. In short, there seems to be some general agreement among highly diverse segments of America's population that a better future for the society can be achieved without radical political change. The contemporary American political scene is quite dramatic, but the political system appears to be remarkably stable.

An extremely important question raised by contemporary political analysts concerns the extent to which there will continue to be any significant cleavages in political ideology in the United States. Daniel Bell (number 28) felt that by the end of the 1950s, political ideologies had lost their force among the intellectuals of the Western world. He argued that "In the Western world there [was] a rough consensus among intellectuals on political issues: The acceptance of the Welfare State; the desirability of decentralized power; a system of mixed economy and of political pluralism."

Perhaps the attitudes of Western intellectuals in the late Fifties will not be reflected in the ideological patterns found among Americans in the late Sixties and in the Seventies. Morris Janowitz and David R. Segal (in number 29) reject the "middle-majority politics model" which emphasizes the decline of dissensus and ideologically based issues in Western, industrial nations. They argue that continuing industrialization will lead to new forms of political conflicts which reflect economic, professional, and bureaucratic interests.

The anxiety of which Arthur M. Schlesinger, Jr., wrote twenty years ago (number 30) is even greater today. The problems generated by "the speed-up of time, the reduction of space and the increase in tension" have multiplied. Many of these problems require political solutions which may be founded upon quite divergent political philosophies. Perhaps it will always be that "Free society and totalitarianism [will] struggle for the minds and hearts of men."

NOTES

[1] See Harold M. Hodges, Jr., *Social Stratification: Class in America* (Cambridge, Massachusetts: Schenkman Publishing Co., Inc., 1964), Chapter I, "The Myth and Creed of Classlessnesss."

[2] For a discussion and documentation of this relationship, see Seymour M. Lipset, *Political Man: The Social Bases of Politics* (New York: Doubleday & Company, Inc., 1960), Chapter 2, "Economic Development and Democracy."

[3] Quoted in Robert A. Dahl, *Modern Political Analysis* (Englewood Cliffs, N.J.: Prentice-Hall, Inc., 1963), p. 79. Dahl presents a concise discussion of the relation of America's economic abundance to the relative peacefulness of her political history.

A. DEMOCRACY AND IDEOLOGY

19. THE MEANINGS OF IDEOLOGY

Robert E. Lane

The science of ideas.
> —*Webster's New International Dictionary,* 2nd ed. (1948).

The integrated assertions, theories, and aims constituting a politico-social program, often with an implication of factitious propagandizing; as, Fascism was altered in Germany to fit the Nazi *ideology.*
> —*Webster's New International Dictionary,* 2nd ed. (1948).
> (additional definition in "New Words" section)

During the Napoleonic Era . . . "ideology" came to mean virtually any belief of a republican or revolutionary sort, that is to say, any belief hostile to Napoleon himself.
> —HENRY D. AIKEN, *The Age of Ideology,* pp. 16–17

What [Marx and Engels] . . . call "ideology" includes not only the theory of knowledge and politics, but also metaphysics, ethics, religion, and indeed any "form of consciousness" which expresses the basic attitudes or commitments of a social class.
> —HENRY D. AIKEN, *The Age of Ideology,* p. 17

We speak of a *particular* and of a *total* conception of ideology. Under the first we include all those utterances the "falsity" of which is due to an intentional or unintentional, conscious, semi-conscious, or unconscious, deluding of one's self or of others, taking place on a psychological level and structurally resembling lies. . . . Since suspicion of falsification is not included in the total conception of ideology, the use of the term "ideology" in the sociology of knowledge has no moral or denunciatory intent. It points rather to a research interest which leads to the raising of the question when and where social structures come to express themselves in the structure of assertions, and in what sense the former concretely determine the latter.
> —KARL MANNHEIM, *Ideology and Utopia,* pp. 238–239

They [ideologies] are compounds of projective systems, in the interest of which

SOURCE: Robert E. Lane, *Political Ideology* (New York: The Free Press of Glencoe, 1962), pp. 13–16. © by The Free Press, a corporation, 1962. Reprinted by permission of The Macmillan Company.

empirical evidence is mobilized, and have therefore the same structure as rationalizations.

—ABRAM KARDINER and associates, *The Psychological Frontiers of Society,* p.34

Ideology is the conversion of ideas into social levers. . . . For the ideologue, truth arises in action, and meaning is given to experience by the "transforming moment."

—DANIEL BELL, *The End of Ideology,* pp. 370–371

Ideology refers to a more or less institutionalized set of beliefs—"the views someone picks up." Belief-disbelief systems contain these too but, in addition, they contain highly personalized pre-ideological beliefs.

—MILTON ROKEACH and associates, *The Open and Closed Mind,* p. 35

The term ideology is used in this book, in the way that is common in current literature, to stand for an organization of opinions, attitudes, and values—a way of thinking about man and society. We may speak of an individual's total ideology or of his ideology with respect to different areas of social life; politics, economics, religion, minority groups, and so forth. Ideologies have an existence independent of any single individual; and those which exist at a particular time are results of both historical processes and of contemporary social events.

—T. W. ADORNO and associates, *The Authoritarian Personality,* p. 2

I have set forth above a number of interpretations of the meaning of "ideology." Even if we limit our interest to political ideology, the range and variety are formidable. I shall use the term "political ideology" to mean a body of concepts with these characteristics:

1. They deal with the questions: Who will be the rulers? How will the rulers be selected? By what principles will they govern?

2. They constitute an *argument;* that is, they are intended to persuade and to counter opposing views.

3. They integrally affect some of the major values of life.

4. They embrace a program for the defense or reform or abolition of important social institutions.

5. They are, in part, rationalizations of group interests—but not necessarily the interests of all groups espousing them.

6. They are normative, ethical, moral in tone and content.

7. They are (inevitably) torn from their context in a broader belief system, and share the structural and stylistic properties of that system.

Most ideologies also have these qualities:

1. They are group beliefs that individuals borrow; most people acquire an ideology by identifying (or disidentifying) with a social group.

2. They have a body of sacred documents (constitutions, bills of rights, manifestos, declarations), and heroes (founding fathers, seers and sages, originators and great interpreters).

And all ideologies, like all other beliefs, imply an empirical theory of cause and effect in the world, and a theory of the nature of man.

In some of the current literature, there is a suggestion that ideology is not so important as it once was. This is neatly reflected in two book titles, one, a volume on nineteenth-century philosophy edited by Henry Aiken, called *The Age of Ideology*,[1] the other, a book of essays by Daniel Bell, called *The End of Ideology*.[2] What is implied in this contrast is, first, that analysis is taking the place of ideology (the comparable volume for the twentieth-century philosophers is called *The Age of Analysis*);[3] second, that at midcentury there is a kind of exhaustion of political ideas in the West, and hence, third, that the transformation of broadly conceived political ideas into social action is no longer the center of an exciting struggle. There is some confirmation of this point. But lest one be deceived by a phrase, there should be no doubt that the common man *has* a set of emotionally charged political beliefs, a critique of alternative proposals, and some modest programs of reform. These beliefs embrace central values and institutions; they are rationalizations of interests (sometimes not his own); and they serve as moral justifications for daily acts and beliefs.

Of course, there is a difference between the articulated, differentiated, well-developed political arguments put forward by informed and conscious Marxists or Fascists or liberal democrats on the one hand, and the loosely structured, unreflective statements of common men. In general, of course, what I have to say has to do with the ideologies of just such common men; but occasionally it is useful to distinguish between these two varieties. In those few cases I distinguish between the "forensic" ideologies of the conscious ideologist and the "latent" ideologies of the common man.

NOTES

[1] Henry D. Aiken, *The Age of Ideology: The Nineteenth Century Philosophers* (New York: Mentor, 1956).

[2] Daniel Bell, *The End of Ideology: On the Exhaustion of Political Ideas in the Fifties* (New York: The Free Press of Glencoe, 1960).

[3] Morton White, *The Age of Analysis: The Twentieth Century Philosophers* (New York: Mentor, 1956).

20. SOME SOURCES OF SUPPORT FOR DEMOCRATIC METHODS

Robert E. Lane

> For the vast majority of Americans the term "democracy" has no connotations beyond "political forms after the American fashion."
> —GEOFFREY GORER, *The American People,* p. 222

> It would be an exaggeration to suggest that the twentieth-century American was more democratic than his nineteenth-century forebears but accurate enough to say that his democracy, having been more effectively challenged, was more self-conscious and rationalized than at any time since Lincoln.
> —HENRY S. COMMAGER, *The American Mind,* p. 408

Some writers employ the term "democracy" in a broad social framework, including within it the relationship between social classes, among ethnic groups, and the general interpersonal relations of a community. In such usages, "equality" is the ingredient that gives the experience of democracy its savor, and "average" is the concept that gives it a certain odor.[1] Others focus more upon the governmental institutions of a polity, seeing in the arrangements for expressing the will of the people, the essence of the idea. Under these circumstances the idea of majority rule is the essential ingredient. A third variety looks to the protection of the rights of the individual, his freedom of expression, and the surrounding freedoms of religion and press and assembly that protect him from trespass, generally from governmental trespass. For these, the idea of minority rights is usually considered to be the jewel for which the democratic setting is valuable.

THE IDEA OF DEMOCRACY IN EASTPORT

What the men of Eastport have in mind, as they focus in an associative and connotative fashion on the term "democracy," is nothing that is quite like any of these. It is, in fact, neither majority rule nor minority rights, but something of a hybrid—majority rights. This concept is a variation of the central theme that was most enthusiastically endorsed in the discussion of freedom: it is the right of the majority to do what is conventionally approved. The word "freedom" is most swiftly, and most usually, associated with the word "democracy" —like this: "The way I look at democracy, the biggest fact is freedom. . . . Everybody is able to voice their opinion, and as long as they're on the right track, be able to do what they—what is right." Woodside, who is speaking here, almost said "do what they *want*" but his conscience intervened. O'Hara, with none of Woodside's Midwestern conscientious inhibitions, says clearly that democracy is to "do pretty much what you want the way you want, without

SOURCE: Robert E. Lane, *Political Ideology* (New York: The Free Press of Glencoe, 1962), pp. 82–97. © by The Free Press, a corporation, 1962. Reprinted by permission of The Macmillan Company.

being forced by the government to do otherwise." But the freedoms he mentions are conventional ones, and he emphasizes the freedom "to get ahead" if you have enough "push." Democracy as a popular concept centers in the freedom of the nondeviant individual to do what the majority thinks right.

Inasmuch as the ideas of equality and of freedom are explored elsewhere, I shall turn to the Eastportian idea of political democracy or popular government, their ideas of the trustworthiness of the electorate, the circumstances when popular government might better be abandoned, the extent to which the rulers can share power with the ruled and get anything done. To bring the matter to a focus, I shall use a measure embracing five criteria for this purpose, a measure that we shall call the "democraticness scale":

1. Willingness or reluctance to deny the franchise to the "ignorant and careless"; degree of elitism or restrictiveness concerning political participation; trust or scorn for "the masses."

2. Patience or impatience with the delays and confusions of democratic processes; appreciation or lack thereof of the protections afforded to minorities involved in these delays; degree of understanding of the policy advantages in "letting everybody have his say."

3. Willingness or reluctance to give absolute authority to a single leader in times of threat; provision or lack of it for ultimate responsibility in Congress and reversion of power to elected officials; relative preference for speed, decisiveness, expedition in contrast to deliberation, consultation, and consensus.

4. Where democratic forms are followed, degree of emphasis (and often disguised approval) of underlying oligarchical methods; appreciation or depreciation of consultative methods; degree of skepticism of popular requests or arguments not backed by sanctions.

5. Belief that the future of democracy in the United States is reasonably secure, or belief that it is uncertain, with various named or nameless contingencies likely to destroy it; appreciation or depreciation of the stability of social institutions, permanence of popular democratic preferences; presence or absence of a "secret" desire to participate in a great personal and social purgative movement.

Judged by these measures, Eastport is a democratic city; these are democratic men. Their views on the quality of the electorate (the first criterion) are sometimes scornful, but except for three men who argued for some kind of screening process to eliminate "the ignorant and careless," they all agreed that everyone regardless of qualification should have the vote. Ruggiero, Eastern State's maintenance clerk, speaks for the others: of the vote by the "ignorant and careless" he says, "There's only one way for democracy . . . we have to trust 'em with it." Ruggiero's view of the nature of man is more like that of Rousseau—basically good, spoiled by the commercialism and selfishness of society.

In addition to their support for the free and open universal franchise, Eastport also accepts with equanimity the confusion and disorderly processes of democracy (with reservations on "bickering" in the Administration) in an age when democracy is challenged to be "efficient." Here again, Woodside is representative (with four exceptions) in his views. He is not the no-nonsense policeman with the impatient night stick. Speaking of democracy, he says: "Oh, definitely it does [create confusion], because everybody has a chance to voice, and the time it is all thrashed out and everything, definitely there is a lot of time wasted—but it's good. It's time not wasted because regardless of how small or how big you are, everybody's opinion is heard, and it's balanced out, and I think that is the most important thing, regardless of time."

Challenged on whether it would not be best, "if there were another war with a threat of atomic bombing of this country," to establish a temporary dictatorship in the hands of the President, most of the men shied away from the notion of even a temporary dictatorship, even in the hands of the President. Costa, an assembly-line operative, thinks his emergency powers and war powers are already strong enough, O'Hara, a maintenance mechanic and oiler, argues "your Congress—that's what you elected them for—they should be able to straighten him out when he's going the wrong way"; and Johnson, the electric-utility mechanic, who says he has often thought of that problem, says, "I don't think any one man should run the show . . . because maybe the wrong man is there—you never know . . . that's too big a decision for one man to make."

When they turn to examine the democracy of their own organizations, the Hilltop Council, the unions, the veterans' organizations—they have some critical things to say, but generally they find the procedures measure up to their somewhat vague ideas of what the democratic process should be. As we shall see in a minute, there is a world of experience of fumbling consensual procedures among these men; and they accept it.

Finally, as to the future of democracy: "Well, I think we'll probably go right along with democracy," says the bookkeeper, McNamara. "It's flexible enough to make the necessary changes in the so-called atomic era." Johnson, a mechanic, agrees, and, like Henry Steele Commager, he finds that democracy "has been tested in quite a few ways in the past years—for instance, this segregation problem." How much of this faith in democracy is based on a want of imagination, a belief that the future will be like the present, or on a simple traditionalism, is hard to say. Sullivan, a truck driver, says of democracy, "I imagine it will always be pretty much the same as now." Of poverty in this country, he says, "I imagine we'll probably always have it [pause] the same as we do now." Although it is certainly true that the twelve who believe in the future of democracy are more likely to be its supporters than the three who do not, yet we must not confuse this dilute traditionalism with a deep and searching confidence in the capacity of democracy to solve its problems or see in it more than a kind of conventional, if useful, support.

Taking into account these and other, perhaps adventitious reasons for the support of democracy and the belief in its future, it is nevertheless true that most, indeed almost all, of the men both understand the frailties of popular government and accept it, with their eyes open. They know that ignorant and careless men, by voting, are helping to direct their own destinies; they acknowledge and accept the confusions and delays of parliamentary procedure; they are concerned over the need for swift, centralized power in emergencies, but they would want such power protected from abuse; they are not cynical about the uses of democratic procedures in their own local organizations; they believe democracy has a future on this continent and perhaps more broadly around the world. They believe these things—why? Why do these Americans, representative of working-class Eastport, and of New Haven, Springfield, Baltimore, Akron, Flint, and a large portion of urban America, adopt the ideology of popular government so completely?

AMERICAN SUPPORT FOR DEMOCRATIC FORMS

There have been many explanations for the hold democratic forms have had on the American mind. At least ten come to mind:

1. The support for popular government is derived from an intellectual lineage tracing back to Montesquieu and Locke and, some would say, Harrington. The men of Eastport are the inheritors of these views, however diluted and "brutalized" the ideas may have become in their passage through time and social strata.

2. The American support of popular government is a product of the American frontier experience, where men learned equality and self-help, and the practices of mutual respect and assistance. If the Turner thesis—that the main product of the frontier was democratic man—has been somewhat eroded of late, it still serves as a focus of attention.[2]

3. Potter has challenged and developed this view,[3] so that it is the abundance of the American economy that has sustained the support of democratic ways and popular government. Where there is abundance—and particularly where there is a growing abundance—it is easier for the privileged to yield and accommodate, for, in absolute terms, they give up nothing. Similarly, it is easier for the underprivileged to contain their political tempers because, after all, they are relatively well off and becoming better off all the time.

4. Germane to this view, but basically different in that it does not rely on growth, is the tracing of American support of popular government to the system of land distribution that prevailed from the earliest colonial (New England) times. The decision, whether forced or not, to permit men to become freeholders, each with his own plot of land, a decision carried out in the West by the Homestead Act and reinforced by irrigation and other policies today, might be said to have given an economic or property basis for an easy growth of popular government. At least Harrington and Jefferson considered a population so based to be a democratic requisite.

5. The geography of continents, not farms, has been said to have provided the continuity of history, the internal peace and security of a nation, the freedom from threat and invasion that permits and encourages the growth of popular government.[4]

6. It has been said that the religious practices of the early nation gave it the initial democratic bent and that these practices have nourished our popular institutions.

The Puritan church in particular and the Protestant churches in general have provided for self-government among the church members or at least among a selected group of elders.[5] Lindsay emphasizes this aspect of the support for representative government in the history of English parliamentary government.[6] It is even more true in the American experience.

7. The relation between self-government in churches and in governments is easier to understand than the relation between what is called free private enterprise and popular government, although it is certainly the case that the men of Eastport are convinced of one aspect of this close relationship. (The one thing they are sure a democratic government should *not* do is to tell a man how to run his business.) Still, it has been argued rather cogently that the experiences men have in choosing among employers, in trying their hand at their own businesses, in assuming responsibility for their own economic destinies leads them to prefer or even insist upon a form of government that gives them some "say" in public affairs.

8. There have been arguments of another kind, ones that turned upon the original "national character" of the English stock. Their emphasis upon rationality (Hume, Locke, Bentham, Smith), their capacity to compromise, their pragmatic tempers, their close relationship to the world of things (that is, mechanical ability), and so forth, are said to have provided the basis for an industrious and stable government; and to have led them to prefer the incremental advantages of a government of compromise as contrasted to the more ephemeral advantages of a government of purer principles.

9. On the other hand, it has been argued that the refreshing admixture of immigrant idealism brought here by men fleeing from tyranny abroad has sustained the American experiment in popular government.

10. Finally, there are current theories of the nature of American child care and early socialization wherein the child is taught his own worth, responsible independence, and how to share in family government, which purport to show why Americans support popular government.[7]

EXPERIENCE WITH DEMOCRATIC FORMS IN EASTPORT

The way in which people behave is all of a piece. . . . It would be impossible suddenly to introduce "democracy," which is a word for a type of behavior and an attitude of mind which runs through our whole culture, through our selection of candidates for office, our behavior in street cars, our schools and our newspapers, into an undemocratic society—as it would suddenly to introduce feudalism into a modern American city.
—MARGARET MEAD, *And Keep Your Powder Dry*, p. 20

One thing is clear: unless a traditional way of looking at things is regularly reinforced by the experience of living men, it will gradually be extinguished. Perhaps this will take generations or longer (Kardiner says that much in the Plainville personality is a dysfunctional residue of what was functional to medieval man);[8] perhaps it will take only a short time; but at the same time that tradition is absorbed, it is eroded, however slightly, and turned into something a little different. One must look, then, not only at what have been the historical forces shaping the American tradition of democracy that, as conventional, culture-bound men, Eastportians absorb, but also at the forces shaping the lives and outlook of these men in their own daily existences.

It is striking how few of the influences said to reinforce the democratic orientation of the American nation over the course of its history can be said to have a firsthand, immediate bearing on the lives of these men. They have not themselves read Locke, Montesquieu, Madison, Jefferson, or their own constitution. As we shall see, the phrase "a government of laws and not of men" leaves them bewildered. They have not lived on a frontier, never, for the most part, in open country at all. They have not owned land, as a homesteader or as a householder; they are not, in this sense, given an independent economic basis for criticism of government or, more important, the corporation. Most of them have not experienced laissez faire as an entrepreneur experiences it, and those that have must report mixed satisfactions. Dempsey tried his hand at a restaurant addition to his house and lost his savings; Ferrera has been in several bankruptcies; Johnson seeks to open up a gardening business on his own, but this is still largely a fantasy in his mind; few of their parents were small businessmen—but Ruggiero's father tried tailoring on an independent basis and lost much of his money, and Ferrera's father had to close down his barbershop because of illness. One or two, it is true, have somewhere in their family backgrounds a successful small businessman: Johnson's aunt has a beauty parlor, Woodside's brother has a radio repair shop, Rapuano's brother has a grocery store—but this is hardly enough to provide these men with those economic experiences that are said to link laissez-faire economics to democracy. They are all now employees, and their experiences here do not help to contribute to a belief in self-government; they apply at factory gates or in employment offices for positions where they have only minimal "say" in what takes place. A union may help, but only a few have been close enough to the processes of union organization and collective bargaining to speak with clarity and feeling about them. Yet for a few, like Sullivan, Costa, DeAngelo, and Woodside, there is something of value in this union experience that deserves examination, and to which we shall shortly return.

Most of these men are Roman Catholics; their churches do not vest much control in lay boards, councilors, vestrymen. Holy Name Societies seem to have elected officers, but they are rather tightly controlled. The Catholic world is caught between the hierarchical medieval vision and the new Western style of life. They have not been protected from the influence of war by the Atlantic ocean; born, for the most part, during or shortly after the First World War, they have lived through the Second World War and the Korean War, and many of them have been in the Armed Forces at one time or another. Five of the men are of Irish descent, six are of Italian descent, two are from Eastern European stock (a Polish Catholic and a Lithuanian Jew), one is half-Scandinavian, and only one is Anglo-Saxon. Thus, at least two-thirds of the men are from Eastern or Southern European gene pools and cannot be said to share in whatever is thought to be inheritable from that cherished Anglo-Saxon—and perhaps Scandinavian and perhaps Irish—temperament. If, on the other hand, it is claimed that their parents came to America in search of freedom, and thus were self-selected for their faith in popular government, it must be said that the Italian-American parents, more than the children, supported Mussolini, and according to some (McNamara is one) the Irish parents were more prejudiced against other racial and ethnic groups than they themselves are.

Finally, turning to the question of early experience, we cannot find any evidence that these men were encouraged, as children, to believe that they were, so to speak, voting members of the family household or that they could control their group destinies by group action. The evidence here is obscure; perhaps many of them were encouraged in this way. We have found only four instances where the sons' relations with their fathers were marked by cold or hostile feelings creating a serious and permanent damage. But in general it is the middle class, and not the working class, that helps a child to internalize the values and capacities congruent with democratic systems.[9] Is it the schools, with their middle-class teachers and value system, both parochial and public, that induct these men into the uses of democracy? Their classrooms may not have had this spirit (although some always will); still, the student councils, the civics events clubs, even elections of team captains may convey a democratic message. Perhaps Ferrera first learned the ways (and pleasures) of democracy in his election to captaincy of the football team in Eastport High.

With a few exceptions, then, must it be said that the forces that shaped the democratic heritage of a nation are now so attenuated, or operate in so different a milieu, that they are no longer serving to reinforce, generation by generation, the democratic ideal among living men? For these men of Eastport, is it largely the absorption of a past not quite their own, and conformity to the present as they find it, that leads them to support the ideal of popular government? Not quite. Here, I think, one must distinguish two different kinds of experience. In one, a person may have a set of experiences in a society that, while not really relevant to the political order, nevertheless create for him a *general* sense of satisfaction that leads him to accept and endorse the political system of his society. This is a little like the "halo effect" in judging persons; if a teacher likes a child's manners, she will see him as brighter and handsomer than she otherwise would. Thus if a person likes the opportunities for education and self-advancement in a society, he may tend to like everything about that society. It is, too, a little like the process of stimulus generalization: if a person, say, responds favorably to a monetary reward, and this is reinforced, he may respond favorably to other rewards that can be seen as having monetary value. Partly it is that the causes of social phenomena are so obscure that any institutions that are associated in one's mind with a satisfactory situation may be thought to have some causal relationship to that situation. In any event, the satisfactions the men of Eastport receive from certain aspects of career and family life do seem, by some one or all of these processes, to generalize to the political and social order in which their careers come to fruition and their families have their existence.

Following this line of argument, perhaps the most important single factor in the Eastportian support of the general society of which popular government is a part is the economic and social position of these men relative to that of their fathers. They are all, with, I think, only two exceptions, markedly better off than their fathers. Each man has not only stepped into his father's shoes; he has ordered a larger size. But it is not only in this comparison that these men of Eastport fare well; they fare well economicaly with respect to their own expectations (except for the dream of a house of their own). It is true that they are in debt, that they were, at the time, seriously worried about unemployment and layoffs, that many had illnesses that caused them long, deep hours of anxiety, that they had postponed a number of gratifications to achieve their respectable status, and that now in some ways, they had forgotten what it was like to "have a good time." But while all these things are true, the rewards in pride, in a sense of responsibilities met, in the companionship at the shop, and the supportive affection of wife and children, and in the small indulgences their budgets permitted, all kept them positively oriented toward the society of which their government is a part. In a rewarding life, however painful it may be at times, convention and the going order are anchored to bedrock.

But there is a second kind of experience, which is more specifically related to an enduring affection for the ways of democracy: it is experience in democratic procedures in small groups. Their church, it seems, leads them into this understanding only a little way; their schools a little way further. The voluntary groups that the men belong to, the labor unions, the veterans' organizations, the community councils and Parent-Teacher Organizations, catch the men at different ages. They mean different things and serve as vehicles for a variety of needs, but almost all of them have elected officers, parliamentary procedures, majority rule tempered by minority rights, and other aspects of what might be said to be popular government. People are often facetious about these aspects of their organizations; sometimes they are cynical. The men of Eastport were neither. Ruggiero, the university maintenance clerk, speaking of the Disabled American War Veterans, says, "I'd say yes [they are democratically run]; because they vote fairly, I mean you have your caucuses . . . you have a little more fight in it than you would be in the, uh, religious organizations." DeAngelo, speaking of his union, says, "I think they're run democratically—don't force any issues on anybody. I mean, like the way we run it, if we have a meeting with the company and they were discussing work practices or something—anything that we agreed upon in there is not binding until we have a meeting with the body, and the body is the deciding factor." Sullivan, a truck driver, who has had his differences with the union, reviews the situation briefly: "I don't know so much about the [democratic] way the union is run. [pause] The national leaders—I guess they don't care what goes on as long as their money keeps coming in. They're not interested with the actual running of it . . . so I guess your local committees and your regional committees are—I think it's run pretty democratic." Sullivan is hard to please, outspoken, and bitter about some of his experiences—his endorsement is, therefore, a meaningful one. This is the most usual view, and it extends even to social clubs. It is so usual that the men sometimes wonder whether there is another way. Sokolsky, speaking of his Young Couples' Club, says, "We have elections once a year and the people we like we vote in. . . . What other way is there?"

At Hilltop there is a Community Council with responsibilities for representing the tenants before the management, for supervising recreational facilities, for taking up matters of general interest such as road repairs and dogs running loose. Some of the men go to these meetings and consider themselves members, while others do not. Sullivan has been on the council, Flynn has been an officer of the organization, and several of the men have supervised sports or have otherwise been associated with it. What do they learn? Sullivan says the Hilltop Council is democratically run. Flynn, a most respected person around Hilltop, says, "I happen to be in a position in the ones [organizations] that I do belong to, to see that they are democratically run. . . . Maybe some people in the same organizations might differ. I think an attempt is made to see that all viewpoints are expressed." Most agree with him; a few, as he says, are skeptical.

On balance, the Legion posts, the lodges and the unions, the PTA's and the community councils are schools for learning, in an enclosed space, what the wider democracy of the nation requires. Not least of all, they teach the imperfections, the hesitations, the halting progress of democracy, and so prepare their members for a more realistic and informed view. At least in part, popular government survives less because men are aware of its crowning virtues than because they are adequately prepared for its galling vices.

CHARACTEROLOGICAL REINFORCEMENT
FOR THE DEMOCRATIC FAITH

But the generalization of satisfaction and the reinforcements of experience are not enough to explain the adoption of democratic ideals by the men. People do not support conventional ideals, with the understanding conviction these men show, without a set of personal qualities congenial to those ideals.

Among these is, first, the assumption of responsibility for their own fates by the men of Eastport, for each believes himself to be the master of some portion of his environment as well as the captain of his soul. A combination of this individualism with the characterological ego-strength that undergirds it leads the men of Eastport to accept self-government as the appropriate form of government. If their own destinies are in their own hands—something they accept—they must be given some "say" in the nature of government.

We said that, in the second place, most of the Eastport men have sufficient tolerance of delay, confusion, and ambiguity to suffer along with a procrastinating, hesitating legislature.[10] Our evidence suggests that one's tolerance differs a good deal with the nature of the matter that is ambiguous and how much you care about it. Although, most of the men (three-fifths) agreed that "bosses should say just what is to be done and exactly how to do it if they expect us to do a good job," they and others think that "people ought to pay more attention to new ideas even if they seem to go against the American way of life," and they are willing to believe that "some of our most deeply held beliefs will be successfully challenged by science someday."

In a more qualitative and impressionistic way, I have reviewed the discussion on political parties, the records of Roosevelt and Eisenhower, the merits of several religions, the treatment of the Little Rock situation, and the attitudes toward urban redevelopment in their home town. The discussion is remarkably balanced; partisanship is held to a low level—almost deprived of its cutting edge; heroes are found to be of human proportion—in short, the ambiguities of life and politics are not only tolerated, they are elaborated upon. These Americans of recent lineage but impeccable pedigree have a high tolerance for ambiguity, a strong preference for hearing more than one side of an issue, and a capacity for accepting delay and confusion in the process of getting what they want.

The support of popular government is realistic; whence this realism? One way to answer this is to say it comes from the application of an established pattern; it is part of a more general way of thinking. This, then, is a third source of democratic support. Of course there are, in Eastport, certain autistic and romantic ways of losing touch with reality and there are milder cases that are not so incapacitating. Some relied upon projective and self-delusive thinking, such as the belief that nationality makes no difference in making friends—denied by the names of their closest friends—or the wish to know less about unpleasant matters—a kind of denial, as in Costa's anger when the Chamber of Commerce published figures on rising unemployment. There were mildly obsessive ideas, such as Johnson's constant reference to people in every situation as, in the first place, "out to make a buck," as though men had only one motive (along with his probably delusory notion that he might come into some money someday). But the remarkable thing is the sturdy sanity of the group. Those who had special hatreds (Rapuano of doctors and Communists, Kuchinsky of Jews) felt grieved and injured rather than persecuted; no one (except Kuchinsky's wife) so far as I could tell had the mild forms of paranoia that one sometimes finds in everyday life. There were few delusions of powerful friends whom a person could call on to solve his problems—if he but chose to do so. The endowment of words like "progress," "democracy," or "Communism" with magical powers with the expectation that by manipulating them one could change one's life position, or the state of the Union, was evident, but only the magic of "education" seemed seriously disruptive of realistic thinking. The autistic inability to "hear" or "understand" what I was saying was present—as the Kuchinsky example will show—but was minimal. I could (when necessary) almost always break into the stream of consciousness and direct its flow to areas of relevance to the topic in hand. In short, these men were "there," and positioned themselves in a real world, dealing with it realistically. This realism, then, permitted them to make a reasonably accurate appraisal of the nature, process, and value of popular government, an appraisal that need not be disappointed, yet avoided cynicism.

Fourth, if popular government is to decide the circumstances of one's life, then not only must the public have the qualities that fit them for their responsibilities; each person must also have faith that others, as well as himself, in fact do have these qualities. Morris Rosenberg, who invented the "faith in people" scale, found that one's disbelief in the helpfulness, trustworthiness, sympathy, and cooperativeness of other people was clearly related to a belief that political authorities (or any authorities) cared little what one wanted or needed to have done, and to a disbelief in the feasibility of democracy.[11] Almond has found that there are substantial differences among several national cultures; with Americans generally *high* in faith of this sort.[12] The small evidence available to me at the moment of writing suggests that such faith in people in the United States is not only high but also fairly constant over geographical and social class ranges. (I compute Rosenberg's mean score based on his sample of about 1,500 Cornell college students to be 3.73; the mean score of the fifteen Eastport men was 3.67.) Moreover, to the statement, "These days a person really doesn't know whom he can count on," eleven of the fifteen men disagreed. Three of the four who agreed with this misanthropic statement (which is, in fact, part of an "anomie scale") are the men who qualify as least supportive of popular government. Thus, the premise seems sound that a confidence in one's fellow men must precede a support for democracy, and in Eastport, as in Plainville,[13] the induction of citizens into society has given them such a trust in the nature of man as to make the postulates of democracy plausible.

There are three men, and only three, who *strongly* disagree with the statement "Nowadays a person has to live pretty much for today and let tomorrow take care of itself." These three men are, again, the undemocrats. Is it, then, that a support for democracy presupposes some appreciation of "today," some sense that life is worth living *now;* that it is not continually a preparation for possible future contingencies? A fifth characterological support for democratic forms may be a capacity for present enjoyment. Such enjoyment, unclouded by the kind of phenomena represented in Kuchinsky's withdrawal, Rapuano's confusions, and Ferrera's moody tempers, may help a man to find congenial the democratic way of life, with its focus on the pursuit of happiness, not honor or glory. This is not hedonism, but rather finding a pivot for the balance of self-indulgence and self-sacrifice that gives a little to indulgence. And, it seems, behind this is the idea that each man is worthy of some modest consideration—even if it is only his own self-consideration.

NOTES

[1] See, for example, Robert and Helen Lynd's report on the advantages of being "average" in their *Middletown in Transition: A Study in Cultural Conflicts* (New York: Harcourt, Brace, 1937), p. 123.

[2] Frederick Jackson Turner, *The Frontier in American History* (New York: Holt, 1920).

[3] David M. Potter, *People of Plenty: Economic Abundance and the American Character* (Chicago: University of Chicago Press, 1954).

[4] Daniel J. Boorstin, *The Genius of American Politics* (Chicago: University of Chicago Press, 1953), pp. 8–35.

[5] See Curtis P. Nettels, *The Roots of American Civilization* (New York: Crofts, 1936), pp. 164–169.

[6] A. D. Lindsay, *The Modern Democratic State* (London: Oxford University Press, 1943), pp. 117–121.

[7] See, for example, Erik H. Erikson, *Childhood and Society* (New York: Norton, 1950).

[8] Abram Kardiner and associates, *The Psychological Frontiers of Society* (New York: Columbia University Press, 1945), pp. 418–448.

[9] See a summary and interpretation of this literature in my *Political Life: Why People Get Involved in Politics* (New York: The Free Press of Glencoe, 1959), pp. 227–228.

[10] On the concept of tolerance of ambiguity, see Else Frenkel-Brunswik, "A Study of Prejudice in Children," *Human Relations,* I (1949), pp. 295–306; and "Intolerance

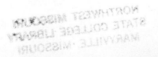

of Ambiguity, as an Emotional Personality Variable," *Journal of Personality,* 18 (1949), pp. 108–143.

[11] Morris Rosenberg, "Misanthropy and Political Ideology," *American Sociological Review,* 21 (1956), pp. 690–695.

[12] Gabriel Almond and Sidney Verba, forthcoming study of socialization in five countries.

[13] See Abram Kardiner and associates, *The Psychological Frontiers of Society,* pp. 345–350.

21. SOCIAL CONFLICT, LEGITIMACY, AND DEMOCRACY

Seymour Martin Lipset

Legitimacy and Effectiveness

The stability of any given democracy depends not only on economic development but also upon the effectiveness and the legitimacy of its political system. Effectiveness means actual performance, the extent to which the system satisfies the basic functions of government as most of the population and such powerful groups within it as big business or the armed forces see them. Legitimacy involves the capacity of the system to engender and maintain the belief that the existing political institutions are the most appropriate ones for the society. The extent to which contemporary democratic political systems are legitimate depends in large measure upon the ways in which the key issues which have historically divided the society have been resolved.

While effectiveness is primarily instrumental, legitimacy is evaluative. Groups regard a political system as legitimate or illegitimate according to the way in which its values fit with theirs. Important segments of the German Army, civil service, and aristocratic classes rejected the Weimar Republic, not because it was ineffective, but because its symbolism and basic values negated their own. Legitimacy, in and of itself, may be associated with many forms of political organization, including oppressive ones. Feudal societies, before the advent of industrialism, undoubtedly enjoyed the basic loyalty of most of their members. Crises of legitimacy are primarily a recent historical phenomenon, following the rise of sharp cleavages among groups which are able, because of mass communication, to organize around different values than those previously considered to be the only acceptable ones.

A crisis of legitimacy is a crisis of change. Therefore, its roots must be sought in the character of change in modern society. Crises of legitimacy occur during a transition to a new social structure, if (1) the *status* of major conservative institutions is threatened during the period of structural change; (2) all the major groups in the society do not have access to the political system in the transitional period, or at least as soon as they develop political demands. After a new social structure is established, if the new system is unable to sustain the expectations of major groups (on the grounds of "effectiveness") for a long enough period to develop legitimacy upon the new basis, a new crisis may develop.

Tocqueville gives a graphic description of the first general type of loss of legitimacy, referring mainly to countries which moved from aristocratic monarchies to democratic republics: ". . . epochs sometimes occur in the life of a nation when the old customs of a people are changed, public morality is destroyed, religious belief shaken, and the spell of tradition broken . . ." The citizens then have "neither the instinctive patriotism of a monarchy nor the

336

reflecting patriotism of a republic; . . . they have stopped between the two in the midst of confusion and distress." [1]

If, however, the status of major conservative groups and symbols is not threatened during this transitional period, even though they lose most of their power, democracy seems to be much more secure. And thus we have the absurd fact that ten out of the twelve stable European and English-speaking democracies are monarchies.[2] Great Britain, Sweden, Norway, Denmark, the Netherlands, Belgium, Luxembourg, Australia, Canada, and New Zealand are kingdoms, or dominions of a monarch, while the only republics which meet the conditions of stable democratic procedures are the United States and Switzerland, plus Uruguay in Latin America.

The preservation of the monarchy has apparently retained for these nations the loyalty of the aristocratic, traditionalist, and clerical sectors of the population which resented increased democratization and equalitarianism. And by accepting the lower strata and not resisting to the point where revolution might be necessary, the conservative orders won or retained the loyalty of the new "citizens." In countries where monarchy was overthrown by revolution, and orderly succession was broken, forces aligned with the throne have sometimes continued to refuse legitimacy to republican successors down to the fifth generation or more.

The one constitutional monarchy which became a fascist dictatorship, Italy, was, like the French Republic, considered illegitimate by major groups in the society. The House of Savoy alienated the Catholics by destroying the temporal power of the Popes, and was also not a legitimate successor in the old Kingdom of the Two Sicilies. Catholics were, in fact, forbidden by the church to participate in Italian politics until almost World War I, and the church finally rescinded its position only because of its fear of the Socialists. French Catholics took a similar attitude to the Third Republic during the same period. Both the Italian and French democracies have had to operate for much of their histories without loyal support from important groups in their societies, on both the left and the right. Thus one main source of legitimacy lies in the continuity of important traditional integrative institutions during a transitional period in which new institutions are emerging.

The second general type of loss of legitimacy is related to the ways in which different societies handle the "entry into politics" crisis—the decision as to when new social groups shall obtain access to the political process. In the nineteenth century these new groups were primarily industrial workers; in the twentieth, colonial elites and peasant peoples. Whenever new groups become politically active (*e.g.,* when the workers first seek access to economic and political power through economic organization and the suffrage, when the *bourgeoisie* demand access to and participation in government, when colonial elites insist on control over their own system), easy access to the *legitimate* political institutions tends to win the loyalty of the new groups to the system, and they in turn can permit the old dominating strata to maintain their own status. In nations like Germany where access was denied for prolonged periods, first to the *bourgeoisie* and later to the workers, and where force was used to restrict access, the lower strata were alienated from the system and adopted extremist ideologies which, in turn, kept the more established groups from accepting the workers' political movement as a legitimate alternative.

Political systems which deny new strata access to power except by revolution also inhibit the growth of legitimacy by introducing millennial hopes into the political arena. Groups which have to push their way into the body politic by force are apt to overexaggerate the possibilities which political participation affords. Consequently, democratic regimes born under such stress not only face the difficulty of being regarded as illegitimate by groups loyal to the *ancien régime* but may also be rejected by those whose millennial hopes are not fulfilled by the change. France, where right-wing clericalists have viewed the Republic as illegitimate and sections of the lower strata have found their expectations far from satisfied, is an example. And today many of the newly independent nations of Asia and Africa face the thorny problem of winning the loyalties of the masses to democratic states which can do little to meet the utopian objectives set by nationalist movements during the period of colonialism and the transitional struggle to independence.

In general, even when the political system is reasonably effective, if at any time the status of major conservative groups is threatened, or if access to politics is denied to emerging groups at crucial periods, the system's legitimacy will remain in question. On the other hand, a breakdown of effectiveness, repeatedly or for a long period, will endanger even a legitimate system's stability.

A major test of legitimacy is the extent to which given nations have developed a common "secular political culture," mainly national rituals and holidays.[3] The United States has developed a common homogeneous culture in the veneration accorded the Founding Fathers, Abraham Lincoln, Theodore Roosevelt, and their principles. These common elements, to which all American politicians appeal, are not present in all democratic societies. In some European countries, the left and the right have a different set of symbols and different historical heroes. France offers the clearest example of such a nation. Here battles involving the use of different symbols which started in 1789 are, as Herbert Luethy points out, "still in progress, and the issue is still open; every one of these dates [of major political controversy] still divides left and right, clerical and anticlerical, progressive and reactionary, in all their historically determined constellations." [4]

Knowledge concerning the relative degree of legitimacy of a nation's political institutions is of key importance in any attempt to analyze the stability of these institutions when faced with a crisis of effectiveness. The relationship between different degrees of legitimacy and effectiveness in specific political systems may be presented in the form of a fourfold table, with examples of countries characterized by the various possible combinations:

	Effectiveness +	−
Legitimacy +	A	B
−	C	D

Societies which fall in box A, which are, that is, high on the scales of both legitimacy and effectiveness, have stable political systems, like the United States, Sweden, and Britain.[5] Ineffective and illegitimate regimes, which fall in box D, are by definition unstable and break down, unless they are dictatorships maintaining themselves by force, like the governments of Hungary and eastern Germany today.

The political experiences of different countries in the early 1930s illustrate the effect of other combinations. In the late 1920s, neither the German nor the Austrian republic was held legitimate by large and powerful segments of its population. Nevertheless, both remained reasonably effective.[6] In terms of the table, they fell in box C. When the effectiveness of various governments broke down in the 1930s, those societies which were high on the scale of legitimacy remained democratic, while such countries as Germany, Austria, and Spain lost their freedom, and France narrowly escaped a similar fate. Or to put the changes in terms of the table, countries which shifted from A to B remained democratic, while those which shifted from C to D broke down. The military defeat of 1940 underlined French democracy's low position on the scale of legitimacy. It was the sole defeated democracy which furnished large-scale support for a Quisling regime.[7]

Situations like these demonstrate the usefulness of this type of analysis. From a short-range point of view, a highly effective but illegitimate system, such as a well-governed colony, is more unstable than regimes which are relatively low in effectiveness and high in legitimacy. The social stability of a nation like Thailand, despite its periodic *coups d'état,* stands out in sharp contrast to the situation in neighboring former colonial nations. On the other hand, prolonged effectiveness over a number of generations may give legitimacy to a political system. In the modern world, such effectiveness means primarily constant economic development. Those nations which have adapted more successfully to the requirements of an industrial system have the fewest internal political strains, and have either preserved their traditional legitimacy or developed strong new symbols.

The social and economic structure which Latin America inherited from the Iberian peninsula prevented it from following the lead of the former English colonies, and its republics never developed the symbols and aura of legitimacy. In large measure, the survival of the new political democracies of Asia and Africa will depend on their ability to meet the needs of their populations over a prolonged period, which will probably mean their ability to cope with industrialization.

Legitimacy and Conflict

Inherent in all democratic systems is the constant threat that the group conflicts which are democracy's life-blood may solidify to the point where they threaten to disintegrate the society. Hence conditions which serve to moderate the intensity of partisan battle are among the key requisites of democratic government.

Since the existence of a moderate state of conflict is in fact another way of defining a legitimate democracy, it is not surprising that the principal factors determining such an optimum state are closely related to those which produce legitimacy viewed in terms of continuities of symbols and statuses. The character and content of the major cleavages affecting the political stability of a society are largely determined by historical factors which have affected the way in which major issues dividing society have been solved or left unresolved over time.

In modern times, three major issues have emerged in Western nations: first, the place of the church and/or various religions within the nation; second, the admission of the lower strata, particularly the workers, to full political and economic "citizenship" through universal suffrage and the right to bargain collectively; and third, the continuing struggle over the distribution of the national income.

The significant question here is: Were these issues dealt with one by one, with each more or less solved before the next arose; or did the problems accumulate, so that traditional sources of cleavage mixed with newer ones? Resolving tensions one at a time contributes to a stable political system; carrying over issues from one historical period to another makes for a political atmosphere characterized by bitterness and frustration rather than tolerance and compromise. Men and parties come to differ with each other, not simply on ways of settling current problems, but on fundamental and opposed outlooks. This means that they see the political victory of their opponents as a major moral threat, and the whole system, as a result, lacks effective value-integration.

The place of the church in society was fought through and solved in most of the Protestant nations in the eighteenth and nineteenth centuries. In some, the United States, for example, the church was disestablished and accepted the fact. In others, like Britain, Scandinavia, and Switzerland, religion is still state-supported, but the state churches, like constitutional monarchs, have ceased to be major sources of controversy. It remains for the Catholic countries of Europe to provide us with examples of situations in which the historic controversy between clerical and anticlerical forces has continued to divide men politically down to the present day. In such countries as France, Italy, Spain, and Austria, being Catholic has meant being allied with rightist or conservative groups in politics, while being anticlerical, or a member of a minority religion, has most often meant alliance with the left. In a number of these countries, newer issues have been superimposed on the religious question. For conservative Catholics the fight against socialism has been not simply an economic struggle, or a controversy over social institutions, but a deep-rooted conflict between God and Satan.[8] For many secular intellectuals in contemporary Italy, opposition to the church legitimizes alliance with the Communists. And as long as religious ties reinforce secular political alignments, the chances for compromise and democratic give-and-take are weak.

The "citizenship" issue has also been resolved in various ways. The United States and Britain gave the workers suffrage in the nineteenth century. In countries like Sweden, which resisted until the first part of the twentieth century, the struggle for citizenship became combined with socialism as a *political* movement, thereby producing a revolutionary socialism. Or, to put it in other terms, where the workers were denied both economic and political rights, their struggle for redistribution of income and status was superimposed on a revolutionary ideology. Where the economic and status struggle developed outside of this context, the ideology with which it was linked tended to be that of gradualist reform. The workers in Prussia, for example, were denied free and equal suffrage until the revolution of 1918, and thereby clung to revolutionary Marxism. In southern Germany, where full citizenship rights were granted in the late nineteenth century, reformist, democratic, and nonrevolutionary socialism was dominant. However, the national Social Democratic party continued to embrace revolutionary dogmas. These served to give ultra-leftists a voice in party leadership, enabled the Communists to win strength after the military defeat, and, perhaps even more important historically, frightened large sections of the German middle class who feared that a socialist victory would end all their privileges and status.

In France, the workers won the suffrage but were refused basic economic rights until after World War II. Large numbers of French employers refused to recognize French trade-unions and sought to weaken or destroy them after every union victory. The instability of the French unions, and their constant need to preserve militancy in order to survive, made the workers susceptible to the appeals of extremist political groups. Communist domination of the French labor movement can in large part be traced to the tactics of the French business classes.

These examples do not explain why different countries varied in the way they handled basic national cleavages. They should suffice, however, to illustrate the way in which the conditions for stable democratic government are related to the bases of diversity. Where a number of historic cleavages intermix and create the basis for ideological politics, democracy will be unstable and weak, for by definition such politics does not include the concept of tolerance.

Parties with such total ideologies attempt to create what the German-American political scientist Sigmund Neumann has called an "integrated" environment, in which the lives of the members are encased within ideologically linked activities. These actions are based on the party's assumption that it is important to isolate its followers from the "falsehoods" expressed by nonbelievers. Neumann has suggested the need for a basic analytic distinction between parties of representation, which strengthen democracy, and parties of integration, which weaken it.[9] The former are typified by most parties in the English-speaking democracies and Scandinavia, plus most centrist and conservative parties other than religious ones. These parties view their function as primarily one of securing votes around election time. The parties of integration, on the other hand, are concerned with making the world conform to their basic philosophy. They do not see themselves as contestants in a give-and-take game of pressure politics, but as partisans in a mighty struggle between divine or historic truth on one side and fundamental error on the other. Given this conception of the world, it becomes necessary to prevent their followers from being exposed to the cross-pressures flowing from contact with outsiders which will reduce their faith.

The two major nontotalitarian groups which have followed such procedures have been the Catholics and the Socialists. In much of Europe before 1939 the Catholics and Socialists attempted to increase intra-religious or intra-class communications by creating a network of social and economic organizations within which their followers could live their entire lives. Austria offers perhaps the best example of a situation in which two groups, the Social Catholics and the Social Democrats, dividing over all three historic issues and carrying on most of their social activities in party or church-linked organizations, managed to split the country into two hostile camps.[10] Totalitarian organizations, fascist and Communist alike, expand the integrationist character of political life to the furthest limit possible by defining the world completely in terms of struggle.

Efforts, even by democratic parties, to isolate their social base from cross-pressures clearly undermine stable democracy, which requires shifts from one election to another and the resolving of issues between parties over long periods of time. Isolation may intensify loyalty to a party or church, but it will also prevent the party from reaching new groups. The Austrian situation illustrates the way in which the electoral process is frustrated when most of the electorate is confined within parties of integration. The necessary rules of democratic politics assume that conversion both ways, into and out of a party, is possible and proper, and parties which hope to gain a majority by democratic methods must ultimately give up their integrationist emphasis. As the working class has gained complete citizenship in the political and economic spheres in different countries, the socialist parties of Europe have dropped their integrationist emphasis. The only nontotalitarian parties which now maintain such policies are religious parties like the Catholic parties or the Calvinist Anti-Revolutionary party of Holland. Clearly the Catholic and Dutch Calvinist churches are not "democratic" in the sphere of religion. They insist there is but one truth, as the Communists and fascists do in politics. Catholics may accept the assumptions of political democracy, but never those of religious tolerance. And where the political conflict between religion and irreligion is viewed as salient by Catholics or other believers in one true church, then a real dilemma exists for the democratic process. Many political issues which might easily be compromised are reinforced by the religious issue and cannot be settled.

Wherever the social structure operates so as to isolate *naturally* individuals or groups with the same political outlook from contact with those who hold different views, the isolated individuals or groups tend to back political extremists. It has been repeatedly noted, for example, that workers in so-called "isolated" industries—miners, sailors, fishermen, lumbermen, sheepshearers, and long-shoremen—who live in communities predominantly inhabited by others in the same occupation usually give overwhelming support to the more left-wing platforms. Such districts tend to vote Communist or socialist by large majorities, sometimes to the point of having what is essentially a "one-party" system. The political intolerance of farm-based groups in times of crisis may be another illustration of this same pattern, since farmers, like workers in isolated industries, have a more homogeneous political environment than do those employed in most urban occupations.[11]

These conclusions are confirmed by studies of individual voting behavior which indicate that individuals under cross-pressures—those who belong to groups predisposing them in different directions, or who have friends supporting different parties, or who are regularly exposed to the propaganda of different groups—are less likely to be strongly committed politically.[12]

Multiple and politically inconsistent affiliations, loyalties, and stimuli reduce the emotion and aggressiveness involved in political choice. For example, in contemporary Germany, a working-class Catholic, pulled in two directions, will most probably vote Christian-Democratic, but is much more tolerant of the Social Democrats than the average middle-class Catholic.[13] Where a man belongs to a variety of groups that all predispose him toward the same political choice, he is in the situation of the isolated worker and is much less likely to be tolerant of other opinions.

The available evidence suggests that the chances for stable democracy are enhanced to the extent that groups and individuals have a number of cross-cutting, politically relevant affiliations. To the degree that a significant proportion of the population is pulled among conflicting forces, its members have an interest in reducing the intensity of political conflict.[14] As Robert Dahl and Talcott Parsons have pointed out, such groups and individuals also have an interest in protecting the rights of political minorities.[15]

A stable democracy requires relatively moderate tension among its contending political forces. And political moderation is facilitated by the system's capacity to resolve key dividing issues before new ones arise. If the issues of religion, citizenship, and "collective bargaining" are allowed to accumulate, they reinforce each other, and the more reinforced and correlated the sources of cleavage, the less likelihood for political tolerance. Similarly, the greater the isolation from heterogeneous political stimuli, the more the background factors "pile up" in one direction, the greater the chances that the group or individual will have an extremist perspective. These two relationships, one on the level of partisan issues, the other on the level of party support, are joined by the fact that parties reflecting accumulated unresolved issues will further seek to isolate their followers from conflicting stimuli. The best conditions for political cosmopolitanism are again those of economic development—the growth of urbanization, education, communications media, and increased wealth. Most of the obviously isolated occupations—mining, lumbering, agriculture—are precisely those whose relative share of the labor force declines sharply with industrialization.[16]

Thus the factors involved in modernization or economic development are linked to those which establish legitimacy and tolerance. But it should always be remembered that correlations are only statements about relative degrees of congruence, and that another condition for political action is that the correlation never be so clear-cut that men feel they cannot change the direction of affairs by their actions. And this lack of high correlation also means that for analytic purposes the variables should be kept distinct even if they intercorrelate. For example, the analysis of cleavage presented here suggests specific ways in which different electoral and constitutional arrangements may affect the chances for democracy. These are discussed in the following section.

Systems of Government

If crosscutting bases of cleavage make a more vital democracy, it follows that, all other factors being constant, two-party systems are better than multi-party systems, that the election of officials on a territorial basis is preferable to proportional representation, and federalism is superior to a unitary state. Of course there have been and are stable democracies with multi-party systems, proportional representation, and a unitary state. In fact, I would argue that such variations in systems of government are much less important than those derived from the basic differences in social structure discussed in the previous sections. Nevertheless, they may contribute to over-all stability or instability.

The argument for the two-party system rests on the assumption that in a complex society parties must necessarily be broad coalitions which do not serve the interests of one major group, and that they must not be parties of integration but must seek to win support among groups which are preponderantly allied to the opposition party. The British Conservative or American Republican parties, for instance, must not basically antagonize the manual workers, since a large part of their votes must come from them. The Democratic and Labor parties are faced with a similar problem vis-à-vis the middle classes. Parties which are never oriented toward gaining a majority seek to win the greatest possible electoral support from a limited base—a "workers" party will accentuate working-class interests, and a party appealing primarily to small business-men will do the same for its group. For these splinter parties, elections, instead of being occasions for seeking the broadest possible base of support by con-vincing divergent groups of their common interests, become events in which they stress the cleavages separating their supporters from other segments of the society.

The proposition that proportional representation weakens rather than strengthens democracy rests on an analysis of the differences between multi-party and majority party situations. If it is true, as suggested above, that the existence of many parties accentuates differences and reduces consensus, then any electoral system which increases the chance for more rather than fewer parties serves democracy badly.

Besides, as the German sociologist Georg Simmel has pointed out, the system of electing members of parliament to represent territorial constituencies rather than groups (as proportional representation encourages), forces the various groups to secure their ends within an electoral framework that involves concern with many interests and the need for compromise.[17]

Federalism increases the opportunity for multiple sources of cleavage by add-ing regional interests and values to the others which crosscut the social structure. A major exception to this generalization occurs when federalism divides a country across the lines of basic cleavage, e.g., between different ethnic, re-ligious, or linguistic areas, as it does in India and Canada. Democracy needs cleavage within linguistic or religious groups, not between them. But where such divisions do not exist, federalism seems to serve democracy well. Besides creat-ing a further source of crosscutting cleavage, it provides the various functions which Tocqueville noted it shared with strong voluntary associations—resistance to centralization of power, the training of new political leaders, and a means of giving the out party a stake in the system as a whole, since both national parties usually continue to control some units of the system.

I might emphasize again that I do not consider these aspects of the political structure essential for democratic systems. If the underlying social conditions facilitate democracy, as they seem to in, say, Sweden, then the combination of many parties, proportional representation, and a unitary state does not seriously weaken it. At most it permits irresponsible minorities to gain a foothold in parliament. On the other hand, in countries like Weimar Germany and France, where a low level of effectiveness and legitimacy weakens the foundations of democracy, constitutional factors encouraging the growth of many parties further reduce the chances that the system will survive.

Contemporary Challenges: Communism and Nationalism

The characteristic pattern of stable Western democracies in the mid-twentieth century is that they are in a "post-politics" phase—that is, there is relatively little difference between the democratic left and right, the socialists are moderates, and the conservatives accept the welfare state. In large measure this situation reflects the fact that in these countries the workers have won their fight for full citizenship.

Representatives of the lower strata are now part of the governing groups, members of the club. The basic political issue of the industrial revolution, the incorporation of the workers into the legitimate body politic, has been settled.[18] The key domestic issue today is collective bargaining over differences in the division of the total product within the framework of a Keynesian welfare state, and such issues do not require or precipitate extremism on either side. However, even though the working class of the Western democracies is incorporated into the society, it still possesses authoritarian predispositions which, under certain conditions, appear in support of extremist political and religious movements.

In most of Latin and Eastern Europe, the struggle for working-class integration into the body politic was not settled before the Communists appeared on the scene, and this fact drastically changed the political game. Communists could not be absorbed in the system in the way that the socialists have been. Communist workers, their parties and trade-unions, cannot possibly be accorded the right of access to actual political power by a democratic society. The Communists' self-image, and more particularly their ties to the Soviet Union, lead them to accept the self-fulfilling prophecy that they cannot secure their ends by democratic means. This belief prevents them from being allowed access, which in turn reinforces the Communist workers' sense of alienation from the government. The more conservative strata in turn are strengthened in their belief that giving increased rights to the workers or their representatives threatens all that is good in life. Thus the presence of Communists precludes an easy prediction that economic development will stabilize democracy in these European countries.

In the newly independent nations of Asia and Negro Africa the situation is somewhat different. In Europe the workers were faced with the problem of winning citizenship from the dominant aristocratic and business strata. In Asia and Africa the long-term presence of colonial rulers has identified conservative ideology and the more well-to-do classes with subservience to colonialism, while leftist ideologies, usually of a Marxist variety, have been identified with nationalism. The trade-unions and workers' parties of Asia and Africa have been a legitimate part of the political process from the beginning of the democratic system. Conceivably such a situation could mean a stable democracy, except for the fact that these political rights predate the development of a stable economy with a large middle class and an industrial society.

The whole system is standing on its head. The left wing in the stable European democracies grew gradually during a fight for more democracy and gave expression to the discontents created by the early stages of industrialization, while the right retained the support of traditionalist elements in the society, until eventually the system came into an easy balance with modifications on both sides. In Asia the left wing is now in power during a period of population explosion and early industrialization, and will have to accept responsibility for all the consequent miseries. And, as in the poorer areas of Europe, the Communists, who capitalize on all these discontents in a completely irresponsible fashion, are currently a major party—the second largest in most Asian states.

Given the existence of poverty-stricken masses, low levels of education, an elongated-pyramid class structure, and the "premature" triumph of the democratic left, the prognosis for political democracy in Asia and Africa is bleak. The nations with the best prospects—Israel, Japan, Lebanon, the Philippines, and Turkey—tend to resemble Europe in one or more major factors: high educational level (all except Turkey), a substantial and growing middle class, the retention of political legitimacy by conservative groups. The others are committed more deeply to a certain tempo of economic development and to national independence, under whatever political form, than they are to the pattern of party politics and free elections which exemplify our model of democracy. It seems likely that in countries which avoid Communist or military dictatorship, political developments will follow the pattern developing in countries such as Ghana, Guinea, Tunisia, or Mexico, with an educated minority using a mass movement and leftist slogans to exercise effective control, and holding elections as a gesture toward ultimate democratic objectives and as a means of estimating public opinion rather than as effective instruments for a legitimate turnover in office.[19] With the pressure for rapid industrialization and the immediate solution of chronic problems of poverty and famine, it is unlikely that many of the new governments of Asia and Africa will be able to support an open party system representing basically different class positions and values.[20]

Latin America, economically underdeveloped like Asia, is politically more nearly like Europe in the early nineteenth century. Most Latin-American countries became independent states before the rise of industrialism and Marxist ideologies and so contain strongholds of traditional conservatism. The countryside is often apolitical or traditional, and the leftist movements secure support primarily from the industrial proletariat. Latin-American Communists, for example, have chosen the European Marxist path of organizing urban workers, rather than the "Yenan way" of Mao, seeking a peasant base.[21] If Latin America is allowed to develop on its own and is able to increase its productivity, there is a good chance that many Latin-American countries will follow in the European direction. Recent developments, including the overthrow of a number of dictatorships, reflect the effects of a growing middle class and increased wealth and education. There is, however, the great danger that these countries may yet follow in the French and Italian direction rather than that of northern Europe, that the Communists will seize the leadership of the workers, and that the middle class will be alienated from democracy. Once a politically active middle class is in existence, the key distinction between "left" and "right" political tendencies no longer suffices as a means of differentiation between supporters and opponents of democracy.

NOTES

[1] Alexis de Tocqueville, *Democracy in America,* Vol. I (New York: Alfred A. Knopf, Vintage ed., 1945), pp. 251–52.

[2] Walter Lippmann in referring to the seemingly greater capacity of the constitutional monarchies than the republics of Europe to "preserve order with freedom" suggests that this may be because "in a republic the governing power, being wholly secularized, loses much of its prestige; it is stripped, if one prefers, of all the illusions of intrinsic majesty." See his *The Public Philosophy* (New York: Mentor Books, 1956), p. 50.

[3] See Gabriel Almond, "Comparative Political Systems," *Journal of Politics,* 18 (1956), pp. 391–409.

[4] Herbert Luethy, *The State of France* (London: Secker and Warburg, 1955), p. 29.

[5] The race problem in the American South does constitute one basic challenge to the legitimacy of the system, and at one time did cause a breakdown of the national order. This conflict has reduced the commitment of many white southerners to the democratic game down to the present. Great Britain had a comparable problem as long as Catholic Ireland remained part of the United Kingdom. Effective government could not satisfy Ireland. Political practices by both sides in Northern Ireland, Ulster, also illustrate the problem of a regime which is not legitimate to a major segment of its population.

[6] For an excellent analysis of the permanent crisis of the Austrian republic which flowed from the fact that it was viewed as an illegitimate regime by the Catholics and conservatives, see Charles Gulick, *Austria from Hapsburg to Hitler* (Berkeley: University of California Press, 1948).

[7] The French legitimacy problem is well described by Katherine Munro. "The Right wing parties never quite forgot the possibility of a counter revolution while the Left wing parties revived the Revolution militant in their Marxism or Communism; each side suspected the other of using the Republic to achieve its own ends and of being legal only so far as it suited it. This suspicion threatened time and time again to make the Republic unworkable, since it led to obstruction in both the political and the economic sphere, and difficulties of government in turn undermined confidence in the regime and its rulers." Quoted in Charles Micaud, "French Political Parties: Ideological Myths and Social Realities," in Sigmund Neumann, ed., *Modern Political Parties* (Chicago: University of Chicago Press, 1956), p. 108.

[8] The linkage between democratic instability and Catholicism may also be accounted for by elements inherent in Catholicism as a religious system. Democracy requires a universalistic political belief system in the sense that it accepts various

different ideologies as legitimate. And it might be assumed that religious value systems which are more universalistic, in the sense of placing less stress on being the only true church, will be more compatible with democracy than those which assume that they are the only truth. The latter belief, which is held much more strongly by the Catholic than by most other Christian churches, makes it difficult for the religious value system to help legitimate a political system which requires as part of its basic value system the belief that "good" is served best through conflict among opposing beliefs.

Kingsley Davis has argued that a Catholic state church tends to be irreconcilable with democracy since "Catholicism attempts to control so many aspects of life, to encourage so much fixity of status and submission to authority, and to remain so independent of secular authority that it invariably clashes with the liberalism, individualism, freedom, mobility and sovereignty of the democratic nation." See "Political Ambivalence in Latin America," *Journal of Legal and Political Sociology*, 1 (1943), reprinted in A. N. Christensen, *The Evolution of Latin American Government* (New York: Henry Holt, 1951), p. 240.

[9] See Sigmund Neumann, *Die Deutschen Parteien: Wesen und Wandel nach dem Kriege* (Berlin: Junker und Dünnhaupt Verlag, 1932) for exposition of the distinction between parties of integration and parties of representation. Neumann has further distinguished between parties of "democratic integration" (the Catholic and Social Democratic parties) and those of "total integration" (fascist and Communist parties) in his more recent chapter, "Toward a Comparative Study of Political Parties," in the volume which he edited: *Modern Political Parties, op. cit.*, pp. 403–5.

[10] See Charles Gulick, *op. cit.*

[11] This tendency obviously varies with relation to urban communities, type of rural stratification, and so forth. For a discussion of the role of vocational homogeneity and political communication among farmers, see S. M. Lipset, *Agrarian Socialism* (Berkeley: University of California Press, 1950), Chap. 10, "Social Structure and Political Activity." For evidence on the undemocratic propensities of rural populations see Samuel A. Stouffer, *Communism, Conformity, and Civil Liberties* (New York: Doubleday & Co., Inc., 1955), pp. 138–39. National Public Opinion Institute of Japan, Report No. 26, *A Survey Concerning the Protection of Civil Liberties* (Tokyo, 1951) reports that the farmers were the occupational group by far the least concerned with civil liberties. Carl Friedrich, in accounting for the strength of nationalism and Nazism among German farmers, suggests similar factors to the ones discussed here; that "the rural population is more homogeneous, that it contains a smaller number of outsiders and foreigners, that it has much less contact with foreign countries and peoples, and finally that its mobility is much more limited." Carl J. Friedrich, "The Agricultural Basis of Emotional Nationalism," *Public Opinion Quarterly*, 1 (1937), pp. 50–51.

[12] Perhaps the first general statement of the consequences of "cross-pressures" on individual and group behavior may be found in a work written over fifty years ago by Georg Simmel, *Conflict and the Web of Group Affiliations* (Glencoe: The Free Press, 1956), pp. 126–95. It is an interesting example of discontinuity in social research that the concept of cross-pressures was used by Simmel, but had to be independently rediscovered in voting research. For a detailed application of the effect of multiple-group affiliations on the political process in general, see David Truman, *The Governmental Process* (New York: Alfred A. Knopf, 1951).

[13] See Juan Linz, *The Social Bases of German Politics* (unpublished Ph.D. thesis, Department of Sociology, Columbia University, 1958).

[14] See Bernard Berelson, Paul F. Lazarsfeld, and William McPhee, *Voting* (Chicago: University of Chicago Press, 1954), for an exposition of the usefulness of cross-

pressure as an explanatory concept. Also, see Chap. 6 for an attempt to specify the consequences of different group memberships for voting behavior, and a review of the literature.

[15] As Dahl puts it, "If most individuals in the society identify with more than one group, then there is some positive probability that any majority contains individuals who identify for certain purposes with the threatened minority. Members of the threatened minority who strongly prefer their alternative will make their feelings known to those members of the tentative majority who also, at some psychological level, identify with the minority. Some of these sympathizers will shift their support away from the majority alternative and the majority will crumble." See Robert A. Dahl, *A Preface to Democratic Theory* (Chicago: University of Chicago Press, 1956), pp. 104–5. Parsons suggests that "pushing the implications of political difference too far activates the solidarities between adherents of the two parties which exist on other, nonpolitical bases so that members of the political majority come to defend those who share other of their interests who differ from them politically." See Parsons' essay "Voting and the Equilibrium of the American Political System," in E. Burdick and A. Brodbeck, eds., *American Voting Behavior* (Glencoe: The Free Press, 1959), p. 93. A recent discussion of this problem in a Norwegian context points up "the integrative functions of cross-cutting conflict . . . [when] the conflict lines between the voter groups cut across the divisions between readers of newspapers of different political tendencies and this places a considerable proportion of the electorate in a situation of cross-pressure . . . In the Norwegian situation there is an interesting two way process of mutual restraints: on the one hand a majority of the Socialist voters are regularly exposed to newspaper messages from the opposition parties, on the other hand the non-Socialist papers, just because they in so many cases dominate their community and address themselves to a variety of politically heterogeneous groups, are found to exercise a great deal of restraint in the expression of conflicting opinions." Stein Rokkan and Per Torsvik, "The Voter, the Reader and the Party Press" (Mimeographed, Oslo: 1959).

[16] Colin Clark, *The Conditions of Economic Progress* (New York: Macmillan, 1940).

[17] Georg Simmel, *op. cit.*, pp. 191–94. Talcott Parsons has recently made a similar point that one of the mechanisms for preventing a "progressively deepening rift in the electorate" is the "involvement of voting with the ramified solidarity structure of the society in such a way, that, though there is a correlation, there is no *exact* correspondence between political polarization and other bases of differentiation," Talcott Parsons, *op. cit.*, pp. 92–93.

[18] T. H. Marshall has analyzed the gradual process of incorporation of the working class into the body politic in the nineteenth century, and has seen that process as the achievement of a "basic human equality, associated with full community membership, which is not inconsistent with a superstructure of economic inequality." See his brief but brilliant book *Citizenship and Social Class* (London: Cambridge University Press, 1950), p. 77. Even though universal citizenship opens the way for the challenging of remaining social inequalities, it also provides a basis for believing that the process of social change toward equality will remain within the boundaries of allowable conflict in a democratic system.

[19] See David Apter, *The Gold Coast in Transition* (Princeton: Princeton University Press, 1955), for a discussion of the evolving political patterns of Ghana. For an interesting brief analysis of the Mexican "one-party" system see L. V. Padgett, "Mexico's One-Party System, a Re-evaluation," *American Political Science Review*, 51 (1957), pp. 995–1008.

[20] As this chapter was being edited for publication, political crises in several poor and illiterate countries occurred, which underline again the instability of democratic government in underdeveloped areas. The government of Pakistan was overthrown peacefully on October 7, 1958, and the new self-appointed president announced that "Western-type democracy cannot function here under present conditions. We have only 16 per cent literacy. In America you have 98 per cent." (Associated Press release, October 9, 1958). The new government proceeded to abolish parliament and all political parties. Similar crises have occurred, almost simultaneously, in Tunisia, Ghana, and even in Burma, since World War II considered one of the more stable governments in Southeast Asia, under Premier U Nu. Guinea has begun political life as a one-party state.

It is possible that the open emergence of military semi-dictatorships without much of a democratic "front" may reflect the weakening of democratic symbols in these areas under the impact of Soviet ideology, which equates "democracy" with rapid, efficient accomplishment of the "will of the people" by an educated elite, not with particular political forms and methods.

[21] Robert J. Alexander, *Communism in Latin America* (New Brunswick: Rutgers University Press, 1957).

22.   ATTITUDE STRUCTURE AND THE PROBLEM OF IDEOLOGY

Angus Campbell, Philip E. Converse, Warren P. Miller,
Donald E. Stokes

The widespread lack of familiarity with prominent issues of public policy, along with confusion on party position that remains even among individuals familiar with an issue, attests to the frailties of the political translation process. This insensitivity to policy controversies seems particularly significant when laid against our data concerning the stability of party identification over time. If the political relevance or, more especially, the partisan relevance of "new" problems is seen but darkly or not at all, it is less surprising that party allegiances gain momentum over time and are rarely derailed by pressures arising outside the political order.

It might be argued that although the "man in the street" may have only a loose idea of what is going on in terms of specific policy, he has a firm sense of the global policy differences between the parties, and relates them with equal firmness to highly generalized values of his own. A hypothesis of this sort could be fitted nicely with findings concerning the stability of party identification over time. Leaders of each party are continually forced to take positions, and from time to time these specific decisions fail to square well with the broader philosophy that normally characterizes the party. But policy as it may be formulated in the most general dimensions of ideology seems fairly stable for a party or tandem of parties throughout long political eras. Parties of the "left" and "right" do not trade positions from election to election. Assuming stability in parallel values in individuals, it would follow that partisan preferences would be pursued for long periods of time.

This suggestion directs our attention to the clusters or "structures" of attitudes involving political issues. We shall scan our data for evidence of this attitude structure, first at the level of the specific policy matters and subsequently at a more abstract level of generalized political values. Since our several modes of procedure reflect some widely held presumptions as to what "attitude structure" is, it is important to make these notions clear at the outset.

"ATTITUDE STRUCTURES" AND IDEOLOGY

We speak of an "attitude structure" when two or more beliefs or opinions held by an individual are in some way or another functionally related. As a simple example, we might encounter a person who is opposed to government activity in the area of low-cost housing. If we question him further as to his attitudes toward government ownership of utilities, he might oppose intervention here as well, and go on to say that in general he dislikes the idea of govern-

SOURCE: Angus Campbell, Philip E. Converse, Warren P. Miller, Donald E. Stokes, *The American Voter: An Abridgement* (New York: John Wiley & Sons, Inc., 1964), pp. 109–123. Reprinted by permission of the authors and publisher.

ment intrusion in economic areas where private industry has traditionally held sway. In such a case, we would feel that we had struck upon a cluster of attitudes that were functionally related, inasmuch as there seems to be interdependence between each opinion and the others. If this individual were to be persuaded that government intervention was generally desirable, we would expect attitudes toward both the housing problem and the utilities problem to change accordingly.

We may imagine a number of types of functional relationship binding attitudes together. There is, for example, a means-end relationship that often emerges clearly in attitude structures. A government activity thus may be favored because it is seen as a stepping stone to some broader goal. Or attitudes may be functionally related if they operate in the service of a similar need. There may be a sharply aggressive cast to all of an individual's foreign policy opinions that would lead us to suspect that out-group objects like foreign peoples and nations were targets for release of hostility.

One property of an attitude that is useful to recognize has to do with the specificity of the object that is evaluated. Affect may be aroused by objects as specific as a clause in a House bill or as general as the abstraction "freedom." Attitude structures are often thought of as hierarchies in which more specific attitudes interact with attitudes toward the more general class of objects in which the specific object is seen to belong.

At the very best, judgment on the presence or absence of a functional relationship between two or more attitudes demands some degree of inference on the part of the investigator. Although any specific person may show congruence of opinions "accidentally," it is generally supposed that correlations between attitudes that are visible in aggregates are reliable evidence of some structuring of the attitudes on the part of individual members.

Ideology. An ideology may be seen as a particularly elaborate, close-woven, and far-ranging structure of attitudes. By origin and usage its connotations are primarily political, although the scope of the structure is such that we expect an ideology to encompass content outside the political order as narrowly defined —social and economic relationships, and even matters of religion, education, and the like.

Any cognitive structure that subsumes content of wide scope and diversity must be capped by concepts of a high order of abstraction. The wider the range of objects so classified, the more remote and general the concept that is necessary to capture their similarity. Perhaps no abstraction has been used more frequently in the past century for political analysis than the concept of a liberal-conservative continuum—the "right" and the "left" of a political spectrum. The generality of this dimension makes it a powerful summary tool. Above the flux of specific domestic issues lie a number of broad controversies regarding the appropriate posture of the national government toward other sectors of the social order, such as the development of resources, industry, and trade; the church; the privileged and the underprivileged; relatively local political bodies; and the world community. Differences between liberal and conservative tend to focus upon the degree to which the government should assume interest, responsibility, and control over these sectors of endeavor.

The nature of the advocacy that is called liberal or conservative comes to depend, within the immediate context, upon what is and what is hoped for. The viewpoint termed conservative may thereby become that which is reluctant to disturb the existing order of relationships, whether they be laissez faire or interventionist. The liberal viewpoint sees room for improvement in the product of social and political process through change in these relationships.

The widespread use of a liberal-conservative distinction in political analysis leads us to focus attention upon it rather heavily in this paper. We shall first consider the evidence for structures of attitudes emerging from our items of relatively specific public policy. Then we shall attempt to improve our grasp of the meaning that may reasonably be attributed to these structures, by assessing their status as "ideology."

ATTITUDE STRUCTURES IN ISSUES OF PUBLIC POLICY

Analysis of the ten domestic issues and six foreign policy items explored in 1956 yields one set of opinions within each area that forms a satisfactory Guttman scale. Five domestic issues contributed to one scale, including the items on aid to education, medical care, employment guarantees, FEPC and Negro housing, and public versus private production of electricity and housing. In primary content these items all have to do with the desirability of governmental action in areas of social welfare. Therefore, although we intend to inquire further into the meaning of this structure, we shall label this the "social welfare" structure.

Similarly, four of the six foreign policy items showed relationships of a sort that qualified the set as a second attitude structure. The content shared across these issues and relatively absent in the two excluded items concerned the desirable degree of United States intervention in international affairs. At one extreme were persons who thought our government should not be concerned with problems in other parts of the world, should not give economic aid to poor countries, should not maintain overseas military installations to fight Communism, and should not offer aid to the so-called neutral nations. At the other end of the continuum were persons favoring American activity in all of these spheres.

There undoubtedly were other issues in 1956 which, had we attempted to measure them, could have qualified as parts of either the social welfare or the foreign structure. Neither of these sets of issues should be considered as more than a selection from the opinions that might be shaped by the same underlying attitude. On the other hand, the fact that the other attitudes that we had measured within each broad policy area failed to fit the major structures located gives us a sense of the boundaries for each structure and hence sets limitations on their meaning. From this viewpoint the data evince a rather slight degree of structure in the attitudes of the mass electorate.

It is important to recognize the degree to which our "normal" or *a priori* expectations in these matters are conditioned by sophisticated views of the parts that make up a coherent political ideology. Locked in this perspective, we may wonder at the low-income person who wants to see government services extended, yet agrees that "the government ought to cut taxes even if it means putting off some important things that need to be done." However, both responses may spring from the same motivation—a simple desire for improvement of one's economic lot. So long as the structure of political attitudes is loose, potential contradictions will not be confronted.

The fact that an issue reaction fails to fit into a larger organization of attitude that seems appropriate for it does not mean that the response is random or in any other sense "uncaused." The problem is rather that the structure imposed on the situation by the analyst turns out in such instances to be inadequate. It may be that the sources of responses to an issue are so diverse from individual to individual that all sense of patterning across an aggregate is lost. More often, clear roots may exist, but the analyst ignores them because they have no place in his preconceptions concerning "logical" or traditional ideological position. His organizing dimensions simply depart from the modes of organization abroad in the general population.

The Interrelationship of Foreign and Domestic Policy Structures. Across our sample as a whole in 1956 there was no relationship between scale positions of individuals on the domestic and foreign attitudinal dimensions. An interventionist position in foreign affairs was as likely to be taken by a domestic conservative as by a domestic liberal, and the relative isolationist was as likely to favor social welfare activities in Washington as he was to oppose them. Whether this seems surprising depends once again on our preconceptions. In terms of elite behavior and party programs there has been some reason to associate parties of the "right" in domestic affairs with nationalism in foreign questions, as opposed to the frequent humanitarian internationalism of "leftist" parties. Yet it is difficult to find evidence for this configuration of attitudes in the general electorate of 1956, and we are forced to conclude once again that the typical American lacks a clearly patterned ideology of such breadth. He may feel strongly about a variety of individual issues, but there are severe limitations on our ability to predict his position in one issue area from his position in another.

Now that we have assessed some of the outer limits of structure visible in the electorate, it becomes important to focus more careful attention on the two major structures that are apparent. What is the nature of the commonality that underlies each of these structures? What political significance may be attributed to them? We may increase our understanding of these attitude patterns by analyzing some of their more important correlates.

THE SIGNIFICANCE OF ATTITUDE STRUCTURES ON POLICY ISSUES

Foreign Policy. Not only do the differences in activism-withdrawal fail to correlate with placement on the social welfare dimension; they fail as well to show a correlation with political partisanship in 1956. People who tended to give internationalist responses to the four foreign policy items were no more likely to express identification with the Democratic Party than with the Republican Party. This finding, when laid against other aspects of our data, is of great interest.

First, the absence of correlation between foreign policy position and partisanship seems to be of much the same cloth as the general confusion as to the foreign policy alignments of the major parties. However, it appears to clash with other findings. For example, in the Eisenhower elections the partisan balance of foreign policy concerns was of considerable benefit to the Republican cause. We must resolve the apparent contradiction by examining more closely the types of response that produce a sense of clear partisan pattern, as opposed to those that produce instead a sense of confusion in perceived partisan implications.

Partisan patterns on foreign concerns developed most clearly in 1956 where the issues were formulated at the simple and global level of getting into war or staying out of it. Such patterns faded out when the issue grounds were shifted to the more *specific* means of attaining the goal. People had feelings about the desirability of American engagement abroad that lent consistency and a sense of structure to their responses on items of this nature. But the "bridge" perceptions were lacking that would meaningfully link activist or withdrawal feelings to one of the parties. Hence the broad public mandate in 1956 could be taken to express, among many other things, a fear of getting into war, and an appreciation of the political *agents* thought best capable of avoiding war. But there was no visible mandate concerning the choice between intervention and isolation as a *means* toward peace. The victorious party drew no greater support from people of either policy persuasion.

The withdrawal activism dimension of foreign policy attitudes did show some association with other dispositions toward politics, a fact that helps to round out our understanding of these opinions. Generally, internationalists were more likely to be politically informed and involved than were those favoring withdrawal from international commitments. The internationalist was more aware of differences in the policy commitments of the two major parties. He was also more likely to be interested in and familiar with a more extensive range of the policy questions that we probed than was his isolationist counterpart. The internationalist, too, tends to register a stronger sense of political efficacy than does the isolationist. People advocating withdrawal from foreign engagements are, by their own assessment, less effective participants in politics; the internationalist feels that he is in control of his political world and that it is responsive to his desires and acts.

The involvement and sense of effectiveness that characterize the internationalists undoubtdly have further political implications. In terms of the actual 1956 election, the mandate of the public on the activism-withdrawal question was rendered unclear by confusion over party lines. However, the rallying of more informed, involved, and active citizens to the internationalist position suggests that this persuasion is likely to be pressed more diligently outside of the immediate election situation than a census or unweighted poll of the national constituency would lead us to expect.

Domestic Policy. The items involved in the domestic issue structure reflect the social welfare controversies of the New Deal-Fair Deal era. They are, by and large, the questions that revealed the clearest consensus as to party differences. Therefore, it is not surprising that although foreign attitudes had lost their partisan element in 1956, position in the domestic issue structure remained clearly associated with partisan preference. Persons who favored social welfare activity by the federal government were likely to be identified with the Democratic Party. They perceived the Democratic Party to be closer than the Republican Party to their own position on other issues, and their voluntary references to domestic issues, within the system of proximal attitudes, were highly favorable to the Democratic cause or critical of the Republican.

The structure of opinions built around the problem of social welfare activity is of intense interest to us for reasons that go beyond its unique partisan implications, however. For this structure is one which has clearest relevance for traditional discussions of the "left" and the "right" in political ideology. Although we can hardly gainsay the significance of these core dimensions of modern ideology in the decision making of political elites, how important may we presume them to be at the level of mass political behavior?

Evidence as to the great momentum of long-standing party loyalties and the vicissitudes of the political translation process where specific matters are concerned have moved us toward the tentative conclusion that events outside the political order impinge only feebly upon the evolution of partisan decisions at the mass level. It would seem to follow that ideology of a sort that binds a broad range of human experience to dynamic evaluations of politics cannot be thought to be widespread in the American population.

This is, however, argument by indirection, and we can now confront the matter directly. We have isolated an attitude structure capturing the core ideological controversies of our epoch. The structure exists empirically, and, moreover, it shows relationships of substantial magnitude with partisan preference in the direction that would be predicted by notions of ideology. That is, people sort themselves into patterns of response that are coherent in terms of a liberal-conservative dimension; and people who choose liberal alternatives tend to identify with the more liberal, or "leftist," Democratic Party, whereas people choosing conservative alternatives tend more often to express loyalty to the conservative, "rightist" Republican Party. Furthermore, we find that people of lower status predominate both among those who rank as "liberal" in their social welfare attitudes and among the adherents of the "liberal" party. Citizens in higher strata tend to prefer the "conservative" alternatives to such questions, and give primary support to the conservative party.

It is common to leap from these bare facts to the conclusion that traditional ideological structures are important parts of the armory of attitudes generally used in political evaluation. For some predictions the social and political outcome is the same whether or not this assumption is warranted. In other cases, however, our expectations may be sorely betrayed if we are not more cautious in our view of ideology at a mass level. It is our contention that this assumption is frequently overdrawn. We shall attempt to demonstrate a number of other facts, equally real, which are inexplicable once this assumption is made. And we shall consider how the basic triangle of relationships laid out above can be generated with very little in the way of full-blown "ideology" in the motives and values of the actors involved.

First it is important to distinguish between behavior impelled by self-interest in a primitive and short-sighted sense, and the operation of self-interest within a structure of attitudes that might reasonably be labeled an "ideology." This discrimination may seem difficult, since it is customary to assume that perceived interest is the primary criterion whereby the individual locates an appropriate ideology. Thus ideology and self-interest become tightly linked in our minds.

We have no quarrel with the view that ideological position is largely determined by self-interest. But we do maintain that it matters whether self-interest proceeds in a simple and naked sense, or has indeed become imbedded in some broader ideological structure. We have suggested, for example, that the possession of ideology equips the individual to perceive the connectedness of many superficially diverse events and relate them to one another coherently. One important implication of such understanding is that the person is sensitized to the existence of "roundabout" routes that, despite a superficial detour, will better secure ultimate gratification.

Political action is, in itself, a roundabout route to the fulfillment of most forms of self-interest. From the point of view of a frontier farmer harassed by price cuts and discrimination in freight rates, the formation of a political organization to send a representative to a distant parliamentary body is a less clear means of remedying evils than burning the grain elevator. Even where it is perceived that the path to a goal is through politics, usually a variety of more and less direct paths are available. Frequently shorter paths are less effectual than the longer. One function of ideology is to maintain the perspective of time and roundabout routes that permit the most effective long-range political evaluations.

We may survey our domestic policy items more generally from this new vantage point. The responses that come to form a coherent "social welfare" structure lending credence to ideological assumptions are at the same time questions in which the path of self-interest for a lower-status person is quite clear, and they are scarcely more obscure for the individual of higher status. Several of the other items that might be comfortably located in a broad liberal or conservatve ideology do not turn out to fit this key structure. In a rough way, we may distinguish two types. First, there are those in which some other dimension than the economic appears primary, or in which the number of steps necessary to link a policy choice to self-interest is multiplied and hence less clear. For a person who fears unemployment, a question concerning government guarantees of employment can be directly related to self-interest. But a question about the role of business in government can only be related to self-interest if one has an understanding of business interests and the advantages conferred by political power. The items of this type show little or no relationship with items in the social welfare structure. The second type, in which there is an actual conflict posed for lower-status persons between immediate financial interest and longer-range, indirect gains, is represented only by the tax item. And in this case alone the visible relationship with items of the social welfare scale runs in a direction perfectly contrary to our ideological expectations.

In sum, then, the pattern of responses to our domestic issues is best understood if we discard our notions of ideology and think rather in terms of primitive self-interest.[1] Of course, the basic triangle of relationships between status, issue "liberalism," and party is no more difficult to account for in these terms than it is when more full-fledged ideology is assumed. Indeed, the fact that these relationships are never overwhelming in magnitude is probably a good deal *more* comprehensible once we have scaled our assumptions down in this fashion. For the possibility of widespread confusion about political means and ends among the least informed seems easier to countenance if we recognize that the level of sophistication about such matters is generally rather low.

There are other points at which we may pit ideological expectations against simpler notions of self-interest. The fact that no mean proportion of lower-status people are Republican and high-status people are Democratic has always occasioned a good deal of comment. Whether we deal in terms of ideology or simpler interest concepts, these people are out of step, for they appear to espouse a political instrument counter to their interest. What forces permit them to maintain this apparent disequilibrium? Perhaps the most familiar explanation is an ideological one, for strongly ingrained ideology is one of the few motivating forces that can be seen to induce a person to act in terms of interest other than his own. The stereotype built up to account for the low-status Republican involves an origin in the tradition-bound individualism of rural America. For high-status Democrats, two types of ideological mechanisms receive attention. The person who has achieved status from modest beginnings may maintain his old ideology because of the deep impressions that past experiences of social inequity have made upon him. The aristocrat by birth, on the other hand, may be motivated to liberal ideals by what is essentially *noblesse oblige*.

There is no doubt that within midcentury America many persons fitting these descriptions could be located. But the question remains whether persons meeting such specifications loom at all large among the low-status Republicans and high-status Democrats to be found in a cross section of the electorate. It is our contention that they do not, but represent instead a deviant few who have attracted attention because of the pleasing manner in which they fill ideological preconceptions.

Several pieces of data may be brought to bear on the question. Figure 1 shows, for example, that low-status Republicans fall rather close to the radical extreme of the social welfare scale.[2] Their attitudes are not greatly different from those held by Democrats of equivalent status. With these findings in hand we are not likely to be impressed by the argument that these low-status people are kept within the Republican ranks by their exceptionally conservative political ideologies.

Figure 1 suggests that the relationship between partisanship and social welfare attitudes noted previously is slightly stronger among persons of higher education levels. In the degree that higher-status Democrats depart from the attitudes of higher-status Republicans there is an indication that ideology of the sort postulated may be playing some role. However, this role appears weak at best. We would not be convinced, for example, that the higher-status liberal maintains his unusual position by any striking commitment to liberal causes. Higher-status Democrats are very substantially more conservative in their attitudes than either low-status Democrats *or* low-status Republicans. Differences in attitude attributable to party, although statistically significant, are thoroughly eclipsed by those differences correlated with status.[3]

If the ideological explanation fails to account for the low-status Republican and the high-status Democrat, what interpretation may be substituted? Figure 1 suggests again that we consider the problem in two parts. The strong attitude-status correlation that appears within each party grouping is now adequately accounted for in simple self-interest terms. The question then remains why people of low or high status with appropriate social welfare attitudes identify themselves with the "wrong" party. We must remember that a variety of other factors influence partisan choice. The importance of this fact increases as we scale down our assumptions about the role of ideological concerns in decisions by the broad electorate. For the sophisticated observer, the ramifications of some of these core domestic policy decisions are so broad that dimensions of attitude relating to them deserve heavy weight in any political choice. But in the

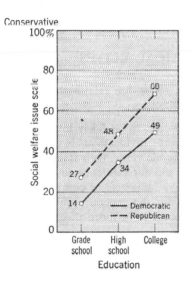

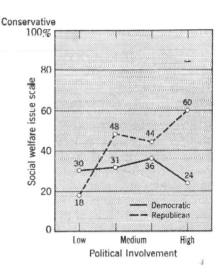

FIG. 1. Relation of education to social welfare attitudes, by party.

FIG. 2. Relation of political involvement to social welfare attitudes, by party.

degree that the public lacks this ideological superstructure, the significance accorded such policy matters must be somewhat less. Consequently, other factors independent of these concerns, such as candidate attractiveness or long-standing party loyalty, increase in relative importance.

Furthermore, although people presented with certain policy alternatives can do a reasonable job of selecting responses that appear to further their self-interest, this fact is in itself no guarantee that they have ever sorted out how the parties stand on the matter. If the person has never been motivated to follow political affairs closely, we can well imagine that he may feel a bond wth a party and may be able to discern self-interest in a set of policy propositions without having established a link between the party and its policy position.

This possibility is supported by Fig. 2, which shows that partisan differences on social welfare attitudes are indeed dependent on political involvement. Differences between adherents of the two parties are sharpest among the most highly involved; where involvement is low, there is no significant variation in social welfare attitude by party. Thus we conclude that one important factor in the choice of a party that is "wrong" in view of the individual's social welfare attitudes and status location is simple indifference and the lack of information thereby implied.

Generally, then, closer examination of some of the connections that have been assumed to exist on the basis of the original triangle of status, attitude, and party relationship reveals a variety of gaps. Although from time to time we catch glints of possible ideology operating, by and large the pattern of relationships that are statistically significant is explicable only in terms of a much more modest self-interest assumption. And even the simple self-interest assumption produces partisan relationships only where there is some degree of formal education and involvement in politics.

IDEOLOGY AND POLITICAL ELITES

Herbert McClosky has written as follows about the relationships between conservation and a range of specific political attitudes:

> The correlation(s) between them tend, however, to be fairly low, suggesting that for the present, at least, many Americans divide in their party preferences, their support of candidates, their economic views, their stands on public issues, or their political self-identifications without reference to their beliefs in liberalism or conservatism. The latter have influence, of course, especially among some of the more articlate groups; for the general population, however, political divisions of the sort named appear to be more affected by group membership factors than by personality.[4]

These findings are clearly corroborated by our data on a national sample. There is no significant correlation between conservatism and party identification, for example, even with Southern respondents excluded. In short, if we focus upon the total range of individuals represented in the national electorate, we find almost no correlation between a general disposition that we would expect to be of prime political relevance and variation in issue attitudes or partisanship. However, we may locate subgroups in the population for which sophisticated expectations do receive some support. These islands of support become highly instructive in assessing the reasons for discontinuity elsewhere. For example, McClosky, before applying his scale to a cross section population, used it with leaders of both political parties. He found that it discriminated at a very satisfactory level between Republican and Democratic elites.[5] Now we can surmise that such party leadership must have differed radically from a "normal" population in a number of ways. First, such people certainly would rank as highly involved in politics. Second, we would suppose them to have a very abnormal command of political events and recent party history. Third, it is likely that they were disproportionately people of high education, for whom conceptual abstractions of the sort used in ideological thinking are relatively common coin.

These traits that distinguish political party elites are traits shared with the several "spectator" elites—journalistic and academic—who tend to apply concepts such as the liberal-conservative continuum to analyses of political motivations and events. The fact that theoretical expectations are borne out within party elites attests once again to the value of such concepts for the understanding of behavior in these circles. But party activists of this type represent such a tiny fraction of the electorate that they are too few to permit analysis even in a relatively large national sample. These data lead to the same conclusion as our preceding analyses: as we depart from the extreme combinations of involvement, background, and education represented by such elites, the significance of familiar ideological frames of reference drops off rapidly. It is not hard to see why the sophisticated observer is readily misled in his analytic constructions. He recognizes of course that individuals differ in the partisan or issue content of their political beliefs, for he sees these differences contested in the daily drama of politics at an elite level. But he falls prey to the assumption that the same basic frames of reference are shared by all citizens who take any interest in politics whatever.

Most citizens tend to locate themselves in a political party at an early point in their adult life, and this identification typically then gains strength throughout life. The party that wins favor appears to depend predominantly upon social transmission from the family or early reference groups. The critical initial decision appears to be taken most frequently under strong social influence early in life, when involvement in politics is at low ebb, and, presumably, political information is most scanty as well. Thus if involvement and background are preconditions for the establishment of meaningful links between basic values and party preference, then we must suppose that in the bulk of cases, the individual is committed to a party at a time when he is least likely to have the wherewithal to bring ideological considerations of this sort into play. Thereafter, the self-reinforcing aspects of a psychological identification progressively reduce the probability of change in partisan allegiance. If the crucial identifications were postponed until the individual had observed the parties for some time with the modest but more active involvement and fuller information of the middle-aged adult, we would expect that ultimate partisanship would show more convincing relationships with underlying values of this sort. Or if the psychological potency of party identification were weaker later in life, so that existing partisanship dictated less thoroughly the interpretation of political events, we might also expect more rearrangement of partisanship to achieve better fit with underlying values. In the absence of these conditions the impression of discontinuity between such values and partisanship remains almost complete.

NOTES

[1] Lipset has pointed out that although lower-status groups favor "liberal" policies on matters of social welfare legislation, then tend at the same time to take anti-liberal or intolerant positions on matters involving treatment of deviants or ethnic minorities. These empirical facts have contributed to Lipset's sense of dissatisfaction with com-

mon assumptions concerning the configuration of beliefs treated generically as "liberalism." He argues for a distinction between "economic" and "noneconomic liberalism." See Seymour Martin Lipset, "Democracy and Working-Class Authoritarianism," *American Sociological Review*, XXIV (August 1959). We are most sympathetic with this critique. However, the data concerning opinions on taxes suggest that even the connotations of the term "economic liberalism" may be unrealistically broad. If these attitudes have internal coherence, they are expressions of self-interest, not "liberal ideologies."

[2] For reasons that will be apparent in the subsequent text, we use education as the criterion of status in this figure. However, other status criteria produce similar patterns.

[3] Although this is clear even on the basis of Fig. 1, the use of a single status criterion understates the full significance of the status dimension in predicting social welfare attitudes. For example, income as a second criterion makes a considerable independent contribution to the prediction of attitudes.

[4] Herbert McClosky, "Conservatism and Personality," *American Political Science Review*, LII (March 1958), pp. 44–45.

[5] *Ibid.*

23. THE STRUCTURE OF PUBLIC OPINION ON POLICY ISSUES

Robert Axelrod

Much has been written about the relationships between various policy issues, but little reliable analysis is available on how the public sees these relationships. Campbell *et al.* report that New Deal–Fair Deal issues scale together, as do several foreign policy issues.[1] There is no relationship between the scales; a liberal on welfare issues is no more likely to be an internationalist than is a conservative on welfare issues. Finally, high identification with a party is associated with a lower than average probability of being a non-scalar individual.[2] These observations hint at the nature of the structure of public opinion on policy issues, but they are only the beginning of an adequate understanding of the question.

METHOD

The method used in this study to determine the structure of public opinion on policy issues is cluster analysis.[3] A set of issues is considered a cluster if every pair in that set has a degree of similarity greater than some fixed threshold value. Thus four issues would form a cluster if each of the six possible pairs of these issues were closely associated. If the measure of association is suitably chosen, the clusters will be equivalent to Guttman scales, and indeed this fact has been used by MacRae as the criterion for acceptance of a scale.[4] To see why this can be done, consider the normal product-moment correlation coefficient ϕ. Two items that scale together perfectly will have one of the entries in the fourfold table equal to zero, but this condition is not sufficient to guarantee that $\phi = 1$. However, this can be rectified by using as the index of association $\phi' = \phi / \phi_{max}$ where ϕ_{max} is the highest value of ϕ possible given the same marginals in the fourfold table.[5]

The data needed for an analysis of the structure of public opinion was gathered as part of the 1956 national survey conducted by the University of Michigan Survey Research Center.[6] Sixteen policy statements were given each respondent:

The government ought to cut taxes even if it means putting off important things that need to be done.

The government in Washington ought to see to it that everybody who wants to work can find a job.

This country would be better off if we just stayed home and did not concern ourselves with problems in other parts of the world.

The government ought to help people get doctors and hospital care at low cost.

The U.S. should give economic help to the poorer countries of the world even if they can't pay for it.

SOURCE: *Public Opinion Quarterly*, XXXI, No. 1 (Spring, 1967), pp. 51–60. Reprinted by permission of the author and publisher.

If the Negroes *are not* getting fair treatment in jobs and housing, the government in Washington should see to it that they do.

The government ought to see to it that big business corporations don't have much say about how the government is run.

The best way for this country to deal with Russia and Communist China is to act just as tough as they do.

If cities and towns around the country need help to build more schools, the government in Washington ought to give them the money they need.

The U.S. should keep soldiers overseas where they can help countries that are against Communism.

The government should leave things like electric power and housing for private businesssmen to handle.

The government ought to see to it that labor unions don't have much say about how the government is run.

The U.S. should be willing to go more than half-way in being friendly with other countries of the world.

The government ought to fire any government worker who is accused of being a Communist even though they don't prove it.

The U.S. should give help to foreign countries even if they are not as much against Communism as we are.

The government in Washington should stay out of the question of whether white and colored children go to the same school.

The special publics used in this analysis are:

1. Total sample (1,762 persons)
2. Completed college (141)
3. Did not complete grade school (276)
4. Actively particated in 1956 campaign (268) by doing any one of the following:
   a. Bought something to help
   b. Went to meetings
   c. Did any work for a party or candidate
   d. Belonged to a political club or organization
5. Knew correct name of the Congressional candidate he voted for (390)
6. Did not vote (477)
7. Cared a good deal which party won (459)
8. Had annual income over $10,000 (134)
9. Had annual income of $1,000 to $3,000 (294)

RESULTS

The array of pairwise scale coefficients, ϕ', for the total sample is shown in Figure 1. The most distinctive and perhaps the most important property of these data is the absence of *any* values above .50. The significance of this is made evident by the fact that a cluster is often defined by a minimum value of .75, and a value of .65 is regarded as being of marginal significance for the purpose of constructing a reliable Guttman scale. Another way to appreciate the meaning of the low values involved is to recall that these values of ϕ' are always larger than the correlation coefficient.

The first scale measures liberalism in terms of five New Deal–Fair Deal domestic issues: government aid to education, insure medical care, government guarantee of jobs, racial equality in jobs and housing, and leave electricity and housing to private industry. This can be regarded as a scale if the threshold value of ϕ' is set at the very low level of .14. If the item on private industry in electricity and housing is removed, the scale becomes considerably more coherent, with the theshold of ϕ' rising to .30.

An array similar to the one shown in Figure 1 for the total population has been constructed for each of the special publics, and hence the clarity of their

FIG. 1. PAIRWISE SCALE COEFFICIENTS FOR THE TOTAL SAMPLE [a]

Government aid to education

44   Insure medical care

42   43   Government guarantee of jobs

30   32   37   Racial equality in jobs and housing

27   38   17   14   Leave electricity, housing to private industry

−28 −38 −36 −20   1 Cut taxes

18   9   9   49   19 0 Segregation of schools

 7   23   8   −0   18 3   20 Influence of unions in government

−7 −16 −18 −12   −14 28   8   27 Influence of big business in government

−37 −26 −27 −11   15 19   15   20 10 Fire suspect Communists

−13 −13 −14   −0   7 23   12   6 5 29   Act tough toward Russia, China

−2   −8   3   6   −16 7   −9   −5 2 1   27 Friendliness toward other
                                              nations

−22 −39 −40 −10   8|38   5   19 24 21   12 12· Avoid foreign involve-
                                                   ·ment

 9   4   5   19 −1| 8   9   8 14 8   7 22· 22 Economic aid to for-
                                                   ·eign countries

 5   2 −9   8 −9|20   −3   5 12 0 −10 7· 22 25 Send soldiers
                                                   ·abroad

14   −7 −12   10 −0|19   4   6 6 15   15 36· .29 45 19 Give aid
                                                   ·to
                                              · · · · · · · · neutral
                                                              countries

[a] The chart is read in the same way as a mileage chart. The polarity of each issue is chosen to maximize the average value of ϕ'.

Liberalism cluster—triangle

Foreign policy cluster—dotted triangle

Welfare cluster crossed with foreign
policy cluster—rectangle

attitudes on welfare issues can be determined. One measure of the coherence or clarity of a scale is the average value of γ' in the cluster that defines that scale, and this value of each of the publics is given in Table 1. The publics that are expected to be more sophisticated (the participants, wealthy, educated, concerned, and informed) exhibit a greater tendency to be consistent on welfare

TABLE 1. COHERENCE OF LIBERALISM SCALE FOR EACH OF THE PUBLICS

Public	Average γ'
Participants	.44
Wealthy	.42
College graduates	.39
Concerned	.37
Informed	.35
Total population	.32
Poor	.32
Uneducated	.28
Nonvoters	.25

issues than does either the total population or the publics expected to be less sophisticated (the nonvoters, uneducated, and poor).

An interesting relationship is exhibited in Figure 1 between the welfare issues and the question on lowering taxes even if it means putting off important things that need to be done. V. O. Key has noticed in his discussion of the same data that those who are in favor of these welfare programs oppose taxation more frequently than those who oppose them. It is difficult to disagree with his comment: "These interrelations suggest melancholy thoughts about the practical politics of the interaction of tax and substantive policy." [7] In examining this relationship for the special publics, the startling result emerges that college graduates show this same inconsistent pattern of attitudes. While welfare programs may be consistent with lowered taxes according to Keynesian economics, this is unlikely to be the reasoning used by even the college graduates. A more likely explanation is that lowered taxes are seen as another way government can promote welfare.

The second scale reported by Campbell et al. consists of four of the six foreign policy questions: avoid foreign involvement, economic aid to foreign countries, send soldiers abroad, and give aid to neutral countries. The dotted triangle in Figure 1 indicates that this set of four issues has positive association, but the relationship is not sufficient to define a very coherent scale. The total sample has a coherence of .27 and even the public with the greatest consistency on these four issues, the people who have never completed grade school, had an index of only .36. These foreign policy questions do evoke a vague pattern reflecting an internationalist-isolationalist dimension, but the extent of this structure is not great.

The relationship between liberalism on the welfare scale and internationalism on the four foreign policy questions is exhibited by the entries in the rectangle in Figure 1. There are as many positive as negative entries, and the average value of ϕ' is $-.03$. In other words, there is no net association between domestic liberalism and internationalism for the American public as a whole. Table 2 shows that this finding holds not only for the total sample, but also for each of the special publics examined.

TABLE 2. ASSOCIATION OF DOMESTIC LIBERALISM AND INTERNATIONALISM FOR EACH OF THE PUBLICS

Public	Average ϕ'
College graduates	.14
Wealthy	.05
Uneducated	.04
Informed	.03
Poor	$-.01$
Total population	$-.03$
Participants	$-.06$
Concerned	$-.07$
Nonvoters	$-.12$

An important advantage of cluster analysis over other methods of constructing Guttman scales is that one can readily search for all possible scales instead of merely testing the few that have been hypothesized. Thus a systematic search through the array of ϕ' given in Figure 1 might lead to the discovery of a new cluster that is at least as distinct as the other two in terms of length, threshold, and average value.

This is indeed the case. There exists a six-item scale that includes three welfare issues, two domestic nonwelfare issues, and a foreign policy issue. This cluster is larger than the welfare or foreign policy scales, has a threshold that is no lower, and has $\overline{\phi'}$ of .33, which is higher than either of the other two scales. The questions in this new scale are: government aid to education, insure medical care, government guarantee of jobs, cut taxes, fire suspect Communists, and avoid foreign commitment. A person at one extreme of the scale favors each of these positions and a person at the other extreme disapproves of each. Agreement with the first three items reflects a liberal attitude on the welfare scale, while agreement with the second three reflects what is currently regarded as a conservative position.[8] Thus the scale measures something very different from the left-right dimension that is so frequently used in commentary on the structure of American public opinion. The cluster that defines this new scale has been extracted from the main array and is presented in Figure 2 with the polarity of the second three items reversed.

An appropriate name for this scale is "populism" because one of its extremes corresponds to many of the attitudes of the American Populist movement of the 1890's.[9] The Populist concern with social reform at home is reflected in the modern populist demand for the improvement of education, medical care, and

FIG. 2. POPULISM CLUSTER.

Government aid to education					
44	Insure medical care				
42	43	Government guarantee of jobs			
28	38	36	Cut taxes [a]		
37	26	27	19	Fire suspect Communists [a]	
22	39	40	38	21	Avoid foreign involvement [a]

[a] Polarity reversed.

job opportunity. The nativism of the original Populist movement is echoed in the anti-civil liberties attitude, and its distaste for foreign involvement is duplicated by the populists in this modern dimension. The absence of many issues is also consistent with the nature of the original movement. A distinction was made between wars of conquest and wars for humanity, and the modern populist, while being against involvement per se, is not necessarily against giving economic aid to poor nations or keeping soldiers overseas to help anti-Communist countries. Just as the Populist movement before the turn of the century had nothing against Negroes or the urban worker, so the modern populist is not necessarily against racial equality in jobs and housing or the strength of the labor union. None of the issue questions allows an exact indication of whether the modern populist sees monopoly trusts as a major problem, but there is a marked and consistent positive association between the populism dimension and the question on whether government ought to see to it that big business corporations do not have much to say about how the government is run.

The dimension of populism is most coherent for the nonvoters ($\overline{\mathscr{S}'} = .38$), and, as would be expected, the dimension has no meaning to college graduates in the sample ($\overline{\mathscr{S}'} = .14$). A comparison of liberalism and populism is shown in Table 3.

TABLE 3. COMPARISON OF LIBERALISM AND POPULISM

	New Deal–Fair Deal Liberalism	Modern Populism
Mean for total population	$\overline{\mathscr{S}'} = .32$	$\overline{\mathscr{S}'} = .33$
Threshold	$\mathscr{S}'_{min} = .14$	$\mathscr{S}'_{min} = .19$
Length	5 items	6 items
Best clients [a]	Participants	Nonvoters
Worst clients	Nonvoters	College graduates

[a] The special public with the highest value of $\overline{\mathscr{S}'}$.

To summarize the results:

1. American public opinion on policy issues has no single clear pattern, and there is hardly a trace of an over-all left-right dimension. This is true for the informed and the concerned, for the well-educated and the uneducated, for the rich and the poor, and for the participant and the nonvoter.

2. There exists a weak welfare cluster that is most meaningful for political participants, the wealthy, and the educated. There is also a weak foreign policy cluster that is most meaningful for the informed. Liberalism on the welfare scale bears no correlation with internationalism on the foreign policy scale.

3. The clearest dimension (in terms of length, threshold, and average value) is populism, defined by an extreme representative who favors Federal improvement of education, medical care, and job opportunity but is against current tax levels, civil liberties, and foreign involvement.[10] The populism dimension is most distinct for nonvoters.

DISCUSSION

The lack of a strong pattern in attitudes on policy implies that no well-defined, widely shared ideology is used by the public to relate these issues to each other. Apparently, people tend to view each issue independently of the others, perhaps, for example, thinking of sick people when asked about government-insured medical care, and about local school facilities when asked about aid to education. To a considerable extent, attitudes are compartmentalized, as illustrated by the inconsistent relation between attitudes on tax policy and substantive policy, and the weak association between attitudes on segregation of schools and racial equality in jobs and housing. Indeed, the greatest product-moment correlation between any two of the issues examined accounts for less than one-fifth of their variance.

This tendency to view each policy issue separately contributes to the low salience of American national politics to the public. If many issues were judged by the criterion of a single attitude, the effect associated with each of these issues would be cumulative. If, as is actually the case, the attitude associated with each policy issue is largely independent of attitudes on other issues, the effects associated with the issues tend to cancel each other. In political terms, an equivalent proposition about current policy attitudes is that, if people were concerned with more than a few issues, then most of them would be indifferent to *any* set of policy stands by a political party.

An implication of this proposition is that recent proposals to make the Democratic and Republican Parties more ideologically distinct would have little significance to the typical voter. Indeed, even the college graduates, who comprise less than 8 per cent of the population, see no significant policy dimension that the parties could use to separate themselves.[11]

Even though no policy dimension is very coherent, populism is the most distinct one that exists. The political scientist and his cousin the political commentator have long relied on the left-right dimension and have only recently begun to digest the fact that for the American public domestic liberalism is not correlated with internationalism.[12] Perhaps less reliance on the analytic constructs that apply only to the most sophisticated segments of society will lead to the discovery that much of the public views policy questions as they were seen in the 1890's and not the 1930's.

A question worthy of further study is whether the modern populist dimension is a continuation of the Populist heritage or whether it is an independent phenomenon that resembles it. Tests would include the extent to which the modern populist tends to share the characteristic beliefs of the Populist movement, such as a perception of cabalism, a tincture of anti-Semitism, and a belief in a golden age in the past.

Richard Hofstadter has said, "While its special association with agrarian reforms has now become attenuated, I believe that Populist thinking has survived in our own time, partly as an undercurrent of provincial resentments, popular and 'democratic' rebelliousness and suspiciousness, and nativism." [13] The case is hardly proven, but cluster analysis of survey data has now provided supporting evidence for what had previously remained a hypothesis untested by systematic data.

NOTES

[1] Angus Campbell, Philip E. Converse, Warren E. Miller, and Donald E. Stokes, *The American Voter* (New York: Wiley, 1960), pp. 194–198.

[2] *Ibid.*, p. 201.

[3] A word is in order about the relationship of cluster analysis to factor analysis. The goal of factor analysis is to explain the observed correlation matrix using as few factors, or "underlying causes," as possible. The goal of cluster analysis is to determine the presence and nature of multivariate dependence. Unfortunately, the precise correspondence between factors and clusters is still a matter of statistical research, but it is known that under certain conditions they are equivalent and that sometimes information retrieved in a cluster analysis is lost through factor analysis (see R. E. Bonner, "On Some Clustering Techniques," *I.B.M. Journal of Research and Development,* Vol. 8, January 1964, pp. 22–32).

Cluster analysis was chosen for this study because the results are easier to interpret and the problem of factor rotation is not present. In addition, cluster analysis is not as sensitive as factor analysis to variations in the domain of issues chosen for analysis.

[4] Duncan MacRae, Jr., "Interparty Division and Cabinet Coalition in the Fourth French Republic," *Comparative Studies in Society and History,* Vol. 5, January 1963, pp. 164–211.

[5] For further details, see Edward E. Cureton, "Note on $\mathscr{S} / \mathscr{S}_{max}$" *Psychometrica,* 24 (March 1959), pp. 89–91.

[6] I would like to thank the Inter-University Consortium for Political Research and Yale University Political Science Research Library for making these data available.

[7] V. O. Key, *Public Opinion and American Democracy* (New York: Knopf, 1961), p. 168.

[8] It may appear that this scale is an artifact of the tendency of some people to be "yea-sayers" and others to be "nay-sayers" regardless of the content of the question. This is refuted by the fact that a "yes" answer on these six questions is not correlated with a "yes" on the other ten questions.

[9] My description of the Populist movement is taken from Richard Hofstadter, *The Age of Reform* (New York: Vintage Books, 1960).

[10] Note that the scale is equally well defined by a representative of anti-populism, and thus the populism scale measures a dimension of cleavage and not a uniform tendency toward pro-populist patterns of attitudes.

[11] Of course, there may be smaller groups who are especially important to the political process and who have a much clearer structure than any of the special

publics examined, but the size of the total sample precludes a cluster analysis of their attitudes.

[12] Many of the "inconsistent" attitudes of some Congressmen might be explained by their conformity to the populism dimension rather than to the liberalism dimen-sion. If so, it would speak well for the ability of American political institutions to adapt to current patterns that do not have a distinct ideology, group identification, set of symbols, or leadership.

[13] Hofstadter, *op. cit.*, p. 5.

B. SOME SOCIAL AND PSYCHOLOGICAL SOURCES OF IDEOLOGICAL DIFFERENCES

24. PERSONALITY AND POLITICAL SOCIALIZATION: THE THEORIES OF AUTHORITARIAN AND DEMOCRATIC CHARACTER

Fred I. Greenstein

The socialization experiences which culminate in adult citizenship can be divided into two rough categories: that learning which is specifically about government and politics, and nonpolitical personal development which affects political behavior. My concern here is with a particularly controversial, but intriguing, portion of the topics arising in the second category—the notions of "authoritarian" and "democratic" character. In addition to reviewing theory and research on these character types, I will discuss briefly several of the problems involved in untangling the complex connections among personal character, political beliefs, political action, and the functioning of political and other social institutions. This is an extensive and extraordinarily craggy intellectual terrain. In a brief essay I can only hope, as it were, to engage in high-altitude aerial reconnaissance—that is, to construct a rather abstract and quite selective map of the phenomena which interest us, illustrating rather than demonstrating my assertions.

Put bluntly, the questions which concern us are: "Can we distinguish types of individuals whose personal make-up—apart from their specifically political beliefs—disposes them to act in a democratic or an authoritarian manner?" "What socialization practices produce such individuals?" "What can be said about the circumstances under which the actual behavior of such individuals will be democratic or authoritarian, and about the aggregate effects which individuals with democratic or authoritarian dispositions may have on the functioning of political institutions?"

THE STUDY OF AUTHORITARIAN AND DEMOCRATIC CHARACTER

There is, by far, more literature on authoritarian than on democratic character. One of the wonders of recent social science scholarship has been the

SOURCE: *The Annals of* The American Academy of Political and Social Science, 361 (September, 1965), pp. 81–95. Reprinted by permission of the author and publisher.

372

profusion of "authoritarianism" research in the past decade and a half. An admittedly selective review of writings on the topic through 1956 contained 260 bibliographical references.[1] Today, anything but the most sparse systematic discussion of the relevant research would require a monograph. Even as interest in this matter begins to fall off, it is rare to find an issue of a journal dealing with personality and attitude research that contains no reference to authoritarianism and no use of the various techniques designed to measure it.

The main immediate stimulus for this explosion of research was the publication in 1950 of a 990-page volume by T. W. Adorno, Else Frenkel-Brunswik, Nevitt Sanford, and Daniel J. Levinson, entitled *The Authoritarian Personality,*[2] which reported the fruits of several years of investigation into the psychology of anti-Semitism. On the basis of a rich but bewilderingly varied and uneven assortment of research procedures, the authors of this work reached a striking conclusion about the psychology of hostility to Jews and other minority groups. Such prejudiced attitudes, they argued, were not simply beliefs which people happened to have acquired. Rather, one could identify what might be called a "bigot personality," [3] a type of individual with deep-seated psychological needs which manifested themselves in a variety of ways over and beyond ethnic prejudice. *The Authoritarian Personality* is a book dealing more with prejudice than with the problem suggested by its title—psychological dispositions toward authority. "The title," as one of the authors points out, "was not thought of until the writing was virtually finished," [4] But it was the title phrase which came to provide the heading under which subsequent investigation proceeded, and, in general, ethnic prejudice has become a secondary issue in research on authoritarianism.

The term "authoritarian" has at least two shortcomings as an analytic tool. First, it is applicable not only to individual psychological dispositions (our concern here), but also to the content of political belief and to the structure of political systems. Because of this we may easily gloss over the possibility that "authoritarianism" at any one of these levels is not necessarily accompanied by authoritarianism at the other levels. For example, democratic beliefs may be imposed in an authoritarian manner. And, within an authoritarian movement, the leadership may include individuals of nonauthoritarian dispositions, and may even conduct its own deliberations in a democratic fashion.

Secondly, the term seems almost inevitably to be a pejorative. In a liberal democracy "authoritarian" equals "bad." The evaluative connotations of the term interfere with our efforts to use it as a neutral instrument for denoting an empirical phenomenon. A historical note on the work of the Nazi psychologist E. R. Jaensch may help to remind us that the term can have meaning independent of its negative connotations. In 1938 Jaensch described a psychological type with remarkable similarities to the typology presented in *The Authoritarian Personality*. But his evaluation of the type was not at all negative. Rather, he saw it as exemplifying the best virtues of National Socialist manhood.[5]

There is, of course, nothing new in the awareness that some people are more deferential toward authority than others and that the same people often are harsh to their subordinates. The fawning underling is a stock character in fiction, as is the tyrannical superior. It is a safe assumption that the readers of Fielding's *Tom Jones* (1747) had no difficulty recognizing the character of Deborah

Wilkins, who "seldom opened her lips either to her master or his sister till she had first sounded their inclinations, with which her sentiments were always strictly consonant," and of whom Fielding says:

> It is the nature of such persons . . . to insult and tyrannize over little people. This being indeed the means which they use to recompense to themselves their extreme servility and condescension to their superiors; for nothing can be more reasonable than that slaves and flatterers should exact the same taxes on all below them which they themselves pay to all above them.[6]

What *is* new in the twentieth-century literature on authoritarianism is the specification of a constellation of psychological correlates of this tendency and the elaboration of a theory of its psychodynamics and genesis. This theory (which I shall shortly summarize) was woven from a number of strands of contemporary social psychological thought. Some of the formulations in *The Authoritarian Personality* were presaged by research in the 1930's and 1940's into "fascist attitudes." [7] Others can be found in the World War II and cold-war national-character literature, particularly the efforts to diagnose German Japanese, and Russian character.[8] The discussion of "authoritarian character" in Erich Fromm's widely discussed *Escape from Freedom* [9] seems to have been particularly influential, as were the various efforts in the 1930's by Fromm and others connected with the Institut für Sozialforschung to blend Freud and Marx in an analysis of the role of the family "in maintaining authority in modern society." [10] Underlying all of these discussions was what still is probably the most revolutionary facet of twentieth-century social science—psychoanalysis —and, particularly, several overlapping elements in Freud's thought: the notion of the anal character, his analyses of obsessional neuroses and of paranoia, and his delineation of the mechanism of projection. (The dependence of the conception of authoritarianism upon a personality theory that places such a great emphasis on the significance of childhood experience makes authoritarianism a particularly strong candidate for discussion in a symposium on political socialization.)

The Authoritarian Personality, therefore, served to focus attention on hypotheses which had been in the air for some time, rather than to suggest completely new hypotheses. But it did something more—and this seems to have been especially important in spurring the subsequent research. The section of the book devoted to "measurement of ideological trends" provided a number of "ready-made tests that had already been taken through many of the technical procedures of validation which every [psychological] test must pass," [11] the most notable and widely used of these being the F- (fascism) scale. The ready-made tests were very conveniently available to subsequent investigators, whereas the fascinating body of theory which guided the research was "in no single place in the volume" [12] conveniently stated. In the long run, this emphasis on certain restricted measurement techniques proved to be most unfortunate, since the authoritarian literature became progressively bogged in what in many respects was a comedy of methodological errors, and a number of the original insights in *The Authoritarian Personality* never received careful attention.[13]

In contrast to the several paragraphs required simply to make peremptory reference to the intellectual history of authoritarian personality study, the state of investigation into democratic personality can be briefly stated. There has been some theorizing on this topic and virtually no research. No one, to my knowledge, has attempted to devise and use a D- (democratic) scale. Our consideration of democratic character, therefore, has far less to go upon. I shall concentrate mainly on what seems to me to be an especially interesting discussion of the topic, an essay by Harold Lasswell which, I think, has not received the attention it merits.[14]

A number of commentators—including the authors of *The Authoritarian Personality*—have expressed skepticism over whether a concept such as "democratic character" corresponds sufficiently to anything found in the "real world" to be worth using.[15] The test of usefulness of a typology—or, in currently fashionable jargon, model—is, however, not merely its correspondence with presently available data. Typologies clarify thinking and guide research. They may serve to summarize aspects of what has already been observed, they may suggest hypotheses for future observations, and they may simply be vehicles for reasoning. What is important is that a typology make sufficient and appropriate distinctions for the purpose at hand.

AUTHORITARIAN CHARACTER

Three general distinctions appropriate for setting forth a typology of personality are: phenomenology, dynamics, and genesis. In other words, first we may take note of all of the psychological characteristics composing the type which, with a minimum of inferential interpretation, are readily observable. Then we summarize our hypotheses about the processes underlying the observables. How are the observed features related to each other? What ties them together? Finally, we assemble the hypotheses which are most relevant to the present essay: What accounts for the development of this type of individual? How does he arise in the socialization process?

These distinctions provide us, in effect, with a logical reconstruction of the process of inquiry: We observe that, although each individual we encounter is in many respects unique, individuals resemble some of their fellows more than they do others. If the pattern of resemblances is particularly striking, we begin to reflect on what makes such a type of individual work, on his inner dynamics. Then we endeavor to find out what made him the way he is. The distinctions also often reflect the state of knowledge. Agreement on matters of phenomenology is relatively easy to come by, even among scholars with quite different intellectual orientations. Interpretations of underlying dynamics are more controversial. Given the paucity of good longitudinal research—that is, studies of the same individuals over a period of time—reliable evidence of genesis may be especially rare.

Phenomenology of the Authoritarian

Some of the dozen or so traits appearing in the various conceptualizations of the authoritarian type are of immediate interest to the student of politics since they assume a form which directly parallels activities commonly performed in the political arena. Others would seem to be of more remote interest. Most central for our purposes is the pair of traits labeled "authoritarian aggression" and "authoritarian submission"—the dominance-submissiveness tendencies of the authoritarian. Such an individual, like Fielding's Mrs. Wilkins, abases himself before those who stand above him hierarchically, or whom he perceives to be powerful, and lords it over whoever seems to be weak, subordinate, or inferior. "German folklore," Adorno relates, "has a drastic symbol for this"— bicyclist's personality (*Radfahrernaturen*): "Above they bow, below they kick." [16]

Also politically relevant is the tendency of such individuals to *think* in power terms, to be acutely sensitive to questions of who dominates whom. Only at a slightly further remove from politics is the pervasive rigidity in the authoritarian's manner of confronting the world. He is, in Else Frenkel-Brunswik's phrase, "intolerant of ambiguity." [17] He likes order and is made uncomfortable by disorder; where the phenomena he is exposed to are complex and subtle, he imposes his own tight categories upon them, ignoring their nuances. His thinking therefore makes more than the usual use of stereotypes. Another of the traits composing the character type is "conventionalism." The authoritarian, much like Riesman's "radar-controlled" other-directed personality,[18] is described as being particularly sensitive to "external agencies" and, especially, to the prevailing standards of his own social group.

The foregoing authoritarian traits, all of which can be seen to have some rather immediate potential bearing on behavior in the political arena, hang together in a fashion which puts little strain on our common sense: dominance of subordinates; deference toward superiors; sensitivity to power relationships; need to perceive the world in a highly structured fashion; excessive use of stereotypes; and adherence to whatever values are conventional in one's setting. We can easily visualize an individual with these complementary attributes. But what is perhaps most intriguing about the authoritarian syndrome is that several further, less obvious, traits are found as a part of the presenting symptoms.

These rather exotic additional concomitants lead us beyond phenomenology to the psychoanalytically based theory of dynamics. For example, the authoritarian is described as being superstitious. (One of the items of the F-scale is "Although many people may scoff, it may yet be shown that astrology can explain a lot of things.") He is preoccupied with virility, tending toward "exaggerated assertion of strength and toughness." (While this trait might be juxtaposed with the authoritarian's interest in power, there is the added element here of being hard-boiled and rugged. The equivalent trait in the less well-developed typology of female authoritarianism is "pseudo-femininity"— a preoccupation with being "feminine and soft.") The authoritarian's assumptions about human nature are generally pessimistic, and he tends to be cynical about the motives of others. He is disposed to believe that "wild and dangerous things go on in the world"—that "the world is a jungle." He shows a puritanical preoccupation with sex—a "concern with sexual 'goings on' " and "a strong inclination to punish violators of sex mores." And, finally, he shows a trait of

which much is made in the theoretical explanation of this pattern—
"anti-intraception." This is "an attitude of impatience with and opposition to the subjective and the tender-minded." One of its more conspicuous
forms is an inability to introspect, to acknowledge one's own feelings and
fantasies.

The authoritarian typology, like Freud's famous juxtaposition of orderliness,
parsimoniousness, and obstinacy in the anal personality type, may well have
the merit of being less obvious to common sense than most of the formulations with which social scientists work. But what is its basis in reality? Are individuals to be found who exhibit these characteristics, or a sufficent proportion
of them, to make the notion of "authoritarian personality" more than an intriguing exercise in reasoning? The answer, I think, is yes, but I cannot even
begin to refer to the elements in the tangled body of authoritarian research on
which such a conclusion might be based. It can, at any rate, be seen that the
question *is* potentially answerable, and much more readily so than the questions
arising at the dynamic and genetic levels.[10]

Dynamics of Authoritarianism

While the typology of dynamics which has been proposed to account for this
pattern of traits also can be elaborated in considerable detail, we must content
ourselves here simply with suggesting its major themes. The authoritarian, it is
argued, is an individual with strong, but ambivalent, dispositions toward figures
of authority. Denial of the negative side of these feelings is central to such an
individual's functioning. The authoritarian is able to conceal from himself his
rage toward those in authority only by the massive defense procedure of reaction formation, involving a total repression of critical and other unacceptable
impulses toward authority and a bending over backwards in excessive praise of
it.[20] But repression has its costs and side-effects, and repressed impulses seek
alternative outlets. Hostility not only is rechanneled toward whoever is perceived
as weak and unauthoritative, but also has a more diffuse effect on the authoritarian's generally negative views of man and his works, as well as contributing to his need to scan his environment for signs of authority relationships, his tendency (via projection) to see the world as full of dangerous things
and people, and his desire to punish others, for example, sex offenders, who have
surrendered to their impulses. Feelings of personal weakness are covered by a
façade of toughness. A side-effect of channeling enormous energy into repression and reaction formation is that the authoritarian's emotional capacities and
even certain of his cognitive capacities are stunted. He is unable to face the
prospect of canvassing his own psyche—for fear of what such introspection
may yield—and therefore becomes highly dependent upon external sources of
guidance.[21]

This general thesis about authoritarian dynamics might be called the ego-
defensive theory of authoritarianism. After the fashion of classical psychoanalysis, the theory places great emphasis on irrationality—on how the self,
in seeking to maintain inner equilibrium (that is, to defend against impulses
and conscience), is flawed in its perception of and response to the environment.

Since the empirical standing of psychoanalysis continues to be controversial, it is not difficult to understand why this aspect of authoritarian theory is less settled than the question of phenomenology.[22]

It is quite possible to accept the phenomenological typology of authoritarianism and reject the ego-defensive thesis of its dynamics. This, in effect, has been done by several commentators who present what might be called a *cognitive* theory of authoritarianism. The cognitive theory holds that the patterns of expression and behavior that have been characterized as authoritarian are based upon simple learning of the conceptions of reality prevalent in one's culture or subculture, and that these patterns also may to some extent be accurate reflections of the actual conditions of adult life faced by some individuals, rather than having the labyrinthine roots in reaction formation suggested by the ego-defensive theory.[23] Recent research suggests that there is some merit in both the cognitive and the ego-defensive formulations. Much of what has been called "working-class authoritarianism" does seem to have its roots in simple cognitive learning, whereas, at the higher socioeconomic levels, authoritarian orientations seem more often to tap less accessible motivational sources.[24]

The Genesis of Authoritarianism

Adorno and his associates, in fact, anticipated the thesis of cognitive authoritarianism by acknowledging that the personality manifestations they were studying could in some instances merely reflect "surface resentment" with a "more or less rational" basis in learning.[25] Subsequent extensions of the cognitive explanation, for example, by Hyman and Sheatsley, have stressed the lack of information available in lower-class subcultures and the lack of opportunity of lower-class individuals to acquire the desire and capacity to manipulate symbols—or, at least, the symbols with which public discourse is conducted—with any degree of sophistication. Such social settings, it is suggested, produce individuals who respond to the F-scale in much the same fashion as would be predicted by the ego-defensive theory of authoritarianism, but who do not show the pathology described in the theory. Furthermore, the lower-class world may, in many respects, really *be* a jungle. Under such circumstances "authoritarianism" reflects little more than learning from one's exemplars and realistic attempts to characterize one's environment.

The Authoritarian Personality, however, concentrates on elucidating the childhood antecedents of ego-defensive authoritarianism. The typical early determinants of this pattern come as no surprise in the light of the theory of underlying dynamics.

> When we consider the childhood situation . . . we find reports of a tendency toward rigid discipline on the part of the parents, with affection which is conditional rather than unconditional, i.e., dependent upon approved behavior on the part of the child. Related to this is a tendency . . . to base [family] interrelationships in rather clearly defined roles of dominance and submission. . . . Forced into a surface submission to parental authority, the child develops hostility and aggression which are poorly channelized. The

displacement of a repressed antagonism toward authority may be one of the sources, and perhaps the principal source, of his antagonism toward out-groups.[26]

The authors derived these and similar conclusions about how ego-defensive authoritarianism arises in the socialization process partly from their subjects' retrospective reports of childhood experiences, but also from direct studies by Frenkel-Brunswik of ethnically prejudiced and unprejudiced children. The studies of children suggested that "warmer, closer and more affectionate inter-personal relationships prevail in the homes of the unprejudiced children" and that prejudice was associated with "strictness, rigidity, punitiveness, rejection vs. acceptance of the child."

In the home with the orientation toward rigid conformity . . . mainte-nance of discipline is often based upon the expectation of external rigid and superficial rules which are bound to be beyond the comprehension of the child. Family relationships are characterized by fearful subservience to the demands of the parents and by an early suppression of impulses not accept-able to the adults.

Since the moral requirements in such a home must appear to the child as overwhelming and at the same time unintelligible, and the rewards meager, submission to them must be reinforced by fear of and pressure from external agencies. Due to the lack of a genuine identification with the parents, the fearfully conforming child does not make the important developmental step from mere social anxiety to real conscience.[27]

I have earlier noted that the authoritarian personality research grew out of an intellectual tradition which drew on both Freudian psychology and Marxian sociology. It is the Freudian emphasis on early childhood socialization that occupies most of the discussion in *The Authoritarian Personality* of how au-thoritarianism is socialized. But occasionally a Marxian explanation of the genesis of authoritarianism appears, as in the final paragraph of the volume where the authors remark that "people are continuously molded from above because they must be molded if the overall economic pattern is to be main-tained." [28] The point being made here is evidently that of Fromm, who in *Escape from Freedom* develops, *inter alia*, a conception of "social character" as that which "internalizes external necessities and thus harnesses human energy for the task of a given economic and social system"; a conception of the au-thoritarian character as the energy source in the development of Western capitalism (in contrast to Weber's Protestant Ethic); and a conception of the family as, in effect, mainly a transmission belt providing the system with the type of personality it "requires." [29] Apart from whatever merit there may be in Fromm's specific historical argument, we have here a further class of ex-planatory factors—overlapping the references to culture in the cognitive model—which may be introduced to explain the genesis of authoritarianism, namely, social structure and social role requirements.[30]

FROM CHARACTER STRUCTURE TO POLITICAL STRUCTURE

The field of culture and personality research, into which the authoritarian literature falls, is not in especially good repute. Particularly suspect are the attempts—perhaps most marked in the wartime national-character literature—to reason from (often imperfect) evidence about early socialization and personality development, rapidly and effortlessly, to explanations of broad social and historical phenomena, such as the rise of Nazism, Japanese militarism, and so forth. The disparaging label "psychologism" has come to be attached to such inferential leaps. These exercises in reducing politics and sociology to psychology often impress no one less than the psychoanalysts themselves. "Shortly after Pearl Harbor," an analyst relates:

> a small group of noted social scientists, intent on studying the cultural roots of German National Socialism, invited a number of refugee scholars and interviewed them about their experiences and ideas on this subject. I was among those invited. I remember that I mentioned among the factors which seemed to me to have disposed the German people for a nationalistic dictatorship, the failure of German nineteenth century liberalism, and the subsequent success of Prussian militarism, in bringing about the much-desired unification of Germany; this experience, I argued, had conditioned the German people to distrust the democratic process and to put their faith in strong-arm methods. I also mentioned the impact of rapid industrialization upon a society still almost feudal in its caste structure, without interceding commercialism and without a strong commercial class such as was already established in Anglo-Saxon countries at the outset of industrialization; such a situation seemed to make people more alert to the possibilities of power, rather than the potentialities of welfare, inherent in industry. I was then interrupted by my host, a noted anthropologist; this was not what I had been expected to contribute. As a psychoanalyst I should point out how Nazism had developed from the German form of child rearing. I replied that I did not think that there was any such relationship; in fact, political opinion did not seem to be determined in early childhood at all. This view was not accepted and I was told that the way the German mother holds her baby must be different from that of mothers in democracies. When we parted, it was clear that my hosts felt that they had wasted their time.[31]

Although there are numerous statements by *Authoritarian Personality* contributors acknowledging that personality factors are neither "the major [n]or exclusive determinants of political or social movements," [32] it is difficult to gainsay the critics who argue that the work is shot through with psychologism. For example, by labeling the personality trends we have been discussing "prefascist" and "potentially fascist," they tended to resolve by definition the complex empirical question of how deeper personality trends articulate with specifically political belief and with actual behavior. And their references to the "great . . . fascist potential" [33] in American society seemed to reflect equally naïve assumptions about the relationship between the distribution of psychological dispositions in a society and its over-all political structure. By very briefly indicating some of the many factors which intervene between character structure and political structure, we can touch upon some of the further questions that have arisen in connection with the study of authoritarianism.

Personality and Belief System

As is often pointed out, persons with similar deep psychological characteristics may entertain different political beliefs, and persons with similar beliefs may differ in personality. This is so because there normally are a variety of alternative channels which can express underlying psychic needs, and also because, given the inattentiveness to politics of most citizens, political orientations often are acquired haphazardly, without engaging deeper personality sources. The original authoritarian personality research was influenced not only by the intellectual traditions to which I referred above, but also by the political climate of the 1930's and 1940's and, in particular, the grim history of German national socialism and the presence in the United States of nativistic radical-right movements. This seems to have been one of the reasons for the insensitivity in the original research to the possibility—which subsequently received a good bit of attention—that authoritarian character traits may be manifested in other than rightist political beliefs.[34] Related to this was a tendency in the original reports to discuss the ethnically prejudiced and politically conservative attitudes of many authoritarians as if these were part of the defining characteristics of the syndrome itself. For some purposes it may be desirable to treat opinions as "an integral part of personality,"[35] but in studying personality and politics we can see that it often is essential to distinguish analytically between character and belief, lest the question of the connections between them be settled in our definitions rather than our research. The research, of course, may well show that authoritarian personality characteristics are associated with authoritarian beliefs, and that these personality characteristics *do* "fit" best with right-wing ideology. But, at best, the relationship is likely to be imperfect.

Effects of Personality and Belief System on Action

The individual with a "potentially fascist" character structure, then, does not necessarily hold "fascist" beliefs. Furthermore, the connections of character structure *and* belief content with action are not necessarily as straightforward as the usage "potential fascist" implies. Action results from the situations in which people find themselves, including the formal and informal roles they are called upon to perform, as well as from their psychological predispositions. The lack of "one-to-one correlation" between psychological dispositions and action is often pointed out. It may be less well appreciated that the correlation can even be negative; in some circumstances an individual's behavior may actually be the *reverse* of what would have been expected if only his predispositions were taken into account. An example of this is to be found in work by Katz and Benjamin on behavior of Northern white college undergraduates toward Negro co-workers. Presumably racially prejudiced "authoritarians were actually more deferential with Negroes than were non-authoritarians," a finding which the investigators felt was "due to the authoritarian's fear of revealing anti-Negro attitudes in a potentially punitive environment." [36] Still further insight into the subtleties of personality-role relationships might have been obtained if the investigators had also looked into whether authoritarians felt more strain in such situations than did nonauthoritarians, or how each group would have responded if sufficient tension and frustration had been introduced to challenge the authoritarians' "inner controls" of "their hostile impulses." [37] The point is that we must employ analytic distinctions which attune us to the possible subleties of our subject.

Aggregate Effects of Individual Predispositions and Actions

So much more than simple addition is involved in moving from the distribution of individual characteristics in a society—for example, its proportion of authoritarians—to questions about over-all political structure that some social scientists are led to a kind of vulgar Durkheimianism, which denies on methodological grounds the relevance of psychology to sociology and political science. At the very least, the addition of personal characteristics is a matter of weighted rather than simple sums.[38] It takes a good many authoritarian voters to equal one authoritarian President of the United States. Moreover, "more than one set of personality characteristics" is needed "to make a political movement. . . . Movements and institutions, even if they are authoritarian, require both more and less than authoritarian personality structures," and even "a liberal democratic society itself could probably not function satisfactorily with only 'democratic liberal personalities' to fill all its roles." [39] Here again, the point is not to deny the significance of the sequelae of socialization (personality and political belief), but to suggest the care necessary to make inferences about the matter.

DEMOCRATIC CHARACTER

Lasswell's essay "Democratic Character," like the discussion which has just preceded, is essentially typological. In effect, he elaborates a hypothetical construct, in part from the existing research on the antidemocratic character, in part by deductions from an analysis of the role requirements of democratic society. The main general features of the psychological topology are a "self-system" (the individual's conscious orientations, which consist of his cognitive assumptions, his preferences, and his identifications), an "energy-system" (roughly equivalent to the Freudian unconscious, composed of conscience, ego ideals, and drives), and a special definition of the term "character," as "the self-system of the person, together with the degree of support, opposition or non-support received from the unconscious parts of the personality." "Character" therefore acquires the dimension of strength and weakness, much as in lay usage. "When we say that a man is of steadfast character it is implied that he has sufficient command of the resources of the whole personality to maintain the self-system despite environing conditions which are adverse." [40]

At the cognitive level, the democratic character believes in the benevolent potentialities of mankind, rejecting the authoritarian's more Hobbesian conception of human nature. The democrat's preferences are consistent with the role requirements in the model of the democratic social system—that is, he *wants* to behave in the ways he should behave, if the functioning of the democratic system is to be successful. Furthermore, he is a "multi-valued" moderate who can weigh alternative goals against each other, rather than an absolutist in pursuit of a single value who, because of his inability to compromise, might endanger the stability of the system. And it is especially important that the democratic character be free of the pursuit of power as a single end-in-itself. In addition, the democrat's identifications are broad and comprehensive—Lasswell speaks of the "open ego"—unlike the good guys-bad guys pattern of the authoritarian.

This pattern of conscious perspectives, Lasswell points out, might well be found among individuals who at the unconscious level had antidemocratic inclinations and, particularly, destructive, power-seeking, or self-punishing tendencies. Referring, in effect, to the curiously labeled "rigid low scorer" of the authoritarian studies, Lasswell acknowledges that

> democratic responses often arise from motivations which are incompatible with . . . [democracy], and signify that the individual has achieved part of his democratic outlook by 'reaction formation' against tendencies of an opposite kind. Many democrats appear to develop in opposition to anti-democratic parents, for example.

While he grants that "the destructive energies of a person may be directed against enemies of the democratic community," he nevertheless excludes the democrat-by-reaction formation from his typology, since "from the point of view of modern personality research, the characters which are achieved by a complex process of balanced defense are viewed as constituting less enduring formations than those which evolve more directly." [41] On the matter of socialization, Lasswell comments that "there is reason to believe that in some cultures the possibility of developing an outgoing democratic character is excluded at an early period. The prevailing patterns of child care appear to induce early despair that profound gratifications can emanate from other human beings." [42] The concluding sections of the essay are directly addressed to the problem of how to socialize democratic characters.

There is a lapidary quality to Lasswell's essay—his formulation, overly condensed in this review, is itself quite elliptically stated. The formulation does, however, offer promising suggestions for expanding the scope of research on personality and political socialization. And the novel conception of character strength he introduces— the capacity to withstand environmental pressure adverse to one's values—raises interesting possibilities for bringing together two hitherto largely unconnected strands in the literature on prerequisites of democracy: the psychological writings we have been discussing here and the currently expanding work on the structural features of democracies and the typical belief systems to be found in them.

SUMMARY AND CONCLUSIONS

In contemporary anthropology the distinction has occasionally been made between the old culture-and-personality literature, which was especially concerned with early childhood socialization and its effects on personality formation, and the new culture-and personality literature, which focuses on systematic exploration of people's cognitive maps of their environment.[43] I have reviewed what might be called the old political socialization literature—itself a strand of the early culture-and-personality movement—in contrast to the recently burgeoning research on the development of specifically political orientations.

At base, these divisions between old and new are an artifact of the history of research. Human beings, at whatever stage of the lifelong socialization process, are not divided into self-contained compartments of personality versus cognitions, "specifically political" versus "non-political but politically relevant" development. What has been adventitiously separated needs to be pulled together. But in the present instance this will call for a good bit of careful conceptualization. We need sets of distinctions which "carve at the joints" for thinking about what intervenes between personality socialization and political systems.

Some of the distinctions suggested in this essay can be summarized in the following statements: Personality formation may be along ego-defensive or more cognitive lines; the connections between personality and political belief need to be examined rather than assumed; both personality and beliefs must be examined *in situations* in order to understand behavior; the ways in which individual predispositions and actions aggregate and affect the political and social system need to be explicated. And, to turn the circle, it is the political and social systems which provide the socializing environment for "political" and "politically relevant" personal development and the situations within which political action takes place. In a newfangled way, this is to suggest no more than was evident to Plato: that politics needs to be understood (and undertaken) in the light of human nature and human development.

NOTES

[1] Richard Christie and Peggy Cook, "A Guide to Published Literature Relating to the Authoritarian Personality through 1956," *The Journal of Psychology,* Vol. 45 (April 1958), pp. 171–199.

[2] T. W. Adorno *et al., The Authoritarian Personality* (New York: Harper, 1950), hereafter cited as *AP.*

[3] A phrase used in a prepublication report of the study to the general public: Jerome Himelhoch, "Is There a Bigot Personality?" *Commentary,* Vol. 3 (March 1947), pp. 277–284.

[4] Nevitt Sanford, "The Approach of the Authoritarian Personality," *Psychology of Personality,* ed. J. L. McCary (New York: Grove Press, 1959), p. 256.

[5] E. R. Jaensch, "Der Gegentypus," *Beiheft zur Zeistschrift für angewandte Psychologie und Charakterkunde,* Beiheft 75 (1938). Just as the *AP* was mainly concerned with the type of individual whose dispositions are antithetical to democracy, Jaensch was most concerned with the "anti-type," whose dispositions were incongruent with National Socialism.

[6] Henry Fielding, *Tom Jones,* Book I, chaps. 6 and 8.

[7] For example, Ross Stagner, "Fascist Attitudes: Their Determining Conditions," *The Journal of Social Psychology,* Vol. 7 (November 1936), pp. 438–454; Allen L. Edwards, "Unlabeled Fascist Attitudes," *Journal of Abnormal and Social Psychology,* Vol. 36 (October 1941), pp. 575–582.

[8] For example, Ruth F. Benedict, *The Chrysanthemum and the Sword* (Boston: Houghton, 1946); Henry V. Dicks, "Personality Traits and National Socialist Ideology," *Human Relations,* Vol. 3 (1950), pp. 111–154; and the same author's "Observations on Contemporary Russian Behavior," *Ibid.,* Vol. 5 (1952), pp. 111–175.

[9] Erich Fromm, *Escape from Freedom* (New York: Holt, Rinehart & Winston, 1941). The authors also acknowledged their indebtedness to A. H. Maslow's essay "The Authoritarian Character Structure," *Journal of Social Psychology,* Vol. 18 (1943), pp. 401–411.

[10] Max Horkheimer (ed.), *Studien über Autorität und Familie* (Paris, 1936), p. 902.

[11] Nathan Glazer, "New Light on 'The Authoritarian Personality,'" *Commentary,* Vol. 17 (March 1954), p. 290.

[12] M. Brewster Smith, Review of *The Authoritarian Personality, Journal of Abnormal and Social Psychology,* Vol. 45 (October 1950), p. 775.

[13] A variety of telling methodological criticisms of *The Authoritarian Personality* appear in the essays of Herbert H. Hyman and Paul B. Sheatsley and of Richard Christie, in Richard Christie and Marie Jahoda (eds.), *Studies in the Scope and Method of "The Authoritarian Personality"* (Glencoe, Ill.: Free Press, 1954), hereafter cited as *SSMAP.* Subsequent investigators may have been discouraged from attending to certain of the original insights because especially severe methodological strictures were raised in connection with the sections of the book based on quasi-clinical psychological techniques, precisely the sections which are richest in hypotheses. A vigorous essay by Edward A. Shils in *SSMAP* arguing that the authors had erroneously equated authoritarianism with "right-wing authoritarianism" and that they had fallen victim to naïve sociological assumptions may also have discouraged attention to certain of the broader themes raised by the volume. Somewhat after the publication of *SSMAP,* an extensive series of papers on "response set" in authoritarian research were published, adding further to the methodologically gnarled quality of the literature. Some of these papers were devoted to showing that, at least in part, many of the findings in the authoritarian literature were attributable to a mechanical shortcoming of the psychological test typically used to measure authoritarianism (the F-scale). The test was worded so that a positive response was scored as "authoritarian," but some subjects (especially people of low education) tended to respond "yes" to *any* question, independent of their authoritarian tendencies. Other of the papers were devoted to developing new, "response-set free" measures. Some of the more interesting of these papers are conveniently reprinted in chapter six of Martha T. Mednick and Sarnoff A. Mednick, *Research in Personality* (New York: Holt, Rinehart & Winston, 1963).

[14] Harold D. Lasswell, "Democratic Character," in *The Political Writings of Harold D. Lasswell* (Glencoe, Ill.: Free Press, 1951), pp. 465–525, hereafter cited as *DC.*

Also see Karl Mannheim, *Freedom, Power and Democratic Planning* (London: Oxford University Press, 1950), pp. 228–245; Christian Bay, *The Structure of Freedom* (Stanford, Calif.: Stanford University Press, 1958), pp. 155–239; Alex Inkeles, "National Character and Modern Political Systems," *Psychological Anthropology,* ed. Francis Hsu (Homewood, Ill.: Dorsey Press, 1961), pp. 172–209; Robert E. Lane, *Political Ideology* (New York: Free Press of Glencoe, 1962), pp. 400–412.

[15] *AP*, p. 1, but see pp. 781–783 for the authors' subtype "the genuine liberal." For a criticism of both the democratic and the authoritarian character typologies in the context of what I take to be the argument that typologies are useless since no individual ever is a pure instance of a type, see David Spitz, "Power and Personality: The Appeal to the 'Right Man' in Democratic States," *American Political Science Review,* Vol. 52 (March 1958), pp. 88–89.

[16] T. W. Adorno, "Freudian Theory and the Pattern of Fascist Propaganda," *Psychoanalysis and the Social Sciences,* ed. Géza Róheim, Vol. VII (New York, 1951), p. 291n. My discussion of authoritarian traits is based on *AP,* chap. 7 and *passim* and the Sanford discussion referred to in note 4. The latter is perhaps the single most concise and comprehensive exposition by an *AP* contributor.

[17] Else Frenkel-Brunswik, "Intolerance of Ambiguity as an Emotional and Perceptual Personality Variable," *Journal of Personality,* Vol. 18 (September 1949), pp. 108–143.

[18] David Riesman, with Nathan Glazer and Reuel Denney, *The Lonely Crowd* (New Haven: Yale University Press, 1950).

[19] Christie makes the following statement at the conclusion of an extensive, rigorous review of authoritarianism research. "Both the strength and weakness of *The Authoritarian Personality* lie in its basic assumptions which are rooted in psychoanalytic theory. Such an orientation has led to the uncovering of a host of data which in all likelihood would not have been discovered by investigators with differing theoretical viewpoints. Despite some methodological weaknesses in the original research, subsequent findings have been predominantly confirmatory," *SSMAP,* pp. 195–196.

[20] The authoritarian type is described as having repressed sexual as well as hostile impulses, but the significance of repressed sexuality in authoritarianism does not seem to have been fully explicated. At points in the *AP,* the implication seems to be simply that the authoritarian has acceded to parental taboos concerning sexuality. At other points (for example, p. 798), the implication is that the repressed sexual impulses are toward the parents and particularly the father. The latter, more classically psychoanalytic construction, is developed in some detail by Fromm in the work cited in note 9 (pp. 77–135, English abstract, pp. 908–911). See especially his discussion of sadomasochism.

[21] Dependence upon external guidance provides the common element in several of the surface manifestations of authoritarianism, which at first glance seem not to be related to each other: conventionality (accepting the prevailing values in one's environment); stereotypy (accepting the prevailing descriptive categories); superstition (belief that we are controlled from without by mysterious agencies); intolerance of ambiguity and use of rigid categories (discomfort when the environment provides few guideposts for thought and action).

[22] For two recent discussions designed to reduce polemic and seek empirical clarification of the issues underlying the controversial status of psychoanalysis, see B. A. Farrell, "The Status of Psychoanalytic Theory," *Inquiry,* Vol. 7 (Spring 1964), pp. 104–123; Peter Madison, *Freud's Concept of Repression and Defense: Its Theoretical and Observational Language* (Minneapolis: University of Minnesota Press, 1961). A number of interesting investigations based on the ego-defensive theory of authori-

tarian dynamics have been reported. For example, Herbert C. Schulberg, "Insight, Authoritarianism and Tendency to Agree," *Journal of Nervous and Mental Disease,* Vol. 135 (December 1962), pp. 481–488.

[23] See the essay by Hyman and Sheatsley in *SSMAP* (esp., p. 91 f.); Herbert H. Hyman, *Political Socialization* (Glencoe, Ill.: Free Press, 1959), p. 47; S. M. Miller and Frank Riessmann, " 'Working-Class Authoritarianism': A Critique of Lipset," *British Journal of Sociology,* Vol. 12 (September 1961), pp. 263–276. I take the ego-defensive versus cognitive distinction from the recent literature on the functions served by opinions for the personality: M. Brewster Smith *et al., Opinions and Personality* (New York: John Wiley & Sons, 1956), chap. 3; Daniel Katz, "The Functional Approach to the Study of Attitudes," *Public Opinion Quarterly,* Vol. 24 (Summer 1960), pp. 163–204.

[24] See, for example, Angus Campbell *et al., The American Voter* (New York: John Wiley & Sons, 1960), pp. 512–515. Also the very interesting attempt by Thomas F. Pettigrew to demonstrate that the amount of personality-based (that is, ego-defensive) prejudice toward Negroes is the same in the American North, the American South, and in South Africa, and that the higher level of anti-Negro sentiment in the latter two areas is due to the cognitive learning which occurs in cultures where race prejudice is prevalent. "Personality and Sociocultural Factors in Intergroup Attitudes: A Cross-National Comparison," *Journal of Conflict Resolution,* Vol. 2 (March 1958), pp. 29–42. The question of cognitive versus ego-defensive authoritarianism is complex, however, and a fuller discussion would engage us in technical matters connected with the instruments used to measure authoritarianism (see note 13).

[25] *AP,* pp. 753–756.

[26] *Ibid.,* pp. 482–483.

[27] Else Frenkel-Brunswik, "Further Explorations by a Contributor to 'The Authoritarian Personality,' " in *SSMAP,* pp. 236–237.

[28] *AP,* p. 976.

[29] See especially the appendix to *Escape from Freedom* on "Character and the Social Process," pp. 277–299.

[30] There is, of course, nothing incompatible between explanations of authoritarianism in terms of family socialization and explanations in terms of social structure. Nor need the latter be exclusively in economic terms. Evidence of the effects of the socioeconomic organization of a society on its members' personality characteristics is now becoming available from a study of personality differences between farmers and herders in four East African tribes. Two preliminary reports are Walter Goldschmidt, "Theory and Strategy in the Study of Cultural Adaptability," *American Anthropologist,* Vol. 67 (April 1965), pp. 402–408 and Robert B. Edgerton, " 'Cultural' vs. 'Ecological' Factors in the Expression of Values, Attitudes, and Personality Characteristics," *Ibid.,* pp. 442–447.

[31] Robert Waelder, *Basic Theory of Psychoanalysis* (New York: International Universities Press, 1960), pp. 53–54.

[32] Frenkel-Brunswik, in *SSMAP,* p. 228.

[33] *AP,* p. 974.

[34] See Shils' discussion of "left authoritarianism" in *SSMAP.* Also see the work of Rokeach, who has attempted to develop a "content-free" alternative to the various approaches to the question of authoritarianism, by stressing the "structure" of people's beliefs. Milton Rokeach, "Political and Religious Dogmatism: An Alternative to the Authoritarian Personality," *Psychological Monographs,* No. 425 (1956) and *The Open and Closed Mind* (New York: Basic Books, 1960). One might say that the Marxian heritage of the original authoritarian research (by discouraging attention to authori-

tarianism on the left) hinders awareness of the diversity of belief consistent with common psychological characteristics, whereas the Freudian heritage (by pointing to ego-defensive rather than cognitive explanations) hinders awareness of the diversity of psychological characteristics consistent with common beliefs. For a discussion in *The Authoritarian Personality* of a personality subtype quite like Shils' notion of left-wing authoritarianism, see the treatment of the "rigid low scorer" on pp. 771–773.

[35] Smith *et al.*, Opinions and Personality, p. 1.

[36] Irwin Katz and Lawrence Benjamin, "Effects of White Authoritarianism in Biracial Work Groups," *Journal of Abnormal and Social Psychology,* Vol. 61 (November 1960), pp. 448–456.

[37] See the remarks of Riesman and Glazer, in response to criticisms of their psychological explanations of social phenomena in *The Lonely Crowd.* "Although we said in *The Lonely Crowd* that different kinds of character could be used for the same kinds of work within an institution, we emphasized the price paid by the character types that fitted badly, as against the release of energy provided by congruence of character and task." David Riesman and Nathan Glazer, "*The Lonely Crowd:* A Reconsideration in 1960," *Culture and Social Character: The Work of David Riesman Reviewed,* ed. Seymour M. Lipset and Leo Lowenthal (New York: Free Press of Glencoe, 1961), p. 438. The same point (that behavior may be inconsistent with personality, but that some people may nevertheless undergo "distinctive burdens" in conforming to role requirements) is made by Reinhard Bendix in a widely quoted essay criticizing the various "psychiatric" explanations of social institutions. "Compliant Behavior and Individual Personality," *American Journal of Sociology,* Vol. 58 (November 1952), p. 297 and p. 300.

[38] A point made by Herbert Hyman in Bjorn Christiansen *et al.* (eds.), *Cross-National Social Research* (Oslo: Institute for Social Research; Mimeographed, 1951), p. 31. On the problem of aggregate effects also see Harry Eckstein, *A Theory of Stable Democracy,* Princton University Center of International Studies, Research Monograph, No. 10 (April 1961).

[39] Shils, in *SSMAP,* p. 45 and p. 48.

[40] *DC,* p. 428.

[41] *Ibid.,* pp. 506–507. On the rigid low scorer, see note 33.

[42] *Ibid.,* p. 497.

[43] Anthony F. C. Wallace, "The New Culture-and-Personality," *Anthropology and Human Behavior* (Washington, D.C.: The Anthropological Society of Washington, 1962), pp. 1–12.

25. ARE CIVIC LEADERS MORE TOLERANT THAN OTHER PEOPLE?

Samuel A. Stouffer

This article compares [a] special sample of 14 kinds of community leaders with a cross-section of the population in the cities of 10,000 to 150,000 from whom these leaders are drawn, and also with a cross-section of the entire United States, with respect to the following question:

Are various types of community leaders more likely, or less likely, than people in the cross-section to respect the civil rights of radicals and other non-conformists, even though they may suspect or disapprove their opinions?

To illustrate: Most business leaders can scarcely be expected to endorse the views of a man who advocates government ownership of the railways or all big business. Neither, presumably, does the rank and file of the population in an American community. But should the views of a Socialist be suppressed? Should he be allowed to make a speech in one's community? Should a book he wrote be eliminated from the public library? Should he be allowed to teach in a college or university?

The findings to be presented here will show that community leaders of all types—including businessmen—are *more likely* than the cross-section to accord a Socialist the right to express his views freely.

Again, consider a man who is against churches and religion. Few Americans would share his views, and even more of them would suspect the atheist of being a Communist than would suspect the Socialist. But our findings will show that community leaders are *more likely* than the rank and file of the public to accord an atheist the right to express his views freely.

Or take quite a different category of person. Consider a man whose loyalty has been criticized by a Congressional investigating committee but who swears under oath he is not a Communist. We find that the community leaders are almost unanimous in granting him the right to speak or teach or the right to have his book read—or the right to hold a job. The majority of the rank and file hold likewise, but there is a large minority in the rank and file who would withdraw such privileges from him.

Finally, a much more drastic case; namely, the man who admits he is a Communist. Many of the community leaders draw a line here. They split about 50–50 on the subject of letting him make a speech in their community or letting a book he writes remain in the public library, and they differ widely in their willingness to let him hold a job. They are overwhelmingly against his holding jobs in government or defense plants and against his teaching in schools or universities, but they tend to be willing to tolerate him in non-sensitive employment. The rank and file, however, is more sweeping and undiscriminating. Only a small minority, for example, would let an admitted Communist make a speech in their community or would let his book remain in the public library.

SOURCE: Samuel A. Stouffer, *Communism, Conformity and Civil Liberties* (Garden City, N.Y.: Doubleday & Co., Inc., 1955), pp. 26–57. Copyright © 1955 by Samuel A. Stouffer. Reprinted by permission of Doubleday & Company, Inc.

Attitudes toward curtailing the civil liberties of the four kinds of nonconformists or suspected nonconformists can be combined in a single summary measure. This is a general scale of willingness to tolerate nonconformity. . . . On this scale, all categories of community leaders, including commanders of the American Legion and regents of the D.A.R., tend on the average to be *more respectful of the civil rights of those of whom they disapprove* than the average person in the general population, either of the same cities from which the leaders come or of the nation as a whole.

What does this mean?

It *does not mean* that the community leaders approve of the nonconformists or suspected nonconformists whose rights they would uphold.

It *does mean* that the community leaders, being especially responsible and thoughtful citizens, are more likely than the rank and file to give a sober second thought to the dangers involved in denying civil liberties to those whose views they dislike.

Tolerance is not absolute. It may be presumed that almost nobody would support the right to cry "Fire!" in a crowded theater; to engage, if a teacher, in sexual relations with students; to conspire, if a government official, with agents of the Soviet Union. The issues before America are not and never have been the preservation of absolute rights of freedom, but rather of *how and where to set the limits.* If the limits are set too high, orderly activity, and even life itself, of the nation might become impossible. If the limits are set too low, all of the Anglo-Saxon heritage of relative freedom may be endangered.

That different Americans would set different limits is to be expected. It is the purpose of the present study to show where different kinds of Americans, as of the summer of 1954, thought those limits should be set.

CIVIL RIGHTS FOR SOCIALISTS

If a person wanted to make a speech in your community favoring government ownership of all the railroads and big industries, should he be allowed to speak, or not?

Chart I compares the answers to this question by our sample of community leaders, by a cross-section of people in those cities, and by a national cross-section, rural and urban.

To give the reader some feeling for error on such a survey as this, the results are also shown separately from each of the two survey agencies, which collected their data independently. Chart I makes it clear that the community leaders, on the average, would be more tolerant than the cross-sections. Looking at the data from both agencies pooled, we see that 84% of the leaders would let the Socialist speak, 61% of the cross-section in the same cities, and 58% of the national cross-section, rural and urban. The absolute figures differ somewhat, but the *pattern* is the same, whichever survey organization's samples are considered.

The "community leaders" are arbitrarily selected. Hence, only in a restricted sense does a figure based on all such leaders have meaning. If, however, we look at individual categories, such as "Mayors" or "Presidents of the Parent-Teachers' Association," we can be more specific. We have two samples, for example, of mayors of cities of 10,000 to 150,000 populations. True, we have only about 50 cases in each sample and therefore, by chance alone, the two samples of mayors will be expected to differ somewhat. In fact, about a third of such samples, according to probability theory, should differ by about 10 percentage points, and about one in 20 should differ by more than 20 percentage points. . . .

CHART I

COMMUNITY LEADERS ARE MORE WILLING THAN THE RANK AND FILE TO GIVE A SOCIALIST A RIGHT TO SPEAK

QUESTION: If a person wanted to make a speech in your community favoring government ownership of all the railroads and big industries, should he be allowed to speak, or not?

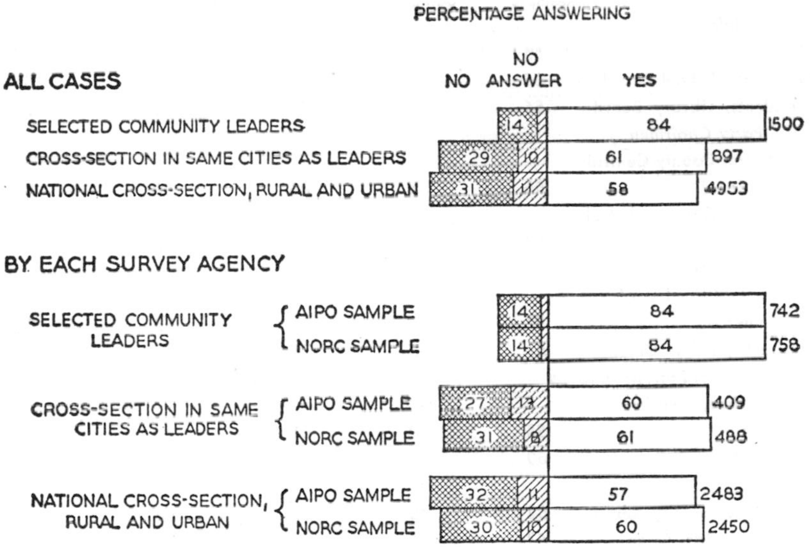

PERCENTAGE ANSWERING

		NO NO ANSWER	YES	
ALL CASES				
SELECTED COMMUNITY LEADERS		14	84	1500
CROSS-SECTION IN SAME CITIES AS LEADERS		29 10	61	897
NATIONAL CROSS-SECTION, RURAL AND URBAN		31 11	58	4953

BY EACH SURVEY AGENCY					
SELECTED COMMUNITY LEADERS	{	AIPO SAMPLE	14	84	742
	{	NORC SAMPLE	14	84	758
CROSS-SECTION IN SAME CITIES AS LEADERS	{	AIPO SAMPLE	27 13	60	409
	{	NORC SAMPLE	31 8	61	488
NATIONAL CROSS-SECTION, RURAL AND URBAN	{	AIPO SAMPLE	32 11	57	2483
	{	NORC SAMPLE	30 10	60	2450

Numbers inside the bars show percentages; numbers at the ends of the bars show the size of sample. AIPO is the American Institute of Public Opinion (the Gallup Poll); NORC is the National Opinion Research Center.

The data are shown in Table I. The important fact in this table is *not any one particular percentage*—comparison of the findings of the two agencies shows how such percentages differ, as would be expected, for any given occupational category. The important fact, rather, is that *without a single exception,* no matter which agency's data we use, each type of community leader was on the averge more likely to be willing to let a Socialist make a speech than was the cross-section of the population.

Community leaders differed by types. At the extremes, the leaders of the women's clubs, the American Legion, and the D.A.R. were less willing to tolerate a Socialist speech than, say, the chairmen of the school board or the presidents of the bar association. If the difference between two types of leaders, based on the combined samples, is about 14% or more, we can be reasonably sure that it is big enough not to be attributable to sampling error.

But, to repeat, the most important finding in Table 1 is the fact that every type of leader, without exception, was more willing to permit a Socialist speech than were the cross-sections of population.

TABLE 1. WILLINGNESS TO GIVE A SOCIALIST THE RIGHT TO SPEAK

(Types of Community Leaders Compared with Cross-Section)

	Number of Cases		Percentage Willing to Let Socialist Speak in Their Community		
	AIPO Sample	NORC Sample	AIPO Sample	NORC Sample	Combined Sample
Public Officials					
Mayors	56	56	79%	80%	80%
Presidents, School Board	53	58	90	85	88
Presidents, Library Board	56	53	93	91	92
Political Party Chairmen					
Republican County Central Committee	55	55	86	88	87
Democratic County Central Committee	53	50	96	87	91
Industrial Leaders					
Presidents, Chamber of Commerce	57	56	82	88	85
Presidents, Labor Union	51	55	77	82	80
Heads of Special Patriotic Groups					
Commanders, American Legion	55	59	81	70	76
Regents, D.A.R.	50	50	76	74	75
Others					
Chmn., Community Chest	52	48	89	98	93
Presidents, Bar Assoc.	53	46	94	96	95
Newspaper Publishers	44	48	97	98	97
Pres., Women's Club	54	55	62	75	68
Presidents, Parent-Teachers' Assoc.	53	59	83	75	79
Average of Community Leaders	742	758	84%	84%	84%
Cross-Section of Same Cities as Leaders	409	488	60	61	61
National Cross-Section Rural and Urban	2483	2450	57	60	58

Similar patterns are found on other specific questions. About the same proportions, and in most instances the same people as were willing to let a Socialist speak, said "No" to the following question:

If some people in your community suggested that a book he wrote favoring government ownership should be taken out of your public library, would you favor removing the book, or not? Responses were as follows:

	Favor	No Opinion	Not Favor	Total
Community Leaders	18%	3%	79%	100%
Cross-Section in Same Cities	35	13	52	100
National Cross-Section	35	13	52	100

A good many people who would let a Socialist speak or would retain his book in the library balked at saying "Yes" to the question: Should such a person be allowed to teach in a college or university, or not? Percentages were:

	No	No Opinion	Yes	Total
Community Leaders	47%	5%	48%	100%
Cross-Section in Same Cities	54	13	33	100
National Cross-Section	54	13	33	100

CIVIL RIGHTS FOR ATHEISTS

For many people, protection of the rights of atheists is a tougher problem than protection of the rights of Socialists. In Chart II and Table 2, answers are tabulated to the question: If a person wanted to make a speech in your community against churches and religion, should he be allowed to speak, or not?

In all groups the percentages saying "Yes" are less than for the corresponding question about a Socialist, but the *pattern* is the same as before. The community leaders, on the average and in every individual category, are more likely than the cross-sections to say "Yes." These findings hold for every type of leader, irrespective of which of the two agencies reported, in spite of some substantial differences between the two agencies.

Two other questions about atheists are of interest:

If some people in your community suggested that a book he wrote against churches and religion should be taken out of your public library, would you favor removing the book or not? Percentages answering:

	Favor	No Opinion	Not Favor	Total
Community Leaders	34%	2%	64%	100%
Cross-Section in Same Cities	60	5	35	100
National Cross-Section	60	5	35	100

Should such a person be allowed to teach in a college or university, or not? The vote, even among leaders, tends to be "No."

	No	No Opinion	Yes	Total
Community Leaders	71%	4%	25%	100%
Cross-Section in Same Cities	85	3	12	100
National Cross-Section	84	4	12	100

CHART II

COMMUNITY LEADERS ARE MORE WILLING THAN THE RANK AND FILE TO GIVE AN ATHEIST A RIGHT TO SPEAK

QUESTION: If a person wanted to make a speech in your community against churches and religion, should he be allowed to speak, or not?

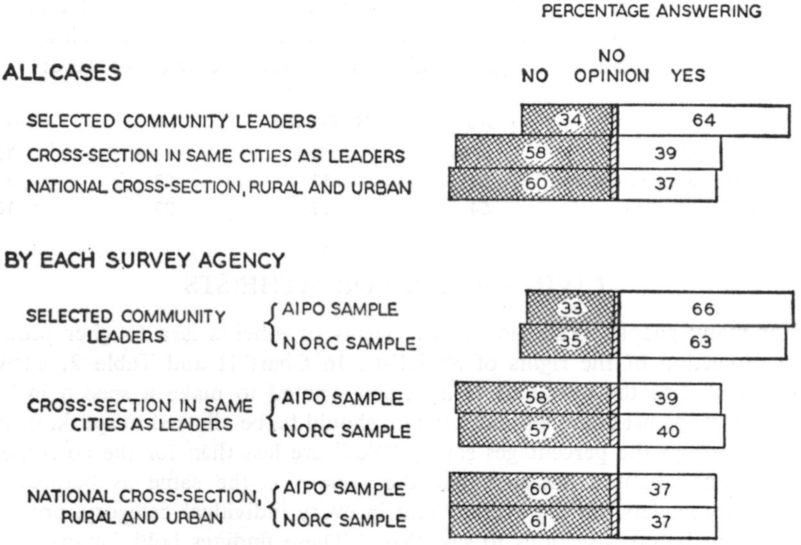

PERCENTAGE ANSWERING

ALL CASES

NO   NO OPINION   YES

	NO OPINION	YES
SELECTED COMMUNITY LEADERS	34	64
CROSS-SECTION IN SAME CITIES AS LEADERS	58	39
NATIONAL CROSS-SECTION, RURAL AND URBAN	60	37

BY EACH SURVEY AGENCY

		NO OPINION	YES
SELECTED COMMUNITY LEADERS	AIPO SAMPLE	33	66
	NORC SAMPLE	35	63
CROSS-SECTION IN SAME CITIES AS LEADERS	AIPO SAMPLE	58	39
	NORC SAMPLE	57	40
NATIONAL CROSS-SECTION, RURAL AND URBAN	AIPO SAMPLE	60	37
	NORC SAMPLE	61	37

Based on same samples as Chart I.

TABLE 2. WILLINGNESS TO GIVE AN ATHEIST THE RIGHT TO SPEAK

(Types of Community Leaders Compared with Cross-Sections)

	Percentage Willing to Let Atheist Speak in Their Community		
	AIPO Sample	NORC Sample	Combined Samples
Public Officials			
Mayors	61%	62%	62%
Presidents, School Board	68	50	59
Presidents, Library Board	84	66	75
Political Party Chairmen			
Republican County Central Com.	70	75	72
Democratic County Central Com.	72	58	66
Industrial Leaders			
Presidents, Chamber of Commerce	69	66	68
Presidents, Labor Union	59	60	59

TABLE 2. WILLINGNESS TO GIVE AN ATHEIST THE RIGHT TO SPEAK
Cont.

(Types of Community Leaders Compared with Cross-Sections)

	Percentage Willing to Let Atheist Speak in Their Community		
	AIPO Sample	NORC Sample	Combined Samples
Heads of Special Patriotic Groups			
Commanders, American Legion	49	44	47
Regents, D.A.R.	56	52	54
Others			
Chairmen, Community Chest	65	85	75
Presidents, Bar Association	80	86	83
Newspaper Publishers	82	83	82
Presidents, Women's Club	43	51	46
Presidents, Parent-Teachers' Assoc.	67	52	59
Average of Community Leaders	66%	63%	64%
Cross-Section of Same Cities as Leaders	39	40	39
National Cross-Section, Rural and Urban	37	37	37

Number of cases in each sample same as in Table 1.

CIVIL RIGHTS FOR A MAN WHOSE LOYALTY HAS BEEN QUESTIONED BUT WHO SWEARS HE IS NOT A COMMUNIST

Consider a man whose loyalty has been questioned before a Congressional committee, but who swears under oath he has never been a Communist. Should he be allowed to make a speech in your community, or not?

Relatively few Americans—community leaders and rank and file alike—were willing to put roadblocks in the way of such a man. But, as in all other cases, the leaders were more tolerant than the rank and file.

Chart III shows the reactions toward letting such a man make a speech in their community. Among the leaders, 87% would accord him the right; in the cross-section of people in the same cities, 71%; in the national cross-section, 70%. The agreement between the findings from the two survey agencies is, again, strikingly close.

Moreover, we see from Table 3 that whichever survey agency's results we look at, each of the 14 types of community leaders is, on the average, more tolerant on this issue than the average of the cross-sections.

Although all of the percentages tend to go up and down together, depending on the particular topic, the *pattern* observed in Chart III holds for a variety of other questions asked about this person whose loyalty has been questioned before a Congressional committee but who swears under oath that he has never been a Communist. For example:

Suppose he wrote a book which is in your public library. Somebody in your community suggests the book should be removed from the library. Would you favor removing the book, or not?

	Favor	No Opinion	Not Favor	Total
Community Leaders	7%	5%	88%	100%
Cross-Section in Same Cities	18	10	72	100
National Cross-Section	17	12	71	100

CHART III

COMMUNITY LEADERS ARE MORE WILLING THAN THE RANK AND FILE TO GIVE RIGHT TO SPEAK TO A MAN WHOSE LOYALTY HAS BEEN CRITICIZED BUT WHO SWEARS HE IS NOT A COMMUNIST

QUESTION: Consider a man whose loyalty has been questioned before a Congressional committee, but who swears under oath he has never been a Communist. Should he be allowed to make a speech in your community, or not?

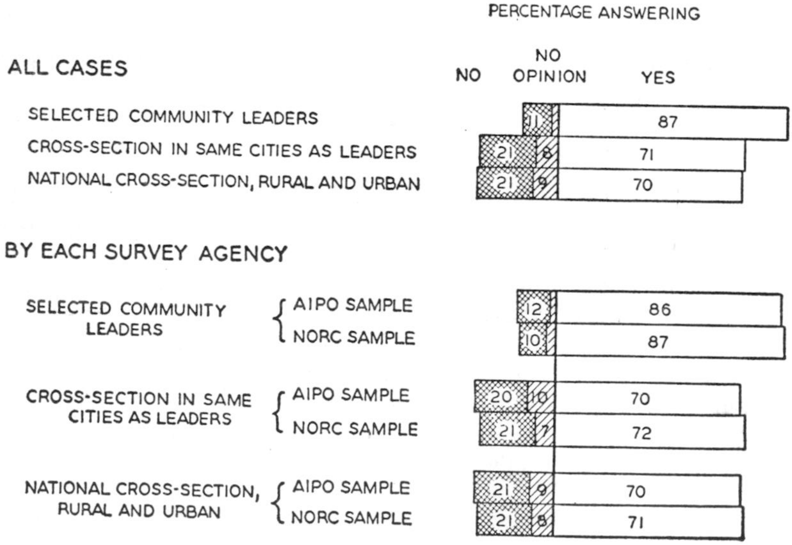

PERCENTAGE ANSWERING

ALL CASES

	NO	NO OPINION	YES
SELECTED COMMUNITY LEADERS		11	87
CROSS-SECTION IN SAME CITIES AS LEADERS	21	8	71
NATIONAL CROSS-SECTION, RURAL AND URBAN	21	9	70

BY EACH SURVEY AGENCY

		NO	NO OPINION	YES
SELECTED COMMUNITY LEADERS	AIPO SAMPLE		12	86
	NORC SAMPLE		10	87
CROSS-SECTION IN SAME CITIES AS LEADERS	AIPO SAMPLE	20	10	70
	NORC SAMPLE	21	7	72
NATIONAL CROSS-SECTION, RURAL AND URBAN	AIPO SAMPLE	21	9	70
	NORC SAMPLE	21	8	71

Based on same samples as Chart I.

TABLE 3. WILLINGNESS TO GIVE RIGHT TO SPEAK TO A MAN WHOSE LOYALTY HAS BEEN QUESTIONED BUT WHO SWEARS HE IS NOT A COMMUNIST

(Types of Community Leaders Compared with Cross-Sections)

	Percentage Willing to Let Him Speak in Their Community		
	AIPO Sample	NORC Sample	Combined Samples
Public Officials			
Mayors	88%	88%	88%
Presidents, School Board	85	88	87
Presidents, Library Board	95	83	89
Political Party Chairmen			
Republican County Central Com.	82	90	86
Democratic County Central Com.	87	92	89
Industrial Leaders			
Presidents, Chamber of Commerce	83	93	88
Presidents, Labor Union	92	82	87
Heads of Special Patriotic Groups			
Commanders, American Legion	89	83	86
Regents, D.A.R.	76	92	84
Others			
Chairmen, Community Chest	88	88	88
Presidents, Bar Association	85	89	87
Newspaper Publishers	93	93	93
Presidents, Women's Club	80	82	81
Presidents, Parent-Teachers' Assoc.	92	80	86
Average of Community Leaders	86%	87%	87%
Cross-Section of Same Cities as Leaders	70	72	71
National Cross-Section, Rural and Urban	70	71	70

Number of cases in each sample same as in Table 1.

Respondents were asked to consider whether such a person should be fired from various jobs. The large majority said "No," but those who would not let him teach in a college or high school or would not let him work in a defense plant were somewhat more numerous, as might be expected, than those who would fire him if he were a clerk in a store or a radio singer:

Suppose this man is a high school teacher. Should he be fired, or not?

	Yes	No Opinion	No	Total
Community Leaders	16%	4%	80%	100%
Cross-Section in Same Cities	21	8	71	100
National Cross-Section	22	9	69	100

Suppose he is teaching in a college or university. Should he be fired, or not?

	Yes	No Opinion	No	Total
Community Leaders	15%	4%	81%	100%
Cross-Section in Same Cities	20	8	72	100
National Cross-Section	22	9	69	100

Suppose he has been working in a defense plant. Should he be fired, or not?

	Yes	No Opinion	No	Total
Community Leaders	13%	5%	82%	100%
Cross-section in Same Cities	16	9	75	100
National Cross-Section	18	10	72	100

Suppose he is a clerk in a store. Should he be fired, or not?

	Yes	No Opinion	No	Total
Community Leaders	4%	3%	93%	100%
Cross-Section in Same Cities	12	7	81	100
National Cross-Section	11	8	81	100

Suppose he is a radio singer. Should he be fired, or not?

	Yes	No Opinion	No	Total
Community Leaders	6%	3%	91%	100%
Cross-Section in Same Cities	12	9	79	100
National Cross-Section	12	8	80	100

The subject of boycott was also brought up. The question was asked about the radio singer: Now suppose the radio program he is on advertises a brand of soap. Somebody in your community suggests you stop buying that soap. Would you stop, or not? The percentages endorsing such a boycott are very small:

	Yes	No Opinion	No	Total
Community Leaders	5%	3%	92%	100%
Cross-Section in Same Cities	10	7	83	100
National Cross-Section	9	8	83	100

CIVIL RIGHTS FOR ADMITTED COMMUNISTS

Everybody has a line which he draws somewhere. There are wide differences in opinion as to the danger of the internal Communist threat but there was almost nobody in any of the samples who expressed sympathy with Communist doctrines. For example, only 5% in the national cross-section thought it possible for a man to believe in Communism and still be a loyal American. And even among this 5% the overwhelming majority supported a firm stand against Russia, most of them saying, for example, that we should fight Russia if necessary to prevent the Communists from taking over the rest of Europe or Asia.

But the lines marking the limits of tolerance of American Communists vary, depending on how clear the risk to society seems in a specific situation.

For example, community leaders and the rank and file alike are generally agreed that Communists have forfeited the right to hold certain kinds of jobs— as teachers in high schools or colleges or as workers in defense plants.

But the community leaders are more likely than others to take the calculated risk of letting Communists speak in their communities or letting their books remain in the public library. And the leaders are more likely than others to support the right of Communists to hold non-sensitive jobs.

Consider first the question: Suppose an admitted Communist wants to make a speech in your community. Should he be allowed to speak, or not? We see in Chart IV that 51% of the community leaders would let him speak, as compared with 29% of the cross-section in the same cities and 27% of the national sample. Moreover, Table 4 shows that each of the 14 selected types of leaders was more willing, on the average, to let a Communist speak than were the cross-sections. This is true, whichever survey agency's findings we look at.

We get much the same picture from the question: Suppose he wrote a book which is in your public library. Somebody in your community suggests the book should be removed from the library. Would you favor removing it, or not?

	Favor	No Opinion	Not Favor	Total
Community Leaders	54%	4%	42%	100%
Cross-Section in Same Cities	66	6	28	100
National Cross-section	66	7	27	100

Community leaders are just as much in favor as the cross-section, if not more so, of getting Communists out of defense plants: Question: Suppose he is working in a defense plant. Should he be fired, or not?

	Yes	No Opinion	No	Total
Community Leaders	93%	2%	5%	100%
Cross-Section in Same Cities	91	4	5	100
National Cross-Section	90	4	6	100

And community leaders are only slightly less likely than the general population to think that a Communist has forefeited his right to teach in schools or colleges.

Suppose he is a high school teacher. Should he be fired, or not?

	Yes	No Opinion	No	Total
Community Leaders	89%	2%	9%	100%
Cross-Section in Same Cities	93	3	4	100
National Cross-Section	91	4	5	100

CHART IV

COMMUNITY LEADERS ARE MORE WILLING THAN THE RANK AND FILE TO GIVE A COMMUNIST THE RIGHT TO SPEAK

QUESTION: Suppose an admitted Communist wants to make a speech in your community. Should he be allowed to speak, or not?

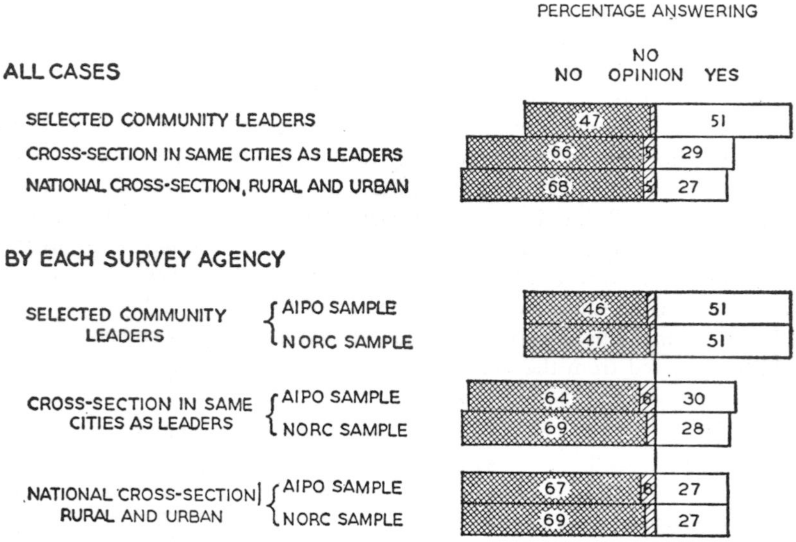

PERCENTAGE ANSWERING

ALL CASES

	NO	NO OPINION	YES
SELECTED COMMUNITY LEADERS	47		51
CROSS-SECTION IN SAME CITIES AS LEADERS	66		29
NATIONAL CROSS-SECTION, RURAL AND URBAN	68		27

BY EACH SURVEY AGENCY

		NO	NO OPINION	YES
SELECTED COMMUNITY LEADERS	AIPO SAMPLE	46		51
	NORC SAMPLE	47		51
CROSS-SECTION IN SAME CITIES AS LEADERS	AIPO SAMPLE	64		30
	NORC SAMPLE	69		28
NATIONAL CROSS-SECTION RURAL AND URBAN	AIPO SAMPLE	67		27
	NORC SAMPLE	69		27

Based on same samples as Chart I.

TABLE 4. WILLINGNESS TO GIVE A COMMUNIST THE RIGHT TO SPEAK

(Types of Community Leaders Compared with Cross-Sections)

	Percentage Willing to Let Communist Speak in Their Community		
	AIPO Sample	NORC Sample	Combined Samples
Public Officials			
Mayors	44%	34%	39%
Presidents, School Board	43	36	40
Presidents, Library Board	74	60	67
Political Party Chairmen			
Republican County Central Com.	54	63	59
Democratic County Central Com.	62	50	56
Industrial Leaders			
Presidents, Chamber of Commerce	42	49	46
Presidents, Labor Union	47	44	45

TABLE 4. WILLINGNESS TO GIVE A COMMUNIST THE RIGHT TO SPEAK *Cont.*

(Types of Community Leaders Compared with Cross-Sections)

	Percentage Willing to Let Communist Speak in Their Community		
	AIPO Sample	NORC Sample	Combined Samples
Heads of Special Patriotic Groups			
Commanders, American Legion	47	47	47
Regents, D.A.R.	36	42	39
Others			
Chairmen, Community Chest	56	68	62
Presidents, Bar Association	60	66	63
Newspaper Publishers	72	73	73
Presidents, Women's Club	42	35	39
Presidents, Parent-Teachers' Assoc.	41	44	43
Average of Community Leaders	51%	51%	51%
Cross-Section of Same Cities as Leaders	28	30	29
National Cross-Section, Rural and Urban	27	27	27

Number of cases in each sample same as in Table 1.

Suppose he is teaching in a college. Should he be fired, or not?

	Yes	No Opinion	No	Total
Community Leaders	86%	3%	11%	100%
Cross-Section in Same Cities	91	5	4	100
National Cross-section	89	5	6	100

On the other hand, community leaders are strikingly more willing to grant Communists the right to hold relatively non-sensitive jobs:

Suppose he is a clerk in a store. Should he be fired, or not?

	Yes	No Opinion	No	Total
Community Leaders	51%	4%	45%	100%
Cross-Section in Same Cities	68	7	25	100
National Cross-Section	68	6	26	100

Suppose this admitted Communist is a radio singer. Should he be fired, or not?

	Yes	No Opinion	No	Total
Community Leaders	48%	4%	48%	100%
Cross-Section in Same Cities	64	8	28	100
National Cross-Section	63	8	29	100

A majority both of the leaders and of the cross-section would not boycott his sponsor. Question: Now, suppose the radio program he is on advertises a brand of soap. Somebody in your community suggests that you stop buying that soap. Would you stop, or not?

	Yes	No Opinion	No	Total
Community Leaders	27%	4%	69%	100%
Cross-Section in Same Cities	37	8	55	100
National Cross-Section	36	8	56	100

Two questions, pertaining to penalties which the public would impose on Communists, are worth noting:

Should an admitted Communist have his American citizenship taken away from him, or not?

	Yes	No Opinion	No	Total
Community Leaders	66%	7%	27%	100%
Cross-Section in Same Cities	80	8	12	100
National Cross-section	77	10	13	100

Should an admitted Communist be put in jail, or not?

	Yes	No Opinion	No	Total
Community Leaders	27%	10%	63%	100%
Cross-Section in Same Cities	52	13	35	100
National Cross-Section	51	15	34	100

Do you or don't you think the government should have the right to listen in on people's private telephone conversations, in order to get evidence against Communists?

	Yes	No Opinion	No	Total
Community Leaders	62%	5%	33%	100%
Cross-Section in Same Cities	66	7	27	100
National Cross-Section	64	9	27	100

It is interesting and perhaps surprising to note that the majority of people, most of whom would be very tough on Communists, say that they would not break their friendship with a man who they discovered had been a Communist *but who is not one now.*

Suppose you discovered that one of your friends today had been a Communist ten years ago, although you are sure he is not now. Would you break your friendship with him, or not?

	Yes	No Opinion	No	Total
Community Leaders	7%	4%	89%	100%
Cross-Section in Same Cities	15	8	77	100
National Cross-Section	14	8	78	100

Suppose you discovered that one of your good friends today had been a Communist until recently, although he says he is not now. Would you break your friendship with him, or not?

	Yes	No Opinion	No	Total
Community Leaders	28%	11%	61%	100%
Cross-Section in Same Cities	35	14	51	100
National Cross-Section	34	14	52	100

Almost half of the cross-section also would be relatively lenient with a man who invoked the Fifth Amendment because he does not want to be forced into testimony against his former friends. The leaders were slightly *less* likely than others to be lenient in this case.

Sometimes a man says he refuses to answer certain questions about Communism because he does not want to be forced to testify against his former friends. Should he be punished very severely, severely, not too severely, or not at all?

	Very Severely	Severely	No Opinion	Not too Severely	Not at all	Total
Community Leaders	6%	33%	11%	32%	18%	100%
Cross-Section in Same Cities	6	24	16	32	22	100
National Cross-Section	6	23	15	34	22	100

On another question dealing with possible personal action against suspected Communists, the picture is somewhat different:

On the whole, do you think it is a good idea or a bad idea for people to report to the F.B.I. any neighbors or acquaintances whom they suspect of being Communists?

	Good Idea	No Opinion	Bad Idea	Total
Community Leaders	65%	3%	32%	100%
Cross-Section in Same Cities	72	8	20	100
National Cross-Section	73	8	19	100

Although most of the leaders, like the cross-section, tended to feel it their duty to report to the F.B.I., the leaders were more likely than the cross-section to see dangers of damage to innocent people. Among leaders who would report to the F.B.I., 27% volunteered in a free-answer question that this might hurt innocent people, and 14% suggested dangers of creating an atmosphere of fear and suspicion. In the national cross-section, the corresponding figures were only 13% and 4%. It might also be noted that a danger mentioned by 5% of the leaders who would report to the F.B.I. and by as many as 25% of the corresponding people in the cross-section was the possibility of personal reprisal by Communists.

A quite general question also differentiates local community leaders from the cross-section. Respondents were handed a card and were asked which, in their opinion, of the two statements printed on the card is more important:

To find out all the Communists even if some innocent people should be hurt.

To protect the rights of innocent people even if some Communists are not found out.

Answers were as follows:

	Find out Communists	Don't Know	Protect Rights	Total
Community Leaders	42%	6%	52%	100%
Cross-Section in Same Cities	60	9	31	100
National Cross-Section	58	10	32	100

HOW MUCH CAN WE TRUST QUESTIONS LIKE THESE?

The problem needs discussion at two levels. First, do people understand the questions and do they answer honestly? Second, even if they do, how seriously should we take a given question as a predictor of action in a concrete future situation?

How Reliable Are the Responses?

There are two kinds of tests as to the first level of problems. If the respondents have difficulty in understanding certain questions or are evasive, the skilled interviewers are likely to notice it (or suspect it). Each interviewer was required to submit a report of such difficulties—and there appears to have been relatively little trouble with most of the questions. There were some misunderstandings but practically no signs of lack of candor. Probably the reason for the candor was the nature of the *rapport* established in the early part of the interview. . . . Furthermore, when one reads questionnaires as a whole he gets no impression of evasiveness, even where he encounters evident errors of understanding.

A second test which can be applied is a systematic statistical check on what we call *internal consistency*. Suppose a respondent says he would let an admitted Communist work in a defense plant, but would fire a store clerk whose loyalty is suspected but who swears he has never been a Communist. He *could* mean both of these things. But it is a good bet that one or the other response is wrong. He probably misunderstood one of the questions. No matter how skilled we are in question wording, people will misunderstand a question here and there and give answers exactly the opposite of what they mean. This can happen through a lack of attention alone. Inconsistencies become especially serious with respect to questions about which opinion is overwhelmingly on one side. For example, only 298 people of the entire national cross-section of 4933 said they would not fire an admitted Communist in a defense plant. But analysis shows that as many as 100 of the 298 who said they would be lenient in this situation said they would *not* be lenient in *a variety* of situations which most people think are far less dangerous. These 100 people constitute only 2% of our entire sample, but they constitute a *third* of all who say they would not fire a worker in a defense plant. Another example: The American people overwhelmingly rejected the idea of boycotting the product of the sponsor of a radio singer who was accused of being disloyal but denied under oath he was a Communist. Indeed, the very suggestion of such an idea was regarded by some as silly enough to laugh at. Yet 433 people were found who said they agreed with the idea. Let us examine these 433 further. Did they mean it? As many as 150 of them—and possibly many more—evidently did not, because they were very lenient on answers to a *considerable variety of questions* which most people thought required serious sanctions. These 150 people constitute only 3% of the entire sample, but their errors are sufficient to damage the reliability of the question, since they constitute over a third of all who said "Yes" to it.

On the other hand, if we have a question to which 60% said "Yes" and 40% said "No," we can permit a considerable margin of error on both sides. The procedure of *scaling,* introduced in the next section, provides an objective statistical test which enables us to reject questions which are misunderstood by too many people.

How Well Can We Predict Action?

The second level of problems with respect to questions like those used in this article has to do with specific predictions which one might wish to make. Obviously one cannot predict the behavior of any small segment of people if a substantial fraction of them misunderstood a question. But let us assume that we are dealing with a question which was quite clearly understood. It still does not follow that most people who say, for example, that they would favor throwing a Socialist's book out of a library would be *active* proponents of such an idea if it were proposed in their town. For many people this is an idea which may never have occurred before. Free, unguided responses to the first part of the questionnaire will show that most people are not thinking very seriously about such matters, let alone worrying about them. All that the answer to such a question describes is what we call a *latent tendency.* If some friends came around to stir such people up it is quite likely that it would be easier to arouse them in favor of throwing out the book than it would be to arouse them against it. But whether they would be stirred at all in an actual life situation would depend on *who did the arousing.* This is why our data on the local community leaders are so crucial. Some of these leaders may have had to face actual problems of this kind, and even more of them may have imagined themselves as involved in such problems. The fact that, on the average, the leaders are more likely than the rank and file to give tolerant answers is highly important, because their own *latent tendencies* are more likely to be activated than those of the rank and file, and indeed it is some of these leaders in turn who would activate responses in others.

In other words, we must not take the answers to any specific question as explicit predictions of action. Rather, we must regard them as indexes of *latent tendencies.* The best such index is one based not on a single question but on a composite of many questions. This composite, which we shall call a scale, tends to cancel out many of the accidental errors of reporting which are bound to attach to the answers to any one particular question. The scale ranks people according to their latent tendencies—leaders as well as others—and this ordering is extremely important. But . . . rank on the scale alone must not be expected to *guarantee* specific future actions.

INTRODUCING A SCALE OF WILLINGNESS TO TOLERATE NONCONFORMISTS

Even if each question were reliable, it would be tediously repetitive to examine it in a variety of contexts. We will want to ask: In the cross-sections of the population, who are relatively the most tolerant toward nonconformists and who are least tolerant? City people or rural people? Easterners, Midwesterners, or Southerners? Older or younger? Men or women? Educated or the less educated? Etc. For sheer economy of presentation as well as for question reliability, we need a single index or scale which will summarize an individual's relative degree of tolerance.

Fortunately, we have such a scale. One of the most important findings in the charts and tables presented is the remarkable consistency in *patterns* of response. The community leaders, on almost all questions, are more willing to respect the rights of the nonconformist than are the rank and file. This is true on questions which 75% favor, or on which people split 50–50, or on questions which only 25% favor. It is true with respect to the rights of Socialists, atheists, suspected Communists who swear to their innocence, or admitted Communists. Further cross-tabulations show that, if a man or woman is one of only 25% who would be tolerant on a given item, he tends to be tolerant on most other items to which a still larger proportion give "tolerant" answers. And vice versa. If a person is one of a minority who would be severe on a Socialist, he tends to be one of a still larger group who would be tough on an atheist or admitted Communist. Not all questions are consistent, in this sense, with other questions, but most of them are.

These facts make a scale possible. Out of the questions here reported, 15 were selected to constitute that scale. Questions on which there was near unanimity were omitted, as were a few others which showed more than average inconsistency. . . .

The scale as originally constructed ranked respondents in one of six ranks. For simplicity of presentation, the scale scores have been recombined into three still broader rank groups with the following labels:

Relatively more tolerant. Constituting about a third of the national cross-section, these people give *tolerant* types of answers on more of the 15 questions than other people.

Relatively less tolerant. Constituting about a fifth of the national cross-section, these people give *intolerant* types of answers on more of the 15 questions than other people.

In-between. Between these two groupings are the rest of the population.

Chart V uses this scale to make a summary comparison just like the comparisons which have already been made for selected individual items.

Now, a word as how *not* to read this chart. It does *not* say that 66% of the community leaders are tolerant as compared with 31% of the national cross-section. Or that only 5% are intolerant as compared with 19% of the cross-section. The scale does not measure tolerance in any absolute sense.

What does Chart V say? It says (1) that we decided on a score on our tolerance scale high enough so that 31% of the national cross-section got that score or a higher one. We call these people our "more tolerant" group. Having set that score, we found that 66% of the community leaders got that score or a higher one. Similarly, (2) that we decided on a score that was low enough so that 19% of the national cross-section got that score or a lower one. We call that group our "less tolerant" group. Having set that score, we found that only 5% of the community leaders got that score or a lower one. . . .

It is so important to see clearly the distinction made here between an unjustifiable *absolute* statement and a justifiable *relative* statement that we venture to illustrate further what we mean by an analogy from baseball. Suppose we found that two thirds of the players on one team batted above .250, as compared with only half the players on another team. We might arbitrarily call

CHART V

COMMUNITY LEADERS ARE RELATIVELY MORE TOLERANT THAN THE RANK AND FILE ON SCALE OF TOLERANCE OF NONCONFORMISTS

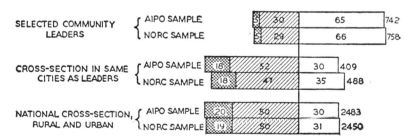

Based on same samples as Chart I.

anybody who hits above .250 a "good hitter," but another person might apply this term only to people who hit above .300. He might think that a mere .250 batter is terrible. Hence he can properly object if we say two thirds of the players on a team are good hitters—just as readers can properly object if we say 66% of the community leaders are tolerant. Many such leaders, by his standards, may be intolerant. But he cannot object if we say that a .250 hitter is usually a *better* hitter than one with a lower batting average. Hence he can agree that one team has a larger proportion of "better hitters" than the other team. Likewise, even if some of the community leaders ranked as "relatively more tolerant" by us are intolerant by a given reader's absolute standards, he still can accept the statement that the community leaders contain a larger proportion of "relatively more tolerant people" than does the cross-section.

As the reader would expect from the previous data in this paper, the two survey agencies agree quite closely in their findings when translated into the summary scale in Chart V.

Table 5, like previous tables, shows that each of the 14 selected categories of community leaders contains a larger proportion of individuals who are classed

TABLE 5. SCALE OF WILLINGNESS TO TOLERATE NONCONFORMISTS

(Types of Community Leaders Compared with Cross-Sections)

	Percentage "Relatively More Tolerant" on Scale		
	AIPO Sample	NORC Sample	Combined Samples
Public Officials			
Mayors	59%	62%	60%
Presidents, School Board	66	59	62
Presidents, Library Board	82	75	79
Political Party Chairmen			
Republican County Central Com.	60	80	70
Democratic County Central Com.	70	58	64
Industrial Leaders			
Presidents, Chamber of Commerce	77	54	65
Presidents, Labor Union	61	63	62
Heads of Special Patriotic Groups			
Commanders, American Legion	45	47	46
Regents, D.A.R.	38	56	48
Others			
Chairmen, Community Chest	77	87	82
Presidents, Bar Association	75	79	77
Newspaper Publishers	85	83	84
Presidents, Women's Club	46	53	49
Presidents, Parent-Teachers' Assoc.	68	68	68
Average of Community Leaders	65%	66%	66%
Cross-Section of Same Cities as Leaders	30	35	32
National Cross-section, Rural and Urban	30	31	31

Number of cases in each sample same as in Table 1.

as "more tolerant" on the scale than are contained in the cross-section in the same cities or in the national cross-section. This result holds without exception even if we base our findings on the samples from each survey agency taken separately.

There is considerable range among the different types of leaders. But a further caution must be exercised in making such comparisons. Even the combined sample for any particular category of leader is small and therefore subject to considerable chance variation. For example, the comparative percentages in Table 5 for presidents of the Chamber of Commerce and for labor unions are 65 and 62, respectively. But in the AIPO sample the difference is in one direction; in the NORC sample the difference is reversed. Moreover, by the rule suggested earlier in this paper, we require differences between two categories of leaders to be at least 14% to be significant. We do see in Table 5 that the commanders of the American Legion are significantly less likely to be at the tolerant end of the scale than most of the other community leaders. Similarly, the regents of the D.A.R. and the presidents of the women's clubs. On the other hand, the presidents of the library board, the chairmen of the Community Chest, the presidents of the bar associations, and the newspaper publishers are significantly more tolerant on this scale than several others on the list.

A final comment may be needed. From one point of view the word "tolerance" as used in the present context may be an unhappy choice. To a careless reader it may imply "approval," which again let us say it does not. If I am tolerant of a kidnaper, it is only in the sense that I want him to have every right to which the laws of the land entitle him. If I am tolerant of a totalitarian, Fascist or Communist, I do not have to approve his views. I can be as implacably against his views as Jefferson was against those of repressive authoritarians a century and a half ago: "I have sworn upon the altar of God eternal hostility against every form of tyranny over the mind of man." But if I am tolerant, there are rights which I will grant, within the law, even to those whom I most condemn. The scale of willingness to tolerate nonconformity is measuring tolerance in this sense. But again let it be pointed out, this scale does not measure such tolerance *in general*. It deals only with attitudes toward certain types of nonconformists or deviants. It does not deal with attitudes toward extreme right-wing agitators, toward people who attack minority groups, toward faddists or cultists, in general, nor, of course, toward a wide variety of criminals. For purposes of this study, the tolerance of nonconformity or suspected nonconformity is *solely* within the broad context of the Communist threat.

A NOTE ON THE TIME SPAN OF THE STUDY AS RELATED TO THESE ATTITUDES

This study went into the field in mid-May 1954, while the Army-McCarthy hearings were still in progress. About a third of the respondents were interviewed in May, about half in the first two weeks of June, and the remainder during the rest of June and July.

There were not many unusually dramatic events during this period. But, in any case, one would not expect the kind of latent tendencies reported here to shift markedly with ups and downs in the news over a period of a few weeks or even of several months.

There is evidence consistent with the probability of little change. The date of all but 51 of the interviews in the cross-section was reported on the questionnaires. The following table compares the tolerance scores of the national cross-section by time of interview:

Time of Interview	Relatively Less Tolerant	In-Between	Relatively More Tolerant	Total	Number of Cases
May 15–31	18%	51%	31%	100%	1476
June 1–15	19	51	30	100	2391
June 16–30	22	47	31	100	533
July 1–31	19	52	29	100	482

The differences in scores by time periods are clearly not significant. In general, the characteristics by education, etc., of those interviewed late were about the same as the characteristics of those interviewed early. We cannot, of course, say that some people's attitudes did not change during this period. But if there were changes, those in the direction of more tolerance were almost exactly balanced by other changes in the direction of less tolerance.

HOW THESE FINDINGS RELATE TO PREVIOUS KNOWLEDGE

No previous studies have compared civic leaders with the general public, as to their attitudes toward nonconformity, in the same kind of systematic detail which the present paper provides. But there is a wide variety of evidence about the public as a whole. . . .

The readiness of most of the American public to limit the civil rights of Communists and the readiness of substantial minorities to restrict the liberties of Socialists, atheists, and other deviant or radical groups find ample support in past survey findings.

As far back as 1937, Gallup found the majority of voters in favor of banning Communist literature and of denying Communists the right to hold public office, to hold public meetings, and to express their views. In 1940 a Roper survey found a majority of the people urging some kind of restriction or punitive action against American Communists. During the war years, when Russia was allied with the United States in the fight against Hitler, tolerance of the rights of Communists in America rose slightly, but even in 1943, after the battle of Stalingrad, two Americans out of five would have prohibited any Communist Party member from speaking on the radio. By 1948 this proportion was up to 57%; by 1952 it had risen to 77%; and in a survey conducted by the NORC in January 1954, the figure was 81%. If it is true that speaking to a potentially nation-wide radio audience is regarded as more dangerous than "making a speech in your community" to a more limited audience (as the question was put in the present survey), our figure of 68% who would deny this right to Communists is not out of line with past findings.

The willingness of minorities (and sometimes majorities) of the public to abridge the civil liberties of groups other than Communists is also documented by earlier research. Even before World War II, for example, Roper found 44% taking the view that freedom of speech should be restricted with respect to certain times, subjects, and groups, while Gallup reported 34% of the opinion that newspapers should not be allowed to take sides during an election campaign and 41% who felt that teachers should not be free to express their views on government and religion in college classrooms. An NORC survey before the war found 25% who would deny Socialists the right to publish newspapers.

By 1953, those who would deny Socialists the right to publish increased from 25% to 45%, and the proportion who opposed unlimited free speech went up from 32% to 45%. Those who would forbid newspapers to criticize our form of government rose from 30% to 42%. The present findings, therefore, showing a considerable intolerance of Socialists, atheists, and other radicals, are strongly supported by all past research.

The reader may have noticed that, while many in the present survey would allow nonconformists to make speeches and to circulate their writings, many fewer would permit them to teach in colleges and universities. This view of the college classroom as an especially sensitive area is also documented by earlier surveys. Back in the thirties Gallup found that two thirds of the public would not allow Communists to speak to student groups, and almost two out of five felt that schools should not teach the facts about Fascism and Communism. Since the war there has been general public support for teacher loyalty oaths, and there has been more opposition to Communist teachers than to permitting Communists to hold "a government job." In general, as also shown in the present study, past research has found that the degree of tolerance of Communists depends upon the perceived risk to the country or the community; and teaching, government jobs, and sensitive jobs in industry have long been barred to Communists by public opinion.

SUMMARY

This paper has shown, on a large variety of individual questions and on a scale of tolerance of nonconformity, the following facts:

1. Without exception, each of the 14 types of community leaders tends to be more willing to respect the civil rights of Socialists, atheists, those suspected of disloyalty who deny they are Communists, and self-avowed Communists than either the rank and file in the same cities as the leaders or the national cross-section. A considerable variety of rights was considered—rights to speak, to hold jobs, and many others.

2. The consistency of the main findings of two different survey agencies adds confidence to the conclusions. On large samples, differences between the two

agencies are negligible. On small samples of individual types of leaders, the two agencies differ considerably in some instances—but the main conclusion is the same, whether based on the samples of each agency alone or whether based on the combined samples.

3. From various points of view, the detailed attitudes reported in this paper —even the attitudes of civic leaders—may not be a pleasant picture. But the fact that responsible community leaders are more likely than the rank and file to give the sober second thought to the civil rights of the nonconformists or suspected nonconformists here studied can be of much significance to America's future. If the reverse had been found, the future might look dark indeed to those who view with anxiety current threats to historic liberties. Plans of public education which aim at building more respect for the American tradition should be able to count on strong support from influential civic leadership at the grass roots.

26. SOCIAL STRAINS IN AMERICA

Talcott Parsons

THE VIEW IN 1955

To the relatively objective observer, whether American or foreign, it seems clear that the complex of phenomena that have come to be known as "Mc-Carthyism" must be symptoms of a process in American society of some deep and general significance. Some interpret it simply as political reaction, even as a kind of neo-fascism. Some think of it as simply a manifestation of nationalism. The present paper proposes to bring to bear some theoretical perspectives of sociology in an attempt to work out an interpretation which goes beyond catch-words of this order.

McCarthyism can be understood as a relatively acute symptom of the strains which accompany a major change in the situation and structure of American society, a change which in this instance consists in the development of the atti-tudes and institutional machinery required to implement a greatly enhanced level of national political responsibility. The necessity for this development arises both from our own growth to an enormous potential of power, and from the changed relation to the rest of the world which this growth in itself, and other changes extraneous to American development, have entailed. The strains to which I refer derive primarily from conflicts between the demands imposed by the new situation and the inertia of those elements of our social structure which are most resistant to the necessary changes.

The situation I have in mind centers on the American position in interna-tional affairs. The main facts are familiar to all. It is not something that has come about suddenly, but the impact of its pressures has been cumulative.

The starting point is the relative geographical isolation of the United States in the "formative" period of its national history, down to, let us say, about the opening of the present century. The Spanish-American War extended our involvements into the Spanish-speaking areas of the Caribbean and to the Philippines, and the Boxer episode in China and our mediation of the Russo-Japanese War indicated rapidly growing interests in the Orient. Then the First World War brought us in as one of the major belligerents, with a brief pos-sibility of taking a role of world leadership. From this advanced degree of inter-national involvement, however, we recoiled with a violent reaction, repudiating the Treaty of Versailles and the League of Nations.

In the ensuing period of "normalcy," until the shock of Pearl Harbor settled the question, it could still be held that the "quarrels" of foreign powers beyond the Americas were none of our concern, unless some "arbitrary" disturbance impinged too closely on our national interests. By the end of the Second World War, however, this attitude could not again be revived by any body of opinion which pretended to depend upon a realistic appraisal of our situation. Our own strength, in spite of our massive disarmament and demobilization, had grown too great; the defeat of France and the disorganization of Germany destroyed

SOURCE: Daniel Bell (ed.), *The Radical Right* (New York: Doubleday & Co., Inc., 1963). Reprinted by permission of the author.

such continental European balance of power as had existed; Britain, though victorious, was greatly weakened in the face of world-wide commitments; and Soviet Russia emerged as a victorious and expanding power, leading with a revolutionary ideology a movement which could readily destroy such elements of stability favorable to our own national values and interests as still remained in the world. Along with all this have come developments in military technology that have drastically neutralized the protections formerly conferred by geographical distance, so that even the elementary military security of the United States cannot now be taken for granted apart from world-wide political order.

The vicissitudes of American foreign policy and its relations to domestic politics over this period show the disturbing effect of this developing situation on our society. We have twice intervened militarily on a grand scale. With a notable difference of degree, we have both times recoiled from the implications of our intervention. In the second case the recoil did not last long, since the beginnings of the Cold War about 1947 made it clear that only American action was able to prevent Soviet domination of the whole continent of Europe. It can, however, be argued that this early and grand-scale resumption of responsibility imposed serious internal strains because it did not allow time for "digesting" the implications of our role in the war.

The outstanding characteristic of the society on which this greatly changed situation has impinged is that it had come to be the industrial society par excellence—partly because the settlement of the continental area coincided with the later industrial revolution, partly because of the immense area and natural resources of the country, but partly too because of certain important differences between American and European society. Since the United States did not have a class structure tightly integrated with a political organization that had developed its main forms before the industrial revolution, the economy has had a freedom to develop and to set the tone for the whole society in a way markedly different from any European country or Japan.

All highly industrialized societies exhibit many features in common which are independent of the particular historical paths by which their developments have taken place. These include the bureaucratic organization of the productive process itself, in the sense that the roles of individuals are of the occupational type and the organizations in which they are grouped are mainly "specific function" organizations. Under this arrangement the peasant type of agricultural holding, where farming is very closely bound up with a kinship unit, is minimized; so too of small family businesses; people tend to look to their productive function and to profit as a measure of success and hence of emancipation from conflicting ties and claims; the rights of property ownership are centered primarily in the organization which carries functional responsibility, and hence permits a high degree of segregation between private life and occupational roles for production purposes; contract plays a central part in the system of exchange, and para-economic elements tend to be reduced in importance.

Outside the sphere which touches the organization of the economy itself, industrialism means above all that the structures which would interfere with the free functioning of the economy, and of their adaptation to it, are minimized. The first of these is family and kinship. The American family system, chiefly characterized by the isolation of the nuclear or conjugal family, has gone farther than in any European society toward removing all interferences with the occupational roles of the breadwinning members, and with occupational mobility. A second field is religion. The American combination of federalism and the separation of church and state has resulted in a system of "denominational pluralism" which prevents organized religion from constituting a monolithic structure standing in the way of secular social developments. The third field concerns the matter of social stratification. The United States of course has a class structure; but it is one which has its primary roots in the system of occupational roles, and in contrast to the typical European situation it acts as no more than a brake on the processes of social mobility which are most important to an industrial type of occupational system. Under an effective family system there must be some continuity of class status from generation to generation, and there cannot be complete "equality of opportunity." In America, however, it is clearly the occupational system rather than kinship continuity that prevails.

Linked to this situation is our system of formal education. The United States was among the pioneers in developing publicly supported education; but this has taken place in a notably decentralized way. Not only is there no Department of Education in the Federal government, but even the various state departments are to a large extent service organizations for the locally controlled school systems. Higher education further has been considerably more independent of class standards which equate the "scholar" with the "gentleman" (in a class sense) than has been the case in Europe. Also a far larger proportion of each age-group attends institutions of higher education than in European countries.

Politically the most important fact about American industrialism is that it has developed overwhelmingly under the aegis of free enterprise. Historically the center of gravity of the integration of American society has not rested in the political field. There came to be established a kind of "burden of proof" expectation that responsibilities should not be undertaken by government unless, first, the necessity for their being undertaken at all was clearly established, and second, there was no other obviously adequate way to get the job done. It is therefore not surprising that the opening up of vast new fields of governmental responsibility should meet with considerable resistance and conflict.

The impact of this problem on our orientation to foreign relations has been complicated by an important set of internal circumstances. It is a commonplace that industrialism creates on a large scale two sets of problems which uniformly in all industrialized countries have required modifications of any doctrinaire "laissez-faire" policy: the problems of controlling the processes of the economy itself, and of dealing with certain social repercussions of industrialization.

As the process of industrialization has developed in America there has been a steady increase in the amount of public control imposed on the economy, with the initiative mainly in the hands of the Federal government. This trend was accelerated in the latter years of the nineteenth century, and has continued, with interruptions, through the New Deal. The New Deal, however, was more concerned with the social repercussions of industrialization, rather than with more narrowly economic problems. The introduction of a national system of social security and legislation more favorable to labor are perhaps the most typical developments. This internal process of government intervention has not gone far enough to satisfy European socialists, but it certainly constitutes a great modification of the earlier situation. Moreover, in broad lines it can be regarded as firmly established. It is significant that the major political parties now tend to vie with each other in promoting the extension of social security benefits, that there is no likelihood of repeal of the Federal Reserve Act, and that there is no strong movement to place the unions under really severe legal restraints.

On the whole, business groups have accepted the new situation and cooperated to make it work with considerably more good faith than in Continental Europe. Nevertheless, these internal changes have been sufficiently recent and far-reaching to keep the strains attendant on them from being fully resolved. Moreover they have created an important part of the problems with which this examination is chiefly concerned, problems touching the composition of the higher strata of the society, where the primary burden of responsibility must fall.

By contrast with European countries, perhaps in some ways particularly Britain, the United States has been conspicuous for the absence or relative weakness of two types of elite elements. The first of these is a hereditary upper class with a status continuous from pre-industrial times, closely integrated with politics and public service. The second is an occupational elite whose roots are essentially independent of the business world—in the independent professions, the universities, the church, or government, including civil and military services.

In America the businessmen have tended to be the natural leaders of the general community. But, both for the reasons just reviewed and for certain others, this leadership has not remained undisputed. On the whole the business community has, step by step, resisted the processes of internal change necessitated by industrialization rather than taken the leadership in introducing them. The leadership that has emerged has been miscellaneous in social origin, including professional politicians, especially those in touch with the urban political machines, leaders in the labor union movement and elements in close touch with them. An important part has been played by men and women who may be said to exhibit a more or less "aristocratic" tinge, particularly in the Eastern cities, President Roosevelt of course having been among them. An important part has been played by lawyers who have made themselves more independent of the business connection than the typical corporation lawyer of a generation ago. Under the pressure of emergency, there has been a tendency for high military officers to play important roles in public life.

Another important group has been composed of "intellectuals"—again a rather miscellaneous assembly including writers, newspapermen, and members of university faculties. In general the importance of the universities has been steadily enhanced by the increasingly technical character of the operations of the economy; businessmen themselves have had to be more highly educated than their predecessors, and have become increasingly dependent on still more highly trained technicians of various kinds.

The important point is that the "natural" tendency for a relatively unequivocal business leadership of the general community has been frustrated, and the business group has had to give way at many points. Nevertheless, a clearly defined non-business component of the elite has not yet crystallized. In my opinion, the striking feature of the American elite is not what Soviet propaganda contends that it is—the clear-cut dominance by "capitalists"—but rather its fluid and relatively unstructured character. In particular, there is no clear determination of where political leadership, in the sense including both "politics" and "administration," is to center.

A further feature of the structure of American society is intimately related to the residual strains left by recent social changes. There is a continuing tendency for earlier economic developments to leave a "precipitate" of upper groups, the position of whose members is founded in the achievements of their ancestors, in this case relatively recent ones. By historical necessity these groups are strongest in the older parts of the country. Hence the cities of the Eastern seaboard have tended to develop groups that are the closest approach we have— though still very different from their European equivalent—to an aristocracy. They have generally originated in business interests, but have taken on a form somewhat similar to the mercantile aristocracies of some earlier European societies, such as the Hanseatic cities. In the perspective of popular democratic sentiments, these groups have tended to symbolize at the same time capitalistic interests and social snobbery. In certain circumstances they may be identified with "bohemianism" and related phenomena which are sources of uneasiness to traditional morality.

As the American social and economic center has shifted westward, such groups in the great Middle Western area and beyond have been progressively less prominent. There the elites have consisted of new men. In the nature of the case the proportional contribution to the economy and the society in general from the older and the newer parts of the country has shifted, with the newer progressively increasing their share. But at the same time there is the sense among them of having had to fight for this share against the "dominance" of the East. A similar feeling permeates the lower levels of the class structure. A major theme of the populist type of agrarian and other radicalism had combined class and sectional elements, locating the source of people's troubles in the bankers and railway magnates of the East and in Wall Street. It must not be forgotten that the isolationism of the between-the-wars period was intimately connected with this sectional and class sentiment. The elder La Follette, who was one of the principal destroyers of the League of Nations, was not a "conservative" or in any usual sense a reactionary, but a principal leader of the popular revolt against "the interests."

It must also not be forgotten that a large proportion of the American population are descendants of relatively recent immigrants whose cultural origins are different from the dominant Protestant Anglo-Saxon elements. A generation and more ago the bulk of the new immigration constituted an urban proletariat largely dominated by the political machines of the great cities. By now a great change has taken place. The children of these immigrants have been very much Americanized, but to a considerable degree they are still sensitive about their full acceptance. This sensitivity is if anything heightened by the fact that on the whole most of these elements have risen rapidly in the economic and social scale. They are no longer the inhabitants of the scandalous slums; many have climbed to lower-middle-class status and higher. They have a certain suscepti-bility to "democratic" appeals which are directed against the alleged snobbery of the older dominant elements.

Finally, the effect of the great depression of the 1930s on the leading business groups must not be forgotten. Such a collapse of the economy could not fail to be felt as a major failure of the expectation that business leaders should bear the major responsibility for the welfare of the economy as a whole and thus of the community. In general it was not the businessmen but the government, under leadership which was broadly antagonistic to business, which came to the rescue. Similarly, the other great class of American proprietors, the farmers, had to accept governmental help of a sort that entailed controls, which in turn inevitably entailed severe conflicts with the individualistic traditions of their history. The fact that the strains of the war and postwar periods have been piled so imme-diately on those of depression has much to do with the severity of the tensions with which this analysis is concerned.

My thesis, then, is that the strains of the international situation have impinged on a society undergoing important internal changes which have themselves been sources of strain, with the effect of superimposing one kind of strain on another. What responses to this compound strain are to be expected?

It is a generalization well established in social science that neither individuals nor societies can undergo major structural changes without the likelihood of producing a considerable element of "irrational" behavior. There will tend to be conspicuous distortions of the patterns of value and of the normal beliefs about the facts of situations. These distorted beliefs and promptings to irrational action will also tend to be heavily weighted with emotion, to be "overdetermined" as the psychologists say.

The psychology of such reactions is complex, but for present purposes it will suffice to distinguish two main components. On the negative side, there will tend to be high levels of anxiety and aggression, focused on what rightly or wrongly are felt to be the sources of strain and difficulty. On the positive side there will tend to be wishful patterns of belief with a strong "regressive" flavor, whose chief function is to wish away the disturbing situation and establish a situation in phantasy where "everything will be all right," preferably as it was before the disturbing situation came about. Very generally then the psychological formula tends to prescribe a set of beliefs that certain specific, symbolic agencies are responsible for the present state of distress; they have "arbitrarily" upset a satis-factory state of affairs. If only they could be eliminated the trouble would dis-appear and a satisfactory state restored. The role of this type of mechanism in primitive magic is quite well known.

In a normal process of learning in the individual, or of developmental change in the social system, such irrational phenomena are temporary, and tend to subside as capacity to deal with the new situation grows. This may be more or less easily achieved of course, and resolution of the conflicts and strains may fail to be achieved for a long period or may even be permanently unsuccessful. But under favorable circumstances these reactions are superseded by an in-creasingly realistic facing of the situation by institutionalized means.

Our present problem therefore centers on the need to mobilize American society to cope with a dangerous and threatening situation which is also intrinsically difficult. It can clearly only be coped with at the governmental level; and hence the problem is in essence a matter of political action, involving both questions of leadership—of who, promoting what policies, shall take the primary responsibility—and of the commitment of the many heterogeneous elements of our population to the national interest.

Consequently there has come to be an enormous increase in pressure to subordinate private interests to the public interest, and this in a society where the presumptions have been more strongly in favor of the private interest than in most. Readiness to make commitments to a collective interest is the focus of what we ordinarily mean by "loyalty." It seems to me that the problem of loyalty at its core is a genuine and realistic one; but attitudes toward it shade all the way from a reasonable concern with getting the necessary degree of loyal cooperation by legitimate appeals, to a grossly irrational set of anxieties about the prevalence of disloyalty, and a readiness to vent the accompanying aggression on innocent scapegoats.

Underlying the concern for loyalty in general, and explaining a good deal of the reaction to it, is the ambivalence of our approach to the situation: The people in the most "exposed" positions are on the one hand pulled by patriotic motives toward fulfillment of the expectations inherent in the new situation; they want to "do their bit." But at the same time their established attitudes and orientations resist fulfillment of the obligation. In the conflict of motives which ensues it is a natural consequence for the resistance to be displaced or projected on to other objects which function as scapegoats. In the present situation it is precisely those parts of our population where individualistic traditions are strongest that are placed under the greatest strain, and that produce the severest resistances to accepting the obligations of our situation. Such resistances, however, conflict with equally strong patriotic motives. In such a situation, when one's own resistance to loyal acceptance of unpalatable obligations, such as paying high taxes, are particularly strong, it is easy to impute disloyal intentions to others.

Our present emotional preoccupation with the problem of loyalty indicates above all that the crisis is not, as some tend to think, primarily concerned with fundamental values, but rather with their implementation. It is true that certain features of the pattern of reaction, such as tendencies to aggressive nationalism and to abdication of responsibilities, would, if carried through, lead to severe conflict with our values. But the main problem is not concerned with doubts about whether the stable political order of a free world is a goal worth sacrificing for, but rather with the question of how our population is rising or failing to rise to the challenge.

The primary symbol that connects the objective external problem and its dangers with the internal strain and its structure is "Communism." "World Communism" and its spread constitute the features of the world situation on which the difficulty of our international problem clearly centers. Internally it is felt that Communists and their "sympathizers" constitute the primary focus of actual or potential disloyalty.

With respect to the external situation, the focus of the difficulty in the current role of Soviet Russia is of course reasonable enough. Problems then arise mainly in connection with certain elements of "obsessiveness" in the way in which the situation is approached, manifested for instance in a tendency to subordinate all other approaches to the situation exclusively to the military, and in the extreme violence of reaction in some circles to the Chinese situation, in contrast to the relative tolerance with which Yugoslavia is regarded.

Internally, the realistic difficulty resides mainly in the fact that there has indeed been a considerable amount of Communist infiltration in the United States, particularly in the 1930s. It is true that the Communist Party itself has never achieved great electoral success, but for a time Communist influence was paramount in a number of important labor unions, and a considerable number of the associations Americans so like to join were revealed to be Communist-front organizations, with effective Communist control behind the public participation of many non-Communists. Perhaps most important was the fact that considerable numbers of the intellectuals became fellow-travelers. In the days of the rise of Nazism and of the popular front, many of them felt that only Soviet Russia was sincere in its commitment to collective security; that there was a Franco-British "plot" to get Germany and Russia embroiled with each other, etc. The shock of the Nazi-Soviet pact woke up many fellow-travelers, but by no means all; and the cause was considerably retrieved by Hitler's attack on Russia.

Two other features of the Communist movement which make it an ideal negative symbol in the context of the present loyalty problem are the combination of conspiratorial methods and foreign control with the progressive component of its ideological system. On the one hand the party has drastically repudiated the procedures of constitutional democracy, and on this issue has broken with all the democratic socialist parties of Europe; it claims the protection of democratic procedures and civil liberties, but does not hesitate to abuse them when this seems to be advantageous. There has further never been any question of the American party determining its own policies by democratic procedures. Perhaps in fact the knowledge of the extent to which the "front" organizations have been manipulated from behind the scenes has been the most disillusioning aspect for liberal Americans of their experience with Communism at home.

At the same time the movement had a large content of professed idealism, which may be taken to account for the appeal of Communism before the Cold War era for such large elements of liberal opinion in the United States, as in other Western countries. Marx was, after all, himself a child of the Enlightenment, and the Communist movement has incorporated in its ideology many of the doctrines of human rights that have formed a part of our general inheritance. However grossly the symbols of democracy, of the rights of men, of peace and brotherhood, have been abused by the Communists, they are powerful symbols in our own tradition, and their appeal is understandable.

Hence the symbol "Communism" is one to which a special order of ambivalence readily attaches. It has powerful sources of appeal to the liberal tradition, but those who are out of sympathy with the main tradition of American liberalism can find a powerful target for their objections in the totalitarian tactics of Communism and can readily stigmatize it as "un-American." Then, by extending their objections to the liberal component of Communist ideology, they can attack liberalism in general, on the grounds that association with Communist totalitarianism makes anything liberal suspect.

These considerations account for the anti-Communist's readiness to carry over a stereotype from those who have really been party members or advanced fellow-travelers to large elements of the intellectuals, the labor movement, etc., who have been essentially democratic liberals of various shades of opinion. Since by and large the Democratic Party has more of this liberalism than has the Republican, it is not surprising that a tendency to label it as "sympathizing" with or "soft toward" Communism has appeared. Such a label has also been extended, though not very seriously, to the Protestant clergy.

But there is one further extension of the association that is not accounted for in these terms, nor is the failure to include certain plausible targets so accountable. The extension I have in mind is that which leads to the inclusion as "pro-Communist" of certain men or institutions that have been associated with political responsibility in the international field. Two symbols stand out here. The first is Dean Acheson. Mr. Acheson has for years served the Democratic Party. But he has belonged to the conservative, not the New Deal wing of the party. Furthermore, the coupling of General Marshall with him, though only in connection with China, and only by extremists, clearly precludes political radicalism as the primary objection, since Marshall has never in any way been identified with New Deal views. The other case is that of Harvard University as an alleged "hot-bed" of Communism and fellow-traveling. The relevant point is that Mr. Acheson typifies the "aristocrat" in public service; he came of a wealthy family, he went to a select private school (Groton) and to Yale and Harvard Law School. He represents symbolically those Eastern vested interests, against whom antagonism has existed among the new men of the Middle West and the populist movement, including the descendants of recent immigrants. Similarly, among American universities Harvard has been particularly identified as educating a social elite, the members of which are thought of as "just the type," in their striped trousers and morning coats, to sell out the country to the social snobs of European capitals. It is the combination of aristocratic associations—through the Boston Brahmins—and a kind of urban-bohemian sophistication along with its devotion to intellectual and cultural values, including precisely its high intellectual standards, which makes Harvard a vulnerable symbol in this context.

The symbol "Communism," then, from its area of legitimate application, tends to be generalized to include groups in the population who have been associated with political liberalism of many shades and with intellectual values in general and to include the Eastern upper-class groups who have tended to be relatively internationalist in their outlook.

A second underlying ambivalent attitude-structure is discernible in addition to that concerning the relation between the totalitarian and the progressive aspects of Communism. On the one hand, Communism very obviously symbolizes what is anathema to the individualistic tradition of a business economy—the feared attempt to destroy private enterprise and with it the great tradition of individual freedom. But on the other hand, in order to rise to the challenge of the current political situation, it is necessary for the older balance between a free economy and the power of government to be considerably shifted in favor of the latter. We must have a stronger government than we have traditionally been accustomed to, and we must come to trust it more fully. It has had in recent times to assume very substantial regulatory functions in relation to the economy, and now vastly enhanced responsibilities in relation to international affairs.

But, on the basis of a philosophy which, in a very different way from our individualistic tradition, gives primacy to "economic interests," namely the Marxist philosophy, the Communist movement asserts the unqualified, the totalitarian supremacy of government over the economy. It is precisely an actual change in our own system in what in one sense is clearly this direction that emerges as the primary focus of the frustrations to which the older American system has been subjected. The leaders of the economy, the businessmen, have been forced to accept far more "interference" from government with what they have considered "their affairs" than they have liked. And now they must, like everyone else, pay unprecedentedly high taxes to support an enormous military establishment, and give the government in other respects unprecedentedly great powers over the population. The result of this situation is an ambivalence of attitude that on the one hand demands a stringent display of loyalty going to lengths far beyond our tradition of individual liberty, and on the other hand is ready to blame elements which by ordinary logic have little or nothing to do with Communism, for working in league with the Communist movement to create this horrible situation.

Generally speaking, the indefensible aspect of this tendency in a realistic assessment appears in a readiness to question the loyalty of all those who have assumed responsibility for leadership in meeting the exigencies of the new situation. These include many who have helped to solve the internal problems of the control of the economy, those who in the uneasy later 'thirties and the first phase of the war tried to get American policy and public opinion to face the dangers of the international situation, and those who since the war have tried to take responsibility in relation to the difficult postwar situation. Roughly, these are the presumptively disloyal elements who are also presumptively tainted with Communism. Here again, admittedly, certain features of our historical record and attitudes provide some realistic basis for this tendency. In fact many elements in both parties have failed lamentably to assess correctly the dangers of the situation, both internally and externally. New Dealers have stigmatized even the most responsible elements of the business world as economic royalists and the like, while many elements in business have clung long past a reasonable time to an outmoded belief in the possibility of a society with only a "night watchman" government. In foreign affairs, some members of the Democratic Party have been slow to learn how formidable a danger was presented by totalitarian Communism, but this is matched by the utopianism of many Republicans about the consequences of American withdrawal from international responsibilities, through high tariffs as well as political isolationism. The necessity to learn the hard realities of a complex world and the difficulty of the process is not a task to be imposed on only part of the body politic. No party or group can claim a monopoly either of patriotic motive or of competent understanding of affairs.

In a double sense, then, Communism symbolizes "the intruder." Externally the world Communist movement is the obvious source of the most serious difficulties we have to face. On the other hand, although Communism has constituted to some degree a realistic internal danger, it has above all come to symbolize those factors that have disturbed the beneficent natural state of an American society which allegedly and in phantasy existed before the urgent problems of control of the economy and greatly enhanced responsibility in international affairs had to be tackled.

Against this background it can perhaps be made clear why the description of McCarthyism as simply a political reactionary movement is inadequate. In the first place, it is clearly not simply a cloak for the "vested interests" but rather a movement that profoundly splits the previously dominant groups. This is evident in the split, particularly conspicuous since about 1952, within the Republican Party. An important part of the business elite, especially in the Middle West and in Texas, the "newest" area of all, have tended in varying degrees to be attracted by the McCarthy appeal. But other important groups, notably in the East, have shied away from it and apparently have come to be more and more consolidated against it. Very broadly, these can be identified with the business element among the Eisenhower Republicans.

But at the same time the McCarthy following is by no means confined to the vested-interest groups. There has been an important popular following of very miscellaneous composition. It has comprised an important part of those who aspire to full status in the American system but have, realistically or not, felt discriminated against in various ways, especially the Mid-Western lower and lower middle classes and much of the population of recent immigrant origin. The elements of continuity between Western agrarian populism and McCarthyism are not by any means purely fortuitous. At the levels of both leadership and popular following, the division of American political opinion over this issue *cuts clean across the traditional lines of distinction between "conservatives" and "progressives,"* especially where that tends to be defined, as it so often is, in terms of the capitalistic or moneyed interests as against those who seek to bring them under more stringent control. McCarthyism is *both* a movement supported by certain vested-interest elements *and* a popular revolt against the upper classes.

Another striking characteristic of McCarthyism is that it is highly selective in the liberal causes it attacks. Apart from the issue of Communism in the labor unions, now largely solved, there has been no concerted attack on the general position of the labor movement. Further, the social program aimed toward the reduction of racial discrimination has continued to be pressed, to which fact the decision of the Supreme Court outlawing segregation in public education and its calm reception provide dramatic evidence. Nevertheless, so far as I am aware there has been no outcry from McCarthyite quarters to the effect that this decision is further evidence of Communist influence in high circles—in spite of the fact that eight out of nine members of the present court were appointed by Roosevelt and Truman.

Perhaps even more notable is the fact that, unlike the 1930s, when Father Coughlin and others were preaching a vicious anti-Semitism, anti-Semitism as a public issue has since the war been very nearly absent from the American scene. This is of course associated with full employment. But particularly in view of the rather large and conspicuous participation of Jewish intellectuals in the fellow-traveling of the 1930s, it is notable that Jewishness has not been singled out as a symbolic focus for the questioning of loyalty. A critical difference from German Nazism is evident here. To the Nazis the Jew was the *primary* negative symbol, the Communist the most prominent secondary one. But it must also be remembered that capitalism was symbolically involved. One of the functions of the Jew was to *link* Communism and capitalism together. This trio were the "intruders" to the Nazis. They symbolized different aspects of the disturbance created by the rapid development of industrialism to the older preindustrial *Gemeinschaft* of German political romanticism. It was the obverse of the American case—a new economy destroying an old political system, not new political responsibilities interfering with the accustomed ways of economic life.

Negatively, then, the use of the symbol "Communism" as the focus of anxiety and aggression is associated with a high order of selectivity among possibly vulnerable targets. This selectivity is, I submit, consistent with the hypothesis that the focus of the strain expressed by McCarthyism lies in the area of political responsibility—not, as Marxists would hold, in the structure of the economy as such, nor in the class structure in any simple, Marxian-tinged sense.

The same interpretation is confirmed by the evidence on the positive side. The broadest formula for what the McCarthyites positively "want"—besides the elimination of all Communist influence, real or alleged—is perhaps "isolationism." The dominant note is, I think, the regressive one. It is the wishful preservation of an old order, which allegedly need never have been disturbed but for the wilful interference of malevolent elements, Communists and their sympathizers. The nationalistic overtones center on a phantasy of a happy "American way" where everything used to be all right. Naturally it is tinged with the ideology of traditional laissez-faire, but not perhaps unduly so. Also it tends to spill over into a kind of irritated activism. On the one hand we want to keep out of trouble; but on the other hand, having identified an enemy, we want to smash him forthwith. The connection between the two can be seen, for example, in relation to China, where the phantasy seems to be that by drastic action it would be possible to "clean up" the Chinese situation quickly and then our troubles would be over.

The main contention of these pages has been that McCarthyism is best understood as a symptom of the strains attendant on a deep-seated process of change in our society, rather than as a "movement" presenting a policy or set of values for the American people to act on. Its content is overwhelmingly negative, not positive. It advocates "getting rid" of undesirable influences, and has amazingly little to say about what should be done.

This negativism is primarily the expression of fear, secondarily of anger, the aggression which is a product of frustration. The solution, which is both realistically feasible and within the great American tradition, is to regain our national self-confidence and to take active steps to cope with the situation with which we are faced.

On the popular level the crisis is primarily a crisis of confidence. We are baffled and anxious, and tend to seek relief in hunting scapegoats. We must improve our understanding and come to realize our strength and trust in it. But this cannot be done simply by wishing it to be done. I have consistently argued that the changed situation in which we are placed demands a far-reaching change in the structure of our society. It demands policies, and confidence, but it demands more than these. It demands above all three things. The first is a revision of our conception of citizenship to encourage the ordinary man to accept greater responsibility. The second is the development of the necessary implementing machinery. Third is national political leadership, not only in the sense of individual candidates for office or appointment, but in the sense of social strata where a traditional political responsibility is ingrained.

The most important of these requirements is the third. Under American conditions, a politically leading stratum must be made up of a combination of business and nonbusiness elements. The role of the economy in American society and of the business element in it is such that political leadership without prominent business participation is doomed to ineffectiveness and to the perpetuation of dangerous internal conflict. It is not possible to lead the American people *against* the leaders of the business world. But at the same time, so varied now are the national elements which make a legitimate claim to be represented, the business element cannot monopolize or dominate political leadership and responsibility. Broadly, I think, a political elite in the two main aspects of "politicians" whose specialties consist in the management of public opinion, and of "administrators" in both civil and military services, must be greatly strengthened. It is here that the practical consequences of McCarthyism run most directly counter to the realistic needs of the time. But along with such a specifically political elite there must also be close alliance with other, predominantly "cultural" elements, notably perhaps in the universities, but also in the churches.

In the final sense, then, the solution of the problem of McCarthyism lies in the successful accomplishment of the social changes to which we are called by our position in the world and by our own domestic requirements. We have already made notable progress toward this objective; the current flare-up of stress in the form of McCarthyism can be taken simply as evidence that the process is not complete.

THE VIEW IN 1962

McCarthyism was essentially a crisis of national solidarity in the face of what, for us as a nation, were accumulating and unprecedented political demands and responsibilities. The precipitating factor was the Korean War, which, acting as a "last straw," frustrated the expectations of relaxation that many Americans held after the end of the big war, a war that itself was entered into only after serious internal division and conflict. The focus of the strain was the problem of national loyalty. But the very insistence on national loyalty created a paradox that Edward Shils, in his *The Torment of Secrecy,* has highlighted more clearly than anyone else, in that the very demand for nearly absolute national loyalty undermined our national capacities for effective action.

One of the most striking features of the McCarthy movement was its intensity while it lasted, and the rapidity with which it subsided when the "bubble" finally burst. Though more deep-rooted and underlying strains may have been involved—and may still be—McCarthyism as a social threat was more clearly analogous to a financial panic, say, than to a long-drawn-out depression. Putting the situation in terms of that analogy may help to clarify the ways in which the strain operated. When there is a run on the bank by depositors the tendency is, in a cumulative regression, to more and more "elementary" monetary transactions. In the ordinary course of business "cash" is only a minor convenience, for most transactions are carried out essentially by exchange of deposits within a credit system. But if too many depositors want payment all at once, these demands cannot be honored and the credit system maintained. "Logically" the end of the line of monetary deflation, of course, is a return to species payments, or the use of metal, the toting of which would make any commercial transaction quite weighty. Such a downward spin can only be checked by a restoration of "confidence," which means willingness to accept payment other than "hard" cash—the return to credit. In short, there has to be a foundation of trust for the credit system to operate.

McCarthyism was such a "deflationary spiral." The "credit" repudiated was the ordinary level of commitment of the citizen to the national interest, which in a pluralistic society is virtually never total. What the McCarthyites demanded of those who claimed to be "trustworthy" was not fulfillment of ordinary obligations, but an absolute guarantee that no other commitment could conceivably compete with what *they* called "loyalty" to the government.

Obviously this pressure generated a special kind of conflict in American society. We have a tradition that the claims of government on the individual are relatively minimal, and the presumptive morality is one of defense of individual rights against government. In the 1950s we were made acutely aware of the serious threats to national security and of the necessity of strengthening the government in ways that, in some sense, involved a sacrifice of private rights.

In such a situation there will necessarily be widespread ambivalence, and it was to be expected that the phenomenon of scapegoating would be prominent. It was my view, as stated in the original (1955) paper, that the most prominent scourgers would be those who had a strong—moral as well as "material"—vested interest in limiting the powers of government, and that the victims would be those who had on the whole taken the initiative in realistic attempts to meet the situation. From this point of view it was not unintelligible that the men who had entered government service were the ones most victimized. (This is perhaps analogous to the banker who, having taken the responsibility for lending "other people's money" is then, by populistic demand, subjected to the most rigorous checking, so that even any minor loss through error of judgment comes to be attributed to his bad faith.)

The question may now be raised whether the most recent (1962) phase of development of the radical right is a repetition of McCarthyism or something different. There is, it seems to me, a common substratum, but in many respects the current flare-up has markedly different features.

The common substratum seems to lie in the tendency to polarization that derives from the main pattern of developmental change in American society. In the broadest sense—which can be made to correspond only approximately to political-party divisions—the "right" is the protest against the fact that American society is changing, and against the direction of change. The United States is a society that has been evolving toward increasing complexities and scale of its organization and functions; a greater concentration of population and activities in complex communities; increasing responsibility in the world political system; and a higher order of technology, knowledge, sophistication, and the like. The conservatives are the read-guard resistance to this trend.

Common to all the multifarious aspects of the right wing is a certain type of "individualism." It has such facets as the individualism of the small unit as against the large—the independent entrepreneur versus the large corporation, and similarly the rural and small town versus the city and the metropolis. As regards international relations, this individualism romanticizes our earlier lack of involvement in the complex world of power relations, when America could be left to work out its own destiny. Most generally perhaps this individualism is the idealization of pristine simplicity as against organizational and other complexity.

In the general picture, the current right seems to be the more regressive of the two, and for that very reason possibly less threatening, since the radical wing of conservatism is likely to be excluded from power. In understanding its salience it should also be remembered that while McCarthyism started during the latter part of the Truman administration, it came to a head under a Republican administration. The so-called "resurgence" of the right in the past year is, in part, undoubtedly a simple function of the Republican Party's again going into opposition.

In spite of this common substratum, in an important sense the current rightist preoccupations, typified perhaps by the John Birch Society, are the obverse of the McCarthyites. The right of the 1960s shares, of course, the symbol of Communism as the source of all evil, but its meaning has been shifted in a way that brings to the fore the other side of an ambivalent motivational complex.

An important symptom of the difference between McCarthyism and Birchism is the shift in the geographical center of gravity.[1] This is a move from the Middle West to the Southwest (Texas, to be sure, is the common sector in both movements, and to some extent the same is true of that perennial hothouse of the exotic, Southern California.) This is no accident; the Southwest is the nearest thing left to a frontier, or, more specifically, Texas and Southern California are the sections that, despite a rapidly burgeoning urban civilization, still cherish the illusion that the old frontier is alive.

The essential point about the frontier is that it was the situation—in legend at least—of the predominance of self-help. Here a man—who was allegedly *really* a man—was most obviously "on his own." If "bad" men were about, he had to defend himself—and of course the good women—with his bare firsts or his six-shooter. He made his living "honestly"—by wrestling with nature in the form of recalcitrant soils, drought, storm, and "ornery" beasts—so that no one could say when he won that it was because he was dependent on anyone.[2]

It seems to me that it is this fierce and hence "defensive" independence which is the hallmark of the most recent right.[3] The good life is to be completely untamed by the disciplines of complex society. From the point of view of this individualism, the income tax is a "tribute" exacted by a "foreign" usurper; namely, the urban, and more or less European, America. The income tax— attacks on which were by no means absent from the ideology of the McCarthy era (cf. the views of the late Representative Carroll Reece)—has been upgraded to become almost the central symbol of evil; i.e., the first entering wedge of "Communism." The reason why it is unexceptionably "Communist" is simply that it presumes to assert the authority of government. By taking away what "belongs to" the taxpayer, it symbolizes the arbitrariness in almost any regulation of the complete freedom of the individual to "do what he will with his own," and defend himself against comers who challenge his rights.

This is the essential structure of the ambivalence. The McCarthyites demanded absolute subordination of all private rights to the government. McCarthy was in effect the most drastically radical "Socialist" imaginable. The Bircher demands nearly absolute immunity from any type of public control over his independence.

In this regard, the image of Communism is somewhat different in the two cases. . . . For the McCarthyites the aggression against the source that called for the development of government was the key to its pattern. To meet the threat of real Communism, there was a strengthening of responsible government and more centralized authority. To fight "Communism," which stands for the total state, McCarthy demanded even more centralized government. This is a motivational mechanism operating analogously to the normal oedipal situation—the resentment against the "father" as the symbolic source of the pressure to grow up, but also an identification with him. The McCarthyites, by demanding absolute loyalty, were in fact promoting a kind of distorted identification with government. The identification was carried out in a destructive way so as to threaten the many altogether legitimate pluralistic loyalties and associations, to subordinate them altogether too drastically to the one national loyalty, and in the process to attack large numbers of completely innocent persons and in general spread an atmosphere of unwarranted distrust.

Except for the readiness in quick anger to deal summarily with sources of frustration, and hence to demand total victory over international Communism, the new right movements seem to lack this element of identification. Hence they are more regressive than McCarthy, in that they apparently seek, without qualification, to preserve the socially "infantile" state of everything "little." Their influence is even more drastically "deflationary" than the McCarthyite, in the constriction of commitments to the more highly organized sectors of society. This includes the extensive functions of government, but it also goes beyond them. Even the large corporation is in some sense felt to be vaguely "Socialistic," in that it interferes with the complete independence of the small man.

In this sense, the Birchers are the extreme wing of a much more ramified complex. The central focus of it seems to be the political rear-guard action (and its roots in the social structure) of the rural and small-town elements in the society, which have been able to "dig in," above all through legislative refusal to redistrict, first for the House of Representatives, but even more for the state legislature. In this connection, the question of "equal protection of the laws" through fair representation is slowly building up to becoming the most important internal political question of the society, a question that crosscuts many of the older bases of political differentiation and segmentation, most conspicuously, of course, underlying the coalition of Republicans and Southern Democrats.[4]

But one must see, too, that "individualism" is by no means confined to a complex of what I have here called "regressive" attitudes. There is an opposite group whose orientation, though "ideological," presents a very different case from that of the reactionary individualists. These are the intellectuals whom Winston White has called the Moralizers.[5] Regarding themselves as liberals, or left of center, they deplore many of the features of contemporary society, in particular what they hold to be the increasing pressures to "conformity," but they also stress the importance of the responsibility of the individual, not for "self-help," but for the welfare of the society, and hence for the collective interest of the nation as a whole. They stand in an obverse relation to the Birchers, but in a quite different direction from that of the McCarthyites. The element of acceptance of the developing social order, of "identification" with it, as described above, is stronger for them than for the McCarthyites. It does not, however, involve a coerced loyalty, but the opposite—a free acceptance of individual responsibility to the point of often being utopian about the necessity for formal organization and for authority that can implement important collective goals. Whereas the Birchers are drastically "deflationary" with respect to any sort of social responsibility, the Moralizers are "inflationary," in that they seem to hold that full commitment of the individual is enough—the practical organization and know-how are secondary.

But there is a third, and indeed, a very different type of individualism that is focal to the whole American pattern of values and attitudes—the strong emphasis on freedom and responsibility of the individual *within* a framework of both normative order and collective organization. This is what on occasion I have called "institutionalized individualism," using Durkheim's famous analysis of the relation between contractual agreements and the "non-contractual" institutional elements of contract as a prototype.[6] In this point of view, we can see society as providing for more complex, more technical, and more "professional" jobs; allowing for more variety of choices, in occupation and in culture, and providing greater diversity within the framework of organization. It is my strong conviction that the main trend of development in the society is individualistic in *this* sense.[7]

The regressive individualism of which the Birchers are the extreme examples is very different from this. Regressive individualism resists the processes of institutional change by virtue of which a more complex and hence more effective division of labor or differentiation has been developing, by which there has developed an increasingly ramified system of pluralistic collective solidarities and enterprises (including, of course, the enterprises of government but by no means confined to them),[8] and, finally, by which there has been developing a more generalized and elaborated system of norms, especially at the level of law, through which the inevitably complex relations of such a society come to be regulated. Seen in this perspective, the Birchers are the generic type of the true "reactionary." The phrase that has already been rather widely applied to them and to groups like them—that they want to "repeal the twientieth century"— seems to sum them up very well indeed.

NOTES

[1] For emphasizing this point, as well as considerable contribution to the general pattern of analysis outlined here, I am indebted to Dr. Winston White.

[2] A paradigmatic case of this frontier mentality is described in E. Z. Vogt, Jr., *Modern Homesteaders* (Harvard University Press), a study of "Texan" migrants into a semi-arid section of New Mexico.

[3] Another interesting manifestation of this complex is the part it plays in the opposition to the fluoridation of water supplies.

[4] The decision of the Supreme Court to restrict the legislatures' freedom to avoid redistricting may prove to be a highly important factor in this situation.

[5] *Beyond Conformity* (Free Press, 1961).

[6] Cf. Emile Durkheim, *The Division of Labor in Society,* Bk. I, Ch. 7.

[7] Perhaps the fullest statement of the sense in which this is the case yet published is Parsons and White, "The Link Between Character and Society," in Lipset and Lowenthal, editors, *Culture and Social Character* (Free Press, 1961).

[8] Durkheim was one of the few to see clearly that the "division of labor" in the private sector must proceed concomitantly with increasing elaboration of the functions of government. Cf. Durkheim, *op. cit.*

27. BLACK NATIONALISM

Gary T. Marx

The white man is by nature a devil and must be destroyed. The black man will inherit the earth; he will resume control, taking back the position he held centuries ago when the white devil was crawling around the caves of Europe on all fours.

—Malcolm X

The Big Niggers as a class don't think. . . . Once a Negro reaches college level he is no good for anybody.

—Black nationalist leader

The Muslims purport to be separationists, but time and again they will lament the failing of integration. Theoretically, as separationists they should be pleased when integration doesn't work.

—W. Haywood Burns

In the late 1950s the mass media began to detect the presence of a new militant force in the Negro community. Almost overnight much concern was expressed over what was heralded as a rising tide of black nationalism. The most prominent nationalist group was the Muslims. Soon millions of Americans knew of Elijah Muhammad, and heard the Muslim program outlined in potent rhetoric by Malcolm X. The significance of the Muslims was thought to be the mood they exemplified rather than their membership, which has remained quite small. Still, signs of rising black nationalism aroused apprehension on the part of many. It seemed a clear portent of a developing impatience and anger.

Any general assessment of the mood of the Negro community and of the current status of racial protest requires an analysis of black nationalism. While much has been written on this subject, very few trustworthy facts are known. Is there considerable support for nationalistic programs and sentiments among Negroes generally, or is support pretty much limited to actual members of nationalist organizations such as the Muslims?

First of all, what does the term black nationalism mean? Broadly speaking, it implies pride in being black—a positive regard for Afro-American origins, history, and culture. One finds much of this spirit in the recent writings of Negro intellectuals. As Lerone Bennett has written: "The mood is, in essence, an affirmation of Negro experience and Negro values. It is not necessarily a rejection of white-ness, but it is quite definitely an acceptance of blackness. . . ." [1] This aspect of black nationalism, coupled with an emphasis on the development of Negro institutions and programs of self-help, is part of the meaning many attach to the concept of black power.

But beyond this general sort of nationalism, or racial pride, lies a more

SOURCE: Gary T. Marx, *Protest and Prejudice* (New York: Harper & Row, 1967), pp. 106–125; revised, with a new postscript, 1969. Copyright © 1967 and postscript © 1969 by Anti-Defamation League of B'Nai Brith. Reprinted by permission of Harper & Row, Publishers.

431

extreme variety built of notions of racial superiority and separatism which, in the case of the Muslims, are grafted onto a radical eschatology. Indeed, the Muslims exemplify the link between present-day black nationalism and the earlier tradition of messianic cult movements among Negroes. The Muslims were one such movement for some decades before the emergence of the civil rights movement gave them new relevance and direction. It is this more radical and racist variety of black nationalism that we shall investigate in this paper. Primary attention will be given to support for the Black Muslims since at the time of our study they were the dominant nationalist group.

INDEX OF SUPPORT FOR BLACK NATIONALISM [2]

In building a measure of support for the Muslims, two issues from their platform (also supported by many other nationalist groups) were used: refusal to fight for the United States in the event of a war, and giving black Americans their own country. The index also included two questions which gave respondents the chance to single out the Muslims as the group doing the most to help Negroes, and Malcolm X, a leading black nationalist spokesman in 1964, as the individual doing the most to help. For each black nationalist response a score of one was given; scores thus ranged from zero to four.

The index is a quite permissive criterion of black nationalist support when contrasted with the Black Muslims' program and occasional statements by their spokesman. Thus it provides an absolutely maximum estimate of Muslim support, registering even the "softest" or mildest pro-Muslim sentiment. For example, to be counted in this study as sympathetic to black nationalism, one need not believe that the white man is a devil in the theological sense or that Negroes are genetically superior to whites or are God's chosen race.

The data in Table 1 show that reports of a "rising tide" of black nationalism,

TABLE 1. SUPPORT FOR BLACK NATIONALISM BY REGION

Score on Index of Support for Black Nationalism	Metro	N.Y.	Chic.	Atl.	Birm.	Total
0	75%	71%	65%	69%	73%	72%
1	21	21	28	28	26	24
2	3	4	6	3	1	3
3	0.0062	3	0	0	0	0.55
4	0	1	1	0	0	0.27
Total	100%	100%	100%	100%	100%	100%
Number	(481)	(174)	(130)	(194)	(199)	1,093[a]

[a] Metro refers to a representative sample of Negroes in non-Southern metropolitan areas of the U.S. Those interviews from the metopolitan area sample which occurred in New York [44 cases] and in Chicago [54 cases] have been reported in both the metropolitan sample and the New York and Chicago samples. Hence the total number reported in this column is less than the total number of respondents for the samples shown separately.

at least in late 1964, were widely misleading; strong and consistent support for the Muslims was at best an infinitesimal ripple in the Negro community. In the summer of 1964, only three persons out of nearly 1,100 interviewed gave a pronationalist response on all four questions. Indeed, less than 1 per cent would accept three of these statements. In fact, less than 4 per cent of the combined sample give a pronationalist answer to two of the four. Thus, 96 per cent of the Negroes sampled rejected all four. Thus, even by this relatively loose definition of black nationalism, only one-third of 1 per cent of our respondents offered strong and consistent support for the Muslims, and only 4 per cent indicated moderate support.[3]

Muslim national headquarters is in Chicago, and according to Malcolm X, New York City is where they have the most members. Table 1 shows that sympathy for black nationalism is a bit higher in Chicago and New York than elsewhere. However, even in these two cities, more than nine out of ten Negroes showed little or no sympathy.

This relative lack of support is consistent with the very small number of black people who have become active members of the Nation of Islam. For example, Essien-Udom states that "the appeal of black nationalism is very special and is not actively supported by the Negro masses," and, in referring to the Muslims as a vocal but insignificant minority, he suggests that active membership is between 5,000 and 15,000.[4] Most observers of the Muslims have seen fit to label them as "secessionist," seeing the more conventional civil rights groups as "pluralistic" or "assimilationist." It is true that much of the Muslim rhetoric is based on vague talk of some "land of our own" and "three, four, or more states." However, relative to the action taken earlier by other secessionist groups such as Garvey's UNIA (Universal Negro Improvement Association) or the Peace Movement of Ethiopia, the Muslims seem to have actually concentrated little effort in this direction. The building of a $20 million center in Chicago, and their investments in the rest of the country, seem to contradict the expectation that they soon hope to have a land of their own. The secessionist emphasis is also somewhat contrary to Muslim leader Elijah Muhammad's statement of "What the Muslims Want." [5] "We want equality of opportunity. We want equal membership in society."

Given these facts, and the Muslim's high degree of racial concern it is not surprising that, in spite of the separatist theme, the black nationalist sympathizers in our sample are at least as high and even higher than others in their concern over integration and in their opposition to discrimination. For example, 56 per cent of this group (those with scores of two, three, or four on the index) [6] felt that the government was pushing integration too slowly, while only 32 and 36 per cent of those with scores of zero or one felt this way (Table 2). Almost nine out of ten of those sympathetic to black nationalism felt that Negroes and whites should go to the same schools; almost eight out of ten, that a restaurant owner should not be allowed to discriminate; and six out of ten, that discrimination in the sale of property should not be permitted. For each of these three discrimination items, the percentage giving the antidiscrimination response was higher or about the same as the percentage giving such a response among those with scores of zero or one.

TABLE 2. CONCERN OVER INTEGRATION BY INDEX OF SUPPORT FOR BLACK NATIONALISM

	Index of Support for Black Nationalism		
	Unsympathetic		Sympathetic
	0	1	(2,3,4,)
Per cent thinking that government is pushing integration too slowly	32	36	56
Per cent thinking white and Negro children should go to the same schools	92	87	86
Per cent disagreeing that a restaurant owner should not have to serve Negroes if he doesn't want to	79	74	77
Per cent disagreeing that an owner of property should not have to sell to Negroes if he doesn't want to	48	47	63
Per cent scored as militant on Index of Conventional Militancy	27	23	44
Number	(788)	(262)	(43)

As a result of this pattern it is not surprising that black nationalist supporters score relatively high on the Index of Conventional Militancy; [7] 44 per cent of this group scored as militant, as against only 23 and 27 per cent of those with scores of one and zero respectively (Table 2).

In spite of the separatist rhetoric of the Muslims, black Nationalist sympathizers in our sample are fairly strong in their opposition to discrimination and concern over integration. This finding does not invalidate our measure.[8] Rather, it suggests that a concern over integration (at least in principle) and support for black nationalism can easily exist together. In fact, for many of our black nationalist sympathizers, their continued frustration, resulting from a deep concern over integration and the lack of radical changes in the Negro's position within American society, may well be the factor that led them to accept black nationalist ideology. Malcolm X himself is reported to have said that what the Muslims really want is equality now, but that they are driven to separatism because their aims are frustrated.[9]

A DESCRIPTIVE PORTRAIT

Groups with different demographic, social, and psychological characteristics differ from each other with respect to the proportion who are militant. Seeing that people born outside the deep South are higher in militancy than people born there suggests that there is something about where one is born that is causally related to militancy. However, in the case of support for the Muslims, the smaller number of sympathizers makes such explanatory analysis much more difficult. Extensive explanatory analysis of Muslim support must be left to a sample drawn from a special universe. The same thing is true when attempting to analyze support for groups such as the Birch Society or the Ku Klux Klan. In a nationally representative sample of ordinary size, too few such supporters would be found. However, the number of black nationalist sympathizers was adequate for a simple descriptive analysis. Descriptive analysis simply means presenting a picture of the black nationalists by showing how they differ from other respondents in a variety of respects. In an explanatory analysis one asks, for example, whether the old and young differ in the extent to which they support black nationalism. In a descriptive analysis, one reverses the question and asks whether black nationalist sympathizers are generally older or younger than nonsympathizers.

The remaining part of this paper will be concerned with how black nationalist sympathizers differ from nonsympathizers. By nonsympathizers is meant that 96 per cent of the sample who rejected three or all four of the index items. Involving as it does almost the entire sample, this is quite a varied group, and one can obtain a much clearer picture by further classifying those not in sympathy according to their position on the Index of Conventional Militancy. Thus, we shall compare black nationalist supporters with persons who scored as militant or conservative. Simply to clarify the discussion, persons scored as moderates on civil rights are excluded from the data. Such persons invariably fell between the militants and the conservatives in the comparisons that follow.

Proceeding in this fashion, we shall compare black nationalist sympathizers with militants and conservatives. Two general comparisons are of central interest. First of all, how do militants and black nationalists differ from conservatives? The first two groups are similar in the sense that they are concerned about contemporary protest, while the third has remained apathetic. Secondly, how do militants differ from nationalists, since the former have retained their commitment to the structure and values of American society, while in many cases the latter have not?

Our descriptive portrait will begin with some questions on civil rights, and then turn to demographic, social, and psychological characteristics.

Some Differences and Similarities Regarding Civil Rights Issues

The Muslims have been critical of the civil rights movement. They have accused it of being a trick, and have called demonstrations ineffective and directed at what they perceive to be rather trivial ends (sitting next to the white man at a lunch counter when they should be more concerned with owning the establishment instead). They state that only token changes have occurred and that in fact no others can occur until Negroes and whites are completely separated. Consequently, it is not surprising that the black nationalist sympathizers in the sample rate the effectiveness of civil rights demonstrations lower than do militants. For example, as seen in Table 3, only 40 per cent, as compared with 67 per cent of the militants, felt that civil rights demonstrations had "helped a great deal." The conservatives, a disproportionate number of whom are older and low in social status and, hence, have had less direct benefit from demonstrations, were only slightly more likely to say that demonstrations had "helped a great deal" than were the black nationalist supporters.

For the black nationalists, this evaluation of the worth of demonstrations may be seen as just one strand of a more general pessimism about the situation of black people in American society. This is not true of the conservatives. For example, a full 40 per cent of the black nationalist supporters felt that things in this country were getting worse for Negroes, while only 6 per cent of the militants and 13 per cent of the conservatives felt this way. And in response to a question about whether Negroes were better off in the North or the South,

TABLE 3. OUTLOOK FOR CIVIL RIGHTS: BLACK NATIONALIST SYMPATHIZERS COMPARED WITH MILITANTS AND CONSERVATIVES

Per Cent Agreeing	Black Nationalist Sympathizers	Militants	Conservatives
Civil rights demonstrations helped a great deal	40%	67%	42%
Things getting worse for Negroes in this country	40	6	13
Situation of Negroes is the same in North and South	53	27	32
The day will come when whites will accept Negroes	63	75	75
Negroes some day are going to rise to the leadership of the world	80	67	66
Negroes are God's chosen people today	24	5	5
Number	(43)[a]	(266)[a]	(220)[a]

[a] All subsequent tables have approximately the same number of respondents unless the contrary is indicated.

more than half of the black nationalist supporters responded "the same" while about one-third of the conservatives and one-fourth of the militants gave this essentially negative response. Nationalists tend to refuse to distinguish matters of degree in the Negro's condition—it's all bad. They were also slightly less likely to agree that "the day will come when Negroes will be fully accepted by whites" than were militants and conservatives.

However, they were more likely to agree with the statement "Negroes are someday going to rise to the leadership of the world." Eight out of ten nationalists agreed with this statement. This kind of optimism is consistent with Muslim ideology in which Allah has determined that the black man is "by nature divine" and is destined to rule, now that the ruling time allotted to whites is almost up.[10] It can also be seen that almost one in four of the black nationalist sympathizers felt that today Negroes were God's chosen people as against one in twenty of the other groups.

Police and Violence

A frequent complaint of the black nationalists is police brutality. The Black Muslims seem to have been subjected to particularly harsh treatment at the hands of the police, as an attack on the Los Angeles mosque indicated. Reflecting this is the finding that seven out of ten of the black nationalist sympathizers in our sample felt that police treated Negroes badly, while for the conservatives less than three in ten gave this response (Table 4).

TABLE 4. ATTITUDES OF BLACK NATIONALIST SYMPATHIZERS, MILITANTS, AND CONSERVATIVES TOWARD POLICE, RIOTS, AND VIOLENCE [a]

	Black Nationalist Sympathizers	Militants	Conservatives
Per cent thinking police treat Negroes badly	72%	53%	28%
Number	(36)	(239)	(194)
Per cent thinking riots do some good	72	48	48
Number	(37)	(258)	(193)
Per cent disagreeing violence will never help Negroes	49	40	24
Number	(39)	(256)	(204)
Per cent high on acceptance of violence	39	24	16
Number	(36)	(248)	(184)

[a] Because for these questions a "don't know" response was more likely to represent a desire not to respond rather than a genuine lack of opinion, the data in these tables omit the "don't knows."

While the Muslims talk in apocalyptic language about the coming Armageddon and the need for self-defense in their utterances to the white community, they do not go nearly as far as the leader of a New York-based black nationalist group who during the Harlem riots screamed for the "blood to flow" and was quoted as saying, "I'm preaching violence . . . the Negroes must be free and the state must be completely and totally smashed. We'll have to kill a lot of cops and judges. No revolution was ever won by peaceful means, so we must fight and then set up a state of our own choosing." Still, the Muslim attitude toward riots and violence at the time of the study was very different from that of the conventional civil rights groups. While the Muslims have been unduly labeled as a violent group, an undercurrent of support for riots and lack of faith in non-violence can easily be detected. More than seven out of ten of those receptive to the Muslim appeal felt that riots do some good, while less than one-half of the militants and conservatives felt this way. Similarly, about half the nationalists denied that "violence will never help Negroes get equal rights." This figure is 40 per cent for militants and only 24 per cent for conservatives. Although the acceptance of violence is relatively high among black nationalist sympathizers, even among this group about half felt that violence would not help, and about three in ten agreed that no good can ever come from riots. When these two questions are combined into a measure of acceptance of violence, only about four out of ten nationalists scored as high on the acceptance of violence in contrast to 24 per cent of militants and 16 per cent of conservatives. That many black nationalist sympathizers do not seem to be high in the acceptance of violence is consistent with the official teachings of the Muslims.[11] In urging his followers to respect law and order the leader of the Muslims states: "Obey those in authority" and "be yourself . . . a righteous Muslim. Follow the Golden Rule. . . . Be polite, courteous and respectful so that you may inspire respect from the police officers." [12]

Black nationalists are often extremely critical of white merchants in Negro ghettoes. They claim these merchants treat Negroes with disrespect, sell inferior goods at quality prices, and, in addition, often employ Negroes only in menial positions at substandard wages. Black nationalist supporters were much more critical of the way white store owners treated Negroes than were nonsupporters of nationalism. Among the former, 44 per cent said that almost all white store owners take advantage of Negroes. This figure drops to only 15 per cent among militants and conservatives.

Criticism of white businessmen is usually matched by a plea for purchasing from black businessmen who don't "put shellac on spoiled meat to make it look fresh" and who "pay a living wage." The Muslims put great emphasis on the development of Negro-owned businesses and themselves own a number of enterprises. This agitation does not seem to have had an important effect on consumer behavior. The percentage of black nationalist sympathizers who report they shop at none or only a few white-owned stores (14) is about the same as the percentage of militants (10) and conservatives (17) who report this. Regardless of what Negroes would like to do, there are relatively few Negro-owned stores in many areas, and those that do exist are not diverse enough to cover all consumer needs, making it almost impossible not to shop at some white-owned stores. This "entrapment" by the white merchant of those already hostile may operate to intensify black nationalist feelings.

Exposure to Protest Values

With regard to a number of variables presumably related to exposure to values legitimizing protest, black nationalist sympathizers and militants are quite similar and differ considerably from conservatives. About seven out of ten of the former two groups were under 44 years of age, as against less than half of the conservatives. A majority of both black nationalist supporters and militants were men, whereas two out of three conservatives were women. Conservatives were also much more likely than the others to have been raised in the deep South and in a rural area. When these factors are observed together in the Index of Exposure to Values Legitimizing Protest, 45 per cent of the black nationalist sympathizers and 46 per cent of the militants scored as high, while only 15 per cent of the conservatives did (Table 5). Thus, regardless of the type of protest, those who show civil rights concern are more likely to be men, younger, and raised in big cities outside the deep South. These four factors may

TABLE 5. DEMOGRAPHIC CHARACTERISTICS OF BLACK NATIONALIST SYMPATHIZERS, MILITANTS, AND CONSERVATIVES

Per Cent Affirmative	Black Nationalist Sympathizers	Militants	Conservatives
Men	72%	54%	31%
Under 44	70	67	45
Raised in a big city	33	40	19
Raised in deep South	27	36	57
High on Index of Exposure to Values Legitimizing Protest	45	46	15

be seen as predisposing an individual to be in a milieu (either temporal, social, or geographical) in which exposure to values legitimizing protest is more likely to occur.

The literature suggests that new immigrants to the city, especially from Southern rural areas, are especially attracted to black nationalism because of their dislocation and the normal tensions of urban slum living [13] However, black nationalist supporters in our sample were less likely to come from rural areas than were conservatives. They were also the least likely to have migrated from the South. Among those now living in the North, 46 per cent of the black nationalist sympathizers had moved from the South as against 65 per cent of the conservatives and 55 per cent of the militants. However, black nationalist sympathizers have been more geographically mobile than the rest of the sample. Thirty per cent of the nationalist sympathizers reported that they had lived in their present city less than six years, as against only 11 per cent of the conservatives and 15 per cent of the militants. Although black nationalist supporters were least likely to have come from the South or from rural areas, they were most likely to have come from some place else recently. For them the tension and strain associated with moving from the South to the North, from a rural area to an urban one, or between urban areas, may facilitate receptiveness to the nationalist appeal.

An additional type of strain, not unrelated to the problems of migration, is the disparity between ambitions and the opportunity for their actualization. Merton suggested that an imbalance between means and ends could lead to various types of deviant behavior, and numerous analysts have pointed out that the frustration of rising expectations is an important impetus for radical social change.[14] In the case of Negroes this strain may be particularly acute. Living in the world's most affluent society and socialized to have the same success values as whites, they are nevertheless largely denied the opportunity for actualizing these values because of discrimination and its bastard offspring, the lack of acquired skills. Our study included two questions which roughly measure the fit between ambition and opportunity. Respondents were asked first, "How important is it to you to get a promotion on your job?" and then, "Would you say your chances of promotion in the next few years are excellent, good, fair, or poor?" Compared to others, black nationalist sympathizers were more likely to evidence frustration. Of this group, 50 per cent reported that a promotion was important to them yet they had a poor or only a fair chance of getting one, while for conservatives this figure drops to 25 per cent and for militants, to 34 per cent (Table 6).

This measure was computed only for those for whom the question of a promotion was relevant, those presently employed. Additional evidence of the greater strains experienced by black nationalists may be seen in the fact that one in four of this group was unemployed or had ben laid off at the time of the interview, while this was the case for only one in ten of the militants and conservatives.

TABLE 6. JOB OPPORTUNITIES OF BLACK NATIONALIST SYMPATHIZERS, MILITANTS, AND CONSERVATIVES

	Black Nationalist Sympathizers	Militants	Conservatives
Per cent for whom a promotion is important yet who report having a poor or only a fair chance to obtain one (Only among those employed)	50%	34%	25%
Number	(18)	(141)	(72)
Per cent unemployed	26%	9%	10%

Social Position

It has been seen that Muslim sympathizers and militants are similar in characteristics which are presumably related to exposure to protest values and that both differ greatly from conservatives in these ways. However, black nationalist supporters are markedly different from militants in social position. Indeed, pronationalists are much more like conservatives than militants in this respect. Analysis showed that a majority of nationalists and conservatives earned less than $4,000 a year while fewer than three in ten of the militants earned this little. They were also somewhat more likely to be in blue-collar occupations than militants. In addition, while 52 per cent of the conservatives and 35 per cent of the black nationalist sympathizers had no more than a grammar school education, this was true for only 22 per cent of the militants. When these factors are combined into an Index of Social Class, 58 per cent of the conservatives and 40 per cent of the black nationalist sympathizers, as opposed to only 22 per cent of the militants, scored as lower class. At the other extreme, 29 per cent of the militants scored as upper class as contrasted with only 7 and 6 per cent of black nationalist supporters and conservatives (Table 7).

The relation of black nationalism to social class noted here is consistent with the reports of contemporary observers about the lower class base of such movements.[15] The failure of the Garvey movement and the Communist Party to gain appreciable support from middle-class Negroes also attests to this group's general rejection of the more radical solutions to the plight of the black man. However, the failure of black nationalism to attract more than a minute pro-

TABLE 7. SOCIAL POSITION OF BLACK NATIONALIST SYMPATHIZERS, MILITANTS, AND CONSERVATIVES

Social Class	Black Nationalist Sympathizers	Militants	Conservatives
Lower	40%	22%	58%
Middle	53	49	36
Upper	7	29	6
Total	100%	100%	100%

portion even of the most disadvantaged indicates the general rejection of radical solutions in the Negro community at the time of the study.

Social Participation

Those who support black nationalism and apathetic conservatives are again similar and differ from militants in their "symbolic" and "actual" social participation. About half of both black nationalist sympathizers and conservatives report they do not read either Negro magazines or general circulation magazines. Among militants, more than four out of five report reading Negro magazines; and about three out of four, general magazines. The pattern for reading Negro and general newspapers is the same. However, in spite of their relative isolation from ordinary communications channels, more than one in four of the black nationalist sympathizers report reading the newspaper of the Nation of Islam, *Muhammad Speaks,* while almost none of the other two groups report reading this paper.

In considering actual participation, seven out of ten of both black nationalists and conservatives report belonging to no organizations, while this is true of only about half of the militants. Black nationalist supporters and conservatives were also similar in the proportion who did not vote in 1960 and the percentage socializing with friends infrequently; on each count, militants were much higher in participation.[16]

When the factors observed here are combined into the Index of Social Participation, more than four out of ten black nationalist sympathizers and conservatives score as very low in social participation compared to only 12 per cent of the militants (Table 8).

TABLE 8. SOCIAL PARTICIPATION OF BLACK NATIONALIST SYMPATHIZERS, MILITANTS, AND CONSERVATIVES

Index of Social Participation	Black Nationalist Sympathizers	Militants	Conservatives
Low	42%	12%	44%
Medium	28	31	34
High	30	57	22
Total	100%	100%	100%

Some Psychological Factors

Given the lower level of social participation and lower class position of both the black nationalist supporters and the conservatives, it is not surprising that on measures of intellectual sophistication these groups were found to be similar and scored much lower than militants (Table 9). For example, about one out of two scored as high on the F-scale items as against less than one in four of the militants.[17] With respect to knowledge about civil rights leaders, only 31 per cent and 23 per cent were able to identify four leaders, compared to 66 per cent of the militants. The pattern is comparable for the other items used in the Index of Intellectual Sophistication—the indexes of awareness of the role of social factors, knowledge of writers, and intellectual values. On this larger measure, almost four in ten of the black nationalists and five in ten of the conservatives but only one in ten of the militants were labeled unsophisticated (Table 9).

In considering the measure of morale, black nationalist supporters and conservatives are again similar and differ from the militants. About one in three

TABLE 9. SOME PSYCHOLOGICAL CHARACTERISTICS OF BLACK NATIONALIST SYMPATHIZERS, MILITANTS, AND CONSERVATIVES

Per Cent Reporting	Black Nationalist Sympathizers	Militants	Conservatives
High score on F scale (4,5)	53%	23%	46%
Correctly identify all four civil rights leaders	31	66	23
Correctly identify two or all three authors	25	44	13
High score on Index of Awareness of How Social Factors Shape Behavior (2,3)	23	57	31
High Score on Index of Acceptance of Intellectual Values (3)	14	29	7
Score as unsophisticated on Index of Intellectual Sophistication (0,1,2,)	39	11	54
Very low morale (0)	36	12	36
Unfavorable self-image (0)	14	6	26

of these groups were found to have a very low morale as against slightly more than one in nine of the militants.

With respect to self-image, only about one in twenty of the militants, as opposed to one in seven of the black nationalist supporters and one in four of the conservatives, had an unfavorable self-image.[18]

Religion

Religion seems to inhibit conventional militancy. It seems reasonable to suppose that commitment to Christianity would particularly inhibit black nationalism, especially the Muslim variety. The Black Muslims constitute a competing religion, and it would make as little sense to speak of a Christian Muslim as to speak of a Baptist Catholic. Muslims are especially aware of their direct contradiction of Christianity and refer to it as a "slave religion" and "white man's religion." The Bible they regard as a "poison book," [19] meant to trick Negroes into accepting their suffering.[20] That support of Christianity and of the Muslims tend to be mutually incompatible is borne out by the data. One out of two black nationalist sympathizers were scored as not at all religious or not very religious within the context of Christian religiosity, while only one out of five of the conservatives and one in three of the militants were scored this way.

In summary, this article has noted that only a small fraction of black Americans in 1964 offered even minimal support for black nationalism of the Muslim variety and, among those who did, many still favored integration, at least in principle.

The rejection of separatist black nationalism is consistent with the whole of the Negro's American experience which, however snail-like in pace, has been a gradual move toward inclusion. Since the enemies of the Negro have traditionally stressed separation, until recently opposition to separation had been a natural objective. In much the same way, Jews have been driven to the political left because the anti-Semites are on the right. Furthermore, as James Baldwin realized in his Parisian exile, whatever else the American Negro may be, he is fundamentally American.[21] Any movement for separation must fly in the face of the American experience and of the changes that have and are taking place.

While black nationalist sympathizers were much more pessimistic about their prospects in American society than were other Negroes, one of the interesting things our data revealed was the optimism of the vast majority of those surveyed. The belief that progress is being made and that a brighter future can come without radical change no doubt hinders receptiveness to the Muslim appeal, as well as to other radical solutions.

Another factor which would seem to hinder the Muslims is the black man's traditional attachment to Christianity. Even in its activist social gospel form, which may provide impetus to race protest, it still preaches nonviolence, the brotherhood of man, and love for one's enemy, and hence seems less likely to inspire support for the nationalists. So long as Christianity either of an otherworldly or a social gospel variety retains its hold over American black men, it will remain an obstacle to this kind of black nationalism.

A major theory of extremist behavior suggests that, in times of severe crisis, those isolated and in lower social positions, being unsophisticated and having little to lose but their degradation, are more likely than the privileged to support movements for radical social change that go outside the framework of established values. However, in normal times, the unsophisticated and alienated are disproportionately apathetic. Consistent with this theory, it was found that a relatively large segment of the more depressed and alienated part of the black community did not score as militant. However, we have now seen that those few who are sympathetic to black nationalism are relatively low in both social position and social participation.

Unless or until a major economic crisis or a series of important and sustained civil rights setbacks shakes the optimism of middle-class Negroes or the apathy of the Negro masses, Negroes will probably continue to be relatively unresponsive to the appeals of the black nationalists. And even then, increased feelings of despair and futility may be the predominant consequence. Such events might well increase acts of racial violence and increase feelings of hostility without this energy becoming channeled into an organized movement for social change. In the event of such an occurrence, however, it seems reasonable to conclude that black nationalists will be disproportionately drawn from the more deprived and isolated segments of the black community and will be predominantly younger males, raised in big cities outside the South.

Barring such catastrophes, the data clearly indicate a number of major impediments to black nationalist, and especially Muslim, aspirations. For the Muslims to gain any appreciable support they probably would have to surrender the eschatological and apocalyptic components of their ideology. They would have to cease to be a religion in order to become a mass movement. Furthermore, they would have to modify their antipathy toward the civil rights struggle, for American Negroes want in, not out. They might also need to ease the puritanical moral demands they impose on members. In short, they would have to become much more like a conventional civil rights organization, perhaps attracting support by being the most militant civil rights group. The movement which Malcolm X tried to get started after his break with the Muslims did in fact embody many of these changes.

POSTSCRIPT

The interviews on which the above study is based were conducted in late 1964. Since that time important changes have occurred on the civil rights scene: the deaths of Malcolm X and Martin Luther King, widespread civil disorders, and the emergence of the black power movement.

Increased awareness of, and frustration over, the massive obstacles to real integration and increased pride in blackness have resulted in important changes at the leadership level and among activists.

As the case of the Jews in Europe clearly indicates, the type of orientation dominant within an ethnic minority group at any one time is to an important extent dependent on the receptiveness of the dominant group. When the dominant group seems receptive, emphasis is placed on inclusion and assimilation. When the dominant group is not receptive, or its supposed receptiveness is illusory, the minority group may increasingly run inward and in a separatist direction.

Other periods in American history show Negro protest movements going toward or away from the dominant society depending on its receptiveness. For example, the hopes raised by the Civil War and World War I led to an initial emphasis on inclusion, yet the shattering of hope soon led to the predominance of separatist leaders such as Booker T. Washington and Marcus Garvey. There are further examples of Negro leaders such as Paul Cuffee and Martin Robinson

Delaney who, like many of today's black power leaders, began strongly favoring integration and then, overwhelmed by a sense of futility, turned to separatist positions.

For black power spokesmen the emphasis is increasingly put on equality, rather than integration, and on developing a strong black community, rather than on dispersing that community throughout the larger society.[22] The main issue is seen as poor schools, houses, and jobs, and not separate ones. The crucial goal then becomes obtaining equality in these areas, and not integration. This is felt to be politically more realistic as well as better for the black self-image.[23] It is ironic that traditional American ethnic pluralism which is conducive to (or at least not incompatible with) a degree of black self-development is also consistent with the white rejection of blacks.

The black power orientation elaborates themes traditionally present (such as nondiscriminatory treatment and equality pursued through organizing the economic and political power of the Negro community and the right of self-defense). It also draws upon black nationalist themes (such as a more explicit orientation toward working-class Negroes, rejection of the established Negro leadership, a strong concern with pride in blackness, an emphasis on developing the Negro community through self-help, a lack of faith in nonviolence and support for urban uprisings, and an angrier, more impatient, tone and style). Furthermore, it addresses itself to new problems and issues not traditionally the concern of civil rights groups. These have to do with pursuing the ethnic interests of black men rather than with questions of civil rights and discrimination per se.

Yet are these changes necessarily incompatible with traditional American pluralism, and has a comparable shift in mass attitudes also taken place? The answer to both questions would seem to be no.

The diverse organizations which operate under the rubric of black power have been unduly labeled as pro-violence and antiwhite. In a country that took its independence and its land in violence, with a strong frontier legacy, Negro talk of self-defense and arming demonstrators, and even veiled threats of future uprisings if change is not forthcoming, is hardly an American version of the Mau Mau. To argue for the strengthening of Negro institutions is not necessarily to be antiwhite, nor to support segregation. It would seem to be a necessary step for psychological, political, and economic independence and equality. This self-assertion is in no way inconsistent with the ethnic solidarity earlier demonstrated by groups such as the Irish, Italians, and Jews,[24] though clearly there is also the potential for violence, racism, and intellectual dishonesty.

In considering mass support for the more extreme kind of black nationalism, numerous studies carried out since 1964 show a high degree of consistency in their descriptive findings and confirm the data reported above.

The 1965 UCLA study of Watts and a 1966 national *Newsweek* survey reached conclusions similar to those reported earlier.[25] A national *Fortune* magazine survey carried out late in 1967 found 15 per cent rejecting integration as a goal for Negroes; it is significant and perhaps a suggestion of things to come, that among those under 25 years of age this figure is 9 per cent, while for those over 25 it drops to 2 per cent. Eighty-three per cent felt that Martin Luther

King "fights for what people want" while this figure for the Muslims dropped to 5 per cent.[26]

A six-city survey undertaken in 1967 for the Lemberg Center for the Study of Violence concludes that "while Negro dissatisfaction is real and intense, it has not driven most Negroes to an extremist approach." The study found overwhelming support for the more moderate civil rights organizations. Seven out of ten blacks questioned felt that the government of their city was doing "too little" to encourage racial integration, while less than one per cent felt it was doing too much.[27]

A 1967 study of black attitudes in Chicago finds 5 per cent thinking Negroes and whites should go to separate schools. Fifty-seven per cent chose Martin Luther King as "closest to what you really think about civil rights" while less than one per cent chose the Muslims.[28]

A 1967 study carried out by the Southern Regional Council on the attitudes of Negro high school youth in Atlanta reports 11 per cent agreeing "I am a strong believer in black power" and 12 per cent agreeing "the more Negroes are separated from whites the better." However only 31 per cent agreed "Black Americans should be proud to be fighting in Vietnam." Seventy-five per cent expressed approval of the NAACP, though for the Nation of Islam this figure drops to 11 per cent.[29]

A 1968 national CBS news poll reports 22 per cent in favor of black control of black communities and 17 per cent in favor of building whole new communities just for Negroes. Only 5 per cent of the blacks questioned felt it would be a good idea for Negroes to have a separate country. Ironically, black nationalists can find far greater support and resources for this position in the white community than in the black, as 33 per cent of the whites questioned felt this to be a good idea.[30]

A 1968 study of Miami Negroes by Philip Meyer, using a three-question index, found one person in 20 strongly supporting, and 6 out of 10 strongly rejecting, separatism. The few supporters included two kinds of person: radical pro-violence youth and passive apathetic older people resigned to separatism as a natural order.[31]

The most comprehensive study of racial attitudes yet undertaken, the 1968 fifteen-city survey carried out for the National Advisory Commission on Civil Disorders, reaches similar conclusions.[32] In a time period dominated by impassioned rhetoric and ever more articulate black demands for separation, it may seem surprising that less than one black in five believes stores in "A Negro neighborhood should be owned and run by Negroes," and even fewer believe schools with mostly Negro children should have Negro principals and mostly Negro teachers. One in twenty favors his child attending a mostly Negro school or a separate black nation (Table 10). Though when broken down by age young people again were somewhat more accepting than older. However, it is significant to note that there is relatively great support for a moderate black nationalist cultural emphasis. Thus more than four out of ten felt Negro school children should study an African language.

Dramatic shifts at the leadership level have not been accompanied by a massive change in black opinion. Although new issues have developed and attiudes toward old issues have shifted slightly, the dominant thrust of black mass opinion seems to have remained about the same.

This relative lack of support at a mass level offers no grounds for complacency. The magnitude of injustice, the intensity of concern felt by many, and the potential for social disruption and reaction cannot be measured by such quantitative means. Everyone's opinion does not count equally, and opinions can change.

Nor does the relative lack of mass support say anything about the significance of black radicalism in forcing change. Extreme demands up the ante and can make moderate black spokesmen seem positively attractive to those in power. Malcolm X stated of the "so-called Negro leaders": "They charge us [with] being extremists but if it was not for the extremists the white man would ignore the moderates."

Furthermore, lack of support is not the same thing as active opposition. Louis Lomax's words about the Muslims apply equally to newer forms of black radicalism. "In the end . . . the Negro masses neither join nor denounce the Black Muslims. They just sit home in the ghetto amid the heat, the roaches, the rats, the vice, the disgrace, and rue the fact that come daylight they must meet the man . . ." [33]

TABLE 10. PERCENTAGE OF NEGROES FAVORING SEPARATIST RESPONSE TO EACH OF TEN QUESTIONS

Believe stores in "a Negro neighborhood should be owned and run by Negroes"	18
Believe school with mostly Negro children should have Negro principal	14
Prefer to live in all Negro or mostly Negro neighborhood	13
Believe school with mostly Negro children should have mostly Negro teachers	10
Agree that "Negroes should have nothing to do with whites if they can help it"	9
Believe whites should be discouraged from taking part in civil rights organizations	8
Prefer own child to go to all or mostly Negro school	6
Believe close friendship beween Negroes and whites is impossible	6
Agree that "there should be a separate black nation here"	6
Prefer child to have only Negro friends, not white friends too	5

As presented in A. Campbell and H. Schuman, *Racial Attitudes in Fifteen American Cities*, Ann Arbor, Michigan, Survey Research Center, 1968, p. 16.

Whether this indifference will remain true in the future depends on many things, not the least of which is the extent to which this society can bridge the gap between its ideals and its practices. However, the continued failure to obtain meaningful integration or significant changes in the life situation of the average Negro may well relegate the findings reported here to a brief episode in a long historical struggle.

NOTES

[1] *Confrontation: Black and White* (Chicago: Johnson Publishing Company, 1965), p. 239.

[2] In the remaining parts of this paper, when the term black nationalism is used, it refers to the separatist variety manifested by the Muslims.

[3] It should be noted that difficulties of drawing a sample representative of unattached black males probably underestimates the degree of support for black nationalism.

[4] E. U. Essien-Udom, *Black Nationalism* (New York: Dell, 1962), pp. 349 and 84. This modest statement stands in marked contrast to the undocumented wild assertions made by journalists and often by social scientists, too, as to the widespread support the Muslims have in the black community.

[5] The ten statements of "What the Muslims Want" and twelve statements of "What the Muslims Believe" appear in each issue of the Muslim newspaper *Muhammad Speaks*.

[6] There are several reasons for considering those with scores of two or more as sympathetic to black nationalism. It offers at least a minimum number of cases to work with and permits some confidence in the statistical inferences to be made. It permits inclusion of those who may support the policies of the Black Muslims and Malcolm X but who did not necessarily single them out as doing the most to help Negroes. It permits inclusion of those few cases who may have responded to the explosive break of Malcolm X from the Muslims in late 1963 by supporting one but not the other. It also permits inclusion of those who may be generally sympathetic toward the Muslims but who disagree with their idea of a separate country for Negroes.

Internal analysis of the index shows that almost all of those with scores of two, three, and four felt that the United States would not be worth fighting for in the event of a war, but only about two in three felt that it would be a good idea to give Negroes their own country. One out of three chose the Muslims as the group doing the most to help Negroes, while one out of five chose Malcolm X as the individual doing the most to help.

[7] This is an index which attempted to capture some of the elements common to the more conventional civil rights groups in the summer of 1964. Built into the eight-item index are questions dealing with a number of dimensions of racial protest such as impatience over the speed of integration, opposition to discrimination in public facilities and the sale of property, perception of barriers to Negro advancement, support of civil rights demonstrations, and expressed willingness to take part in a demonstration. Those giving the militant response to five or more of the questions are considered militant, those giving such a response to three or four of the questions, moderate, and to less than three, conservative.

Most of the conservatives did not hold to well-thought-out points of view and might be said to be conservative by omission rather than commission. The comment of a midwestern housewife who failed to give any militant responses was typical: "I don't keep up with these things. My eyes are bad and I don't read much. I take care of my grandchildren, so I just don't keep up with what's going on." The conservatism of this group was not related to support for separatist black nationalism.

[8] Evidence of the external validity of the index may be seen in the fact that as scores increase from zero to four the percentage indicating disapproval of the Muslims decreases from 58 per cent to 0 per cent. The situation is similar for disapproval of Malcolm X. The percentage reading the Muslim newspaper, *Muhammad Speaks,* also increases with score on the index.

⁹ W. H. Burns, *Voices of Negro Protest in America* (New York: Oxford University Press, 1963), p. 80.

To the extent that the Muslims are driven to their "radical" proposals by the frustration of "respectable goals," they are clearly "extremists" of a very different nature from the KKK and the American Nazi party, with whom they are often wrongly compared. In a complete reversal, it is the partial realization of "respectable goals" (nondiscriminatory treatment and the integration of the Negro into the mainstream of American life) that drive these white extremists to their separatist positions. The Muslims also do not wish to deprive whites of their rights while the white extremists clearly wish to deprive Negroes of theirs.

¹⁰ This emphasis in Muslim ideology may help explain why a majority of the black nationalist sympathizers agreed that the day would come when whites would accept Negroes, in spite of their greater pessimism about the current situation of the black man within American society. One of the few Muslims in the sample, in agreeing that the day will come when Negroes will be accepted by whites, added, "If they (Negroes) have their own government." Malcolm X stated that "it is not the Negroes but the whites who are a race because they are racing with time."

¹¹ However, these questions have some limitations.

¹² Essien-Udom, *op. cit.*, p. 292.

¹³ *Ibid.*, p. 23; Burns, *op. cit.*, p. 65.

¹⁴ Robert Merton, *Social Theory and Social Structure* (New York: Free Press, 1962), pp. 131–160.

¹⁵ C. Eric Lincoln, *The Black Muslims in America* (Boston: Beacon Press, 1961), p. 22; Essien-Udom, *op. cit.*, pp. 32 and 201; Burns, *op. cit.*, p. 65.

¹⁶ In spite of their civil rights concern and racial awareness, one might predict that black nationalists would be relatively low in voting, in part because of their lower status and social isolation, in part because of a sense of futility in electing a white man or a middle-class Negro to office. In addition, until recently the Muslims have not shown much interest in politics and have generally refrained from voting. (Lincoln, *op. cit.*, p. 18; Essien-Udom, *op. cit.*, p. 312).

¹⁷ The *F* scale is considered here as a measure of breadth of perspective rather than of deep-lying authoritarian personality characteristics. However, one of the original intentions of the authoritarian personality studies was to document the existence of a fascist or authoritarian personality, which presumably was especially likely to be attracted to antidemocratic authoritarian social movements. The finding that a sizable percentage of black nationalist sympathizers are high on the *F* scale is consistent with this as with Essien-Udom's assertion that "many turn to the Nation of Islam because they feel a need for a strong leader and an important personality with whom to identify" (*op. cit.*, p. 110).

Unlike the participatory democracy found among other civil rights organizations in 1964 (where virtual anarchy occasionally marked the relationship between local groups and the national office), the Muslims are very tightly organized and "authority in the Nation of Islam on all matters of ideology, theology, and policy rests solely in the Messenger of Allah" (*ibid.*, p. 160).

¹⁸ In exploring group image among black nationalists, one finds opposing tendencies. On the one hand, one of the most significant aspects of black nationalism is its attempt to create a sense of pride and dignity in being black. For the Muslims, black is beautiful, and black men are God's chosen people. However, when one makes a distinction between the Negro potential and his current situation, a much more negative self-image emerges. Negroes who are as yet "unredeemed" are referred to as "dead" and severely criticized for their complacency. Of them, the Muslim leader states, "You cannot find any other people in the world whose morals are so low" (*ibid.*, p. 91).

[19] Although the Muslims are critical of the Bible, they frequently quote from it to support the veracity of their prophecies.

[20] Elijah Muhammad states: "No one after death has ever gone any place but where they were carried. There is no heaven or hell other than on earth for you and me, and Jesus was no exception. His body is still . . . in Palestine and will remain there" (Lincoln, *op. cit.,* p. 123).

It is interesting to note that although the black nationalists are strong in rejecting Christianity and its otherworldly emphasis, their heavy reliance on a deterministic Allah may nevertheless lead to political inactivity. Essien-Udom notes: "The attainment of black power is relegated to the intervention of Almighty Allah sometime in the future . . . Not unlike other religionists the Muslims too may wait for all eternity for the coming of the Messiah, the predicted apocalypse in 1970 notwithstanding" (*op. cit.,* pp. 313–314). Opposition to this policy of non-engagement was a factor in Malcolm X's breaking with the Muslims.

In order for religion to be socially relevant it must place heavy emphasis on the here and now and in addition involve the notion that men, as opposed or in addition to, a deterministic God, may play a crucial role in the structuring of human affairs.

[21] A recent remark of Baldwin's is also relevant in this context: "I remember coming home from school, you can guess how young I must have been, and my mother asked me if my teacher was colored or white, and I said she was a little bit colored and a little bit white . . . And as a mattter of fact I was right. That's part of the dilemma of being an American Negro; that one is a little bit colored and a little bit white, and not only in physical terms but in the head and in the heart" (James Baldwin in Kenneth Clark, ed., *The Negro Protest,* Boston: Beacon Press, 1963). Parenthetically, although few realize it, "white" Americans are also a little bit colored.

[22] For example, see S. Carmichael and C. Hamilton, *Black Power* (New York: Random House, 1967).

[23] It is argued that emphasis on the token integration that has occurred only served to focus attention away from the problems of millions still remaining in the ghetto. It has been suggested that those few Negro children in integrated Southern settings may have been psychically scared by having to face howling mobs and daily ostracism and humiliation from their fellow white students.

It is emphasized, and I think wrongly, that integration implies that there is nothing of worth within the black community. It is further suggested that integration must be a two-way street and will be meaningless until it is voluntarily initiated by whites. The white concerned with integration is welcomed to come live in Watts, yet few whites speaking the language of universal brotherhood have chosen this option.

For some the questioning of integration implies a broader critique of American society. Stokeley Carmichael states, "I've never seen myself fighting to get into a country that's bombing hell out of Vietnam or a country that sees money as its only raison d'etre. The fight of the civil rights movement is to get white people off our backs."

[24] For an extended discussion of these issues, see Gary T. Marx, *Protest and Prejudice,* pp. 205–213.

[25] Institute of Government and Public Affairs, UCLA, and *Newsweek,* August 22, 1966.

[26] *Fortune Magazine,* January, 1968.

[27] Roper Research Associates, "What to Do About Riots," *The Public Pulse,* October, 1967, No. 25.

[28] The Interuniversity Social Research Committee, *Militancy For and Against Civil Rights and Integration in Chicago: Summer 1967* (Chicago: Community and Family Study Center, University of Chicago, 1967).

[29] James E. Conyers and William J. Farmer, *Black Youth in a Southern Metropolis* (Atlanta: Southern Regional Council, 1968).

[30] *White and Negro Attitudes Toward Race-Related Issues and Activities* (Princeton, N.J.: Opinion Research Corporation, 1968).

[31] P. Meyer, J. Greene, G. Kennedy, *Miami Negroes: A Case Study in Depth* (Miami, Fla.: *Miami Herald,* 1968).

[32] A. Campbell and H. Schuman, *Racial Attitudes in Fifteen American Cities* (Ann Arbor, Michigan: Survey Research Center, 1968).

[33] Louis Lomax, *When the Word Is Given* (New York: New American Library, 1964), p. 67. Our data did indicate that, when an individual or organization was disapproved of, it was almost certain to be Malcolm X and the Black Muslims. Still, consistent with the above statement, about one-half of those questioned did not offer disapproval of either.

C. THE END OF IDEOLOGY?

28. THE END OF IDEOLOGY IN THE WEST

Daniel Bell

Men commit the error of not knowing when to limit their hopes.—Machiavelli

There have been few periods in history when man felt his world to be durable, suspended surely, as in Christian allegory, between chaos and heaven. In an Egyptian papyrus of more than four thousand years ago, one finds: ". . . impudence is rife . . . the country is spinning round and round like a potter's wheel . . . the masses are like timid sheep without a shepherd . . . one who yesterday was indigent is now wealthy and the sometime rich overwhelm him with adulation." The Hellenistic period as described by Gilbert Murray was one of a "failure of nerve"; there was "the rise of pessimism, a loss of self-confidence, of hope in this life and of faith in normal human effort." And the old scoundrel Talleyrand claimed that only those who lived before 1789 could have tasted life in all its sweetness.

This age, too, can add appropriate citations—made all the more wry and bitter by the long period of bright hope that preceded it—for the two decades between 1930 and 1950 have an intensity peculiar in written history: world-wide economic depression and sharp class struggles; the rise of fascism and racial imperialism in a country that had stood at an advanced stage of human culture; the tragic self-immolation of a revolutionary generation that had proclaimed the finer ideals of man; destructive war of a breadth and scale hitherto unknown; the bureaucratized murder of millions in concentration camps and death chambers.

For the radical intellectual who had articulated the revolutionary impulses of the past century and a half, all this has meant an end to chiliastic hopes, to millenarianism, to apocalyptic thinking—and to ideology. For ideology, which once was a road to action, has come to be a dead end.

Whatever its origins among the French *philosophes,* ideology as a way of translating ideas into action was given its sharpest phrasing by the left Hegelians, by Feuerbach and by Marx. For them, the function of philosophy was to be critical, to rid the present of the past. ("The tradition of all the dead generations weighs like a nightmare on the brain of the living," wrote Marx.) Feuerbach, the most radical of all the left Hegelians, called himself Luther II. Man would be free, he said, if we could demythologize religion. The history of all thought was a history of progressive disenchantment, and if finally, in Christianity, God had been transformed from a parochial diety to a universal abstraction, the

SOURCE: Daniel Bell, *The End of Ideology* (New York: The Free Press of Glencoe, 1960), pp. 369–375. © by The Free Press, a corporation, 1960. Reprinted by permission of The Macmillan Company.

function of criticism—using the radical tool of alienation, or self-estrangement —was to replace theology by anthropology, to substitute Man for God. Philosophy was to be directed at life, man was to be liberated from the "specter of abstractions" and extricated from the bind of the supernatural. Religion was capable only of creating "false consciousness." Philosophy would reveal "true consciousness." And by placing Man, rather than God, at the center of consciousness, Feuerbach sought to bring the "infinite into the finite."

If Feuerbach "descended into the world," Marx sought to transform it. And where Feuerbach proclaimed anthropology, Marx, reclaiming a root insight of Hegel, emphasized History and historical contexts. The world was not generic Man, but men; and of men, classes of men. Men differed because of their class position. And truths were class truths. All truths, thus, were masks, or partial truths, but the real truth was the revolutionary truth. And this real truth was rational.

Thus a dynamic was introduced into the analysis of ideology, and into the creation of a new ideology. By demythologizing religion, one recovered (from God and sin) the potential in man. By the unfolding of history, rationality was revealed. In the struggle of classes, true consciousness, rather than false consciousness, could be achieved. But if truth lay in action, one must act. The left Hegelians, said Marx, were only *littérateurs*. (For them a magazine was "practice.") For Marx, the only real action was in politics. But action, revolutionary action as Marx conceived it, was not mere social change. It was, in its way, the resumption of all the old millenarian, chiliastic ideas of the Anabaptists. It was, in its new vision, a new ideology.

Ideology is the conversion of ideas into social levers. Without irony, Max Lerner once entitled a book "Ideas Are Weapons." This is the language of ideology. It is more. It is the commitment to the consequences of ideas. When Vissarion Belinsky, the father of Russian criticism, first read Hegel and became convinced of the philosophical correctness of the formula "what is, is what ought to be," he became a supporter of the Russian autocracy. But when it was shown to him that Hegel's thought contained the contrary tendency, that dialectically the "is" evolves into a different form, he became a revolutionary overnight. "Belinsky's conversion," comments Rufus W. Mathewson, Jr., "illustrates an attitude toward ideas which is both passionate and myopic, which responds to them on the basis of their immediate relevances alone, and inevitably reduces them to tools."

What gives ideology its force is its passion. Abstract philosophical inquiry has always sought to eliminate passion, and the person, to rationalize all ideas. For the ideologue, truth arises in action, and meaning is given to experience by the "transforming moment." He comes alive not in contemplation, but in "the deed." One might say, in fact, that the most important, latent, function of ideology is to tap emotion. Other than religion (and war and nationalism), there have been few forms of channelizing emotional energy. Religion symbolized, drained away, dispersed emotional energy from the world onto the litany, the liturgy, the sacraments, the edifices, the arts. Ideology fuses these energies and channels them into politics.

But religion, at its most effective, was more. It was a way for people to cope with the problem of death. The fear of death—forceful and inevitable—and more, the fear of violent death, shatters the glittering, imposing, momentary dream of man's power. The fear of death, as Hobbes pointed out, is the source of conscience; the effort to avoid violent death is the source of law. When it was possible for people to believe, really believe, in heaven and hell, then some of the fear of death could be tempered or controlled; without such belief, there is only the total annihilation of the self.

It may well be that with the decline in religious *faith* in the last century and more, this fear of death as total annihilation, unconsciously expressed, has probably increased. One may hypothesize, in fact, that here is a cause of the breakthrough of the irrational, which is such a marked feature of the changed moral temper of our time. Fanaticism, violence, and cruelty are not, of course, unique in human history. But there was a time when such frenzies and mass emotions could be displaced, symbolized, drained away, and dispersed through religious devotion and practice. Now there is only this life, and the assertion of self becomes possible—for some even necessary—in the domination over others.* One can challenge death by emphasizing the omnipotence of a movement (as in the "inevitable" victory of communism), or overcome death (as did the "immortality" of Captain Ahab) by bending others to one's will. Both paths are taken, but politics, because it can institutionalize power, in the way that religion once did, becomes the ready avenue for domination. The modern effort to transform the world chiefly or solely through politics (as contrasted with the religious transformation of the self) has meant that all other institutional ways of mobilizing emotional energy would necessarily atrophy. In effect, sect and church became party and social movement.

A social movement can rouse people when it can do three things: simplify ideas, establish a claim to truth, and, in the union of the two, demand a commitment to action. Thus, not only does ideology transform ideas, it transforms people as well. The nineteenth-century ideologies, by emphasizing inevitability and by infusing passion into their followers, could compete with religion. By identifying inevitability with progress, they linked up with the positive values of science. But more important, these ideologies were linked, too, with the rising class of intellectuals, which was seeking to assert a place in society.

The differences between the intellectual and the scholar, without being invidious, are important to understand. The scholar has a bounded field of knowledge, a tradition, and seeks to find his place in it, adding to the accumulated, tested knowledge of the past as to a mosaic. The scholar, qua scholar, is less involved with his "self." The intellectual begins with *his* experience, *his* indi-

---

* The Marquis de Sade, who, more than any man, explored the limits of self-assertion, once wrote: "There is not a single man who doesn't want to be a despot when he is excited . . . he would like to be alone in the world . . . any sort of equality would destroy the despotism he enjoys then." De Sade proposed, therefore, to canalize these impulses into sexual activity by opening universal brothels which could serve to drain away these emotions. De Sade, it should be pointed out, was a bitter enemy of religion, but he understood well the latent function of religion in mobilizing emotions.

vidual perceptions of the world, *his* privileges and deprivations, and judges the world by these sensibilities. Since his own status is of high value, his judgments of the society reflect the treatment accorded him. In a business civilization, the intellectual felt that the wrong values were being honored, and rejected the society. Thus there was a "built-in" compulsion for the free-floating intellectual to become political. The ideologies, therefore, which emerged from the nineteenth century had the force of the intellectuals behind them. They embarked upon what William James called "the faith ladder," which in its vision of the future cannot distinguish possibilities from probabilities, and converts the latter into certainties.

Today, these ideologies are exhausted. The events behind this important sociological change are complex and varied. Such calamities as the Moscow Trials, the Nazi-Soviet pact, the concentration camps, the suppression of the Hungarian workers, form one chain; such social changes as the modification of capitalism, the rise of the Welfare State, another. In philosophy, one can trace the decline of simplistic, rationalistic beliefs and the emergence of new stoic-theological images of man, e.g. Freud, Tillich, Jaspers, etc. This is not to say that such ideologies as communism in France and Italy do not have a political weight, or a driving momentum from other sources. But out of all this history, one simple fact emerges: for the radical intelligentzia, the old ideologies have lost their "truth" and their power to persuade.

Few serious minds believe any longer that one can set down "blueprints" and through "social engineering" bring about a new utopia of social harmony. At the same time, the older "counter-beliefs" have lost their intellectual force as well. Few "classic" liberals insist that the State should play no role in the economy, and few serious conservatives, at least in England and on the Continent, believe that the Welfare State is "the road to serfdom." In the Western world, therefore, there is today a rough consensus among intellectuals on political issues: the acceptance of a Welfare State; the desirability of decentralized power; a system of mixed economy and of political pluralism. In that sense, too, the ideological age has ended.

And yet, the extraordinary fact is that while the old nineteenth-century ideologies and intellectual debates have become exhausted, the rising states of Asia and Africa are fashioning new ideologies with a different appeal for their own people. These are the ideologies of industrialization, modernization, Pan-Arabism, color, and nationalism. In the distinctive difference between the two kinds of ideologies lies the great political and social problems of the second half of the twentieth century. The ideologies of the nineteenth century were universalistic, humanistic, and fashioned by intellectuals. The mass ideologies of Asia and Africa are parochial, instrumental, and created by political leaders. The driving forces of the old ideologies were social equality and, in the largest sense, freedom. The impulsions of the new ideologies are economic development and national power.

And in this appeal, Russia and China have become models. The fascination these countries exert is no longer the old idea of the free society, but the new one of economic growth. And if this involves the wholesale coercion of the population and the rise of new elites to drive the people, the new repressions are justified on the ground that without such coercions economic advance cannot take place rapidly enough. And even for some of the liberals of the West, "economic development" has become a new ideology that washes away the memory of old disillusionments.

It is hard to quarrel with an appeal for rapid economic growth and modernization, and few can dispute the goal, as few could ever dispute an appeal for equality and freedom. But in this powerful surge—and its swiftness is amazing—any movement that instates such goals risks the sacrifice of the present generation for a future that may see only a new exploitation by a new elite. For the newly-risen countries, the debate is not over the merits of Communism—the content of that doctrine has long been forgotten by friends and foes alike. The question is an older one: whether new societies can grow by building democratic institutions and allowing people to make choices—and sacrifices—voluntarily, or whether the new elites, heady with power, will impose totalitarian means to transform their countries. Certainly in these traditional and old colonial societies where the masses are apathetic and easily manipulated, the answer lies with the intellectual classes and their conceptions of the future.

Thus one finds, at the end of the fifties, a disconcerting caesura. In the West, among the intellectuals, the old passions are spent. The new generation, with no meaningful memory of these old debates, and no secure tradition to build upon, finds itself seeking new purposes within a framework of political society that has rejected, intellectually speaking, the old apocalyptic and chialistic visions. In the search for a "cause," there is a deep, desperate, almost pathetic anger. The theme runs through a remarkable book, *Convictions*, by a dozen of the sharpest young Left Wing intellectuals in Britain. They cannot define the content of the "cause" they seek, but the yearning is clear. In the U.S. too there is a restless search for a new intellectual radicalism. Richard Chase, in his thoughtful assessment of American society, *The Democratic Vista*, insists that the greatness of nineteenth-century America for the rest of the world consisted in its radical vision of man (such a vision as Whitman's), and calls for a new radical criticism today. But the problem is that the old politico-economic radicalism (pre-occupied with such matters as the socialization of industry) has lost its meaning, while the stultifying aspects of contemporary culture (e.g., television) cannot be redressed in political terms. At the same time, American culture has almost completely accepted the avant-garde, particularly in art, and the older academic styles have been driven out completely. The irony, further, for those who seek "causes" is that the workers, whose grievances were once the driving energy for social change, are more satisfied with the society than the intellectuals. The workers have not achieved utopia, but their expectations were less than those of the intellectuals, and the gains correspondingly larger.

The young intellectual is unhappy because the "middle way" is for the middle-aged, not for him; it is without passion and is deadening. Ideology, which by its nature is an all-or-none affair, and temperamentally the thing he wants, is intellectually devitalized, and few issues can be formulated any more, intellectually, in ideological terms. The emotional energies—and needs—exist, and the question of how one mobilizes these energies is a difficult one. Politics offers little excitement. Some of the younger intellectuals have found an outlet in science or university pursuits, but often at the expense of narrowing their talent into mere technique; others have sought self-expression in the arts, but in the wasteland the lack of content has meant, too, the lack of the necessary tension that creates new forms and styles.

Whether the intellectuals in the West can find passions outside of politics is moot. Unfortunately, social reform does not have any unifying appeal, nor does it give a younger generation the outlet for "self-expression" and "self-definition" that it wants. The trajectory of enthusiasm has curved East, where, in the new ecstasies for economic utopia, the "future" is all that counts.

And yet, if the intellectual history of the past hundred years has any meaning—and lesson—it is to reassert Jefferson's wisdom (aimed at removing the dead hand of the past, but which can serve as a warning against the heavy hand of the future as well), that "the present belongs to the living." This is the wisdom that revolutionists, old and new, who are sensitive to the fate of their fellow men, rediscover in every generation. "I will never believe," says a protagonist in a poignant dialogue written by the gallant Polish philosopher Leszek Kolakowski, "that the moral and intellectual life of mankind follows the law of economics, that is by saving today we can have more tomorrow; that we should use lives now so that truth will triumph or that we should profit by crime to pave the way for nobility."

And these words, written during the Polish "thaw," when the intellectuals had asserted, from their experience with the "future," the claims of humanism, echo the protest of the Russian writer Alexander Herzen, who, in a dialogue a hundred years ago, reproached an earlier revolutionist who would sacrifice the present mankind for a promised tomorrow: "Do you truly wish to condemn all human beings alive today to the sad role of caryatids . . . supporting a floor for others some day to dance on? . . . This alone should serve as a warning to people: an end that is infinitely remote is not an end, but, if you like, a trap; an end must be nearer—it ought to be, at the very least, the labourer's wage or pleasure in the work done. Each age, each generation, each life has its own fullness. . . ."

29. SOCIAL CLEAVAGE AND PARTY AFFILIATION: GERMANY, GREAT BRITAIN, AND THE UNITED STATES [1]

Morris Janowitz and David R. Segal

Empirical research on the political sociology of the multiparty nations of western Europe has been pursued with great vigor and a sense of historical perspective in part because some of the major propositions of the leading theorists could be explored by means of a growing body of sample-survey data. One dominant theme has been to marshal evidence describing the decline of a clear-cut and sharply differentiated social-class basis of party affiliation, that is, the modulation of "class conflict" politics. With the emergence of advanced industrialism, the social basis of mass political behavior becomes more complex and more heterogeneous.[2] In this view, correspondingly, the content of politics has been transformed from an ideologically defined and diffuse struggle to a set of demands for concrete bargaining. Granting this political change in selected industrialized societies, the actual extent and process of the transformation remains to be determined, especially in terms of cross-national comparisons.

ALTERNATIVE MODELS

Two different models are central for dealing with these issues. The most widely publicized approach for analyzing the decline of class-conflict politics in western Europe (and its relative absence in the United States) is the notion of "middle majority" politics. Fundamentally, this orientation gives priority to changes in social stratification derived from economic growth and accordingly places lesser importance on the independent and autonomous roles of political institutions. Central importance is placed on economic growth and economic affluence, although the complexities of political change are acknowledged.[3] Particularly, changes in economic levels—that is, the rising standard of living—produce greater equality in the social structure, which in turn produces changes in political demands and a broadening of political citizenship. Socioeconomic position, and, more concretely, occupation, is taken as the crucial measure of social stratification. The social structure of a middle-majority society is seen as one in which the number of persons in the upper working class and the lower middle class exceed those in the end groups, the upper middle class and the lower working class. It is a society in which the line between working and middle class is not very distinct, and there is a fusion into the life style of the middle stratum.

In this approach, the social groups who still accept ideological or class-conflict politics are holdouts or residues, and the future decline of their political impact is explicitly asserted as the future growth of class-conflict politics once was. Thus,

SOURCE: *The American Journal of Sociology*, 72, Number 6 (May, 1967), pp. 601–618. Copyright 1967 by The University of Chicago. Reprinted by permission of The University of Chicago Press.

Lipset writes, "In the long run, however, the remaining bases of ideologically intrinsic politics will continue to decline due to the contradictions between reality and their definition of the situation, and because of the irrelevance of their call to action in terms of a situation which will no longer exist." [4] The politics of the "middle majority" implies, of course, not the end of party divisions, but a narrowing of party differences and a transformation in the political consequences of these divisions.

The alternative model is that of "consensus and cleavage." [5] Politics and political behavior are still seen as derived from the conflicts of social strata, but political affiliations are more than a by-product of social stratification. Political institutions and political leadership are more autonomous elements in the process of change. The social-stratification system is itself molded by political decisions and the action of political parties.

The "consensus and cleavage" approach postulates a more complicated pattern of social stratification, in which political conflict is manifested by new and more differentiated social groupings which reflect economic, professional, and bureaucratic interests. Likewise, religious, ethnic, and linguistic differences can persist or emerge as bases of political cleavage which include ideological elements. Advanced industrialization produces a changing stratification system which alters older forms of political conflict and provides the basis for newer forms. These new conflicts are more delimited in scope, but they have deep consequences on collective problem-solving, and they may be so aggregated as to produce pervasive strains. Because there are built-in limitations in the trend toward greater social equality, in this view what is crucial is not only the persistence of the social-structural basis of cleavages but also the capacity of the political institutions to adjust and to create the conditions for political consensus.

Moreover, in contrast to the middle-majority model the emphasis on strain places greater importance on the international context and on the impact of foreign affairs. For Western Europe, bargaining politics is an expression not only of changes in internal social structure but of the recent history of adjustment, after intense struggle, with the Soviet Union. The emerging phase of international relations is already producing new bases of internal cleavage in Western Europe, both as nationalistic orientations become more dominant and as neutralist sentiments protrude into domestical political debate. Thus, the "consensus and cleavage" model is not limited to an extrapolation of the elements of the recent past that have produced an increase in political bargaining. Instead it seeks to identify those changes in social structure, in political institutions, and in the international context that have the possibility of introducing new rigidities and new conflicts into the language of politics.

The difference between the middle-majority and the consensus-and-cleavage positions can be briefly summarized along one crucial dimension of political change in an advanced industrial society. The middle-majority outlook assumes that the social sources of rigid ideological orientation or of political extremism are residues or holdouts which, with additional economic expansion, will be incorporated into the political structure. The consensus-and-cleavage approach sees the sources of rigid ideological orientation and political extremism as also being the products of social change and political leadership. It is therefore oriented toward the detection of new sources of resistance to political integration.

These two approaches of political sociology do not exhaust the debate, although they encompass the basic issues investigated by those who make use of sample surveys. Traditional conceptions of social-class conflict, adapted to deal with new issues, still have currency in polemical political writing that makes use of sociological categories.[6] One derivative of these traditional class-conflict notions is applicable to sample-survey data. The argument runs that increased skill and technique in mass manipulation make it possible for the economic elites to pervert and inhibit the political expression of social-class interests. The processes of mass communications, which are particularly overlooked by the middle-majority model, need not be tied to social-class-conflict categories. These issues are still worthy of the most careful investigation, although contemporary survey data do not necessarily assist in the pursuit of this goal.[7] Obviously, our approach included traditional social-class-conflict variables, and it emerged that these variables were as relevant as any particular and delimited source of cleavage, although they hardly supplied the basis for an over-all interpretation of the processes of political change in industrialized societies.

SAMPLE-SURVEY DATA

Sample-survey data supplies a basis for exploring these models. But the investigator who seeks to make use of national sample surveys for the purposes of cross-national comparisons faces a pervasive dilemma. On the one hand he has the option of utilizing for secondary analysis a body of disparate and uncoordinated surveys which have at least the advantage that they were designed to take into acount the historical and institutional setting of each specific country. However, this approach presents extensive problems because of the lack of comparability in the measurement of key variables. More serious limitations operate to the extent that available surveys do not necessarily contain adequate coverage of similar or theoretically related topics so that systematic comparisons are difficult to make. The result is that the existing literature contains many insightful propositions but analysis is often discursive and incomplete.

On the other hand, individual investigators have sought to be both comparable and systematic by organizing a single unified research design and applying it to a number of nations. Such a strategy runs the risk of being criticized as "intellectual imperialism," namely, projecting the political assumptions and definitions of one nation onto another. In this approach there is a danger of searching for uniform variables and failing to develop a survey instrument appropriate for the historical and institutional setting of each country.

This paper is a report of an effort to make national sample-survey materials more relevant for cross-national analysis and to reduce the dilemmas of working in this field. The approach was applied to existing bodies of data, but it could equally be used in planning and developing new research efforts. We were not interested primarily in studying the same variables in each country but in analyzing variables that had comparable meaning and significance in each country. First, this meant it was necessary to state the particular problematic issue of comparative politics under study in general terms. We were concerned with the consequences of different patterns of social stratification on party affiliation. Second this meant developing operational measures that reflected the national social structure and its sociopolitical balance but organizing the data in such a fashion as to permit the maximum comparability.

National sample surveys are particularly well suited for cross-national research on the social-stratification bases of party affiliation and political partisanship. Sampling procedures in the United States and in western European countries are based on national parameters and therefore produce data about the nation-state as a whole, at the expense of understanding regional and metropolitan differences. But our comparisons are precisely at the national level.

This type of comparative analysis should include the widest possible range of multi-party states with similar levels of economic development. However, we chose Great Britain, West Germany, and the United States because the stability of their postwar competitive party systems has been similar enough to permit useful paired comparison, and our analysis relies heavily on paired comparisons. The degree of precision in the sample surveys of these countries is great enough to record the relatively small differences that characterize both political change within a nation and numerous types of cross-national differences.

Nevertheless, notions such as middle-majority politics or the politics of consensus and cleavage present complex problems when applied to a specific body of survey data. The variables derived from these frameworks are not readily operationalized and measured. Despite our efforts at explicit definitions, they are overlaid with implicit and subtle political and ideological preferences. Which of the three nations most closely approximates the model of middle-majority politics? Of all the possible measures of social cleavage, which are most politically relevant for each of these three countries? Such questions we shall postpone until we examine the data on the association between social-class position and party affiliation. However, it should be pointed out that our preference was for the "consensus and cleavage" model both on the basis of theoretical considerations and existing data. The results of this empirical investigation served only to strengthen our assumption.

Comparison of these nations involved three paired comparisons. In particular, we believed that Great Britain would reveal a much higher level of partisan polarization on the basis of socioeconomic stratification than the United States.[8] Existing studies indicated this pattern. It seemed reasonable to assume that the Germans would be more polarized than the United States and less polarized than Great Britain. Moreover, in placing Germany between Great Britain and the United States, it would be important to know whether Germany was markedly closer to Great Britain or closer to the pattern in the United Sates. Yet, as we shall argue, each of these assertions about the relative degree of socioeconomic stratification of party affiliation, if correct, could best be explained and amplified by the consensus-and-cleavage model.

National surveys of political opinion are typically based on rather small probability samples, which produce relevant data on the over-all distribution of voting behavior, party affiliations, and attitudes but are limited for purposes of detailed analysis. This paper is based on the accumulation of similar-type national surveys in each of the three countries. For Germany, the 12,676 cases used were collected by the Institut für angewandte Sozialwissenschaft during a one-year period in 1963–64 and involved seven surveys. For Great Britain, the data were based on 5,628 interviews carried out by Research Services, Ltd., by means of four national surveys during the period before the general election of 1964. In the case of the United States, there were 11,146 cases based on eight national surveys completed during the period of 1961 and 1964, two by the National Opinion Research Center.

The cumulation of cases from a series of national samples is justified on the basis of two assumptions. First, previous research has indicated that political partisanship and its correlates are relatively persistent and stable. Therefore, we assumed that the summation of data collected over a short period of time would not distort the findings encountered.[9] Second, there is the question of sampling points, and again it was assumed that, if the probability bases of the samples were similar, it would be possible to cumulate independent national samples without introducing significant distortion for our purposes.

SOCIOECONOMIC STRATIFICATION AND PARTY AFFILIATION

The first step in our analysis was to determine the degree of polarization of party affiliation in the three nations. In order to measure on a comparable basis the relation between socioeconomic position and party affiliation, it was necessary to (a) have a general conceptualization of class structure that would be applicable to all three countries and (b) to construct operational measures that would accurately reflect each national setting. This task is greatly simplified by the overriding limitation of national probability surveys, which do not collect relevant data on the "upper" or very top social stratum. The actual size of this group is so limited that the procedures of sample surveying do not produce analyzable numbers, and thereby one of the most difficult sociological questions in social stratification is avoided by simple exclusion.

Both the middle-majority model and the consensus-and-cleavage approach emphasize the growing differentiation of the occupational structure. A large and refined number of occupational categories are required to describe the skill structure of an industrialized society. Despite the fact that we have used the largest sized samples to be assembled for comparative political analysis, our categories of analysis remain limited and reflect present practices in national-survey work. These data were classified by the overriding distinction between blue collar (working class) and white collar (middle class). Further differentiation within each of these groupings was both essential and possible. Much comparative research into social mobility has been conducted on the basis of movement from blue- to white-collar positions and vice versa, but the results are indeed oversimplified, and current methodology of the national sample survey at least permits a four-group stratification pattern.

We believed that differentiation within both the working class and the middle class should reflect "style of life," and this could be measured by education level or income or a combination of both. More subtle categorization by content of education, work setting, life cycle, etc., was not possible. However, education and income are highly intercorrelated, and in fact it makes little or no difference which of these criteria are used as the basis for separating the middle-class group into upper-middle and lower-middle strata or for making the equivalent distinction in the working-class group.

The relevant issue is to locate the appropriate cutting points for each specific country which would still produce the most comparable or equivalent patterns of socio-economic stratification. For West Germany, a monthly income of DM. 1,000 or more separated the upper middle class from the lower middle class, while a monthly income of DM. 600 was the dividing line for the upper working class from the lower working class. On an equivalent basis, for the United States an annual income of $10,000 was used to divide the upper middle class from the lower-middle-class group, and for the working class a $5,000 or more annual income was used to to differentiate between upper and lower strata. The data in Great Britain were collected on a somewhat different basis, namely, by social-strata grades as judged by the interviewer. These categories were directly translated into the four-strata hierarchy.

The diffuse term "party affiliation" supplied an appropriate measure for cross-national analysis. Differences as to how the electoral systems operate to create a national "regime" cannot, of course, be overlooked. In Germany, the national electoral decision is between parties directly. The national candidates are not on the ballot, and the voter selects a district candidate. In Great Britain the voter makes a similar decision, but the candidate is more of a district representative of the national party leadership. In the United States, the citizen decides between national candidates.

However, party affiliation has a relatively standard meaning in all three nations because the parties are mass parties and are seeking to develop the broadest political allegiance. Party affiliation refers to the diffuse commitment to one or another of the political parties. It is the base from which political parties mobilize electoral support. It is a measure that varies slowly, and it persists between elections when these surveys were conducted.

"Party affiliation" was, in effect, operationalized with slight differences in each country in order to reflect national meanings. For the United States, because national elections are held at regular intervals, respondents were asked, "Generally speaking, do you usually think of yourself as a Republican, a Democrat, an Independent, or what?" Because of the high cultural value in answering "Independent," those who gave this response were probed for their leanings. The category "Independent" was reserved for persons who did not lean to either the Republican or the Democratic party.

For Great Britain, because elections are not periodic, the measure of party affiliation was based first on the question of party voting intention in the event an election were to be held. The relatively large number of undecided were probed as to their party leanings. In Germany, the respondent was asked to express his preference among the various political parties.[10] (See Table 1 for the distribution of reported party affiliation in Germany, Great Britain, and the United States.)

In developing these measures a research strategy was employed that is at

TABLE 1. DISTRIBUTION OF PARTY AFFILIATION (BASED ON CUMULATED NATIONAL SURVEYS)

	Total Sample	
	N	%
Germany:		
Social Democrat	4,393	34.6
Christian Democrat	5,135	40.5
Other	908	7.2
D.K.; N.A.*	2,240	17.7
Total	12,676	100.0
Great Britain:		
Labor	2,030	36.1
Conservative	1,775	31.5
Other	433	7.7
D.K.; N.A.	1,390	24.7
Total	5,628	100.0
United States:		
Democratic	6,080	54.6
Republican	3,416	30.6
Neither †	1,650	14.8
Total	11,146	100.0

* D. K. = don't know; N. A. = no answer.
† The category "Neither" for the United States was composed of approximately equal parts of declared independent and D.K. or N.A. responses.

variance with the contemporary data bank and retrieval systems. The current emphasis in the reanalysis of survey data is to store data in electronic data-processing systems and to develop common categories for retrieval. This approach has the advantage of speeding the process of data-handling but removes the analyst further and further from direct contact with and understanding of his data. A general set of categories is developed which is designed to be relevant for all types of analysis. Because of the widely different systems of collection and coding, risks in excessive and rigid standardization are likely.

Instead, these data were handled by a confrontation approach in which procedures for comparison were developed for each research problem. The original data from all of the studies of the three nations were collected at the Institut für angewandte Sozialwissenschaft. In terms of the specific hypothesis to be tested, rubrics that were functionally equivalent but reflected relevant national differences were created. The data were then recoded for each country.

The data presented in Table 2 reveal that party affiliation is the most highly associated with socioeconomic status in Great Britain, less so in West Germany and least in the United States. The measure of association employed was that of Cramér's V, which was calculated in each country for those persons on whom there was adequate data to locate their positions in this schema of social stratification. The resulting statistics were: for America, $V = .171$; for Germany, $V = .246$; and for England, $V = .372$. As mentioned above, an alternative definition of socioeconomic position (Table 3) based on a more refined eight-strata schema (four categories of occupation, each divided on the basis of income) produced the same relative pattern of polarization of party affiliations (the association was found to be weakest in the United States, $V = .162$; intermediate for West Germany, $V = .284$; highest for Great Britain, $V = .394$). By both schemata of social stratification, these differences are large and noteworthy. Moreover, it appears that Germany falls midway between the United States and Great Britain and is not merely a variant of the pattern in one or the other nation.

These detailed breakdowns reveal in all three countries that the "Left"-oriented party failed to increase in concentration among the lower-working-class group as compared with the upper working class. This is not because of defection to a third party. It is, rather, the result of an ability in all three countries (but particularly in Germany) of the "conservative" party to penetrate this group and reduce its expected losses or the result of the increase in non-partisanship in the lower-working-class group.

TABLE 2. SOCIOECONOMIC STATUS AND PARTY AFFILIATION: UNITED STATES, GERMANY, GREAT BRITAIN (BASED ON CUMULATED NATIONAL SURVEYS)

Party Affiliation	Social Status							
	Middle Class				Working Class			
	High Income		Low Income		High Income		Low Income	
	N	%	N	%	N	%	N	%
United States:								
Democrat	518	47	1,436	51	1,416	61	1,242	61
Republican	446	40	1,003	35	554	24	418	20
Neither	147	13	388	14	346	15	363	18
Total	1,111	100	2,827	100	2,316	100	2,023	100
Germany:								
Social Democrat	340	25	871	28	1,086	50	1,117	49
Christian Democrat	677	49	1,485	47	724	33	720	31
Other	185	14	299	9	85	4	88	4
N.A.*	166	12	493	16	277	13	367	16
Total	1,368	100	3,148	100	2,172	100	2,292	100
Great Britain:								
Labor	109	11	229	23	846	45	846	47
Conservative	542	56	388	40	451	24	394	22
Other	76	8	99	10	140	8	118	6
D.K., N.A.	237	25	259	27	433	23	461	25
Total	964	100	975	100	1,870	100	1,819	100

* D.K. = don't know; N.A. = no answer.

TABLE 3. SOCIOECONOMIC STATUS AND PARTY AFFILIATION
A. UNITED STATES

Social Status	Party Identification							
	Democrat		Republican		Neither		Total	
	N	%	N	%	N	%	N	%
Upper middle:								
High income	180	44	172	42	55	14	407	100
Low income	314	46	271	39	105	15	691	100
Lower middle:								
High income	338	48	274	39	92	13	704	100
Low income	1,122	53	731	34	283	13	2,136	100
Upper working:								
High income	1,253	61	493	24	305	15	2,051	100
Low income	905	62	313	21	251	17	1,469	100
Lower working:								
High income	163	62	61	23	41	15	265	100
Low income	337	61	105	19	111	20	553	100

B. GERMANY

	Social Democrat		Christian Democrat–Christian Social Union		Other		N.A.*		Total	
	N	%	N	%	N	%	N	%	N	%
Upper Middle:										
High income	84	16	282	54	104	20	54	10	524	100
Low income	129	23	272	49	78	14	76	14	555	100
Lower middle:										
High income	256	30	395	47	81	10	112	13	844	100
Low income	742	29	1,213	47	221	8	417	16	2,593	100
Upper working:										
High income	588	49	402	33	52	4	167	14	1,209	100
Low income	523	53	283	28	46	5	144	14	996	100
Lower working:										
High income	498	52	322	34	33	3	110	11	963	100
Low income	594	46	437	34	42	3	223	17	1,296	100

* N.A. = no answer.

C. GREAT BRITAIN

	Conservative		Labor		Other		N.A. Ineligible		Total	
	N	%	N	%	N	%	N	%	N	%
Upper middle	542	56	109	11	76	8	237	25	964	100
Lower middle	388	40	229	23	99	10	259	27	975	100
Upper working	451	24	846	45	140	8	433	23	1,870	100
Lower working	394	22	846	47	118	6	461	25	1,819	100

* N.A. = no answer.

SOCIAL-SYSTEM CLEAVAGES

The second step in the analysis involves additional dimensions of stratification. The consensus-and-cleavage approach implies that beyond social class the other major social-system cleavages related to party affiliation vary from nation to nation. Moreover, the consequences of these cleavages for political change depend on whether they work to reduce or to heighten the strains generated by socioeconomic stratification. For the United States, first, race was taken as a dominant source of party affiliation and then religious affiliation. For Germany, because of the absence of racial division, religion supplied a majority dimension, while for Great Britain, in the absence of racial or religious divisions, sex and age differences were assumed to operate as potential bases of political cleavage.[11] This is not to be taken as meaning that racial issues are absent in British politics, as they are significant. Rather, racial minorities are so small that in general they do not constitute a significant socioeconomic voting group to which political leaders make appeals. In Table 4 the polarization of party affiliation by socioeconomic position is presented for each nation holding constant the above relevant variable of political cleavage.

These data indicate the different consequences of social cleavages for party affiliation in each of the nations. Is the socio-economic polarization higher or

TABLE 4. SOCIOECONOMIC STATUS, SOCIAL CLEAVAGE, AND PARTY AFFILIATION: UNITED STATES, GERMANY, AND ENGLAND

	Total Sample	Social Cleavage	
United States	$V = .162$	White Non-white	$V = .149$ $V = .011$
Germany	$V = .284$	Catholic Non-Catholic	$V = .297$ $V = .251$
Great Britain	$V = .397$	Males Females	$V = .412$ $V = .387$

lower among these social divisions? For the United States, the white population reveals a pattern of polarization similar to the total sample; namely, Democratic affiliation is negatively associated with socioeconomic position at a level just below that for the total sample (Cramér's $V = .149$). By contrast, Negro affiliation is markedly unpolarized because it is unrelated to socioeconomic position. At each level, Negroes hold predominantly Democratic affiliation (Cramér's $V = .011$). In addition, we explored the relevance of religion as a secondary basis of polarization. The Protestant figure is somewhat greater than for the United States as a whole (Cramér's $V = .18$). The difference between Protestants (.18) and non-Protestant (.12) is less than the difference between Negroes and whites. Thus, religion in the United States operates as a basis of polarization but not as much as race. For Germany, religion operates to produce some additional polarization among the Catholics (Cramér's $V = .297$), while among the Protestants socioeconomic polarization of party affiliation is somewhat lower (Cramér's $V = .251$). In Great Britain, sex operates in the same fashion but with rather slight magnitude. Males are more polarized on the basis of socioeconomic position in their party affiliation, while women are less (Cramér's $V = .412$ for males and $.387$ for women). This represents a greater commitment of women to the Conservative party against their socioeconomic position. Alternatively, in Great Britain age serves as another basis of polarization, since the Conservative party has the advantage among old people, both male and, especially, female.

Insofar as party affiliation is an expression of social attachment within the context of economic self-interest, these data reveal with some precision the extent to which specific additional social variables create a base of political cleavage. A simple measure is the difference in the scores measuring polarization of party affiliation within socioeconomic groups; the greater the difference, the more the control variable operates as a basis of political cleavage. Thus the greatest difference is for the United States, where the data demonstrate the obvious reality that Negroes have a political affiliation as a racial group rather than dividing between Democrats and Republicans on the basis of their socioeconomic position. The amount of dissensus introduced by religion in Germany is much less and by sex in Great Britain is even less (differences in scores: for race in United States, $.138$; for religion in Germany $.046$; for sex in Great Britain $.025$). These data underline the obvious reality that the higher consensus on socioeconomic bases in the United States should not overlook the greater degree of polarization on other social bases.

INSTITUTIONAL FACTORS AND POLITICAL INTEGRATION

The third step in the analysis of this body of comparative survey data is to probe further the underlying social-structural variables accounting for party affiliation. It should not be overlooked that even the simple schema of socioeconomic stratification plus *one* selected variable produces social groupings with immensely wide differences in political-party preferences. Among the respondents who expressed party preference, the social-structural variation was as follows:

Great Britain:
Upper-middle-class women   74% Conservative
Lower-working-class men   25% Conservative
                           $\Delta = 49\%$

Germany:
Upper-middle-class Catholics   71% Christian Democrat
Lower-working-class Protestants   27% Christian Democrat
                           $\Delta = 44\%$

United States:
Upper-middle-class white   47% Republican
Lower-working-class Negro   17% Republican
                           $\Delta = 30\%$

This array seems to give further support to the relevance of the "consensus and cleavage" model. In addition, it seemed relevant to examine on a wide empirical basis whether other variables, especially institutional associations, would also be revealing of the underlying social-structural basis of party affiliation.

In order to maximize the meaningful reduction of unexplained variance in party affiliation, the statistical technique used was based on the non-symmetric splitting of social groups, the so-called tree technique.[12] By this process the ordering of variables and their dichotomizing is based on the results of computer operations.

Our effort was to maintain, as in the other phases of the analysis, an optimal balance of variables which would take into consideration national differences and maintain a basis for comparability among the three countries.

Despite the enormous effort in collecting these studies, standardizing the variables, and analyzing the data by the procedures of the tree analysis, the results indicate that political sociologists do not yet have adequate bodies of data for cross-national analysis, and our goal still must emphasize the collection of adequate empirical materials. Interestingly enough, this is probably due more to the limitations on the available data from the United States and Great Britain than from Germany. It needs to be emphasized that only in the case of Germany are the data sufficiently comprehensive to produce meaningful results, but for comparative purpose even the initial branches in the tree analysis are revealing. In the case of Germany, on the basis of previous analysis, a tree of many branches was constructed which explained more of the variance than could be explained by standard methods of analysis (see Table 5). But even these preliminary findings help clarify the patterns of convergence and diversity in social stratification that underlie party affiliation.

For Great Britain, the tree analysis reaffirms that the most important single variable is the split on social-class position. (This variable accounted for 13.2 per cent of the variance.) Only within the working class, the next most important split was the size of household; persons living in large households—those of more than three people—were more prone to be affiliated with the Labor party than those in smaller households. (This variable accounted for only 2.1 per cent additional explanation of the variance.) The high degree of consensus underlying party affiliation can be inferred from the absence of additional bases of cleavage in these data. No other available variable included in surveys to which we had access increased the amount of explained variance by 1 per cent or more.

In the United States, a similar type of simple model emerges with religious affiliation as the most important initial split. Democratic affiliation was linked to "minority religion" (Catholic, Baptist, Jewish, or no preference) in contrast to the core Protestants with Republican affiliation. (This variable reduced the unexplained variance by 6.8 per cent.) The second step came in dichotomizing the Protestant groups on the basis of occupation as between a group of working-class occupations and a group of middle-class occupations (this variable reduced the variance by only 1.6 per cent).[13] In the case of the United States, the tree analysis did not serve to differentiate the respondents to the same degree as for Great Britain.

TABLE 5. PARTY AFFILIATION BY SOCIAL-STRATIFICATION GROUPING BASED UPON "TREE ANALYSIS": UNITED STATES, GREAT BRITAIN, AND GERMANY

Group Definition	Size of Group		(%) Affiliation with Major Left Party
	N	%	
	United States		
1. "Minority Religions"/or no preference	2,932	31.0	78
2. 'Core Protestants"/working-class occupations	2,139	22.7	67
3. 'Core Protestants"/middle-class occupations	4,360	46.3	52
Total	9,431	100.0	
	Great Britain		
1. Working-class strata/large households	1,074	28.1	72
2. Working-class strata/small households	1,485	38.8	64
3. Middle-class strata	1,267	33.1	27
Total	3,826	100.0	
	Germany		
1. Union affiliation/non-practicing Catholics	2,520	26.5	72
2. Working-class strata/no union affiliation/non-Catholics	1,775	18.7	60
3. Working class/union affiliation/Catholics	531	5.6	41
4. Middle-class strata/no union affiliation/non-Catholics	2,562	27.0	31
5. Practicing Catholics/no union affiliation	2,105	22.2	18
Total	9,493	100.0	

For Germany, the tree analysis resulted in five social groupings which were built initially on the basis of social-class position (occupation) and religion. But the increased explanatory power of the model was the result of the fact that it was able to incorporate institutional variables, such as trade-union affiliation and church attendance.[14] The extreme groups, based upon unionism and religion, were on the "Left," union-affiliated non-practicing Catholics, 72 per cent of whom supported the Social Democratic party, and on the "Right," non-union-affiliated practicing Catholics, of whom only 18 per cent supported the Social Democratic party.

The tree-analysis procedure for Germany highlighted the importance of the religion variable as a basis of political cleavage, in part because the measure included actual religious behavior as well as denomination. Further, the effort to explore institutional variables proved rewarding because trade-union affiliation had a general nation-wide relevance. Thus, for example, middle-class persons who were not practicing Catholics, but who had family trade-union affiliations, expressed a 62.1 per cent preference for the Social Democratic party and were subsumed under the "Left"-oriented group. In contrast, the similar social groupings without family affiliation to trade unions only reached 49.3 per cent in their Social Democratic preference.

For Germany trade-union membership is a simple but meaningful measure of integration into the larger political system. For the United States, the equivalent integrating structures are so variegated that sample surveys do not easily permit their precise identification. Finally, for none of the samples was there adequate basis to analyze the mass media as another integrative mechanism to the political system.

POLITICAL CHANGE

What relevance do these data have in helping to understand the processes of political stability and change in advanced industrial societies? How can these findings be integrated with institutional studies of politics?

1. These data reaffirm the conclusion that the degree of social-class polarization of party affiliation varies considerably even among these three nations with relatively comparable social structures. The observation in and of itself that Great Britain is more polarized than the United States or Germany, and, on the basis of other studies, that it has been since 1945, raises important questions about "middle majority" theories of political change. It would seem that the persistently higher the degree of party affiliation (and party vote) along socioeconomic lines, the less ideologically based social class-conflict politics decline and the less a nation conforms to a model of bargaining-type politics. But on the basis of this analysis this is not the case in a paired comparison of Great Britain with Germany or with the United States.

Our data dealt with mass political orientations and not with elite perspectives. However, there is no reason to argue that Great Britain has a more ideologically based electorate than Germany or the United States. In fact, we would argue that British mass politics is less ideological and based more on mass consent than Germany.[15] For a comparison of Great Britain with the United States the same holds true, or at least there is no noticeable gap.[16]

For example, we can make use of a series of specific comparisons about mass predisposition as presented by Gabriel Almond and Sidney Verba to indicate that Germany has distinctly less of a "democratic" culture based on consent and political integration, while the differences they report between the United States and Great Britain are at best minor. Popular sentiments toward the national government as measured by positive attitudes on the theme that the national government improves conditions were equal in Great Britain and the United States (76 per cent, 77 per cent), while they were distinctly lower for Germany (61 per cent).[17] The same pattern of attitudes was encountered on expectations of equal treatment by the public bureaucracy and the police.[18] Even for information on refusal to report voting decision, a crude but revealing measure of consent politics, the results were negligible for Great Britain and the United States but reached 15 per cent of the respondents for Germany.[19]

More important, feelings of civic competence were equal at the national level in the United States (77 per cent) and Great Britain (78 per cent), while for

Germany the figure was lower (62 per cent).[20] If the Almond-Verba measures of political competence are combined with expectations of equal treatment by administrative agencies, the United States drops below Britain and Germany. Finally, many of these measures of consent toward the political and electoral system are influenced by educational level, thereby giving the United States a reported over-all advantage. However, when education is held constant, lower-class Americans have lower scores than those for Great Britain. It is frequently argued that the process of social change and the growth of affluence weaken ideological commitment by creating greater equality. However, this process of social change does not guarantee the comparable development of positive commitments to the rules of the "bargaining" game. Here we are dealing with cultural traditions and the impact of political institutions on social structure.

2. In interpreting these findings on socioeconomic position and party affiliation, it is necessary to re-emphasize the limitations in sample-survey data, especially in relating these data to historical trends. Undoubtedly, there are important elements of convergence in occupational and socioeconomic stratification patterns in the United States, Great Britain, and West Germany, but they have not yet converged, nor is their convergence predetermined.[21] Moreover, the present patterns of convergence are not necessarily the result of similar historical sequences. The emergence of industrialism has not followed the same pattern in Great Britain and Germany as compared with the United States, since the development of occupational systems does not conform to a single "ideal" or "type" pattern. In Great Britain and Germany industrial processes were introduced into a society that had a relatively well-developed middle stratum of commercial and governmental occupations and a traditional agricultural labor force. In the United States industrialization was grafted onto a social structure with a much less well-developed commercial and administrative structure and a very different agricultural base.

These differences in patterns of socioeconomic stratification, together with absolute differences in living standards, constitute a central theme in the comparative political sociology of the United States and western Europe. These differences help explain the persistently higher relevance in Great Britain and Germany of socioeconomic position as a basis of political cleavage and the greater polarization of party affiliation as compared with the United States. But, as indicated above, greater socioeconomic polarization of party affiliation does not necessarily mean more class conflict or more ideological politics if we are dealing with the comparative analysis of the United States, Great Britain, and West Germany.

3. Our data indicate that a consensus-and-cleavage model that includes both socioeconomic and other structural variables, plus institutional affiliations, supplies a relevant basis of organizing comparative national survey data. The tree analysis, in particular, highlighted the process of social change and the new sources of political cleavages as the older basis of social-class conflict declines.

But survey data supply only a partial basis for examining patterns of social change in order to identify these new sources of political cleavage. On the macro-social-system level, available research, for example, indicates that during the last two decades the built-in trends toward income redistribution associated with the first and earlier developments of the welfare state in Great Britain and the United States have slowed, and may even have reversed themselves.[22] Such trends, unless altered by drastic changes in taxation and wage policies, are likely to contribute new elements of political cleavage.

Likewise, there is every reason to believe that, with the growth of a more complex division of labor and of a more differentiated educational system, the categories of social stratification we used in this analysis become too un-differentiated to capture the realities of social change. Despite the relative success we have had with simple variables in accounting for party affiliation, we agree with Wilensky's formulation of the neeed for a more refined approach to study mass ideology and mass political references. In fact this is precisely what the tree analysis indicates:

> Our data suggest that we need to slice up social structure in ways that capture both the persistence of older divisions (age, religion, occupation) and the emergence of newer ones (the quality and content of education) and to do it more precisely than usual. To say "white collar" or "working class" is to obscure most of what is central to the experience of the person and the structure of society. To say "professional, technical, and kindred" captures more of social life but not much more. "Lawyer" and "engineer" moves us closer to social reality, for these men develop quite different styles of life, rooted in diverse professional schools, tasks, work schedules, and organizational contexts. To say "independent practitioner" is to say even more, and finally, to particularize the matter with "solo lawyer" vs. "firm lawyer" is to take account of the sharp contrasts in recruitment base (social origins, religion, quality of professional training), career pattern and rewards which divide the two.[23]

One important consequence of such social differentiation on political behavior is observable from the available data. On the basis of the findings of this research and others generally, there is an over-all inverse relationship between higher socioeconomic position and affiliation with the Labor party, the Social Democratic party, and the Democratic party. Within the upper-middle stratum, however, persons from non-business occupations and professions are more likely to hold partisan affiliation with these political parties than persons in the upper-middle socioeconomic stratum who are business affiliated. This is particularly the case for the United States and Great Britain.[24] The administrative, professional, and scientific personnel who are employed in educational, governmental, health and welfare institutions, tend to become politically polarized from their counterparts in industrial and commercial hierarchies. Clearly, differences in recruitment, educational experience, and, most important, in group interest generated by employment in a different work setting are all operative factors.[25]

The notion of status crystallization, or more precisely status congruence, can be used to describe this linkage between social stratification and political partisanship.[26] Status congruence refers to gross characteristics and can involve large discrepancies in social position such as the case of a person with "lower class" educational achievement who is earning a very high income; or it can involve more subtle and smaller but nevertheless politically important differences. This is what appears to be at work within the upper-middle-class stratum. The business-connected persons have less education than their professional and technical counterparts (some college or college, as compared with college and postcollege education), while their income level is on the average higher. This pattern of status incongruence sets the social context within which their political polarization develops.

Survey research can incorporate such more refined variables in order to capture the greater complexity of contemporary work settings. However, there is an inherent limitation in national surveys with limited numbers of cases as currently practiced. If the sequential influence of social origin, education, work experience, and institutional ties is to be probed, even the cumulation of repeated national samples will have to be augmented by subsamples of crucial age and occupational groupings selected on more purposive and theoretical criteria.[27]

4. As stated above, the "consensus and cleavage" model does not assume that the social sources of rigid ideological political orientation or the sources of political extremism are residues or holdouts which additional economic expansion will incorporate into the political structure and therefore eliminate or contain. Instead, it is oriented to identifying new sources of political cleavage and political conflict as well as to transforming old sources. For example, from our data it is clear that in all three societies there is a tendency for persons in the lower working class to have a higher degree of non-party affiliation than in the other strata of society. While the magnitude is not large, it reflects a persistent vulnerability produced by advanced industrialism. The underlying configuration that generates this lack of effective participation is not to be seen in terms of education or income per se but as a series of life experiences which produce persons and families without adequate institutional links to the political system. But we are not dealing only with a lower-class phenomenon, for such disruption can occur at various points in the social structure, for example, among elderly men and women living outside family units or among the downwardly mobile. What is important is that the sources of such disruption persist with the development of an advanced industrial society.

Alternatively, language and ethnic differences have emerged in the last decade in particular regions of Western Europe as important sources of sharp political cleavage. Ethnic and language differences can constitute independent sources of political polarization, but they can be specific manifestations of a more comprehensive process of political conflict under conditions of advanced industrialism, namely, the cleavage between the center and the periphery. In Great Britain, ethnic and regional feelings fuse together to support political cleavages based on reactions to differential rates of economic progress. There is a division between England on the one hand and Scotland and Wales on the other, which have experienced slower rates of economic development. For each comparable social grouping the Conservative party has more partisans in England than in Scotland and Wales.

In Germany, regionalism has been obscured or repressed as a result of the basic division into East and West Germany. There is still a basis of polarization between the central urban metropolitan centers and the less industrialized hinterlands. In the United States, regional differences are pervasive and complex. Regionalism in the South is based on historical and racial factors and a lag in economic development; a markedly different type of western regionalism is linked to very rapid and very special forms of economic development. As a result, ideological and conflict politics has important regional variations, both in the South and in the Far West.

5. This analysis of the sources of party affiliation has focused on domestic politics. This is what is implied in the transformation of social-class struggles into bargaining politics. But beyond our findings, consensus and cleavage more and more come to involve foreign affairs on a mass basis as literacy grows and as the nature of warfare becomes completely destructive. In fact, one can make the argument that the decline in ideological politics since 1945 has been influenced not only by changes in internal social stratification but also because in all three societies the overriding concerns with the Cold War made possible the management of the national economy so as to inhibit political conflict and created a situationally based consensus. We prefer at a minimum to see mass perceptions of the threat of war and international tensions as a relevant and emerging basis for political cleavage.

For the recent past, survey data gives conservative-type parties in both the United States and Great Britain an advantage in that they are seen as being more effective and skillful in international relations and foreign policy. In Great Britain this issue helps account for the difficulty of the Labor party in translating its popular support into electoral success. In the United States this issue is even more pronounced in that the Democratic party is viewed as more aggressive in international relations and even characterized by some as the "war party." In Germany, the differences in public perceptions about the skill and posture of the two parties in international relations do not vary to any noteworthy extent. As international relations are transformed away from the patterns of the last twenty years, foreign policy is likely to supply a basis of political polarization, since the range of alternative policies is certain to become broader and more complex.

In summary, we would conclude that existing quantitative survey data, with all their limitations, make a contribution to comparative political sociology that goes well beyond common sense and "well-informed" bases of judgment. For comparative analysis, measures from one nation cannot be mechanically imposed on another even if they have highly similar social structures. The analysis of sample-survey data requires both a concern for national differences and a reliance on equivalent categories. As a result of a series of paired comparisons we found that partisan affiliations were most polarized on the basis of socioeconomic positions in Great Britain, less in Germany, and the least in the United States. In each country, there were different secondary social bases of political cleavage. Our initial assumption was that differences in social stratification per se cannot explain comparative party affiliation or, in turn, differing levels of political consensus. It is obvious that political institutions play an active role in fashioning such mass orientations. The model of consensus and cleavage, which attributes an element of independence to political arrangements, not only helps explain the transformation of social-class conflict but helps avoid overlooking the persistent and emerging sources of political conflict in an advanced industrial society.

NOTES

[1] This paper is the outgrowth of our collaborative efforts with Klaus Liepelt of the Institut für Angewandte Sozialwissenschaft, Bad Godesberg, West Germany. We wish to acknowledge the National Opinion Research Center, University of Chicago; the Survey Research Center, University of Michigan; and Research Services, Ltd., London, for access to their national sample data. The Institut für angewandte Sozialwissenschaft undertook the computational work.

[2] See especially the work of the Committee on Political Sociology of the International Sociological Association. Stein Rokkan, "International Cooperation in Political Sociology: Current Efforts and Future Possibilities," in Erik Allardt and Yrjo Littunen (eds.), *Cleavages, Ideologies and Party Systems* (*Transactions of the Westermarck Society,* Vol. X), pp. 5–18.

[3] S. M. Lipset, "The Changing Class Structure and Contemporary European Politics," *Daedalus,* XCIII (Winter, 1964), 271–303.

[4] *Ibid.,* pp. 295–96. See also Robert E. Lane, "The Politics of Consensus in an Age of Affluence," *American Political Science Review,* LIX, No. 4 (December, 1965), 874–95.

[5] Morris Janowitz, "Political Sociology," in *International Encyclopedia of the Social Sciences* (New York: Macmillan Co., in press); William Kornhauser, *The Politics of Mass Society* (New York: Free Press, 1959).

[6] See George Lichtheim, "Class and Hierarchy: A Critique of Marx?", *European Journal of Sociology,* V, No. 1 (1964), 101–11.

[7] See Morris Janowitz and Dwaine Marvick, *Competitive Pressure and Democratic Consent: An Interpretation of the 1952 Election* (Chicago: Quadrangle Books, 1965), for an effort to probe these issues.

[8] Philip E. Converse defines status polarization as "the strength of the relationship between status and relevant politico-economic variables" (see "The Shifting Role of Class in Political Attitudes and Behavior," in Eleanor Maccoby, Theodore M. Newcomb, and Eugene L. Hartley [eds.], *Readings in Social Psychology* [New York: Holt, Rinehart & Winston, 1958], p. 394. Robert R. Alford, in *Party and Society* (Chicago: Rand McNally, 1963), p. 102, assigns Great Britain a mean index of class voting of 40. The magnitude of the same statistic for the United States was 16. For further information on class and partisanship in England see J. Blondel, *Voters, Parties, and Leaders: The Social Fabric of British Politics* (Baltimore, Md.: Penguin Books, 1963), p. 91, and Richard Rose, *Politics in England* (Boston: Little, Brown & Co., 1964), p. 73. See also J. Bonham, *The Middle Class Vote* (London: Faber & Faber, 1954), and Mark Abrams and Richard Rose, *Must Labour Lose?* (Baltimore, Md.: Penguin Books, 1960).

[9] A computer simulation of the 1960 presidential election using poll data collected in the course of an entire decade has claimed, "The benefits of large numbers and broadly based coverage proved to be greater than the benefits of timeliness" (Ithiel de Sola Pool, Robert P. Abelson, and Samuel L. Popkin, *Candidates, Issues, and*

Strategies [Cambridge, Mass.: M.I.T. Press, 1964], pp. 65–67). However, the purposes of the analysis and the variables employed must be kept in mind, and there are obvious limits to the time span that can be involved. The Research Services Ltd., surveys were studies J. 4104, J. 4285, J. 4380, and J. 4475; the National Opinion Research Center studies were S. 110 and S. 640, and those conducted by the Survey Research Center were numbers 706, 714, 720, 734, and 736.

[10] "Num einmal ganz allgemein: Welche der politischen Parteien gefallt Ihnen zur Zeit am besten? (Soweit man das sagen kann). (Welche ist denn gerade noch der beste?)"

[11] Blondel, *op. cit.,* p. 91, and Rose, *op. cit.,* p. 63, point out that in England women are the politically handicapped group. Robert McKenzie and Allan Silver attribute disproportionate Tory leanings among English women to a deferential ideology (see "Conservatism, Industrialism and the Working Class Tory in England," *Transactions of the Fifth World Congress of Sociology,* III [1964], 191–202).

[12] John A. Sonquist and James N. Morgan, "The Detection of Interaction Effects" (Ann Arbor: Survey Research Center, University of Michigan, 1964). The specific technique applied was that developed by J. H. G. Seegers ("De Contrasgroepen-Methode: Nadere Uitwerking en eel Tweetal Toepassinger," *Sociale Wetenschappen,* No. 3 [1964], pp. 194–225). Because the analysis could be carried out only on those respondents who had expressed a party affiliation, the case base was reduced; United States, 9,431 cases; Great Britain, 3,826; Germany, 9,493.

[13] These findings were not unexpected. Analyzing data from American Institute of Public Opinion Survey no. 636K (1960), Alford computed indexes of class voting that for Protestants were +19 and for Catholics only +6. It should be pointed out that Roper Survey no. 78 for the same year provides figures of +18 and +10 for the same indexes. The difference in magnitude serves to demonstrate the variability among small samples on such matters. See Alford, *op. cit.,* p. 243.

[14] In connection with a study of the 1965 German elections, the analysis of German data has been expanded to include a great number of cases and a set of sociopsychological variables. These data will be presented in a forthcoming paper by Klaus Liepelt and Friederike Golzem.

[15] Gabriel Almond and Sidney Verba, *The Civic Culture* (Princeton, N.J.: Princeton University Press, 1963), e.g., pp. 82 ff.

[16] See James B. Christoph, "Consensus and Cleavage in British Political Ideology," *American Political Science Review,* LIX, No. 3 (September, 1965), 629–42.

[17] Almond and Verba, *op. cit.,* p. 82.

[18] *Ibid.,* p. 108.

[19] *Ibid.,* p. 116.

[20] *Ibid.,* p. 226.

[21] S. M. Lipset and Reinhard Bendix, *Social Mobility in Industrial Society* (Berkeley: University of California Press, 1959); S. N. Miller, "Comparative Social Mobility: A Trend Report and Bibliography," *Current Sociology,* Vol. IX, No. 1 (1960); see also Morris Janowitz, "Social Stratification and Mobility in West Germany," *American Journal of Sociology,* Vol. XLIV, No. 1 (1958), 6–24.

[22] See Richard Morris Titmuss, *Income Distribution and Social Change* (Toronto: University of Toronto Press, 1962), and Herman P. Miller, *Rich Man, Poor Man* (New York: Thomas Y. Crowell Co., 1964).

[23] Harold L. Wilensky, "Mass Society and Mass Culture," in Bernard Berelson and Morris Janowitz (eds.), *Reader in Public Opinion and Communication* (2d ed.; New York: Free Press, 1966), pp. 317–18.

[24] Angus Campbell, Philip E. Converse, Warren E. Miller, and Donald E. Stokes,

The American Voter (New York: John Wiley & Sons, 1960), pp. 482–83; Mark Abrams, Research Services, Ltd., London, unpublished report, 1966.

[25] The distinction suggested by Daniel R. Miller and Guy E. Swanson, between entrepreneurial and bureaucratic groups, is applicable (see *The Changing American Parent* [New York: John Wiley & Sons, 1958]).

[26] Gerhard Lenski, "Status Crystallization: A Non-Vertical Dimension of Social Status," *American Sociological Review*, XIX (August, 1954), 405–13.

[27] The design of the German 1965 election study of the Institut für angewandte Sozialwissenschaft is a step in this direction.

30. POLITICS IN AN AGE OF ANXIETY

Arthur M. Schlesinger, Jr.

Western man in the middle of the twentieth century is tense, uncertain, adrift. We look upon our epoch as a time of troubles, an age of anxiety. The grounds of our civilization, of our certitude, are breaking up under our feet, and familiar ideas and institutions vanish as we reach for them, like shadows in the falling dusk. Most of the world has reconciled itself to this half-light, to the reign of insecurity. Even those peoples who hastily traded their insecurities for a mirage of security are finding themselves no better off than the rest. Only the United States still has buffers between itself and the anxieties of our age: buffers of time, of distance, of natural wealth, of national ingenuity, of a stubborn tradition of hope.

A nation which has made a religion of success ought to find it hard to acclimate itself to the middle of the twentieth century. For frustration is increasingly the hallmark of this century—the frustration of triumphant science and rampant technology, the frustration of the most generous hopes and of the most splendid dreams. Nineteen hundred looked forward to the irresistible expansion of freedom, democracy and abundance; 1950 will look back to totalitarianism, to concentration camps, to mass starvation, to atomic war. Yet for the United States the world tragedy still has the flickering unreality of a motion picture. It grips us as we see it; but, lingering over the familiar milkshake in the bright drugstore, we forget the nightmare in the resurgence of warmth and comfort. Anxiety is something we hear about. It is not yet part of our lives—not of enough of our lives, anyway, to inform our national decisions.

The world tragedy, as it impinges upon Americans, strikes us in relatively simple terms. It is we or they; the United States or the Soviet Union; capitalism or Communism; let us resolve this conflict, and all problems will be solved. These choices are, indeed, the terms of the immediate problem; and it is only in these terms that steps can be taken toward enduring solutions. But let us not deceive ourselves into regarding the American-Russian rivalry as the source of world troubles.

Neither capitalism nor Communism is the cause of the contemporary upsurge of anxiety. Indeed, to a considerable degree, unhappy people have registered the same complaints against both. Each system is charged with having dehumanized the worker, fettered the lower classes and destroyed personal and political liberty. Before the First War, the case against Communism was generally made in terms of efficiency, the case against capitalism in terms of morality; that is, Communism was conceded to be enlightened in principle but was held not to work; capitalism was conceded to work but was held not to be enlightened in principle. After the Soviet experience, the Great Depression and the Second War, we see a reverse tendency—a disposition to admit the inefficiency of capitalism and justify it as providing the margin on which liberty and democracy subsist;

SOURCE: Arthur M. Schlesinger, Jr., *The Vital Center* (Boston: Houghton Mifflin Co., 1949), pp. 1–10. Reprinted by permission of the author and publisher.

a disposition to believe that the very completeness of Communist control necessarily squeezes out freedom.

In a sense, the arguments are interchangeable, the indictments cancel out. Does not this suggest that both sides have indulged in what Whitehead calls the "fallacy of misplaced concreteness"—the error of mistaking abstractions for concrete realities? We have seen identical criticisms lodged with heat and fervor against the abstractions "capitalism" and "Communism." But these criticisms may perhaps be lodged more profoundly, not against any particular system of ownership, but against industrial organization and the post-industrial state, whatever the system of ownership.

The human race in the last three centuries has been going through a global change-of-life. Science and technology have ushered man into a new cycle of civilization, and the consequence has been a terrifying problem of adjustment. In two centuries science and technology have narrowed the seas, ravaged the forests and irrigated the deserts. They had leveled national frontiers, undermined national self-sufficiencies and infinitely increased man's power to build and to destroy. The velocity of life has entered into a new phase. With it has come the imperative need for a social structure to contain that velocity—a social structure within which the individual can achieve some measure of self-fulfillment.

This new social structure must succeed where the ancient jurisdictions of the family, the clan, the guild and the nation-state have failed. It must solve the problems created by the speed-up of time, the reduction of space and the increase in tension. It must develop new equivalents for the sanctions once imposed by custom and by religion. The specifications for the new society cannot but strain to the utmost the emotional and moral resources of the individual and the community.

In restrospect, these demands seem to have been too severe and exhausting. Civilization has not met them, which is why today it is consumed by anxiety and fear. Failing to create a new social structure, it has become the victim rather than the master of industrialism. The liberation of the individual during the Renaissance and Reformation set the Industrial Revolution in motion; in its course, industrialism has given people new freedom and opportunity. Yet its ultimate tendency under whatever system of ownership—a tendency inherent in its very technical structure—is to impersonalize economic relationships. In the end industrialism drives the free individual to the wall.

A static and decentralized society, based on agriculture and handicraft, was a society dependent on personal ties and governed by a personal ethic. Industrialism shattered the ties and consequently the ethic. A new code arose to cope with the remote and statistical units of the modern economy; and the gap between economic practice and personal morality widened swiftly and alarmingly. The industrial manager dealt, not in familiar personal relationships, but in impersonal magnitudes over great stretches of time and distance. The corporation was almost as much a device to solve moral as economic problems. It gave the new impersonality an institutional embodiment; a corporation, as the saying went, had neither a body to be kicked nor a soul to be damned. "Corporations will do what individuals would not dare to do," the richest man in

Boston wrote with candor a century ago. "—Where the dishonesty is the work of *all* the Members, every *one* can say with Macbeth in the murder of Banquo 'Thou canst not say I did it.' " [1]

The impersonality of the new economic system meant, in brief, that no one had to feel a direct responsibility for the obvious and terrible costs in human suffering. Doubtless there was a lurking sense of guilt; but the very mechanism of organization provided solace and remission. As organization became more elaborate and comprehensive, it became increasingly the instrumentality through which moral man could indulge his natural weakness for immoral deeds. All organization suffered from this internal tendency. What was true of the competitive corporation became all the more true of the monopoly; and what was true even to a degree of the democratic state (which, after all, was responsive to popular control as the corporation was not) became horribly true of the totalitarian state. "A crime which would press quite heavily on the conscience of one man, becomes quite endurable when divided among many." [2]

The impersonality of the system, in other words, brought out, not the best, but the worst in the men who operated it. Industrialism, at the same time that it released vast new energies, imposed on the world a sinister new structure of relationships. The result was to give potent weapons to the pride and the greed of man, the sadism and the masochism, the ecstasy in power and the ecstasy in submission; and it thereby increased man's sense of guilt. The result was to create problems of organization to which man has not risen and which threaten to engulf him; and it thereby multiplied man's anxieties. The result was to devitalize the old religions while producing nothing new capable of controlling pride and power; and it thereby heightened both guilt and anxiety.

Man today must organize beyond his moral and emotional means: this is the fundamental cause of our distempers. This basic dilemma projects itself to us in the middle of the twentieth century in terms of the conflict between the United States and the Soviet Union. But the USA and the USSR are not the alternatives today because either nation has solved the basic problem—because either nation has succeeded in squaring the temptations of power and the corruptions of organization with the weaknesses of man. They are centers of hope because they are centers of power; and they are centers of power, less because of political or social wisdom than because of natural endowments in population, in fertility of the soil and in treasures beneath it, in geographical size and geographical remoteness. Their power makes them the inevitable focus of the tensions of the age. But they are not the cause of the tensions. Nor does either nation have the secret of their solution. Nor will the destruction of one by the other usher in utopia.

The fact that the contest between the USA and the USSR is not the source of the contemporary crisis does not, however, alter the fact that the crisis must be met in terms of this contest. Enthusiasts have suggested other strategies. If organization is the basic trouble, for example, one can sympathize with the anarchist rejection of organization. One can dally with the distributist dream of decentralization and the restoration of feudalism. One can admire the serenity of those who follow Gandhi's faith in non-violence. But one must face the fact that none of these "solutions" solves very much except the complexes of the individual who adopts them. They raise questions which must be raised; they provide the basis perhaps for a searching moral criticism of the existing order; but they leave the main forces of social chaos untouched. A Thoreau or a Gandhi, who has gone himself through intense moral ordeals, has earned the most profound moral respect. But it is a far cry from Thoreau or Gandhi to the ineffectual escapists who in their name engage in such practices as conscientious objection in time of war.

You cannot flee from science and technology into a quietist dreamworld. The state and the factory are inexorable: bad men will run them if good abdicate the job. The USA, the USSR, the strength of industrialism and the weakness of man cannot be evaded; they make up the problem; and there is no point, in General Marshall's phrase, in "fighting the problem." We must understand that the terms of the problem do not exhaust the dilemma of history; but we must understand equally that men in the middle of the twentieth century can strike at the dilemma of history only in terms of the problem.

We can act, in consequence, only in terms of imperfect alternatives. But, though the choice the alternatives present may be imperfect, it is nonetheless a real choice. Even if capitalism and Communism are both the children of the Industrial Revolution, there remain crucial differences between the USA and the USSR. These can be defined as basically the differences between free society and totalitarianism. This is a choice we cannot escape.

The conception of the free society—a society committed to the protection of the liberties of conscience, expression and political opposition—is the crowning glory of western history. Centuries of struggle have drawn a ring of freedom around the individual, a ring secured by law, by custom and by institutions. Here is a classic statement of the tests of freedom:

1. Is there the right to free expression of opinion and of opposition and criticism of the Government of the day?
2. Have the people the right to turn out a Government of which they disapprove, and are constitutional means provided by which they can make their will apparent?
3. Are there courts of justice free from violence by the Executive and free of all threats of mob violence and all association with any particular political parties?
4. Will these courts administer open and well-established laws which are associated in the human mind with the broad principles of decency and justice?
5. Will there be fair play for poor as well as for rich, for private persons as well as Government officials?
6. Will the rights of the individual, subject to his duties to the state, be maintained and asserted and exalted?
7. Is the ordinary peasant or workman, earning a living by daily toil and striving to bring up his family, free from the fear that some grim police organization under the control of a single party, like the Gestapo, started by the Nazi and Fascist parties, will tap him on the shoulder and pack him off without fair or open trial to bondage or ill-treatment? [3]

A conception of unequaled grandeur (modern liberals will, I trust, forgive the fact that the quotation is from Winston Churchill)—yet this conception has broken down at vital points under the pressures of industrial organization. Its failure has created its totalitarian enemy—which professes to meet these needs and moves to do so, proudly and even flagrantly, at the expense of the liberties which define free society.

Is there reason to believe that totalitarianism will be any more effective a master of the pressures of industrial society? The evidence suggests rather that the totalitarian enterprise brings in its wake a whole series of new and intolerable evils. Far from solving the problems of organization, totalitarianism raises them to a climax. A man like Thoreau could find the liberal state of free society a "semihuman tiger or ox, stalking over the earth, with its heart taken out and the top its brain shot away." [4] But the liberal state acknowledged many limitations in its demands upon men: the total state acknowledges none. It systematically annihilates the gaps and rivalries which make for freedom in a more loosely organized society. It dispenses with liberty without providing security. If organization corrupts, total organization corrupts totally.

Free society and totalitarianism today struggle for the minds and hearts of men. If the USA and the USSR were in entire ideological agreement, the imperatives of power—of geography and of economic competition—would still tend to create rivalries; but the ideological conflict has now detonated the power conflict. There is no easy answer to this double polarization. If we believe in free society hard enough to keep on fighting for it, we are pledged to a permanent crisis which will test the moral, political and very possibly the military strength of each side. A "permanent" crisis? Well, a generation or two anyway, permanent in one's own lifetime, permanent in the sense that no international miracle, no political sleight-of-hand will do away overnight with the tensions between ourselves and Russia.

Indeed, we have no assurance that any solution is possible. The twentieth century has at least relieved us of the illusion that progress is inevitable. This age is straining all the capacities of man. At best, it is an age of transition; at worst, an age of catastrophe. And even an age of transition, as John C. Calhoun has reminded us, "must always necessarily be one of uncertainty, confusion, error and wild and fierce fanaticism." [5] There is no more exciting time in which to live—no time more crucial or more tragic. We must recognize that this is the nature of our age: that the womb has irrevocably closed behind us, that security is a foolish dream of old men, that crisis will always be with us.

Our own objective is clear. We must defend and strengthen free society. The means are somewhat more difficult. Surrender to totalitarianism—whether the surrender of military strong points or the surrender of standards and values—is the most certain road to the destruction of free society. War is the next most certain road. The first question is: how to protect free society short of war? The answer will involve all dimensions of activity—political, economic, moral and military.

NOTES

[1] Peter C. Brooks to Edward Everett, July 15, 1845, Everett Papers, Massachusetts Historical Society.

[2] William M. Gouge, *A Short History of Paper Money and Banking in the United States*, Philadelphia, 1833, Part I, p. 43.

[3] Winston Churchill, London *Times*, August 29, 1944.

[4] H. D. Thoreau, "Plea for Captain John Brown," *Works*, Boston, 1894, vol. iv, p. 429.

[5] John C. Calhoun, *A Disquisition on Government*, New York, 1854, p. 90.